GROC's CANDID GUIDE TO THE
DODECANESE
ISLANDS

Including

RHODES, CHALKI, KASTELLORIZO, KARPATHOS, KASOS, SIMI, TILOS, NISIROS, KOS, KAMIMNOS, LEROS, PATMOS & LIPSOS

with excursion details to

PSERIMOS, YIALOS, ANGATHONISI, ARKI & MARATHI

As well as

Athens City & Piraeus

For the package, villa, backpacker &
ferry-boating holiday-maker,
whether travelling by air, car, coach or train

by

Geoffrey O'Connell

Published by
Ashford Press Publishing
1 Church Road
Shedfield
Hampshire
SO3 2HW

CONTENTS

Grikos. ROUTE THREE: Ormos Agriolivado, Kampos, Ormos Kampou, Vagia, Lampi. EXCURSION TO ARKI & MARATHI ISLANDS; ANGATHONISI ISLAND.

ILLUSTRATIONS

Please do not forget that prices are given as a guide only, especially accommodation and restaurant costs which are subject to fluctuation, almost always upwards. In the last year or so, not only lodging and 'troughing' costs, but also transport charges, particularly ferry-boat fees, have escalated dramatically. The increased value of most other currencies to the Greek drachmae has compensated, to some extent, for apparently inexorably rising prices.

In an effort to keep readers as up-to-date as possible regarding these and other matters, I have introduced **GROC's GREEK ISLAND HOTLINE**. See elsewhere for details.

The series is entering its sixth year of publication and I would appreciate continuing to hear from readers who have any additions or corrections to bring to my attention. As in the past, all correspondence (except that addressed to 'Dear filth' or similar endearments) will be answered.

I hope readers can excuse errors that creep (well gallop actually) into the welter of detailed information included in the body text. In order to keep the volumes as up-to-date as possible, the period from inception to publication is kept down to some six months which does result in the occasional slip up....

GROC's Candid Guides
introduce to readers

Suretravel '88

A comprehensive holiday insurance plan that 'gives cover that many other policies do not reach', to travellers anywhere in the world. In addition to the more usual cover offered, the **SURETRAVEL HOLIDAY PLAN** includes (where medically necessary):
24 hour World Wide Medical Emergency Service including, where appropriate, repatriation by air ambulance.

Additionally, personal accident, medical and emergency expenses EVEN while hiring a bicycle, scooter or car.

An example premium, in 1988, for a 10-17 day holiday in Greece is £13.40 per person.

Note: All offers & terms are subject to the Insurance Certificate Cover

For an application form please complete the cut out below and send to:

Willowbridge Enterprises, Bridge House, Southwick Village, Nr Fareham, Hants. PO17 6DZ

Mr/Mrs/Miss...Age.......................

of...

....

request a **SURETRAVEL** application form.

Date of commencement of holiday...............................Duration ....

Signature...Date.....................

The Candid Guides
unique
'GROC's Greek Island Hotline'

Available to readers of the guides, this service enables a respondent to receive a bang up-to-the-minute, update to the extensive information contained in a particular Candid Guide.

To obtain this paraphrased computer print-out, covering the Introductory Chapters, Athens, Piraeus & the Mainland Ports as well as any named islands, up to twenty five in number, all that is necessary is to:-

Complete the form below, enclosing a payment of £1.50 (to include postage), and send to:-

Willowbridge Enterprises, Bridge House, Southwick Village, Nr.Fareham, Hants. PO17 6DZ

Note: The information will be of little use to anyone who does not possess the relevant GROC's Candid Greek Island Guide.

Mr/Mrs/Miss ....

of...

....

I have read/possess GROC's Candid Greek Island Guide to the...

& require a **GROC's Greek Island Hotline.**

to include the following, other islands:- ....

....

and enclose a fee of £1.50. Signature...Date ....

Note. I appreciate that the 'Hotline' may not be dispatched for up to 7-10 days from receipt of this application.

INTRODUCTION

This volume is the second edition of Rhodes, one of six in the popular and proven series of GROC's Candid Guides to the Greek Islands. The rationale, the raison d'etre behind their production is to treat each island grouping on an individual and comprehensive basis, rather than attempt overall coverage of the 100 or so islands usually described in one volume. This obviates attempting to do justice to, say, Leros in amongst an aggregation of many other, often disparate islands.

Due to the vast distances involved very few, if any, vacationers can possibly visit more than a number of islands in a particular group, even if spending as much as four weeks in Greece.

It is important for package and villa holiday-makers to have an unbiased and relevant description of their planned holiday surroundings rather than the usual extravagant hyperbole of the glossy sales brochure. It is vital for backpackers and ferry-boat travellers to have on arrival, detailed and accurate information at their finger tips. With these differing requirements in mind factual, 'straight-from-the-shoulder' location reports have been combined with detailed plans of the major port, town and or city of each island in the group as well as topographical island maps.

Amongst the guides available there are earnest tomes dealing with Ancient and Modern Greece, a number of thumbnail travel booklets and some worthy, if often out-of-date books. Unfortunately they rarely assuage the various travellers' differing requirements. These might include speedy and accurate identification of one's position on arrival; the situation of accommodation as well as the whereabouts of a bank, the postal services and the tourist offices. Additional requisites embrace a swift and easy to read resumé of the settlement's main locations, cafe-bars, tavernas and restaurants; detailed local bus and ferry-boat timetables as well as a full island narrative. Once the traveller has settled in, then and only then, can he or she feel at ease, making their own finds and discoveries.

I have chosen to omit lengthy accounts of the relevant, fabulous Greek mythology and history. These aspects of Greece are, for the serious student, very ably related by authors far more erudite than myself. Moreover, most islands have a semiofficial tourist guide translated into English, and for that matter, French, German and Scandinavian. They are usually well worth the 300 to 400 drachmae (drs) they cost, are extremely informative in 'matters archaeological' and are quite well produced, if rather out of date, with excellent colour photographs. Admittedly the English translation might seem a little quaint (try to read Greek, let alone translate it), and the maps are often unreliable but cartography is not a strong Hellenic suit!

Each **Candid Guide** finally researched as close to the publication date as is possible. Naturally, any new ideas are incorporated but in the main the guides follow a now well-tried formula. Part One deals with the preliminaries and describes in detail the different aspects of travelling and enjoying to the full the unforgettable experience of a Greek islands sojourn. Part Two details a full and thoroughly redrafted account of Athens City, still the hub for Greek island travel, and the relevant mainland ports for connections to the island group in question. Part Three introduces the island chain, followed by a detailed description of each island, the layout being designed to facilitate quick and easy reference.

The exchange rate has fluctuated quite violently in recent years and up-to-date information must be sought prior to departure. For instance at the time of writing the final draft of this guide, the rate to the English pound (£) was hovering about 230drs. Unfortunately prices are subject to fluctuation, usually upward with annual increases varying between 10-20%. Fortunately the drachma tends to devalue by approximately the same amount.

Recommendations and personalities are almost always based on personal observation and experience, occasionally emphasised by the discerning comments of readers or colleagues. They may well change from year to year and be subject to different interpretation by others.

The series incorporates a number of innovative ideas and unique services introduced over the years including:

The Decal: Since 1985 some of the accommodation and eating places recommended in the guides display a specially produced decal to help readers identify the particular establishment.

GROC's Greek Island Hotline: A new and absolutely unique service to readers of the **Candid Guides**. Application to **The GROC's Greek Island Hotline** enables purchasers of the guides to obtain a summary which lists all pertinent and relevant comments that have become available since the publication of the particular guide – in effect, an up-to-date update.

A payment of £1.50 (incl. postage) enables a respondent to receive the paraphrased computer print-out incorporating bang up-to-the-moment information in respect of the Introductory Chapters, Athens, Piraeus & the Mainland Ports as well as any named islands, up to twenty five in number. All it is necessary to do is for a reader to complete the form, or write a letter setting out the request for **GROC's Greek Island Hotline**, enclose the fee and post them to Willowbridge Enterprises, Bridge House, Southwick Village, Nr Fareham, Hants PO17 6DZ. Tel (0705) 375570.

Travel Insurance: A comprehensive holiday insurance plan that 'gives cover that many other policies do not reach....' See elsewhere for details.

The author (and publisher) are very interested in considering ways and means of improving the guides and adding to the backup facilities, so are delighted to hear from readers with their suggestions.

Enjoy yourselves and 'Ya Sou' (welcome). *Geoffrey O'Connell* 1988

ACKNOWLEDGMENTS

Every year the list of those to be formally thanked grows and this edition shows no diminution in their number which has forced the original brief entry from the inside front cover to an inside page.

There are those numerous friends and confidants we meet on passage as well as the many correspondents who are kind enough to contact us with useful information, all of who, in the main, remain unnamed.

Rosemary who accompanies me, adding her often unwanted, uninformed comments and asides (and who I occasionally threaten not to take next time), requires especial thanks for unrelieved, unstinting (well almost unstinting) support despite being dragged from this or that sun kissed beach.

This second edition of The Dodecanese is the result of close collaboration between myself and Anne Merewood who was herself aided and abetted by her husband Mike Mikrigiorgos, when his army duties permitted. To them my grateful thanks.

Although receiving reward, other than in heaven, some of those who assisted me in the production of this edition require specific acknowledgement for effort far beyond the siren call of vulgar remuneration! These worthies include Graham Bishop, who drew the maps and plans, and Viv Hitié, who controls the word processor.

Lastly, and as always, I must admonish Richard Joseph for ever encouraging and cajoling me to take up the pen – surely the sword is more fun?

The cover picture of Simi Harbour is produced by kind permission of GREEK ISLAND PHOTOS, Willowbridge Enterprises, Bletchley, Milton Keynes, Bucks.

PART ONE

1 Packing, insurance, medical matters, climatic conditions, conversion tables & a starter course in Greek

Leisure nourishes the body and the mind is also fed thereby; on the other hand, immoderate labour exhausts both.
Ovid

Vacationing anywhere on an organised tour allows a certain amount of latitude regarding the amount of luggage packed, as this method of holiday does not preclude taking fairly substantial suitcases. On the other hand, ferry-boating and backpacking restricts the amount a traveller is able to carry and the means of conveyance. This latter group usually utilise backpacks and or roll-bags, both of which are more suitable than suitcases for this mode of travel. The choice between the two does not only depend on which is the more commodious, for at the height of season it can be advantageous to be distinguishable from the hordes of other backpackers. To promote the chances of being offered a room, the selection of roll-bags may help disassociation from the more hippy of 'genus rucksacker'. If roll-bags are selected they should include shoulder straps. These help alleviate the discomfort experienced whilst searching out accommodation on hot afternoons with arms just stretching and stretching and stretching.

In the highly populous, oversubscribed months of July and August, it is advisable to pack a thin, foam bedroll and lightweight sleeping bag, just in case accommodation cannot be located on the occasional night.

Unless camping out, I do not think a sweater is necessary between the months of May and September. A desert jacket or lightweight anorak is a better proposition and a stout pair of sandals or training shoes are obligatory, especially if very much walking is contemplated. Leave out the evening suit and cocktail dresses, as the Greeks are very informal. Instead take loose-fitting, casual clothes, and do not forget sunglasses and a floppy hat. Those holiday-makers staying in one place in the hottest months and not too bothered about weight and encumbrances might consider packing a parasol or beach umbrella. It will save a lot of money in daily rental charges.

Should there be any doubt about the electric supply (and you shave) include a pack of disposable razors. Ladies might consider acquiring one of the small, gas cylinder, portable hair-curlers prior to departure. Take along a couple of toilet rolls. They are useful for tasks other than that with which they are usually associated, including mopping up spilt liquid, wiping off plates, and blowing one's nose. It might be an idea to include a container of washing powder, a few clothes pegs, some string for a washing line and a number of wire hangers.

Those visitors contemplating wide ranging travel should consider packing a few plastic, sealed-lid, liquid containers, a plate and a cup, as well as a knife and fork, condiments, an all-purpose cutting/slicing/carving knife as well as a combination bottle and tin opener. These all facilitate economical dining whilst on the move as food and drink, when available on ferry-boats and trains, can be comparatively expensive. Camping out requires these elementary items to be augmented with simple cooking equipment.

Mosquito coils can be bought in Greece but a preferable device is a small two prong, electric heater on which a wafer thin tablet is placed. They can be purchased locally for some 1000drs and come complete with a pack of the capsules. One trade name is *Doker Mat* and almost every room has a suitable electric point. The odourless vapour given off certainly sorts out the mosquitoes and is (hopefully) harmless to humans. Mark you we did hear of a tourist who purchased one and swore by its efficacy, not even aware it was necessary to place a tablet in position.

Whilst discussing items that plug in, why not pack an electric coil. This enables the brew up of a morning 'cuppa'. Tea addicts can use a slice of lemon instead of milk. Those who like their drinks sweet may use those (often unwanted) packets of sugar that accompany most orders for Nes meh ghala or a spoonful of the honey that will be to hand for the morning yoghurt – won't it?

Consider packing a pair of tweezers, some plasters, calamine lotion, after-sun and insect cream, as well as a bottle of aspirin in addition to any pharmaceuticals usually required. It is worth noting that small packets of soap powder are now cheaper in Greece than much of Europe and shampoo and toothpaste cost about the same. Sun-tan oil which was inexpensive has now doubled in price and should be 'imported'. Including a small phial of disinfectant has merit, but it is best not to leave the liquid in the original glass bottle. Should it break, the disinfectant and glass mingled with clothing can prove not only messy but will leave a distinctive and lingering odour. Kaolin and morphine is a very reliable stomach settler. Greek chemists dispense medicines and prescriptions that only a doctor would be able to mete out in many other Western European countries, so prior to summoning a medico, try the local pharmacy.

Insurance & medical matters

While touching upon medical matters, a national of an EEC country should extend their state's National Health cover. United Kingdom residents can contact the local *Department of Health and Social Security* requesting form number *E111 UK*. When completed, and returned, this results in a *Certificate of Entitlement to Benefits in Kind during a stay in a Member State*. Well, that's super! In short, it entitles a person to medical treatment in other EEC countries. Do not only rely on this prop, but seriously consider taking out a holiday insurance policy covering loss of baggage and money; personal accident and medical expenses; cancellation of the holiday and personal liability. Check the exclusion clauses carefully. It is no good an insured imagining he or she is covered for 'this or that' only to discover the insurance company has craftily excluded claims under a particular section. Should a reader intend to hire a scooter ensure this form of 'activity' is insured and not debarred, as is often the case. Rather than rely on the minimal standard insurance cover offered by many tour companies, it is best to approach a specialist insurance broker. For instance, bearing in mind the rather rudimentary treatment offered by the average Greek island hospital, it is almost obligatory to include *Fly-Home Medicare* cover in any policy. A couple of homilies might graphically reinforce the argument. Firstly the Greek hospital system expects the patient's family to minister and feed the inmate 'out-of-hours'. This can result in holiday companions having to camp in the ward for the duration of any internment. Perhaps more thought-provoking is the homespun belief that a patient is best left the first night to survive, if it is God's will, and to pass on if not! After a number of years hearing of the unfortunate experiences of friends and readers, who failed to act on the advice given herein, as well as the inordinate difficulties I experienced in arranging cover for myself, I was prompted to offer readers an all embracing travel insurance scheme. Details are to be found elsewhere in the guide. **DON'T DELAY, ACT NOW**.

Most rooms do not have rubbish containers so why not include some plastic bin liners which are also very useful for packing food as well as storing dirty washing. A universal sink plug is almost a necessity. Many Greek sinks do not have one but, as the water usually drains away very slowly, this could be considered an academic point.

Take along a pack of cards, and enough paperback reading to while away sunbathing sojourns and long journeys. Playing cards are subject to a government tax, which makes their price exorbitant, and books are expensive but some shops and lodgings operate a book-swap scheme.

Many flight, bus, ferry-boat and train journeys start off early in the morning, so a small battery-operated alarm clock may well obviate sleepless, fretful nights prior to the dawn of a departure. A small hand or wrist compass can be an enormous help orientating in towns and if room and weight allow, a torch is a useful addition to the inventory.

Readers must not forget their passport which is absolutely essential to (1) enter Greece, (2) book into most accommodation as well as campsites, (3) change money and (4) hire a scooter or car.

In the larger, more popular, tourist orientated resorts *Diners* and *American Express (Amex)* credit cards are accepted. Personal cheques may be changed when accompanied by a Eurocheque bank card. Americans can use an *Amex* credit card at their overseas offices to change personal cheques up to $1000. They may also, by prior arrangement, have cable transfers made to overseas banks, allowing 24hrs from the moment their home bank receives specific instructions.

It is wise to record and keep separate the numbers of credit cards, travellers's cheques and airline tickets in case they should be mislaid. Incidentally, this is a piece of advice I always give but rarely, if ever, carry out myself. Visitors are only allowed to import 3000drs of Greek currency (in notes) and the balance required must be in traveller's cheques and or foreign currency. It used to be 1500drs but the decline in the value of the Greek drachma has resulted in the readjustment. Despite which, with only 3000drs in hand, it is often necessary to change currency soon after arrival. This can be a problem at weekends or if the banks are on strike, a not uncommon occurrence during the summer months. *See* **Banks, Chapter Seven** for further details in respect of banks and money.

Imported spirits are comparatively expensive (except on some of the duty free Dodecanese islands) but the duty free allowance allowed into Greece, is up to one and a half litres of alcohol. So if a person is a whisky or gin drinker, and partial to an evening sundowner, they should acquire a bottle or two before arrival. Cigars are difficult to buy on the islands, so it may well be advantageous to take along the 75 allowed. On the other hand, cigarettes are so inexpensive in Greece that it hardly seems worthwhile 'importing' them. Note the above applies to fellow members of the EEC. Allowances for travellers from other countries are 1 litre of alcohol and 50 cigars. Camera buffs should take as much film as possible as it is more costly in Greece than in most Western European countries.

Officially, the Greek islands enjoy some 3000 hours of sunshine per year, out of an approximate, possible 4250 hours. The prevailing summer wind is the northerly *Meltemi* which can blow very strongly, day in and day out during July and August, added to which these months are usually dry and very hot for 24 hours a day. The sea in April is perhaps a little cool for swimming, but May and June are marvellous months, as are September and October.

For the statistically minded:

The monthly average temperatures in the Dodecanese include:

	Jan	Feb	Mar	Apr	May	June	July	Aug	Sept	Oct	Nov	Dec
Average air temperature Rhodes	C*11.6	12	13.3	16.6	20.6	25	27.2	27.6	24.9	20.4	16.4	13.2
	F*52.9	53.5	55.9	61.0	69.1	77	81	81.7	76.8	68.7	61.5	55.8
Sea surface temperature (at 1400hrs) RhodesC*	16	15	16	18	19	23	24	25	24	23	19	16
	F*60.8	59	60.8	64.4	66.2	73.4	75.2	7 7	75.2	73.4	66.2	60.8

The best time of year to holiday

The above charts indicate that probably the best months to vacation are May, June, September and October, the months of July and August being too hot. Certainly, the most crowded months, when accommodation is at a premium, are July, August and the first two weeks of September. Taking everything into account, it does not need an Einstein to work the matter out.

Conversion tables & equivalent

Units	Approximate conversion	Equivalent
Miles to kilometres	Divide by 5, multiply by 8	5 miles = 8km
Kilometres to miles	Divide by 8, multiply by 5	
Feet to metres	Divide by 10, multiply by 3	10 ft = 3m
Metres to feet	Divide by 3, multiply by 10	
Inches to centimetres	Divide by 2, multiply by 5	1 inch = 2.5 cm
Centimetres to inches	Divide by 5, multiply by 2	
Fahrenheit to centigrade	Deduct 32, divide by 9 and multiply by 5	77°F = 25°C
Centigrade to fahrenheit	Divide by 5, multiply by 9 and add 32	
Gallons to litres	Divide by 2, multiply by 9	2 gal = 9 litres
Litres to gallons	Divide by 9, multiply by 2	

Note: 1 pint = 0.6 of a litre and 1 litre = 1.8 pints

Pounds (weight) to kilos	Divide by 11, multiply by 5	5 k = 11 lb
Kilos to pounds	Divide by 5, multiply by 11	

Note: 16 oz = 1 lb; 1000g = 1 kg and 100g = 3.5 oz

Tyre pressures
Pounds per square inch to kilometres per square centimetre

lb/sq.in	kg/cm	lb/sq.in	kg/cm
10	0.7	26	1.8
15	1.1	28	2.0
20	1.4	30	2.1
24	1.7	40	2.8

The Greeks use the metric system but most 'unreasonably' sell liquid (i.e. wine, spirits and beer) by weight. Take my word for it, a 640g bottle of wine is approximately 0.7 of a litre or 1.1 pints. Proprietary wines such as *Demestica* are sold in bottles holding as much as 950g, which is 1000ml or 1¾ pints and represents good value.

Electric points in the larger towns, smarter hotels and holiday resorts are 220 volts AC and power any American or British appliance. A few older buildings in out-of-the-way places might still have 110 DC supply. Remote pensions may not have any electricity, other than that supplied by a generator and even then the rooms might not be wired into the system. More correctly they may well be wired but not connected!

Greek time is 2 hours ahead of GMT, as it is during British Summer Time, and 7 hours ahead of United States Eastern Time. That is except for a short period when the Greek clocks are corrected for their winter at the end of September, some weeks ahead of the United Kingdom alteration.

Basics & essentials of the language

These notes and subsequent **Useful Greek** at the relevant chapter endings are not, nor could be, intended to substitute for a formal phrase book or three. Accent marks have been omitted.

Whilst in the United Kingdom it is worth noting that the *British Broadcasting Co.* (Marylebone High St, London WIM 4AA) has produced an excellent book, *Greek Language and People*, accompanied by a cassette and record.

For the less committed a very useful, pocket-sized phrase book that I always have to hand is *The Greek Travelmate* (Richard Drew Publishing, Glasgow) costing £1.99. Richard Drew, the publisher, recounts a most amusing, if at the time disastrous, sequence of events in respect of the launch of this booklet. It appears the public relations chaps had come up with the splendid idea of sending each and every travel writer a preview copy of the book complete with an airline tray of the usual food and drink served mid-flight. This was duly delivered at breakfast time but, unlike Bob Newhart's record of the *HMS Codfish's* shelling of Miami Beach, this was not a 'slow newsday'. No, this was the day that Argentina chose to invade the Falklands, which dramatic event drove many stories off the pages for good, including the phrase book launch!

The Alphabet

Capitals	Lower case	Sounds like
A	α	Alpha
B	β	Veeta
Γ	γ	Ghama
Δ	δ	Dhelta
E	ε	Epsilon
Z	ζ	Zeeta
H	η	Eeta
Θ	θ	Theeta
I	ι	Yiota
K	κ	Kapa
Λ	λ	Lamtha
M	μ	Mee
N	ν	Nee
Ξ	ξ	Ksee
O	ο	Omikron
Π	π	Pee
P	ρ	Roh
Σ	σ	Sighma
T	τ	Taf
Y	υ	Eepsilon
Φ	φ	Fee
X	χ	Chi
Ψ	ψ	Psi
Ω	ω	Omegha

Groupings

αι	'e' as in let
αυ	'av/af' as in have/haff
ει/οι	'ee' as in seen
ευ	'ev/ef' as in ever/effort
ου	'oo' as in toot
γγ	'ng' as in ring
γκ	At the beginning of a word 'g' as in go
γχ	'nks' as in rinks
μπ	'b' as in beer
ντ	At the beginning of a word 'd' as in deer
	In the middle of a word 'nd' as in send
τζ	'ds' as in deeds

Useful Greek

English	Greek	Sounds like
Hello/goodbye	Γειά σου	Yia soo (informal singular said with a smile)
Good morning/day	Καληµέρα	Kalimera
Good afternoon/evening	Καλησπέρα	Kalispera (formal)
Good night	Καληνύχτα	Kalinikta
See you later	Θα σε δω αργοτερα	Tha se tho argotera
See you tomorrow	Θα σε δω αύριο	Tha se tho avrio
Yes	Ναι	Ne (accompanied by a downwards and sideways nod of the head)
No	Οχι	Ochi (accompanied by an upward movement of the head, heavenwards & with a closing of the eyes)
Please	Παρακαλώ	Parakalo
Thank you	(Σαζ) Ευχαριστώ	(sas) Efkaristo
No, thanks	Οχι ζυχαριστώ	Ochi, efkaristo
Thank you very much	Ευχαριστώ πολύ	Efkaristo poli
After which the reply may well be:-		
Thank you (& please)	Παρακαλώ	Parakalo
Do you speak English?	Μιλάτε Αγγλικά	Milahteh anglikah
How do you say....	Πως λενε...	Pos lene...
...in Greek?	...στα Ελληνικά	...sta Ellinika
What is this called?	Πως το λένε	Pos to lene
I do not understand	Δεν καταλαβαίνω	Then katahlavehno
Could you speak more slowly (slower?)	Μπορειτε να µιλάτε πιο αργά	Boreete na meelate peeo seegha (arga)
Could you write it down?	Μπορειτε να µου το γράψετε	Boreete na moo to grapsete

Numbers

One	Ενα	enna
Two	Δύο	thio
Three	Τρία	triah
Four	Τέσσερα	tessehra
Five	Πέντε	pendhe
Six	Εξι	exhee
Seven	Επτά	eptah
Eight	Οκτώ	ockto
Nine	Εννέα	ennea
Ten	Δέκα	thecca
Eleven	Εντεκα	endekha

Twelve	Δώδεκα	thodhehka
Thirteen	Δεκατρία	thehka triah
Fourteen	Δεκατέσσερα	thehka tessehra
Fifteen	Δεκαπέντε	thehka pendhe
Sixteen	Δεκαέξι	thekaexhee
Seventeen	Δεκαεπτά	thehkaeptah
Eighteen	Δεκαοκτώ	thehkaockto
Nineteen	Δεκαεννέα	thehkaennea
Twenty	Εικοσι	eeckossee
Twenty-one	Εικοσι ένα	eeckcossee enna
Twenty-two	Εικοσι δύο	eeckcossee thio
Thirty	Τριάντα	treeandah
Forty	Σαράντα	sarandah
Fifty	Πενήντα	penindah
Sixty	Εξήντα	exhindah
Seventy	Εβδομήντα	evthomeendah
Eighty	Ογδόντα	ogthondah
Ninety	Ενενήτα	eneneendah
One hundred	Εκατό	eckato
One hundred and one	Εκατόν ένα	eckaton enna
Two hundred	Διακόσια	theeakossia
One thousand	Χίλια	kheelia
Two thousand	Δύο χιλιάδες	thio kheeliathes

Mandraki High St, Nisiros.

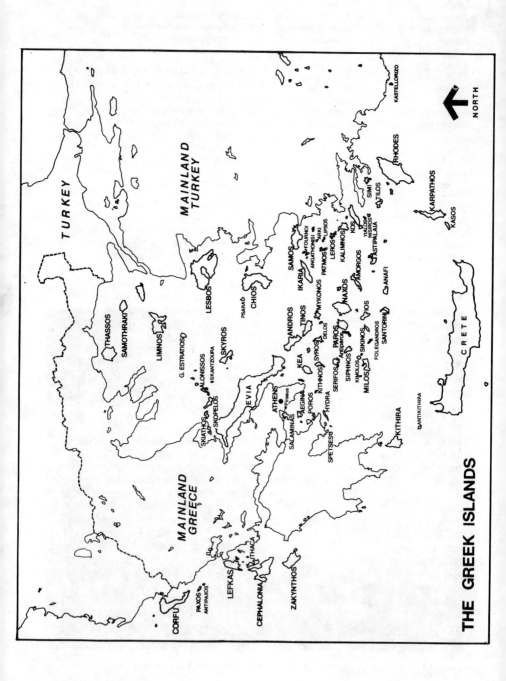

THE GREEK ISLANDS

2 Getting to & from the Dodecanese & Athens

If all the year were playing holidays, to sport would be as tedious as work. William Shakespeare

To start this chapter off, first a word of warning. Whatever form of travel is utilised, travellers must not pack money or travellers cheques in luggage that is to be stowed away, out of sight. Some years ago, almost unbelievably, we met a young lady who had at the last moment, prior to checking-in at the airport, stuffed some drachmae notes in a zipped side pocket of one of her suitcases. On arrival in Greece, surprise, surprise, she was minus the money.

BY AIR
From the United Kingdom

Scheduled flights The choice of airline access to the Dodecanese Islands rests between direct flight to Rhodes or via Athens East (international) airport. From here, transfer by bus to Athens West (domestic) airport and then, by Olympic Airways, on to the islands of Karpathos, Kos, Leros or Rhodes. Olympic Airways international and domestic flights use the West airport. If this were not enough, thanks to the Greek government's policy to open up the more inaccessible islands, there are also flights available from Rhodes to Karpathos, Kasos, Kastellorizo and Kos; a Kos to Leros flight and a Karpathos to Kasos connection. This latter inter-island flight opens up the possibility of flying direct to Iraklion (Crete), catching a bus to Sitia and taking the Sitia to Rhodes flight via Kasos and or Karpathos. Confusing is it not? There is also a Thessaloniki(M) to Rhodes flight.

Heathrow to Athens (3¼hrs): daily, non-stop via *British Airways, Olympic* and others.
Scheduled air fare options include: 1st class return, economy, excursion, APEX (Advanced Purchase Excursion Fare), PEX (instant purchase, and the cheapest scheduled fare) and Eurobudget.

Charter flights & package tours Some package tour operators keep a number of seats available on each flight for, what is in effect, a charter flight. A nominal charge is made for accommodation (which need not be taken up but read on...), the cost of which is included in the return air fare. These seats are substantially cheaper than scheduled APEX fares and are known as 'Charter Cheapies'. Apart from the relatively low price, the normal two week holiday period can be extended by a further week or weeks for a small surcharge. There are a variety of United Kingdom departure airports including Birmingham, Gatwick, Luton, Manchester and Newcastle. But, as one correspondent has pointed out, the frequency of charter flights tails off dramatically between October and March, as does the choice of airport departure points. Do not forget this when contemplating an out-of-season holiday.

An increasing tide of near penniless British youngsters taking a charter flight to Athens and causing various sociological problems, prompted the Greek authorities to announce their intention, from 1988, to carefully monitor charter flight arrivals. Those who did not have irrefutable proof of authorised accommodation, as well as enough money to survive, would be repatriated immediately at the carriers expense. In the consequent muddle of internecine squabbling between the charter companies and the Greeks, the authorities agreed to relax the originally stringent threat, but only for 1988. Despite this, it would be best for independent travellers to have proof of some booked accommodation and sufficient money to see them through their planned length of stay.

To ascertain what is on offer, scan the travel section of the Sunday papers as well as the weekly magazine *Time Out* and, possibly, *Private Eye*. There are many, varied packaged holidays available from the large tour operators whilst some of the smaller, more personal companies offer a bewildering array of multi-centre, fly-drive, budget-bed, self-catering and personally tailored holidays, in addition to the usual hotel accommodation.

Exceptionally reasonable charter flights, with the necessary accommodation vouchers, are available from *Owners Abroad Ltd*, Ilford, who also have offices in Manchester, Birmingham and Glasgow. Examples of their fares and destinations for 1988 include:

Two week return fares	Low Season	Mid-season	High Season
Athens leaving Gatwick Thursday, Friday & Sunday	From £98.75	£111.75	£117.75
Athens leaving Manchester Thursday & Friday	From £109.75	£122.75	£128.75
Athens leaving Birmingham Thursday	From 106.75	£119.75	£126.75
Athens leaving Newcastle Friday	From £123.75	£137.75	£143.75
Kos leaving Gatwick Wednesday	From £129.75	£143.75	£148.75
Kos leaving Birmingham Wednesday	From £138.75	£152.75	£156.75
Kos leaving Manchester Wednesday	From £139.75	£154.75	£159.75
Rhodes leaving Gatwick Wednesday	From £107.75	£121.75	£127.75
Rhodes leaving Luton Wednesday	From £132.75	£145.75	£151.75
Rhodes leaving Birmingham Wednesday	From £138.75	£151.75	£156.75
Rhodes leaving Manchester Wednesday	From £118.75	£132.75	£137.75
Rhodes leaving Newcastle Wednesday	From £146.75	£159.75	£165.75

These rates are subject to inexcusable surcharges and airport taxes totalling £14.95 per head. The fares for three weeks are those above plus £25, for four weeks plus £30 and for five or six weeks, an additional 50 per cent is charged. Note that the total number of weeks allowed in Greece for travellers who arrive and depart by charter flights is six, not twelve weeks.

Perhaps the least expensive flights available are *Courier Flights*. These scheduled seats start off at about £65 return to Athens for the low season period. BUT passengers can only take a maximum of 10kg of hand luggage, one holdall measuring no more than 1ft x 2ft – no other baggage. Other restrictions result in only one passenger being able to travel at a time and for a minimum period of ten or fourteen days. The *cognoscenti* assure that these seats are booked well ahead.

It is a pity, if inevitable, that the Olympic Airways subsidiary, *Allsun Holidays* has had to drop their selected island-hopping holidays. There were too many complaints! I can imagine.

Olympic Airways offer their 'Love-A-Fare' service, yes, 'love-a-fare' which is an APEX option in summer dress. The London to Athens return flight costs from £166 but the booking must be made at least two weeks in advance and allows a maximum of four weeks stay. There are Olympic offices in London as well as Manchester, Birmingham and Glasgow.

Amongst companies offering interesting and slightly off-beat holidays are the *Aegina Club Ltd* and *Ramblers Holidays*. *Aegina* offer a wider range of tours, three different locations in up to three weeks, and additionally, will tailor a programme to fit in with client's requirements. *Ramblers*, as would be imagined, include walking holidays based on a number of locations with half-board accommodation. More conventional inclusions, many in smaller, more personal hotels, pensions and tavernas than those used by the larger tour companies, are available from:

Timsway Holidays. Their brochure includes many of the Dodecanese resorts including the less tourist ravaged islands of Karpathos and Pserimos. Other selective locations are offered by *Laskarina Holidays* whose islands neatly dovetail with *Timsway* as they include comparatively unexploited Chalki and Tilos.

For those to whom money is no object *The Best of Greece* include a Rhodes hotel. *See* **Travel Agents, A To Z, Athens, Chapter Nine.**

Mind you the firm with the most complete coverage of the Dodecanese must be *Twelve Islands*. They can offer package holidays at locations on islands that other firms simply 'haven't reached'. Twelve islands also offer a range of interesting variations including 'Castaways', 'Painting', 'Botanical', 'Take-A-Chance', 'Two-and Multi-Centre' and 'Island Hopping' holidays.

Students Young people lucky enough to be under 26 years of age (oh to be 26 again) should consider contacting *STA Travel* who market a number of inexpensive charter flights (for adults as well). Students of any age or scholars under 22 years of age (whatever mode of travel is planned) should take their *International Student Identity Card (ISIC)*. This ensures discounts are available whenever they are applicable, not only in respect of travel but also for entry to museums, archaeological sites and some forms of entertainment.

If under 26 years of age, but not a student, it may be worthwhile applying for membership of *The Federation of International Youth Travel Organization (FIYTO)* which guarantees discounts from some ferry and tour operators.

From the United States of America
Scheduled flights
Olympic flights include departures from:

Atlanta (via John F Kennedy (JFK) airport, New York (NY): daily
Boston (via JFK or La Guardia, NY): daily
Chicago (Via JFK): daily
Dallas (via JFK): daily
Houston (via JFK): daily
Los Angeles (via JFK): daily
Miami (via JFK): daily, 15 hours
Minneapolis (via JFK): daily
New York (JFK:) daily direct, approx. 10½ hours
Norfolk (via JFK): daily, except Saturday

Philadelphia (via JFK:) daily, about 11 hours
Rochester (via JFK): daily
San Francisco (via JFK): daily, approx. 14½ hours
Seattle (via JFK or London): daily
Tampa (via JFK): daily
Washington DC (via JFK or La Guardia): daily

Note that flights via New York's John F Kennedy airport involve a change of plane from, or to, a domestic American airline.

USA domestic airlines, also run a number of flights to Greece and the choice of air fares is bewildering. These include economy, first class return, super APEX, APEX GIT, excursion, ABC, OTC, ITC, and others, wherein part package costs are incorporated.

Charter/standby flights & secondary airlines As in the United Kingdom, scanning the Sunday national papers' travel section, including the *New York Times*, discloses various companies offering package tours and charter flights. Another way to make the journey is to take a standby flight to London and then fly, train or bus on to Greece. Alternatively, there are a number of inexpensive, secondary airline companies offering flights to London, and the major Western European capitals.

Useful agencies, especially for students, include *Let's Go Travel Services*.

From Canada
Scheduled Olympic flights include departures from:
Montreal: twice weekly direct
or (via Amsterdam, JFK and/or La Guardia NY): daily except Mondays
Toronto (via Montreal): twice weekly
or (via Amsterdam, JFK and or La Guardia NY): daily except Monday and Friday
Winnipeg (via Amsterdam): Thursday and Sunday only.

As for the USA, not only do the above flights involve a change of airline but there is a choice of domestic and package flights as well as a wide range of differing fares.

Student agencies include *Canadian Universities Travel Service*.

From Australia
There are Australian airline scheduled flights from Adelaide (via Melbourne), Brisbane (via Sydney), Melbourne and Sydney to Athens. Flights via Melbourne and Sydney involve a change of plane from, or to, a domestic airline. Regular as well as excursion fares and affinity groups.

From New Zealand
There are no scheduled flights.
Various connections are available as well as regular and affinity fares.

From South Africa
Scheduled Olympic flights include departures from:
Cape Town (via Johannesburg): Fridays and Sundays only.
Johannesburg: direct, Thursday, Friday and Sunday.

Flights via Johannesburg involve a change of plane from, or to, a domestic airline. South African airline flights from Johannesburg to Athens are available as regular, excursion or affinity fares.

From Ireland
Scheduled Olympic flights from:
Dublin (via London) daily, which involves a change of airline to *Aer Lingus*.

Note that when flying from Ireland, Australia, New Zealand, South Africa, Canada and the USA there are sometimes advantages in travelling via London or other European capitals on stopover and taking inexpensive connection flights to Greece.

From Scandinavia
including:
Denmark Scheduled Olympic flights from:
Copenhagen (via Frankfurt): daily, involving a change of aircraft as well as non-stop flights on Wednesday, Friday, Saturday and Sunday.
Sweden Scheduled Olympic flights from:
Stockholm (via Copenhagen and Frankfurt): Tuesday, Wednesday, Friday and Saturday.
Norway Scheduled Olympic flights from:
Oslo (via Frankfurt or Copenhagen): daily.

All the Scandinavian countries have a large choice of domestic and package flights with a selection of offerings. Contact *SAS Airlines* for *Olympic Airways details*.

AIRPORTS
United Kingdom
Do not forget if intending to stay in Greece longer than two weeks, the long-stay car parking fees tend to mount up – and will the battery last for a 3 or 4 week laver? Incidentally, charges at Gatwick are about £32.00 for two weeks, £42.00 for three weeks and £52.00 for four weeks. The difficulty is that most charter flights leave and arrive at rather unsociable hours, so friends and family may not be too keen to act as a taxi service.

Athens
Hellinikon airport is split into two parts, West (Olympic domestic and international flights) and East (foreign airlines). There are coaches to make the connection between the two airports, and Olympic buses to Athens centre as well as city buses.

At the Western or domestic airport, city buses pull up alongside the terminal building. Across the road is a pleasant cafe/restaurant but the service becomes fairly chaotic when packed out. To the left of the cafe (facing) is a newspaper kiosk and further on, across a side road, a Post Office is hidden in the depths of the first building.

The Eastern airport is outwardly quite smart but can, in reality, become an expensive, very cramped and uncomfortable location if there are long delays. (Let's not beat about the 'airport', the place becomes a hell-hole). Suspended flights occur when, for instance, air traffic controllers strike elsewhere in Europe. So remember when leaving Greece to have enough money and some food left for an enforced stay. Flight departures are consistently overdue and food and drink in the airport are costly with a plastic cup of coffee costing 115drs. Furthermore, there are simply no facilities to accommodate a lengthy occupation by a plane load of passengers. The bench seats are very soon fully occupied – after which the floor of the concourse fills up with dejected travellers sleeping & slumped for as long as it takes the aircraft to arrive. You have been warned.

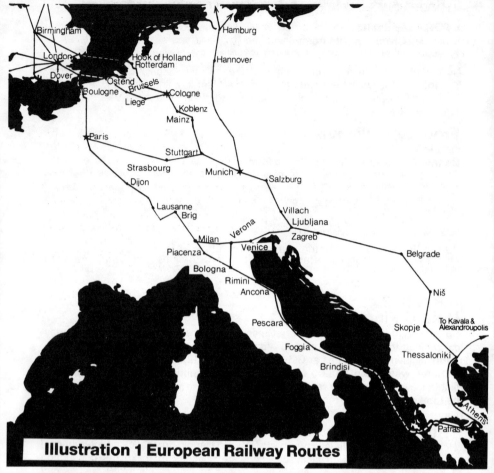

Illustration 1 European Railway Routes

BY TRAIN
From the United Kingdom & European countries
(Illustration 1).

Recommended only for train buffs and masochists but one of the alternative routes to be considered when a visitor intends to stay in Greece in excess of 6 weeks. The quickest journey of the three, major scheduled overland routes takes about 60 hours, and a second-class return fare costs in the region of £266. Tickets are valid for two months. One advantage of rail travel is that travellers may break the journey along the route (a little difficult on an airline flight), and another is that it is possible to travel out on one route and back by an alternative track (if you will excuse the pun). It is important to take along basic provisions, toilet paper and to wear old clothes.

A fairly recent return to the 'day of the train' reinforced my general opinion and introductory remarks in respect of this particular method of travel, bringing sharply back into focus the disadvantages and difficulties. The list of drawbacks should be enough to deter any but the most determined.

Try not to have a query which involves making use of the overseas information desk at *Victoria Station* as the facility is undermanned and the wait to get to a counter averages ⅓hr. The staff are very willing but it is of interest that they overcome the intricacies of the official British Rail European timetable ('it's all Greek to me guvnor') by overtly referring to the (infinitely) more manageable *Thomas Cook* publication.

The channel crossing is often on craft that would not be pressed into service if we declared war on the Isle of Wight; the sea journey is too short for any cabins to be available; the duty free goods on offer are very limited and there are inordinate delays between train, boat and train.

The French trains that ply between the coast and Paris are of an excellent standard. On the other hand changing trains at the 'black hole' of *Gare du Nord* sharply focuses travellers' attention on a whole subculture of human beings who exist in and around a number of European railway stations. My favourite example of this little known branch of the human race is the 'bag-shuffler' – usually a middle-aged lady. The genus is initially recognisable by the multitudinous paper and plastic bags festooned about their person. Once at rest the contents are constantly and interminably shuffled from one bag to another, and back again, the ritual being accompanied by low mutterings. French railway stations, which are heated to a temperature relating to gentle simmer on a domestic cooker, have perfected a waiting room seating arrangement that precludes any but a drunk contortionist stretching out for a nap. In common with most other railway stations, food and drink are expensive and credit cards impossible to use, even at the swanky station restaurants. The railway station's toilet facilities are minuscule and men are charged for other than the use of a urinal and washbasin. Ladies have to pay about 2 Francs (F), a private closet costs 6F and a shower 12F. Potential users must not imagine they will be able to sneak in for a crafty stand-up wash using a basin – the toilets are intently watched over by attendants who would only require knitting needles to irresistibly remind one of the women who sat at the foot of the guillotine.

The Metro connection between the railway stations of *Gare du Nord* and *Gare de Lyon* is not straightforward and involves a walk. The *Gare de Lyon* springs a minor trap for the unwary in that the inter-continental trains depart from platforms reached by a long walk up the far left platforms (facing the trains). Don't some of the French trains now resemble children's rocket drawings?

Although it may appear to be an optional extra, it is obligatory to purchase a couchette ticket for the train journey. This is a Catch 22 situation brought about by the rule that only couchette ticket holders have the right to a seat! Yes, well, not so optional. It is also necessary to pack food and drink, at least for the French part of the journey, as usually there are no refreshment services. In Italy most trains are met, at the various station stops by trolley pushing vendors of (rather expensive) sustenance.

Venice station, signed *Stazione St Lucia*, is most conveniently sited bang-on the edge of the Grand Canal waterfront with shops and restaurants to the left. Some of the cake shops sell slabs of pizza pie for about 1000 lira (L) which furnishes good standby nourishment. The scheduled stopover here will have to be adjusted for any (inevitable) delay in arrival. Venice (on the outward journey) is the watershed where Greek, and the occasional Yugoslavian, carriages are coupled up. After this passengers can be guaranteed to encounter a number of nasties. The replacement compartments are seedier and dirtier than their French and Italian counterparts. The lavatories vary between bad to unspeakable and faults include toilets that won't flush (sometimes appearing to mysteriously fill up); Greek style toilet paper (which apart from other deficiencies lacks body and – please excuse the indelicacy – through which fingers break); no toilet paper at all (which is worst?); no soap dispenser; a lack of coat hooks; water taps that don't and all very grimy.

From Venice the term 'Express' should be ignored as the train's progress becomes slower and slower and slower with long, unscheduled stops and quite inordinate delays at the Yugoslavian frontiers. During the Yugoslavian part of the journey it is necessary for passengers to lock themselves into their compartment as some of the locals have an annoying habit of entering and determinedly looting tourists' luggage. There have even been 'totally unsubstantiated rumours', in the last year or two of callow fellows spraying an aerosol knockout gas through the keyholes, breaking in and at leisure relieving passengers of their belongings. I must stress I have not actually met victims and the story may be apocryphal. It is inadvisable to leave the train at *Belgrade* for a stopover as the accommodation available to tourists is extremely expensive, costing in the region of £60 plus for a double room, per night. Additionally, it is almost impossible to renegotiate a couchette for the remainder of the onward journey. There are trolley attendants at the major Yugoslavian railway stations but the innards of the rolls proffered are of an 'interesting' nature resembling 'biltong' or 'hardtack' burgers. Certainly when poked by the enthusiastic vendors I'm sure their fingers buckle. Another item of 'nutriment' on offer are large, but rather old cheese curd pies. A railway employee wanders the length of the train twice a day with a very large aluminium teapot ostensibly containing coffee. Nobody appears to be interested in payment with Yugoslavian dinars, but American dollars or English pounds sterling almost cause a purr of satisfaction. Travellers lucky enough to have the services of a Greek attendant may well find he keeps a cache of alcoholic drinks for sale. An aside is that Yugoslavians are obsessed by wheel-tapping and at all and every stop (almost at 'the drop of a sleeper'), appear and perform. Much of the journey beyond Belgrade is on a single line track and should, for instance, a cow break into a trot the animal might well overtake the train. At the frontier passengers may be reminded of the rigours of Iron Curtain countries, as they will be subjected to rigorous, lengthy baggage and documents checks by a swamp of officials, whose numbers include stern faced, unsmiling, gun-toting police.

In stark contrast the friendly Greek frontier town of *Idomeni* is a tonic. Even late at night the station's bank is open as is the taverna/snackbar with a scattering of tables on the platform and a buzz of brightly lit noise and activity.

To avoid the Yugoslavian experience a very pleasant alternative is to opt for the railway route that travels the length of Italy to *Brindisi Port*. Here international ferry-boats can be caught to the mainland Greek ports of Igoumenitsa or Patras, from either of which buses make the connection with Athens, whilst Patras offers the possibility of another train journey on to Athens. Brindisi (Italy), contains several traps for the unwary. Unfortunately the Maritime Railway Station and the quay for the Italy-Greek ferryboats are some 200m apart, which on a hot day... The railway station has no formal ticket office or barrier. It is only necessary to dismount, turn left along the platform, left again, beside the concrete wall supporting the first floor concourse (which stretches over and above the platforms), across the railway lines and left again down the sterile dockland street romantically named Via del Mare, to the ferry-boat complex. The road, hemmed in by a prefabricated wall on the right, curves parallel to the seawall on the left, from which it is separated by a high chain link fence, a number of railway lines and tarmacadam quay. But, before leaving the station, stop, for all the ticket offices and necessary officials are situated in the referred to upper storey buildings or in the 'Main Street', Corso Garibaldi. My favourite tour office is across the road from the station, alongside a bank on the corner formed by Corso Garibaldi and Via del Mare. The staff are very helpful and most informative. Diagonally across the bottom of this end of the 'Main St' is a small, tree edged square, Plaza Vittorio Emanuele. As it is well endowed with park benches, it has become an unofficial waiting room with travellers and backpackers occupying most of the available seating. Do not forget when booking rail tickets to ask for *Brindisi Maritime*, as the town railway station is some kilometres inland.

The international ferry-boats on this route generally divide neatly into two. The expensive, but rather shambolic Greek ferries and the expensive, but luxurious and well-appointed Italian ferries. The Greek boats are really nothing more than an inter-island ferries of 'middling' quality, with the 'threat' of a cabaret and casino. They can be in appalling condition and the reception staff are often rude. The Italian boats may well include in the trappings, a sea-water swimming pool, a ladies' hairdresser and beauty salon, a number of restaurants, a self-service cafeteria, a coffee bar and a disco. Food and drink is simply expensive. Examples include coffee at 135drs, a beer 120drs, a *petit dejeuner* for two of coffee and cake 520drs and dinner 1300-1900drs a head. On the Greek craft the gourmet standards are average and the service poor whilst the Italian service and offerings are excellent, all at about the same price. Moral, try not to eat on board. Fares range from about 7500drs for a simple, 2 berth cabin to 14000drs for a splendid two berth cabin with a generous en suite bathroom. Don't rely on the purser to carry out normal currency exchange transactions.

Travellers under 26 years of age can take advantage of *British Rail's Inter-Rail pass* by applying to Victoria Travel Centre while Americans and Canadians may obtain an *Eurorail pass* prior to reaching Europe. There is also the *Transalpino ticket* available from the London office of the firm of the same name. All these offers hold out a substantial discount on standard train and ferry fares, but are subject to various terms and conditions. Another student outfit offering cut-price train, coach and airline flights is *London Student Travel (& Eurotrain)*.

Certainly it must be borne in mind that the Greek railway system is not extensive and, unless travelling around other European countries, a concessionary pass might not represent much of a saving. On the other hand discounts in respect of the Greek railways extends to travel on some of the State Railway buses (OSE).

Examples of the various tickets, costs and conditions are as follows:-

Inter-Rail ticket	Under 26 years of age, valid one month for use in 21 countries (and also allows half fare travel in the UK on *Sealink* and *B & I* ships as well as *P & O* ferries via Southampton and Le Havre).	£139	
Transalpino ticket	Under 26, valid for two months and allows stopover en route to the destination. London to Athens via Brindisi or Yugoslavia from	Single £107.35	Return £188.40

Other ticket options include B.I.G.E., Eurotrain and 'Athens Circle'.

Timetables & routes (Illustration 1)

This section caused me as much work as whole chapters on other subjects. *British Rail*, whose timetable I had the greatest difficulty deciphering and *Thomas Cook*, whose timetable I could understand, were both helpful.

Example routes include:

(1) London (Victoria Station), Dover (Western Docks), (jetfoil), Ostend, Brussels, Liege, Aachen, Cologne (change train, ¾hr delay), Mainz, Mannheim, Ulm, Munich (change train ½hr delay) Salzburg, Jesenice, Ljubljana, Zagreb, Belgrade (Beograd), Skopje, Gevgelija, Idomeni, Thessaloniki to Athens. An example of the journey is as follows:
Departure: 1300hrs, afternoon sea crossing, evening on the train, late night change of train at Cologne, night on the train, morning change of train at Munich, all day and night on the train arriving Athens very late, some 2½ days later at 2314hrs.

(2) London (Charing Cross/Waterloo East stations), Dover Hoverport, (hovercraft), Boulogne Hover-point, Paris (du Nord), change train (and station) to Paris (de Lyon), Strasbourg, Munich, Salzburg, Ljubljana, Zagreb, Belgrade (change train 1¾hrs delay), Thessaloniki to Athens.

An example:
Departure: 0955hrs and arrive 2½ days later at 2315hrs.
Second class single fare from £147 and return fare from £271.30.

(3) London (Victoria), Folkestone Harbour, (ferry-boat), Calais, Paris (du Nord), change train (and station) to Paris (de Lyon), Venice, Ljubljana, Zagreb, Belgrade, Thessaloniki to Athens.
An example:
Departure: 1415hrs and arrive 2¼ days later at 0840hrs.

Second class single fare from £135.20 and return fare from £266.

(4) London (Liverpool St), Harwich (Parkeston Quay), ferry-boat, Hook of Holland, Rotterdam, Eindhoven, Venlo, Cologne (change train), Mainz, Mannheim, Stuttgart, Ulm, Munich, Salzburg, Jesenice, Ljubljana, Zagreb, Belgrade, Nis, Skopje, Gevgelija, Idomeni, Thessaloniki to Athens.
An example:
Departure: 1940hrs, night ferry crossing, change train at Cologne between 1048 and 1330hrs, first and second nights on the train and arrive at Athens middle of the day at 1440hrs.

An alternative is to take the more pleasurable train journey through Italy and make a ferry-boat connection to Greece as follows:
(5) London (Victoria), Folkestone Harbour, Calais, Boulogne, Amiens, Paris (du Nord), change train and station to Paris (de Lyon), Dijon, Vallorbe, Lausanne, Brig, Domodossala, Milan (Central), Bologna, Rimini, Ancona, Pescara, Bari to Brindisi.
   (5a) Brindisi to Patras sea crossing.
   (5b) Patras to Athens.
An example:
Departure: 0958hrs, day ferry crossing, change of train at Paris to the Parthenon Express, one night on the train and arrive at Brindisi at 1850hrs. Embark on the ferry-boat departing at 2000hrs, night on the ferry-boat and disembark at 1300hrs the next day. Take the coach to Athens arriving at 1600hrs.
   The second class single fare costs from £163.30. and the return fare from £324.10.

Note it is possible to disembark at Ancona and take a ferry-boat but the sailing time is about double that of the Brindisi sailing. *See* **By Ferry-boat**.

On all these services children benefit from reduced fares, depending on their age. Couchettes and sleepers are usually available at extra cost and Jetfoil sea crossings are subject to a surcharge.

Details of fares and timetables are available from *British Rail Europe* or *The Hellenic State Railways (OSE)*. One of the most cogent, helpful and informative firms through whom to book rail travel must be *Victoria Travel Centre*. I have always found them to be extremely accommodating and it is well worth contacting *Thomas Cook Ltd*, who have a very useful range of literature and timetables available from their Publications Department.

From the Continent & Scandinavia to Athens
Pick up one of the above main lines by using the appropriate connections detailed in Illustration 1.

Departure terminals from Scandinavia include Helsinki (Finland); Oslo (Norway); Gothenburg, Malmo and Stockholm (Sweden); Fredrikshavn and Copenhagen (Denmark).

The above are only a guide and up-to-date details must be checked with the relevant offices prior to actually booking.

BY COACH
This means of travel is for the more hardy voyager and or young. If the description of the train journey has caused apprehension, the tales of passengers of the less luxurious coach companies should strike terror into the listener/reader. Common 'faults' include lack of 'wash and brush up' stops, smugglers, prolonged border custom investigations (to unearth the smugglers), last minute changes of route and breakdowns. All this is on top of the forced intimacy with a number of widely disparate companions, some wildly drunk, in cramped, uncomfortable surroundings.

For details of the scheduled *Euroway Supabus* apply c/o *Victoria Coach Station* or to the *National Express Company*. A single fare costs from £79 and a return ticket from £137 via Italy or £140 via Germany. This through service takes 4 days plus, with no overnight layovers but short stops at Cologne, Frankfurt and Munich, where there is a change of coach. Fares include ferry costs but exclude refreshments. Arrival and departure in Greece is at the Peloponissos Railway Station, Athens.

The timetable is as follows:

Departure from London, Victoria Coach Station, Bay 20: Friday and Saturday at 2030hrs arriving at 1100hrs, 4½ days later.
Return journey
Departure from Filellinon St, Syntagma Sq, Athens: Wednesday and Friday at 1300hrs arriving London at 0800hrs, 4 days later.
Note this company offers a special one month return fare of £127.

Eurolines Intercars (Uniroute) runs a national coach service that shuttles between Athens and Paris on a three day journey. The buses depart twice a week at 1030hrs, Wednesday and Saturday, at a cost of about 13,000drs, but note that baggage costs an extra 200drs. The French end of the connection is close by the Metro station *Porte Vincennes* and the Athens terminus is alongside the *Stathmos Larissis* railway station. These buses are comfortable with air conditioning but no toilet so the leg-stretching stops are absolutely vital, not only for passengers to relieve themselves but to purchase victuals. To help make the journey acceptable passengers must pack enough food and drink to tide them over the trip. It is a problem that the standard of the 'way-station' toilets and snackbars varies from absolutely awful to luxurious. And do not forget that the use of the lavatories is usually charged for in Greece and Yugoslavia. There are sufficient stops in Greece at, for instance, Livadia, Larissa and Thessaloniki, as well as at the frontier. The frontier crossing can take up to some 2¾hrs. The Yugoslavian part of the route passes through Belgrade and at about two-thirds distance there is a lunchtime motorway halt. At this sumptuous establishment even Amex credit cards are accepted and the lavatories are free – a welcome contrast to the previous, 'mind boggling' Yugoslavian stop where even the Greeks blanched at the sight of the toilets! The bus and driver change at Trieste which is probably necessary after the rigours of the Yugoslavian roads.

Use of the lavatories in the bus station has to be paid for and they are very smelly with a 'lecher' in the ladies. One of the two Italian stops is at a luxurious motorway complex. It is worth noting that all purchases at Italian motorway cafe-bars and restaurants have to be paid for first. A ticket is issued which is then exchanged for the purchaser's requirements. This house rule even applies to buying a cup of coffee.

The route between Italy and France over the Alps takes a tediously long time on winding, narrow mountain roads with an early morning change of driver in France. It may well be necessary to 'encourage' the driver on this section to make an unscheduled halt in order to save burst bladders. The bus makes three Paris drop-offs, at about midday, three days after leaving Athens. The best disembarkation point depends on a traveller's plans. Devotees of the *Le Havre* channel crossing must make for the *Gare St Lazare* railway station. The Metro, with one change, costs about 5 francs (F) each and the coach's time of arrival allows passengers to catch a Paris to Le Havre train. This departs on the three hour journey at 1630hrs and the tickets cost some 100 F each. No information in respect of cross-Channel ferries is available at the Paris railway station, despite the presence of a number of tourist information desks.

Illustration 2 European Car Routes & Ferry-boat connections

Incidentally, the walk from the Le Havre railway terminus to the cross-Channel embarkation point is a long haul but there are reasonably priced taxis between the two points. The superb restaurant *Le Southampton*, conveniently across the street from the Ferry-boat Quay, may well compensate for the discomfort of the trudge round, especially as they accept payment by *Amex*.

'Express' coach companies include *Consolas Travel*. This well-established company runs daily buses during the summer months, except Sunday, and single fares start at about £59 with a return ticket costing from £99.

Other services are run by various 'pirate' bus companies. The journey time is about the same and, again, prices, which may be slightly cheaper, do not include meals. The cheaper the fare the higher the chance of vehicle breakdowns and or the driver going 'walkabout'. On a number of islands, travel agents signs still refer to the *Magic Bus*, or as a fellow traveller so aptly put it

– the 'Tragic Bus', but the company that ran this renowned and infamous service perished some years ago. Imitators appear to perpetuate the name.

In the United Kingdom it is advisable to obtain a copy of the weekly magazine *Time Out*, wherein the various coach companies advertise. For return trips from Athens, check shop windows in Omonia Sq, the *American Express* office in Syntagma Sq, or the *Students Union* in Filellinon St, just off Syntagma Sq.

See **Travel Agents, A To Z, Athens, Chapter Nine**

BY CAR (Illustration 2)

Motoring down to Greece is usually only a worthwhile alternative method of travel if there are at least two adults who are planning to stay for longer than three weeks, as the journey from England is about 1900 miles and takes approximately 50hrs non-stop driving.

People taking cars to Greece should ensure that spares are likely to be plentiful. An instance will illuminate. Recently I drove to Greece in a Mazda camping van and the propshaft went on the 'blink'. It transpired there was only one propshaft in the whole of Greece – well that was the story. Spare parts are incredibly expensive and our replacement finally cost, with carriage and bits and pieces, 36,000drs. The ½hr labour required to fit the wretched thing was charged at 2,000drs plus tax or about £18 an hour. At the time the total worked out at approximately £194 which seemed a bit steep, even when compared to English prices. This cautionary tale prompts me to remind owners to take out one of the vehicle travel insurance schemes. The *AA* offers an excellent *5 Star Service Travel Pack* and other motoring organisations have their own schemes. At the time of making the decision the insurance premium might seem a trifle expensive but when faced with possibly massive inroads into available currency, the knowledge that a pack of credit vouchers is available with which to effect payment, is very reassuring.

The motoring organisations will prepare routes from their extensive resources. Certainly the *AA* offers this service but individual route plans now take 2-3 weeks to prepare.

One of the shortest routes from the United Kingdom is via car-ferry to Ostend (Belgium) on to Munich, Salzburg (Germany), Klagenfurt (Austria) and Ljubljana (Yugoslavia). There the Autoput E94 is taken on to Zagreb, Belgrade (Beograd) and Nis on the E5, where the E27 and E55 are used via Skopje to the frontier town of Gevgelija/Evzonoi. Major rebuilding works can cause lengthy delays on the road between Zagreb and Nis.

Drivers through France have a number of possible routes but those choosing to skirt Switzerland will have to cross over into Italy, usually angling down through Lyon and heading in the general direction of Turin. One of the loveliest Franco-Italian frontier crossings is effected by driving through Grenoble to Briancon for the Alpine pass of Col de Montgenevre. Across the border lies Turin (Torino), which bypass, and proceed to Piacenza, Brescia, Verona, Padua (Padova), Venice and cut up to Trieste. I say bypass because the ordinary Italian roads are just 'neat aggravation' and the sprawling towns and cities are almost impossible to drive through without a lot of problems and exhausting delays. Although motorways involve constant toll fees they are much quicker and less wearing on the nerves. Note that Italian petrol stations have a 'nasty habit' of closing for a midday siesta between 1200 and 1500hrs. *See* **By Coach** for hints in respect of Italian motorway cafes and restaurants.

Possibly the most consistently picturesque drive down Italy is that using the incredibly engineered, audaciously Alpine tunnelled toll road that hugs the Mediterranean. This route can provide a check list of famous resorts. Proceed to Cannes and then via Nice, Monaco, and San Remo to Geneva and La Spezia. It is possible to detour to Pisa, Florence (Firenze) and Siena or simply continue on along the coast but this magnificent, often breathtaking motorway, terminates at Livorno. Whatever road is used, this route enables the Tuscany region to be driven through, which probably the only area of Southern Italy not defaced by indiscriminate factory building and urban sprawl, and on to Rome (Roma). After which it is possible to continue on past Naples – drivers should ensure that it is past Naples – to cut across the toe of Italy via Salerno, Potenza and Taranto and on to Brindisi Port. An alternative route is via Turin, Milan, Bergamo, Brescia, Verona and on to Trieste which leads around the southern edge of a few of the lakes, in the area of Brescia. Excursions to Padua and Venice are obvious possibilities.

From Trieste the most scenic (and winding) route is to travel the Adriatic coast road via Rijeka, Zadar and Split to Dubrovnik. This latter, lovely medieval inner city is well worth a visit. At Petrovac the pain starts as the road swings up to Titograd around to Kosovska Mitrovika, Pristina, Skopje and down to the border at Gevgelija. The stretch from Skopje to the Greek frontier can be rather unnerving. Signposting in Yugoslavia is usually very bad; always obtain petrol when the opportunity crops up and lastly but not least, city lights are often turned off during the hours of darkness (sounds a bit Irish to me!), making night driving in built-up areas extremely hazardous. To save the journey on from Petrovac, it is possible, at the height of the season, to catch a ferry from Dubrovnik to Igoumenitsa or Patras on the Greek mainland. (*See* **By Ferry-boat**)

Detailed road reports are available from the *Automobile Association*, but I would like to stress that in the Yugoslavian mountains, especially after heavy rain, landslips can (no will!) result in parts of the road disappearing at the odd spot as well as the surface being littered with rocks. There you go! Also note that the very large intercontinental lorries can prove even more of a dangerous hazard in Yugoslavia where they appear to regard the middle of the sometimes narrow roads as their own territory.

The main road through Greece, to Athens via Pirgos, Larissa and Lamia, is wide and good but the speed of lorries and their trailer units can prove disquieting. Vehicles being overtaken are expected to move right over and tuck well into the wide hard shoulders. From Evzonoi to Athens, via Thessaloniki, is 340 miles (550km) and some of the major autoroute is now a toll road.

Drivers approaching Athens via the Corinth Canal should use the Toll road as the old route is murderously slow, especially in bad weather.

My favourite choice of route used to be crossing the Channel to Le Havre to drive through France, which holds few perils for the traveller, via Evreux, Chartres, Pithiviers, Montargis, Clamecy, Nevers, Lyon and Chambery to the Italian border at Modane. Here the fainthearted take the tunnel whilst the adventurous wind their way over the Col du Mont Cenis. That was until I 'discovered' the Briancon route.

In Italy rather than face the rigours of the Yugoslavian experience, it is worth considering, as for the alternative train journey, cutting down the not-all-that attractive Adriatic seaboard to one of the international Italian ferry-boat ports of Ancona, Bari, or Brindisi where boats connect to Igoumenitsa or Patras on the Greek mainland (*See* **By Ferry-boat & Train**).

General Vehicle & Personal Requirements

Documents required for travel in any European country used to include an *International Driving Licence*, and a *Carnet de Passages* en Douanes (both issued by the AA and valid for one year) but these are not now necessary in many European countries including France, Italy, Switzerland, Germany, Greece and Yugoslavia. Drivers must have their United Kingdom driving licence. One document not to be forgotten is the *Green Insurance Card* and it is recommended to take the vehicle's registration documents as proof of ownership. The vehicle must have a nationality sticker of the approved pattern and design.

Particular countries' requirements include:

Italy Import allowances are as for Greece but the restriction on the importation of Italian currency equals about £100.

All cars entering Italy must possess both right and left hand external driving mirrors. Divers' licences must be accompanied by an Italian translation.

Switzerland If intending to drive through Switzerland remember that the Swiss require the vehicle and all the necessary documents to be absolutely correct. (They would.) The authorities have a nasty habit of stopping vehicles some distance beyond the frontier posts in order to make thorough checks.

Yugoslavia A valid passport is the only personal document required for citizens of, for example, Denmark, West Germany, Finland, Great Britain and Northern Ireland, Republic of Southern Ireland, Holland and Sweden. Americans and Canadians must have a visa and all formalities should be checked with the relevant Yugoslavian Tourist Office.

It is compulsory to carry a warning triangle, a first aid kit and a set of replacement vehicle light bulbs. The use of spotlights is prohibited and drivers planning to travel during the winter should check the special regulations governing the use of studded tyres.

Visiting motorists do not now have to have petrol coupons in order to obtain petrol. But it is still advantageous to purchase them as they are the most cost effective method of buying fuel. The coupons are available at the frontier. Carefully calculate the number required for the journey and pay for them in foreign currency. Not only is the currency rate allowed very advantageous, compared to that if the coupons are paid for in Yugoslavian dinars, but their acquisition allows for 10% more fuel. Petrol stations are often far apart, closed or have run out of fuel, so fill up when possible.

Photographers are only allowed to import five rolls of film; drinkers a bottle of wine and a quarter litre of spirits and smokers 200 cigarettes or 50 cigars. Each person may bring in unlimited foreign currency but only 1500 Yugoslavian dinars.

Fines are issued on the spot and the officer collecting one should issue an official receipt.

To obtain assistance in the case of accident or breakdown dial 987 and the *SPI* will come to your assistance.

Greece It is compulsory to carry a first aid kit as well as a fire extinguisher in a vehicle and failure to comply may result in a fine. It is also mandatory to carry a warning triangle and it is forbidden to carry petrol in cans. In Athens the police are empowered to confiscate and detain the number plates of illegally parked vehicles. The use of undipped headlights in towns is strictly prohibited.

Customs allow the importation of 200 cigarettes or 50 cigars, 1 litre of spirits or 2 lites of wine and only 3000drs but any amount of foreign currency. Visitors from the EEC may import 300 cigarettes or 75 cigars, $1\frac{1}{2}$ litres of spirits or 4 litres of wine.

Speed Limits

See table below – all are standard legal limits which may be varied by signs.

	Built-up areas	Outside built-up areas	Motorways	Type of Vehicle affected
Greece	31 mph (50 kph)	49mph (80 kph)	62 mph (100 mph)	Private vehicles with or without trailers

Yugoslavia	37 mph	49 mph	74 mph	Private vehicles
	(60 kph)	(80 kph)	(120 mph)	without trailers
	62 mph*			
	(100 kph)*			

*Speed on dual carriageways

FERRY-BOAT (Illustration 2).

Some of the descriptive matter under the heading **By Train** in this chapter refers to inter-country, ferry-boat travel, especially that relating to Brindisi Port and the international ferry-boats.

Due to the popularity of Brindisi, height of the season travellers must be prepared for crowds, lengthy delays and the usual ferry-boat scrum (scrum not scum). Other irritants include the exasperating requirement to purchase an embarkation pass, with the attendant formalities which include taking the pass to the police station on the second floor of the port office to have it punched! Oh, by the way, the way the distance between the railway station and the port is about 200m and it is absolutely necessary to 'clock in' at least 3hrs before a ferry's departure otherwise passengers may be 'scratched' from the fixture list, have to rebook and pay again.

That is why the knowledgeable head for the other departure ports, more especially Ancona. Motorists should note that the signposting from the autoroute runs out failing to indicate the turn off to Ancona for the Ferry-boat Quay – it is the south exit. But once alongside the quay all the formalities for purchasing a ferry-boat ticket and currency exchange are conveniently to hand in the concourse of the very large, square Victorian, 'neo something' building, alongside the quay-side.

Those making the return boat journey from Greece to Italy must take great care when purchasing the ferry-boat tickets, especially at Igoumenitsa (Greek mainland). The competition is hot and tickets may well be sold below the published price. If so, and a traveller is amongst the 'lucky ones', it is best not to 'count the drachmae' until on board. The port officials carefully check tickets and if they find any that have been sold at a discount then they are confiscated and the purchaser is made to buy replacements at the full price. Ouch!

Passengers must steal themselves for the monumentally crass methods employed by the Italian officials to marshall the passengers prior to disembarking at the Italian ports. The delays and queues that stretch throughout the length of the boat's corridors appear to be quite unnecessary and can turn normally meek and mild people into raging psychopaths.

Sample Ferry-boat Services From Italy & Yugoslavia

From Italy:

Brindisi to Patras: (& vice versa)	(April-Oct) daily	Companies include:- Anco Ferries, 33 Akti Miaouli, 185 35 Piraeus. Tel(010301)4116917/4520135. CF Flavia & Flavia II

Sample ferry-boat fees To Patras:-		Low season	High season
per person:	deck from	5500drs	7500drs
	aircraft seats	6000drs	8500drs
	2/4 berth cabin c/w washbasin	7500drs	11000drs
	2 berth cabin c/w bathroom	12/15000drs	16/20000drs
cars (over 4¼m) Duration: 20hrs.		5000drs	8/10000drs

Brindisi to Igoumenitsa: (April-Oct) daily
& Patras: (& vice versa)

Companies include:-
Fragline, 5a Rethymnou St,10682 Athens
Tel(010301) 8214171/8221285.

Nausimar, 9 Filellinon St, 185 36 Piraeus.
Tel(010301) 452490
CF Igoumenitsa Express

Adriatic Ferries, 15-17 Hatzikyriakou Ave
185 37 Piraeus. Tel(010301) 4180584.
CF Adriatic Star

Agapitos Lines, 99 Kolokotroni St, 185
35 Piraeus. Tel(010301) 4136246.
CF Corfu Diamond & Sea.

HML, 28 Amalias Ave, Athens.
Tel (010301)3236333/4174341.
CF Egnatia, Castalia, Corinthia & Lydia.

Adriatica Naviagazione, 97 Akti Miaoili,
Piraeus. Tel(010301)4181901/3223693.
CF Appia & Espr. Grecia

Sample ferry-boat fees
To Igoumenitsa:-

per person:			Low season	High season
	deck	from	4/5000drs	6500drs
	aircraft seats		5500drs	7500drs
	2/4 cabin c/w washbasin		6/7000drs	10000drs
	2 berth cabin c/w bathroom		10/14000drs	14/19000drs
cars (over 4¼m) Duration; 11½ hrs			5000drs	8000drs

Ancona to Patras:
(& vice versa)

(April-Oct) Monday,
Wednesday, Friday
& Saturday

Karageorgis Lines, 26-28 Akti-Kondyli,
Piraeus. Tel (010301)4110461/4173001.
CF Mediterranean Sea & Sky

Sample ferry-boat fees
To Patras:-

per person:			Low season	High season
	deck	from	5700drs	7000drs
	aircraft seats		-	-
	2/4 berth cabin c/w washbasin		10400drs	12400drs
cars (over 4¼m) Duration: 35 hrs	2 berth cabin c/w bathroom		21400drs	25600drs

Ancona to Igoumenitsa
& Patras (& vice versa)

(May-June) Wednesday,
& Saturday
(June-Oct) Wednesday,
Thursday, Saturday,
& Sunday.
(May-Sept) Wednesday,
& Saturday
(July-Aug) Additionally
Sunday, Thursday,
& Friday
(April-May & October)
Monday,Tuesday,
& Thursday
(June-September)
Monday,Thursday
& Saturday
(July-Aug)
Monday,Tuesday,
Thursday & Saturday

Companies include:-
Minoan Lines, 2 Leoforos Vasileos,
Konstantinou, Athens.
Tel (010301) 7512356.
CF El Greco & Fedra

Marlines, 38 Akti Possidonos, 185 31
Piraeus. Tel (010301) 4110777
CF Princess M, Countess M & Queen M

Strintzis Lines, 26 Akti Possidonos,
185-31 Piraeus.Tel(010301)4129815
CF Ionian Sun, Star & Glory.

Sample ferry-boat fees
To Igoumenitsa:-

per person:			Low season	High season
	deck	from	4/5700drs	5/7000drs
	aircraft seats		5/6600drs	7/8000drs
	2/4 cabin c/w washbasin		7400drs	9400drs
	2 berth cabin c/w bathroom		12/16000drs	15/19600drs

cars (over 4¼m)
Duration: 24 hrs

Bari to Igoumenitsa & Patras:(& vice versa)	(mid-April) Wednesday & Friday (May)Friday & Sunday (June & Oct)Wednesday, Friday & Sunday (July-Sept) daily	Ventouris Ferries, 7 Efplias St, 185 37 Piraeus. Tel (010301) 4181001 CF Bari, Patra & Athens Express

Sample ferry-boat fees
To Igoumenitsa:-

per person:			Low season	High season
	deck	from	3400drs	5100drs
	aircraft seats		4100drs	6100drs
	2/4 cabin c/w washbasin		6800drs	9500drs
	2 berth cabin c/w bathroom		11500drs	15600drs
cars (over 4¼m)			4200drs	7500drs

Duration: 13 hrs.

Sample ferry-boat fees
To Patras:-

per person:			Low season	High season
	deck	from	4700drs	5800drs
	aircraft seats		5400drs	6800drs
	2/4 cabin c/w washbasin		7500drs	10800drs
	2 berth cabin c/w bathroom		12200drs	17700drs
cars (over 4¼m)			4200drs	9500drs

Duration: 20½ hrs.

From Yugoslavia

Dubrovnik to Igoumenitsa:(& vice versa)	(July-Aug) Monday, Tuesday & Thursday	Jadrolinja Line, c/o Hermes en Greece, 3 Iassonos St,185 37 Piraeus. Tel (010301)4520244.

Duration: 20 hrs.

Rijeka to Igoumenitsa:　　(July-Aug) Monday, Wednesday & Sunday

Duration; 43 hrs

Split to Igoumenitsa:　　(July-Aug) Monday. Tuesday & Thursday

Duration: 29 hrs.

Zadar to Igoumenitsa:　　(July-Aug) Tuesday

Duration: 36 hrs

Ferries that dock at Igoumenitsa can connect with Athens by scheduled bus services and those that dock at Patras connect with Athens by both scheduled bus and train services.

The Greek mainland ports of Igoumenitsa and Patras are detailed in **GROC's Candid Guide to Corfu & The Ionian Islands.**

Note the above services are severely curtailed outside the summer months, many ceasing altogether.

USEFUL NAMES & ADDRESSES
The Automobile Association, Fanum House, Basingstoke, Hants. RG21 2EA.   Tel (0256) 20123
AA Routes   Tel (0256) 492182
The Greek National Tourist Organisation, 195-197 Regent St, London WIR 8DL.
   Tel (01) 734 5997
The Italian State Tourist Office, 1 Princess St, London W1R 8AY.   Tel (01) 408 1254
The Yugoslavian National Tourist Office, 143 Regent St, London WIR 8AE.   Tel (01) 734 5243
British Rail Europe, PO Box 303, London SW1 1JY.
   Tel (01) 834 2345 *(Author's note – keep ringing)*
The Hellenic State Railways (OSE), 1-3 Karolou St, Athens, Greece. Tel (010301) 01 5222 491
Thomas Cook Ltd, Publications Dept, PO Box 36, Thorpewood, Peterborough PE3 6SB.
   Tel (0733) 63200

Other useful names & addresses mentioned in the text include:
Time Out, Southampton St, London WC2E 7HD.
Courier Flights/Inflight Courier, 45 Church St, Weybridge, Surrey KT13 8DG.
   Tel (0932) 857455/56
Owners Abroad Ltd, Valentine House, Ilford Hill, Ilford, Essex IG1 2DG.   Tel (01) 514 8844
Olympic Airways, 164 Piccadilly, London W1V 9DE.   Tel (01) 846 9080
Ref. 'Love-a-Fare'   Tel (01) 493 3965
Aegina Club Ltd, 25A Hills Rd, Cambridge CB2 1NW.   Tel (0223) 63256
Ramblers Holidays, 13 Longcroft House, Fretherne Rd, Welwyn Garden City, Herts AL8 6PQ.
Timsway Holidays, Penn Place, Rickmansworth, Herts. WD3 IRE   Tel (02404) 5541
Laskarina Holidays, St Mary's Gate, Wirksworth, Derbyshire, DE4 4DQ   Tel (062 982) 2203/4
Twelve Islands, Angel Way, Romford, Essex RM1 1AB   Tel (0708) 752653
The Best of Greece (Travel) Ltd, Rock House, Boughton Monchelsea, Maidstone, Kent ME17 4LY
   Tel (0622) 46678
STA Travel, 39 Store St, London WC1E 7BZ.   Tel (01) 580 7733
Victoria Travel Centre, 52 Grosvenor Gdns, London SW1   Tel (01) 730 8111
Transalpino, 214 Shaftesbury Ave, London WC2H 8EB.   Tel(01) 379 6735
London Student Travel, (Tel (01) 730 3402/4473) & Eurotrain, Tel (01) 730 6525), both at 52
Grosvenor Gdns, London SW1N 0AG.
Euroways Supabus, c/o Victoria Coach Station, London, SW1.   Tel (01) 730 0202
or c/o National Express Co.
The Greek address is: 1 Karolou St, Athens.   Tel (010301) 5240 519/6
Eurolines Intercars (Uniroute), 102 Cours de Vincennes, 75012 Paris (Metro Porte Vincennes)
National Express Co, Westwood Garage, Margate Rd, Ramsgate CT12 6S1.   Tel (0843) 581333
Consolas Travel, 29-31 Euston Rd, London NW1.   Tel (01) 833 2026
The Greek address is: 100 Eolou St, Athens.   Tel (010301) 3219 228

Amongst others the agencies and offices listed above have, over the years and in varying degrees, been helpful in the preparation of the guides. I would like to extend my sincere thanks to all those concerned. Some have proved more helpful than others!

Olympic Airways Overseas office addresses are as follows:
America: 647 Fifth Ave, New York, NY 10022.   Tel (0101 212)
   (Reservations) 838 3600
   (Ticket Office) 735 0290
Canada: 1200 McGill College Ave, Suite 1250, Montreal, Quebec H3B 4G7.
   Tel (0101 418) 878 9691
   80 Bloor St West, Suite 406 Toronto ONT M552VI.   Tel (0101 416) 920 2452
Australia: 44 Pitt St, 1st Floor, Sydney, NSW 2000.   Tel (01061 2) 251 2044
South Africa: Bank of Athens Buildings, 116 Marshall St, Johannesburg.
   Tel (010127 11) 836 5951
Denmark: 4 Jernbanegade DK 1608, Copenhagen.   Tel (010451) 126-100
Sweden: 44 Birger Jalsgatan, 11429 Stockholm.   Tel (010468) 113-800

More useful overseas names & addresses include:
Let's Go Travel Services, Harvard Student Agencies, Thayer Hall B, Harvard University; Cambridge,
MA02138 USA   Tel 617 495 9649
Canadian Universities Travel Service, 187 College St, Toronto ONT M5T IP7 Canada.
   Tel 417 979 2406
Automobile Association & Touring Club of Greece (ELPA), 2 Messogion Street, Athens.
   Tel (010301) 7791 615

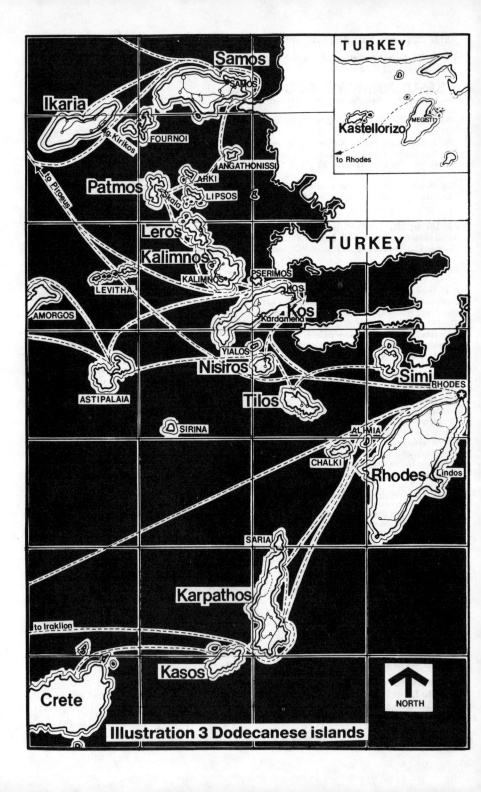

Illustration 3 Dodecanese islands

3 Travel Between Athens & the Dodecanese Islands

I see land. I see the end of my labour. Diogenes

The Greek islands are very thick on the water, numbering between 1000 and 3000, depending upon which authority you wish to believe. Approximately 100 are inhabited of which some 16 are located in the Dodecanese islands that I have chosen to agglomerate in the group. (Illustration 3).

In the past, the only way of setting foot on an island was to make for the relevant port and board a ferry-boat. Over the years a specialised and efficient system of water-borne travel developed. Apart from the advent of international air flights direct to the larger islands of Kos and Rhodes, the opening of a number of smaller airfields to take domestic flights has made it possible to fly to Athens and take a flight to the island of Karpathos, Kasos and Leros in addition to the aforementioned, larger islands. From Rhodes it is also possible to fly on to Kastellorizo.

BY AIR

It can prove difficult to obtain a seat for domestic flights on the spot, especially at the height of the tourist season as Greeks now utilise the services extensively. It may be preferable to forward book through a local Olympic office prior to arrival. Ferry-boat travel was always much cheaper than air flight but in recent years this differential all but disappeared. In some cases flying was even cheaper than a 3rd class ferry-boat ticket and certainly less expensive than a 2nd class fare. A savage price hike in air fares in mid-1986 restored the ferries economic advantage.

Travellers arriving in Athens, other than by aircraft, and wanting a domestic flight from the West airport, can catch one of the Olympic coaches or city buses to the airport. These depart from the Olympic terminal and offices, 96-100 (Leoforos) Sygrou and Syntagma Square – day and night at a cost of 80-120drs depending on the hour, compared to the 400-550drs charged by a taxi (*See* **Arrival By Air, Athens, Chapter Nine**). An irate reader has taken me to task for not pointing out that approximately an hour must be allowed between catching the airline bus and the relevant plane check-in time.

Many travellers do not wish to stop over in Athens. If this is the case, and arriving other than on an Olympic flight, it is possible to travel from the East to the domestic, West, airport using the connecting bus service.

The staff of Olympic, the Greek airline, are usually very helpful and their English good, although occasionally it is possible to fall foul of that sporadic Greek characteristic, intransigence. I remember arriving, heavily laden and tired, at the Athens Olympic offices very early one morning. On asking for advice about the location of a hotel, any hotel, I was politely directed, by the girl at the enquiries desk, to the Tourist police, which would have involved an uphill walk of at least 1¼km weighed down by an assortment of bags. There was a hotel, in which we stayed, immediately around the corner from the terminal!

It is worth considering utilising internal flights on one leg of a journey, especially if Athens is the point of arrival or departure. The possible extra cost of the flight, over and above the overland and ferry fares, must be balanced against the time element. For instance, Athens to Rhodes takes some 55 mins by air whilst the ferry takes about 19 hours. One other advantage of domestic air travel is that the fares can be paid for by the use of *American Express, Diners* or *Access Mastercard*, possibly saving precious drachmae, especially towards the end of a holiday. On the other hand, the cost of domestic flights has been steeply increased over the last couple of years, as have ferry-boat fares. The air fares uplift is such as to restore the old differentials of ferry-boat travel being about 50% cheaper than flying.

BY FERRY

In the following comments I am calling on my experience of travelling third and tourist class on any number of ferry boats.

In general, where sleeping arrangements are available and necessary they will prove satisfactory if certain basic rules are followed. First claim a bunk by depositing luggage on the chosen berth, it will be quite safe as long as money and passports are removed. The position of a berth is important and despite the labelling of 'Men' and 'Women' sleeping areas, a berth can usually be selected in either. Try to choose one adjacent to stern deck doors to ensure some ventilation. Due to the usual location of the third and tourist class accommodation beneath decks, it can get very hot and stuffy. A last tip is to lay a towel over plastic bunk covering to alleviate what otherwise would prove to be a sticky, uncomfortable night. Some ferries only have aircraft type, fold back seats in the 3rd/tourist class decks. Travellers should attempt, where possible, to find a lounge in which the television is muted.

The third class lavatories are often in an unsightly condition even prior to a craft's departure. To help enjoy reasonable surroundings and have the use of a shower, quietly proceed into the next class and use their facilities (but don't tell everybody). Both the toilets and the showers suffer from the usual deficiencies listed under **Greek Bathrooms, Chapter Four**, so be prepared.

Important points to take into account when inter-island ferry-boating include the following:

1. The ferries are owned by individual steamship companies and an employee of one line will be unable or unwilling to give enquirers information in respect of another company's timetable. Incidentally, this individual ownership results in a wide disparity in quality of service and general comfort between different ferry-boats.

2. The distances and voyage times are quite often lengthy and tiring. Additionally the duration of the overall passage sometimes (no always) results in the timetable going awry, with delays in scheduled departure times at islands well into a ferry's voyage.

3. There are usually four basic fare classes: first, second, tourist and third/deck class. The published fares on scheduled ferries are government controlled and the third/deck class option represents extremely good value. Purchasers must ensure that they state the fare class required as failure to do so may well result in a more expensive, tourist ticket being bought instead of the cheaper, deck class. Apart from the aforementioned four categories, there can be a variety of first and second-class sleeping accommodation, including private and shared cabins.

There are a number of 'Express' ferries and tourist trip boats, usually plying a particular island-to-island journey, on which charges are considerably higher.

4. Food and drink on the ferries used to be comparatively expensive, but price rises on the land have not been mirrored at sea. On the other hand the service on the older boats is often discourteous and inefficient, so it may be advantageous to pack provisions for a long voyage.

Wholesome and inexpensive ferry-boat picnic food includes: tomatoes, cucumber, bread, salami, ham, *Sunfix* orange juice and a bottle of wine (or two!).

Take some bottled water. Greek chocolate (especially with nuts) is very good but does not keep well in the ambient daytime temperatures.

5. The state of the toilets and the lack of basic supplies makes it mandatory that one or two lavatory rolls are packed, easily to hand as it were. The usual lack of washroom facilities commends the stowage of a pack of 'wipes'.

Quite frankly, on some occasions it will be necessary to stand on the rim of the toilet bowl as the only way of using the facility. Sorry!

6. Tickets should be purchased from a ticket agency prior to a voyage, as they can cost more when bought on board. Ticket agency offices vary from 'the plush' to boxed-in back stairs. Clients who have checked the scheduled prices should not go wrong. On the other hand they must be sure their price list is up to date as fare increases over recent years have been very large. For instance the 3rd class Piraeus to Rhodes charge increased from 1545drs to 2133drs between April 1985 and June 1987.

7. At the height of the season, the upper deck seats are extremely hot during the day and uncomfortably chilly at night. It is advisable to stake a claim to a seat as early as possible because the ferries are usually very crowded during the summer months. Voyagers who intend to lay out a sleeping bag and sleep the night away on the deck would do well to remember to occupy a seat, not the deck itself which is more often than not sluiced down in the night hours.

8. Travellers should ensure they have a good fat book and a pack of cards to while away the longer sea voyages. Despite the awesome beauty of the islands and the azure blue sea, there are often long, unbroken periods of Mediterranean passage to endure, interrupted only by the occasional passing ship and the dramatic activity and ructions that take place during a port call.

9. Travellers sensitive to discordancy, and who find disagreeable a cacophony, a clamour of sound, may well find unacceptable the usual raucous mix experienced in the average 3rd class lounge. This is auditory assault often embodies two televisions (tuned to different programmes, the picture constantly flickering, suffering a snowstorm or horizontally high jumping in a series of stills) overlaid by the wail of Greco-Turkish music piped over the ship's tannoy system. Best to fly!

One delight is to keep a weather eye open and hope to observe some dolphins diving and leaping in the ship's wake. Their presence is often made discernible by the loud slapping noise they make when re-entering the water.

Ferry-boaters must take care when checking the connections, schedules and timetables as they can, no do, change during the year, especially outside the inclusive months of May to September, as well as from one year to another. So be warned.

Do not forget, when the information is at it's most confusing, the Port police are totally reliable, but often a little short on English. Their offices are almost always on, or adjacent to the quayside.

For some years the Government, in an effort to promote tourism to selected, 'backwater' islands (who are the lucky ones), have offered free tickets during the out-of-season months of April/May and September/October. The Dodecanese passages included in this scheme are as follows:-

Rhodes to Chalki, Kasos, Kastellorizo and Tilos; Kalimnos to Pserimos (and Astipalaia); Patmos to Angathonisi and Lipsos as well as Kos to Nisiros. Be sure to enquire for these offers as they may well not be thrust upon one! The Rhodes to Kastellorizo 'freeby' applies from April all the way through to October.

Please refer to **Piraeus..., Chapter Ten**, and individual island chapters for full details of ferry-boat timetables.

Perhaps the most 'individual' craft that floats in the Dodecanese waters is the **FB Kyklades**, a stablemate of the 'incredible' **Miaoulis** delicensed in 1987 and about which I have written in more detail in **GROC's Candid Guide to the Cyclades**. This 'African Queen', no, no the redoubtable **Kyklades** describes a vast semicircular Aegean peregrination, setting out from Piraeus to finally dock at Kavala (M) some days later, only to retrace its 'footsteps'. Comparable to a modern-day, manned, *Flying Dutchman*, the **Kyklades** looms out of the sea only to as mysteriously disappear again. Due to the distances and numbers of ports involved in this weekly schedule, the craft tends to fall behind the official timetable, and that's being kind. In 1986 and some of 1987 this particular ferry-boat was out of action for a time and its promises, like those of a reluctant virgin, should be regarded with caution, if not disbelief! Well certainly all the information relating to the craft must be regarded with circumspection.

The **FB Nireas** has shabby Third class accommodation, in stark contrast to the lightly used and well-appointed First and Second class accommodation. It might be worth noting that tickets are rarely, if ever, checked... Additionally the decks are left very dirty. This is due to the lackadaisical attitude of the somewhat menacing and piratical crew who prefer to mingle with the passengers. They occasionally display their 'showbiz' abilities by swinging through the deck awning supports, and exhibit their romantic proclivities by pressing their attentions on some of the 'likely-looking' female travellers. On re-reading this cavil I realise it sounds rather old-maidish, but I can assure readers none of the gang made-off with my girl! The ridiculously small Third class snackbar does now serve a wider range of pies and pastries than a few years ago. To round off this 'state of the ferry art', the deck seating backrests have been cunningly installed in such a way as to ensure the maximum discomfort. In comparison the **CF Omiros** and **Alcaeos** are very pleasant, spacious, comfortable craft with a large cafeteria serving a variety of meals at reasonable prices. The **CF Kamiros** and **Ialysos** are acceptable apart from the toilets which quickly degenerate into a disgusting shambles. There are good TV lounges, as well as reasonably priced bars and self-service cafeterias on both craft. The **FB Panormitis** is a small, hardy, tough little ship, rather more like a cargo boat than a passenger ferry. Passengers, for whom facilities are minimal, tend to be crammed into the few seats, rather like cattle. On the other hand it is difficult not to take to the craft. Certainly the inhabitants of the smaller islands in the Dodecanese chain regard the Panormitis as a lifeline – so much so that they cross themselves, saying 'God speed the Panormitis' as it sails out of port. The captain and crew manage to stick rigidly to the timetable – a most unusual feat. The **CF Golden Vergina** was probably built for international journeys as it possesses an aft deck swimming pool (unfortunately out of commission) as well as many other larger craft facilities.

FLYING DOLPHINS (Hydrofoils – Ceres)

These speedy craft cut the ferry-boat timetables in half but the fares are about double.

CRUISE SHIPS

Fly/cruise packages on offer are usually rather up-market and, in the main, are based on seven days or multiples thereof. The cruise ships call in at selected islands for a part or full day, with excursions where applicable.

Other holiday-makers should note that the large influx of this 'genus' of fun loving tourist can have quite an impact on an island, and the *cognoscenti* normally vacate the particular port of call for that day.

GREEK ISLAND PLACE NAMES

This is probably the appropriate place to introduce the forever baffling problem which helps to bedevil the traveller – Greek place names. For instance, the island of Rhodes may well be designated Rodos. The reason for the apparently haphazard nomenclature lies in the long and complicated territorial ownership of Greece and its islands, more especially the latter. The base root may be Greek, Latin, Turkish or Venetian. Additionally the Greek language has three forms – Demotic (spoken), Katharevousa (literary) and Kathomiloumeni (compromise), of which Demotic and Katharevousa have each been the official linquistic style. Even as recently as 1967-74 the *Colonels* made Katharevousa, once again, the authorised form, but Demotic is now the approved language. Help!

Street names can be equally confusing and I have plumped for my personal choice sometimes stating the alternatives, but where this is not possible, well, there you go! I mean how can Athens' main square, Syntagma be spelt Syntagina, Sintagma or Syntagmatos?

Hotel and pension titles often give rise to some frustration where a Guide has listed the Roman scripted appellation. For instance to the (vast majority of the) uninitiated, *Hotel* Αυλη does not at first, second or third sight look like *Avli*, does it?

Due to scholastic, critical comments I must defend my habit of mixing Roman and Greek script when referring to establishment and street names. For example, I may write the Greek ΑΚΤΗ ΕΘΝΙΚΗΣ ΑΝΤΙΣΤΑΣΗΣ, which translates to the Roman *Akti Ethnikis Antistasis*. My only defence is that 99.9% of readers transmit that which they see to the brain without being able to make the mental gymnastics necessary to substitute the different letters. This is markedly so in respect of those letters that have no easy or direct equivalent. Will my more erudite friends excuse the rest of us dyslexic Grecophiles!

Street names are subject to some obscurity as the common noun Odhos (street) is often omitted, whilst Leoforos (avenue) and Plateia (square) are usually kept in the name. The prefix Saint or St is variously written as Agios, Ayios, Ag or Ai. A *nome* approximates to a small English county, a number of which make up a province such as the Peloponnese or Thessaly.

At this stage, without apologies, I introduce my own definition to help identify an unspoilt Greek town as follows: *where the town's rubbish is collected by donkey, wooden panniers slung across its back, slowly clip-clopping up a stepped hillside street, the driver, not even in sight but probably languishing in a stray taverna!*

Map nomenclature	Greek	Translation
Agios/Ag/Ayios/Aghios	Αγιος	Saint
Akra/Akrotiri	Ακρωτηρι	Cape/headland
Amoudia		Beach
Ano	Ανω	Upper
Archeologikos (horos)	Αρχαιολογικος	Ancient (site)
Cherssonissos		Peninsula
Chora/Horo/Horio/khorio	Χωριο	Village
Kato	Κατω	Lower
Kiladi		Valley
Klimaka		Scale
Kolpos	Κολπος	Gulf
Leoforos	Λεωφορος	Avenue
Limni	Λιμνη	Lake/marsh
Limani	Λιμανι	Harbour
Lofos		Hill

Moni/Monastiri	Μοναστηρι	Monastery
Naos	Ναος	Temple
Nea/Neos	Νεο	New
Nissos/Nissi	Νησος	Island
Odhos/Odos	Δρομος (Οδος)	Street
Ormos	Ορμος	Bay
Oros	Ορος	Mountain
Palios/Palaios	Παλιος	Old
Paralia		Seashore/beach
Pediada		Plain
Pelagos		Sea
Pharos		Lighthouse
Pigi		Spring
Plateia	Πλατεια	Square
Potami	Ποταμι	River
Prokimea		Quay
Spilia	Σπηλια	Cave
Steno		Straight
Thalassa		Sea
Vuno	Βουνο	Mountain

Useful Greek

English	Greek	Sounds like
Where is...	Που ειναι	Poo eene...
...the Olympic Airways office	τα γραφεια της Ολυμπιακης	...ta grafia tis Olimbiakis
...the railway station	ο σιδηροδρομικος σταθμος	...sidheerothromikos stathmos
...the bus station	ο σταθμος των λεωφορειων	...stathmos ton leoforion
...the boat	το πλοιο	...to plio
...the nearest underground station	ο πλησιεοτερος σταθμος του ηλεκτρικοο	...o pleessiestehros stathmos too eelektrikoo
...the ticket office	το εκδοτηριο των εισιτηριων	...to eckdhoterio ton eessitirion
...the nearest travel agency	το πλησιεστεπο πρακτορεον ταξιδιων	...to pleessiestehro praktorion taxidion
I'd like to reserve...	Θελω να κρατησω	Thelo na kratiso
...seat/seats on the	θεση/θεση για	...thessee/thessis ghia
...to	για	...ghia
...plane	αεροπλανο	...aeroplano
...train	τραινο	...treno
...bus	λεωφορειο	...leoforio
...ferry-boat	πλοιο	...plio
When does it leave/arrive	Ποτε φευγει/φθανει	Poteh fehvghi/fthanee
Is there...	Υπαρχει	Eeparhee...
...from here to	απ εδωστο	...Apetho sto
...to	στον	...ston
Where do we get off	Που κατεβαινομε	Poo katevenomhe
I want to go to	Θελω να παω στους	Thelo na pao stoos...
I want to get off at	Θελω να κατεβω στο	Thelo na katevo sto...
Will you tell me when to get off	Θα μου πειτε που να κατεβω	Thah moo peete poo nah kahtevo
I want to go to...	Θελω να παω στους	Thelo na pao stoos
Stop here	Σταματα εδω	Stamata etho
How much is it	Ποσο ειναι	Posso eene
How much does it cost ...to	Ποσο κανει η μεταφορα στο	Posso kani i metafora ...sto
Do we call at	Θα σταματησωμε στην	Tha stamatissome stin

Signs often seen affixed to posts & doors

Greek	English
ΑΦΙΞΙΣ	ARRIVAL
ΑΝΑΧΩΡΗΣΙΣ	DEPARTURE
ΣΤΑΣΙΣ	BUS STOP
ΕΙΣΟΔΟΣ	ENTRANCE
ΕΞΟΔΟΣ	EXIT
ΚΕΝΤΡΟ	CENTRE (as in town centre)
ΕΙΣΟΔΟΣ ΕΛΕΥΘΕΡΑ	FREE ADMISSION
ΑΠΑΓΟΡΕΥΕΤΑΙ Η ΕΙΣΟΔΟΣ	NO ENTRANCE
ΕΙΣΙΤΗΡΙΑ	TICKET
ΠΡΟΣ ΤΑΣ ΑΠΟΒΑΘΡΑΣ	TO THE PLATFORMS
ΤΗΛΕΦΩΝΟΝ	TELEPHONE
ΑΝΔΡΩΝ	GENTLEMEN
ΓΥΝΑΙΚΩΝ	LADIES
ΑΠΑΓΟΡΕΥΕΤΑΙ ΤΟ ΚΑΠΝΙΣΜΑ	NO SMOKING
ΤΑΜΕΙΟΝ	CASH DESK
ΤΟΥΑΛΕΤΕΣ	TOILETS
ΑΝΟΙΚΤΟΝ	OPEN
ΚΛΕΙΣΤΟΝ	CLOSED
ΩΘΗΣΑΤΕ	PUSH
ΣΥΡΑΤΕ	PULL

4 Island Accommodation

How doth man by care oppressed, find in an inn a place of rest. Combe

Package villa and tour organised holiday-makers will have accommodation arranged prior to arrival in Greece. In contrast, the most important matter to the independent traveller, is undoubtedly the procurement of lodgings, especially the first overnight stay on a new island or at an untried location.

The choice and standard of accommodation is bewildering, ranging from extremely simple Rooms, in private houses (usually clean but with basic bathroom facilities), even to luxury class, almost indecently plush hotels able to hold their own with the most modern counterpart, almost anywhere else in the world. The deciding factor must be the budget and a person's sensibilities. My comments in respect of standards reflect comparisons with Western European establishments. Those referring to prices are usually in relation to other Greek options.

Travellers stepping off a ferry-boat are usually part of a swarming throng made up of Greeks, tourists and backpackers engulfed by a quayside mass of Greeks, tourists and backpackers struggling to get aboard the same craft. Visitors may well be approached by men, women and youngsters offering accommodation. It is a matter of taking pot-luck there and then, or searching around the town to make an independent selection. The later in the day, the more advisable it is to take an offer, unseen, but it is obligatory to establish the price, if the rooms are with or without a shower, is the water hot and how far away they are located. It can prove unnerving to be 'picked up' and then commence on an ever-lengthening trudge through the back streets of a strange place, especially as Greek ideas of distance are rather optimistic.

Any accommodation usually requires a traveller's passport to be relinquished. As a passport is also required to change money and to hire a car or a scooter, it is a good idea, if married or travelling with friends, to have separate documents. Then, if necessary, one passport can be left with the landlord and another kept for other purposes, as required.

Official sources and many guidebooks lay much emphasis on the role of the Tourist police in finding accommodation, but this cannot be relied upon as the offices may well be closed on arrival. Moreover changes in the structure of the various police forces over the last few years has resulted in the once separate and independent Tourist police being integrated with the Town police. I for one regard this as a very retrograde step. Such a pity that the Greeks, innovators of this excellent service, should now abandon the scheme, more especially in the light of the ever increasing number of tourists. Perhaps having achieved their goal of ensuring Greece is a number one holiday spot, the authorities are allowing the tour guides and couriers (that go 'hand in sand' with the ever increasing number of package tourists) to take over the Tourist police role in an *ex officio* capacity? Preposterous! I hope so.

A fruitful source of accommodation leads are tavernas, which more often than not, result in an introduction to a Room or pension owner. Failing that, they usually send out for someone.

BEDROOMS
Greek bedrooms tend to be airy, whitewashed and sparsely furnished. The beds are often hard, as are the small pillows, and unyielding mattresses may well be laid directly on to bed-boards, not springs.

It is advisable to inspect bedroom walls for the evidence of blood-red splats. These indicate flattened, but once gorged, mosquitoes and result from a previous occupant's night-time vigil. Well designed rooms usually have a top-opening window screened off with gauze so that they can be left ajar without fear of incursions by winged, creepy-crawlies. Where no gauze is in evidence, it is best to keep the windows tightly closed at night, however alien this may be. Those not in possession of a proprietary insect repellent may well have to reconcile themselves to a sleepless night. Tell-tale buzzing echoing in the ears indicates one has already been bitten. It is comparable to being attacked by Lilliputian Stuka night-fighters.

Hanging points are noticeable by their absence. Often there will be no wardrobe but if present, there is unlikely to be any hangers, not even the steel-wire type, and the cupboard doors may be missing. A rather idiosyncratic feature is that clothes hooks, when present, are often very inadequate, looking as if they have been designed, and are only suitable for, hanging coffee mugs by the handles.

Even more maligned and even more misunderstood than Greek food is:

THE GREEK BATHROOM

I use the descriptive word bathroom, rather than refer simply to the toilets, because the total facility requires some elucidation. The following will not apply to Luxury, Class A or B hotels – well, it should not!

The plumbing is quite often totally inadequate. Instead of the separate wastes of the bath, shower and sink being plumbed into progressively larger soil pipes, thus achieving a 'venturi' effect, they are usually joined into a similar diameter tube to that of the individual pipes. This inevitably causes considerable back pressure with inescapable consequences. If this were not sufficient to cause a building inspector (who?) nightmares, where 'Mama' owns a washing machine it is invariably piped into the same network. That is why the drain grill, cunningly located at the highest point of the bathroom floor, often foams. The toilet waste is almost always insufficient in size and even normal, let alone excessive, use of toilet paper results in dreadful things happening, not only to the bathroom, but probably to a number of bathrooms in the building, street and possibly the village. If this were not enough... the header tank rarely delivers sufficient 'flush'. It has to be pointed out that Greeks have had, for many years, to be economic in the use of water and some islands ration it, turning off the supply for a number of hours per day, in the height of the summer.

Common faults are to find the lavatory without a seat; flooded to a depth of some inches; the bathroom light not working; no toilet roll; door locks not fitted as well as dirty WC pans and or any combination of the above. Furthermore, the wash basin may well be without a drain plug. Amongst other reasons, the lack of a plug is to stop flooding if a sink tap is accidently left turned on when the mains water is switched off, and not turned off when the water supply is resumed!

The most common type of en suite bathroom is an all purpose lavatory and shower room. Beware! Years of research reveals that the shower head is usually positioned in such a way as to not only wash down the occupant but to drench the (amazingly) absorbent toilet roll as well as the bathers clothes, towel and footwear. Incidentally, the drain point is usually located in such a way as to ensure that the bathroom is kept awash to a depth of between 1' and 3' ... and the resultant pool invariably lies where a toilet sitter's feet fall – if you read my meaning.

It is not unusual for there to be no hot water, even if a heating system is in evidence. Government energy conservation methods, the comparatively high cost of electricity and the use of moderately sized solar heating panels, all contribute to this state of affairs. Where solar panels are the means of heating the water, remember to beat the rush and shower as early as possible, for the water soon loses its heat. Why not share with a friend? If hot water is available, but it is not heated by solar energy, then it will be necessary to locate the relevant electric switch. This is usually a 4 way position, ceramic knob hidden away behind a translucent panel door. On the other hand... To be fair to owners of accommodation, it is standard practice to charge for the use of hot water showers so it pays the landlord to have the switch out of sight and reach. Room charges may well be increased by 50 to 100drs per day, per head, for the use of a shower, but this ought to be detailed on the Government controlled price list that should be displayed, and is usually suspended on the back of the bedroom door.

One stipulation on water-short islands that really offends the West European (and North American?) sense of delicacy, is the oft present, hardly legible sign, requesting guests to put their 'paper' in the wastebin supplied, and not down the pan! I must own up to not always obeying this dictum and have had to make a hurried departure from a number of islands, let alone a pension or village, when the consequences of my profligate use of toilet paper have become apparent.

THE BEACH
Some backpacking youngsters utilise the shore for their night's accommodation. In fact all island ferry-boaters must be prepared to consider the beach as a standby at the more crowded locations during the months of July and August. I have only had to spend two or three nights on the beach in the eight or nine years of island excursions but admit to steering clear of the height of season months of late July, August and early September. Certainly the weather could not be more ideal for sleeping under the stars, the officials are generally not too fussed and may well direct travellers to a suitable spot. Beware of mosquitoes and tar.

CAMPING
In direct contrast to *ad hoc* sleeping on the beach beneath the stars, camping, except at approved sites, is strictly forbidden. The law is not always rigorously applied. The restriction comes about from a wish to improve general hygiene, to prohibit and discourage abuse of private property and as a precaution against forest fires. The NTOG operate most of the licensed sites, some of which are spectacularly located, but there are some authorised, privately run camping grounds, which are also price controlled. A *Carnet-Camping International*, although not normally requested, affords campers worldwide, third-party liability cover and is available to United Kingdom residents from the AA and other, similar organisations.

If moved on by any official for sleeping out on the beach or illegally camping, it is advisable not to argue and go quietly. The Greek police have fairly wide, autonomous powers and it is preferable not to upset them unnecessarily.

As a guide, overnight campsite fees are charged as follows:
Adults 290-400drs; children $\frac{1}{2}$ adult rate and tent hire 400-550drs.

YOUTH HOSTELS (ΞΕΝΩΝΑΣ ΝΕΩΝ)
Establishments in Athens include the *YMCA (XAN)* and *YWCA (XEN)* as well as the *YHA*, which also has one or three outposts on the islands. The appellation more often than not is applied to ethnic private pensions catering for young travellers. They are habitually are rather down-at-heel and tend to be operated in a somewhat Spartan, slovenly manner.

It is preferable to have YHA membership, taking the Association's card along.

Approximate prices per night at the YMCA and YWCA are 900drs and in a Youth Hostel 400-450drs.

ROOMS

The story goes that as soon as a tourist steps off the ferry, he (or she) is surrounded by women crying *Rooms* (*Dhomatio*), and whoops, within minutes the traveller is ensconced in some wonderful Greek family's private home.

History may well have been like that, and in truth the ferries are still met at almost every island, the inhabitants offering not only rooms but pensions and the lower category hotels. Rooms are the cheapest accommodation and are generally very clean, sometimes including the option of breakfast, which is ordinarily charged extra. Prices reflect an island's popularity and the season, but the average 1987 mid-season cost in the Dodecanese was 1500drs for a double room, depending upon the classification.

Government approved and categorised rooms are subject to an official tariff, and are slightly more expensive than freelance householders. A general point relates to a cautionary tale told us by a delightful French couple. They were in the habit of replying to a room owner's enquiry as to how many nights they wished to stay by saying 'Tonight'. One lady room owner interpreted this to mean two nights! Beware the inaccurate translation.

At the more tourist popular island resorts a new, unwelcome phenomena has reared 'his' ugly head. This is the long stay, enterprising layabout who rents a large double or triple bedroom for the summer season from a hapless, unsuspecting owner of accommodation. The 'entrepreneur', a species to be avoided, then daily sublets out the room, cramming in some 5 or 6 a night.

Apart from a prospect being approached leaving the ferry, the Tourist police would, in the past, advise about available accommodation but their role is being drastically reduced in their amalgamation with the Town police. The Tourist police offices were signed, if at all; 'ΤΟΥΡΙΣΤΙΚΗ ΑΣΤΥΝΟΜΙΑ'. Householders display the sign 'ΕΝΟΙΚΙΑΖΟΝΤΑΙ ΔΩΜΑΤΙΑ' or simply 'ΔΩΜΑΤΙΑ', when they have a room to rent.

PENSIONS ('PANSION, ΠΑΝΣΙΟΝ')

This type of lodging was a natural progression from Rooms and now represents the most often found and reasonably priced accommodation on offer.

The older type of pension is rather reminiscent of those large Victorian English houses, split up into bed-sits. In the main though they have been purpose built, usually during the Colonels' regime (1967-74) when government grants were freely available for the construction of tourist quarters. The owner usually lives in the basement and acts as concierge. The rooms are functional and generally the guests on each level share a bathroom and shower and (a rather nice touch when provided) a communal refrigerator in which visitors can store their various provisions and drinks. Mid-season charges for 1987 varied between 1500 and 2000drs for a double room.

Sometimes a breakfast of coffee, bread and jam, perhaps butter and a boiled egg, is available for about 150drs and represents fair value compared with the cost of a cafe breakfast.

TAVERNAS (ΤΑΒΕΡΝΑ)

Tavernas are, first and foremost, eating places. Some tavernas, especially those situated by, or near, beaches, also have accommodation available. The only drawback is that the more popular the taverna, the less likely guests are to get a full night's sleep, but of course the more involved they will be with the taverna's social life which often continues into the small hours. Charges are similar to those of a Pension.

HOTELS (ΞΕΝΟΔΟΧΕΙΟΝ)

Shades of difference and interpretation can be given to the nomenclature by variations of the bland, descriptive noun hotel. For instance ΞΕΝΟΔΟΧΕΙΟΝ ΥΠΝΟΥ indicates a hotel that does not serve meals and ΠΑΝΔΟΧΕΙΟΝ a low grade hotel.

Many independent travellers would not consider hotels as a first choice. The high classification ones are more expensive than Pensions and the lower grade hotels often cost the same, but may well be rather seedy and less desirable than the equivalent class pension. Greek hotels are classified L (Luxury) A, B, C, D and E and the prices charged within these categories (except L) are controlled by the authorities.

It is unfortunately almost impossible to neatly pigeon-hole and differentiate between hotels and their charges as each individual category is subject to fairly wide standards, and charges are dependent on a multitude of possible percentage supplements and reductions as detailed below:

Shower extra (C, D and E hotels); number of days stayed less than three, plus 10 per cent; air conditioning extra (A and B hotels); out of season deductions (enquire); high season extra (ie months of July, August and the first half of September, plus 20 per cent; single occupancy of a double room, about 80 per cent of the double room rate. The higher classification hotels may well insist on guests taking demi-pension terms, especially in high season.

The following table must be treated as a guide only but is based on 1988 prices.

Class	Comments	Indicated mid-season, double-bedroom price
L	All amenities, a very high standard and price. Probably at least one meal in addition to breakfast will have to be purchased. Very clean. Very hot water.	
A	High standard and price. Most rooms have an en suite shower or bath. Guests may well have to accept demi-pension terms. Clean Hot water.	6000-8000 drs
B	Good standard. Many rooms have an en suite shower or bath. Clean. Hot water.	4000-6000 drs
C	Usually an older hotel. Faded elegance, shared bathroom. Cleanish. Possibly hot water.	2000-4000 drs
D	Older, faded hotel. Shared bathroom, which may well be 'interesting'. A shower, if available, will be an 'experience' and the water cold.	1500-2500 drs
E	Old, faded and unclean. The whole stay will be an 'experience'. Only very cold water.	1200-1600 drs

The prices indicated include government taxes, service and room occupancy until noon.

Where in the text reference is made to 'official rates', these are the prices listed in the *Guide to the Greek Hotels*. Generally prices detailed throughout this guide are those applicable to 1987.

THE XENIAS

Originally government owned and promoted to ensure the availability of high standard accommodation at important tourist centres but now often managed by private enterprise. Only A, B and C rated categories, they are usually of a better standard than hotels in a similar class.

FLATS & HOUSES

During the summer months this type of accommodation, referred to by travel agents and package tour operators as villas, is best booked prior to arriving in Greece. Not only will pre-booking be easier but, surprisingly, works out cheaper than flying out and snooping around.

The winter is a different matter, but probably not within the scope of most of our readers.

Further useful names & addresses
The Youth Hostel Association, 14 Southampton St, London WC2E 7HY.   Tel. 01 836 8541

Useful Greek

English	Greek	Sounds like
I want...	Θελω	Thelo...
...a single room	ενα μονο δωματιο	...enna mono dhomatio
...a double room	ενα διπλο δωματιο	...enna thiplo dhomatio
...with a shower	με ντουζ	...me doosh
We would like a room for...	Θα θελαμε ενα δωματιο για...	Tha thelame ena dhomatio ghia...
two/three days/a week/ until	δυο/τρειζ μερεζ/μια εβδομαδα/μεχρι	thio/trees meres/meea evthomatha/mekhri
Can you advise of another...	Ξερετε κανενα αλλο...	Xerete kanena alo...
house with rooms	σπιτι με δωματιο	speeti meh dhomatio
pension	πανσιον	panseeon
inn	πανδοχειο	panthokheeo
hotel	ξενοδοχειο	ksenodhokheeo
youth hostel	ξενωναζ νεων	xenonas neon
How much is the room for a night?	Ποσο κανει το δωματιο για τη νυχτα	Poso kanee dho dhomatio ghia ti neektah
That is too expensive	Ειναι πολυ ακριβα	Eene polee akriva
Have you anything cheaper?	Δεν εχετε αλλο πιο φθηνο	Dhen ekhete ahlo pio ftheeno
Is there...	Υπαρχει	Eeparkhee
a shower	ενα ντουζ	doosh
a refrigerator	ενα ψυγειο	psiyeeo
Where is the shower?	Που ειναι το ντουζ	Poo eene dho doosh
I have to leave...	Πρεπει να φυγω	Prepee na feegho...
today	σημερα	simera
tomorrow	αυριο	avrio
very early	πολυ νωρις	polee noris
Thank you for a nice time	Ευχαριστω για την συμπαθητικη ωρα*	Efkareesto ghia tin simpathitiki ora

*This is the exact translation, which would never be used, however, in Greek. An expression meaning rather: 'thanks for the fun' is:

	Ευχαριστω για την διασκεδαση	Efkaristo ghia tin thiaskethasi

5 Travelling around an island

A man is happier for life from having once made an agreeable tour. Anon

A few introductory remarks may well be apposite in respect of holiday-makers' possessions and women in Greece. The matter is discussed elsewhere but it is not out of place to reiterate one or two points (Rosemary calls it 'carrying on').

PERSONAL POSSESSIONS

Do not leave airline tickets, money, travellers' cheques and or passports behind at the accommodation. A man can quite easily acquire a wrist-strap handbag in which to conveniently carry these items. The danger does not, even today, lie with the Greeks, but with fellow tourists, down-and-outs and professional thieves working a territory.

WOMEN

There has been, in recent years, a movement towards the 'Spanish-Costa' percentage ploy. Young Greek men, in the more popular tourist areas, have succumbed to the prospects offered by the sexually liberated overseas women holiday-makers, especially those openly courting sun, sand and sex. Greek girls are still subject to rigorous parental control so it is not surprising that the local lads turn their attentions to other, possibly more fruitful, pastures. Greeks who indulge in this pastime are derogatorily referred to as *Kamaki* – 'spearers of game', after the traditional fishing trident. It's up to you girls, there is no menace, only opportunities!

Now back to the main theme of the chapter but before expanding on the subject a few words will not go amiss in respect of:

BEACHES

A surprisingly large number of beaches are polluted in varying degrees, mainly by seaborne plastic and some tar. Incidentally, olive oil is an excellent medium with which to remove this black menace which sticks to towels, clothes and shoes better than the proverbial .... to a blanket.

Lack of anything but a small rise and fall of tide removes the danger of swimmers being swept out to sea but, on windy days, the tug of the sea's undertow can be very strong.

Jellyfish and sea urchins can occasionally be a problem in a particular bay, jellyfish increasingly so. One of my Mediterranean correspondents advises me that cures for the jellyfish sting include ammonia, urine (ugh) and a paste of meat tenderiser (it takes all sorts I suppose).

The biggest headache (literally) to a tourist is the sun, or more accurately, the heat of the sun at the height of the summer season. To give an example of the extreme temperatures sometimes experienced, in Athens a few years ago birds were actually falling out of the trees, and they were the feathered variety! Every year dozens of tourists are carted off, suffering from acute sunburn. A little often, (sun that is), must be the watchword. The islands benefit from the relief of the prevailing summer wind, the *Meltemi*.

Whereas nudism was once severely punished by puritanical authorities, as long as tourists, who wish to sunbathe topless, bottomless or both, utilise those beaches allocated for the purpose, there will be no trouble. Over the years, as Greek families have increasingly appreciated the delights of the beach, even the young women have taken to going topless. It is very pleasant to observe more and more middle-aged Greek ladies taking to the sea, often in all enveloping black costumes and straw hats. Some, to preserve their modesty, appear to swim in everyday clothes.

Despite the utterly reasonable condemnation of modern day advances in technology by us geriatrics, one amazing leap forward for all travelling and beach bound mankind is the *Walk-Master* personal stereo-casettes. No more the strident, tinny beat of the transistor (or more commonly the 'ghetto-blaster'), now simply the jigging silence of ear-muffed and transfixed faces. Splendid!

It may well be that a reader is a devoted sun worshipper and spends every available minute on the beach, patio or terrace; if so there is no need to read any further. On the other hand when a holiday-maker's daytime interests range beyond conversion of the sun's rays into painful, peeling flesh, and there is a wish to travel around a particular island, then the question of *modus operandi* must be given some thought.

First, purchase an island map and one of the colourful and extremely informative tourist guides available on the larger islands. *Clyde Surveys* of Maidenhead produce an excellent map of Rhodes and the Dodecanese islands that can be purchased prior to departure. This series is now marketed by Bartholomews.

Having purchased the maps and guides it is necessary to consider the alternative methods of travel and appraise their value.

ROADS

The main roads of most islands are passable but asphalted country lanes often degenerate alarmingly, becoming nothing more than heavily rutted and cratered tracks. Generally much road building and reconstruction is under way. Beware as not all roads, indicated as being in existence on the maps, are anything more than, at the best, donkey tracks or are simply non-existent. Evidence of broken lines marking a road must be interpreted as meaning there is no paved highway at all.

ON FOOT

Owing to the hilly terrain of the islands and the daytime heat encountered, readers may well have had enough walking without 'looking for trouble'. A quick burst down to the local beach, taverna. shop or restaurant, and the resultant one hundred or so steps back up again, may well go a long way to satiating any desire to go 'walkies'. If needs be, walking is often the only way to negotiate the more rugged donkey tracks and the minimum footwear is a solid pair of sandals or 'trainers'. Plan not to walk during the midday hours, wear a hat, at least take along sufficient clothes to cover up should the sun prove too hot and pack a bottle of drinking water.

HITCHING

The comparative paucity of privately owned cars makes hitch-hiking an unsatisfactory mode of travel. On the other hand, if striking out to get to, or return from a particular village on a dead end road, most Greek drivers stop when thumbed down. It may well be a lift in the back of a Japanese pick-up truck, possibly sharing the space with some chickens, a goat or sheep or all three!

DONKEY

Although once a universal 'transportation module', now usually only available for hire on specific journey basis in particular locations. A personal prejudice is to consider donkey rides part of the unacceptable face of tourism, added to which it tends to be exorbitantly expensive.

BUSES

Buses (and taxis) are the universal method of travel in Greece, so the services are widespread if, naturally enough, a little Greek in operation. Generally they run approximately on time and the fares are, on the whole, extremely reasonable. Passengers must expect to share the available space with fairly bulky loads and occasionally, livestock.

The trick is to first find the square on which the buses terminus. Then locate the bus office where the tickets are pre-purchased and on the walls or windows of which might be stuck the timetable and the fares structure. The real fun starts if the bus is not only 'sardine packed', but fares are collected by a conductor who has to somehow make his way through, round and over the passengers. Be available well prior to the scheduled departure times as buses have a 'nasty habit' of departing early. Ensure any luggage is placed in the correct storage compartment for the particular destination otherwise it may go missing.

Buses are often crowded, especially when a journey coincides with a ferry-boat disgorging its passengers. The timetables are usually scheduled so that a bus or buses await a ferry-boat's arrival, except perhaps very early or late arriving craft. A bus rarely leaves a potential client standing, they just encourage everyone aboard.

Do not fail to observe the decorations festooned around and enveloping the driver. Often these displays resemble a shrine, which taking account of the way some of the drivers propel their bus, is perhaps not so out of place. Finally, do have some change available as coins are always in short supply. It is helpful to know that local buses may be labelled TOPIKO (ΤΟΠΙΧΟ).

A critic recently took me to task for not stressing that the summer bus schedules listed throughout the text are the subject of severe curtailment, if not total termination during the winter months from October through to May. So, smacked hand Geoffrey and readers please note.

TAXIS

As indicated in the previous sub-heading, taxis are the 'other' mode of island travel. They are usually readily available and can be remarkably modern and plush. On the other hand...

Ports and towns nearly always have a main square on which the taxis rank but come the time of a ferry-boat's arrival they queue on the quayside. Fares are governed by the local authorities and, at the main rank, are often displayed giving examples of the cost to various destinations. Charges are reasonable by European standards, but it is essential to establish the cost prior to hiring.

It may come as a shock for a 'fare' to have his halting, pidgin Greek answered in 'pure' Australian or American. But this is not surprising when one considers that many island Greeks have spent their youth on merchant ships or emigrated to the New World for 10 to 15 years. On their return home, with the future relatively financially secure, many take to taxi driving to supplement their income (and possibly to keep out of the little woman's way?).

BICYCLE, SCOOTER & CAR HIRE

Be very careful to establish what (if any) insurance cover is included in the rental fee, and that the quoted hire charge includes any compulsory taxes.

On the whole, bicycles are very hard work and poor value in relation to, say the cost of hiring a *Vespa* scooter – an option endorsed when the mountainous nature of most islands, and the midday heat, is taken into consideration. The once popular Italian machines are progressively being replaced by the ubiquitous, semi-automatic

Japanese motorcycles. Although the latter do away with the necessity to fight the gears and clutch, they are not entirely suited to transporting two heavyweights. I have had the frightening experience, when climbing a steep mountainside track, of the bike jumping out of gear, depositing my passenger and I on the ground leaving the scooter whirling found like a crazed mechanical Catherine wheel.

It is amazing how easy it is to get a good tan while scootering. The moderate wind draws the sun's heat, the air is laden with the smell of wild sage and oleanders and with the sun on one's back... marvellous!

Very rarely is a deposit requested when hiring a bike or motorbike but a passport is required. Always shop around to check out various companies' charges: the nearer to a port, town or city centre a hirer is, the more expensive the machines will be. Take a close look over the chosen mode of transport before settling up, as maintenance of any mechanical unit in Greece is poor to non-existent. Bicycles and scooters, a few years old, will be 'pretty clapped out'. A client must check the brakes, they will be needed, and should not allow the hirer to fob him off without making sure there is a spare wheel.

Increasingly, the owners of two wheeled vehicles are hiring out dubious looking crash helmets. Flash young Greek motorbike riders usually wear their 'Space Age' headgear on the handlebars, where no doubt it will protect them (that is the handlebars) from damage. A useful tip when hiring a scooter is to take along a towel! It doubles up as useful additional padding for the pillion passenger's bottom on rocky roads and saves having to sit on painfully hot plastic seating should a rider forget to raise the squab when parked. Sunglasses are necessary to protect the eyes from airborne insets. Out of the height-of-season and early evening it becomes very chilly so a sweater or jumper is a good idea and females may well require a headscarf, whatever the time of day or night.

Fuel is served in litres and five litres of two-stroke costs about 320-340drs. Fill up as soon as possible as fuel stations are in fairly 'short supply' outside the main towns. Increasingly the gap between the scooter and the car is being filled with more sophisticated machinery which include moon-tyred and powerfully engined Japanese motorbikes and beach-buggies.

Typical daily hire rates are: for a bicycle 250drs; a Vespa scooter 1500-2000drs; a car from 5000drs including full insurances and taxes but mileage may cost extra, calculated at so much per kilometre. Out of season and period hire for all forms of conveyance can benefit from 'negotiation'. Car hire companies require a daily deposit, which now starts off at 20,000drs per day, as well as a hirer's passport and driving licence details. Due to this large outlay it is almost mandatory to pay by credit card, which all car hire companies 'gratefully grab'. It is noticeable that I and many readers regard car hire as a legalised rip-off. One contentious area that causes unpleasant disputes is the increasing habit of the hire companies to charge comparatively expensively for any damage incurred, and I mean any damage, however slight. A hirer's detailed reasons for the causes of an accident, the damage and why it should not cost anything falls on deaf ears. Furthermore it is no use threatening to involve the police as they will not be at all interested in the squabble.

Several other words of warning might not go amiss. Taking into account the uncertain state of the roads, do not hire a two-wheeled conveyance if not thoroughly used to handling one. There are a number of very nasty accidents every year, involving tourists and hired scooters. Additionally the combination of poor road surfaces and usually inadequate to non-existent vehicle lights should preclude any night-time scootering. A hirer must ensure he (or she) is fully covered for medical insurance, including an unscheduled, *Medicare* flight home, and do check, before leaving the home shores, that a general holiday policy does not exclude accidents incurred on hired transport, especially scooters.

The glass-fronted metal framed shrines mounted by the roadside are graphic reminders of a fatal accident at this or that spot. Incidentally, on a less macabre note, if the shrine is a memorial to a man, the picture and bottle often present (more often than not of Sophia Loren and whisky) represent that person's favourite earthbound desires.

But back to finger-wagging. The importance of the correct holiday insurance cover cannot be over-stressed. The tribulations I have encountered in obtaining inclusive insurance, combined with some readers' disastrous experiences, have resulted in the inclusion in the guide of an all embracing scheme. This reminder should be coupled with the strictures in **Chapter One** drawing attention to the all-inclusive policy devised for readers of the **Candid Guides**. Enough said!

More useful names & addresses

Clyde Surveys Ltd, Reform Road, Maidenhead, Berks SL6 8BU   Tel (0628) 21371
Efstathiadis Group, 14 Valtetsiou St, Athens   Tel 3615 011

Useful Greek

English	Greek	Sounds like
Where can I hire a...	Που μπορώ να νοικιάσω ένα	Poo boro na neekeeaso enna...
...bicycle	ποδήλατο	...pothilato
...scooter	σκούτερ	...sckooter
...car	αυτοκίνητο	...aftokinito
I'd like a...	Θα ήθελα ένα	Tha eethela enna...
I'd like it for...	Θα το ήθελα για	Tha dho eethela ghia...
...a day	μία μέρα (or: μιά)	...mia mera
...days	μέρες	...meres
...a week	μία εβδομάδα	...mia evthomadha
How much is it by the...	Πόσο κάνει την	Poso kanee tin...
...day	μέρα	...mera
...week	εβδομάδα	...evthomadha
Does that include...	Συμπεριλαμβάνονται σαυτό	Simberilamvanonte safto
...mileage	τα χιλιόμετρα	...tah hiliometra
...full insurance	μικτή ασφάλεια	...meektee asfaleah
I want some	Θέλω	Thelo
...petrol (gas)	βενζίνης	...vehnzini
...oil	λάδι	...lathi
...water	νέρο	...nero
Fill it up	Γεμίστε το	Yemiste to
...litres of petrol (gas)	λίτρα βενζίνης	...litra vehnzinis
How far is it to...	Πόσο απέχει	Poso apechee
Which is the road for...	Ποιός είναι ο δρόμος για	Pios eene o thromos ghia
Where are we now	Που είμαστε τώρα	Poo eemaste tora
What is the name of this place	Πώς ονομάζεται αυτό το μέρος	Pos onomazete afto dho meros
Where is...	Που είναι	Poo eene...

Road Signs

ΑΛΤ	STOP
ΑΠΑΓΟΡΕΥΕΤΑΙ Η ΕΙΣΟΔΟΣ	NO ENTRY
ΑΔΙΕΞΟΔΟΣ	NO THROUGH ROAD
ΠΑΡΑΚΑΜΠΤΗΡΙΟΣ	DETOUR
ΕΛΑΤΤΩΣΑΤΕ ΤΑΧΥΤΗΤΑΝ	REDUCE SPEED
ΑΠΑΓΟΡΕΥΕΤΑΙ Η ΑΝΑΜΟΝΗ	NO WAITING
ΕΡΓΑ ΕΠΙ ΤΗΣ ΟΔΟΥ	ROAD REPAIRS
ΚΙΝΔΥΝΟΣ	BEWARE (Caution)
ΑΠΑΓΟΡΕΥΕΤΑΙ ΤΟ ΠΡΟΣΠΕΡΑΣΜΑ	NO OVERTAKING
ΑΠΑΓΟΡΕΥΕΤΑΙ Η ΣΤΑΘΜΕΥΣΙΣ	NO PARKING

6 Island Food & Drink

Let us eat and drink for tomorrow we die. Corinthians

It is a pity that many tourists, prior to visiting Greece, have, in sundry restaurants throughout Europe and North America, 'experienced' the offerings masquerading as Greek food. Greek food and drink does not appear to cross its borders very well. I do not think it is possible to recreate the unique quality of Greek cooking in foreign lands. Perhaps this is because they owe much of their taste to, and are in sympathy with, the very air laden with the scent of the flowers and herbs, the very water, clear and chill, the very soil of the plains and scrub clad mountains, the ethereal and uncapturable quality that is Greece. Incidentally, many critics would postulate that it was impossible to create Greek food, full stop, but be that as it may...

Salad does not normally send me into ecstasy but, after a few days in Greece, the very thought of a peasant salad, consisting of endive leaves, sliced tomatoes and cucumber, black olives, olive oil and vinegar dressing, all topped off with feta cheese and sprinkled with oregano, parsley or fennel, sends me salivating to the nearest taverna.

Admittedly, unless you are lucky enough to chance across an outstanding taverna, the majority are surprisingly unadventurous and the choice of menu limited. Mind you there are one or two restaurants serving exciting and unusual meals, if the spelling mistakes are anything to go by. For instance I have observed over the years the following no doubt appetising dishes: *omeled, spachetti botonnaise, shrings salad, bowels entrails, lump cutlets, limp liver, mushed pot, shrimps, crambs, kid chops, grilled meatbolls, spar rips, wine vives, fiant oven, swardfish, pork shops, staffed vine leaves, wild greens, string queens, wildi cherry, bater honi, gregg goti (!), mate with olive oil, bruised meat, forced meat balls, Creek salad, lamp kebab ....with rise, personal shrimps, mutton bowels served with pice, beef shoup, lame liver, intest liver, cububer, scorpines, chickey, greef beans, fried pataroes, bems giauts, veal roast in kettle, loveubrawn, walout kake, honey boiles, various complex (in the coffee section) and et cetera* – don't they sound interesting.

On a more positive note, whilst the usual dishes will be known to readers, a recommendation, a mention of a dish I haven't seen before and a 'musing' may not go amiss. As to the recommendation, where an eating house serves up a good creamy tzatziki and a Greek salad it makes a very refreshing dish to combine the two. Latterly I came across a meal I have not encountered previously, saganaki. This is a very tasty dish of scrambled egges/omelette in which are mixed sliced bacon and or sausage, all cooked in an olive oil greased 6' pan. The ruminative, brown study relates to the humble potato. Why, oh why, taking into account the copious plates of *patatas* available (thus proving the existence in quantity of the aforesaid tuber), are there no variations on the theme? Where are, oh where are mashed, roast or creamed potatoes to, once in a while usurp the omnipresent, universal chip?

A FEW HINTS & TIPS

Do not insist upon butter, the Greek variant is not very tasty to the European palate, is expensive and in the heat tends to dissolve into greasy pools.

Sample the retsina wine and after a bottle or two a day for a few days there is every chance you will enjoy it. Moreover, retsina is beneficial (well that's what I tell myself), acting as a splendid anti-agent to the comparative oiliness of some of the food.

Bread is automatically served with a meal – and charged for – unless a diner indicates otherwise. It is very useful for mopping up excess olive oil and thus requires no butter to make it more greasy. It has become a noticeable, and regrettable, feature in recent years that the charge for bread has increased to between 10 and 30drs per head, and I have seen it as high as 40drs. Naughty! Many eateries have developed the nasty little habit of lumping an extra tax calculation in with the bread charge, that is extra to the usual tax inclusive prices listed on the menu.

Greek food tends to be served on the 'cool' side. Even if the meal started out hot, and by some mischance is speedily served, it will arrive on a thoroughly chilled plate.

The selection of both food and drink is almost always limited and unenterprising unless diners elect to frequent the more international restaurants (but why go to Greece?). On the other hand the choice of establishments in which to eat and or drink is unlimited, in fact the profusion is such that it can prove very confusing. If in doubt about which particular restaurant or taverna to patronise, use the well tried principle of picking one frequented by the locals. It will invariably serve good quality food at reasonable prices. It is generally a waste of time to ask a Greek for guidance in selecting a good taverna or restaurant as he will be reluctant to give specific advice in case the recommendation proves unsatisfactory.

Especially in the more rural areas, do not be shy, ask to look over the kitchen to see what's cooking. If denied this traditional right, be on your guard as the food may well be pre-cooked, tasteless and plastic, particularly if the various meals available are displayed in a neon-lit showcase. Do not order the whole meal all at once, as would be usual at home. If you do it will be served simultaneously and or in the wrong sequence. Order course by course and take your time, everyone else does. Diners are not being ignored if the waiter does not approach the table for anything up to 20 minutes, he is just taking his time and is probably overworked. At first the blood pressure may inexorably rise as your presence appears to be continually disregarded but it makes a visitor's stay in Greece very much more enjoyable if all preconceived ideas of service can be forgotten. Lay back and settle into the glorious and indolent timelessness of the locals' way of life. If in a hurry, pay when the order arrives for if under the impression that it took a disproportionate time to be served, just wait until it comes to settling up. It will probably take twice as long to get the bill (*logariasmo*) as it did to receive the food.

Chicken, when listed, is usually served with some chips. Fish, contrary to expectations, appears very expensive, even in comparison with European prices, so you can imagine the disparity with the cost of other Greek food. When ordering fish it is normal to select the choice from 'the ice' and, being priced by weight, it will be put on the scales prior to cooking. This is the reason that fish is listed at so many drachmae per kilo, which does reduce the apparently outrageous price just a little. If seeking 'cost conscious' meals, and wishing for a change from the ubiquitous moussaka, beef steak, or for that matter, chicken and chips, why not plump (!) for *kalamari* (squid). Even at present day, inflated prices they usually provide a filling, tasty, low budget cost meal at 250-350drs. It has to be admitted that demand has resulted in the more popular locations and areas serving up imported Mozambique squid. These can often be recognised by their regular shape and sweet taste – probably suiting less demanding palettes very well. From the late summer months locally caught kalamares tend to be large and knobbly.

Government price lists are a legal necessity for drinking and eating places. They should state the establishment's category and the price of every item served. Two prices are shown, the first being net is not really relevant, the second, showing the price actually charged, includes service and taxes.

Food is natural and very rarely are canned or any frozen items used, even if available. When frozen foods are included in the meal the fact must be indicated on the menu by addition of the initials *KAT*. The olive oil used for cooking is excellent, as are the herbs and lemons, but it can take time to become accustomed to the different flavours imparted to food. Before leaving the subject of hints and tips, remember that olive oil can be pressed into service for removing unwanted beach tar from clothes.

A most enjoyable road, quayside or ferry-boat breakfast is to buy a large yoghurt (*yiaorti*) and a small pot of honey (*meli*), mix the honey into the yoghurt and then relish the bitter-sweet delight. If locally produced, natural yoghurt (usually stored in cool tubs and spooned into a container) cannot be purchased, the brand name *Total* is an adequate substitute being made from cow's or sheep's milk. I prefer the sheep derived product and, when words fail, break into a charade of 'baa-ing'. It keeps the other shoppers amused if nothing else. The succulent water melon, a common and inexpensive fruit, provides a juicy, lunchtime refreshment.

Apart from waving the tablecloth in the air, or for that matter the table, it is usual to call *parakalo* (please). It is also permissible to say *gharkon* or simply 'waiter'.

A disturbing habit, becoming more prevalent in recent years, is the increasing use of the word *Special/Spezial*. This is simply to enable establishments to charge extra for a dish or offering that would have, in the past, been the 'norm'. A good example is 'Special souvlaki pita' which is nothing more than a normal giro meat souvlaki. The 'standard', inferior substitute is a slab of meat. Oh dear.

THE DRINKS
Non-alcoholic beverages Being a cafe (and taverna) society, coffee is
drunk at all times of the day and night. Greek coffee (*kafe*) is in fact a leftover from the centuries long Turkish influence, being served without milk in small cups and always with a glass of deliciously cool water. Unless specified otherwise it will be served sickly sweet or *varigliko*. There are many variations but the three most usual are *sketto* (no sugar), *metrio* (medium) or *glyko* (sweet). Beware not to completely drain the cup, the bitter grains will choke an imbiber. Except in the most traditional establishments (*kafeneions*), you can ask for *Nes-kafe* or simply *Nes* which, rationally is an instant coffee. This home-grown version often has a comparatively muddy taste. If you require milk with your coffee it is necessary to ask for *meh ghala*. A most refreshing version is to order Nes chilled or *frappé*. French coffee (*ghaliko kafe*), served in a coffee pot with a separate jug of hot milk, espresso and cappuccino are found in the larger, provincial towns, ports and international establishments. However, having made a detailed request, you may well receive any permutation of all the possibilities listed above, however carefully you may think you have ordered.

Tea, (*tsai*), perhaps surprisingly, is quite freely available, made of course with the ubiquitous teabag, which is not so outrageous since they have become universally commonplace. In more out of the way places herbal tea may be served.

Purchasing bottled mineral waters is not always necessary as, generally, island water is superb but should you wish to have some stashed away in the fridge, brand names include *Loutraki, Nigita,* and *Sariza. Sprite* is fizzy and *lemonade/lemonatha* a stillish lemonade. Orangeade (*portokaladha*), cherry soft drink (*visinatha*) and fruit juices are all palatable and sold, as often as not, under brand names, as is the universal *Koka-Kola*. A word of warning comes from a reader who reported that, in the very hot summer months, some youngsters drink nothing but sweet, fizzy beverages. This can result in mouth ulcers caused by fermenting sugar, so drink some water every day. A blot on the general 'aqua pura standard' are most of the islands that make up the Sporades (that is all accept Skyros). The tap water on these is more than likely contaminated. As one Skiathos pharmacist exploded 'Why, when we have the finest water in the world, are we Greeks forced to buy bottled water?'. He went on to elaborate that he regarded the H_2O totally unreliable, not only on Skiathos but Skopelos and Alonissos. This by the way, was as he doled out the drugs necessary to cure a very, very bad bout of *Montezuma's Revenge* that I was suffering – the first time in some 10 years. Generally the cost of bottled water is between 65-75drs.

Alcoholic beverages
They are generally sold by weight. Beer comes in 330g tins, very occasionally a small bottle or more usually the large 500g bottles – have the 500g, it is a good value measure. Wine is sold in 340/430g (half bottle), 680/730g (1.1 pints) and 950g (1¾ pints) sized bottles.

Beer Greek brewed or bottled beer represents good value except when served in cans, which are the export version and, I regard, a 'swindle'. This European habit should be resisted for no other reason than it means the cost, quantity for quantity, is almost doubled. Now that *Fix Hellas* is not obtainable, due to the founder's death, the only other widely available, bottled beers are *Amstel* and *Henninger*. Draught lager is insidiously creeping in to various resorts and should be avoided, not only or purist reasons, but because it is comparatively expensive, as are the imported, stronger bottled lagers. No names, no pack drill but *Carlsberg* is one that springs to mind. A small bottle of beer is referred to as a *mikri bira* and a large one *meghali bira*.

Wine Unresinated (*aretsinoto*) wine is European in style, palatable and popular brands include red and white *Demestica*, *Cambas* and *Rotonda*. More refined palates will approve of the dry white wines (*aspro*) of Rhodes island, including *Rhodos*. Greek wine is not so much known for its quality but if quantity of brands can make up for this then the country will not let you down. Red wine (*Krasi kokino*), dark wine (*Krasi mavro*) as well as white wine (*Krasi aspro*) are best ordered draught (*huna*) or from the barrel (*apo vardi*) which are much less expensive than the overpriced bottles.

Resinated wine is achieved, if that can be considered the expression, by the barrels, in which the wine is fermented, being internally coated with pine tree resin. The resultant liquid is referred to as retsina, most of which are white, with a *kokkineli* or rosé version sometimes available. Some consider the taste to be similar to chewing wet, lead pencils but this is patently obviously a heresy. Retsina is usually bottled, but some tavernas serve 'open' (*apo vareli*) retsina in metal jugs. When purchasing for personal consumption it can be found dispensed into any container a client might like to press into service, from large vats, buried in side-street cellars. The adjective 'open' (*apo vareli*) is used to describe retsina available on draught or more correctly from the barrel. Asking for *Kortaki* ensures being served the traditional, economically priced small bottle of retsina, rather than the expensive full sized bottle. Rumour has it that the younger retsinas are more easily palatable, but that is very much a matter of taste. A good 'starter' kit is to drink a bottle or two twice a day for three or four days and if the pain goes...

Spirits & others As elsewhere in the world, sticking to the national drinks represents good value.

Ouzo, much maligned and blamed for other excesses, is, in reality, a derivative of the aniseed family of drinks (which include *Ricard* and *Pernod*) and, taken with water, is a splendid 'medicine'. Ouzo is traditionally served with *mezethes* (or *mezes* – the Greek equivalent of Spanish tapas). This is a small plate of, for instance, a slice of cheese, tomato, cucumber, possibly smoked eel, octopus and an olive. When served they are charged for, costing some 20 to 30drs, but the tradition of offering them is disappearing in many tourist locations. If you specifically do not wish to be served mezes then make the request *ouzo sketto*. *Raki* is a stronger alternative to ouzo, often 'created' in Crete.

Metaxa brandy, available in three, five and seven star quality, is very palatable but with a certain amount of 'body', whilst Otys brandy is smoother. Greek aperitifs include *Vermouth, Mastika* and *Citro*.

DRINKING PLACES

Prior to launching into the various branches of this subject, I am at a loss to understand why so many cafe-bar and taverna owners select chairs that are designed to cause the maximum discomfort, even suffering. They are usually too small for any but a very small bottom, too low and made up of wickerwork or raffia that painfully impresses its pattern on the sitter's bare (sun-burnt?) thighs.

Kafeneion (ΚΑΦΕΝΙΟΝ) Greek cafe, serving only Turkish coffee. Very Greek, very masculine and in which women are rarely seen. They are similar to a British working man's club, but with backgammon, worry beads and large open windows allowing a dim view of the smoke-laden interior.

Ouzeries (ΟΥΖΕΡΙ) As above, but the house speciality is (well, well) ouzo.

Cafe-bar (ΚΑΦΕ ΜΠΑΡ) As above, but serving alcoholic beverages as well as coffee, and women are to be seen.

Pavement cafes French in style, with outside tables and chairs sprawling over the road as well as the pavement. Open from mid-morning, throughout the day, to one or two o'clock the next morning. Snacks and sweet cakes are usually available. Inside any of the above, the locals chat to each other in that peculiar Greek fashion which gives the impression that a full-blooded fight is about to break out at any moment. In reality, they are probably just good friends, chatting to each other over the blaring noise of a televised football match, a sickly American soap opera or a ghastly English 'comic' programme, the latter two with Greek subtitles.

Drinks can always be obtained at a taverna or restaurant, but you may be expected to eat, so read on.

It is of course, possible to sup at hotel cocktail bars, but why leave home!

EATING PLACES

At the cheapest end of the market, and more especially found in Athens, are pavement-mounted stands serving doughnut-shaped bread (*koulouri*) which make for an inexpensive nibble at about 7-10drs.

Pistachio nut & ice-cream vendors They respectively push their wheeled trolleys around the streets, selling a wide variety of nuts in paper bags for 50-100drs or ice-creams in a variety of flavours and prices.

Galaktopoleio (ΓΑΛΑΚΤΟΠΩΛΕΙΟ) Shops selling dairy products including milk, butter, yoghurt, bread, honey and sometimes omelettes and fritters with honey (*loukoumades*). These are for 'take-away' or consumption on the premises and is a traditional but more expensive alternative to a restaurant/bar at which to purchase breakfast.

Zacharoplasteion (ΖΑΧΑΡΟΠΛΑΣΤΕΙΟΝ) Shops specialising in pastries, cakes (*glyko*), chocolates and soft drinks as well as, sometimes, a small selection of alcoholic drinks.

Galaktozacharoplasteion A combination of the two previously described establishments.

Snackbar (ΣΝΑΚ ΜΠΑΡ, **Souvlatzidika** & **Tyropitadika**) Snackbars are not so numerous in the less touristy areas, often being restricted to one or two in the main town. They represent good value for a stand-up snack. The most popular offering is *souvlaki pita* – pita bread (or a roll) filled with grilled meat or kebab (*doner kebab* – slices off a rotating, vertical spit of an upturned cone of meat also called *giro*) and garnished with a slice of tomato, chopped onion and a dressing, all wrapped in an ice-cream shaped twist of greaseproof paper. Be careful, as *souvlaki* is not to be muddled with *souvlakia* which, when served at a snackbar, consists of wooden skewered pieces of lamb, pork or veal meat grilled over a charcoal fire. These are almost indistinguishable from *shish-kebab*, or *souvlakia*, served at a sit-down meal where the metal skewered meat pieces are interspersed with vegetables.

Note that in touristic locations the adjective *Special*, when applied to souvlaki, usually indicates an average, correctly made offering for which a comparatively extortionate price is charged. The cheaper alternative will be simply a slab of meat in place of the slices of giro meat.

Other 'goodies' include *tiropites* – hot flaky pastry pies filled with cream cheese; *boogatsa* – a custard filled pastry; *spanakopita* – spinach filled pastry squares or pies; a wide variety of rolls and sandwiches (*sanduits*) with cheese, tomato, salami and other spiced meat fillings, as well as toasted sandwiches (*tost*).

This reminds me to point out to readers that if 'toast' is ordered it is odds on that a toasted cheese sandwich will be served.

Creperies These are intruding in the most concentrated package tourist resorts, Aristotle reminding me of the film version of the American milk shake bar. Compared to the more traditional Greek establishments they serve very expensive sandwiches, pies and other 'exotica' including thin pancakes or crepes, thus the name.

They are a rather chic, smooth, smart version of their chromium, brightly neon lit 'cousins', the:-

Fast food joint A surely unwelcome import selling ice-creams, hot-dogs and hamburgers.

Pavement cafes Serve snacks and sweets.

Pizzerias Seem to be on the increase and are restaurants specialising in the imported Italian dish which prompts one to ask why not go to Italy? To be fair they usually represent very good value and a large serving often feeds two.

Tavernas (ΤΑΒΕΡΝΑ), **Restaurants** (ΕΣΤΙΑΤΟΡΙΟΝ), **Rotisserie** (ΨΗΣΤΑΡΙΑ) & **Rural Centres** (ΕΞΟΧΙΚΟΝ ΚΕΝΤΡΟΝ) Four variations on a theme. The traditional Greek taverna is a family concern, frequently only open in the evening. More often than not, the major part of the eating area is outside, under a vine trellis covered patio, along the pavement and or on a roof garden.

Restaurants tend to be more sophisticated, possibly open all day and night but the definition between the two is rather blurred. The price lists may include a chancy English translation, the waiter might be smarter and the tablecloth and napkins could well be linen, in place of the taverna's paper table covering and serviettes.

As tavernas often have a spit-roasting device tacked on the side, there is little, discernible difference between a rotisserie and a taverna. A grilled meat restaurant may also be styled ΨΗΣΤΑΡΙΑ.

The Rural Centre is a mix of cafe-bar and taverna in, you've guessed it, a rural or seaside setting.

Fish tavernas (ΨΑΡΟΤΑΒΕΡΝΑ) Tavernas specialising in fish dishes.

Hotels (ΞΕΝΟΔΟΧΕΙΟΝ), ΞΕΝΟΔΟΧΕΙΟΝ ΥΠΝΟΥ is a hotel that does not serve food, ΠΑΝΔΟΧΕΙΟΝ, a lower category hotel and ΧΕΝΙΑ, a Government-owned hotel. Xenias are usually well run, the food and drink international, the menu written in French and the prices reflect all these 'attributes'.

An extremely unpleasant manifestation (to old fogeys like me) is illustrated by the prolification of menus in the more popular holiday resorts, namely Greek bills of fare set out Chinese restaurant style. You know, 'Set Meal A' for two, 'Meal B' for three and Meal 'C' for four and more...!

THE FOOD
Some of the following represents a selection of the wide variety of menu dishes available.

Sample menu

Ψωμί (Psomi)	Bread
ΠΡΩΙΝΟ	BREAKFAST
Αυγά τηγανιτα με μπέικον και τομάτα	Fried egg. bacon & tomato
Τοστ βούτυρο μαρμελάδα	Buttered toast & marmalade
Το πρόγευμα (to pro-ye-vma)	English (or American on some islands) breakfast
ΑΥΓΑ	EGGS
Μελάτα	soft boiled
Σφικτά	hard boiled
Τηγανιτά	fried
Ποσσέ	poached
ΤΟΣΤ ΣΑΝΤΟΥΙΤΣ	TOASTED SANDWICHES
Τοστ με τυρί	toasted cheese
Τοστ (με) ζαμπόν και τυρί	toasted ham & cheese
Μπούρκερ	burger
Χαμπουρκερ	hamburger
Τσίσμπουρκερ	cheeseburger
Σάντουιτς λουκάνικο	hot dog
ΟΡΕΚΤΙΚΑ	APPETIZERS/HORS D'OEUVRES
Αντσούγιες	anchovies
Ελιές	olives
Σαρδέλλες	sardines
Σκορδαλιά	garlic dip
Τζατζίκι	tzatziki (diced cucumber & garlic in yoghurt)
Ταραμοσαλάτα	taramosalata (a fish roe pate)
ΣΟΥΠΕΣ	SOUPS
Σούπα φασόλια	bean
Αυγολέμονο	egg & lemon
Ψαρόσουπα	fish
Κοτόσουπα	chicken
Ντοματόσουπα	tomato
Σούπα λαχανικών	vegetable

ΟΜΕΛΕΤΕΣ	OMELETTES
Ομελέτα μπέικον	bacon
Ομελέτα μπέικον τυρί τομάτα	bacon, cheese & tomato
Ομελέτα τυρί	cheese
Ομελέτα ζαμπόν	ham
Ομελέτα ουκωτάκια πουλιών	chicken liver

ΣΑΛΑΤΕΣ	SALADS
Ντομάτα Σαλάτα	tomato
Αγγούρι Σαλάτα	cucumber
Αγγουροτομάτα Σαλάτα	tomato & cucumber
Χωριάτικη	Greek peasant/village salad

ΛΑΧΑΝΙΚΑ (ΛΑΔΕΡΑ*)	VEGETABLES
Πατάτες	potatoes **
Πατάτες Τηγανιτές	chips (french fries)
φρέσκα φασολάκια	green beans
Υιγαντες	(large) white beans
Σπαράγκια	asparagus
Κολοκυθάκια	courgettes or zucchini
Σπανάκι	spinach

*indicates cooked in oil.
**usually served up as chips

Note various methods of cooking include:
Baked – στο φούρνο; boiled – βραστά; creamed – με ασπρη σαλτσα; fried – τηγανιτα; grilled – στη σχαρα; roasted – ψητά; spit roasted – σούβλας.

ΚΥΜΑΔΕΣ	MINCED MEATS
Μουσακάς	moussaka
Ντομάτες Γεμιστές	stuffed tomatoes (with rice or minced meat)
Κεφτέδες	meat balls
Ντολμαδάκια	stuffed vine leaves (with rice or minced meat)
Παπουτσάκια	stuffed vegetable marrow (rice or meat)
Κανελόνια	canelloni
Μακαπόνια με κυμά	spaghetti bolognese (more correctly with mince)
Παστίτσιο	macaroni, mince and sauce
Σουβλάκι	shish-kebab

ΡΥΖΙ	RICE
Πιλάφι	pilaff
Πιλάφι (με) γιαούρτι	with yoghurt
Πιλάφι συκωτάκια	with liver
Σπανακόριζο	with spinach
Πιλάφι κυμά	with minced meat

ΠΟΥΛΕΡΙΚΑ	POULTRY
Κοτόπουλο	chicken, roasted
Πόδι κότας	leg of chicken
Στήθος κότας	chicken breast
Κοτόπουλο βραστό	boiled chicken
Ψητο κοτοπουλο στη σούβλα	spit-roasted chicken

ΚΡΕΑΣ	MEAT
Νεφρά	kidneys
Αρνϊ	lamb†
Αρνίσιες Μπριζόλες	lamb chops
Παιδάκια	lamb cutlets
Συκώτι	liver
Χοιρινδ	pork†
Χοιρινές Μπριζόλες	pork chops
Λουκάνικα	sausages
Μπιφτέκι	steak (beef)

Μοσχαρίσιο	veal
Μοσχαρίσιες Μπριζολες	veal chops
Μοσχάρι	grilled veal
Ψητό Μοσχαράκι	roast veal

† often with the prefix suffix to indicate if roasted or grilled as above.

ΨΑΡΙΑ	FISH
Σκουμπρί	mackerel
Συναγρίδα	red snapper
Μαρίδες	whitebait
Οκταπόδι	octopus
Καλαμάρια	squid
Μπαρμπούνι	red mullet
Κέφαλος	mullet
Αυθρίνι	grey mullet

ΤΥΡΙΑ	CHEESE
Φετα	feta (goat's-milk based)
Γραβιέρα	gruyere-type cheese
Κασέρι	cheddar-type (sheep's-milk based)

ΦΡΟΥΤΑ	FRUITS
Καρπούζι	water melon
Πεπόνι	melon
Μήλα	apple
Πορτοκάλι	oranges
Σταφύλια	grapes
Κομπόστα φρούτων	fruit compote

ΠΑΓΩΤΑ	ICE-CREAM
Σπέσιαλ	special
Παγωτό βανίλλια	vanilla
Παγωτό σοκολάτα	chocolate
Παγωτό λεμονι	lemon
Γρανίτα	water ice

ΓΛΥΚΙΣΜΑΤΑ	DESSERTS
Κέικ	cake
φρουτοσαλάτα	fruit salad
Κρέμα	milk pudding
Κρεμ καραμελέ	cream caramel
Μπακλαβας	crisp pastry with nuts & syrup or honey
Καταίφι	fine shredded pastry with nuts & syrup or honey
Γαλακτομπούρεκο	fine crispy pastry with custard & syrup
Γιαούρτι	yoghurt
Μέλι	honey

ΑΝΑΨΥΚΤΙΚΑ	COLD DRINKS/SOFT DRINKS
Πορτοκάλι	orange
Πορτοκαλάδα	orangeade
Λεμονάδα	lemonade made with lemon juice
Γκαζόζα (Gazoza)	fizzy lemonade
Μεταλλικό νερό	mineral water
Κόκα κολα	Coca-cola
Πέψι κολα	Pepsi-cola
Σέβεν-απ	Seven-Up
Σόδα	soda
Τονικ	tonic
Νερό (Nero)	water

ΚΑΦΕΔΕΣ	COFFEES
Ελληνικός (Καφὲς)	Greek coffee (sometimes called Turkish coffee ie. Toupkikos Καφε)
σκὲτο (skehto)	no sugar
μετριο (metrio)	medium sweet
γλυκὸ (ghliko)	sweet (very)

(Unless stipulated it will turn up 'ghliko'. Do not drink Turkish coffee before the grouts have settled.)

Νες καφὲ	Nescafe
Νες (με γαλα) (Nes me ghala)	Nescafe with milk
Εσπρὲσσο	espresso
Καπουτσίνο	cappuccino
φραπὲ	chilled coffee is known as 'frappe'
Τσὰι	tea
Σοκαλάτα γάλα	chocolate milk

ΜΠΥΡΕΣ	BEERS
ΦΙΞ (ΕΛΛΑΣ) Μπύρα	Fix (Hellas) beer
φιάλη	bottle
κουτί	can
ΑΜΣΤΕΛ (Αμστελ)	Amstel
ΧΕΝΝΙΝΓΕΡ (Χέννινγκερ)	Henninger

(300g usually a can, 500g usually a bottle)

ΠΟΤΑ	DRINKS
Οὐζο	Ouzo
Κονιάκ	Cognac
Μπράντυ	Brandy
Μεταξά	Metaxa
3 ΑΣΤ	3 star
5 ΑΣΤ	5 star
Ουίσκυ	Whisky
Τζιν	Gin
Βότκα	Vodka
Καμπάρι	Campari
Βερμούτ	Vermouth
Μαρτίνι	Martini

ΚΡΑΣΙΑ	WINES
Κόκκινο	red
Ασπρο	white
Ροζε Κοκκινέλι	rose
Ξηρό	dry
Γλυκό	sweet
Ρετσίνα	resinated wine
e.g. Θεόκριτος	Theokritos
Αρετσίνωτο	unresinated wine
e.g. Δεμέστιχα	Demestica

340g is a ½ bottle, 680g is a bottle, 950g is a large bottle

Useful Greek

English	Greek	Sounds like
Have you a table for...	Εχετε ένα τραπέζι για	Echete enna trapezee ghia...
I'd like...	Θὲλω	Thelo...
We would like...	Θὲλουμε	Thelome...
a beer	μιά μπύρα	meah beerah
a glass	ένα ποτήρι	ena poteeree

a carafe	μιά καράφα	meea karafa
a small bottle	ένα μικρό μπουκάλι	ena mikro bookalee
a large bottle	ένα μεγάλο	ena meghalo bookalee
bread	ψωμί	psomee
tea with milk	τσάι με γάλα	tsai me ghala
with lemon	τσάι με λεμόνι	me lemoni
Turkish coffee (Greek)	Τούρκικος καφές	Tourkikos kafes
sweet	γλυκός	ghleekos
medium	νέτριος	metreeo
bitter (no sugar)	πικρό	pikro
Black coffee	Nescafe xwpis γάλα	Nescafe horis ghala
Coffee with milk	Nescafe με γάλα	Nescafe me ghala
a glass of water	ενα ποτήρι νερό	enna poteeree nero
a napkin	μιά πετσέτα	mia petseta
an ashtray	ένα σταχτοδοχείο	enna stachdothocheeo
toothpick	μιά οδοντογλυφίδα	mea odontoglifidha
the olive oil	το ελαιόλαδο	dho eleolatho
Where is the toilet?	Που είναι η τουαλέττα	Poo eene i(ee) tooaleta?
What is this?	Τι είναι αυτό	Ti ine afto
This is...	Αυτό είναι	Afto eene
cold	κρύο	kreeo
bad	χαλασμένο	chalasmeno
stale	μπαγιάτικο	bayhiatiko
undercooked	άψητο	apseeto
overcooked	παραβρασμένο	paravrasmeno
The bill please	Το λογαριασμό παρακαλώ	To loghariasmo parakalo
How much is that?	Πόσο κάνει αυτό	˙Poso kanee afto?
That was an excellent meal	Περίφημο γεύμα	Pereefimo yevma
We shall come again	Θα ξανάρθουμε	Tha xanarthoume

Lindos Acropolis under reconstruction, strangely to recount not by the Italians -- possibly Trafalgar House. Rhodes.

7 Shopping & Public Services

Let your purse be your master Proverb

Purchasing items in Greece is still quite an art form or subject for an *Open University* degree course. The difficulties have been compounded by the rest of the western world becoming nations of supermarket shoppers, whilst the Greeks have stubbornly remained traditionally and firmly with their individual shops, selling a fixed number of items and sometimes only one type of a product. Shopping for a corkscrew, for instance, might well involve calling at two or three seemingly look-alike ironmongers, but no, they each specialise in certain lines of goods and do not stock any items outside those prescribed, almost as if by holy writ.

On the other hand Greece is adopting many of the (retrograde?) consumer habits of its Western European neighbours. In cosmopolitan towns and cities and tourist exposed islands credit cards, including *Visa, Access Mastercharge, Diners* and *American Express*, are accepted at the more expensive restaurants and classier gift/souvenir shops. The more popular areas of Rhodes and Kos sport the credit card symbols.

The question of good and bad buys is a rather personal matter but the items listed below are highlighted on the basis of value for money and quality.

Clothing and accessories that are attractive and represent good value include embroidered peasant dresses, leather sandals, woven bags, tapestries and furs. Day-to-day items that are inexpensive take in Greek cigarettes, drinks including *ouzo, Metaxa* brandy and selected island wines. Suitable gifts for family and friends embraces ceramic plates, sponges, Turkish delight and worry beads (*komboloe*). Disproportionately expensive items include camera film, toiletries, sun oils, books and playing cards. Do not forget to compare prices and preferably shop in the streets and markets, not in airport and hotel concessionary outlets, which are often much more expensive.

Try not to run short of change. Everybody else does, including bus conductors, taxi drivers and shops.

Opening hours

Strict or old fashioned summer shop hours are:

Monday, Wednesday and Saturday: 0830-1400hrs; Tuesday, Thursday and Friday: 0830-1330hrs & 1730-2030hrs.

Generally, during the summer months, shops in tourist areas are open Monday to Saturday from 0800-1300hrs. They then close for the siesta until 1700hrs, after which they open again until at least 2030hrs, if not 2200hrs. Sundays and Saints' days are more indeterminate, but there is usually a general shop open, somewhere. In very popular tourist resorts and busy ports, many shops often open seven days a week.

Drink

Available either in the markets from delicatessen meat/dairy counters or from 'off licence' type shops.

Smokers

Imported French, English and American cigarettes are inexpensive, compared with European prices, at between 100 and 150drs for a packet of twenty. Greek cigarettes, which have a distinctive and different taste, are excellent. Try *Karellia* which cost about 68drs for twenty and note that the price is printed around the edge of the packet. Even Greek cigars are almost unheard of on the islands, while in Athens they cost 10-15drs each. Dutch cigars work out at 25-30drs each, so, if a cigar smoker, take along your holiday requirements.

Newspapers & magazines

The Athens News is published daily, except Mondays, in English and costs 50drs. Overseas newspapers are available up to 24 hours after the day of publication, but note that all printed matter is comparatively expensive. Quality English papers cost 200drs.

Photography (Fotografion – ΦΩΤΟΓΡΑΦΕΙΟΝ)

Photographers should carry all the film possible as, being imported, it is comparatively expensive. Despite the allure of the instant print shops that have sprung up on the more popular islands, it is probably best to wait until returning home. The quality of reproduction and focus of the development is 'variable'. That is not to say that the back-at-home 'bucket-print' outfits, whose envelopes fall out of almost every magazine one cares to purchase, are infallible. I had a long drawn out experience with a Shropshire company who managed to 'foul up' the development of five rolls of film. The problem is that a holiday-maker who only has two or three films to develop and receives back the complete batch rather blurred might consider it to be an 'own goal'. On the other hand it might be the print company who have botched the job.

To counter the very bright sunlight, when using colour film, blue filters should be fitted to the lens.

Radio

To receive the English language overseas broadcasts tune to 49m band on the *Short Wave*. In the evening try the *Medium Wave*. English language news is broadcast by the Greek broadcasting system at 0740hrs on the *Medium Wave* (AM), somewhere between 700-800 Khz.

Tourist Guides & Maps

Shop around before purchasing either, as the difference in price of the island guides can be as much as 150drs, that is between 300-450drs. Island maps cost from 80-100drs. Some major ports and towns have one authentic, well stocked bookshop, usually positioned a little off the town centre. The proprietor often speaks adequate English and courteously answers most enquiries.

SHOPS
Bakers & bread shops (ΑΡΤΟΠΟΙΕΙΟΝ, ΑΡΤΟΠΩΛΕΙΟΝ or ΠΡΑΤΗΡΙΟΝ ΑΡΤΟΥ)

For some obscure reason bakers are nearly always difficult to locate, often being hidden away, in or behind other shops. A pointer to their presence may well be a pile of blackened, twisted olive wood, stacked up to one side of the entrance, and used to fuel the oven fires. They are almost always closed on Sundays and Saints days, despite the ovens often being used by the local community to cook their Sunday dinners. Bread shops tend to be few and far between. Both may also sell cheese and meat pies.

The method of purchasing bread can prove disconcerting, especially when sold by weight. Sometimes the purchaser selects the loaf and then pays but the most bewildering system is where it is necessary to pay first then collect the goods.

·Difficult if the shopper's level of Greek is limited to grunts, 'thank you' and 'please'!

Greek bread has another parameter of measure, that is a graduation in hours – 1 hour bread, 4 hour bread and so on. After the period is up, the loaf is usually completely inedible, having transmogrified into a rock-like substance.

Butcher (ΚΡΕΟΠΩΛΕΙΟΝ)

Similar to those at home but the cuts are quite different (surely the Common Market can legislate against this deviation!).

Galaktopoleio et al.

Cake shops (*Zacharoplasteion*) may sell bottled mineral water (ask for a cold bottle). *See* **Chapter Six**.

Markets

The smaller ports and towns may have a market street and the larger municipalities often possess a market building. These are thronged with locals and all the basic necessities can be procured relatively inexpensively. Fruit and vegetable stalls are interspersed by butchers and dairy delicatessen shops. During business hours, the proprietors are brought coffee and a glass of water by waiters carrying the cups and glasses, not on open trays, but in round aluminium salvers with a deep lid, held under a large ring handle, connected to the tray by three flat arms.

Supermarkets (ΥΠΕΡΑΓΟΡΑ/ΣΟΥΠΕΡΜΑΡΚΕΤ)

Very much on the increase and based on small town, self-service stores but not to worry, they inherit all those delightful, native Greek qualities including quiet chaos. It has to be admitted every so often one does come across a 'real supermarket' recognisable by the check-out counters, but this still does not mean it is a Western European equivalent – more an organised shambles.

Mini-Market

The nomenclature usually indicates a well stocked store in a small building.

Speciality shops

Found in some big towns and Athens while pavement browsing. The little basement shops can be espied down flights of steps, specialising, for instance, in dried fruit, beans, nuts and grains.

Street Kiosks (Periptero/ΠΕΡΙΠΤΕΡΟ)

These unique, pagoda-like huts stay open remarkably long hours, often from early morning to after midnight. They sell a wide range of goods including newspapers, magazines (surprisingly sometimes in the larger cities porno-graphic literature), postcards, tourist maps, postage stamps, sweets, choc-olates, cigarettes and matches. Additionally they form the outlet for the pay phone system and, at the cost of 5drs, a local call may be made. It is rather incongruous, to observe a Greek making a possible important business call, in amongst a rack of papers and magazines, with a foreground of jostling pedestrians and a constant stream of noisy traffic in the background. Owner-ship is often a family affair – vested as a form of Government patronage and handed out to deserving citizens.

Alternate ways of shopping

Then there are the other ways of shopping: from handcarts, their street-vendor owners selling respectively nuts, ice-cream, milk and yoghurt; from the back of a donkey with vegetable-laden panniers or from two wheeled trailers drawn by fearsome sounding, agricultural rotovator power units. Often the donkey or powered trailer has an enormous set of scales mounted on the back end, swinging like a hangman's scaffold.

If the vegetable/fruit is being sold by 'gypsy-types' then it is advisable to only purchase from those who have their prices written up, usually on a piece of cardboard. Even locals admit to being 'ripped off' by, say, a roadside banana seller. These free market entrepreneurs are often prosecuted for breaking the law.

Frequently used shops include:

ΒΙΒΛΙΟΠΩΛΕΙΟΝ – bookshop; ΚΡΕΟΠΩΛΕΙΟΝ – butcher; ΙΧΘΥΟΠΩΛΕΙΟΝ – fishmonger; ΟΠΩΡΟΠΩΛΕΙΟΝ – greengrocer; ΠΑΝΤΟΠΩΛΕΙΟΝ – grocer; ΚΟΥΡΕΙΟΝ – hairdresser; ΚΑΠΝΟΠΩΛΕΙΟΝ – tobacconist. Readers may observe that the above all have a similar ending and it is worth noting that shop titles that terminate in 'ΠΩΛΕΙΟΝ/πωλειον' are selling something, if that's any help.

SERVICES
The Banks & Money (ΤΡΑΠΕΖΑ)

The minimum opening hours are 0800-1300hrs Monday to Thursday and 0800-1300hrs on Friday. Some banks, in the most tourist ravaged spots, open in the evenings and or on Saturdays. Some smaller towns, villages or, for that matter, islands do not have a bank, in which case there may be a local money changer acting as agent for this or that country-wide bank. Do not forget that a passport is almost always required to change travellers' cheques. In the larger cities personal cheques may be changed at a selected bank when backed by a *Eurocheque* (or similar) bank guarantee card. A commission of between $\frac{1}{4}$–$1\frac{1}{2}$% is charged on all transactions, depending upon I know not what! Whereas Eurocheques used to be changed in sums of no more than £50, English sterling, the arrangement now is that a cheque is cashed in drachmae, up to a total of 25,000drs. As the charges for changing cheques are based on a sliding scale weighted against smaller amounts, this new arrangement helps save on fees.

The service is usually discourteous and generally only one employee, if at all, reluctantly speaks English, so make sure the correct bank is selected to carry out a particular transaction (such as changing a personal cheque). Each bank displays a window sticker giving an indication of the tourist services transacted. There is nothing worse, after queuing for half an hour or so, than to be rudely told to go away. I once selected the wrong bank to carry out some banking function, only to receive a loud blast of abuse about a long-departed foreigner's bouncing cheque. Most embarrassing.

Change offices can be used for cashing travellers cheques, as can the larger hotels, but naturally enough at a disadvantageous rate compared with the banks. For instance, the commission charged is 2%, or up to double that charged by the banks. Ouch! *See* **Post Office** for another interesting and less expensive alternative.

The basis of Greek currency is the drachmae. This is nominally divided into 100 lepta and occasionally price lists show a price of, say 62.60drs. As prices are rounded up (or down), in practice the lepta is not now encountered. Notes are in denominations of 50, 100, 500 and 1000drs and coins in denominations of 1 and 2drs (bronze), 5, 10, 20 and 50drs (nickel). Do not run out of change, it is always in demand. Repetitious I know, but well worth remembering.

Museums

The following is a mean average of the entry information but each museum is likely to have its own peculiarities. In the summer season (1st April-31st Oct) they usually open daily 0845-1500/1900hrs, Sundays and holidays 0930-1430/1530hrs and are closed Mondays or Tuesdays. They do not open for business on 1st January, 25th March, Good Friday, Easter holiday and 25th December. Admission costs range from nothing to 100/250drs, whilst Sundays and holidays are sometimes free.

Post Offices (ΤΑΧΥΔΡΟΜΕΙΟΝ/ΕΛΤΑ)

Stamps can be bought from kiosks (plus a small commission) and shops selling postcards as well as from Post Offices. Post boxes are scattered around, are usually painted yellow, are rather small in size and often difficult to find, being fixed, high up, on side-street walls. In 1987 postage rates for cards to the United Kingdom were 40drs for a small card and between 45 & 50drs for a large one. When confronted by two letter-box openings, the inland service is marked ΕΣΩΤΕΡΙΚΟΥ/Εσωτερικου and the overseas ΕΞΩΤΕΡΙΚΟΥ/Εξωτερικου. Letters can be sent for poste restante collection, but a passport will be required for them to be handed over.

Most major town Post Offices are modern and the service received is only slightly less rude than that handed out by bank staff.

Post Offices are usually open Monday to Friday between 0730-2030hrs for stamps, money orders and registered mail; 0730-2000hrs for poste restante and 0730-1430hrs for parcels, which have to be collected.

In recent years the range of Post Office services has been expanded to include cashing *Eurocheques* and *Travellers Cheques* as well as currency exchange. All but the most out-of-the-way island offices now offer these facilities. This can prove very useful knowledge, especially on busy tourist islands where foreign currency desks are usually subject to long queues. More importantly the commission charged can be up to half that of the banks. Another interesting source of taking currency abroad, for United Kingdom residents, is to use *National Giro Post Office* cheques which can be cashed at any Post Office in Greece. Detailed arrangements have to be made with the international branch of Giro.

Telephone Office (OTE)

A separate organisation from the Post Office. To accomplish an overseas or long-distance call it is necessary to go to the OTE office where there are a number of booths from which to make calls. Offices in busy locations are likely to have long queues. The counter clerk indicates which compartment is to be used and alongside him are mounted the instruments to meter the cost. Payment is made after completion of the call at a current rate of 5drs per unit, so ensure that the meter is zeroed prior to making a connection. Opening days and hours vary enormously. Smaller offices may only open weekdays for say 7 hours between 0830-1530hrs whilst some of the larger city offices are open 24 hours a day, seven days a week.

Overseas dialling codes		Inland services	
Australia	0061	Directory enquiries	131
Canada & USA	001	Provincial enquiries	132
New Zealand	0064	General information	134
South Africa	0027	Time	141
United Kingdom & Ireland	0044	Medical care	166
Other overseas countries	161	City police	100
		Gendarmerie	109
		Fire	199
		Tourist police	171
		Roadside assistance	104
		Telegrams/cables	165

To dial England, drop the '0' from all four figure codes. Thus making a call to, say, Portsmouth, for which the code is 0705, dial 00 44 705 ...
The internal service is both very good and reasonably priced. Local telephone calls can be made from some bars and the pavement kiosks (periptero) and cost 5drs, which is the 'standard' coin. Some phones take 10 and 20drs coins. The presence of a telephone is often indicated by the sign ΕΔΩΤΗΛΕΦΩΝΕΙΤΕ, a blue background denotes a local phone, and an orange one an inter-city phone. Another sign, Εδω Τηλεφωνειτε (the lower case equivalent), signifies 'telephone from here'. The method of operation is to insert the coin and dial. If a connection cannot be made, place the receiver back on the cradle and the money is returned.

Telegrams may be sent from either the OTE or Post Office.

Useful Greek

English	Greek
Stamps	ΓΡΑΜΜΑΤΟΣΗΜΑ
Parcels	ΔΕΜΑΤΑ

English	Greek	Sounds like
Where is...	Που είναι	Poo eenne...
Where is the nearest...	Που είναι η πλησιέστερη	Poo eenne i pleesiesteri
baker	ο φούρναρης/ψωμας	foornaris/psomas
bakery	Αρτοποιείον	artopieeon
bank	η τράπεζα	i(ee) trapeza
bookshop	το βιβλιοπωλείο	to vivleeopolieo
butchers shop	το χασάπικο	dho hasapiko
chemist shop	το φαρμακείο	to farmakio
dairy shop	το γαλακτοπωλείο	galaktopolieon
doctor	ο γιατρός	o yiahtros
grocer	το μπακάλης	o bakalis
hospital	το νοσοκομείο	to nosokomio
laundry	το πλυντήριο	to plintirio, (plintireeo, since i = ee)
liquor store	το ποτοπωλείο	to potopolio (potopoleeo)
photographic shop	το φωτογραφείο	to fotoghrafeeo
post office	το ταχυδρομείο	to tahkithromio
shoe repairer	το τσαγκαράδικο	to tsangkaradiko
tailor	ο ραπτης	o raptis
Have you any...	Εχετε	Ekheteh...
Do you sell...	Πουλάτε	Poulate...
How much is this...	Πόσο κάνει αυτό	Posso kanee afto...
I want...	Θέλω	Thelo...
half kilo/a kilo	μισό κιλό/ένα κιλό	miso kilo/ena kilo
aspirin	η ασπιρίνη	aspirini
apple(s)	το μήλο/μήλα	meelo/meela
banana(s)	η μπανάνα/μπανάνες	banana/bananes
bread	το ψωμί	psomee
butter	το βούτυρο	vutiro
cheese	το τυρί	tiree
cigarettes (filter tip)	το τσιγάρο (με φίλτρο)	to tsigharo (me filtro)
coffee	καφές	cafes
cotton wool	το βαμβακι	to vambaki
crackers	τα κρακεράκια	krackerakia
crisps	τσιπς	tsseeps
cucumbers	το αγγούρι	anguree

disinfectant	το απολυμαντικό	to apolimantiko
guide book	ο τουριστικός οδηγός	o touristikos odhigos
ham	το ζαμπόν	zambon
ice-cream	το παγωτό	paghoto
lemons	το λεμόνια	lemonia
lettuce	το μαρούλι	to marooli
map	το χάρτης	o khartis
a box of matches	ενα κουτί σπίρτα	ena kuti spirta
milk	το γάλα	to ghala
pate	πατέ	pate
(ball point) pen	το μπικ	to bik
pencil	το μολύβι	to molivi
pepper	το πιπέρι	to piperi
(safety) pins	μια παραμάνα	mia (meea) paramana
potatoes	οι πατάτες	patates
salad	η σαλάτα	i salatah
salami	το σαλάμι	salahmi
sausages	το λουκάνικα	lukahniko
soap	το σαπούνι	to sapooni
spaghetti	σπαγγέτο	spayehto
string	ο σπαγκος	o spangos
sugar	η ζάχαρη	i zakhahree
tea	το τσάι	to tsai
tomatoes	η ντομάτες	domahdes
toothbrush	η οδοντόβουρτσα	odhondovourtsa
toothpaste	η οδοντόκρεμα	odhondokrema
writing paper	το χαρτι γραψίματος	to kharti grapsimatos

Simi Harbour.

A chapel within the confines of Antimachia Castle, Kos.

8 Greece: History, Mythology, Religion, Present-day Greece, Greeks & their Holidays

All ancient histories, as one of our fine wits said, are but fables that have been accepted. Voltaire

HISTORY

Excavations have shown the presence of Palaeolithic man up to 100,000 years ago. Greece's history and mythology are, like the Greek language, formidable to say the least, with legend, myth, folk tales, fables and religious lore often inextricably mixed up. Archaeologists are now establishing that some mythology is based on ancient facts.

Historically Greeks fought Greeks, Phoenicians and Persians. Under Alexander the Great they conquered Egypt and vast tracts of Asia Minor. Then they were in turn conquered by the Romans. After the splitting of the Roman Kingdom into Western and Eastern Empires, the Greeks, with Constantinople as their capital, were ruled by the Eastern offshoot, only to fall into the hands of the Franks about AD 1200, who were followed by the Turks. The Venetians, Genoese and finally the Turks ruled most of the islands.

In 1821 the War of Independence commenced, which eventually led to the setting up of a Parliamentary Republic in 1928. Incidentally, Thessaly, Crete and the Dodecanese islands remained under Turkish rule. By the time the Dodecanese islanders had thrown out the Turks, the Italians had taken over. If you are now confused, give up, because it gets even more difficult to follow.

The Greek monarchy, which had come into being in 1833, and was related to the German Royal family, opted in 1913 to side with the Axis powers. The chief politician Eleftherios Venizelos, disagreed, was dismissed and set up a rival government, after which the King, under Allied pressure, retired to Switzerland. In the years following the end of the First World War the Turks and Greeks agreed, after some fairly bloody fighting, to exchange a total of one and a half million people.

In 1936 a General Metaxas became dictator and achieved immortal fame by booting out Mussolini's representative. This came about when, in 1940, Mussolini demanded permission for Italy's troops to traverse Greece, and received the famous *Ochi* (No). (This day has become a national festival known as *Ochi Day*, celebrated on 28th October). The Italians demurred and marched on Greece, the soldiers of whom, to the surprise of everybody including themselves, reinforced the refusal by routing the invaders. The Italians were only saved from total humiliation by the intervention of the Germans who then occupied Greece for the duration of the Second World War. At the end of hostilities, all the Italian held Greek islands were reunited with mainland Greece.

As the wartime German ascendancy declined, the Greek freedom fighters split into royalist and communist factions and proceeded to knock even more stuffing out of each other than they had out of the Germans. Until British intervention, followed by large injections of American money and weapons, it looked as if Greece would go behind the Iron Curtain. A second civil war broke out between 1947 and 1949 and this internal strife was reputed to have cost more Greek lives than were lost during the whole of the Second World War.

In 1951, Greece and Turkey became full members of NATO, but the issue of the ex-British colony of Cyprus was about to rear its ugly head, with the resultant, renewed estrangement between Greece and Turkey. The various political manoeuvrings, the involvement of the Greek monarchy in domestic affairs and the worsening situation in Cyprus, led to the *coup d'etat* by the *Colonel's Junta* in 1967, soon after which King Constantine II and his entourage fled to Italy. The extremely repressive dictatorship of the Junta was apparently actively supported by the Americans and condoned by Britain. Popular country-wide feeling and, in particular, student uprisings between 1973-1974, which were initially put down in Athens by brutal tank attacks, led to the eventual collapse of the regime in 1974. In the death-throes of their rule, the Colonels, using the Cyprus dream to distract the ordinary people's feeling of injustice, meddled and attempted to overthrow the vexatious priest, President Makarios. The net result was that the Turks invaded Cyprus and made an enforced division of that unhappy, troubled island.

In 1974, Greece returned to republican democracy and in 1981 joined the EEC.

RELIGION

The Orthodox Church prevails everywhere but there are small pockets of Roman Catholicism as well as very minor enclaves of Muslims on the Dodecanese islands and mainland, western Thrace. The schism within the Holy Roman Empire, in 1054, caused the Catholic Church to be centred on Rome and the Orthodox Church on Constantinople.

The Turkish overlords encouraged the continuation of the indigenous church, probably to keep their bondsmen quiet, but it had the invaluable side effect of keeping alive Greek customs and traditions during the centuries of occupation.

The bewildering profusion of small churches, scattered 'indiscriminately' all over the islands, is not proof of the church's wealth, although the Greek people are not entirely convinced of that fact. It is evidence of the piety of the families or individuals who paid to have them erected, in the name of their selected patron saint, as thanksgiving for God's protection. The style of religious architecture changes between the island groups.

Many churches only have one service a year, on the name day of the particular patron saint, and this ceremony is named *Viorti* or *Panayieri*. It is well worth attending one of these self-indulgent extravaganzas to observe and take part in celebratory village religious life and music. One and all are welcome to the carnival festivities which include eating and dancing in, or adjacent to, the particular churchyard.

The words *Byzantine* and *Byzantium* crop up frequently with especial reference to churches and appertain to the period between the fourth and fourteenth centuries AD. During this epoch Greece was, at least nominally, under the control of Constantinople (Istanbul), built by the Emperor Constantine on the site of the old city of Byzantium. Religious paintings executed on small wooden panels during this period are called icons. Very very few original icons remain available for purchase, so beware if offered an apparent 'bargain'.

When visiting a church, especially noticeable are the pieces of shining, thin metal, placed haphazardly around or pinned to wooden carvings. These *tamata* or *exvotos* represent limbs or portions of the human body and are purchased by worshippers as an offering, in the hope of an illness being cured and or limbs healed.

Male and female visitors to all and every religious building must be properly clothed. Men should wear trousers and a shirt. Ladies clothing should include a skirt, or if unavoidable trousers, a blouse and if possible a headscarf. Many monasteries simply will not allow entrance to scantily or 'undressed' people. With that marvellous duality of standards the Greeks evince, there is quite often a brisk clothes hire business transacted on the very entrance steps. But it is not wise to rely on this arrangement being in force.

GREEKS

In making an assessment of the Greek people and their character, it must be remembered that, perhaps even more so than the Spaniards or the Portuguese, Greece has only recently emerged into the twentieth century. Unlike other countries 'discovered' in the 1960s by the holiday industry, they have not, in the main, degraded or debased their principles or character, despite the onrush of tourist wealth. For a people to have had so little and to face so much demand for European 'necessities', would have strained a less hardy and well-balanced people.

Greece's recent emergence into the western world is evidenced by the still patriarchal nature of their society, a view supported for instance, by the oft-seen spectacle of men lazing in the taverna whilst their womenfolk work in the fields (and why not).

Often the smallest village, on the remotest island, has an English-speaking islander who has lived abroad at some time in his life, earning a living through seafaring, as a hotel waiter, or as a taxi driver. Thus, while making an escape from the comparative poverty at home, for a period of good earnings in the more lucrative world, a working knowledge of English, American or Australian will have been gained. *Greek strine* or, as usually contracted, *grine* simply has to be heard to be believed.

The greatest hurdle to understanding is undoubtedly the language barrier, especially if it is taken into account that the Greeks appear to have some difficulty with their own language in its various forms. Certainly, they seem, on occasions, not to understand each other and the subject matter has to be repeated a number of times. Perhaps that is the reason for all that shouting!

There can be no doubt that the traditional Greek welcome to the *Xenos* or *Singrafeus*, now increasingly becoming known as *touristas*, has naturally, become rather lukewarm in the more 'besieged' areas. It is often difficult to reconcile the shrugged shoulders of a seemingly disinterested airline official or bus driver, with being stopped in the street by a gold-toothed, smiling Greek proffering some fruit. But remember the bus driver may realise the difficulty of overcoming the language barrier, may be very hot, he has been working long hours earning his living and he is not on holiday. Sometimes a drink appears mysteriously at one's taverna table, the donor being indicated by a nod of the waiter's heard, but a word of warning here. Simply smile and accept the gift graciously. Any attempt to return the kindness by 'putting one in the stable' for your new-found friend only results in a 'who buys last' competition which will surely be lost. I know, I am speaking from 'battle-weary' experience. Greeks are very welcoming and may well invite a tourist to their table. But do not expect more, they are reserved and have probably had previous unhappy experiences of ungrateful, rude, overseas visitors.

Women tourists can travel quite freely in Greece without fear, except perhaps from other tourists. On the other hand, females should not wear provocative attire or fail to wear sufficient clothing. This is especially so when in close social contact with Greek men, who might well be inflamed into 'action' or Greek women, whom it will offend, probably because of the effect on their men! Certainly all the above was the case until very recently but the constant stream of 'available' young tourist ladies on the more popular islands has resulted in the local lads taking both a 'view' and a chance. It almost reminds one of the *Costa Brava* in the early 1960s. The disparate moral qualities of the native and tourist females has resulted in a conundrum for young Greek women. To compete for their men's affections they have to loosen their principles with an unheard of and steadily increasing number of speedily arranged marriages, if you know what I mean.

Do not miss the *Volta* (Βολγα), the traditional, family evening walkabout on city, town and village square. Dressed for the event, an important part of the ritual is for the family to show off their marriageable daughters. Good fun and great watching, but the Greeks are rather protective of their family and all things Greek... you may comment favourably, but keep adverse criticism to yourself.

It is interesting to speculate on the influence of the early Greek immigrants on American culture. To justify this hypothesis consider the American habit of serving water with every meal, the ubiquitous hamburger (which is surely a poorly reproduced and inferior souvlaki and which is now being reimported) and some of the official uniforms, more particularly the flat, peaked hats of American postmen and policemen.

THE GREEK NATIONAL HOLIDAYS

Listed below are the national holidays and on these days many areas and islands hold festivals, but with a particular slant and emphasis.

1st January	New Year's Day/The Feast of Saint Basil
6th January	Epiphany/Blessing of the Waters – a cross is immersed in the sea, lake or river during a religious ceremony.
The period 27th Jan to 17th February	The Greek Carnival Season
25th March	The Greek National Anniversary/Independence Day
April – movable days	Good Friday/Procession of the 'Epitaph'; Holy Week Saturday/Ceremony of the Resurrection; Easter Sunday/open air feasts
1st May	May/Labour Day/Feast of the Flowers
1st to 10th July	Greek Navy Week
15th August	Assumption Day/Festival of the Virgin Mary, especially in the Cycladian island of Tinos (beware travelling at this time, anywhere in the area)
28th October	National Holiday/'Ochi' Day
24th December	Christmas Eve/Carols Evening
25th December	Christmas Day
26th December	St Stephen's Day
31st December	New Year's Eve carols, festivals

In addition to these national days, each island has its own particular festivals and holidays which are listed individually under each island.

A word of warning to ferry-boat travellers will not go amiss here – DO NOT travel to an island immediately prior to one of these festivals NOR off the island immediately after the event. It will be almost impossible to do other than stand, that is if one has not already been trampled to death in the various stampedes to and from the ferry-boats.

PART TWO

9 ATHENS CITY (ATHINA, AΘHNAI)

There is no end of it in this city, wherever you set your foot, you encounter some memory of the past. Marcus Cicero

Tel prefix 01

The capital of Greece and major city of Attica (Illustrations 4, 5 & 6). Previously the springboard for travel to most of the Greek islands, but less so since a number of direct flights have become available to the larger islands. Experienced travellers flying into Athens airport, often try to arrange their arrival for early morning and head straight to either the West airport (for a domestic flight), Piraeus port (*See* **Chapter Ten**), the railway station or bus terminal, so as to be able to get under way immediately.

ARRIVAL BY AIR
International flights other than *Olympic Airways* land at the:

East airport
Public transport facilities include:

Bus No. 18:   East airport to Leoforos Amalias almost as far as Syntagma Sq. Going to the airport the bus stop is on the right (*Syntagma Sq. behind one*) just beyond the East airport Olympic stop. Say every 30 mins from 0600-2400hrs and after midnight every hour on the half hour i.e. 0030, 0130, 0230hrs.
Fare 120drs. Yellow express bus.*

Bus No. 121:   East airport to Leoforos Olgas. 0630-2250hrs.
Fare 120drs.

Bus No. 19:   East airport to Plateia Karaiskaki/Akti Tselepi, Piraeus. Every hour from 0800-2000hrs.
Fare 120drs. Yellow express bus.*

Bus No. 101:   East airport via Leoforos Possidonos (coast road) to Klisovis/Theotoki St, Piraeus. Every 20 mins from 0500-2245hrs.
Fare 50drs.

Don't jump for the bus without obtaining tickets first from the office adjacent to the bus terminus.

One correspondent advised that for those not wanting to trek into Athens centre, it is worth considering staying in a hotel close by the airport. One drawback is the proximity of the flight-path. A recommended hotel that is a short distance away and not in a direct line with the runway is the:-

Hotel Avra (Class C) 3 Nireos, Paleon Faliro   Tel 981 4064
Directions: Proceed north (in the direction of Piraeus) along the coastal avenue of Leoforos Vasil Georgiou II which at Paleon Faliro becomes Leoforos Possidonos. A No. 101 bus travels the route. Proceed past the Marina to the area where the road cuts inland from the coastline, an overall distance of some 6km. Nireos St is a branch off the Esplanade Road.

The hotel is close to a beach and not outrageously expensive, in comparison to other Athens and Piraeus hotels. Singles sharing the bathroom start at 1220drs and en suite 1720drs while a double en suite costs 2150drs. These prices rise to 1460, 2060 and 2600drs respectively (1st June-31st Oct). Breakfast costs an extra 220drs.

Domestic and all Olympic flights land at the:

West airport
Public transport facilities include:

Bus No. 133:   West airport to Leoforos Square, Leoforos Amalias, Filellinon & Othonos Sts (Syntagma Sq). Every ½ hour from 0530-0030hrs.
Fare 50drs. Blue bus.

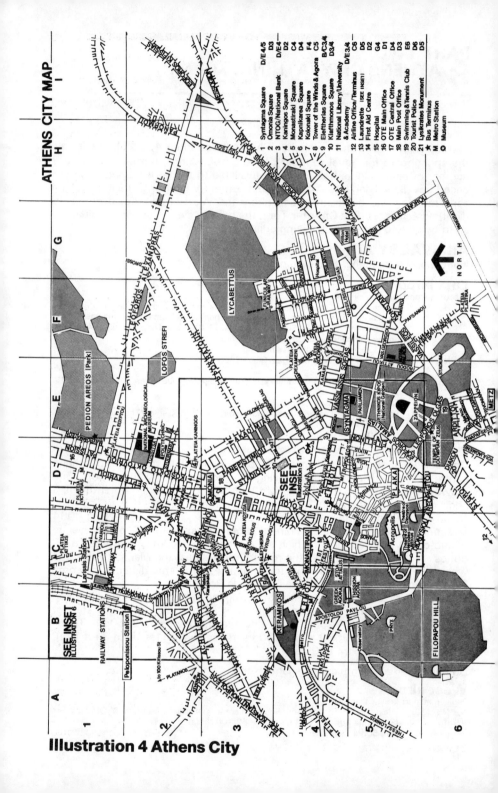

ATHENS CITY MAP

1	Syntagma Square	D/E 4/5
2	Omonia Square	D3
3	NTOG/National Bank	D/E4
4	Kaningos Square	D2
5	Monastiraki Square	C4
6	Kapnikarea Square	D4
7	Kolonaki Square	F4
8	Tower of the Winds & Agora	C5
9	Eleftherias Square	B/C3/4
10	Klafthmonos Square	D3/4
11	National Library/University	
	& Academy	D/E 3/4
12	Airline Office/Terminus	C6
13	Laundrette	(SEE INSET) D5
14	First Aid Centre	D5
15	Hospital	G4
16	OTE Main Office	D1
17	OTE Central Office	D4
18	Main Post Office	D3
19	Swimming & Tennis Club	E6
20	Tourist Police	D6
21	Lysikrates Monument	D5
★	Bus Terminus	
M	Metro Station	
O	Museum	

Illustration 4 Athens City

Bus No. 122:   West Airport to Leoforos Olgas. Every 20mins between 0600-2300hrs.
               Fare 50drs. Blue bus.
Buses No.   West airport via Leoforos Possidonos (coast road) to Klisovis St, Piraeus.
  107 & 109:

In addition there are Olympic buses connecting West and East airports as well as Olympic buses from the West airport to the Olympic offices (*Tmr* 12C5), on Leoforos Sygrou, and Syntagma Sq. Every 20 mins between 0600-2000hrs. Fare 100drs.

ARRIVAL BY BUS
Inter-country coaches usually decant passengers at Syntagma Sq (*Tmr* 1D/E4/5), Stathmos Larissis station (*Tmr* B/C1) or close to one of the major city bus terminals.

ARRIVAL BY FERRY
See **Piraeus, Chapter Ten**

ARRIVAL BY TRAIN
See **Trains, A To Z**

GENERAL (Illustrations 4 & 5)
Even if a traveller is a European city dweller, Athens will come as a sociological and cultural shock to the system. In the summer it is a hot, dusty, dry, crowded, traffic bound, exhaust polluted bedlam, but always friendly, cosmopolitan and ever on the move.

On arrival in Athens, and planning to stay over, it is best to select the two main squares of Syntagma (*Tmr* 1D/E4/5) and Omonia (*Tmr* 2/D3). These can be used as centres for the initial sally and from which to radiate out to the other streets and squares.

There is no substitute for a city map which is issued free (yes, free) from the Tourist Board desk in the National Bank of Greece on Syntagma Sq (*Tmr* 3/D/E4). *See* **NTOG, A To Z.**

Syntagama Square (Constitution or Parliament Sq)
(*Tmr* 1D/E4/5). The airport and many other buses stop here. It is the city centre with the most elite hotels, airline offices, international companies, including the American Express headquarters, smart cafes and the Parliament building, all circumscribing the central, sunken square. In the bottom, right-hand (or south-east) corner of the plateia, bounded by Odhos Othonos and Leoforos Amalias, are some very clean, attendant-minded toilets. There is a charge for the use of these 'squatties'.

To orientate, the *Parliament* building and *Monument to the Unknown Warrior* lie to the east of the square. To the north-east, in the middle, distance, is one of the twin hills of Athens, *Mt Lycabettus (Lykavittos, Lykabettos* & etc, etc). The other hill is the *Acropolis*, to the south-west, and not now visible from Syntagma Sq due to the high-rise buildings. On the west side of the square are the offices of *American Express* and a battery of pavement cafes, with Ermou St leading due west to Monastiraki Sq. To the north are the two parallel, main avenues of Stadiou (a one-way street down to Syntagma) and Venizelou or Panepistimiou (a one-way street out of Syntagma) that both run north-west to:

Omonia Square (Concorde or Harmony Sq) (*Tmr* 2D3) The
'Piccadilly Circus' or 'Times Square' of Athens but rather tatty really, with a constant stream of traffic bludgeoning its way round the large central island which is crowned by an impressive fountain. Visitors trying to escape the human bustle on the pavements by stepping off into the kerbside should beware that they are not mown down by a bus, taxi or car.

There is constant activity night and day, with the racial admixture of people cheek by jowl lending the square a cosmopolitan character all of its own. On every side are hotels. These vary from the downright seedy to the better-class tawdry, housed in rather undistinguised, 'neo-city-municipal' style, nineteenth century buildings, almost unique to Athens.

Various Metro train entrance/exits emerge around the square, spewing out and sucking in travellers. The Omonia underground concourse has a Post Office, telephones, a bank and, by the Dorou St entrance, a block of 'squatty' toilets for which the attendant charges 10drs for two sheets of paper.

Shops, cafes and booths fill the gaps between the hotels and the eight streets that converge on the Square.

To the north-east side of Omonia, on the corner of Dorou St, is a taxi rank and beyond, on the right, a now rather squalid, covered arcade brimful of reasonably priced snackbars. Through this covered passageway, and turning to the left up 28 Ikosiokto Oktovriou (28th October St)/Patission St, and then right down Veranzerou St, leads to:

Kaningos Square (*Tmr* 4D2) Serves as a Bus terminal for some routes.

To the south of Omonia Sq is Athinas St, the commercial thoroughfare of Athens. Here every conceivable item imaginable, including ironmongery, tools, crockery and clothing, can be purchased, and parallel to which, for half its length, runs Odhos Sokratous, the city street market during the day and the red-light district by night.

Athinas St drops due south to:

Monastiraki Square (*Tmr* 5C4) This marks the northernmost edge of the area known as the *Plaka* (*Tmr* D5) bounded by Ermou St to the north, Filellinon St to the east, and to the south by the slopes of the Acropolis.

Many of the alleys in this area follow the course of the old Turkish streets, most of the houses are mid-nineteenth century and represent the 'Old Quarter'.

Climbing the twisting maze of streets and steps of the lower north-east slopes of the Acropolis requires the stamina of a mountain goat. The almost primitive, island-village nature of some of the houses is very noticeable, due, it is said, to a Greek law passed after Independence. This was enacted to alleviate a housing shortage and allowed anyone who could raise the roof of a building, between sunrise and sunset, to finish it off and own the dwelling. Some inhabitants of the Cyclades island of Anafi (Anaphe) were reputed to have been the first to benefit from this new law and others followed to specialist in restoration and rebuilding, thus bringing about a colony of expatriate islanders within the Plaka district.

From the south-west corner of Monastiraki Sq, Ifestou St and its associated byways house the *Flea Market*, which climaxes on Sunday into stall upon stall of junk, souvenirs, junk, hardware, junk, boots, junk, records, junk, clothes, junk, footwear, junk, pottery and junk. Where Ifestou becomes Odhos Astigos and curves round to join up with Ermou St, there are a couple of extensive second-hand bookshops with reasonably priced (for Greece that is), if battered, paperbacks for sale. From the south-east corner of Monastiraki, Pandrossou St, one of the only enduring reminders of the Turkish Bazaar, contains a better class of antique dealer, sandal and shoe makers, and pottery stores.

Due south of Monastiraki Sq is Odhos Areos. The raggle-taggle band of European and Japanese drop-outs selling junk trinkets from the pavement kerb appear to have been replaced by a few local traders. Climbing Odhos Areos skirts the *Roman*

Agora, from which various streets lead upwards, on ever upwards, and which contain a plethora of stalls and shops, specialising in leather goods, clothes and souvenirs. The further you climb, the cheaper the goods become. This interestingly enough does not apply to the tavernas and restaurants which seemingly become more expensive as one ascends.

The Plaka (*Tmr* D5) The 'chatty' area known as the Plaka is littered with eating places, a few good, some bad, some tourist rip-offs. The liveliest street, Odhos Kidathineon, is, at its lowest end, jam-packed with cafes, tavernas and restaurants and at night attracts a number of music-playing layabouts. The class, tone and price of the establishments improves proceeding in a north-eastwards direction. I have to admit to gently knocking the Plaka over the years but it must be acknowledged that the area offers the cheapest accommo-dation and eating places in Athens and generally appears to have been cleaned up in recent years. In fact, since the 1986 'Libyan' downturn in American tourists, the area has become positively attractive. Early and late in the year, once the glut of overseas invaders have gone away, the Plaka returns to being a super place to visit. The shopkeepers become human, shopping is inexpensive and the tavernas revert to being 'Greek' and lively. In the last three weeks of February the *Apokria Festival*, a long running 'Halloween' style carnival, is centred on the Plaka. The streets are filled with dozens of revellers dressed in fancy dress, masks and funny hats wandering about, throwing confetti, and creating a marvellous atmosphere. For this event all the tavernas are decorated.

To the east of Monastiraki Sq is Ermou St which is initially lined by clothes and shoe shops. One third of the way towards Syntagma Sq and Odhos Ermou opens out into a small square on which there is the lovely *Church of Kapnikarea* (*Tmr* 6D4). Continuing eastwards, the shops become smarter with a preponderance of fashion stores whilst parallel to Ermou St is Odhos Ploutonos Kteka, which becomes Odhos Mitropoleos. Facing east, on the right is the City's Greek Orthodox Cathedral, *Great Mitropolis*. The church was built about 1850, from the materials of 70 old churches, to the design of four different architects resulting, not unnaturally, in a building of a rather 'strange' appearance. Alongside, and to the south, is the diminutive, medieval *Little Mitropolis* Church or Agios Eleftherios, dating back to at least the twelfth century but which has materials, reliefs and building blocks probably originating from the sixth century AD. A little further on is the intriguing and incongruous site of a small Byzantine church, built over and around by a modern office block, the columns of which tower above and beside the tiny building.

Leaving Syntagama Sq by the north-east corner, along Vassilissis Sofias, and turning left at Odhos Irodou Attikou, runs into:

Kolonaki Square (*Tmr* 7F4) The most fashionable square in the most fashionable area of Athens, around which most of the foreign embassies are located on the square, as are some expensive cafes, restaurants and boutiques.

To the north of Kolonaki, across the pretty, orange tree planted Dexameni Sq, is the southernmost edge of *Mt Lycabettus* (*Tmr* F/G3). Access to the summit can be made on foot by a number of steep paths, the main one of which, a stepped footpath, advances from the north end of Loukianou St, beyond Odhos Kle-omenous. A little to the east, at the top of Ploutarchou St, which breaks into a sharply rising flight of steps, is the cable car funicular railway. This runs in a 213m long tunnel emerging near to the nineteenth century chapel, which caps the fir tree covered outcrop, alongside a modern and luxuriously expensive restaurant. There are some excellent toilets. The railway service runs continuously as follows:

Winter: Wednesday, Saturday, Sunday 0845-0015hrs; Thursday 1030-0015hrs; Monday, Tuesday, Friday 0930-0015hrs.
Summer: As for winter but the opening hours extend daily to 0100hrs every night.
The trip costs 65drs one-way and 100drs for a return ticket.

A more relaxed climb, passing the open air theatre, can be made from the north end of Lycabettus.

The topmost part of the mountain, where the funicular emerges, is surprisingly small if not doll-like. The spectacular panorama that spreads out to the horizon, the stupendous views from far above the roar of the Athens traffic, are best seen in the early morning or late afternoon. Naturally the night hours are the time to see the city's lights.

Leaving Plateia Kolonaki from the south corner and turning right at Vassilissis Sofias, sallies forth to the north corner of:

The National Garden (Ethnikos Kipos) (*Tmr* E5) Here peacocks,
waterfowl and songbirds blend with a profusion of shrubbery, subtropical trees, ornamental ponds, various busts and cafe tables through and around which thread neat gravel paths.

To the south of the gardens are the *Zappeion Exhibition Halls*. To the north-west, the Greek Parliament buildings, the old Royal Palace and the Tomb or Monument to the Unknown Warrior, guarded by the traditionally costumed *Evzones*, the Greek equivalent of the British Buckingham Palace Guards (*See* **Places of Interest, A To Z**).

South-east of the National Gardens is the *Olympic Stadium* erected in 1896 on the site of the original stadium, built in 330 BC, and situated in a valley of the Arditos Hills.

South-west across Leoforos Olgas are the Olympic swimming pool and the *Tennis and Athletic Club*. To the west of these sporting facilities is the isolated gateway known as the *Arch of Hadrian* overlooking the busy traffic junction of Leoforos Olgas and Leoforos Amalias. Through the archway, the remains of the Temple of Olympian Zeus are outlined, 15 only of the original 104 Corinthian columns remain standing.

Leaving Hadrian's Arch, westwards along Odhos Dionysiou Areopagitou leads to the south side of:-

The Acropolis (Akropoli) (*Tmr* C5) A 10-acre rock rising 229m
above the surrounding city and surmounted by the Parthenon Temple, built in approximately 450 BC, the Propylaia Gateway, the Temple to Athena Nike and the triple Temple of Erechtheion. Additionally, there has been added the modern Acropolis Museum, discreetly tucked away, almost out of sight.

At the bottom of the southern slopes are the *Theatre of Dionysos*, originally said to seat up to 30,000 but more probably 17,000, and the smaller, second century AD, *Odeion of Herodes Atticus*, which has been restored and is used for plays and concerts during the summer festival. It is thought provoking to consider that the Dionysos Odeion is the original theatre where western world drama, as we know it, originated. The west slope leads to the *Hill of Areopagos* (*Areios Pagos*) where, in times of yore, a council of noblemen dispensed supreme judgements. Across

Apostolou Pavlou St lie the other tree covered hills of *Filopapou* (*Philopappos/ Mouseion*), or *Hill of Muses*, from whence the views are far-reaching and out-standing; *Pynx* (*Pynka*), where The Assembly once met and a *son et lumiere* is now held, and the *Asteroskopeion* (*Observatory*), or the *Hill of Nymphs*, whereon stands, surprise, surprise, an observatory.

Descending from the Asteroskopeion towards and across Apostolou Pavlou St is:

The Greek Agora (*Tmr* B/C4) The gathering place from whence the Athenians would have approached the Acropolis. This marketplace cum-civic centre is now little more than rubble, but the glory that once was is recreated by a model.

Nearby the *Temple of Hephaistos* or *Thission* (*Theseion*) sits on a small hill overlooking the Agora and to one side is the reconstructed marketplace, *Stoa Attalus*, the cost of which was met from private donations raised by American citizens.

A short distance to the east of the Greek Agora is the site of:-

The Roman Forum (or Agora) (*Tmr* C5) Close by is the *Tower of the Winds* (*Tmr* 8C5) a remarkable, octagonal tower, probably built in the first century BC and which served as a combination water clock, sundial and weather vane. Early descriptions say the building was topped off with a bronze weather vane represented by the mythological Triton complete with a pronged trident. The carved eight gods of wind can be seen, as can traces of the corresponding sundials, but no interior mechanism remains and the building is now used as a store for various stone antiquities.

A short distance to the north-west is an area known as *The Keramikos* (*Tmr* B4), a cemetery or graveyard, containing the *Street of the Tombs*, a funeral avenue laid out about 400 BC.

In a north-easterly direction from Keramikos, along Pireos St, via Eleftherias Sq Bus terminal (*Tmr* 9C3), turning right down Evripidou St, across Athinas and Eolou Sts, leads to:-

Klafthmonos Square (Klathmonos) (*Tmr* 10D3/4) Supposedly the most attractive Byzantine church in Athens, Aghii Theodori, is positioned in the west corner of the Square.

Looking north-east across Stadiou St, up Korai St and across Panepistimiou Ave, reveals an imposing range of neo-classical buildings (*Tmr* 11D/E3/4), fronted by formal gardens. These comprise the *University* flanked by, to the left (facing), the *National Library*, and to the right, the *Academy*. Behind and running parallel to Stadiou and Panepistimiou, is Akadimias St, on which is another Bus terminal. Just off Akadimias St, in Massalias St, is the *Hellenic-American Union*, many of whose facilities are open to the general public. These include an English and music library, as well as a cafeteria.

North-west of Klafthmonos Sq, to the left of Eolou St, is:-

Kotzia Square (*Tmr* D3) A very large plateia around which, on Sunday at least, a profusion of flower sellers' stalls circle the square.

The once paved area has now been dug up by archaeologists who have unearthed a veritable treasure trove of ancient Athens city walls. At the time of writing the fate of the site is in the hands of the opposing and seemingly irreconcilable tugs of the modernists, who have a vision of a vast underground car park, and the traditionalists, who quite rightly, wish to see the 'dig' preserved for posterity.

Fokionos Negri Actually a street, if not an avenue, rather than a square. It is somewhat distant from the city centre, almost in the suburbs to the north, and usually just off the street plans of Athens. To reach Fokionos Negri from Omonia Square, proceed up 28 Ikosiokto Oktovriou, which runs into Patission St, on past the *National Archaeological Museum* and *Green Park* (*Pedion Areos*), both on the right, to where Agiou Meletiou St runs across Patission St. Fokionos Negri starts as a fairly narrow side-street to the right, but widens out into a tree lined. short, squat ˇvenue with a wide, spacious, centre pedestrian way once gravelled but now extensively resurfaced. Supposedly the *Dolce Vita* or *Via Veneto* of Athens but not out of the ordinary, if quiet wealth is normal. Extremely expensive cafes edge the square halfway up on the right and it certainly becomes extremely lively after nightfall.

Trolley-buses 5, 11, 12 or 13, going north, trundle past the turning.

THE ACCOMMODATION & EATING OUT

The Accommodation On the islands the haul of accommodation includes even 'E' Class hotels but in Athens I have erred on the side of caution and stuck with 'B', 'C' and some better 'D' class hotels and pensions. No doubt there are some acceptable Class 'E' hotels but...

On Adrianou St (*Tmr* D5), in the Plaka district, are a few, very cheap dormitories and students' hostels, where a certain amount of rooftop sleeping is allowed, costing upwards of 500drs per night. Unless set well back from the main road, a set of earmuffs or plugs is almost obligatory to ensure a good night's sleep.

On a cautionary note, since the end of 1981 the Greek authorities have been closing a number of the more 'undesirable', unlicensed hotels, so a particular favourite overnight stop from years gone by may no longer be in business.

Most of the hotel charges listed in this book are priced at the 1987 rates but these will average out for 1988 as follows:

Class	Single	Double	
A	5000-6300	6200-8600drs	) en suite bathroom
B	3000-4500	4000-6200drs	) & breakfast included.
C	1900-3000	2500-4000drs	) sharing bathroom &
D	1000-1500	1500-2500drs	) room rate only.
E	850-1000	1000-1500drs	

See **Arrival By Air, East airport, Introduction**

SYNTAGMA AREA (*Tmr* D/E4/5)
Festos Guest House (*Tmr* D/E5) 18 Filellinon St   Tel 323 2455
Directions: From Syntagma Sq, walk up the rise of Odhos Filellinon past a number of cut-price ticket joints. The entrance is very nearly opposite Ag Nikodimos Church, on the right.

Ethnic guest house with dormitories, triples and quadruple rooms working out at between 500 and 1000drs per person. Hot showers cost an extra 100drs but luggage is stored free. The bar not only serves drinks but simple snacks. For the indiscriminately young at heart.

Hotel Cleo (Cleopatra) (*Tmr* D4) 3 Patroou St   Tel 322 9053
Directions: Leaving Syntagma Sq, walk down Mitropoleos St, towards Monastiraki Sq and take the fourth turning left.

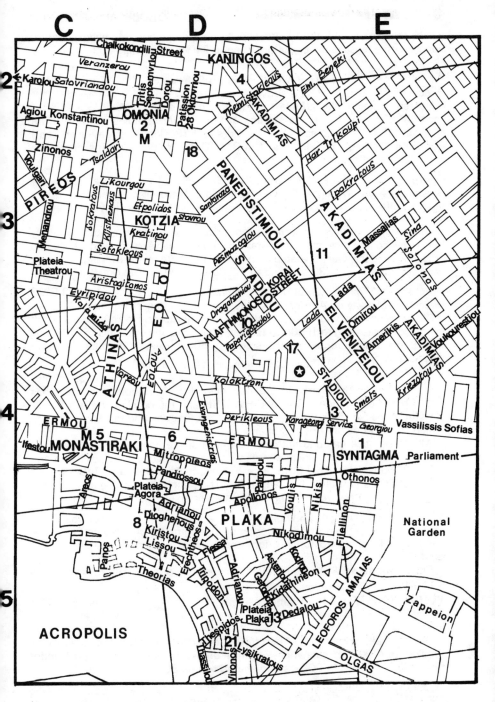

Illustration 5 Athens City inset - The Plaka

Well recommended if threadbare. Ground floor dormitory, free baggage store. Double rooms en suite cost 1650drs rising to 2400drs (1st May-30th Sept). *NB The owners also have a guest house nearby in 18 Apollonos St.*

Pension John's Place (*Tmr* D4) (Class C) 5 Patroou St   Tel 322 9719
Directions: As for *Hotel Cleo* above.

Not surprisingly, the affable old Papa is named John. Well looked after accommodation with singles starting at 900drs and doubles from 1400drs (1st Jan-30th April) increasing to 1200drs and 1800drs (1st May-30th Sept) and 1000drs and 1500drs (1st Oct-31st Dec). Naturally rooms share the bathroom facilities.

George's Guest House (*Tmr* D4) (Class B) 46 Nikis St   Tel 322 6474
Directions: From Syntagma Sq, walk west along Mitropoleos St and turn down the first left-hand turning. The guest house is on the right, beyond the first side-street.

Calls itself a *Youth Hostel with student prices*. It was recommended to me by four Texas college girls, met on the train to Patras some years ago and whose first stop in Greece this was. Shared bathroom and hot water in the evening, if you are quick. Doubles from 1230drs rising to 2200drs (1st April-10th Oct).

Hotel Kimon (*Tmr* D5) (Class D) 27 Apollonos   Tel 323 5223
Directions: Midway on Apollonos St, one block down from Mitropoleos St.

Old but renovated with all rooms sharing the bathrooms. Single rooms start off at 1000drs increasing to 1630drs (1st May-30th Sept) and en suite 1250drs rising to 1750drs. Double rooms en suite start at 1250drs rising to 1875drs.

Hotel Plaka (*Tmr* D4) (Class C) 7 Kapnikareas/Mitropoleos Sts
                                                        Tel 322 2096
Directions: From Syntagma Sq proceed west along Mitropoleos. Kapnikareas St lies between Evangenistrias and Eolou Sts and the hotel is on the left.

Listed because the hotel accepts *American Express* and or *Diners* despite which the charges are not exorbitant.

All rooms have en suite bathrooms with a single costing 1750drs a night and a double 2400drs which charges increase respectively to 2000drs and 2700/3300drs (1st April-30th June & 1st Oct-31st Dec) and 2400drs and 3300/3900drs (1st July-30th Sept). Breakfast might have to be an inclusive, charged extra at between 280 and 350drs per head.

YMCA (XAN) (*Tmr* E4) 28 Omirou St   Tel 362 6970
Directions: From the north-east corner of Syntagma Sq proceed up Panepistimiou St, take the third turning right and across Akadimias Avenue, on the right.

Closed for some years for renovations and may open in 1987... then again it may not.

YWCA (XEN) (*Tmr* E4) 11 Amerikis St.   Tel 362 4291
Directions: All as above but second turning off Panepistimiou St and on the left.

Don't forget, women only. Apart from accommodation there is a cafe serving breakfasts (200drs), sandwiches, a hair dressing salon, library and laundry facilities. Singles from 900drs and shared rooms 800drs per head.

OMONIA AREA (*Tmr* 2D3)
Any hotel or pension rooms facing Omonia Square must be regarded as very noisy.

Hotel Omonia (*Tmr* D3) (Class C) 4 Omonia Sq.　　　　　Tel 523 7210
Directions: Just stand on Omonia Sq, swivel on your heels and on the north side of the Square.
　The reception is on the first floor, as is a cafe-bar and terrace, overlooking the square and its action. Modern but 'worn international' look to the place. Clients may well have to take demi-pension terms. All rooms have en suite bathrooms. Singles start at 1200drs and a double room 1750drs rising, respectively, to 1400drs and 1750drs (1st April-14th July & 15th Sept-31st Oct) and 1700drs and 2100drs (15th July-14th Sept). Breakfast costs 250drs and a meal from 850drs.

Hotel Banghion (*Tmr* D3) (Class C) 18b Omonia Sq.　　　　Tel 324 2259
Directions: As for *Hotel Omonia*, but on the south side of the square.
　Elegant and ageing. Rooms sharing a bathroom cost 1250drs for a single and 1900drs for a double and with en suite bathrooms 1800drs and 2450drs. These charges rise respectively to 1500/2300drs and 2100/2950drs (16th July-30th Sept). Breakfasts costs 280drs increasing to 330drs (16th July-30th Sept).

Hotel Carlton (*Tmr* D3) (Class C) 7 Omonia Sq.　　　　　Tel 522 3201
Directions: As for *Hotel Omonia*.
　Very Greek, provincial and old fashioned. All rooms share bathrooms with single rooms from 1000drs and double rooms 1250drs, increasing to 1200drs and 1350drs (1st April-31st May) and 1350drs and 1500drs (1st June-31st Dec).

Hotel Europa (*Tmr* D2) (Class C) 7 Satovriandou St　　　　Tel 522 3081
Directions: North of Omonia Sq and the second main street up, lying east/west. This is often listed as Chateaubriandou St but the local authorities either have, or have not been notified of the change. Whatever, the street is now a pedestrian precinct.
　Another 'Greek provincial' hotel, the remarkably ancient lift of which creaks its way up and down to the various floors. The rooms are adequate but dingy, there are wardrobes and the floors are covered with brown linoleum. To use the shower the concierge must be asked for the relevant key, in mime if a guest's Greek is as sketchy as the staff's knowledge of English. When produced, the key might well be adjudged large enough to open the doors of the Bastille. Weighted down by this instrument, the moment of truth dawns, for when the door is opened, sheer disbelief may well be the first reaction, especially if it is the first ever stopover in Athens, as it was mine many years ago. A cavernous and be-cobwebbed room reveals plumbing that beggars description. Enough to say the shower is most welcome even if the lack of a point to anchor the shower head, whilst trying to soap oneself down, requires interesting body contortions. The rate for a single room is 1000drs and for a double 1500drs sharing the bathrooms.

Hotel Alma (*Tmr* D2/3) (Class C) 5 Dorou·　　　　　　Tel 524 0858
Directions: Dorou St runs north from the north-east corner of Omonia Sq.
　Modern and the rooms with a balcony are on the seventh and eighth floors. Single rooms sharing a bathroom start at 1200drs and en suite 1400drs while double rooms cost 1400drs and 1750drs, which rates respectively rise to 1500/1700drs and 1800/2000drs (1st April-15th Oct) and 1300/1500drs and 1500/1800drs (16th Oct-31st Dec).

Hotel Orpheus (*Tmr* C/D2) (Class C) 58 Chalkokondili St   Tel 522 4996
Directions: North of Omonia Sq.
  Stolid, studentish and provincial in character. Very well recommended and
reasonably priced with a mix of accommodation available. For 1988 rooms (&
rates) include single (1300drs), double (1800drs), triple (2400drs), quadruple
(2800drs), quintuple (3000drs) and dormitory (500drs per person). There is
a TV lounge, outdoor patio and bar. Continental breakfast is available at 250drs
and an English breakfast at a cost of 400drs. Bar prices are reasonable with
a Nes meh ghala costing 90drs, an ouzo 60drs, Metaxa 3 star brandy 60drs
and an Amstel beer 100drs. Overseas phone calls can be made.

Hotel Eva (*Tmr* C2) (Class D) 31 Victoros Ougo   Tel 522 3079
Directions: West of Omonia as far as Plateia Karaiskaki and to the north,
parallel with and two blocks back from Ag Konstantinou.
  Well recommended, all rooms have en suite bathrooms. Single rooms start
at 1200drs and double rooms 2130drs rising to 1480drs and 2780drs (1st
June-30th Sept). Breakfast costs 250drs.

Hotel Marina (*Tmr* C3) (Class C) 13 Voulgari   Tel 523 7832/3
Directions: South-west from Omonia Sq along Odhos Pireos and 4th turning
to the right.
  Single rooms cost from 1150drs, double rooms 1450drs, both sharing the
bathroom, while rooms with en suite bathrooms cost from 1400drs and
1950drs respectively. These rates rise (16th March-30th June & 16th Oct-
31st Dec) to 1300drs and 1700drs (single and doubles sharing) and 1600drs
and 2350drs (singles and doubles en suite) and again (1st July-15th Oct) to
1400/1900drs and 1750/2650drs. Breakfast is charged at 200drs.

Hotel Vienna (*Tmr* C3) (Class C) 20 Pireos   Tel 524 9143
Directions: South-west of Omonia Sq.
  New, clean and noisy. All rooms have en suite bathrooms with singles
starting at 1700drs and doubles 2250drs, increasing to 2000drs and 2650drs
(1st July-31st Oct). A breakfast costs 250drs.

Hotel Athinea (*Tmr* C2) (Class C) 9 Vilara   Tel 524 3884
Directions: Westwards along Ag Konstantinou and situated on one side of the
small square of Agiou Konstantinou.
  Old but beautifully positioned although cabaret night life may intrude. A
restaurant and cake shop are close by as is a taxi rank. All rooms have en
suite bathrooms. A single room starts off at 1460drs and a double 2000drs
rising to 1830drs and 2400drs (1-15th June & 1-31st Oct) and again to
2000drs and 2850drs (11-30th April & 16th June-30th Sept). Breakfast is
priced at 400drs.

Hotel Florida (*Tmr* C3) (Class C) 25 Menandrou   Tel 522 3214
Directions: Third turning left, south-west along Pireos St.
  Single rooms from 790/1055drs and doubles 1530drs, both without a
bathroom, whilst en suite rooms cost 1220drs and 1865drs. These charges
rise respectively to 990/1320drs and 1910drs, and 1525drs and 2330drs
(1st June-30th Sept). Breakfast is charged at 230drs.

Hotel Alcestis (Alkistis) (*Tmr* C3) (Class C) 18 Plateia Theatrou
                                                          Tel 321 9811
Directions: From Pireos St, south down either Sokratous or Menandrou Sts
and across Odhos Sofokleous St.

Despite its chromium-plated appearance, all glass and marble with a prairie-sized lobby, it is a Class C hotel in a commercial square. Popular and all rooms have en suite bathrooms. Singles start off at 1870drs and doubles 2400drs rising to 2100drs and 2800drs (1st July-30th Sept). Breakfast costs 300drs and lunch/dinner 1000drs.

MONASTIRAKI AREA (*Tmr* C4)

Hotel Tembi/Tempi (*Tmr* C/D4) (Class D) 29 Eolou (Aiolu/Aeolou)
Tel 321 3175
Directions: A main street north of Ermou St, opposite the Church of Ag Irini.
Pleasant rooms with singles sharing the bathroom starting at 800drs rising to 950drs (16th May-31st Oct). Double rooms sharing cost from 1200drs and en suite 1500drs advancing to 1500drs and 1800drs respectively.

Hotel Ideal (*Tmr* C/D4) (Class D) 39 Eolou/2 Voreou Sts.   Tel 321 3195
Directions: On the left of Eolou, walking northwards from Odhos Ermou, and on the corner with Voreou St.
A perfect example of a weather-worn, 19th century, Athens neo-classical building complete with an old fashioned, metal and glass canopy entrance and matchbox sized, wrought iron balconies. The accommodation lives up to all that the exterior promises! The management are helpful, there is a telephone, TV room, a bar and luggage can be stored. Tourist information is freely available as are battered paperbacks for guests. The rooms are clean and the bathroom facilities are shared but there is 24 hour hot water – they promise! Singles start at 800drs and doubles 1200drs rising to 950drs and 1500drs (16th May-31st Oct).

Hotel Hermion (*Tmr* C/D4) (Class D) 66c Ermou St   Tel 321 2753
Directions: East of Monastiraki, adjacent to Kapnikarea Church/Square (*Tmr* 6D4).
Old but clean with the reception up the stairs. All rooms share bathrooms with the single room rate starting off at 900drs and the double rooms 1300drs increasing to 1050drs and 1600drs, respectively (1st July-30th Sept).

Hotel Attalos (*Tmr* C3/4) (Class C) 29 Athinas   Tel 321 2801
Directions: North from Monastiraki Sq.
Recommended to us by a splendidly eccentric English lady artist who should know – she has been visiting Greece for some 20 years. Singles sharing the bathroom start from 1200drs and en suite 1410drs while doubles cost 1500drs and 1750drs. These charges increase to (singles) 1500/1765 and (doubles) 2000/3150drs (1st June-15th Oct). Breakfast is charged at 275drs.

Hotel Cecil (*Tmr* C3/4) (Class D) 39 Athinas   Tel 321 7079
Directions: North from Monastiraki Sq and two buildings up from the Kalamida St turning, on the left-hand side. This is the other side of the road from a very small chapel, incongruously stuck on the pavement. The 'informative' sign outside the hotel is no help.
Clean looking with a single room costing 1200drs and a double 1800drs. The bathrooms are shared.

PLAKA/METZ STADIUM AREAS (*Tmr* D5 & D/E6)
The Plaka is rich in accommodation, as it is in most things!

Hotel Phaedra (*Tmr* D5) (Class D) 4 Adrianou/16 Herephontos Tel 323 8461
Directions: Situated close by a multi-junction of various streets including Lysikratous, Galanou, Adrianou and Herephontos, opposite the Byzantine Church of Ag Ekaterini and its small, attractive gardens.
Pretty area by day, noisy by night. A family hotel with a ground floor bar. All rooms share the bathrooms with a single room costing 1300drs and doubles 1600drs which rates increase respectively to 2000drs and 2500drs (1st April-15th Oct). Breakfast costs 250drs.

Students' Inn (*Tmr* D5) (Class C) 16 Kidathineon St   Tel 324 4808
Directions: On the left of the liveliest stretch of Kidathineon St, walking up from the Adrianou St junction, and almost opposite the front garden of a Japanese eating house.
Hostelish and classified as a pension but recommended as good value with hot showers 'on tap' (sorry) and an English-speaking owner. There is a rooftop, a passable courtyard, a snackbar, the use of a washing machine (which does not always work) and a baggage store costing 50drs per day. The clean but basic rooms, which all share the bathrooms, are complete with a rickety, oilcloth covered table and a mug. Singles cost 1200drs and doubles 1500drs. This latter price increases to 1700drs (2nd May-30th Sept). Breakfast costs 250drs, but I would have to wander out to 'breathe in' the Plaka. The doors are locked at 0200hrs.

Left off Kidathineon Street, climbing towards Syntagma Sq, is Odhos Kodrou on which are two clean, agreeable hotels in a very pleasant area, the:
Hotel Adonis *(Tmr* D5) (Class B) 3 Kodrou/Voulis Sts   Tel 324 9737
Directions: As above and on the right.
Actually a pension so the rates are not outrageous. All rooms have en suite bathrooms with singles starting off at 1800drs and doubles 1900drs rising respectively to 2250drs and 2400drs (1st July-30th Sept) and the:

Acropolis House (*Tmr* D5) (Class B) 6-8 Kodrou   Tel 322 2344
Directions: As above and on the left.
Highly recommended and once again officially classified as a pension with a choice of rooms sharing or complete with en suite bathrooms. Between April and October the expensive single room rates commence at 2375drs and doubles 2880drs while en suite singles cost 2630drs and doubles 3170drs.

Closer to Kidathineon St, and on the right is the:
Kourous Pension (*Tmr* D5) (Class C) 11 Kodrou   Tel 322 7431
Directions: As above.
Rather more provincial than the two establishments detailed above, which lack of sophistication is reflected in the lower prices (and standards). All rooms share the bathrooms and the single room rate starts at 900drs and a double 1400drs climbing to the dizzy heights (!) of 1200drs and 1800drs (1st May-30th Sept).

Hotel Solonion (*Tmr* D5) (Class E) 11 Sp Tsangari/Dedalou   Tel 322 0008
Directions: To the right of Kidathineon St (*facing Syntagma Sq*) between Dedalou St and Leoforos Amalias. Odhos Tsangari is a continuation of Asteriou St.
I did start out by pronouncing I would not list any E class hotels but... Run by a rather stern faced lady who is assisted by a varied collection of part-time assistants to run the old, faded but refurbished building. If a guest strikes lucky

the night porter will be a delightful old boy who was once a merchant in the Greek community resident in Turkey, and caught up in the huge population resettlement of 1922/23. The accommodation is 'student provincial' quality, the rooms being high ceilinged with the rather dodgy floorboards overlaid and hidden beneath brown linoleum. The bathrooms are distinctly ethnic and Victorian in style but hot water is promised all day. On a fine day.... it is possible to espy the Acropolis... well a bit of it. No single rooms are available. A double room sharing the bathroom costs from 1200drs, including one bath a day, which rises to 1400drs (1st April-15th Oct).

Close by the *Hotel Solonion* are the:-
Hotel Kekpoy (Cecrops) *(Tmr* D5) (Class D) 13 Sp Tsangari   Tel 322 3080
Directions: On the same side as and similar to the *Solonion* but a building or two towards Leoforos Amalias.
   All rooms share the bathrooms with singles costing 1300drs and doubles 1390drs (1st April-15th Oct).
Hotel Phoebus (Fivos) *(Tmr* D5) (Class C) Asteriou/12 Peta Sts
Tel 322 0142
Directions: Back towards Kidathineon St, on the corner of Odhos Asteriou and Peta.
   Rather more up-market than the three previously listed hotels, all rooms have en suite bathrooms. A single room is charged at 1950drs and a double room costs 2500drs. These rates rise respectively to 2300drs and 3000drs (1st June-30th Sept). Breakfast costs 300drs.

A few side streets towards the Acropolis is the:-
Hotel Ava *(Tmr* D5) 9 Lysikratous St   Tel 323 6618
Directions: As above.
   I have no personal experience but the establishment has been mentioned as a possibility and is in an excellent, central but quiet situation although it is rather expensive. All rooms have en suite bathrooms, are heated and air conditioned. Single rooms cost from 2800drs and doubles from 3600drs. There are family suites complete with kitchen and refrigerator (sic).

New Clare's House *(Tmr* E6) (Class C Pension) 24 Sorvolou St
Tel 922 2288
Directions: Rather uniquely, the owners have had a large compliments slip printed with a pen and ink drawing on the face and, on the reverse side, directions in Greek saying *Show this to the taxi driver*. This includes details of the location, south of the Stadium, on Sorvolou St between Charvouri and Voulgareos Sts. The pension is on the right, half-way down the reverse slope with the description *white building with the green shutters*. From Syntagma proceed south down the sweep of Leoforos Amalias, keeping to the main avenue hugging the Temple of Olympian Zeus and along Odhos Diakou. Where Diakou makes a junction with Vouligmenis and Ardittou Avenues, Odhos Anapafseos leads off in a south-east direction and Sorvolou St 'crescents' off to the left. Trolley buses 2, 4, 11 & 12 drop travellers by the Stadium. It is quite a steep climb up Sorvolou St, which breaks into steps, to the pretty and highly recommended area of Metz (highly regarded by Athenians that is). Plus points are that the narrow nature of the lanes, which suddenly become steps, keeps the traffic down to a minimum and the height of the hill raises it above the general level of smog and pollution.

The pleasant, flat-fronted pension is on the right and has a marble floor entrance hall. Inside, off to the left, is a large reception/lounge/bar/breakfast/common room and to the right, the lift. Apart from the usual hotel business, the establishment 'beds' some tour companies clients overnighting in Athens, and en route to other destinations. Thus the hotel can be fully booked so it is best to make a forward booking or telephone prior to journeying out here. The self confident English speaking owner presides over matters from a large desk in the reception area and is warily helpful. The lady staff receptionists do not exactly go wild in an orgy of energy sapping activity, tending to indulge in a saturnalia of TV watching. Guests in the meantime can help themselves to bottles of beer and Coke from the bar, paying when convenient to them, and the receptionist. Despite the inferred aura of excellence the usual collection of faults crop up from time to time including: cracked loo seats; no hot water, despite being assured that there is 24 hours hot water (and for longer no doubt were there more hours in the day!); missing locking mechanism on the lavatory door; toilets having to be flushed using a piece of string and the television on the blink. I do not mean to infer that these irritating defects occur all at once – just one or two, every so often. Double rooms sharing a bathroom cost 2100drs and en suite 3000drs which rates increase, respectively, to 2300drs and 3400drs (1st June-31st Dec). Incidentally, where the well appointed bathrooms are shared, the pleasant rooms only have to go fifty-fifty with one other room. The charges, which include breakfast with warm bread every day, may at first impression (and for that matter second and third impression) appear on the expensive side. The 'pain' might be eased by the realisation that the 4th floor has a balcony and a self-catering kitchen, complete with cooker and a fridge, and the 5th floor a laundry room with an iron and 2 rooftop clothes lines. These facilities must of course be taken into account when weighing up comparative prices. The management creates an atmosphere that will suit the young, very well behaved student and the older traveller but not exuberant rowdies. Hands are 'smacked' if guests lie around eating a snack on the front steps, hang washing out of the windows or make a noise, especially between the hours of 1330 and 1700 and after 2330hrs. You know, lights out boys and no smoking in the 'dorms'. Clare's House was originally recommended by pension owner Alexis on the island of Kos and in recent years has been included in one or two of the smaller tour companies' brochures for the Athens overnight stop. Certainly an old friend of ours, Peter, who 'has to put up with yachting round the Aegean waters during the summer months', almost always spends some of his winter Athens months at Clare's and swears by the place.

Before leaving the area there is an intriguing possibility, accommodation that is, in a very quiet street edging the west side of the Stadium.
Joseph's House Pension (*Tmr* E6) (Class C) 13 Markou Moussourou
                                                                    Tel 923 1204

Directions: From the region of Hadrian's Arch/the Temple of the Olympian Zeus (*Tmr* D6) proceed up Avenue Arditou in a north-easterly direction towards the Stadium. Odhos Markou Moussourou climbs steeply off to the right, immediately prior to the wooded hillside of Arditos. The pension is on the left, beyond Meletiou Riga St. On the other hand, it is just as easy to follow the directions to *Clare's House* and proceed east along Charvouri St until it bumps into Markou Moussourou.

The bathrooms are shared with single rooms charged at 1000drs and doubles at 1400drs, which rates rise to 1000drs and 1500drs (1st May-30th Sept).

THISSION AREA (THESION) (*Tmr* B/C4/5)
First south-bound Metro stop after Monastiraki and a much quieter area than, say, the Plaka.
Hotel Phedias (*Tmr* B4) (Class C) 39 Apostolou Pavlou   Tel 345 9511
Directions: South of the Metro station.

Modern and friendly. All rooms share en suite bathrooms with singles costing 1800drs and double rooms 2300drs, rising to 2100drs and 2700drs (1st July-31st Dec). Breakfast is charged at 250drs per head.

OLYMPIC OFFICE AREA (*Tmr* C6)
Hotel Karayannis (*Tmr* C6) (Class C) 94 Leoforos Sygrou   Tel 921 5903
Directions: On the corner of Odhos Byzantiou and Leoforos Sygrou, opposite the side exit of the Olympic terminal office.

'Interesting', tatty and noisy, but very necessary for travellers arriving late at the terminal. Rooms facing the main road should be avoided. The Athenian traffic, which roars up and down the broad avenue non-stop round the clock, gives every appearance of making the journey along Leoforos Sygrou via the hotel balconies, even three or four storeys up. There are picturesque views of the Acropolis from the breakfast and bar rooftop terrace, even if they are through a maze of television aerials. Single rooms with an en suite bathroom cost 1410drs. Double rooms sharing a bathroom cost 1910drs, and en suite 1990drs. These prices increase respectively to 1615drs and 2190/2285drs. Breakfast for one costs 250drs. Best to splash out for the en suite rooms as the hotel's shared lavatories are of a 'thought' provoking nature with a number of the unique features detailed under the general description of bathrooms in **Chapter Four**.

Whilst in this area it would be a pity not to mention the:-
Super-bar Restaurant Odhos Faliron
Directions: As for the *Hotel Karayannis* but behind the Olympic office.

Not inexpensive but very conveniently situated, even if it is closed on Sundays. Snackbar food with 2 Nes meh gala, a toasted cheese and ham sandwich and boiled egg costing 280drs. On that occasion I actually wanted toast...

Youth Hostel 57 Kypselis St and Agiou Meletiou 1   Tel 822 5860
Directions: Located in the Fokionos Negri area of North Athens. Proceed along 28 Ikosiokto Oktovriou/Patission Street from Omonia Sq, beyond Pedion Areos Park to Ag Meletiou St. Turn right and follow until the junction with Kypselis St. Trolley buses 3, 5, 11, 12 & 13 make the journey.

This proclaims itself as *The Official Youth Hostel* and does fulfil the require-ments of those who require very basic, cheap accommodation, albeit in dormitories. The overnight charge is 500 drs.

Taverna Youth Hostel (*Tmr* G2) 1 Drossi St/87 Leoforos Alexandra
Tel 646 3669
Directions: East of Pedion Aeros Park along Leoforos Alexandra almost as far as the junction with Ippokratous St. Odhos Drossi is on the left. It is possible to catch trolley-bus No. 7 from Panepistimiou Avenue or No. 8 from Kanigos

Sq (*Tmr* 4D2) or Akadimias St.

Actually a taverna that 'sprouts' an 'unofficial Youth Hostel' for the summer months only.

If only to receive confirmation regarding the spurious Youth Hostels, it may be worth visiting the:-

YHA Head Office (*Tmr* D3/4) 4 Dragatsaniou   Tel 323 4107

Directions: The north side of Plateia Klafthmonos in a street on the left-hand side of Stadiou St.

Only open Monday-Friday, 0900-1500hrs. They advise of vacancies in the youth hostels and issue international youth hostel cards.

LARISSIS STATION AREA (*Tmr* B/C1)
See **Trains, A To Z.**

CAMPING
Sample daily site charges per person vary between 290-400drs (children half-price) and the hire of a tent between 350-550drs.

Sites include the following:-

Distance from Athens	Site Name	Amenities
8km	**Athens Camping.** 198 Athinon Ave. On the road to Dafni (due west of Athens). Tel 581 4101	Open all year, 25km from the sea. Bar, shop & showers.
10km	**Dafni Camping.** Dafni. On the Athens to Corinth National Road. Tel 581 1562	Open all year, 5km from the sea. Bar, shop, showers & kitchen facilities.

For the above: Bus 853, Athens – Elefsina, departs Koumoundourou Sq/Deligeorgi St (*Tmr* C2/3) every 20 mins between 0510-2215hrs.

14.5km	**Patritsia.** Kato Kifissia, N. Athens. Tel 801 1900 Closed 'temporarily' for 1987, query 1988?	Open June-October. Bar, shop, showers, laundry & kitchen facilities.
16km	**Nea Kifissia.** Nea Kifissia, N. Athens. Tel 807 5544	Open April-October, 20km from the sea. Bar, shop, showers, swimming pool & laundry.
18km	**Dionyssiotis.** Nea Kifissia N. Athens. Tel 807 1494	Open all year
25km	**Papa-Camping.** Zorgianni, Ag Stefanos. Tel 803 3446	Open June-October, 25km from the sea. Laundry, bar & kitchen facilities.

For the above (sited on or beside the Athens National Road, north to Lamia): Lamia bus from 260 Liossion St (*Tmr* C1/2), every hour from 0615 to 1915hrs & at 2030hrs.

35km	**Marathon Camping.** Kaminia, Marathon. NE of Athens. Tel 0294 5577	On a sandy beach & open April-October. Showers, bar restaurant & kitchen facilities.
35km	**Nea Makri.** 156 Marathonos Ave, Nea Makri. NE of Athens just south of Marathon. Tel 0294 92719	Open April-October, 220m from the sea. Sandy beach, laundry, bar & shop.

For the above: The bus from Odhos Mavrommateon, Plateia Egyptou (*Tmr* D1), every ½ hour from 0530 to 2200hrs.

26km	**Cococamp.** Rafina. East of Athens. Tel 0294 23413	Open all year. On the beach, rocky coast. Laundry, bar, showers, kitchen facilities, shop & restaurant.
29km	**Kokkino Limanaki Camping** Kokkino Limanaki, Rafina Tel 0294 31602	On the beach. Open April-October.

29km   **Rafina Camping.** Rafina. East of Athens. Open May-October, 4km from the sandy beach.
Tel 0294 23118   Showers, bar, laundry, restaurant & shop

For the above: The Rafina bus from Mavrommateon St, Plateia Egyptou (*Tmr* D1). Twenty-nine departures from 0550 to 2200hrs.

20km   **Voula Camping.** 2 Alkyonidon St, Voula. Open all year. On the sandy beach. Showers,
Just below Glyfada & the Airport. Tel laundry, shop & kitchen facilities.
895 2712

27km   **Varkiza Beach Camping.** Varkiza. Open all year, by a sandy beach. Bar, shop,
Coastal road Athens-Vouliagmeni-Sou- supermarket, taverna, laundry & kitchen facili-
nion. Tel 897 3613   ties.

60km   **Sounion Camping.** Sounion Tel 0292 Open all year, by a sandy beach. Bar, shop,
39358   laundry, kitchen facilities & a taverna.

76km   **Vakhos Camping.** Assimaki nr Sounion. Open June-September, on the beach.
On the Sounion to Lavrion road. Tel 0292
39263

For the above: Buses from Mavrommateon St, Plateia Egyptou (*Tmr* D1) every hour from 0630 to 1730hrs. Note, to get to Vakhos Camping catch the Sounion bus via Markopoulo and Lavrion.

The Eating Out

Where to dine out is a very personal choice and in a city the size of Athens there are so many restaurants and tavernas from which to choose that only a few recommendations are made. In general, steer clear of Luxury and Class A hotel dining rooms, restaurants offering international cuisine and tavernas with Greek music and or dancing*, all of which may be very good but are usually on the expensive side. Gongoozling from one of the chic establishments, such as a *Floka's*, at one of the smart squares has become an expensive luxury with a milky coffee (Nes meh ghala) or a bottle of beer costing anything up to 150drs, and an ouzo 200drs. In contrast it is possible to 'coffee' in the Plaka at, say *Kafeneion To Mainalon* (on the junction of Odhos Geronda, also named Monisasteriou, and Kidathineon St) where prices are much more reasonable at about 80drs for a Nes meh ghala or an ouzo. It is on an inside wall of *To Mainalon* that two preserved price lists vividly highlight the effect of inflation in Greece. One of them dates back to 1965 and the other to 1968. They are priced in drachmae and lepta – one hundred lepta made up one drachma. A bottle of beer cost 2.50drs in 1965 and 3drs in 1968, a good brandy 3drs and 3.50drs respectively and an ouzo 3drs in both years. Well there you go.

In Athens and the larger, more cosmopolitan, provincial cities, it is usual taverna practice to round off prices, which proves a little disconcerting at first.

In despair it is noted that some restaurants and tavernas climbing the slopes of the Acropolis up Odhos Markou Avriliou, south of Eolou St, are allowing 'Chinese menu' style collective categories (A, B, C etc.) to creep into their menu listings.

*Note the reference to Greek dancing and music is not derogatory – only an indication that it is often the case that standards of cuisine may not be any better and prices often reflect the 'overheads' attributable to the musicians. But See **Palia** & **Xnou Tavernas**.

PLAKA AREA (*Tmr* D5)
A glut of eating houses ranging from the very good and expensive, the very expensive and bad, to some inexpensive and very good.

Taverna Thespis 18 Thespidos St   Tel 323 8242
Directions: On the right of a lane across the way from Kidathineon St, towards the bottom or south-east end of Adrianou St.

Recommended and noted for its friendly service. The house retsina is served in metal jugs. A two hour, slap-up meal of souvlakia, Greek salad, fried zucchini, bread and two carafes of retsina costs in excess of 1600drs for two.

Plaka Village 28 Kidathineon
Directions: On the left (*Adrianou St behind one*), in the block edged by the streets of Adrianou and Kidathineon.

Once an excellent souvlaki snackbar but.... the offerings are now so-so at a cost of 85drs. Added to which, to sit down costs an extra 16drs per head. Price lists do not make this plain and the annoying habit can cause, at the least, irritation. (This practice is also prevalent in the Omonia Square 'souvlaki arcade'). Even more alarming is the 'take it or leave it' attitude that also extends to customer's money. The staff err towards 'taking' it, having to be badgered to return any change. A large bottle of beer costs 80drs, the home-made tzatziki is good, the service is quick and they even remain open Sunday lunchtimes.

Committed souvlaki pita eaters do not have to despair as any number of snackbars are concentrated on both sides at the Monastiraki Square end of Mitropoleos St. Perhaps the most inexpensive souvlaki in the area are to be found by turning right at the bottom of Kidathineon St and wandering down Adrianou in the direction of Monastiraki Sq. Prices fall as low as 58-65drs.

ΟΥΖΕΡΙ Ο ΚΟΥΚΛΗΣ (or **PEPAVI**) 14 Tripodon St　　　　Tel 324 7605
Directions: Up the slope from the Thespidos/Kidathineon junction, one to the left of Adrianou (*facing Monastiraki Sq*), and on the left.

Recognising the establishment used not to be at all difficult as the 1st floor balcony was embellished with a large, stuffed bird and two, big, antique record player horns mounted on the wrought iron balustrade. I write 'used not' because the mounted heron has disappeared, the owners of the taverna maintaining that it has flown away to Mykonos! Mind you the 'HMV' style trumpets are still prominent thus easily distinguishing the old ouzerie/wine shop. The vine continues to grow well.

The taverna, standing on its own, evokes a provincial country atmosphere. It is necessary to arrive early as the ouzerie is well patronised by the locals, which patronage is not surprising considering the inexpensive excellence of one or two of the dishes which include salvers of dolmades and meatballs. Another 'standard' is 'flaming sausages'. These cook away on stainless steel plates set in front of the diner. They are served with a large plateful of hors d'oeuvres, amongst which are a meatball, beans, lettuce, feta, chilli, new potatoes, Russian salad and etc etc, at a cost of 1000drs for two. Great value, very filling indeed but watch the napkins don't go up in flames and bear in mind the house wine is pretty rough. The popularity is vouchsafed by the taverna being full by 2000hrs.

Eden Taverna 3 Flessa St
Directions: Off Adrianou St, almost opposite Odhos Nikodimou, and on the left.

Mentioned because their menu includes many offerings that excellently cater (sorry) for vegetarian requirements. Open 1200hrs to 0100hrs every day except Tuesdays.

Palia Plakiotiki Taverna (Stamatopoulos) (*Tmr* D5) 26 Lissiou St
　　　　　　　　　　　　　　　　　　　　Tel 322 8722
Directions: Proceed up Lissiou St, which parallels Adrianou St, in the general direction of Monastiraki Sq. The open-air taverna is behind a perimeter wall to the right on a steep slope at the junction with Erechtheos St.

Claims to be one of Athens' oldest tavernas. The large terraced area is laid out with clean gravel chippings. Not particularly cheap but a super place at which to have an 'atmospheric' evening as there is a resident group. Note this recommendation, despite my usual caveats regarding joints at which music 'is on score'. (Those remarks are usually attributed to establishments that advertise live bouzouki). Here it is a major attraction in the shape of a huge, spherical man, with a name to match, Stavros Balagouras. He is the resident singer/accordionist/electric pianist and draws tourists and Greeks alike with his dignified and heartfelt performance. Besides traditional, national songs there is year-round dancing, if customers are so moved, on the one square metre floor space! The taverna is particularly Greek and lively at festival times, added to which the food is good and much cheaper than similar establishments. Cheese and meat dishes, with salad and wine for two, costs just 1500drs. The dolmades are stuffed with meat and served in a lemon sauce so cost 350drs and meat dishes average 450/500drs. The wine is rather expensive with a bottle of Cambas red costing 350drs and a large bottle of retsina 292drs. A bottle of Lowenbrau costs a reasonable 92drs. and the bread and head tax works out at only 14drs.

Michiko Restaurant 27 Kidathineon St　　　　　　　Tel 324 6851
Directions: On the right, beyond the junction with Asteriou St proceeding in a north-east direction (*towards Syntagma Sq*), close to a small square and church.

Japanese, if you must, and extremely expensive.

Xynou/Xynos 4 Arghelou Geronda (Angelou Geronta)　　　Tel 322 1065
Directions: Left off the lower, Plaka Square end of Kidathineon St (*facing Syntagma Sq*) and on the left, towards the far point of the short pedestrian way. The unprepossessing entrance door is tucked away in the corner of a recess and can be missed.

One of the oldest, most highly rated Plaka tavernas and well patronised by Athenians. Evenings only and closed on Saturdays and Sundays. A friend advises me that it is now almost obligatory to book in advance although I have managed to squeeze a table for two early on in the evening. Mention of its popularity with Athenians prompts me to stress these are well-heeled locals – you know shipowners, ambassadors and ageing playboys. Xynou is definitely on the 'hotel captains' list of recommended eateries and the tourists who eat here tend to look as if they have stepped off the stage-set of Dallas. But it is not surprising that the cognoscenti gather here because, despite being in the heart of Athens, the premises evoke a rural ambience. The single storey, shed-like, roof tiled buildings edge two sides of a high wall enclosed gravel area, on which are spread the chairs and tables. The food is absolutely excellent and, considering the location, the prices are not that outrageous. A meal of two plates of dolmades in lemon sauce, a plate of moussaka, a lamb fricassee in lemon sauce, a tomato and cucumber salad, a bottle of kortaki retsina and bread for two costs 1530drs. It seems a pity that the bread has to be charged at 50drs but then the ample wine list does include an inexpensive retsina. Three guitarists serenade diners, the napkins are linen, and the service is first class. Readers are recommended to save up and try Xynou's at least once, an experience that will not be easily forgotten.

To Fragathiko Taverna (*Tmr* D5)
Directions: On the left of Adrianou St (*proceeding towards Kidathineon St*) on the junction of Adrianou and Ag Andreou Sts.

Clean, reasonably priced and popular with the younger generation, some of whom may not be entirely wholesome, but their enthusiasm is not surprising considering the inexpensively priced dishes on offer. These include moussaka special 325drs; moussaka special served with 4 kinds of vegetable 425drs; lamb special served with 4 kinds of vegetable 425drs and a vegetarian dish costing 240drs.

Plateia Agora is a lovely, elongated, chic Plaka Square formed at the junction of the bottom of Eolou and the top of Adrianou and Kapnikarea Sts. The square spawns a number of cafe-bar restaurants, including the *Posidion* and *Appollon*, the canopies, chairs and tables of which edge the street all the way round the neat, paved plateia. Don't forget that prices reflect the square's modishness with a bottle of beer at the *Posidion* costing 200drs. There is a spotless public lavatory at the top (Monastiraki) end. The *Appollon* has a particularly wide range of choice and clients can sit at the comfortable tables for an (expensive) hour or so over a coffee (120drs), a fried egg breakfast (300drs) or a full blown meal, if anyone can afford the same. On this tack it is becoming commonplace for some of the smarter places such as the *Posidion* to display unpriced menus. Hope your luck is in and the organ grinder wanders through the square.

From the little square formed by a 'junction of the ways', adjacent to the Lysikrates Monument (*Tmr* 21D5), Odhos Vironos falls towards the south Acropolis encircling avenue of Dionysiou Areopagitou.

Snackbar Odhos Vironos
Directions: As above and on the right (*Plaka behind one*) of the street.
More a small 'doorway' souvlaki pita shop but small is indeed splendid.

Restaurant Olympia 20 Dionysiou Areopagitou
Directions: Proceed along Dionysiou Areopagitou, from the junction with Odhos Vironos, in a clockwise direction. The restaurant is on the right, close to the junction with Thassilou Lane (that incidentally climbs and bends back up to the top of Odhos Thespidos) hard up against the foot of the Acropolis. Between Thassilou Lane and the sun-blind-shaded lean-to butted on to the side of the restaurant, is a small grassed area and an underground Public toilet.
The prices seem reasonable and the place appears to portend good things but....I can only report the promise was in reality, disappointing. The double Greek salad was in truth only large enough for one, the moussaka was 'inactive', the kalamares were unacceptable and the roast potatoes (yes roast potatoes) were in actuality nothing more than dumpy wedges. Oh dear! They do serve a kortaki retsina.

STADIUM (PANGRATI) AREA (*Tmr* E/F6)
Karavitis Taverna (ΚΑΡΑΒΙΤΗΣ) 4 Pafsaniou (Paysanioy).
Directions: Beyond the Stadium (*Tmr* E/F6) going east (*away from the Acropolis*) along Vassileos Konstantinou, and Pafsaniou is the 3rd turning to the right. The taverna is on the left.
A small, leafy tree shaded gravel square fronts the taverna, which is so popular that there is an extension across the street, through a pair of 'field gates'. Our friend Paul will probably berate me (if he was less of a gentleman) for listing this gem. Unknown to visitors but extremely popular with Athenians, more especially those who, when college students, frequented this jewel in

the Athens taverna crown. A meal for four of a selection of dishes including lamb, beef in clay, giant haricot beans, garlic flavoured meatballs, greens, tzatziki, 2 plates of feta cheese, aubergines, courgettes, bread and 3 jugs of retsina, from the barrel, for some 2400drs. Beat that. But some knowledge of Greek is an advantage and the taverna is only open in the evening.

Instead of turning off Vassileos Konstantinou at Odhos Pafsaniou, take the next right proceeding further eastwards.

ΜΑΓΕΜΕΝΟΣ ΑΥΛΟΣ **(The Magic Flute)** Odhos Aminda (Amynta).
Directions: As above and the restaurant is 20m up on the right.
　　Swiss dishes including fondue, schnitzels and salads. Despite being rather more expensive than its near neighbours it is well frequented by Athenians including the composer Hadzithakis (so I am advised).

Virinis Taverna, Archimedes St
Directions: Prior to the side-streets to the two restaurant/tavernas last detailed, the second turning to the right off Vassileos Konstantinou, beyond the Stadium (*Tmr* E/F6) proceeding in an easterly direction, is Odhos Eratosthenous. This climbs up to Plateia Plastira. To the right of the square is Archimedes Street. The taverna is about a 100m along on the left. Incidentally, if returning to the centre of Athens from hereabouts, it is possible to continue along this street and drop down Odhos Markou Moussourou back to Vassileos Konstantinou.
　　A good selection of bistro dishes at reasonable prices, including, for instance, beef in wine sauce at a cost of 350drs. It has been indicated that I might find the place rather 'up market' as there were no souvlaki pitas on offer. Cheeky! It's only that I have learnt through expensive experience over the years that, in Greece, gingham tablecloths and French style menus tend to double the prices!

SYNTAGMA AREA (*Tmr* D/E4/5)
Corfu Restaurant 6 Kriezotou St　　　　　　　　　　　　Tel 361 3011
Directions: North of Syntagma Sq and first turning right off Panepistimiou (El Venizelou).
　　Extensive Greek and European dishes in a modern, friendly restaurant.

Delphi Restaurant 15 Nikis St　　　　　　　　　　　　Tel 323 4869
Directions: From the south-west corner of Syntagma Sq, east along Mitropoleos and the first turning left.
　　Modern, reasonably priced food from an extensive menu and friendly service.

Sintrivani Restaurant 5 Filellinon St
Directions: South-west corner of Syntagma Sq and due south.
　　Garden restaurant serving a traditional menu at reasonable prices.

Vassillis Restaurant 14A Voukourestiou.
Directions: North of Syntagma Sq and the second turning off Panepistimiou St, to the right, along Odhos Smats and across Akadimias St.
　　Variety, in traditional surroundings.

Ideal Restaurant 46 Panepistimiou St.
Directions: Proceed up Panepistimiou from the north-east corner of Syntagma Sq and the restaurant is on the right.
　　Good food at moderate prices.

YWCA 11 Amerikis St.
Directions: From Syntagma Sq proceed north-west along either Stadiou or Panepistimiou St and second or third road to the right, depending which street is used.
Cafeteria serving inexpensive sandwiches.

There are many cafes in and around Syntagma Square. Recommended, but expensive, is the:-
Brazilian Coffee Cafe
Directions: Close by Syntagma Sq, in Voukourestiou St.
Serves coffee, tea, toast, butter and jam, breakfast, ice-creams and pastries.

OMONIA AREA (*Tmr* D3)

Ellinikon Taverna (*Tmr* D2/3) Dorou St.
Directions: North of Omonia Sq, along Dorou St and almost immediately on the left down some steps to a basement.
A cavernous, 'greasy spoon' well frequented by workmen and sundry officials, as well as a sprinkling of tourists. Inexpensive fare and draught retsina available.

Taverna Kostoyannus 37 Zaimi St.
Directions: Leave Omonia northwards on 28 Ikosiokto Oktovriou, turn right at Odhos Stournara to the nearside of the Polytechnic School, and Zaimi St is the second road along. The taverna is to the left approximately behind the National Archaeological Museum.
Good food, acceptable prices and comes well recommended. As in the case of many other Athenian tavernas, it is not open for lunch or on Sundays.

Snackbars
Probably the most compact, reasonably priced 'offerings' but in grubby surroundings, lurk in the arcade between Dorou St and 28 Ikosiokto Oktovriou, off Omonia Sq. Here are situated cafes and stalls selling almost every variety of Greek convenience fast food. A 'standard'* souvlaki costs 70drs and a 'spezial'*, or de luxe, 90drs BUT do not sit down unless you wish to be charged an extra 15-20drs per head. A bottle of beer costs 80drs.
*Note the 'standard' is a preheated slab of meat whilst the 'spezial'(sic) is the traditional, giro meat-sliced offering.

Cafes
Everywhere of course, but on Omonia Sq, alongside Dorou St and adjacent to the *Hotel Carlton*, is a magnificent specimen of the traditional kafeneion.
Greek men sip coffee and tumble their worry beads, as they must have done since the turn of the century.

Bretania Cafe
Directions: Bordering Omonia Square, on the left hand side (*Acropolis behind one or more easily facing the Hotel Omonia*) of the junction with Athinas St.
An excellent, very old-fashioned, Greek, 'sticky' sweet cake shop which is more a galaktozacharoplasteion than a cafe. Renowned for its range of sweets, yoghurt and honey, cream and honey, rice puddings and so on, all served with sugar sweet bread and drinks until 0200hrs every morning. A speciality is 'Flower of the Milk', a cream and yoghurt dish costing 200drs per head.

Continuing on down Athinas St, beyond Plateia Kotzia, leads past the covered meat market building on the left and a number of:-
'Meat Market' Tavernas
Directions: As above and towards the rear of the building. It has to be admitted that it is necessary for prospective diners to pick their way through piles of bones and general market detritus after dark.

Open 24 hours a day and a find for those who like to slum it in less expensive establishments of some note.

LYCABETTUS (LYKAVITOS) AREA (*Tmr* F/G4)
As befits a high priced area,, these listings are very expensive.
Je Reviens Restaurant 49 Xenokratous St.
Directions: North-east from Kolonaki Sq, up Patriachou Ioakim St to the junction with and left on Odhos Marasli, up a flight of steps until it crosses Xenokratous St.

French food, creditable but expensive. Open midday and evenings.

L'Abreuvoir 51 Xenokratous St
Directions: As for *Je Reviens* as are the comments, but even more expensive.

Al Convento Restaurant (*Tmr* G4) 4 Anapiron   Tel 723 9163
Directions: North-east from Kolonaki Sq along Patriachou Ioakim to Marasli St. Turn left and then right along Odhos Souidias and Anapiron St is nearly at the end.

Bonanza Restaurant 14 Voukourestiou
Directions: From the north-west corner of Plateia Kolonaki, take Odhos Skoufa, which crosses Voukourestiou St.

Once known as the *Stage Coach*. Not only Wild West in decor, air-conditioned and serving American style food but very expensive with steaks as a house speciality. Why not to to the good old US of A? Lunch and evening meals, open 1200 to 1600hrs and 1900 to 0100hrs.

THE A TO Z OF USEFUL INFORMATION
AIRLINE OFFICE & TERMINUS (*Tmr* 12C6) Referred to in the introductory paragraphs, as well as under **The Accommodation**. The busy offices are to the left (*facing Syntagma Sq*) of the traffic frantic Leoforos Sygrou. As with other Olympic facilities the office doubles as a terminus for airport buses arriving from and departing to the East and West Airports. Passengers who land up here should note that the most convenient, combined bus stop to Syntagma Square, the centre of Athens, is (*with the building behind one*), across the busy thoroughfare and some 50m up the incline of Leoforos Sygrou. This 'hosts' any number of buses and trolley-buses while the stop directly across the road serves only one or two trolley-buses.

Aircraft timetables. *See* **Chapter Three** for general details of the airports serviced from Athens described in this guide and the individual chapters for details of the timetables.

BANKS (Trapeza – ΤΡΑΠΕΖΑ) Note that if a bank strike is under way (apparently becoming a natural part of the tourist season 'high jinks'), the National Bank on Syntagma Sq stays open and in business. However, in these circumstances, the place becomes even more than usually crowded. Banks include the:

National Bank of Greece (*Tmr* 3D/E4) 2 Karageorgi Servias, Syntagma Sq.

All foreign exchange services: Monday to Thursday 0800-1400hrs, Friday 0800-1330hrs, Saturday, Sunday & holidays 0900-1600hrs; travellers cheques & foreign cash exchange services: weekdays 0800-2000hrs, Saturday, Sunday & holidays 0900-1600hrs.

Ionian & Popular Bank (*Tmr* D/E/4/5) 1 Mitropoleos St.

Only open normal banking hours.

Commercial Bank of Greece (*Tmr* E4) 11 Panepistimiou (El Venizelou).

Normal banking hours.

American Express (*Tmr* D/E4/5) 2 Ermou St, Syntagma Sq   Tel 3244975/9

Carries out usual Amex office transactions and is open Monday to Thursday 0830-1400hrs, Friday 0830-1330hrs and Saturday 0820-1230hrs.

BEACHES Athens is not on a river or by the sea, so to enjoy a beach it is necessary to leave the main city and travel to the suburbs. Very often these beaches are operated under the aegis of the NTOG, or private enterprise in association with a hotel. The NTOG beaches usually have beach huts, cabins, tennis courts, a playground and catering facilities. Entrance charges vary from 25-100drs.

There are beaches and or swimming pools at:

Paleon Faliron/ Faliro	A seaside resort	Bus No. 126: Departs from Odhos Othonos, south side of Syntagma Sq (*Tmr* E5).
Alimos	NTOG beach	Bus No. 133: Departs from Odhos Othonos, south side of Syntagma Sq (*Tmr* E5).
Glyfada (Gllfada)	A seaside resort	Bus No. 129: Departs from Leoforos Olgas, south side of the Zappeion Gardens (*Tmr* E5/6).
Voula	NTOG beach Class A	Bus No. 122: Departs from Leoforos Olgas, south side of the Zappeion Gardens (*Tmr* E5/6).
Voula	NTOG beach Class B	Bus No. 122: Adults 60drs, children 40drs.
Vouliagmeni	A luxury seaside resort & yacht marina. NTOG beach	Bus No. 118: Departs from Leoforos Olgas, south side of the Zappeion Gardens (*Tmr* E5/6). Adults 100drs, children 50drs.
Varkiza	A seaside resort & yacht marina. NTOG Beach	Bus No. 115: Departs from Leoforos Olgas, south side of the Zappeion Gardens (*Tmr* E5/6). Adults 100drs, children 50drs.

There are beaches all the way down to Cape Sounion (Sounio) via the coast road. *See* **Bus timetables, A To Z**.

BOOKSELLERS Apart from the second-hand bookshops in the Plaka Flea Market (*See* **Monastiraki Square, Introduction**), there are three or four on Odhos Nikis (west of Syntagma Sq) and Odhos Amerikis (north-west of Syntagma Sq) as well as one on Lysikratous St, opposite the small church (*Tmr* 21D5).

Of all the above it is perhaps invidious to select one but here goes...

The Compendium Bookshop (& Computers) 28 Nikis St   Tel 322 1248

Directions: On the left of Nikis St (*facing Syntagma Sq*).

Well recommended for a wide range of English language publications. As well as new books they sell some good condition 'used' books. The owner, Rick Schulein, is happy to buy books back into stock that he has sold to a client.The *Transalpino* travel office is in the basement.

BREAD SHOPS In the more popular shopping areas. Descending along Odhos Adrianou, in the Plaka (*Tmr* D5), from the Odhos Thespidos/Kidathineon end, advances past many shops, general stores and a bread shop (or two). They make way for souvenir and gift shops on the way towards Monastiraki.

BUSES & TROLLEY-BUSES These run variously between 0500 and 0030hrs (half an hour past midnight), are usually crowded but excellent value with a 'flat rate' charge of 30drs. Travel between 0500 and 0800hrs is free, not only on the buses but the Metro as well. Also *See* **Access to the Stations, Trains, A To Z.**

Buses The buses are blue (and green) and bus stops are marked *Stasis* (ΣΤΑΣΙΣ). Some one-man-operated buses are utilised and a few have an honesty box for fares.

Trolley-Buses Yellow coloured vehicles and bus stops. Entered via a door at the front marked *Eisodos* (ΕΙΣΟΔΟΣ), with the exit at the rear, marked *Exodos* (ΕΞΟΔΟΣ). Have the correct money to put into the fare machine as there are no tickets or change disgorged.

Major city terminals & turn-round points (*See* footnote at the end of this section).
Kaningos Sq: (*Tmr* 4D2) North-east of Omonia Sq.
Stadiou/Kolokotroni junction: (*Tmr* D/E4). This has replaced the Korai Sq terminus now that Korai has been pedestrianised.
Kifissou St: West-north-west of Omonia Sq. The depot on this major highway lies between the junctions of Lenorman and Leoforos Athinon.
Liossion St: (*Tmr* C2) North-west of Omonia Sq.
Eleftherias Sq: (*Tmr* 9C3) North-west of Monastiraki Sq.
Leoforos Olgas: (*Tmr* D/E5/6) South of the National Garden.
Mavrommateon St*: (*Tmr* D/E1) West of Pedion Areos Park, north of Omonia Sq.
* *The tree shaded north-south street is lined with bus departure points.*

Egyptou Place (Aigyptou/Egiptou): (*Tmr* D1) Just below the south-west corner of Pedion Areos Park, alongside 28 Ikosiokto Oktovriou.
Ag Asomaton Square: (*Tmr* B/C4) West of Monastiraki Sq.
Koumoundourou St: (*Tmr* C2/3) West of Omonia Sq, third turning off Ag Konstantinou.

Trolley-bus timetable
Some major city routes include:
No. 1:   Plateia Attikis (Metro station) (*Tmr* C1), Leoforos Amalias, **Stathmos Larissis** (railway station), Karaiskaki Place, Ag Konstantinou, **Omonia Sq, Syntagma Sq,** Kallithea suburb (SW Athens). Every 10 mins from 0505-2350hrs.
No. 2:   Pangrati (*Tmr* G6), Leoforos Amalias (Central), **Syntagma Sq, Omonia Sq,** 28 Ikosiokto Oktovriou/Patission St, Kipseli (N Athens). From 0630-0020hrs.
No. 10:   N. Smirni (S Athens), Leoforos Sygrou, Leoforos Amalias, **Syntagma Sq,** Panepistimiou St, Stadiou/Kolokotroni junction (*Tmr* D/E4). From 0500-2345hrs.
No. 12:   Leoforos Olgas (*Tmr* D/E5/6), Leoforos Amalias, **Syntagma Sq, Omonia Sq,** 28 Ikosiokto Oktovriou/Patission St (N Athens). From 0630-2235hrs.
Other routes covered by trolley-buses include:
No. 3:   Patissia to Erythrea (N to NNE Athens suburbs). from 0625-2230hrs.
No. 4:   Odhos Kypselis (*Tmr* E1) (North of Pedion Areos Park), **Omonia Sq, Syntagma Sq,** Leoforos Olgas to Ag Artemios (SSE Athens suburbs). From 0630-0020hrs.
No. 5:   Patissia (N Athens suburb), **Stathmos Larissis** (railway station), **Omonia Sq, Syntagma Sq,** Filellinon St, Koukaki (S Athens suburb). From 0630-0015hrs.
No. 6:   Ippokratous St (*Tmr* E3), Panepistimiou St, **Omonia Sq** to N Filadelfia (N Athens suburb). Every 10mins from 0500-2320hrs.
No. 7:   Panepistimiou St (*Tmr* D/E3/4), 28 Ikosiokto Oktovriou/Patission St to Leoforos Alexandras (N of Lycabettus). From 0630-0015hrs.
No. 8:   Plateia Kaningos (*Tmr* 4D2), Odhos Akadimias, Vassilissis Sofias, Leoforos Alexandras, 28 Ikosiokto Oktovriou/Patission St. From 0630-0020hrs.
No. 9:   Odhos Kypselis (*Tmr* E1) (North of Pedion Areos Park), 28 Ikosiokto Oktovriou/Patission St, Stadiou St, **Syntagma Sq,** Petralona (W Athens suburb – far side of Filopapou). Every 10mins from 0455-2345hrs.
No. 10:   Stadiou/Koloktoroni junction (*Tmr* D/E4), Stadiou St, **Syntagma Sq,** Filellinon St, Leoforos Sygrou, Nea Smirni (S Athens suburb). Every 10mins from 0500-2345hrs.
No. 11:   Koliatsou (NNE Athens suburb), **Stathmos Larissis** (railway station), 28 Ikosiokto Oktovriou/Patission St, Stadiou St, **Syntagma Sq,** Filellinon St, Plastira Sq, Eftichidou St, N Pangrati (ESE Athens suburb). Every 5mins from 0500-0010hrs.

No. 13: 28 Ikosiokto Oktovriou/Patission St, Akadimias St, Vassilissis Sofias, Papadiaman-topoulou St, Leoforos Kifissias, Labrini (just beyond Galatsi suburb – NE Athens suburb). Every 10mins from 0500-2400hrs.

No. 14: Leoforos Alexandras, 28 Ikosiokto Oktovriou/Patission, Patissia (N Athens suburb).

Bus timetable

Bus numbers are subject to a certain amount of confusion, but here goes! Some of the routes are as follows:

No. 022: Kaningos Sq (*Tmr* 4D2), Akadimias, Kanari, Patriarchou Ioakim, Marasli, Genadiou St (SE Lycabettus). Every 10mins from 0520-2330hrs.

No. 023: Kaningos Sq (*Tmr* 4D2), Lycabettus.

No. 024: Leoforos Amalias (*Tmr* D/E5), **Syntagma Sq**, Panepistimiou St, **Omonia Sq**, Tritis Septemvriou, Stournara, Sourmeli, Acharnon, Liossion St. Every 20mins from 0530-2400hrs.

NB This is the bus that delivers passengers to 250 Liossion St (Tmr C2), one of the main bus terminals

No. 040: Filellinon St (close to **Syntagma Sq** – *Tmr* D/E4/5), Leoforos Amalias, Leoforos Sygrou to Vassileos Konstantinou, Piraeus. Every 10mins, 24 hours a day. Green bus.

No. 045: Kaningos Sq (*Tmr* 4D2), Akadimias St, Vassilissis Sofias, Leoforos Kifissias to Kefalari and Politia (NE Athens suburb). Every 15mins from 0600-0100hrs.

No. 047: Menandrou St (SW of **Omonia Sq**), **Stathmos Larissis** (railway station).

No. 049: Athinas St (*Tmr* C/D3), (S of Omonia Sq), Sofokleous, Pireos, Sotiros, Filonos St, Plateia Themistokleous, Piraeus. Every 10mins, 24 hours a day. Green bus.

No. 051: Off Ag Konstantinou (*Tmr* C2/3), W of **Omonia Sq**, Kolonou St, Lenorman St, Kifissou St. Every 10mins from 0500-2400hrs.

NB This is the bus that connects to the 100 Kifissou St (Tmr A2), a main bus terminal.

No. 115: Leoforos Olgas (*Tmr* D/E5/6), Leoforos Sygrou, Leoforos Possidonos (coast road) to Vouliagmeni & Varkiza. Every 20mins, 24 hours a day.

No. 116,117 Leoforos Olgas, Varkiza.

No. 118: Leoforos Olgas, Leoforos Sygrou, Leoforos Possidonos (coast road) to Vouliagmeni. Every 20mins from 1245-2015hrs.

No. 121, 128,129: Leoforos Olgas (*Tmr* E6), Glyfada (SSE coastal Athens suburb).

No. 122: Leoforos Olgas, Leoforos Sygrou, Leoforos Possidonos (coast road) to Voula. Every 20mins from 0530-2400hrs.

No. 132: Othonos St (B) Syntagma Sq – *Tmr* D/E4/5), Filellinon St, Leoforos Amalias, Leoforos Sygrou to Edem (SSE Athens suburb). Every 20mins from 0530-1900hrs.

No. 153: Leoforos Olgas, Vouliagmeni (SSE coastal Athens suburb).

No. 224: Polygono (N Athens suburb), 28 Ikosiokto Oktovriou/Patission St, Kaningos Sq, Vassilissis Sofias, Democratias St (Kessariani, E Athens suburb). Every 20mins from 0500-2400hrs.

No. 230: Ambelokipi (E Athens suburb), Leoforos Alexandras, Ippokratous St, Akadimias St, **Syntagma Sq**, Leoforos Amalias, Dionysiou Areopagitou, Apostolou Pavlou, Thission. Every 10 mins from 0500-2320hrs.

No. 405: Leoforos Alexandras, **Stathmos Larissis** (railway station).

No. 510: Kaningos Sq (*Tmr* 4D2), Akadimias St, Ippokratous St, Leoforos Alexandras, Leoforos Kifissias to Dionyssos (NE Athens suburb). Every 20mins from 0530-2250hrs.

No. 527: Kaningos Sq, (*Tmr* 4D2) Akadimias St, Leoforos Alexandras, Leoforos Kifissias to Amaroussion (NE Athens suburb). Every 15mins from 0615-2215hrs.

No. 538, 539: Kaningos Sq, Kifissia (NNE Athens suburb).

No. 603: Akadimias St (*Tmr* E 3/4) to Psychiko (NE Athens suburb).

No. 610: Akadimias St to Filothei (NE Athens suburb).

No. 853, 862, 864: Plateia Eleftherias (*Tmr* 9B/C 3/4), Elefsina (Elefsis – West of Athens, beyond Dafni).

No. 873: Plateia Eleftherias, Dafni (W Athens suburb).

Attica bus timetable (orange buses)

Athens – Rafina: 29, Mavrommateon St (*Tmr* D/E1).
Athens – Nea Makri: 29, Mavrommateon St.
Athens – Marathon: 29, Mavrommateon St.
Athens – Lavrion*: 14, Mavrommateon St.
*See Athens – Sounion route.
All above depart every hour on the half hour between 0630-1730hrs.
One-way fare 130drs, duration 1 hour.

Athens –	Sounion – West coast road: 14 Mavrommateon St
	Every hour on the half hour between 0630-1730hrs.
Return	Every hour on the hour between 0600-1900hrs.
	One-way fare 350drs, duration 1 ½hrs.
Athens –	Sounion – via Markopoulo & Lavrio: 14 Mavrommateon St.
	Every hour on the hour, 0600-1700hrs.
Return	Every hour on the half hour, 0630-1930hrs.
	One-way fare 310drs, duration 2hrs.
Athens –	Vravron: Take either the 0600hrs Sounion bus via Markopoulo orthe 1330hrs Lavrio bus, get off at Markopoulo & catch a local bus to Vravron.

NB The Athens-Attica bus services detailed above cover the city and its environs

The rest of Greece is served by:
1) **KTEL** A pool of bus operators working through one company from two terminals. 260 Liossion St* and 100 Kifissou St**
2) **OSE** (The State Railway Company) Their buses terminus alongside the main railway stations of Stathmos Peloponissou and Larissis. Apart from the domestic services, there is a terminal for other European capitals, including Paris, Istanbul and Munich, at Stathmos Larissis station.
***Liossion St** (*Tmr* C2) is to the east of Stathmos Peloponissou railway station. This terminus serves Halkida, Edipsos, Kimi, Delphi, Amfissa, Kamena Vourla, Larissa, Thiva, Trikala (Meteora) Livadia, Lamia. **Refer to bus route No. 024 for transport to this terminus.**
****Kifissou St** (*Tmr* A2) is to the west north-west of Omonia Sq, beyond the 'steam railway' lines, across Leoforos Konstantinoupoleos and up either Leoforos Athinon, and turn right, or Odhos Lenorman, and turn left. This terminus serves Patras, Pirgos (Olympia), Nafplio (Mikines), Adritsena (Vasses), Kalamata, Sparti (Mistras), Githio,(Diros), Tripolis, Messolongi, Igoumenitsa, Preveza, Ioanina, Corfu, Zakynthos, Cephalonia, Lefkas, Kozani, Kastoria, Florina, Grevena, Veria, Naoussa, Edessa, Seres, Kilkis, Kavala, Drama, Komotini, Korinthos, Kranidi, Xilokastro. **Refer to bus route No. 051 for transport to this terminus.**

For any bus services connecting to the islands detailed in this guide, also refer to the Mainland Ports, Chapter Ten, and the relevant Island chapters.

CAMPING *See* **The Accommodation.**

CAR HIRE As any other capital city, numerous offices, the majority of which are lined up in the smarter areas and squares, such as Syntagma Sq and Leoforos Amalias. Typical is:
Pappas, 44 Leoforos Amalias   Tel 322 0087
There are any number of car hire (and travel) firms on the right of Leoforos Sygrou, descending from the 'spaghetti junction' south of the Temple of Olympian Zeus (*Tmr* D6).

CAR REPAIR Help and advice can be obtained by contacting:
The Automobile & Touring Club of Greece (ELPA), (*Tmr* I/3) 2 Messogion St   Tel 779 1615
   For immediate, emergency attention dial 104.

There are dozens of back street car repairers, breakers and spare part shops parallel and to the west of Leoforos Sygrou, in the area between the Olympic office and the Temple of Olympian Zeus.

CHEMIST *See* **Medical Care**

CINEMAS There are a large number of outdoor cinemas. Do not worry about a language barrier as the majority of the films have English (American) dialogue with Greek subtitles.

Aigli in the Zappeion is a must and is situated at the south end of the National Garden. Other cinemas are bunched together on the streets of Stadiou, Panepistimiou and 28 Ikosiokto Oktovriou/Patission.

Note that the cinemas in Athens, of which there are vast numbers, generally show poor quality films complete with scratches, hisses, jumps, long black gaps and or loss of sound, especially between reels. However a recommendation is the:

Radio City 240 Patission St.

Directions: North of Omonia Sq.

Large screen, good sound and knowledgeable operators.

CLUBS, BARS & DISCOS Why leave home? But if you must, there are enough to satiate the most voracious desires.

COMMERCIAL SHOPPING AREAS During daylight hours a very large street market ranges up Odhos Athinas (*Tmr* C3/4), Odhos Sokratous and the associated side streets from Ermou St, almost all the way up to Omonia Sq. After dark the shutters are drawn down, the stalls canvassed over and the 'ladies of the night' appear.

Plateia Kotzia (*Tmr* C/D3) spawns a flower market on Sundays whilst the Parliament Building side of Vassilissis Sofias (*Tmr* E4) is lined with smart flower stalls that open daily.

Monastiraki Sq (*Tmr* 5C4) and the various streets that radiate off are abuzz, specialising in widely differing aspects of the commercial and tourist trade. Odhos Areos contains a plethora of leather goods shops; the near end of Ifestou Lane is edged by stall upon stall of junk and tourist 'omit-abilia' (forgettable memorabilia); Pandrossou lane contains a better class of shop and stall selling sandals, pottery and smarter 'memorabilia', while the square itself has a number of handcart hawkers.

The smart department stores are conveniently situated in or around Syntagma Sq, and the main streets that radiate off the square, including Ermou, Stadiou and Panepistimiou.

Tapestries are an extremely good buy. A reliable shop is sited close to and on the far side (*from Syntagma Sq*) of Kapnikarea Church (*Tmr* 6 D4), on Ermou St.

In the area south of Syntagma Sq, on the junction of Apollonos and Pendelis Sts, close by Odhos Voulis, there are three small but obliging fruit and greengrocery shops. Apollonos St is useful to shoppers because, close by the junction with Odhos Nikis, on the right-hand side, is a combined fruit and butcher's shop. Next door is a stick souvlaki snackbar and across the road an ironmongers.

See **Bread Shops & Trains, A To Z** for details of other markets and shopping areas.

DENTISTS & DOCTORS *See* **Medical Care, A To Z.**

EMBASSIES

Australia: 15 Messogion Av.	Tel 775 7650
Belgium: 3 Sekeri St.	Tel 361 7886
Canada: 4 Ioannou Gennadiou St.	Tel 723 9511

Denmark: 15 Philikis Etairias Sq.	Tel 724 9315
Finland: 1 Eratosthenous & Vas. Konstantinou Sts.	Tel 751 9795
France: 7 Vassilissis Sofias	Tel 361 1663
German Federal Republic (West Germany): 3 Karaoli/Dimitriou Sts.	Tel 369 4111
Great Britain: 1 Ploutarchou & Ypsilantou Sts.	Tel 723 6211
Ireland: 7 Vassileos Konstantinou.	Tel 723 2771
Netherlands: 5-7 Vassileos Konstantinou.	Tel 723 9701
New Zealand: 15-17 Tshoa St.	Tel 641 0311
Norway: 7 Vassileos Konstantinou St.	Tel 724 6173
South Africa: 124 Kifissias/latridou.	Tel 692 2125
Sweden: 7 Vassileos Konstantinou St.	Tel 722 4504
USA: 91 Vassilissis Sofias.	Tel 721 2951

FERRY-BOAT & FLYING DOLPHIN TICKET OFFICES
Apart from the headquarters, most, if not all, ferry-boat ticket offices are down in Piraeus Port.

On the other hand whilst the main *Ceres Flying Dolphin* booking office is in Piraeus, there is a first floor office in the building immediately to the left of the *National Bank* (*Tmr* 3D/E4) (Syntagma Sq behind one). Despite the staff being disinterested, they are able to hand over a comprehensive timetable and prices.

HAIRDRESSERS No problems with sufficient in the main shopping areas.

HOSPITALS *See* **Medical Care, A To Z.**

LAUNDERETTES There may be others but a good, central recommendation must be:
Coin-op (*Tmr* 13D5) Angelou Geronda.
Directions: From Kidathineon St (*proceeding towards Syntagma Sq*), at the far end of Plateia Plaka turn right down Angelou Geronda, towards Odhos Dedalou, and the launderette is on the right-hand side.

A machine load costs 200drs, 9 mins of dryer time 20drs and a measure of powder 30drs. In respect of the detergent, why not pop out to Kidathineon St and purchase a small packet of Tide for 38drs. For customers who are busy and are prepared to leave the laundry behind, the staff supervise the wash and dry operation at an extra cost of 400drs. Open in the summer daily 0800-2100hrs.

The more usual Athens style is for customers to leave their washing at any one of the countless laundries, collecting it next day dry, stiff and bleached (if necessary).

Note that my lavatorial obsession would not be satisfied without mentioning the Public toilet sited on Plateia Plaka.

LOST PROPERTY The main office is situated at 33 Ag Konstantinou (Tel 523 0111), the Plateia Omonia end of Ag Konstantinou. The telephone number is that of the Transport police who are now in charge of lost property (or *Grafio Hamenon Adikimenon*). Another 'lost & found' telephone number is 770 5771. It is still true to say that you are far more likely to 'lose' personal belongings to other tourists, then to Greeks.

LUGGAGE STORE There is one at No. 26 Nikis St (*Tmr* D5) advertising the service at a cost of 50drs per day per piece, 250drs per week and 750drs per month. Many hotels, guest houses and pensions mind a clients' bags, quite a number at no charge.

MEDICAL CARE
Chemists/Pharmacies (Farmakio – ΦΑΡΜΑΚΕΙΟ) Identified by a green or red

cross on a white background. Normal opening hours and a rota operates to give a 'duty' chemist cover.

Dentists & Doctors Ask at the **First Aid Centre** for the address of the School of Dentistry where free treatment is available. Both dentists and doctors advertise widely and there is no shortage of practitioners.

First Aid Centre (KAT) (*Tmr* 14D2) 21 Tritis Septemvriou St, beyond the Chalkokondili turning and on the left.　　　　　　　　　　　　　Tel 150

Hospital (*Tmr* 15G4) Do not proceed direct to a hospital but initially attend the **First Aid Centre**. When necessary they direct patients to the correct destination.

Medical Emergency:　　　　　　　　　　　　　　　　　　　　　Tel 166

METRO/ELEKTRIKOS (ΗΣΑΜ) The Athens underground or subway system, which operates below ground in the heart of the city and overground for the rest of the journey. It is a simple, one track layout from Kifissia (north-east Athens suburb) to Piraeus (south-west of Athens), and represents marvellous value with two rates of fare at 30 and 60drs. Passengers must have the requisite coins to obtain a ticket from the machine, prior to gaining access to the platforms. Everyone is most helpful and will, if the ticket machine 'frightens' a chap, show how it should be operated. Take care, select the ticket value first, then put the coins in the slot and keep the ticket so as to be able to hand it in at the journey's end. The service operates every 10 mins between 0500 and 2400hrs and travel before 0800hrs is free. Keep an eye open for the old-fashioned wooden carriages.

Station Stops There are 21 which include Kifissia (NE suburb), Stathmos Attiki (for the main railway stations), Plateia Victorias (N Athens), Omonia Sq, Monastiraki Sq (Plaka), Plateia Thission (for the Acropolis) and (Piraeus) Port. From the outside, the Piraeus terminus is rather difficult to locate, the entrance being in the left-hand corner of what appears to be an oldish, waterfront building. There used to be 20 stations but the new 'Peace Stadium' has 'acquired' a stop called Irene.

MUSIC & DANCING *See* **Clubs, Bars & Discos & The Eating Out, A To Z.**

NTOG (EOT) The headquarters of the National Tourist Organisation (NTOG) or, in Greek, the EOT (Ellinikos Organismos Tourismou – ΕΛΛΗΝΙΚΟΣ ΟΡΓΑΝΙΣΜΟΣ ΤΟΥΡΙΣΜΟΥ) is on the 5th floor at 2 Amerikis St (*Tmr* E4), close by Syntagma Sq. But this office does not normally handle the usual tourist enquiries, although the commissionaires manning the desk do hand out bits and pieces of information.

The information desk, from whence the free Athens map, advice, information folders, bus and boat schedules and hotel facts may be obtained, is situated inside and on the left of the foyer of the:

National Bank of Greece (*Tmr* 3D/E4) 2 Karageorgi Servias, Syntagma Sq
　　　　　　　　　　　　　　　　　　　　　　　　　　　　　　Tel 322 2545
Directions: As above.

Do not hope to obtain anything other than pamphlets and a snatch of guidance as it would be unrealistic to expect personal attention from staff besieged by wave upon wave of tourists of every creed, race and colour. The Athens hotel information sheets handed out now include a list of Class D & E establishments. Open Monday-Friday, 0800-2000hrs, Saturdays 0900-1400hrs.

There is now a sign requesting, if there are long queues, that enquirers use the tourist information office inside the **General Bank** situated at the corner

of Ermou St, where it joins Syntagma Square.
There is also an NTOG office conveniently sited at the East Airport.

OPENING HOURS (Summer months) These are only a guideline and apply to Athens (as well as the larger cities). Note that in country and village areas, it is more likely that shops are open from Monday to Saturday inclusive for over 12 hours a day, and on Sundays, holidays and Saints days, for a few hours either side of midday. The afternoon siesta is usually taken between 1300/1400hrs and 1500/1700hrs.

Trade Stores & Chemists Monday, Wednesday and Saturday 0800-1430hrs; Tuesday, Thursday and Friday 0900-1300hrs and 1700-2000hrs.

Food Stores Monday, Wednesday and Saturday 0800-1500hrs; Tuesday, Thursday and Friday 0800-1400hrs and 1730-2030hrs.

Art & Gift shops Weekdays 0800-2100hrs and Sundays (Monastiraki area) 0930-1445hrs.

Restaurants, Pastry shops, Cafes & Dairy shops Seven days a week.

Museums *See* **Museums, Places of Interest, A To Z**

Public Services (including Banks) Refer to the relevant **A To Z** heading.

OTE There are offices at: No. 85, 28 Ikosiokto Oktovriou/Patission St (*Tmr* 16D1) (open 24hrs a day); 15 Stadiou St (*Tmr* 17D4) (open Monday to Friday 0700-2400hrs, Saturday and Sunday 0800-2400hrs); 53 Solonos (*Tmr* E3) and 7 Kratinou (Plateia Kotzia) (*Tmr* C/D3) (open between 0800 and 2400hrs). There is also an office at 45 Athinas St (*Tmr* C/D3).

PHARMACIES *See* **Medical Care, A To Z.**

PLACES OF INTEREST
Parliament Building (*Tmr* E4/5) Syntagma Sq. Here it is possible to watch the Greek equivalent of the British 'Changing the Guard at Buckingham Palace'. The special guards (*Evzones*) are spectacularly outfitted with tasselled red caps, white shirts (blouses do I hear?), coloured waistcoats, a skirt, white tights, knee-garters and boots topped off with pom-poms. The ceremony officially kicks off at 1100hrs on Sunday morning but seems to falter into action at about 1045hrs. Incidentally, there is a band thrown in for good measure.

Museums The seasons are split as follow: Winter (1st November-31st March) and Summer (1st April-31st October). Museums are closed on: 1st January, 25th March, Good Friday, Easter Day and Christmas Day. Sunday hours are kept on Epiphany, Ash Monday, Easter Saturday, Easter Monday, 1st May, Whit Sunday, Assumption Day, 28th October and Boxing Day. They are only open in the mornings on Christmas Eve, New Year's Eve, 2nd January, Easter Thursday and Easter Tuesday. Museums are closed on Tuesdays unless otherwise indicated. Students with cards will achieve a reduction in fees.

Acropolis (*Tmr* C5). The museum exhibits finds made on the site. Of special interest are the sixth century BC statues of Korai women. Entrance charges are included in the admission fee to the Acropolis, which costs 500drs per head and is open Summer weekdays 0730-1930hrs, Sunday and holidays 0800-1800hrs. The museum hours are 0730-1930hrs, Tuesdays 1200-1800hrs, Sundays and holidays 0900-1700hrs.

Benaki (*Tmr* E/F4) On the corner of Vassilissis Sofias and Koubari (Koumbari) St, close by Plateia Kolonaki. A very interesting variety of exhibits made up from private collections. Particularly diverting is a display of national costumes. Weekday Summer hours: 0830-1400hrs, Sundays and holidays 0830-1400hrs and closed Tuesdays. Entrance 150drs.

Byzantine (*Tmr* F4/5) 22 Vassilissis Sofias. As one would deduce from the name – Byzantine art. Summer hours: daily 0900-1700hrs; Sunday and holidays, 0900-1400hrs; closed Mondays. Entrance costs 300drs.

Goulandris 13 Levidou St, Kifissia, N Athens. Natural History. Summer hours: daily 0900-1400hrs; Sunday and holidays 0900-1530hrs; closed Fridays. Entrance costs 30drs.

Goulandris (*Tmr* F4) 4 Neophitou Douka St (off Vassilissis Sofias). The second or 'other' Goulandris Museum. The situation is not helped by the little quirk of some people referring to the Natural History Museum as 'Goulandris'. Help! This Goulandris, that is the Cycladic and Ancient Greek. Art Goulandris Museum is open daily in the summer 1000-1600hrs; closed Tuesday, Sunday and holidays. Entrance costs 150drs.

Kanelloupoulos (*Tmr* C5) On the corner of Theorias and Panos Sts in the Plaka. A smaller version of the Benaki Museum and located at the foot of the northern slope of the Acropolis, at the Monastiraki end. Summer hours: daily 0845-1500hrs; Sunday and holidays 0930-1430hrs. Entrance costs 100drs (and is charged Sundays and holidays).

Keramikos (*Tmr* B4) 148 Ermou St. Finds from Keramikos cemetery. Summer hours: daily 0845-1500hrs; Sunday and holidays 0930-1430hrs and closed on Tuesdays. Entrance to the site and museum costs 200drs.

National Gallery & Alexandros Soutzos (*Tmr* G4) 46 Vassileos Konstantinou/Sofias. Mainly 19th and 20th century Greek paintings. Summer hours: 0900-1500hrs; Sunday and holidays 1000-1400hrs and closed on Mondays. Admission is free.

National Historical & Ethnological (*Tmr* D4) Kolokotroni Sq, off Stadiou St. Greek history and the War of Independence. Summer hours: 0900-1400hrs; Saturday, Sunday and holidays 0900-1300hrs and closed Mondays. Entrance costs 100drs.

National Archaeological (*Tmr* D/E2) 1 Tossitsa St, off 28 Ikosiokto Oktovriou/Patission St. The largest and possibly the most important Greek museum, covering a wide variety of exhibits. A must if you are a museum buff. Summer hours: 0800-1900hrs; Sunday and holidays 0800-1800hrs and closed on Mondays. Entrance costs 400drs, which includes entrance to the *Santorini* and *Numismatic* exhibitions (*See* below).

Numismatic In the same building as the National Archaeological and displaying, as would be imagined, a collection of Greek coins, spanning the ages. Summer hours: 0830-1330hrs; Sunday and holidays 0900-1400hrs and closed on Tuesdays. Admission is free.

Also housed in the same building are the:
Epigraphical Collection: Summer hours: 0830-1330hrs; Sunday and holidays 0900-1400hrs and closed Tuesdays.
Santorini Exhibition: Summer hours: 0930-1500hrs every day but closed on Mondays
and

The Casts and Copies Exhibition: Summer hours: 0900-1400hrs daily but closed Sunday and Mondays.

Popular (Folk) Art (Tmr D5) 17 Kidathineon St, The Plaka. Folk art, folklore and popular art. Summer hours: 1100-1400hrs; Sunday and holidays 1000-1400hrs and closed on Mondays. Entrance free.

War (Tmr F4/5) 2 Rizari St, off Leoforos Vassilissis Sofias. Warfare exhibits covering a wide variety of subjects. Summer hours: daily 0900-1400hrs and closed on Mondays. Entrance is free.

Theatres & Performances For full, up-to-date details enquire at the NTOG office (*Tmr* 3D/E4). They should be able to hand out a pamphlet giving a precise timetable for the year. As a guide the following are performed year in and year out:
Son et Lumiere. From the Pynx hillside, a *Son et Lumiere* features the Acropolis. This show is produced from early April up to the end of October. The English performance starts at 2100hrs every evening, except when the moon is full, and takes 45 minutes. There are French versions at 2215hrs daily, except Tuesdays and Fridays when a German commentary is provided at 2200hrs.

Tickets and information are available from the *Athens Festival booking office* (*See Athens Festival*) or at the Pynx, prior to the outset of the show. Tickets cost 350drs (students 120drs), and are also available at the entrance of the Church, Ag Dimitros Lombardiaris, on the way to the show. Catch a No. 230 bus along Dionysiou Areopagitou St getting off one stop beyond the Odeion (Theatre) of Herodes Atticus and follow the signposted path on the left-hand side.

Athens Festival This prestigious event takes place in the restored and beautiful Odeion of Herodes Atticus. This was built in approximately AD 160 as a Roman theatre, seating about 5000 people and situated at the foot of the south-west corner of the Acropolis. The festival lasts from early June to the middle of September, and consists of a series of plays, ballet, concerts and opera. The performances usually commence at 2100hrs and tickets, which are on sale up to 10 days before the event, are obtainable from the Theatre 1 hour prior to the commencement of the show or from the Athens Festival booking office (*Tmr* D/E4), 4 Stadiou St, Tel 322 1459.

Dora Stratou Theatre (Tmr A6) A short stroll away on Mouseion or Hill of Muses. On the summit stands the Monument of the Filopapou (Philopappos) and nearby the Dora Stratou Theatre, where an internationally renowned troupe of folk dancers, dressed in traditional costumes, perform a series of Greek dances and songs. The theatre group operates daily from about the middle of May to the end of September. The show starts at 2215hrs, that is except Wednesday and Sunday when they perform at 2015 & 2215hrs. Ticket prices vary from 450-750drs (students 350drs) and are available between 0900-1400hrs (Tel 324 4395) and 1830-2300hrs (Tel 921 4650).

Performances are timed to coincide with the ending of the *Son et Lumiere*, on the Pynx.

Lycabettus Theatre On the north-east side of Lycabettus Hill. Concerts and theatrical performances take place at the hillside open-air theatre, between the middle of June and the first week of September, from 2100hrs. Tickets can be purchased from the theatre box office, one hour before the event, or from the *Athens Festival booking office*, referred to previously under Athens Festival.

Wine Festival Held daily at Dafni from the middle of July to the end of August, between 1900-0030hrs. Ticket price 220drs per head. Information and tickets from the *Athens Festival booking office*.

POLICE *See* **Tourist Police, A To Z.**

POST OFFICES (Tachidromio – ΤΑΧΤΔΡΟΜΕΙΟΞ) Weekday opening hours, as a guide, are 0800 to 1300hrs. The Central Post Office at 100 Eolou St (*Tmr* 18D3), close by Omonia Sq, is open Monday-Saturday, 0730-1500hrs. Branch offices are situated on the corner of Othonos and Nikis Sts (Syntagma Sq); at the Omonia Sq underground Metro concourse and on Dionysiou Areopagitou St, at the corner of Tzireon St (*Tmr* D6).

The telephone and telegraph system is run by a separate state organisation. *See* **OTE.**

SHOPPING HOURS *See* **Opening Hours, A To Z.**

SPORTS FACILITIES
Golf. There is an 18 hole course, the *Glifida Golf Club* close by the East Airport. Changing rooms, restaurant and refreshment bar.
Swimming. There is a *Swimming (and Tennis) Club* on Leoforos Olgas (*Tmr* 19E6), across the way from the Zappeion National Gardens. *The Hilton Hotel* (*Tmr* G4) has a swimming pool but, if you are not staying there, use of it costs the price of an (expensive) meal. *See* **Beaches, A To Z.**
Tennis. There are courts at most of the NTOG beaches (*See* **Beaches, A To Z**) as well as at the *Ag Kosmas Athletics Centre*, close by the West airport.

TAXIS (ΤΑΞΙ) Used extensively and, although they seem to me to be expensive, are 'officially' the cheapest in Europe. The Athens drivers are, now, generally without scruples. The metered fares are costed at about 23drs per kilometre. But they are subject to various surcharges including 15drs for each piece of baggage, 240drs per hour of waiting time and 30drs for picking up at, or delivering to, public transport facilities. There is also an extra charge for the hours between midnight and daylight. When a prospective fare is standing at a taxi rank, drivers must pick them up, but are not obliged to do so when cruising, for which there is an extra 'flag falling' charge of 25drs. The sign ΕΛΕΤΘΕΡΟΝ indicates a cab is free for hire. The minimum fare is 110drs and sample fares include:
Syntagma/Omonia Square to the East airport 500drs and to the West airport 400drs; the East airport to Piraeus 500drs and the West airport to Piraeus 350drs. The Syntagma taxi station telephone number is 323 7942.

TELEPHONES *See* **OTE.**

TOURIST OFFICE/AGENCIES *See* **NTOG & Travel Agents & Tour Offices, A To Z.**

TOURIST POLICE (*Tmr* 20D6) I understand, despite the reorganisation of the service, that the Athens headquarters is to remain in operation. This is situated at 7 Leoforos Sygrou (Sygrou/Syngrou/Singrou Av). Open daily 0800-2200hrs. Tel 923-9224. Tourist information in English is available on the telephone number 171.

There are also Tourist police offices close by and just to the north of Larissis Railway Station (open 0700-2400hrs, tel 821 3574) and the East airport (open 0730-2300hrs, tel 981 4093/969 9500).

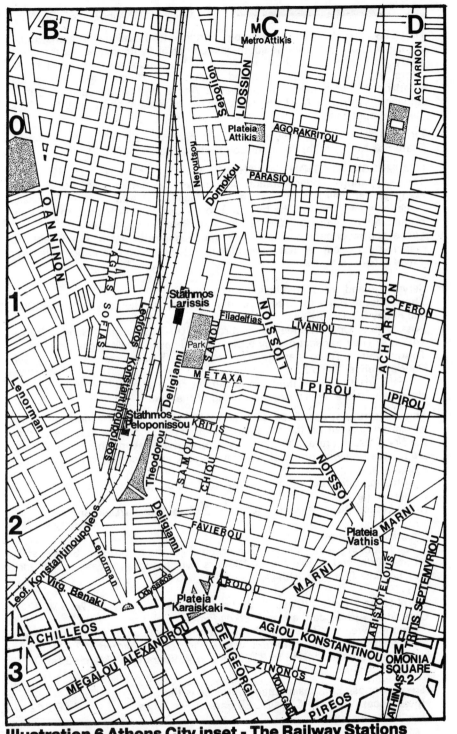

Illustration 6 Athens City inset - The Railway Stations

TOILETS Apart from the various bus termini and the railway stations, there is a super Public toilet on the south-east corner of Syntagma Sq, as there is a pretty grim 'squatty' in the Omonia Sq Metro concourse. This latter costs 20drs. The Plaka is well 'endowed' with one at Plateia Plaka, (on Odhos Kidathineon) and another on the Plateia Agora at the other end of Odhos Adrianou. Visitors to Mt. Lycabettus will not be 'caught short' and the toilets there are spotless.

TRAINS (Illustration 6) They arrive at (or depart from) either (a) Larissis Station (Stathmos No. 1) or (b) Peloponissou Station (Stathmos No. 2).

(A) LARISSIS STATION (STATHMOS No. 1) (*Tmr* B/C1)   Tel 821 3882
The main, more modern station of the two. Connections to the Western European services and the northern provinces of Central Greece, Thessaly, Macedonia and Thrace. The bus stop to the centre of Athens is to the right of the station (*station building behind one*). Refer to **Buses** below.

One correspondent has reminded me to reiterate that it is advisable to reserve return seats at the International 'hatch' as soon as is possible after arrival in Greece by train.

Services in and around the building include:
The National Bank of Greece. Opens Monday to Thursday 0830-1400hrs and Friday 0830-1330hrs.
Post Office. Open Monday to Saturday 0700-2000hrs and Sunday 0900-1400hrs. They transact money exchange and cash travellers cheques.
Tourist police. There is an office just to the north of the station building. *See* **Tourist Police, A To Z**.

To the front of the station is a pavement cafe-bar (a coffee 56drs) and an elongated square, well more a widening of the road.

The Accommodation Even early and late in the summer a number of the hardier stretch out on the pavements around and about the stations (and at the *Hotel Oscar's* rates I'm not surprised). Arrivals, even whilst on the train, are bombarded with offers of accommodation, so much so that the touts are a nuisance.

With the station behind one, to the right, across the concourse and on the corner, is the:
Hotel Lefkos Pirgos (*Tmr* C1) (Class E) 27 Leof.Metaxa/Deligianni
                                                                Tel 821 3765
Directions: As above.
Seedy looking establishment. All rooms share the bathrooms. Singles start off at 840drs and double rooms 1380drs, which prices increase to 1050drs and 1725drs (1st July-10th Oct).

Hotel Nana (*Tmr* C1) (Class B), 29 Leof.Metaxa   Tel 884 2211
Directions: Alongside the *Hotel Lefkos Pirgos*.
Smarter (well it is B class) with the charges reflecting this pre-eminence. All rooms have an en suite bathroom with a single room charged at 2290drs and a double at 3205drs rising to 3205drs and 4395drs (16th March-31st Oct).

Directly opposite the main station entrance is the:
Hotel Oscar (*Tmr* C1) (Class B), 25 Samou/Filadelfias   Tel 883 4215
Directions: As above.

I hardly dare detail the room rates, which for a double room kicks off at 4415drs rising to 5195drs, en suite naturally. Breakfast costs 340drs. I must own up to staying at the Oscar. But it was at the end of a long stint on the Greek islands, added to which there were a couple of other (good) reasons. Firstly they accept payment by *Amex* which, as I have written before, may be of great assistance in eking out dwindling funds, and secondly, the hotel is conveniently close to the railway and the inter-country coach station. Thus the comforts of this hotel, or similar, can be put to good use in order to build up the bodily reserves prior to a planned long distance bus or railway journey! That is not to say that even this luxurious establishment does not escape some of the common faults oft experienced as a 'norm' when staying at its lower classified 'cousins'. The en suite bathroom of our room had a loose lavatory seat, the bath plug had no chain attached (there was a chain but it was not attached), and the small bathroom window was tied up with string. The bedroom sliding balcony window would not completely shut – there was no locking mechanism and the air conditioning didn't. Mind you I must admit to making a reservation without Rosemary, who guarded our backpacks whilst I sorted out the formalities. It may have been the sight of the two, towering, aforementioned packs reversing through the swing doors into reception that resulted in our being allocated this particular 'downtown' room, at the rear of the hotel, overlooking and overlooked by the backsides of a block of flats.

Hotel Elena (Helena) (*Tmr* B/C1) (Class C) 2 Psiloriti/Samou Tel 881 3211
Directions: Along Samou St, south from Leof. Metaxa St, and on the right.
    Single rooms sharing the bathroom cost 1135drs and en suite 1670drs; double rooms sharing are charged at 1870drs and en suite 2270drs.

Hotel Louvre (*Tmr* C2) (Class D) 9 Chiou/Favierou Sts   Tel 522 9891
Directions: Next street back from and parallel to Samou St, towards the south end of Chiou St.
    Greek provincial in outward appearance, despite the grand and evocative name. Single rooms sharing a bathroom cost 1190drs; double rooms sharing 1720drs and en suite 2200drs.

Joy's Hotel (*Tmr* D1) 38 Feron St   Tel 823 1012
Directions: Proceed up Odhos Filadelfias, almost directly opposite the main station, across Odhos Liossion continuing along Livaniou St as far as Odhos Acharnon. Turn left and then first right on to Feron St.
    Reputedly a good value, busy, Youth Hostel style establishment complete with a bar/cafeteria and offering accommodation ranging from a dormitory (500drs) to quadruples. A single bed starts off at 900drs and a double 1600drs. A hot shower costs an extra 100drs.

Street Market Whilst in this area it is worth noting that Odhos Chiou, between Kritis and Favierou Sts, is host to an extensive street market where almost everything is sold from fish to meat and hardware to clothing.

Bread shop & Supermarket (*Tmr* B/C1/2) On the corner of Samou St and Eratyras St. A bit disorganised but very useful.

Snackbar (*Tmr* B/C1) Odhos Samou.
Directions: Across the street from the Park, on the stretch of Odhos Samou between Filadelfias and Leof. Metaxa Sts.
    A small, convenient, souvlaki pita snackbar, run by a very friendly chap. A souvlaki and a bottle of beer costs 125drs.

Buses: Trolley-bus No. 1 pulls up to the right of the station, as do the No's 2 & 4. The fare to Syntagma Sq is 30drs.

(B) PELOPONISSOU STATION (STATHMOS NO. 2) (*Tmr* B1/2)

Tel 513 1601

The station for trains to the Peloponnese, the ferry connections for some of the Ionian islands and international ferries to Italy from Patras.

TRAINS (General)

Tickets: The concept behind the acquisition of a ticket is similar to that of a lottery. On buying one ticket a compartment seat is also allocated. In theory this is a splendid scheme, but in practice the idea breaks down in a welter of bad tempered argument over whom is occupying whose seat. Manners and quaint old-fashioned habits of giving up one's seat to older people and ladies are best avoided. I write this from the bitter experience of offering my seat to elderly Greek ladies, only for their husbands to immediately fill the vacant position. Not what one had in mind! Find your seat and stick to it like glue and if you have made a mistake feign madness, admit to being a foreigner, but do not budge.

At Peloponissou Station the mechanics of buying a ticket take place in organised bedlam. The ticket office 'traps' open half an hour prior to the train's departure. Scenes reminiscent of a Cup Final crowd develop, with prospective travellers pitching about within the barriers of the ticket hatch, and all this in the space of about 10m by 10m. To add to the difficulty, there are two hatch 'slots' and it is anybody's guess which one to select. It really is best to try and steal a march on the 'extra-curricula' activity, diving for a hatch whenever one opens up.

Travellers booking a return journey train ticket to Europe, and routing via Italy, must ensure the tickets are to and from Patras, not Athens. (Yes, Patras). Then the purchase of the separate Patras to Athens (and vice versa) ticket, ensures a seat. A voyager boarding the train with an open ticket will almost surely have to stand for almost the whole of the four hour journey. Most Athens – Patras journeys seem to attract an 'Express' surcharge of between 100-150drs which exacted by the ticket collector.

Incidentally, the general architecture of the Peloponissou building is delightful, especially the ceiling of the booking office hall, centrally located, under the main clock face. To the left, on entering the building, is a glass-fronted information box with all the train times listed on the window. The staff manning this desk are extremely helpful and speak sufficient English so pose no problems in communication (the very opposite of the disinterest shown at the NTOG desk in the National Bank of Greece, on Syntagma Sq).

Advance Booking Office. Information and advance booking for both stations is handled at:
No. 6 Sina (*Tmr* E3) off Akadimias St (Tel 363 4402/4406); No. 1 Karolou (Satovriandou) (*Tmr* C2) west of Omonia Sq. (Tel 524 0647/8) and No. 17 Filellinon (*Tmr* D/E5) (Tel 323 6747/6273).

Toilets The station toilets usually, well always, lack toilet paper.

Sustenance (on the train) An attendant brings inexpensive drinks and snacks around from time to time and hot snacks are available from platform trolleys at the major railway stations.

Railway Head Office (*Tmr* C2) Hellenic Railways Organisation (OSE) 1-3 Karolou St. Tel 522 2491
Directions: One back from the far end of Ag Konstantinou, west from Omonia Sq.

Provisions Shopping in the area of the railway stations is made easy by the presence of the Street Market on Odhos Chiou (*See* **Larissis Station, Trains**).

Access to the stations
Bus/Trolley-bus. From the Airport, travel on the Olympic bus to the terminal at 96-100 Leoforos Sygrou (which at a cost of 100drs is good value). Then catch a bus (Nos. 133, 040, 132, 155, 903 and 161 amongst others) across the street from the terminus to Syntagma Sq, after which a No. 1 or No. 5 (via Omonia Sq) or a No. 11 trolley-bus to the Stathmos Larissis railway station. Instead of making a change of bus at Syntagma Sq, it is also possible to walk west from the terminal on Leoforos Sygrou across Falirou and Odisseos and Androutsou Sts to the parallel street of Odhos Dimitrakopoulou and catch a No. 1 trolley-bus all the way to the stations.
     From Piraeus Port catch the No. 40 (green) bus on Leoforos Vassileos Konstantinou (parallel to the quay) to Syntagma Sq, or the No. 049 from Plateia Themistokleous to Athinas St, close by Omonia Sq. For other possibly conflicting information *See* **Arrival by Air, Introduction; Airline offices & terminus & Buses & Trolley-buses, A To Z.**

Metro The metro station for both railway stations is Attiki, close to Plateia Attikis. From the platform, assuming a traveller has come from the south, dismount and turn right down into the underpass to come out the far or west side of the station on Odhos Liossion. Turn left and walk to the large irregular Plateia Attikis (*with the Hotel Lydia on the right*). Proceed down Domokou St (the road that exits half-right on the far side of the square), which spills into Plateia Deligianni edged by Stathmos Larissis. A more long-winded alternative is to get off the Metro at Omonia Sq, walk west along Ag Konstantinou to Karaiskaki Sq and then up Odhos Deligianni, or catch a No. 1 trolley-bus.

Taxi A reasonable indulgence, if in a hurry, although it must be noted that in the crowded traffic conditions of Athens it is often quicker to walk than catch a cab. *See* **Taxis, A To Z.**

Station to Station To get from one to the other, say Stathmos Larissis to Peloponissou, it is necessary to turn right out of the station and climb the steps over the railway line turning left at the bottom of the far side of the steps and walk some 100m to the forecourt in front of Stathmos Peloponissou. Almost, but not quite adjacent, as some guides put it, if 150m on a very hot day, laden down with cases seems contiguous.

TRAIN TIMETABLES
Peloponissou Station It is easy to read the Peloponissou timetable and come to the conclusion that a large number of trains are leaving the station at the same time. On seeing the single-line track, a newcomer cannot be blamed for feeling apprehensive that it may prove difficult to select the correct carriages. The mystification arises from the fact that the trains are detailed separately from Athens to say Korinthos, Mikines, Argos, Tripolis, Pirgos and etc, etc. There is no mention that the railway line is a circular layout, with single trains circumscribing the route and that each place name is simply a stop on the journey.

Making changes for branch lines can be 'exciting'! Stations are labelled in demotic script and there is no comprehensible announcement from the guard, thus it is easy to fail to make an exit on cue!

Peloponissou Station
Athens to Patras:
Depart　0640, 0826, 1020, 1305, 1542, 1820, 2139 hrs
Arrive　1055, 1206, 1430, 1653, 2005, 2153, 0149 hrs

Patras to Athens:
Depart　0630, 0811, 1105, 1350, 1705, 1842, 2013, 0210 hrs
Arrive　1002, 1257, 1457, 1832, 2118, 2239, 0010, 0636 hrs
One-way fare: Athens to Patras: B Class 545drs, A Class 820drs.

Larissis Station
Athens to Thessaloniki & on to Alexandroupoli:
Depart　0700, 0800, 1100, 1425, 1900, 2110, 2310 hrs
Thessaloniki
Arrive　1448, 1550, 1806, 2217, 0336, 0553, 0750 hrs
Depart　1532,　-　1832, 2316,　-　0617, 0924 hrs
Drama (for Kavala)
Arrive　1854,　-　-　0302,　-　1023, 1338 hrs
Alexandroupoli
Arrive　2216,　-　-　0655,　-　1412, 1738 hrs
One-way fares:
　　Athens to Thessaloniki　　　:B Class 1265drs, A Class 1895drs.
　　Athens to Drama　　　　　　:B Class 1650drs, A Class 2475drs.
　　Athens to Alexandroupoli　　:B Class 1955drs, A Class 2930drs.
Surcharge on Express trains from 170-300drs.

TRAVEL AGENTS & TOUR OFFICES There are offices selling tickets for almost anything to almost anywhere, which include:
ABC 58 Stadiou St. Tel 321 1381
American Express 2 Ermou St, Tel 324 4975/9
On the first floor is an excellent retail travel service. Admittedly they are mainly involved in the sale of tours and excursions but the assistants are extremely efficient and helpful. They will, for instance, telephone round to locate all or any hotels that accept an Amex card, if they have a room and the cost.
CHAT 4 Stadiou St. Tel 322 2886
Key Tours 5th Floor, 2 Ermou St. Tel 323 3756
Viking 3 Filellinon St. Tel 322 9383
Probably the agency most highly regarded by students for prices and variety.
International Student & Youth Travel Service (SYTS) 11 Nikis St
　　　　　　　　　　　　　　　　　　　　　　Tel 323 3767
For FIYTO membership. Second floor, open Monday-Friday 0900-1900hrs and Saturday from 0900-1200hrs.

Filellinon and the parallel street of Odhos Nikis (to the west of Syntagma Sq), all the way south and up as far as Nikodimou St are jam-packed with tourist agencies and student organisations. These include one or two express coach and train fare companies. A sample, going up the rise from Syntagma Square, includes:

Budget Student Travel On the right, opposite a church.
Stafford Travel On the corner of Filellinon and Kidathineon Sts.

An example of the packaged tours on offer, in this instance from **Key Tours** but representatives of most, includes:-

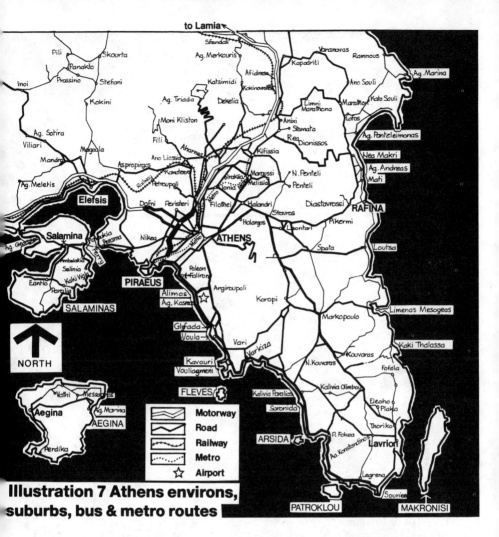

Illustration 7 Athens environs, suburbs, bus & metro routes

One day to Delphi from 4200drs; two days to Epidauras & Mycenae 10,900drs; three days to Delphi & Meteora from 26,150drs & a one day cruise to Aegina, Poros & Hydra, 4000drs.

Callers at the National Bank (*Tmr* 3D/E4/5) usually have to run the gauntlet of 'tours from touts' even if some may only be offering advice ('...I know this white woman?). They are best brushed aside otherwise the unwary might well be borne along on an unstoppable tide.

Sample 'charter' air & bus fares available from Athens to various European capitals include (as quoted by **Economy Travel**, 18 Panepistimiou St, Athens Tel 363 4045):

Air to London 25,000drs; Paris 24,000drs; Rome 17,500drs; Munich 20,000; Berlin 21,000drs; New York 40,000drs; Stockholm 29,000drs.

Bus to London 13,000drs; Paris 12,000drs; Venice 9000drs; Munich 11,000drs; Istanbul 4500drs.

YOUTH HOSTEL ASSOCIATION *See* **The Accommodation.**

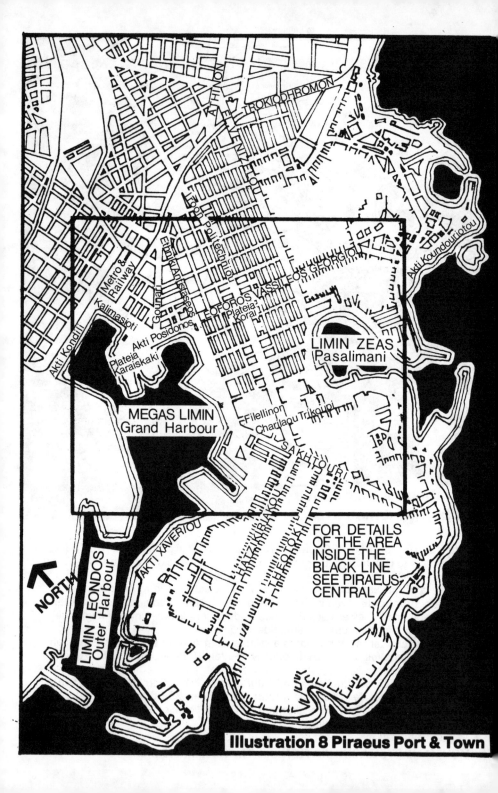

Illustration 8 Piraeus Port & Town

10 PIREAUS (Pireas, Pireefs) & other Mainland Ports (where applicable)

Fortune and hope farewell! I've found the port you've done with me; go now with others sport. From a Greek epigram

Tel prefix 01

Piraeus is the port of Athens (Illustrations 8, 9 & 10) and the usual ferry-boat departure point for most of the Aegean islands. A confusing town on first acquaintance, but very unlike the old Piraeus portrayed in the film *Never on a Sunday*. The bawdy seaport cafes, tavernas and seedy waterfront have been replaced by smart shipping offices, respectable banks and tree planted thoroughfares, squares and parks.

Arrival at Piraeus will usually be by Metro or bus if coming from inland, or by ferry-boat if arriving by sea. (Well, it would be a long tiring swim, wouldn't it?).

ARRIVAL BY BUS

From Syntagma Sq (Athens), Bus No. 40 arrives at Plateia Korai (*Tmr* C3) but in truth that is rather an over simplification. For a start the bus is absolutely crammed early morning and it is very difficult to know one's exact whereabouts, which is germane as the bus hurtles on down to the end of the Piraeus peninsula. The first indicator that the end of the $\frac{3}{4}$ hour journey is imminent is when the bus runs parallel to the Metro lines. The second is crossing a wide avenue at right-angles (Leoforos Vassileos Georgiou) after which signs for the *Archaeological Museum* indicate that it is time to bale out.

From Plateia Korai, north-west along Leoforos Vassileos Georgiou (Yeoryiou) leads to the Main (Grand or Central) Harbour (*Tmr* D2); south-east progresses towards Limin Zeas (Pasalimani) (*Tmr* C/D4) and east towards Limin Mounikhias (Tourkolimano) (*Tmr* B5), the latter two being the marina harbours. Limin Zeas is where the Flying Dolphins dock.

From Omonia Sq (Athens) Bus No. 49 arrives at Ethniki Antistaseos (*Tmr* C2); from the East airport, (a yellow) Bus No. 19 (but often numberless), arrives at Karaiskaki Sq (*Tmr* C/D2). Karaiskaki (Akti Tzelepi) Sq is a main bus terminal. The note in brackets regarding the No. 19 bus should be expanded to point out that all the other buses are blue.

Another service (Bus No. 101) arrives at Theotoki St (*Tmr* E/F3/4) from whence head north-east towards Sakhtouri St and turn left in a northerly direction to reach the southern end of the Main Harbour quay front.

ARRIVAL BY METRO

Piraeus Metro station (*Tmr* 1C1/2), the end of the line, is hidden away in the corner of a large but rather inconspicuous building, flanked by Plateia Roosevelt. It could well be a warehouse, an empty shell of an office block, in fact almost anything but a Metro terminus. Passengers emerge opposite the quayside, at the north end of the waterfront.

If catching a ferry almost immediately, it is probably best to make a temporary headquarters by turning right out of the entrance, following the quay round to the left and 'falling' into one of the three or so cafe-bars set in the harbour-facing side of a sizeable quayside block of buildings. The importance of establishing a shore base, or bridgehead, becomes increasingly apparent whilst attempts are made to locate the particular ferry-boat departure point.

To obtain tickets turn to the left (*Fsw*) out of the Metro station and follow the quayside round. One of the first major landmarks is Karaiskaki (or Akti Tzelepi) Sq (*Tmr* C/D2), fronted by large, shipping office buildings surmounted by a number of neon lit signs. These advertising slogans change from year to year but the point is that they are eye-catching. Proceed along the quay road (Akti Posidonos), between the Streets of Gounari and Ethniki Antistaseos, (*Tmr* C2), keeping the waterfront to the right. Reference to **Ferry-Boat Ticket Offices, A To Z** gives details of various ticket offices. The Port police are located in a quayside shed and must be regarded as favourites to dispense fairly accurate information about ferry-boats. Any information received though is best tucked away for future comparison with the rest of the advice acquired.

ARRIVAL BY FERRY
Reorientate using the above information, but bearing in mind that ferries dock all the way round the Grand Harbour, from the area of the Metro Station (*Tmr* 1C1/2) as far down as the Olympic office (*Tmr* 8D3).

ARRIVAL BY FLYING DOLPHIN
The hydrofoils dock at Limin Zeas Harbour. *See* **Flying Dolphins, A To Z.**

ARRIVAL BY TRAIN
If passengers have not alighted at Athens, Peloponnese trains pull up at the same terminus building as the Metro (*Tmr* 1C1/2) and the Northern Greece trains on the far (north-west) side of the Grand Harbour (*Tmr* 19D/E1/2).

THE ACCOMMODATION & EATING OUT
The Accommodation General remarks for Athens also apply here. Although I have never had to doss (or camp) out in Piraeus, I am advised that it is not to be recommended. There are just too many disparate (desperate?) characters wandering about.

Close by the Metro Station are the:
Hotel Ionion (*Tmr* 4C2) (Class C) 10 Kapodistrion   Tel 417 0992
Directions: Turn left from the Metro station and or Roosevelt Sq (*Fsw*) down the quay road, Kalimasioti St, and left again at the first turning.
   The hotel, halfway up on the right, is noticeable by the prominent sign promising *Family Hotel and from now on Economical Prices*. But is it, with a single room sharing a bathroom charged at 1600drs and a double room, also sharing, 2845drs (1st April-14th Oct)?
The Delfini (*Tmr* 5C2) (Class C) 7 Leoharous St   Tel 412 3512
Directions: As above, but the second turning left.
   Singles cost 2500drs and doubles 3500drs, both with bathroom en suite.
Hotel Helektra (*Tmr* 6C2) (Class E) 12 Navarinou   Tel 417 7057
Directions: At the top of Leoharous St, turn right on to Navarinou St and the hotel is at the end of the block.
   During the season a single room costs 1020drs and a double 1400drs, both sharing the bathroom.

Follow the quay road of Akti Posidonos round to the right, along the waterfront of Akti Miaouli as far as Odhos Bouboulina, the side street prior to Odhos Merarkhias. Turn up Bouboulina St.

Youth Hostel No. 1 (*Tmr* 24D3) 8 Filonos St.
Directions: As above and on the right between the 3rd and 4th lateral street, including the Esplanade.
   A large, very seedy looking establishment.

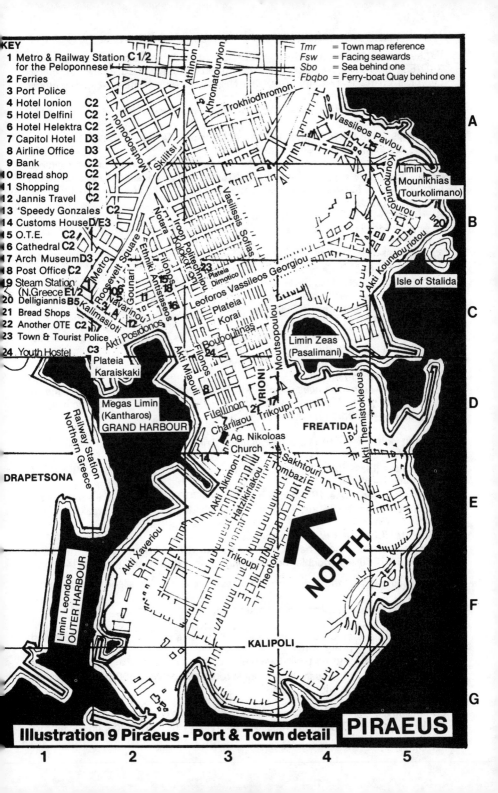

Illustration 9 Piraeus - Port & Town detail   **PIRAEUS**

Further on along the waterfront Esplanade towards the Custom's office (*Tmr* 14D/E3), and close by the Church of Ag Nikolaos, advances to the bottom of Leoforos Charilaou Trikoupi (*Tmr* D3). This street runs south-east and is amply furnished with cheaper hotels including the:

Capitol Hotel (*Tmr* 7D3) Class C) Ch. Trikoupi/147 Filonos Sts   Tel 452 4911
Directions: As above.
   A single room costs 1500drs and a double room 2000drs, both en suite.
Glaros Hotel (Class C) 4 Ch. Trikoupi   Tel 452 7887
A breakfast costs 220drs. Single rooms are en suite and start at 1300drs while a double room sharing a bathroom cost 1500drs and en suite 1750drs. These charges rise to 1370drs for a single room and 1570/1840drs for a double room (1st July-31st Dec).
Serifos Hotel (Class C) 5 Ch. Trikoupi   Tel 452 4967
A single room costs 1200drs and a double room 1750drs, both with en suite bathrooms.
Santorini Hotel (Class C) 6 Ch. Trikoupi   Tel 452 2147
Prices as for the *Serifos Hotel*.
Homeridion Hotel (Class B) 32 Ch. Trikoupi   Tel 451 9811
Rather expensive but all rooms have an en suite bathroom with singles costing 2700drs and a double room 3900drs.

Forming a junction with Leoforos Charilaou Trikoupi is Notara St up which turn left. On this street is sited the:
Faros Hotel (Class D) 140 Notara St   Tel 452 6317
Directions: As above.
   More down-to-earth prices despite which all rooms have en suite bathrooms. A single room costs 1050drs and a double 1350drs which rise respectively to 1100drs and 1450drs (1st July-31st Dec).

Again at right angles to Leoforos Charilaou Trikoupi, is Kolokotroni St on which are situated:
Park House (Class B) 103 Kolokotroni St   Tel 452 4611
Directions: As above.
   A single room costs 1950drs and a double 2700drs, both with en suite bathrooms increasing to 2250drs and 3100drs (16th May-31st Oct). A breakfast costs 350drs.
Aris Hotel (Class D) 117 Kolokotroni St   Tel 452 0487
A single room sharing a bathroom is charged at 880drs and with an en suite bathroom 1100drs. A double room sharing costs 1200drs and en suite 1460drs.

Also leading off to the left is Iroon Politechniou (once Vassileos Konstantinou) whereon:
Noufara Hotel (Class B) 45 Iroon Politechniou   Tel 411 5541
Directions: As above.
   All rooms have an en suite bathroom with singles costing 2315/2845drs and doubles 3115/3915drs. (Phew!)
Savoy Hotel (Class B) 93 Iroon Politechniou   Tel 413-1102
Guests will have to be 'flush' with a single room charged at 3590drs and a double room 4810drs, both with en suite bathrooms.

Continuing along Iroon Politechniou, turn right (*or south-east*) at Plateia Korai along Leoforos Vassileos Georgiou (Vassileos Yeoryiou) which proceeds, on the left, to:

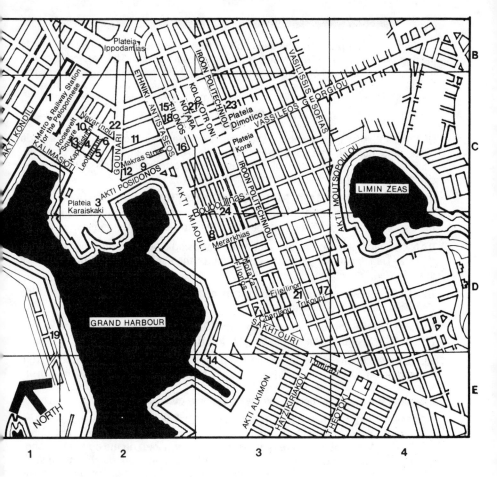

Illustration 10 Piraeus inset

Diogenis Hotel (Class B) 27 Leoforos Vassileos Georgiou   Tel 412 5471
Directions: As above.

Within a few hundred drachmae of the Savoy.

The Eating Out
For eating out read the Athens comments as a general guide. Piraeus is not noted for outstanding rendezvous around the Grand Harbour and its encircling terrain, despite the numerous restaurants, tavernas and cafes along the quayside roads. On the other hand there are some excellent eating places in the area bordering the eastern coastline of the Piraeus peninsula, bounded by Akti Moutsopoulou (*Tmr* C/D3/4) and Akti Koumoundourou (*Tmr* B5) encircling (respectively) the Zeas and Mounikhias harbours.

Especially recommended is the classy:

Delligiannis (*Tmr* 20B5) 1 Akti Koundouriotou   Tel 413 2013
Directions: A very pleasant setting in the 'pretty' part of Piraeus up on the hill to the south-west of Limin Mounikhias. This overlooks a few million pounds worth of private yachts lying to anchor in the most attractive harbour.

Apart from the position, the selection of food is excellent and there is outside seating while the inside resembles a high-class saloon bar. The service is quick, friendly and honest. For instance, enquirers will be advised that the 'souvlaki flambe' is nothing more than souvlaki on fire! 'Inside information' advises that the 'birds liver in wine' is delicious, despite being listed as a starter. Costing 450drs, the portions are larger than most main courses at other tavernas.

On Plateia Karaiskaki, a number of cafe-bar/restaurants stretch along the quayside of the large building that dominates the square. A white van sometimes parks up, early in the day, on the edge of the square, selling from the back of the vehicle, small pizzas and feta cheese pies for about 80drs.

THE A TO Z OF USEFUL INFORMATION

AIRLINE OFFICE & TERMINUS (*Tmr* 8D3) The Olympic office is halfway down the Esplanade of Akti Miaouli, at the junction with Odhos II Merarkhias.

BANKS The most impressive is the vast, imposing emporium housing the *Macedonia & Thrace* situated opposite the corner of the Esplanade roads of Posidonos and Miaouli (*Tmr* 9C2).

BEACHES Between Zeas and Mounikhias harbours, opposite Stalida island. Also *See* **Beaches, A To Z, Athens**.

BREAD SHOPS One on Roosevelt Sq (*Tmr* 10C2) and others on Odhos Kolokotroni (*Tmr* 21C2/3) and Charilaou Trikoupi (*Tmr* 21D3).

BUSES Two buses circulate around the peninsula of Piraeus. One proceeds from Roosevelt Sq to Limin Mounikhias, and on to Neon Faliron, and the other from Korai Sq (*Tmr* C3) via the Naval Cadets College to Limin Zeas. Bus No. 905 connects the Metro station to the Flying Dolphin quay, Limin Zeas.

COMMERCIAL SHOPPING AREA (*Tmr* 11C2) There is a flourishing and busy Market area behind the bank mentioned above, hemmed in by the streets of Gounari and Ethniki Antistaseos. There is an excellent supermarket on the corner of Odhos Makras Stoas, if a shopper cannot be bothered to visit the various shops and stalls of the market. Prices in Piraeus are generally higher than elsewhere in Greece and shop hours are as for Athens.

FERRY-BOATS Most island ferry-boats leave from the area encompassed by Akti Kondili, to the north of the Grand Harbour, Karaiskaki Sq, Akti Posidonos and Akti Miaouli, to the west of the Grand Harbour. As a general rule the Aegean ferries depart from the area of Karaiskaki Square and International ferries leave from the south or far end of the Akti Miaouli quay road.

See **Chapter Eleven** for a synopsis of the islands and ports and the individual islands for details of the timetables.

FERRY-BOAT TICKET OFFICES Yes well, at least they lie extremely thick on the waterfront. It is probably best to make enquiries about the exact location of a particular ferry's departure point when purchasing the tickets. It has to be admitted the vendors tend to refer to a ship's point of departure with any airy wave of the hand. Ticket sellers 'lie in wait', all the way along the quayside streets of Kalimasioti and Akti Posidonos, that is from the Metro station, past the Gounari St turning to the bottom of Ethniki Antistaseos.

My two favourite offices lie at opposite ends of the spectrum, as it were, and are:

Jannis Stoulis Travel (*Tmr* 12C2) 2 Gounari St   Tel 417 9491
Directions: Situated on the right (*Sbo*) of Gounari St.
   The owner, who wears a rather disinterested air, is extremely efficient and
speaks three languages, including English. This business is usually closed outside
'office' hours.

His fast talking, 'speedy Gonzales' counterpart occupies a wall-to-wall stairway on
Kalimasioti St (*Tmr* 13C2). My regard for the latter operator may well be coloured
by the fact that he was the man who sold me my first ever Greek island ferry-boat
ticket.

There are two ticket offices on the harbour side of the large building on Plateia
Karaiskaki, beyond the cafes, two of almost dozens of ticket offices spaced around
this edifice. An enterprising vendor of tickets lurks, from early morning, amongst
the ferry-boat stalls on Akti Posidonos.
   When searching the quayside for the correct ferry-boat, do not go beyond the
Port offices and Custom house (*Tmr* 14D/E3), towards the south end of the
harbour, as these berths are for cruise ships only.

METRO *See* **Arrival by Metro, Introduction.**

NTOG Somewhat inconveniently situated at Limin Zeas Harbour (*Tmr* C/D4) and
only open weekdays between 0700-1500hrs.

OTE The main office (*Tmr* 15C2) is north of the Post Office with another on Odhos
Navarinou (*Tmr* 22C2).

PLACES OF INTEREST
Archaeological Museum (*Tmr* 17D3) Situated between Filellinon and
Leoforos Charilaou Trikoupi Sts. Reopened in the last few years and reportedly
well laid out, with easy to identify exhibits. Opening hours Mondays to
Saturday, 0845-1500hrs, Sunday 0930-1430hrs and closed Tuesdays. Only
Greeks are allowed free admission here, as elsewhere in Greece, foreigners
having to pay 100drs.

Ag Triada (*Tmr* 16C2) The Cathedral was rebuilt in the early l960s, having been
destroyed in 1944. Distinctive, mosaic tile finish.

Zea Theatre Adjacent to the Archaeological Museum, the remains date from about
the second century BC.

Limin Zeas (Pasalimani) (*Tmr* C/D4) This semicircular harbour is of great antiquity.
Now it is lined by high-rise buildings, shelters fishing boats and caiques, provides
a yacht basin for larger, modern yachts, is the location for the Naval Museum of
Greece, contains a Flying Dolphin (hydrofoil) terminal as well as a base for yacht
charterers. Excavations have shown that, in ancient times, several hundred boat
sheds radiated out around the edge of the harbour housing the triremes, the great,
three-banked warships of antiquity.

The Naval Museum of Greece Adjacent to Zeas Harbour with a varied and
interesting series of exhibits down through the ages.

Limin Mounikhias (Tourkolimano or Mikrolimano) (*Tmr* B5) From Limin Zeas,
continue on north-east round the coast cliff road, past the bathing beach (*facing
the tiny island of Stalida*), and the Royal Yacht Club of Greece, to reach this
renowned, 'chatty', picturesque and again semicircular harbour of Mounikhias.

From here racing yachts are believed to have departed for regattas in Saroniko Bay as far back as the 4th century BC, as they do now. The quayside is ringed with tavernas, cafes and restaurants forming a backcloth to the multi-coloured sails of the assembled yachts crowded into the harbour.

The Hill of Kastela overlooks the harbour and has a modern, open-air, marble amphitheatre, wherein theatre and dance displays are staged, more especially during the Athens Festival (*See* **Places of Interest, A To Z, Athens**).

Filonos Street (*Tmr* B/C/D2/3) The 'Soho' of Piraeus, espousing what's left of the old *Never on a Sunday* atmosphere of the town.

POLICE
Port On the quay bounded by Akti Posidonos.
Tourist & Town (*Tmr* 23C3) Dimotico Square.

POST OFFICE (*Tmr*18C2) On Filonos St, north-west of the Cathedral.

RAILWAY STATIONS *See* **Arrival by Metro & Arrival by Train, Introduction.**
Metro (Underground) (*Tmr* 1C1/2).
'Steam' Station (*Tmr* 1C1/2) The Peloponnese terminus is alongside and the far side of the Metro station.
'Steam' Station (*Tmr* 19D/E/2) The terminus for Northern Greece is situated on the far, north-west side of the Grand Harbour.

SWIMMING POOL Adjacent to Limin Zeas Harbour.

TELEPHONE NUMBERS & ADDRESSES

NTOG (*Tmr* C/D4) Zeas Marina	Tel 413 5716
Port Authorities	Tel 451 1311
Taxi station	Tel 4178138

PART THREE
11 INTRODUCTION TO THE DODECANESE ISLANDS (Dodecanese, Dodekanes, Dhodhekanisos)

You asked me for the beauty of ages past, for the beauty of land and sea, for the beauty of human beings, for the beauty of tradition, for the beauty of contemporary luxury, for every kind of beauty, and I brought you to the Dodecanese.

Of all the island groupings perhaps the Dodecanese can be 'all islands to all men' (and women!). From the monastic overlay of Patmos; the curious Italian art deco architecture of Leros; the bustling port activity of Kalimnos; the frantic tourist hustle and bustle of Kos; the quaint island charm of Nisiros, the rather granite quietude of Tilos; the frenzied day-trip invasion of Simi; the old medieval city charm of Rhodes; the burgeoning tourist desirability of Karpathos and forlorn, abject Kasos.

Other, smaller islands in the agglomeration include Arki and Marathi, Angathonisi, Lipsos, Yialos, Pserimos, Chalki and Kastellorizo, all of which are covered in their own right or as excursions from the most adjacent island. This is despite Kastellorizo being a political absurdity, tucked away some 120km east of Rhodes, beneath the southern coastline of Turkey. The restricted and subsidised ferry-boat connection does not strictly reflect the island's requirements, more the pressing necessity to keep the resident population intact and ensure a steady flow of tourists, thus discouraging the Turks from any territorial ambitions. Towards this end, free ferry-boat trips are available to the island all the year round.

The official grouping referred to as the Dodecanese, which means the twelve islands (and confusingly covers at least seventeen), includes Astipalaia. The latter's official inclusion owes more to the niceties of 'administrative illogicality' than coadjacency as Astipalaia is Cycladian in nature and location, with only a twice weekly Dodecanese ferry connection. For these reasons Astipalaia is to be found in the GROC's Candid Guide to the Cyclades, and not the Dodecanese.

Generally ferry-boat travel between the Dodecanese islands is relatively easy with a regular number of ferries travelling the length of the island group. The Greek government's decision to encourage tourism to the lesser known islands has resulted in the long established, scheduled air services to and from Rhodes and Kos being supplemented by selected, small island airfields. These allow flights, on smaller aircraft, from Athens to Karpathos, Kasos, Kastellorizo and Leros. Flying Dolphin hydrofoil services link Rhodes with Kos, Patmos and Simi.

The proximity to the Turkish mainland has, not unnaturally, resulted in the Dodecanese being strongly influenced, over the decades, by their close neighbour. To add spice to the chronicles, the Knights of St John ruled over the islands for some two hundred years, before finally being evicted by the Turks. The Knights' occupation resulted in their building fortifications on most of the islands. The history of the Dodecanese is one of almost constant invasion and conquest starting with the reliably documented Phoenicians, then the Minoans of Crete (2500 and 1440 BC), followed by the Achaians of the Peloponnese (1550-1150 BC). The Dorians ruled from 1150-1000 BC and promulgated the change-over from female dominated gods to a more chauvin-

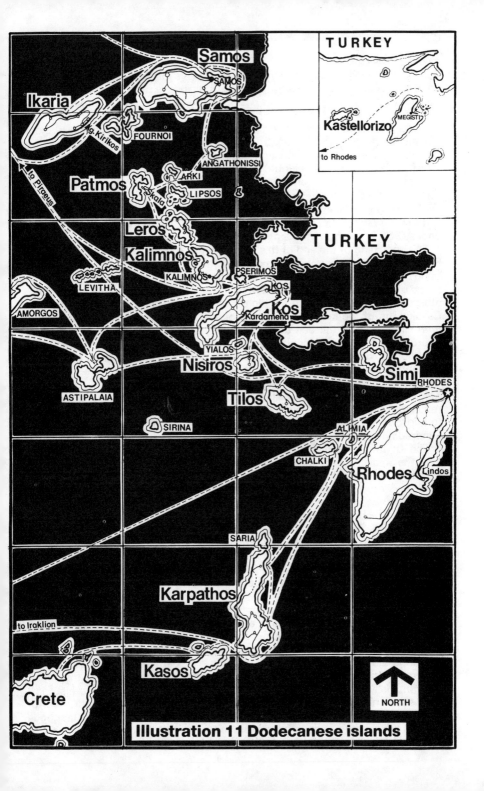

Illustration 11 Dodecanese islands

istically masculine role for the divinity. After Rhodes had sided with the losing Persians, the Athenians took over in 480 BC. This relationship changed to that of allies, after which the Rhodians, by judicious sitting on the fence and constant switching of allegiances, managed to build a position of wealth and power. The eminence of Rhodes was such that even Alexander the Great allowed the island to engage in flourishing trade with the Egyptians, without hindrance. On Alexander's death, Rhodes was powerful enough to rebuff a Macedonian siege, despite the first documented use by the attackers of a nine storey siege tower, the Helepolis. To celebrate this victory over the invaders, the Colossus of Rhodes, one of the Seven Wonders of the ancient world, was built in 341 BC, the original construction costs being supplemented by the sale of the abandoned and obsolescent Helepolis. The unique Colossus was laid low by an earthquake, only to lie in ruins, for approximately 800 years, until AD 654, when the remains were sold off to the Syrians.

The beginning of the end of this period of pre-eminence was heralded when Rhodes signed a treaty with Rome in the second century BC. The Romans, to bring their wealthy and independent island ally into line, declared the Cycladean island of Delos a free port. From here on it was downhill for Rhodes culminating, after the death of Caesar, in the plundering, sacking and firing of the island by Cassius (he of the lean and hungry look!) after Rhodes had declined to side with him. The first thirteen hundred or so years of anno Domini were not to improve for the island, despite coming under Byzantium rule. Forts were built but Rhodes was the subject of endless raids and invasions by, amongst others, the Goths, Arabs, Saracens, Venetians, Franks and Genoese. After a visit to the island by the Crusaders in 1097 and Richard Coeur-de-Lion in 1191, the Knights of St John of Jerusalem, who had been ousted from Jerusalem, requested that the then Genoese overlords allowed them to settle. On being turned down, the Knights conquered the island in 1309 and ruled for two hundred and thirteen years.

The Knights were divided into three divisions; the Military Knights, enlisted from the aristocracy, Soldiers-cum-nurses, from more pedestrian backgrounds and the Brothers, who carried out the religious duties. The order was divided, originally, into seven, then eight Houses, named Tongues. The nomenclature Tongues related to the language, or nationality, of the particular House and included French, Auvergne and Provence (both separate countries from France at that time), Spanish (consequently subdivided into Aragon and Castilian), Italian, German and English. The English were recruited at the Clerkenwell Priory, still extant in the form of the Gate House in St John's Lane, the last remaining London medieval gate. Interestingly the English Tongue, which ceased after Henry VIII's Reformation, was revived about 1830 as the British Order of St John of Jerusalem.

The Knights repulsed two serious sieges in 1444 and 1480 but, in 1522, the Turkish plenipotentiary, Suleiman 1st or The Magnificent, decided to sort out once and for all 'those turbulent Knights (to thoroughly misquote Henry II). Mind you, the magnificent Turk required some 100,000 men (one report mentions 200,000) to overcome the Rhodes garrison. This totalled 650 Knights, assisted by about 400 Candians (from Crete, despite my typist lady originally inking in Canadians, which would have resulted in a historical reassessment methinks), 200 Genoese, 50 Venetians and an assortment of town citizens. After six months, weakened but not bowed, the courageous Knights are reputed to have been betrayed by one of their own, a Portuguese Knight. Suleiman's regard for the besieged was such that the surviving 180

Knights and their supporters were allowed to leave unmolested. This was a rare privilege, for the Turks normally rewarded the vanquished with such 'Turkish delights' as death at the sword, boiling and skinning alive or simple, straightforward burning. The Knights retired, at first to Crete and then to Malta, in 1530, where they remained as a force to be reckoned with until the French took over in 1748.

Recently, in 1988, the order received a certain amount of publicity, with the promotion of an English Benedictine schoolmaster to the pre-eminence of Grand Master. He now presides over a couple of acres and a Roman palace, that is the Knights country, within sight of Vatican City.

Turkish dominance over the Dodecanese islands lasted 390 years but, surprisingly, their influence would appear to have been restricted to a mosque here and a minaret there. Arguably their 400 or so years of rule had less impact and influence than 31 years of Italian occupation in the early 20th century. Certainly the Turks were overtaken by a gentle, slow, languid decline, presiding over the gradual deterioration of the islands' infrastructure and buildings. Mind you, it was fortunate that, as elsewhere, the Turks allowed the Greek religion to continue and distanced themselves from the indigenous population by, for instance, excluding the Greeks from living in the Old Quarter of Rhodes Town. The natives were made to live beyond the walls, setting up the Nea Chora, now submerged in modern-day Rhodes City. The result of this partition was to help preserve the Greek identity and way of life.

The Turkish occupation ended in 1912, when the Italians drove them out of the Dodecanese, during a Turko-Italian conflict resulting from Italian expansionary aggrandisement. A number of international conferences failed to unseat the Italians who, although the Greeks may not see it from their 'taverna seat' quite this way, on balance must be considered to have benefited the islands during their occupation. The undue repression experienced throughout the Fascist part of this period should be weighed against the civil engineering, architectural and archaeological works put in hand by the Italians. Unfortunately the Second World War collapse of the Italians, in 1943, left an 'overlord void' for which the German and British forces fought a number of bitter and costly battles, with much suffering incurred by the locals. After the collapse of the Third Reich, in 1945, the Dodecanese were freed by British and Greek troops, to be formally acceded to Greece in 1947.

Greek Orthodoxy is the religion of the islands with very small enclaves of Turkish Muslims and Jews on Rhodes and Turks on Kos.

At the end of this chapter there is an alphabetical list of the islands included in the book, their major town and port(s), as well as a quick reference resumé of ferry-boat and hydrofoil connections.

The island chapters follow a format which has been devised and developed, over the years, to make the layout as simple to follow as is possible, without losing the informative nature of the text. Each island is treated in a similar manner, allowing the traveller easy identification of his (or her) immediate requirements. The text is faced by the relevant port and town maps, with descriptions tied into the various island routes.

Symbols, Keys & Definitions

Below are some notes in respect of the few initials and symbols used in the text, as well as an explanation of the possibly idiosyncratic nouns, adjectives and phrases that are to be found scattered throughout the book.

Where and when inserted, a star system of rating indicates my judgement of an island, and possibly its accommodation and restaurant standards, by the inclusion of one to five stars. One star signifies bad, two basic, three good, four very good and five excellent. I must admit the ratings are carried out on whimsical grounds and are based purely on personal observation. For instance, where a place, establishment or island receives a detailed 'critique' I may consider that sufficient unto the day... The absence of a star, or any mention at all, has no detrimental significance and might, for instance, indicate that I did not personally inspect this or that establishment.

Keys The key *Tmr*, in conjunction with grid references, is used as a map reference to aid easy identification of this or that location on port and town plans. Other keys used in the text include *Sbo* – 'Sea behind one'; *Fsw* – 'Facing seawards'; *Fbqbo* – 'Ferry-boat quay behind one' and *OTT* – 'Over The Top'.

GROC's definitions, 'proper' adjectives & nouns: These may require some elucidation, as most do not appear in 'official' works of reference.

Backshore: the furthest strip of beach from the sea's edge. The marginal rim edging the shore from the surrounds. *See* **Scrubbly**

Benzina: a small fishing boat.

Chatty: with pretention to grandeur or sophistication.

Dead: an establishment that appears to be 'terminally' closed, and is not about to open for business.

Donkey-droppings: as in 'two donkey-droppings', indicates a very small, 'one-eyed' hamlet. *See* **One-eyed.**

Doo-hickey: an Irish based colloquialism suggesting an extreme lack of sophistication and or rather 'daffy' (despite contrary indications in the authoritative and excellent *Partridges Dictionary of Slang!*).

Downtown: a rundown/derelict area of a settlement – the wrong side of the 'railway tracks'.

Ethnic: very unsophisticated, Greek indigenous and, as a rule, applied to hotels and pensions. *See* **Provincial**.

Gongoozle: borrowed from canal boat terminology, and is the state of very idly and leisurely, but inquisitively, staring at others who are involved in some busy activity.

Greasy spoon: a dirty, unwholesome cafe-bar, restaurant or taverna.

Great unwashed: the less attractive, modern day mutation of the 1960s hippy. They are usually Western European, inactive loafers and layabouts 'by choice', or unemployed drop-outs. Once having located a desirable location, often a splendid beach, they camp under plastic and in shabby tents, thus ensuring the spot is despoiled for others. The 'men of the tribe' tend to trail a mangy dog on a piece of string. The women, more often than not, with a grubby child or two in train, pester cafe-bar clients to purchase items of jewellery.

Note the above genre appears to be incurably penniless (but then who isn't?).

Grecocilious: necessary to describe those Greeks, usually tour office owners, who are making a lot of money from the tourists but are disdainful of the 'hand that feeds them'. They appear to consider holiday-makers as being some form of small intellect, low-browed, tree clambering and inferior relation to the Greek homo-sapiens. They usually can converse passably in two or three foreign languages (when it suits them) and display an air of weary sophistication.

Hillbilly: another adjective or noun, similar to 'ethnic', often applied to describe countryside or a settlement, as in 'backwoods'.

Hippy: those who live outside the predictable, boring (!) mainstream of life and are frequently genuine, if sometimes impecunious travellers. The category may include students or young professionals taking a sabbatical and who are often 'negligent' of their sartorial appearance.

Icons: naturally, a religious painting of a holy person or personages, usually executed on a board. During the Middle Ages the Mediterranean would appear to have been almost awash with unmanned rowing boats and caiques mysteriously ferrying icons hither and thither.

Independents: vacationers who make their own travel and accommodation arrangements, spurning the siren calls of structured tourism, preferring to step off the package holiday carousel and make their own way.

Krifo Scholio: illegal, undercover schools operated during the Turkish occupation, generally run by the inmates of religious orders to educate Greek children in the intricacies of the Orthodox religion and the traditional ways of life.

Mr Big: a local trader or pension owner, an aspiring tycoon, a small fish trying to be a big one in a 'smaller pool'. Sometimes flashy with shady overtones, his lack of sophistication is apparent by his not being Grecocilious!

Noddies or nodders: the palpable evidence of untreated sewage discharged into the sea.

One-eyed: small. *See* **Donkey-droppings.**

Poom: a descriptive noun 'borrowed' after sighting on Crete, some years ago, a crudely written sign advertising accommodation that simply stated POOMS! This particular place was basic with low-raftered ceilings, earth-floors and windowless rooms, simply equipped with a pair of truckle beds and rickety oilcloth covered washstand – very reminiscent of typical Cycladean cubicles of the 1950/60s period.

Provincial: usually applied to accommodation and is an improvement on **Ethnic**. Not meant to indicate, say, dirty but should conjure up images of faded, rather gloomy establishments with a mausoleum atmosphere; high ceilinged Victorian rooms with worn, brown linoleum; dusty, tired aspidistras as well as bathrooms and plumbing of unbelievable antiquity.

Richter scale: borrowed from earthquake seismology and employed to indicate the (appalling) state of toilets, on an 'eye-watering' scale.

Rustic: unsophisticated, unrefined.

Schlepper: vigorous touting for customers by restaurant staff. It is said of a good schlepper, in a market, that he can 'retrieve' a passer-by from up to thirty or forty metres beyond the stall.

Scrubbly: usually applied to a beach or countryside and indicating a rather messy, shabby area.

Squatty: A Turkish or French style ablution arrangement. None of the old, familiar lavatory bowl and seat. Oh no, just two moulded footprints edging a dirty looking hole, set in a porcelain surround. Apart from the unaccustomed nature of the exercise, the Lord simply did not give us enough limbs to keep ones shirt up and control wayward trousers that constantly attempt to flap down on to the floor, which is awash with goodness knows what! All this has to be enacted whilst gripping the toilet roll in one hand and wiping one's 'botty' with the other hand. Impossible! Incidentally the ladies should perhaps substitute blouse for shirt and skirt for trousers, but then it is easier (I am told) to tuck a skirt into one's waistband!

Way-station: mainly used to refer to an office or terminus, stuck out in the sticks and cloaked with an abandoned, unwanted air.

Dodecanese islands described include:

Island name(s)	Capital	Ports (at which inter-island ferry-boats & Flying Dolphins dock)	Ferry-boat/Flying Dolphin connections (FB=ferry-boat; FD=Flying Dolphin; EB=excursion boat; M=Mainland).
Angathonisi (Agathonisi, Gaidaros, Gaidharos)	Megalo Chorio	Ag Georgios	**FB:**Arki,Patmos,Lipsos,Leros, Kalimnos,Kos,Nisiros,Tilos, Simi,Rhodes;Samos. **EB:**Samos,Leros,Patmos.
Arki		Port Augusta	**FB:**Angathonisi,Samos;Patmos, Lipsos,Leros,Kalimnos,Kos, Nisiros,Tilos,Simi,Rhodes.
Chalki (Chalkis, Khalkia, Khalki, Halki)	Nimborio (Emborio, Skala)	Nimborio	**FB:**Rhodes,Simi,Tilos,Nisiros, Kos,Karpathos,Astipalaia, Piraeus(M);Diafani(Karpathos), Karpathos,Kasos,Sitia(Crete), Ag Nikolaos(Crete);Kamiros Skala(Rhodes).
Kalimnos (Kalymos, Calymnos)	Kalimnos (Pothia)	Kalimnos	**FB:**Leros,Lipsos,Patmos,Arki, Angathonisi,Samos;Kos,Nisiros, Tilos,Simi,Rhodes,Karpathos, Kasos,Sitia(Crete),Ag Nikolaos (Crete);Astipalaia,Amorgos, Paros,Piraeus(M). **EB:**Pserimos,Kos,Mastichari (Kos),Patmos,Turkey. **EB:**Xerokampos(Leros),Telentos.
Karpathos (Scarpanto)	Karpathos (Pighadia)	Myrtes Karpathos	**FB:** Kasos,Sitia(Crete), Ag Nikolaos(Crete),Anafi, Santorini,Folegandros,Milos; Diafani(Karpathos),Chalki, Rhodes,Simi,Tilos,Nisiros,Kos, Kalimnos,Astipalaia,Amorgos, Paros,Piraeus(M).
		Diafani	*See* Karpathos.
Kasos (Kassos)	Fry (Phry, Fri, Ophrys)	Fry/Emborio	**FB:** Sitia(Crete),Ag Nikolaos (Crete),Anafi,Santorini, Folegandros,Milos,Piraeus(M); Karpathos,Diafani(Karpathos), Chalki,Rhodes,Simi,Tilos,Nisiros, Kos,Kalimnos,Astipalaia, Amorgos,Paros,Piraeus(M).
Kastellorizo (Kastelorizo, Kastellorizon, Kastelloriso, Castelorizo, Megisti)	Kastellorizo (Kastellorizon, Megisti)	Kastellorizo	**FB:** Rhodes.
Kos (Cos)	Kos	Kos	**FB:** Kalimnos,Leros,Lipsos, Patmos,Arki,Angathonisi,Samos, Chios,Mitilini(Lesbos),Limnos, Kavala(M);Astipalaia,Amorgos, Paros,Piraeus(M);Nisiros,Tilos, Simi,Rhodes.

Island	Main town	Port	Connections
			FD: Simi,Rhodes;Patmos.
			EB: Nisiros,Kalimnos,Pserimos.
		Mastichari	**EB:** Kalimnos,Pserimos.
		Kardamena	**EB:** Nisiros.
Leros	Platanos	Lakki	**FB:** Lipsos,Patmos,Arki,Angathonisi,Samos;Kalimnos,Kos,Nisiros,Tilos,Simi,Rhodes;Patmos,Piraeus(M).
		Ag Marina	**EB:** Lipsos,Patmos,Angathonisi.
		Xerokampos	**EB:** Myrtes(Leros).
Lipsos (Lipsi, Lipso, Lipsoi)	Lipsos	Lipsos	**FB:** Patmos,Arki,Angathonisi,Samos;Leros,Kalimnos,Kos,Nisiros,Tilos,Simi,Rhodes. **EB:** Patmos.
Marathi (Marathos, Maranthi)		Marathi	**EB:** Patmos.
Nisiros (Nisyros, Nissiros)	Mandraki	Mandraki	**FB:** Tilos,Simi,Rhodes;Kos,Kalimnos,Leros,Lipsos,Patmos,Arki,Angathonisi,Samos;Patmos,Piraeus(M).
Patmos	The Chora	Skala	**FB:** Arki,Angathonisi,Samos,Chios,Mitilini(Lesbos),Limnos,Kavala(M);Lipsos,Leros,Kalimnos,Kos,Nisiros,Tilos,Simi,Rhodes;Piraeus(M);Katakolon(M),Venice. **FD:** Kos,Rhodes. **EB:** Kos,Samos,Lipsos,Leros,Ikaria,Paros,Kalimnos.
Pserimos	Pserimos	Pserimos	**EB:** Kos,Mastichari(Kos),Kalimnos.
Rhodes (Rhodhos, Rodos)	Rhodes	Rhodes	**FB:** Simi,Tilos,Nisiros,Kos,Kalimnos,Leros,Lipsos,Patmos,Arki,Angathonisi,Samos,Chios,Mitilini(Lesbos),Limnos,Kavala(M);Astipalaia,Amorgos,Paros,Piraeus(M);Chalki,Karpathos,Kasos,Sitia(Crete),Ag Nikolaos(Crete),Anafi,Santorini,Folegandros,Milos;Megisti(Kastellorizo); **FD:** Kos,Simi,Patmos. **EB:** Lindos(Rhodes),Simi.
		Kamiros Skala	**FB:** Chalki
Simi (Symi, Syme)	The Chora	Gialos/Simi	**FB:** Tilos,Nisiros,Kos,Kalimnos,Leros,Lipsos,Patmos,Arki,Angathonisi,Samos;Astipalaia,Amorgos,Piraeus(M);Rhodes. **FD:** Kos,Rhodes. **EB:** Rhodes.
Tilos (Telos, Episkopi)	Megalo Chorio	Livadia (Levadhia)	**FB:** Nisiros,Kos,Kalimnos,Leros,Lipsos,Patmos,Arki,Angathonisi,Samos;Simi,Rhodes;Astipalaia,Amorgos,Paros,Piraeus(M).
Yialos (Giali)			**EB:** Nisiros.

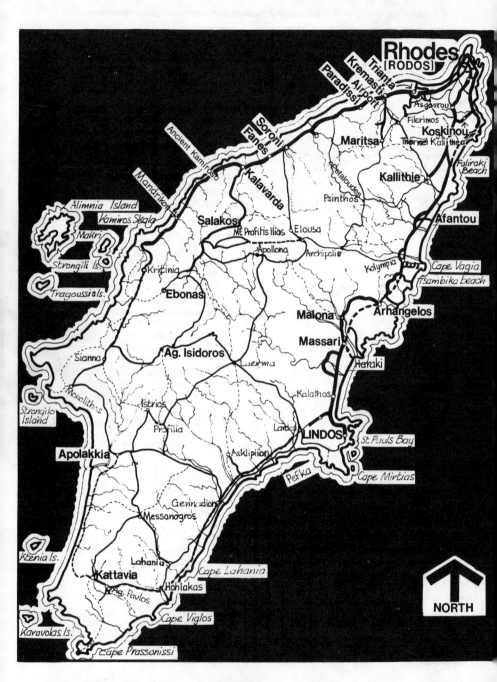

Illustration 12 Rhodes island

12 RHODES, (Rhodos, Rodos)
Dodecanese Islands

North island **

South island ***

FIRST IMPRESSIONS
Mass tourism (second to none); an unrivalled, living medieval Old Quarter; soft, agricultural countryside; still native island Greece below a line from Monolithos to Gennadion; lack of churches, donkeys and any of the great unwashed; traffic lights and No Parking zones; an abundance of public toilets; sun-beds and umbrellas (as Crete is to plastic, so Rhodes is to....).

SPECIALITIES
Fur coats (I know it is not food but you will realise why they are listed when you visit....); pasta dishes; very inexpensive spirits including Scotch whisky and French brandy (due to the duty-free status of the island).

RELIGIOUS HOLIDAYS & FESTIVALS
include: 7th January – Feast of St John the Baptist; 23rd April – Feast of St George, Afantou; 15th June – Ag Amos, nearby Faliraki; 17th June – festival at Asgourou, Koskinou and Paradissi (Paradision); 29th-30th July – Ag Soulas, Soroni; 6th-31st August – dance festivals at Ebonas, Kallithea and Maritsa; 26th August – Ag Fanourios, Rhodes Old Quarter; 8th September – Fertility festival, Tsambika Monastery; 14th September – Feast, Apollona, Damatria and Malona.

VITAL STATISTICS
The island, largest of the Dodecanese, is 77km from top to bottom, up to 37km wide with an area of some 1400sqkm. There is a population of approximately 80,000 of which about 35,000 are domiciled in the capital.

HISTORY
The history section in Chapter Eleven refers mainly to Rhodes island which, as the largest, most prominent and important of the group, is natural enough. All but Patmos island were as 'planets to the sun' of Rhodes, and this subject is expanded on in the relevant text.

Enough to comment and perhaps enquire why, when the Turks did not interfere with the infrastructure of Greek life in an occupation lasting some four hundred years, the Italians should make themselves so very unpopular with the natives by ordering the banning of the Orthodox church and the imposition of Italian as the official language? It just didn't do a lot for their esteem.

GENERAL
Rhodes may either confirm your worst fears or delight and confound one's expectations. It is possible that a holiday-maker's senses will be subject to opposing forces. That is, on the one hand, annoyance and antipathy with the worst manifestations of the tourist trade and its trappings, balanced by constant delight at the almost unexpected evocations of Greek island charm. Certainly the hotel development has been reasonably well contained and not subject to the haphazard growth seen on many islands.

Rhodes must vie with Corfu as the most international holiday target of all the Greek islands. The constant coming and going of aircraft is supplemented by a tidal wave of cruise liners, which daily disgorge and 'hoover' back on board 'mega-waves' of all manner of shipborne sightseers. Incidentally, one of the more languid Rhodian pastimes is to lounge at a convenient cafe-bar and 'spot the tourist', a pursuit shared with the island of Patmos. My own particular variant is to mentally award a prize to the most incongruously attired of these transient pleasure-seekers. Without bias (cross my heart) the prize usually has to be awarded to a North American, but the reader may well regard this as patronising and egocentric!

Perhaps the most unacceptable manifestation of the worldly-wise nature of the inhabitants occurs in Socratous St, the Old Quarter, Rhodes City. The length of this pedestrian way appears to be lined with predatory, schlepping shopkeepers selling mainly furs but also a full range of 'tourist-abilia'. On the other hand the mass market, tourist packaging of Lindos or the wall to wall, high-rise hotels of Faliraki Beach may be regarded as better (or worse) examples. To counter the most glaring excesses of the holiday industry, to restore not only a sense of balance but of great enjoyment and pleasure, it is only necessary to wander through the quieter backwaters of Rhodes City medieval Old Quarter, perhaps taking in the Turkish Baths and meander across the almost bomb-site archaeological waste ground of Plateia Athinas. A definite uplift can be experienced by visiting most of the island south of a line drawn from the breathtaking Monolithos Castle, in the west, to say Gennadion on the east coast. It is much to be regretted that the ubiquitous beach-buggy has put most of the island within the reach of seemingly almost everyone. At least below this 'tourist line', the passage of the fun-seeking, pleasure searching hedonists is, in the main, transitory.

Rhodes is a green and pretty island of comparatively low mountains and relatively flat land in nearly all the areas bordering the coastline. The richness of the architecture owes much to the *Knights*, some to the Turks and a lot to the Italians, who had an insatiable desire to build and reconstruct.

Rhodes is historically famed for roses and deer but the latter are now limited to a few herds penned in enclosures on the slopes of Mt Profitis Ilias and in a section of the Old Quarter moat, close to the Marine Gate.

RHODES (Rhodos, Rodos): capital city & main port

(Illustration 13 & 14) Tel prefix 0241. Really two towns, one the large, rambling, 'four star', medieval Old Quarter encircled by the other, the new 'two star' development – New Town or Nea Chora. This all makes for a rather confusing layout and some initial difficulties in getting about, more especially as the Old Quarter can only be entered via a number of Gates, spaced out around its periphery.

The flourishing Old Quarter appears, at first and possibly second glance, to be a maze of incoherent, directionless narrow lanes, passages, alleys and streets which drunkenly wind their way in between a glorious admixture of dwellings of all descriptions, shapes and sizes. This cocktail is 'stirred' (not shaken) with a mix of squares, churches, mosques and the occasional minaret, crowded and packed inside the great walls encircling the Old Quarter. The almost lifeless, tomb-like Street of the Inns of the Knights (Odhos Ippoton) contrasts absurdly with the crowded, constantly shifting, dawdling, scurrying and harried swarm of tourists who ebb and flow up and down Socratous St, parallel to and only three streets to the south of Odhos Ippoton.

Much of the City acknowledges its debt to the Italians, reflecting a cosmo-politan, Western European ambience rather than that of a traditional Greek island city. For instance the occasional department store is scattered about the inner zone and the suburban outskirts degenerate into high-rise sprawl.

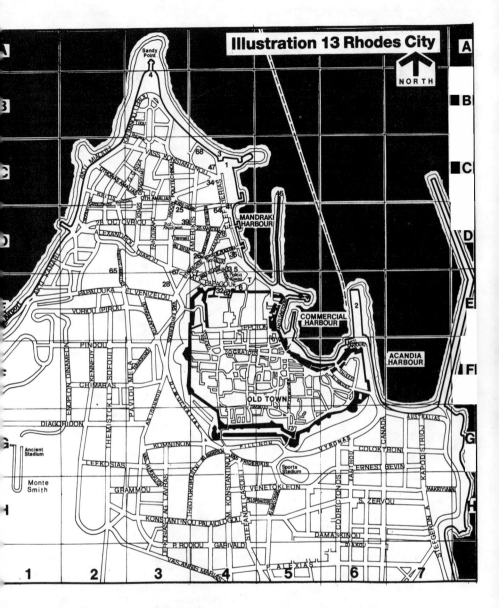

Illustration 13 Rhodes City

Both New and Old town are, on the east side, edged by the waterfront Esplanade. This runs from the small bluff alongside Kountouriotou Sq (*Tmr* 1C4) all the way down to Acandia Harbour (*Tmr* E/F6/7). In Mandraki Harbour (*Tmr* D4/5) small inter-island ferry-boats dock, followed (in a southerly direction) by fishing caiques, then private yachts. The latter are moored all the way round the quayside and along the substantial mole, closing off the eastern side of the Harbour. Three ancient, but now redundant windmills still remain standing on this mole, as does the Fort of St Nicholas. (*Tmr* 46C/D5). The

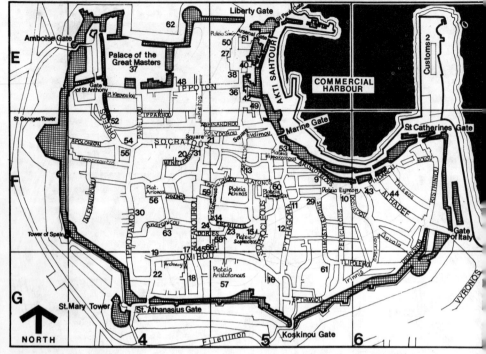

Illustration 14 Rhodes Old Quarter

Tmr = Town map reference
Fsw = Facing seawards
Sbo = Sea behind one
Fbqbo = Ferry-boat Quay behind one

Tmr
1   Kountouriotou Square C4
2   Customs Hall Quay
    & inter-island ferries E6
3   Elli Club & Beach C4
4   The Aquarium A/B3
5   New Market - Bus station D/E4
6   City Tourist office E4
7   NTOG D/E3/4
8   Hall of Justice D4
9   Pension Nikos F5
10 Pension - 15 Ipapanti F5/6
11 Pension Athinaea F5
12 Pension Rena/Taverna Kostas F5
13 Hotel Sydney F5
14 Pension Dora F4/5
15 Hotel Teherani F5
16 Pension Appollon G5
17 Hotel Paris F/G4
18 Pension Massari G4
19 Steve's Pension F/G4
20 Pension Mamas F4
21 Souvlaki snackbar F4/5
22 Rooms No.77 G4
23 Pandesia Restaurant F5
24 Spilia Taverna F4/5
25 Olympic Airways C/D3/4
26 National Bank D3/4
27 Ionian & Popular Bank E5
28 Scooter & bicycle hire/Hotel Thermai E3
29 Mandar Scooters F5
30 Bakery F4
31 Express bakery, cake & pie shop F4
32 Bus station (East side) E4
33 Bus station (West side) D/E4
34 National Theatre C4
35 Bank of Greece D4
36 Archaeological Museum E5
37 Palace of the Grand Masters E4
38 Museum of Decorative Art E5
39 OTE D3/4
40 OTE E5
41 Church of St John the Evangelist C/D4
42 Byzantine Museum E5
    (Orthodox Cathedral of St Mary)
43 Church of St Marie du Bourg F6
44 Hospice of St Catherine F6
45 Church of St Fanourios F/G4/5
46 St Nicholas Fort C/D5
47 Mosque of Murad Reis C4
48 Italian Vice-Consulate E4
49 Inn of England E/F5
50 Municipal Art Gallery E5
51 Temple of Aphrodite E5
52 Clock Tower E/F4
53 Tribune of Commerce F5
54 Mosque of Suleiman F4
55 The Turkish Library F4
56 The Turkish Baths F4
57 Bourouzan Mosque G4/5
58 Retjep Pasha Mosque F/G4/5
59 Kavakly Mosque F4/5
60 Ibrahim Pasha Mosque F5
61 Dolaplee Mosque G5
62 Son et Lumiere E4
63 Folk Theatre F4
64 Post Office/Police C/D4
65 Hospital D/E2/3
66 Archangelos Cafe-bar Restaurant F/G4/5
67 Swimming Pool D/E3
68 Tennis Club B/C3/4
T = Taxi ranks

windmills have been fitted with sails for the titallation of tourists. Beyond St Paul's Gate (*Tmr* E5), the quay road borders the Commercial Harbour and is edged by massive fort walls pierced only by the Marine Gate (*Tmr* F5) and St Catherines Gate (*Tmr* F6). The first, north section of the Commercial Harbour is host to local craft whilst the east side, alongside the Customs Hall Quay (*Tmr* 2E6), is utilised by the larger, inter-island ferry-boats and cruise liners. The most southerly harbour is Acandia (*Tmr* E/F7) where the hydrofoils berth, beyond which the City degenerates into an industrial mess, or 'East End', with a large wine making factory at the centre of the activity and squalor.

North of Mandraki Harbour, Rhodes peaks out to a narrow bluff, Sandy Point, around which the most popular beach wraps itself. The very sandy foreshore commences alongside the Elli Club (*Tmr* 3C4) and continues round the point of the headland, whereon is The Aquarium (*Tmr* 4A/B3), and down the west side of the City. The west shore is narrow, more pebbly and is edged by the main road which is bordered by high-rise buildings with, naturally enough, a fair sprinkling of hotels.

The western avenue, Akti Miaouli, is probably the busiest on the island leading, as it does, down the coast to the international airport (as distinct from the military airfield tucked away inland). Holiday-makers along this stretch should bear in mind that to reach the beach, the umbrellas and the sun-beds requires crossing the traffic laden, noisy highway. Nasty!

Unlike Kos island, where the entire waterfront is an integral part of the town, the seaboard cafe society of Rhodes only fronts Mandraki Harbour, due to the long spread of the harbour facilities. When I say only, that is an unfairly pejorative word, as the excellent cafes line the ground floor of an immense building. This is not so grand as the Liston of Corfu Town, but good, very good news. A coffee can be spun out for an hour or more, from dawn to early the following morning, with the constant harbour, road and pavement activity providing more than adequate entertainment.

ARRIVAL BY AIR

The airport is some 13km out of the city, on the west coast road, immediately prior to the village of Paradissi (Paradision). I cannot but feel that paradise may have been a suitable description in the days before the construction of the airport, but this once pretty village now lies just beyond and to one side of the take-off flight path.

A bus from the airport to Rhodes City stops across the main road. Turn left out of the main airport concourse, up the access slip road and there, across the thoroughfare, is the bus shelter. A single fare costs 120drs and buses run every half-hour to forty five minutes from 0630hrs to 2230hrs. At Rhodes City, the bus pulls in alongside the New Market (*Tmr* 5D/E4). It is doubtful if accommodation will be offered at the Bus terminals, due to the large number of arrivals, departures and general confusion, but to one side is the **City Tourist office** (*Tmr* 6E4), on Plateia Rimini. Turning up (I mean 'up', as it is a fairly steep climb) the main road of Alexandrou Papagou and after four side-streets, to the right of the traffic light junction, is the **NTOG** office (*Tmr* 7D/E3/4).

Taxis tick over 'in wait' outside the airport building, but charge more than those cabs which randomly pull up by the bus shelter. The latter will take up to four passengers to Rhodes for as little as 650drs. Passengers should request the driver to proceed to the vicinity of the NTOG or City Tourist offices, if no definite destination is in mind.

ARRIVAL BY BUS

See **Arrival by Air.**

ARRIVAL BY FERRY

The main inter-island ferries berth in the Commercial Harbour against the Customs House Quay (*Tmr* 2E6), whilst the smaller, island excursion/trip boats dock in Mandraki Harbour, usually in the region of the Hall of Justice (*Tmr* 8D4). Naturally the direction to proceed depends at which Harbour a visitor lands and moreover whether or not seeking accommodation in the Old Quarter.

Those disembarking at the Commercial Harbour should note that St Catherines Gate (*Tmr* F6) is reached by turning right at the bottom of the Quay, then almost immediately left. This Gate allows immediate access to the medieval city. Otherwise follow the Esplanade round to the area of the New Market (*Tmr* 5D/E4). Rooms will usually be offered at both points.

THE ACCOMMODATION & EATING OUT

The Accommodation The prodigious number of tourists, including swarms of backpackers, places a great strain on accommodation at the height of the season. Reference to my introductory remarks in Chapter One should, where at all possible, have dissuaded visitors from travelling in July, August and early September.

Neither the NTOG nor the City Tourist office hand out a list of accommodation, though the former's brochure does list some hotels. On the other hand they do operate a splendid service, establishing an enquirer's requirements and price bracket and then telephoning round to locate a room and book the same. Magic!

The choice rests between the New Town and the Old Quarter. Most of the hotels are located in the New Town, but are tour operator block booked, whilst most of the *Rooms* are scattered about the Old Quarter.

New Town An area rich with D and E class hotels is the truncated wedge created by the streets of Othonos Amalias and Apolloniou Rodiou (*Tmr* C/D2/3). Hotels herein include, in alphabetical order, the *Ambassadeur* (Class C, tel 24679), *Aphrodite* or, confusingly the *Venus* (Class C, tel 24668), *Atlas* (Class D, tel 24022) and *D'Or* (Class D, tel 22911), all from about 2550-3680drs for a double room, as well as the highly regarded and (comparatively) very reasonably priced *Efrossyni* (Class D, tel 24629), with single rooms sharing a bathroom costing 1350drs, a double room sharing 1980drs and double room with en suite bathroom 2450drs.

Old Quarter Very well endowed with reasonably priced hotels, pensions and *Rooms*.

Centred around the Square of the Jewish Martyrs (Plateia Martiron Eyreon – *Tmr* F5/6), the Square with a round, panelled drum surmounted by sea-horse statues, are the:

Pension Nikos (*Tmr* 9F5) No 45A Odhos Aristotelous   Tel 23423
Directions: Overlooking Plateia Martiron Eyreon.

Well kept, clean and recommended. A double room costs from 1500drs and a triple room from 2200drs with the bathroom facilities shared and showers charged extra.

To the left of Plateia Martiron Eyreon (*Acandia Harbour behind one*), a step or three along Odhos Pericleous is a :-

Pension (*Tmr* 10F5/6) 15 Ipapanti St.

Further up the road is the:-
Hotel Spot (Class E) 21 Pericleous St.
Directions: As above.
   All rooms share bathrooms with a single room charged at 600drs per night
and a double room 1200drs. These rate rise, respectively, to 800drs and
1600drs.

The next street to the west of Odhos Pericleous includes the:-
Pension Aleka 8 Dimosthenous St
and the:-
Pension Artemis Pissa 12 Dimosthenous.
Directions: As above.
   Inexpensive but shared rooms.

From Plateia Martirion Eyreon proceed along Odhos Aristotelous to Plateia
Hippokratous (*Tmr* F5). On the left (*Acandia Harbour behind one*) is the paved
Odhos Pythagora which climbs, not so gently, upwards towards Koskinou
Gate (*Tmr* G5) and past the:-

Pension Athinaea (*Tmr* 11F5) (Class C) 45 Pythagora/Palea Agora
Tel 23221

Directions: Up Pythagora St, under the curved archway that spans the lane,
and the entrance is to the left, along a narrow, closed-in alley, with the entrance
on the right.
   Not to be recommended. The rooms are small and stuffed full of excess
furniture, resulting in the strong impression of sleeping in a store cupboard. It
is a mystery why bedside lamps are included in the fittings and fixtures as
there aren't any electric sockets! This of course precludes the use of a travellers
plug-in, electric 'frying pan' with the result that mosquitoes have a free rein.
Our winged insect 'friends' are aided and abetted in destroying a nights sleep
by a nearby cockerel who gets into 'full crow' at about 4.30am, and sounds
as if he is actually on the windowsill. This wretched rooster, mindful that he
is supposed to herald dawn, but in doubt as to the exact moment, keeps up
his 'cock-a-doodle-doo' until about midday. The shared bathroom is very small
and inadequate. A single box room, sorry room, costs 800drs and a double
room 1200drs.

Pension Rena (*Tmr* 12F5) 62 Pythagora   Tel 26217
Directions: Further along Odhos Pythagora from *Pension Athinaea* and on the
right-hand side.
   Shares the frontage with the *Taverna Kostas*, both run by the friendly Mr
Costa Hagicotsas who, with good English, enthusiastically 'encourages' both
prospective diners and 'overnighters' to patronise his establishments.
   A double room costs from 1500drs, sharing a bathroom with one other
bedroom. Breakfast, if taken, costs 200drs.

Pension Lia (Class C) 66c Pythagora   Tel 20371/26209
Directions: In the next turning off to the left, beyond the *Pension Rena*.
   Only double rooms sharing the bathroom which cost 1250drs per night.

In detailing the whereabouts and approach to the following accommodation it
is easiest to take the reader back to the 'main' streets which bisect the Old
Quarter. Naturally, access can be made via the diverse alleys without going
back to the starting blocks, as it were, but....

From Plateia Hippokratous (*Tmr* F5), Odhos Socratous leads off and up in a westward direction.

Hotel Sidney (*Tmr* 13F5) (Class E) 41 Apellou   Tel 25965
Directions: One-third of the way along Socratous St turn left into Apellou St and the hotel is on the left.

A good example of an E class establishment with the added 'delight' of having the Gregoris Disco lurking in the basement. A double room with shower en suite costs 2000drs rising to 2800drs (1st July-30th Sept). Breakfast is available for 250drs.

A little further to the south, Apellou St opens out into the Rhodes equivalent of a wartime bomb site. To be strictly accurate this is Plateia Athinas on to which spill an amalgamation of various truncated lanes. The use of the word square is rather grandiose, similar to titling a road sweeper 'public amenities and highways attendant'. Bits of ancient and modern ruins litter the area. Diagonally opposite Apellou St is Odhos Aristofanous, a narrow lane that swings left into the small Plateia Aristofanous.

Pension Dora (*Tmr* 14F4/5) (Class C) 37 Aristofanous
                                     Tel (Home 25214) 24523
Directions: As above and on the left-hand side, prior to the lane describing a sharp left-hand turn.

The gate opens on to a pretty, profusely flowered and be-shrubbed patio and the entrance to the pension is up the stairs. All rooms share the bathrooms with a single room charged at 760drs and a double room 1110drs, which rates rise to 850drs and 1330drs (1st May-10th Oct).

Pension Sokrates
Directions: From the *Pension Dora*, a few metres further on and the lane turns sharp left to edge the back of a large, pleasant building signed *RENT ROOMS*. Access is gained from Odhos Dorieos via Plateia Aristofanous.

Beyond Aristofanous Square, Plateia Sophocleous accommodates (sorry!) the:-
Hotel Teherani (*Tmr* 15F5) (Class E) 41B Sophocleous   Tel 27594
Directions: As above and on the edge of a Square, almost hidden behind the large *Taverna Trata*, in an ethnic, rather noisy area. It is not only surrounded by four tavernas but borders almost a small park in which are a couple of bench seats. On these the Greek equivalent of the 'Euston Station winos' often carouse and slurp the evenings away.

A clean and comfortable hotel in which only double rooms are available, sharing bathrooms. Prices start off at 1150drs, rising to 1300drs (1st July-31st Oct).

Pension Apollon (*Tmr* 16G5) No 28C
Directions: Continuing along Odhos Sophocleous in a southerly direction, the street joins Odhos Omirou, almost directly across from which junction a small turning leads to the whitewashed steps of the pension, on the left. The signboard includes, *CLEANING. REND ROOMS (sic) BAR WITH MUSIC & GARDEN*.

Inexpensive, if rather basic accommodation. The patrons are often not present so it is best to make oneself at home. A double room costs 1400drs, sharing the toilet and hot showers. Laundry facilities are available.

Right, or westwards along Omirou St advances to the junction with Ag Fanouriou, alongside which is the:-

Hotel Paris (*Tmr* 17F/G4) (Class D) 88 Ag Fanouriou/Omirou   Tel 26356
Directions: As above, on the corner of Ag Fanouriou and Odhos Omirou.

A pleasant hotel, agreeably situated in the Old Quarter, with a large patio garden to one side of the building but the rates are astronomic bearing in mind the establishment's rating. The single rooms have to share a bathroom at a cost of 2000drs, which charge rises to 2600drs (1st July-31st Dec). A double room sharing starts at 2600drs and with an en suite bathroom 3000drs, which prices rise to 3500/4000drs
and:-

Rooms Odhos Omirou
Directions Next door to and owned by the *Hotel Paris*, but after the Lord Mayors show... The presence of this 'doss' house is advertised by a large sign *Rooms for Rent*.

Definitely not recommended, for,apart from the appalling state of the place, the manageress is,without doubt, a 'nutter'. Building defects include lack of window panes, dripping taps, unswept corners hosting little families of bugs and only thin hardboard divisions between rooms – so insubstantial that the breathing of occupants in adjacent rooms can easily be monitored. Even the sofa on the landing has bed bugs and the bed sheets do not smell very fresh. The landlady, who stalks about the landing following guests into the bathroom and their rooms, appears to be convinced that all incumbents are about to wreck the place and or run off without paying. In an effort to forestall any possible miscreant behaviour she repeatedly demands to know 'How many nights are you staying?' and 'How many people are there in the room?', added to which the 'dear thing' demands payment in advance. Plus points are that the only bathroom (shared by all six rooms) is clean and there is a communal fridge on the landing. A double room costs 1400drs, but to be avoided.

Pension Massari (*Tmr* 18G4) (Class C) 42E Irodotou   Tel 22469
Directions: From the junction of Odhos Ag Fanouriou with Omirou St, proceed westwards along Omirou. The first, narrow turning to the left leads beneath a massive archway to an area where the lane opens out. The pension is on the left. A small waste lot opposite is used as a meeting place, battlefield, leisure and recreation area, kitchen, hunting ground and, occasionally, a bathroom by the hordes of neighbourhood cats.

Maria is a friendly, matronly Mama and the the spotless establishment is laid out on two floors, in a square around the small ground floor courtyard. The simple rooms share the bathroom facilities and the showers are very hot. A single room costs 1330drs, a double room 1880drs and a triple room 2300drs per day.

Steve's Pension (*Tmr* 19 F/G4) 60 Omirou   Tel 24357
Directions: Situated further along Omirou St, on the right-hand side, close by the point at which the lane turns sharply left. The signboard proclaims *Pension Steve* and the accommodation is down a small alley beneath a large, beautiful ibiscus tree overhanging the entry passage.

Steve Kefalas, the mild and very pleasant proprietor, spent a number of years in North America as a floor show manager and speaks excellent 'Canadian'. The ground floor rooms and bathrooms are haphazardly arranged throughout the building, beyond which is a pleasant, shaded courtyard. This is the prime feature of Steve's, making an attractive meeting place for the polyglot and cosmopolitan clients. The windows of the somewhat shabby rooms are, in the main, without mosquito screens which is a pity as these winged marauders are a great nuisance in this area. When accommodation is at a premium Steve may place a bunk on one of the flower beds of the courtyard and drape it around with a blanket!

He also owns not entirely equivalent nor totally satisfactory overflow facilities at both:-

No. 77 (*Tmr* 22G4). This house is just around the corner. There is a 'downstairs' bedroom to be traversed to gain the rickety stairs, which have to be negotiated to reach the two cell-like rooms on the first floor. The large door key for these 'cubby holes' seems rather superfluous as neither has any glass in the large window frames. On the other hand the absence of a window pane does assist with the ventilation, but this must be further aided by ensuring that the roof top door, approached by an even more unsafe flight of steps, is left open. The one fairly squalid, shared bathroom is also on the first floor, but the hot water supply is noticeable by its absence.

No. 65 θ. Another 'interesting' but 'friendly' location... The rooms are all on the ground floor. The toilet (or what's left of it) and the shower are the other side of a small, pleasant courtyard which has the usual clutter of tables, chairs as well as a washing line, complete with clothes pegs. The rickety bathroom is home for lots of spiders besides which it is rather public, with a hole for a window. The waste shower and sink water drain into the courtyard, via a hole in the floor – and why not? As with other 'quadrangle' accommodation this facility allows friendly social intercourse (one hopes that's all) with fellow guests. It is axiomatic that the more rustic the setting, the friendlier are the inhabitants.

Steve charges 400drs for 'open air' singles in the courtyard and 1400drs for a double room, but rates for long term stay guests can be the subject of negotiation.

Proceeding in a northerly direction, Ag Fanouriou spills on to Odhos Socratous at a crossroads and tree shaded square. Turning left, facing up the steeply inclined Socratous, and almost immediately left again, alongside the pie, cake and bread shop, leads on to Odhos Menecleous. This winds along to the fascinating Plateia Arionos, in the middle of which a large, crippled tree has part of its tortured trunk supported by a foreshortened Doric column! One flank of the Square is bordered by the splendid, communal Turkish Baths.

Pension 'Mamas' (*Tmr* 20F4) No. 28 Odhos Menecleous.
Directions: Situated on the right, in a widened section of the street before the climb on to Plateia Arionos and immediately prior to the Moustafa Mosque, to the left.

There is a torn curtain shielded shower in the corner of the ethnic courtyard, across which the rooms are reached. The shower is hot and the rooms are acceptable if somewhat expensive at 1500drs for a double room. Mama only communicates in Spanish or French, apart from her native Greek, and an interpreter often has to be drawn into any conversation.

Hotel Kastro (*Tmr* F4) (Class E) 14 Plateia Arionos   Tel 20446
Directions: On the right of Plateia Arionos (*Facing the Turkish Baths*), beyond the *Kastro Taverna*. An interesting situation. There is much local colour and

general 'coming and going' for, apart from a couple of tavernas and a fur 'sweat' shop, around the corner, there is, of course, the Turkish Baths.

A standard but rather expensive E class hotel. Only double rooms are available, those sharing the bathroom cost from 1300drs and en suite 1500drs, which per night charges increase to 1800drs and 2000drs.

The Eating Out
There is no shortage of eating places, in fact there is a surfeit of poor, average and expensive quality establishments. The trick is to sort out the 'rare wheat from the overwhelming chaff'. Rhodes is a comparatively expensive place to 'break bread' and many restaurants take *Diners* and *Amex* credit cards. Enough said!

Cafe-crawling can also prove extremely costly so I have detailed a few establishments where the prices are acceptable, as well as one or two that are extortionate. Not all need be gloom and dyspepsia though.

Half-way up Odhos Socratous (or down, depending on the starting point) is a 'Main Square'. To the left (*facing down the slope of the thoroughfare, which battles through the massed fur shops*) is a popular, tree shaded cafe. A Nes meh ghala costs a reasonable 81drs but alcoholic drinks are expensive.

Two or three buildings further along Odhos Lahetos is a small Kafeneion, on the same side as the tree shaded cafe and a less expensive proposition.

Back at Spocratous Sq, to the right, on the junction with Menecleous St, is the *Express* (*Tmr* 31F4), a very good value baker, cake and pie shop.

A few metres down Odhos Socratous and on the left is a traditional, men only Kafeneion at No. 76 and four shops further on, in an easterly direction, is the:-

Souvlaki Snackbar (*Tmr* 21F4/5)
Once excellent value and popular but now expensive and popular, with a souvlaki pita costing 110drs. The painfully thin Papa obviously does not eat his own fare, otherwise he would be as large as his wife.

Further on down Odhos Socratous is another souvlaki stall, *Fast Food*, also sited on the left, close by the junction with Odhos Apellou. At one of the Plateia Hippokratous cafe-restaurants, two coffees and a breakfast of toast, butter and jam can cost 500drs – but only once!

The shaded Square (*Tmr* E/F5), formed by the streets of Apellou and Evdimou, shelters two dirty and expensive tavernas, cheek by jowl, where the service is rude and slow. They also practice a form of chicanery in which the waiter informs clients that the establishment has 'run out' of bottled orange or lemon drinks, usually costing about 40drs, and offers a medium sized can of juice priced at 180drs.

The International Cafe-bar on Plateia Martiron Eyreon (*Tmr* F5/6) proffers a limited but good value menu. This establishment is a splendid 'loafing milieu' (2 lemonades 80drs) from which to watch the antics of the cruise liner clients. Some of them, when on their 'run ashore', wander up to this Square in order to hire a scooter from one of the outfits spread around the periphery.

The best location at which to enjoy a coffee, have a snack or sandwich and or watch the hurly-burly of commercial life must be within the very large, many sided:-

New Market (*Tmr* 5D/E4).
'New' must be a comparative description, as the place would appear to have

been *in situ* for a fair amount of time. Within the big, inner courtyard there are a number of fast food snackbars as well as a plethora of cafe-bars and kafeneions in amongst the stalls, shops and the fish market. A cognac and Nes meh ghala costs an average 170drs.

The 'Nes' (instant coffee) is often made using individual packets, which make a rather unpleasant tasting 'cuppa'. For an excellent coffee, and if feeling 'flush', wander around to the arcaded exterior of the Market that borders the Esplanade. Here a row of cafe-bars and restaurants, cafe-table to cafe-table, are open from morning to early the next morning, serving the full range of requisites as well as truly enormous ice-creams. They become less regal progressing from left to right (*Sbo*) and my own favourite is the *Cafe Bar Remvee*, fourth from the left, where two white coffees are not overly expensive, considering the location, at a cost of 180drs.

Despite the shortage of reasonable priced eating places, those that receive the *GROC's Stamp of Approval* really do make up for the paucity – small in number they may be, but my goodness one or three of them are really excellent! I hope readers agree.

Taverna Kostas (*Tmr* 12F5)
Directions: *See Pension Rena,* **The Accommodation**.
   Kostas is very friendly and the menu is good value. Two Greek salads, a portion of sole with patatas, a beer, Coke and bread costs 1100drs.

Pandesia Restaurant (*Tmr* 23F5) Plateia Aristofanous.
Directions: Located to one side of the Square and approached from either the direction of Odhos Ag Fanouriou or Odhos Sophocleous. A sign fastened to the wall facing the Square proclaims *Souvlaki Pandesia*.
   The patron, a wild-eyed, high cheek-boned, moustachioed gentleman gets increasingly bothered as the split-level patio of his taverna fills with clients. This is a family concern with the women, wearing traditional costume, working in the kitchen, tucked away a door or two along the narrow side-street, and the young children helping to serve at the tables. A chubby, favoured son often serenades unwary patrons, many of them Greeks, with his scratchy, unattractive violin play. The value and the food are excellent. The service and George's English becomes more and more chaotic as the evening wears on, so it is best to dine here early. Examples of the menu and costs include a meal for two of tzatziki, a Greek salad, two potato omelettes, bread and a bottle of retsina for 600drs and another of aubergines, peppers, one potato omelette, (well they are good), one beefsteak, a bottle of retsina and bread for 580drs. One bean soup, 2 plates of stuffed tomatoes, 1 dolmades, a portion of chips, a portion of feta cheese, bread and 2 bottles of kortaki retsina for two cost 1000drs.

Just around the corner, on the elbow of Eschilou St and behind the *Sea Star Taverna* is the:-
Spilia Taverna (*Tmr* 24F4/5) 24 Eschilou.
Directions: As above.
   At first sight this is an unremarkable little taverna but just hope your luck is in and the music starts. The Patron's neat wife cooks good, freshly prepared food and their daughter, sometimes in evidence and in her twenties, speaks excellent English. If 'Paganini' turns up it will most likely become a very lively evening, with 'your actual dancing in the streets!'. When this bespectacled

virtuoso plays the violin and sings, the patron reaches for his accordion. The action really swings if their bouzouki playing friend arrives, for the trio may well play right through the night. It is best to 'bag' a table on the tiny patio, just across the narrow lane from the taverna building, before the action gets underway, at about 2200hrs. After this patrons flood in and tables and chairs fill the street. Incidentally, Paganini's liver condition prevents him drinking anything more potent than a bottle of lemon. The menu is individually cooked and no one night is a particular dish available, although kalamares are a house speciality, and are they good? A Greek salad, a plate of beans, two large plates of kalamares, two bottles of retsina and bread costs about 1000drs. A meal for three of a souvlakia, a plate of kalamares, a plate of liver, two tzatzikis, patatas, bread, a plate of feta and 3 bottles of retsina costs 1800drs.

Archangelos Cafe-bar Restaurant (*Tmr* 66F/G4/5) Plateia Aristofanous.
Directions: Just to the left of the junction of Omirou St with Plateia Aristofanous.
A very reasonably priced establishment with a wide choice and a rather taciturn owner, who reveals a nice, inner personality to clients of whom he approves. He may hand out little gifts of appreciation – such as wine glasses. A breakfast and meal location. A large *petit dejeuner* (pardon!) for two of yoghurt and honey for one, bacon and eggs for one and 2 Nes meh ghala costs 400drs. An evening meal for two of vegetable and sausage stew, potatoes (yes potatoes not chips), stuffed courgettes (delicious), bread and a large bottle of red wine cost 980drs. The restaurant possesses a microwave, a piece of equipment that rather clashes with the 'hole in the wall' kitchen. It is used to hot up the 'metal tray' dishes.

Both Omirou and Ag Fanouriou Sts spawn a number of night-time tavernas that are invisible during the day, being nothing more than caverns and or cellars. Their offerings are reasonable in quality and price.
I cannot leave the subject of eateries without mentioning (only for the record):-

The Kontiki Mandraki Harbour.
Directions: A very fashionable floating restaurant moored to the south side of the Harbour.
The impossibly high prices purchase nicely presented, but small portions from an extensive menu. To further spoil the fun the meals are served in strict European order and on hot plates! Examples from the bill of fare include avocado with shrimps 1250drs (and this is a starter), tzatziki 278drs, Greek salad 334drs, lamb chops at 1250drs, moussaka 780drs, fillet steak 1550drs and bread 79drs (I thought it was expensive elsewhere). Mark you, they accept various credit cards!

THE A TO Z OF USEFUL INFORMATION
AIRLINE OFFICE & TERMINUS (*Tmr* 25C/D3/4). The Olympic premises are on the left of Odhos Ierou Lochou, beyond the *Plaza Hotel*.
There are pleasant, clean toilets down the stairs as well as a cold drinking water fountain. The Olympic bus fare (120drs) must be paid before getting on the bus but the man does not pull his desk out and start dispensing tickets until the bus is about to leave, so it can prove to be a bit of a scramble. The buses depart approximately every 45 minutes.

Aircraft timetable (Mid-season)

Rhodes to Athens (& vice versa)
A minimum of five flights a day, every day with an extra flight on Tuesday & Thursday.
One-way fare: 8400drs; duration 55mins.

Rhodes to Santorini
Tuesday, Thursday & Saturday	1100hrs
Return	
Tuesday, Thursday & Saturday	0940hrs

One-way fare: 6710drs; duration 1hr.

Rhodes to Thessaloniki
Tuesday & Thursday	1705hrs
Return	
Tuesday & Thursday	1900hrs

One-way fare: 1274drs; duration 1hr 10mins

Rhodes to Iraklion (Crete)
Daily	2150hrs
Return	
Daily	2030hrs

One-way fare: 6470drs; duration 40mins

Rhodes to Karpathos (& vice versa)
A minimum four flights a day, with five on Monday, Tuesday, Wednesday, Thursday & Friday.
One-way fare: 4510drs; duration 40mins.

Rhodes to Kasos
Monday, Wednesday, Friday & Sunday	0705hrs
Return	
Monday, Wednesday, Friday & Sunday	0805hrs

One-way fare: 4420drs; duration 40mins.

Rhodes to Kastellorizo
Thursday & Sunday	0910hrs
Return	
Thursday & Sunday	1015hrs

One-way fare: 4420drs; duration 45mins

Rhodes to Kos
Daily	1340hrs
Return	
Daily	1430hrs

One-way fare: 4070drs; duration 30mins

Rhodes to Mykonos
Monday, Wednesday, Friday & Sunday	1440hrs
Return	
Monday, Wednesday, Friday & Sunday	1310hrs

One-way fare: 7270drs; duration 50mins

Rhodes to Lesbos (Mitilini)
Monday, Wednesday & Friday	1835hrs
Return	

Monday, Wednesday   1645hrs
  & Friday
One-way fare; 10460drs; duration 1hr 30mins.

Rhodes to Paros
Daily   1120hrs
Return
Daily   0750hrs
One-way fare: 8770drs; duration 1hr.

Rhodes to Sitia (Crete)
Saturday   0645hrs
Return
Saturday   0800hrs
One-way fare: 8770drs; duration 55mins

BANKS
The National Bank (*Tmr* 26D3/4)
Directions: On the apex of Vassilisis Sofias and Ethnarchou Sts.

The bank has extended opening hours including: Monday to Thursday 0800-1400 & 1430-2030hrs; Friday 0800-1330 & 1430-2000hrs; Saturday 0800-1400hrs; Sunday 0800-1200hrs. Not only changes travellers cheques but also Eurocheques.   .

Other banks include:-
The Ionian & Popular (*Tmr* 27E5)
Directions: On Plateia Simi, entered from St Paul's Arsenal and Liberty (Eleftherias) Gates.
The Bank of Greece (*Tmr* 35D4)
Directions: Across the Esplanade from the Mandraki Harbour.

BEACHES
Beach 1: Starting at the Elli Club (*Tmr* 3C4), a splendid but very, very crowded beach wraps its way round the Sandy Point headland. The sand is intermixed with very fine, grey pebbles but it is necessary to keep an eye open for tar globules, which are widely spread about. There are beach showers and a diving board in the sea, as well as sun-beds and umbrellas (250drs per person) set out in regimented lines on the fairly narrow strip of sand. The Elli Club buildings include a restaurant, a small first-aid office and very clean *No Pay* toilets, tucked into the corner. Unfortunately these latter, excellent facilities run out of toilet paper by midday so 'clients should carry their own or it may be necessary to 'borrow' some paper napkins from the adjoining taverna. Beyond the Elli Club is a well organised, *Municipal Cantina* selling reasonably priced hot food, rolls, fruit, soft drinks and beer. The Rhodes Tennis Club is just across the road (*See* **Tennis, Sports Facilities, A To Z**).

Beaches 2 & 3: Two other local, small, sandy beaches are located, one each, in the Commercial and Acandia Harbours. The Commercial Harbour beach is signposted *Swimming Prohibited* and there is possibly a sewerage outfall here.

The sandy beach at the bottom of Acandia Harbour, beyond the liner quay, despite sporting another swimming prohibited sign, has a beach shower and toilets. An interesting boatyard lies to the right-hand side, in the corner of the curve created by the large finger pier that forms the east side of this Harbour.

BICYCLE, SCOOTER & CAR HIRE All rental charges are expensive on Rhodes but firms are plentiful enough, although cars often have to be booked ahead. Bike and scooter hire outfits in the New Town include one alongside the 1930s *Thermai Hotel* (*Tmr* 28E3), to one side of a grandiose gate structure, and another on Odhos Alexandrou Diakou. Car hire firms include international companies such as *Avis* and *Hertz*, as well as RETCA at 26 Dodekannision St (*Tmr* D4). One of the less winning sights is when up to twenty cars, from for instance Avis Cars, are hired on behalf of Scandinavian holiday-makers for a 'Safari'. Oh dear! To observe this exciting event it is necessary to keep an eye on the forecourt of the *Thermai Hotel* where they foregather.

Generally car hire costs 4500-5000drs per day, with a damage deposit of up to 12,000drs, whilst a scooter costs from 1400-1500drs a day.

Scooter hire in the Old Quarter is centred to the Dimosthenous St side of the Square of the Jewish Martyrs (*Tmr* F5/6). The firm alongside the *International Cafe-bar*, run by a large, smiling old rogue, is 100drs cheaper than his neater rival:-

I Mandar Scooters (*Tmr* 29F5), 2 Dimosthenous, Old Town, Rhodes Tel 30665
Directions: Operates from a waste lot at the Dimosthenous St end of the Square.

The young man's scooters are modern, in very good condition and the inventory includes a spare wheel as well as a secure locker for valuables. On the other hand his vehicles are a little more expensive than the competition at 1500drs a day. Best to negotiate a week's hire, when the rate tumbles to an average of about 1100drs per day.

BOOKSELLERS Nothing special but one or two dotted about the periphery of the New Market (*Tmr* 5D/E4). Overseas newspapers are sold from two kiosks. These face each other across the wide entrance way into the inner courtyard of the Market, on the seafront side of the building.

BREAD SHOPS There is a bread shop hidden away on Palama St, one up from Odhos Averoff which circles the New Market (*Tmr* 5D/E4). There is no need to go round on to Alexandrou Papagou as a little side-street leads to a flight of steps which emerge alongside the shop. This is not a baker, simply a bread shop.

Bakers include one at No. 41 Ippodamou, The Old Quarter (*Tmr* 30F4). A flat, round wholemeal loaf costs 50drs (possibly four hour bread though!). There is another, *Express* (*Tmr* 31F4), situated on the junction of Menecleous and Socratous Sts. This is not only a baker but a cake, pastry and pie shop.

BUSES The bus service is excellent, the depots are centrally located and information is easy to come by (that is compared to most other islands) from various tourist offices.

Bus timetable
A. The East (side of the island) Terminal (KTEL) (*Tmr* 32E4)
Situated on Odhos Alexandrou Papagou, alongside the Park in which the *Son et Lumiere* takes place.
NB All fares are quoted per person, one-way unless otherwise stated, AND Sunday/holiday schedules are subject to variation from these listings.

Rhodes City to Lindos
Daily   0830, 0900, 0930, 1000, 1030, 1100, 1130, 1300, 1500, 1615hrs
Return journey
Daily   0700, 0735, 0945, 1030, 1130, 1300, 1430, 1500, 1630, 1830hrs
One-way fare: 300drs

Rhodes City to Arhangelos via Afantou.
Daily   0700, 0900, 1000, 1130, 1300, 1430, 1500, 1615, 1700, 1930, 2100hrs
Return journey
Daily   0600, 0630, 0700, 0730, 0800, 1030, 1100, 1200, 1330, 1530, 1830hrs
One-way fare: 180drs

Rhodes City to Tsambika Beach
Daily   0900hrs
Return journey
Daily   1530hrs
One-way fare: 170drs

Rhodes City to Kallithie via Faliraki Beach
Daily   0600, 0700, 0800, 1010, 1210, 1310, 1410, 1510, 1610, 1700,
                      1930, 2100hrs
Return journey
Daily   0630, 0700, 0830, 1040, 1240, 1340, 1440, 1540, 1640, 1830, 2015hrs
One-way fare: 130drs

Rhodes City to Psinthos via Kallithie.
Daily   0600, 1510, 1700hrs
Return journey
Daily   0645, 1610, 1810hrs
One-way fare: 130drs

Rhodes City to Laerma via Malona, Massari, Kalathos, Pilon, Lardos.
Daily   1500hrs
Return journey
Daily   0700, 0715hrs
One-way fare: 330drs

Rhodes City to Messanagros via Malona,Massari,Kalathos,Lardos,Asklipiion Lahania, Kattavia.
Daily   1500hrs
Return journey
Daily   0630hrs
One-way fare: 540drs

Rhodes City to Apolakkia.
Daily   1500hrs
Return journey
Daily   0700hrs
One-way fare: 460drs

Rhodes City to Haraki.
Daily   1300hrs
Return journey
Daily   0700hrs
One-way fare: 220drs

B.The West (side of the island) Terminal (Roda)(*Tmr* 33D/E4)
On Averoff St, alongside the New Market

Rhodes City towards Faliraki Beach as far as the Hotel Calypso.*
Daily   0655, 0745, 0800, 0830, 0900, 1000 & every half-hour until 2400hrs.
Return journey
Daily   0715, 0815, 0830, 0900, 0930, 1030 & every half-hour until 0030hrs.
One-way fare: 80drs

Rhodes City to Koskinou*
Daily   0535, 0640, 0655, 0730, 0840, 1020, 1210, 1340, 1410, 1515, 1610,
                      1710, 1810, 1910, 2000, 2110, 2200hrs
Return journey
Daily   0600, 0705, 0735, 0755, 0905, 1045, 1235, 1405, 1435, 1540, 1635,
                      1735, 1835, 1935, 2025, 2135, 2225hrs

One-way fare: 80drs
I realise that these destinations are on the East side, but we are in Greece aren't we?

Rhodes City to Paradissi (Airport) via (Ialossos) Trianta, Kremasti.
Daily   0655, 0725, 0835, 0900, 0930, 1000, 1030, 1100, 1200, 1225, 1300,
               1400, 1430, 1630, 1700, 1725, 1800, 1830, 2000, 2030, 2100, 2130,
               2200, 2235, 2315hrs
Return journey
Daily   0730, 0800, 0910, 0935, 1005, 1035, 1105, 1135, 1235, 1300, 1335,
               1445, 1520, 1705, 1735, 1800, 1835, 1910, 2035, 2105, 2135, 2235,
               2310, 2350hrs
One-way fare: 70drs

Rhodes City to Ancient Kamiros
Daily   0845, 1010, 1130, 1230, 1440, 1815hrs
Return journey
Daily   0950, 1135, 1230, 1335, 1545, 1925hrs
One-way fare: 180drs

Rhodes City to Petaloudes (Valley of the Butterflies)
Daily   0905, 1015, 1105, 1240hrs
Return journey
Daily   1000, 1110, 1220, 1335hrs
One-way fare: 250drs

Rhodes to Ebonas
Daily   1340hrs (via Kritinia) & 1445hrs (via Salakos)
Return journey
Daily   0600hrs (via Salakos) & 0715hrs (via Kritinia).
One-way fare: 280drs

Rhodes City to Kamiros Skala
Sunday   1010hrs
Return journey
Sunday   1500hrs
One-way fare: 280drs

Rhodes City to Apollona via Archipolis
Daily   1315, 1530hrs
Return journey
Daily   0620, 0710hrs
One-way fare: 240drs

Rhodes City to Maritsa via Pastida
Daily   0805, 1005, 1140, 1310, 1340, 1435, 1510, 1610, 1710, 1840, 1940,
               2040, 2210hrs.
Return journey
Daily   0845, 1045, 1220, 1420, 1515, 1550, 1650, 1750, 1915, 2020, 2120,
               2250hrs.
One-way fare: 80drs

Rhodes City to Kalavarda
Daily   0700, 1215, 2050hrs
Return journey
Daily   0530, 0800, 2150hrs
One-way fare: 180drs

Rhodes City to Monolithos
Daily   1320hrs
Return journey
Daily   0615hrs

Rhodes City to Filerimos
Daily   0910, 1035, 1150hrs
Return journey

Daily   0950, 1115, 1230hrs
One-way fare: 150drs

Rhodes City Buses
No.1 City Tour   0630-2130hrs, every half-hour
No.3 Rodini Park   0530-2230hrs, every half-hour
No.4 St Dimitrios   0615-2145hrs, every half-hour
No.5 St John/   0530-2230hrs, every half-hour
    Monte Smith
No.6 Analipsi,   0615-2245hrs, every 45 mins
    Megavli
One-way fare: 40drs

CAMPING *See* **Faliraki & Lardos, Route One.**

CINEMAS Up to six in the Nea Chora (New Town) including the Rodon, to the rear of the National Theatre, (*Tmr* 34C4), the Esperia (*Tmr* D4) on 25 Martiou, the Metropol (*Tmr* G/H4/5) on variously Vyronos, Vass Friderikis, Dimocratias and the junction with Stefanou Casouli, and the Titania on Colocotroni St (*Tmr* G6/7), east of the Stadium, between the *Hotels Sylvia* and *Aegli*. The usual mix of Greek and foreign films, accompanied by Greek subtitles, with entrance costing about 200drs.

COMMERCIAL SHOPPING AREA
The New Market (Nea Agora) (*Tmr* 5D/E4). Here can be purchased almost all the needs of any shopper. The many sided building encloses a large area crammed with fruit and vegetable stalls. kafeneions, fast food cafeterias, a sprinkling of tatty souvenir shops and, to one side of the tree shaded internal courtyard, the raised rotunda building of the Fish Market. A number of feral cat families occupy the building after the fish sellers have packed their wares. Any approach is met by snarling, spitting, naked aggression.

The shops that occupy the arcaded, columned front facing Mandraki Harbour are, in the main, cafes and cake shops. Around the remaining sides of the external periphery of the building are liquor, grocery and gift shops, as well as a number of small supermarkets. Entry to the inner courtyard is through various alleyways that pierce the facade of the building. A number of public lavatories are also accessible from the courtyard.

In the Nea Chora, or New Town, the occasional smart stores are centred on the streets of Vassilissis Sofias, Gallias and Ethnarchou Makariou.

One reader has advised that there is an excellent momento/souvenir shop on Leoforos Vassileos Konstantinon (*Tmr* C3/4), opposite an ex-Italian period hotel relic, currently being restored to put the building back to work in its former guise. The proprietor sells superb, inexpensive imitation bronze pottery as well as facsimile faces of Greek gods, urns, pots and jugs. An example is a large orange sized, half full face of Adonis at a cost of 300drs. The owner claims his father spent forty years perfecting the process – oh, yes!

In the Old Quarter the total world's output of furs (well it seems that way) are concentrated on the streets of Socratous, Polydorou and Aghisandrou. These three streets and Odhos Orfeos (*Tmr* E/F4) also house a multitude of dress and souvenir shops.

DISCOS No shortage with a number centred on and around Plateia Akadimias (also known as Plateia Vass Georgiou A) (*Tmr* D3) as well as Iroon Politechniou (also known as Vassilopedos Marias) which branches north of Plateia Akadimas and nearby Odhos Alexandrou Diakou.

EMBASSIES, CONSULATES & VICE CONSULS

Austria: 25th Martiou St	Tel 20831
Belgium: 35-37 Odhos Kos	Tel 24661
British: 23, 25th Martiou St	Tel 24963
France: 12 Karpathou St	Tel 22318
Germany, West: 43 Kennedy St	Tel 29730
Holland: Al Diakou St (c/o Ialyssos Travel)	Tel 31571
Italy: Ippoton St	Tel 33980
Norway: Alexia Hotel, Ibiscus St	Tel 34285
Spain: 11-13 Amerikis	Tel 22460
Sweden: Amerikis/Kazouli	Tel 31822
USA: c/o Voice of America	Tel 24731

FERRY-BOATS & FLYING DOLPHINS Yes, well. The scheduled 'main line' ferry-boats dock in The Commercial Harbour against the Customs Hall Quay (*Tmr* 2E6). The summer schedules that follow are subject to all sorts of variations, but (hopefully) give an indication of the excellent coverage.

Excursion and trip boats arrive and depart from Mandraki Harbour.

Personal opinions regarding certain individual ferry-boats are set out in **Chapter Three**.

Ferry-boat timetable (Mid-season)

Day	Departure time	Ferry-boat	Ports/Islands of Call
Monday	1100hrs	Panormitis	Simi,Tilos,Nisiros,Kos,Kalimnos, Leros,Lipsos,Patmos,Arki,Angathonisi, Pythagorion(Samos).
	1200hrs	Ialysos/Kamiros	Kos,Kalimnos,Leros,Patmos,Piraeus(M).
Tuesday	1200hrs	Ialysos/Kamiros	Kos,Kalimnos,Leros,Patmos,Piraeus(M).
	2100hrs	Nireas	Chalki,Karpathos,Kasos,Sitia(Crete), Ag Nikolaos(Crete).
Wednesday	1100hrs	Panormitis	Megisti(Kastellorizo).
	1200hrs	Ialyos/Kamiros	Kos,Kalimnos,Leros,Patmos,Syros, Piraeus(M).
	2400hrs	Golden Vergina	Karpathos,Kasos,Sitia(Crete),Ag Nikolaos(Crete),Anafi,Santorini, Piraeus(M).
Thursday	0200 or 0300hrs(!)	Nireas	Simi,Tilos,Nisiros,Kos,Kalimnos, Astipalaia,Amorgos,Paros,Piraeus(M).
	0900hrs	Panormitis	Simi,Tilos,Nisiros,Kos,Kalimnos.
	1000 or 1130hrs(!)	Alcaeos/Omiros	Kos,Patmos,Vathy(Samos),Chios, Mitilini(Lesbos),Limnos,Kavala(M).
	1200hrs	Omiros	Kos,Kalimnos,Leros,Patmos,Piraeus(M).
	1200hrs	Ialysos/Kamiros	Kos,Kalimnos,Leros,Patmos,Piraeus(M).
Friday	1100hrs	Panormitis	Chalki,Diafani(Karpathos),Karpathos, Kasos.
	1200hrs	Ialysos/Kamiros	Kos,Kalimnos,Leros,Patmos,Piraeus(M).
Saturday	1200hrs	Ialysos/Kamiros	Kos,Kalimnos,Leros,Patmos,Piraeus(M).
	2400 or 0030hrs(!)	Golden Vergina	Chalki,Diafani(Karpathos),Karpathos, Kasos,Sitia(Crete),Ag Nikolaos(Crete), Anafi,Santorini,Folegandros,Milos, Piraeus(M).
Sunday	0900 or 1700hrs(!)	Panormitis	Kastellorizo.

Ferry-boat sailing durations:

Rhodes to			Rhodes to		
	Astipalaia	10½hrs		Simi	2hrs
	Chalki	2½hrs		Tilos	4½hrs
	Kastellorizo	7hrs		Nisiros	7hrs
	Kos	4½-9½hrs		Kalimnos	7-11hrs
	Karpathos	7¼hrs		Leros	11hrs
	Diafani(Karpathos)	5½hrs		Patmos	15hrs
	Kasos	9¼hrs		Angathonisi	17¾hrs
	Piraeus	circa 18hrs		Arki	16¼hrs
	Lipsos	13hrs			

Please *See* individual island details for further details of ferry-boats.

In addition to the above there are expensive (that is expensive in comparison to the scheduled ferry-boat fees) scheduled excursions, trip boats and ferry-boats departing from:

Mandraki Harbour to:

Daily	0900hrs	Lindos(Rhodes)
	0900hrs	Simi
Tuesday, Wednesday & Friday	1830hrs	Simi
Saturday(Lindos)	1330hrs	Simi

One-way fare: Rhodes to Lindos 1600drs
             to Simi 560-2000drs.

Flying Dolphin timetable (Mid-season)

Daily	0730/0800hrs	Kos
Daily	1000hrs	Simi
Monday & Wednesday	0730/0800hrs	Patmos (via Kos)

One-way fare: Rhodes to Kos 6300drs

FERRY—BOAT & FLYING DOLPHIN TICKET OFFICES
These offices are gathered together in an area radiating out from Plateia Kyprou(*Tmr* D4).

FB Panormitis	Kozas Agency, Odhos Kyprou Michail (behind the Bank of Greece - *Tmr* 35D4). Tel 24046
FB Kamiros/Ialysos	DANE Agency (*Tmr* D3/4), 95 Amerikis St.Tel 30930
FB Omiros/Alcaeos	Red Sea Agency, 11 Amerikis St.Tel 27721/22683
FB Kyklades/Nireas	Kydon Agency, Dodekannision Ethelonton St.Tel 23000
FB Golden Vergina	Kouros Agency (*Tmr* D/E4), 34 Karpathou St, (Haile Selassie St) Tel 24377/22400
Flying Dolphin Craft	Kouros Agency (*Tmr* D/E4), 34 Karpathou St, (Haile Selassie St) Tel 24377/22400

HAIRDRESSERS At last three, with shops on the streets of Amerikis, Themeli and Iroon Polytechnou.

LAUNDRY Apart from a number of Dry Cleaners there is a launderette:-

Lavomatic 32, 28th Octovriou St.
Directions: From Plateia Akadimias (*Tmr* D3) proceed westwards along Odhos 28th Octovriou. The shop is located between the side-streets of Fanouraki and Ionos Dragoumi.
    Open daily between 0730-2230hrs. A machine load costs 300drs and a dry 50drs.

LUGGAGE STORE The City Tourist office (*Tmr* 6E4) operates a service, charging 100drs per piece, per day. Luggage is docketed and safely stored.

MEDICAL CARE
Chemists & Pharmacies As many as you like. A rota system is in operation for emergencies.
Dentists Antony Alaxouzos, 40 Amerikis St.
Doctors Dr J Sotiriou, 55 Amerikis St.
Hospital (*Tmr* 65D/E2/3). An out-patient clinic is open 24 hours a day.

NTOG (EOT) (*Tmr* 7D/E3/4). The office is located on the crossroads of Alexandrou Diakou, Alexandrou Papagou, Ethnarchou and Vass. Friderikis. A neat, clean and efficient outfit housed in a 1930s building. The staff offer very helpful, if rather impersonal attention, much in the same style as the Corfu office. They operate an excellent service to accommodate travellers and, once having established a client's particular requirements, telephone around to locate rooms. Only open Monday to Friday between 0830-1430hrs.
When the office is closed contact the City Tourist office (*Tmr* 6E4) who are extremely helpful and friendly. Open for business Monday to Saturday between 0800-2000hrs, Sunday and holidays 0900-1200hrs.

OTE (*Tmr* 39D3/4) The busy, main office is on the junction of Amerikis and 25th Martiou and open daily between 0600-2400hrs.
There is another, small, characterful office (*Tmr* 40E5). This is tucked away beyond the first floor Police Price Control office, alongside a decorative gateway and to one side of 'Museum' Square, diagonally across from Odhos Ippoton. This facility is open Monday to Friday between 0730-2200hrs.

PETROL No shortage, with two petrol stations in the area of the KTEL bus terminus (*Tmr* 32E4).

PLACES OF INTEREST
Aquarium (*Tmr* 4A/B3) This Italian built structure stands at the northern end of the sandy bluff of Rhodes City. Down the staircase leads to very large tanks full of (surprise, surprise) fish and associated underwater vertebrates. Open daily between 0900-2100hrs and entrance costs 150drs.

Churches & Cathedrals
Church of St John the Evangelist, (*Tmr* 41/C/D4) Nea Chora. The present seat of the Archbishop and built by the Italians in 1925 (or was it designed by monkeys, built by robots and driven by Italians? Surely not...!). Modelled upon the St Johns Church that originally stood in the Old Quarter, opposite The Palace of the Grand Masters, but destroyed in the 1850s.

Orthodox Cathedral of St Mary (*Tmr* 42E5) Old Quarter. Across from the bottom of the Street of the Knights (Odhos Ippoton). This 13th century Byzantine church, which became the first Cathedral of the Knights, was converted into a mosque (Enderoum Mosque) by the all-conquering Turks. They replaced the steeple with a minaret. Now a Byzantine Museum.

Church of St Marie du Bourg (*Tmr* 43F6) Odhos Pindarou, Old Quarter. The road from the Square of the Jewish Martyrs, which has been laid through parts of this particular church, makes a junction with Odhos Alhadef.
To the left leads down to an arched opening in the City wall, close by the Commercial Harbour.
Nearby, on Alhadef St, is the:-

Hospice of St Catherine (*Tmr* 44F6) Old Quarter. Built in 1392 to provide accommodation for Italian pilgrims.

On towards St Catherine's Gate, beyond the Church of St Panteleimon, are a few ruins that are all that remain of the:-

Church of the Madonna of Victory, Old Quarter. Built to celebrate a famous victory over the invading Turks at this part of the fortress wall. The inhabitants made a spirited defence after a vision of the Madonna appeared to them in 1480. The building was demolished sometime around 1520.

Church of St Fanourios (*Tmr* 45F/G4/5) Old Quarter. On the right of Odhos Ag Fanouriou (*facing north*), beyond the junction with Omirou St. Entered via a narrow, wooden corridor and today a regular place of worship. The original Byzantine church and its frescoes were taken over by the Turks who, at first, used the building as stables, thus destroying the lower wall paintings. Later it was converted into the Pial-el-Din Mosque, only for the Greeks to take it back and reconvert it to the Orthodox faith. The Italians restored the paintings, towards the end of their occupation.

Gates, Harbours & Walls The Walls of the Old Quarter are continuous and there are two guided tours a week, Monday and Saturday. These start out at 1445hrs from the Palace of the Grand Masters (*Tmr* 37E4), take approximately 1½ hours and cost 300drs. The medieval military wall, towers, gates and ditches were built, and the moats excavated, by the Knights. All were heavily modified during their 213 years of occupation (1309-1522), having been constructed, in part, on Byzantine foundations. After 1465 the fortress was divided into eight sectors or bulwarks which were allocated, for defence purposes, to the eight *Tongues*, or nationalities. After repulsing the Turkish siege of 1480, Italian engineers were commissioned to assist the then Grand Master (Pierre d'Aubusson) to strengthen the fortifications which, in places, resulted in wall thicknesses up to 12 metres. The number of gates were reduced and the moat widened to some 20 metres.

The busiest Gate must be Liberty or Eleftherias (once also named the New Gate), constructed as recently as 1924 and renamed, in 1947, on the reunification of the Dodecanese with Greece.

To the left is the medieval St Paul's Gate leading to the edge of the Commercial Harbour, which was defended by two moles. The north mole stretches out from close by St Paul's Gate, and was fortified by the siege Tower of Naillac, prior to its destruction in the middle 1800s. The eastern mole, on which stood, variously and depending on which authority you believe, thirteen to fifteen windmills, has sadly been replaced by the Customs Quay. The Esplanade roadway skirts the Commercial Harbour and is dominated by the exceedingly massive walls which are pierced by three Gates. These are Arsenal, Marine (sometimes mistakenly annotated St Catherines) and St Catherines (also known as Mills Gate, for obvious reasons), as well as an arched roadway driven through from Alhadef St. Particularly worth inspection is the bas-relief over the attractive Marine or Naval Base Gate. This includes figures of the Virgin Mary, St Peter, St Paul and the arms of Pierre d'Aubusson and of France. This section of wall is reputed to have 'acted' (sorry) as the backcloth for some scenes in the film *Guns of Navarone*.

The battlements run from the Customs Hall Quay along the west side of Acandia Harbour to the Gate of Italy, built in 1924 as part of the orgy of aggrandisement indulged in by the Italians. From hereon the fortifications turn the corner to advance past the Tower of Italy in the direction of Koskinou or St John's Gate, the gate through which the Italians triumphantly marched (in 1912) into the Old Quarter. The section, or bulwark, between this latter Gate and St Athanasius Gate, alongside St Mary's Tower, was that allocated to the English order or *Tongue*. The tower has a bas-relief of The Virgin Mary and child. The Gate of St Athanasius (or St Athun), one of the weakest points of the walled city, was the place where Suleiman, the all-conquering Turk, breached the defences in 1522. Some say his redoubled efforts were due to the duplicity of a Portuguese Knight who let Suleiman know just how ill the Knights were faring, exactly at the time when the Turks were considering giving up the siege.

The Wall now turns past the Tower of Spain and on to the large Tower of St George, once also a Gate. Naturally, I suppose, there is a bas-relief of St George above the old entrance as well of those of a Pope, a Grand Master and the Order of the Knights. The next fortified entrance, the grandest, is Amboise Gate which leads, via a triple arched bridge, over the outer moat and through the main part of the Gate, bedded in the enormous walls. Here the roadway snakes to a bridge over the inner moat and through an inner Gate, which opens out, at right angles on to the tree shaded avenue of Odhos Orfeos. This traffic free thoroughfare is towered over by the walls of the Palace of the Grand Masters (*Tmr* 37E4), on the left, and leads to the last Gate, that of St Anthony, at the top of Odhos Orfeos. Left through this Gate leads to the large, paved courtyard to one side of the Palace and the top of Odhos Ippoton, the Street of the Inns of the Knights.

Mandraki Harbour Outside the Old Quarter walls. The title is Greek for sheep-fold, a pointer to one of the previous uses of the Harbour. Mandraki hosts a yacht marina, the local, fishing boat fleet, the trip boats and small inter-island ferries. At the narrow entrance are two pillars supporting, respectively, a statue of a stag and a doe, one of which has replaced the Italian she-wolf that once graced one of the columns.

It is popular belief that, in ancient times, the famous Colossus of Rhodes stood in the place of the more modest, modern-day pillars, but this theory is questioned by many experts. One of the Seven Wonders of the Ancient World, the bronze statue of the Sun God Apollo, or Helios, supposedly some 30m tall, was erected by Chares of Lindos, about 300 BC. The abandoned Helepolis siege towers, which funded the construction costs of the Colossus, were left behind when a certain Demetrios Poliorketes abandoned an abortive campaign to teach the citizens of Rhodes a lesson for failing to support his father's campaign (it's an ill wind that blows somebody some good, isn't it?). Supposedly the head of the Colossus was surrounded by sunrays and one hand held a torch which, when lit, acted as a guiding light and signal for sailors. Unfortunately, some 70 years after its erection, an earthquake brought the remarkable statue to its knees, the broken remains lying around for eight hundred years. In the 7th century AD the twenty tons of bronze scrap was sold to a Syrian merchant and contemporaneous reports suggest that nine hundred camels were required to remove the booty. More recent calculations have suggested that ninety would have been a more likely figure. Perhaps the original historian was also a fisherman...! It has also been propounded, by a wag no doubt, that the Rhodians received their erstwhile scrap back in kind, for it is rumoured that the Turkish cannon balls were made of the very same material...

To protect the outer mole of Mandraki Harbour, St Nicholas Fort (*Tmr* 46C/D5) was constructed in 1464, on the site of an old chapel. This connection is maintained by the small church built within the walls of the Fort and dedicated to St Nicholas, the Greek Orthodox patron saint of sailors. Over the years the structure was supplemented by a lighthouse and modified to accommodate Second World War gun positions, so maintaining an on and off war footing for nearly five hundred years. This eastern mole also supported three windmills, still extant, dating back to the late 1400s and once used to grind corn. The landward side of the Harbour 'benefited' from the Italian treatment, but the Greeks maintain that the resultant buildings are alien in appearance. For my part, I am sure, that, were it not for the Italians, Rhodes City would present a very 'shambolic' appearance and not the magical and magnificent effect that must, surely, please most eyes. The guide books are, in general, dismissive of the majestic, 1930s, 'neo-municipal' Italian architecture, which buildings include the Harbour Master's office, the Post Office, the Town police, the Town Hall, two theatres, Government House (or the 'Governors Palace') and St John's Church. I admit there is an air of strange unreality about the buildings, as if they have been constructed for a film set or as a marzipan cake decoration, but nonetheless they have style.

One building in this vicinity, not reconstructed or newly built by the Italians, is the delightful and elegant Turkish mosque of Murad Reis (*Tmr* 47C4) and its cemetery. The minaret is particularly attractive and the tree shaded burial ground is littered with quaintly carved headstones. The type and fashion of the stone headwear is supposed to denote the dead man's trade or profession. The circular tomb, adjacent to the mosque, is the burial place of Murad Reis, Admiral to Suleiman the Magnificent, who met his death towards the end of the historic siege of 1522.

The Jewish Quarter Located in the south-east sector of the Old Quarter. The most touching memorials to the haphazard, but deadly quirks of Second World War fate are the Plateia Matiron Eyreon (Square of the Martyrs) and the Synagogue on Odhos Dosiadou, or more correctly the plaque on the wall of this dignified building. The Square, complete with a circular, tiled fountain topped off with three cast sea-horses, was renamed after the Second World War. This act of remembrance commemorates the tragic twist of fortune that befell the Jewish population in July 1943, after the Nazis of the Third Reich unexpectedly took over the administration of Rhodes, from the Italians. The poignant plaque, on the wall of the Synagogue, records that the two thousand Jews, still resident after the European apocalypse, were, in one year, transported by the Germans to concentration camps in the 'Fatherland'. Some fifty survived. Need one say more?

On a brighter note the 15th century Archbishops Palace overlooks the Square and was (not surprisingly) the residence of the Archbishops, prior to the Turkish take-over.

The Knights Quarter The two most attractive ways into this sector of the Old Quarter are either through Liberty or Freedom Gate (*Tmr* E5) to Plateia Simi or via Amboise Gate and St Anthony's (*Tmr* E3/4). On the other hand many cruise liner tourists wander in from the direction of the Commercial Harbour. As it is difficult to describe both routes, simultaneously, I have chosen to wander down the Street of the Knights from the:-

Palace of the Grand Masters (*Tmr* 37E4) The Palace, to the left of the large, paved Plateia Kleovoulou, is a splendid and imposing pile, if possessed of a rather sanitised appearance. This is not so surprising as it was completely rebuilt by the Italians, only being completed a short time prior to their hurried and sudden departure.

The Knights originally completed this magnificent edifice in the 14th century. It served the dual purpose of a fort, in time of war, and the home of the Grand Master, the 'top dog', in times of peace. Surely a rather opulent and oversized domicile for a man who was subject to vows of penury? Despite the ravages inflicted by Suleiman the Magnificent's siege, the Palace suffered very little during the battles. On the other hand, whilst in the possession of the languid Turks, over the next few centuries, the Palace acceleratingly deteriorated, which dilapidation climaxed in a horrendous explosion in 1856. Some absent-minded dolts had stowed away explosives, possibly a long time previously, in the vaults of the Palace and or the Loggia or Church of St John. Wherever and whatever, the initial blast and resultant holocaust destroyed much of this part of the City, killing some eight hundred people and reducing the Palace to ruins. The Italian reconstructed Palace was intended to be used for state visits by their pre-war King, Emmanuel III, and El Duce, Benito Mussolini. In keeping with the grandeur of these personages, the rebuilding allowed for concealed lifts, central heating and electric lighting, modern prerequisites that I am sure the Knights would have found puzzling, to say the least.

The courtyard, hallways and rooms, that are open to the public, exhibit a number of Roman statues and display so many magnificently restored mosaics, mostly from the island of Kos, that it is surprising there are any left elsewhere. The most famous of the mosaics is probably that titled the Nine Muses, dating from the 1st century AD. Naturally, purists berate the restoration, not only for pedantic, ideological reasons but because it is thought to be built over the remains of an ancient temple site. It has to be admitted that the classicists objections do have a point in respect of the disparate collection of antiquities 'borrowed' from other, scattered localities. Open daily between 0800-1900hrs, Sunday and holidays 0800-1800hrs and closed Tuesdays. Entrance costs 300drs.

Street of the Knights (Odhos Ippoton) Turning left out of the Palace entrance gates leads down the almost unbelievably quiet, almost stately, almost funereal street. The buildings seem to crowd the narrow, cobbled lane that falls steeply towards the Commercial Harbour. It takes some longer than others to realise that there are no shops, no traders, no 'schleppers' and, unbelievably, often no tourists. Can this be Rhodes City?

The Knights were divided into the *Tongues* of their native language and each *Tongue* had its own hall of residence or *Inn* which were located on either side of the Street of the Knights. Descending, the street advances past the side-street of Panetiou, on the right, then beneath an archway spanning the thoroughfare which, with its counter-part further down, appears to draw the walls of the buildings even closer together. The structure on the right, on the corner of Panetiou St, is The Loggia of St John, or more correctly, the partly restored Loggia. This used to connect the Palace with St John's Church and was destroyed, in 1856, by the 'big bang'. Much of the site is now occupied by a garden which is followed by the Inn of Spain, dating from the 15th century and edging Ipparhou St, and the other archway. Opposite the Inn of Spain is the Inn of Provence, bordered by entrance ways to gated gardens, the furthest one of which has a small church built over the remains of a Temple to Dionysius.

Once through the archway, the building on the left, which is now the official residence of the Italian Vice Consulate (*Tmr* 48E4), was once the French Chaplain's House. Next door is the Chapel of France (or more correctly the Chapel of the *French Tongue*), complete with a statue of the Virgin and child and the arms of a Grand Master of the period 1365-1374. Next along is the large Inn of France, well endowed with various coats of arms and probably the most eye-catching of all the buildings in the Street. Incidentally, the reason for the preponderance of French associated buildings is that they were the most numerous of the Knights. In fact the French supplied fourteen or so Grand Masters (you know, senior prefect) out of nineteen elected in the two hundred and thirteen years of their rule (and this was prior to the Common Market oligarchy, or was it the forerunner?). Certainly the Inn of France, the construction of which started in 1492, is the grandest of the Inns and possesses the most heavily decorated facade, with various coats of arms and a very noticeable fleur-de-lis and crown. Opposite the French Inn is the 'Edifice of Unknown' (as one of the official guide books quaintly puts it) followed by the side-street, Odhos Lahetos, and a lovely, serene Turkish garden framed by the surrounding walls in which is set a wrought iron gate. The tree shaded and shadowy garden attracts attention, if only because the mute tranquillity of the Street is delightfully disturbed by the bubbling and splashing of the garden's fountain. Across the thoroughfare is the Palace of Villiers de L'Isle Adam, the last Grand Master of Rhodes, who finally had to concede defeat to Suleiman. Next down is the Inn of Italy, with the arms of the Italian Grand Master, Fabrizio del Carretto, who caused the structure to be rebuilt in 1519. The last building on the left is now utilised by The Commercial Bank of Greece.

It is thought that most of the Inns' ground floors, in the days of the Knights, were used as stables or warehouses, the first floors being accessed by open stairs. The Turks, during their long occupation, festooned the buildings with rickety, wooden, upper storey balconies as was their wont. The last structure on the right, the original door of which faced the Street of The Knights, at the far end of the building, was the:-

Hospital of the Knights (*Tmr* 36E5) A museum since 1916, and now the Archaeological Museum, fronting on to Plateia Moussiou (Museum Square). In common with most of the Street of the Knights, it was restored in the early 1900s, the original Hospital having been completed by 1489. The entrance archway opens on to a courtyard, enclosed on all sides by a vaulted frontage. The first floor housed the original infirmary. There are seven pillar roof supports and one wall contains a number of small rooms without windows, the use of which has never been conclusively deduced. The courtyard display includes a marble crouching lion, some 2000 years old; piles of cannon balls from the time of the Turkish invasion; catapult shot, supposedly dating back to the siege of Demetrios Poliorketes, and a mosaic, circa 650 BC, from Arkasa on the island of Karpathos. Other notable exhibits, amongst a number of interesting items, include the Aphrodite of Rhodes, a statue of a woman kneeling and holding out the strands of her hair; the head of the Sun God Helios and the Marine Venus, a statue of Aphrodite, dating back to the 3rd century BC and found on the foreshore off Sandy Point. Splendid public lavatories and a pleasant first floor garden all help to make the Museum well worth a visit. Open daily between 0800-1900hrs, Sundays and holidays between 0800-1800hrs and closed Tuesdays. Entry costs 300drs.

Also on the periphery of Museum Sq, well really a small plateia off the Square, is the totally restored Inn of England (*Tmr* 49E/F5). Built in 1482, the Inn was all but demolished, rebuilt in the early 1900s and restored by the British after the Second World War.

Backtracking across Museum Sq, which bustles with people, towards Liberty Gate progresses past The Inn of Auvergne, the first floor of which is occupied by the Price Control police. From here, beneath an archway, advances on to the very busy pedestrian and vehicle 'ridden' Plateia Simi, a pleasant area with the small Plateia Argyrokastron to the left. This latter Square has a pleasant fountain, based on a font, positioned by the Italians (and thus naturally the subject of modern day debate) and is edged by Armeria Palace. This building was possibly the first infirmary of the Knights, but now houses offices of the Archaeological Department of the Dodecanese.

The Museum of Decorative Arts (*Tmr* 38E5) This building borders another side of the small square and was probably an Arsenal. If time allows, this exhibition merits a visit. On show are a collection of clothes and costumes, embroidery, woodwork, including furniture, china, ceramics and plates as well as the reconstruction of a typical, Greek village room. Open daily between 0800-1300hrs, Sundays 0900-1300hrs and closed Tuesdays. Entrance costs 200drs.

On the Square, as elsewhere throughout the Old Quarter, there are piles of cannon balls, leftovers from the 1522 siege. Across Argyrokastron Sq, and on the same side of the larger Plateia Simi, is a long building in which is situated the Ionian Popular Bank (*Tmr* 27E5) and steps climbing to the:-

The Municipal Art Gallery (*Tmr* 50E5) Here are displayed works of modern Greek painters. Open daily between 0730-1500hrs as well as between 1700-2000hrs on Tuesday, Wednesday, Thursday and Friday. Closed Sunday. Entrance costs 150drs.

Opposite, in the direction of the Arsenal Gate, are the remains of the:-

Temple of Aphrodite (*Tmr* 51E5) These date back to the 3rd century BC.

Two other buildings belong in this section, the:-
Clock Tower (*Tmr* 52E/F4) This was erected on the top of the wall edging Orfeos St. The structure steeples upwards and was once used as a watch tower or signal post.

From the Clock Tower the Knights built an inner wall down to the seafront that separated the Knight's Quarter (Collachium) from the rest of the Old Quarter
and the:-

Tribune of Commerce (*Tmr* 53F5) This was also known as the Palace of Castellania and is on the left of the Square of Hippokratous (*Facing towards Acandia Harbour*). Completed in 1507, it was the Court House of the Knights. The first floor is reached by wide, external stone steps and supported by columns which form a ground level arcade. The doorway is decorated with carved coats of arms.

Mosques (& the Turkish Sector of the Old Quarter) Probably the most noteworthy of the mosques was the:-

Mosque of Suleiman (Tmr 54F4) This is situated at the top of Socratous St, alongside the junction with Orfeos St. The Mosque was constructed in honour of and, no doubt, on the instructions of the Turkish Conqueror, in 1522. This pleasing mosque and minaret was rebuilt in 1808, with materials from a number of other buildings as well as the earlier mosque and, possibly, a church that had stood on the site, prior to 1522. The interior is well kept and spacious.

Across the road from the Suleiman Mosque is the:-

Turkish Library (Tmr 55F4) Built towards the end of the 1700s, the Persian and Arabic exhibits include two Korans, one of 1412, and the other, exquisitely illuminated, dated 1540.

Mosque of Chourmali Medresse This is to be found down Odhos Apolonion, alongside the Turkish Library, and towards St George Tower. A Turkish adaption of a Byzantine church, now in a ruined state. As with many other 'conversions', the traditional Byzantium dome shows up above and topping off the building.

Takkedji (Takkeci) Mosque This was originally a Byzantine church and was also known as the Mosque of the Dervishes. It is sited alongside Ippodamou St, but not now in use.

Hamza Bey Mosque On Odhos Timocreomtos, which branches off Ippodamou St, and once again not in use.

Moustafa (Mustupha) Mosque Also known as Sultan Moustafa Mosque, it was completed in 1765 to one side of Plateia Arionos. This Mosque is now locked and deteriorating but is still of pleasing appearance.

Arionos Square would appear to have more names than usual, which include Plateia Archelaou and the 'Square of the Baths', which is fair enough as one side is edged by the:-

Turkish Baths (Tmr 56F4) Also built in 1765, the building was very badly damaged during the Second World War and subsequently rebuilt. The old marble floor remains and the reconstruction was sympathetically carried out. Unfortunately no 'mixed saunas', the sexes being strictly segregated. Open Monday to Saturday between 0500-1900hrs, entrance costs 150drs, except Wednesday and Saturday, when the cost is 50drs. Rated as a definite experience but the cockroaches are very large.

Abdul Djelil Mosque (Tmr F4) Located on the edge of a small square on Andronicou St. A Byzantine church, prior to conversion, and in a poor state of repair.

Bab Mestoud Mosque Built alongside St Athanasius Gate and once again originally a Byzantine church.

Bourouzan Mosque (Tmr 57G4/5) South of Odhos Omirou, close by the walls and complete with a minaret.

Retjep Pasha Mosque (Tmr 58F/G4/5) On Dories Sq, behind St Fanourios Church, which was once the Pial-el-Din Mosque. The elongated Square has a row of three trees, planted in a rectangular bed. The now abandoned Mosque, built in 1588, was once one of the principal and most decorative of the Turkish religious buildings. It was constructed using, in part, bits and pieces of various Byzantine churches. Now the abandoned forecourt is a playground for the children of the area. There is a small rotunda fountain to the front of the Mosque.

Kavakly Mosque (Tmr 59F4/5) The pleasant little minaret stretches up from behind a stone wall, to one side of the ruined Square of Athinas.

Demerli Mosque Along Odhos Thoucididou Platonos, to the east of Ag Fanouriou. The building was once a large Byzantine church and is now in a bad state of repair.

Ibrahim Pasha Mosque (Tmr 60F5) On the side of the small Plateia Damagitou, located between Sophocleous and Pythagora Sts and their junction with Odhos Platonos. Originally built in 1531, it was restored by the Italians, in the 1930s, who also rebuilt the minaret. A very attractive interior which may be inspected as this Mosque is open to visitors. A large plane tree alongside the building is said to have been the site for summary executions during Turkish rule.

Dolaplee Mosque (Tmr 61G5) Situated at the City wall end of Dimosthenous St, which runs parallel and two streets to the east of Sophocleous St. Once a Byzantine church with the curious feature, shared with one or two others, of having longer cross arms than the nave and apse.

Ilk Mihrab Mosque Also known as Mihram Mosque and sited on Pericleous St, close by the Dolaplee Mosque. Very little now remains of this originally Byzantine church, once possessed of some very fine frescoes.

Agha Mosque On the junction of Socratous and Ag Fanouriou Sts, mounted on wooden pillars, and named after an erstwhile Turkish Commander.

Chadrevan Mosque Close by the Marine Gate, on Socratous St.

The Mosque of Murad Reis is described under Mandraki Harbour.

Son et Lumiere (*Tmr* 62E4) The performances take place in a municipal garden, edged on two sides by sections of the original City wall. They commence at 2015hrs, take approximately one hour, entrance costs 350drs and tickets are available from the NTOG (*Tmr* 7D/E3/4) or at the gate. An English language version is performed every night, except Sunday, with Swedish, German, French and Greek versions on alternative evenings (sounds rather like an obliquely referred to Blue Movie, doesn't it?)

Theatre (*Tmr* 63F4) More exactly the Folk Theatre, situated on Odhos Andronicou in the Old Quarter. Performances last a couple of hours and entrance costs 1000drs. The evening of Greek folk dances and songs commences at 2115hrs every evening, except Saturdays.

There is also the National Theatre (*Tmr* 34C4) bordering the Esplanade, Eleftherias St.

POLICE
Port (*Tmr* 64C/D4) To the right (*Fsw*) of the Post Office.
Town (*Tmr* 64C/D4) In the same Municipal buildings as the Post Office.

POST OFFICE (*Tmr* 64C/D4) The main Post Office is a splendid affair reached by ascending the grand flight of steps of an Italianesque building. This edges Eleftherias St, at the far end of Mandraki Harbour. The rumour that the Scandinavians have a postal slot all of their own is just not true! This office stays open until 2000hrs weekday evenings.

There is another Post Office (*Tmr* F4) on Orfeus St, in the Old Quarter. Open weekdays between 0800-2000hrs as well as Saturday and Sunday between 0900-1800hrs.

SPORTS FACILITIES Possibly a wider choice than anywhere else in Greece, other than Athens. There is a Casino but does gambling count as a sport?

Boating Apply to the Nautical Club of Rhodes (NOR) (*Tmr* 1/C4) at 9 Kountouri-otou Sq (Tel 23287), close by the Elli Club.

Golf Not exactly Rhodes City but there is an 18 hole Golf Club (Tel 51255) at Afantou village, some 20½km out of town, next to the *Xenia Hotel*. A club house, changing rooms and hire of clubs.

Horse Riding 'Mikes Stables', inland from Kallithie village, approximately 15km from the City.

Swimming There is a pleasant outdoor swimming pool (*Tmr* 67D/E3) in the small park across the street from the *Hotel Thermai*, opposite which is an entrance. There is another entrance approximately across the way from the NTOG office (*Tmr* 7D/E3/4). The pool is surrounded by bars and restaurants but it costs 200drs to get in.

Tennis There are a number of tennis courts attached to various hotels, as well as a few public courts. The Rhodes Town Tennis Club (*Tmr* 68B/C3/4 – tel 25705), at 20 Vassileos Konstantinou, faces onto Elli Beach and is about 300m north of the Elli Club. The Tennis Club welcomes all non nationals who wish to play. The courts are open between 0900-2000hrs and fees are 1600drs for two players and 2000drs for four, per hour. Hire of a racquet costs 200drs and three balls 200drs. Players must wear tennis clothes and swimsuits are not allowed. There is a bar and cafe facing the beach road.

Water Sports All sorts. Apply to the Nautical Club of Rhodes (*See* **Boating**). Most of the popular island beaches offer wind surfing, water skiing and para-skiing.

TAXIS The main taxi rank (*Tmr* D/E4/5) is on Plateia Hristoforou (or Alexan-drias), the south side of the New Market (*Tmr* 5D/E4).

A large board indicated various example prices but these were crossed out some three years ago! Sample one-way fares include:-
Rhodes City to Lindos 2200drs, to the Airport 650drs, to the Valley of the Butterflies 1200drs, to Filerimos 800drs and to Kamiros 1500drs.

TELEPHONE NUMBERS & ADDRESSES

British Consulate, 17, 25th Martiou	Tel 27306
Bus Offices, RODA	Tel 24192/27462
KTEL	Tel 27706
City Tourist office (*Tmr* 6 E4)	Tel 24888
Hospital (*Tmr* 65D/E2/3), Erithrou Stavrou (sometimes listed as Helvetas St)	Tel 22222
NTOG (*Tmr* 7D/E3/4)	Tel 23255
Olympic Airways (*Tmr* 25 C/D3/4), 9 Ierou Lochou	Tel 24571/5
Police	Tel 27423
Taxis (*Tmr*T.D/E4/5)	Tel 27666/32452

TOILETS Rhodes possesses a profusion, indeed a plethora of public lavatories including several in the New Market; on Alexandrou Papagou, by the Bus terminus (*Tmr* 32E4); at the Olympic Airways office (*Tmr* 25C/D3/4); opposite the *Hotel Sydney* (*Tmr* 13F5); on Orfeos St, between the Grand Palace Gates and the Clock Tower; one on Acandia Beach as well as the facility alongside the Elli Club (*Tmr* 3C4).

TRAVEL AGENTS & TOUR OFFICES There are a number of firms located on Odhos N. Plastira and Amerikis St, in addition to those listed under **Ferry-boat Ticket Offices, A To Z.**

EXCURSIONS TO RHODES CITY SURROUNDS

Excursion to Monte Smith (1½km) A small anomaly is the persistence of the Greeks in keeping this name for the hill, previously or also known as Mt Ag Stephanos. The English seeming name is due to the fact that one Sydney Smith, an English Admiral, used the prominence as a lookout, during 1802, whilst on the watch for Napoleon's fleet.

The area, rich in archaeological remains, is best approached via Vass Friderikis, taking the right-hand fork into Ag Ioannou then turning right along Odhos Diagoridon. To the left of Diagoridon St is the heavily restored Theatre, which is alongside and almost on the same plane as the Stadium, both set in a grove of olive trees. Above the Theatre, which was possibly a School of Rhetoric, and on a terrace reached up a large flight of steps, is the Temple of Pythios Apollo, marked by three restored columns. Above the Temple, the summit of Monte Smith, site of an ancient Acropolis, gives magnificent views, especially at dusk when the setting sun makes a resplendent sight as it dips dramatically beneath the far horizon.

From the crown (120m) of the hilltop in a northerly direction, and turning east along Odhos Voriou Ipirou, leads past scattered remains, including a few discs of once huge pillars, lying around the Temple of Athena Polias.

Bus No. 5 saves the walk.

Excursion to Rodini Park (3km) A No. 3 City Bus and most east side buses take the Asgourou village road out of Rhodes City past the Park. Rodini was formally laid out by the Italians on an ancient site which included the remains of a Roman aqueduct. Another pretender to the mantle of being the location of the legendary Rhodes School of Rhetoric, the wooded park is criss-crossed with streams, shallow canals, paths, rustic bridges and laced with grottoes and ponds, all set in richly planted grounds. Naturally enough (!) there is a restaurant as well as a night club.

Some 15 minutes walk further on, in a south-west direction, is a burial place, the Tomb of the Ptolemies. This is probably a misnomer as Ptolemy and his progeny were Kings of Egypt. The tomb is of the Hellenistic era with columns carved into the rock.

Excursion to Thermei Kallithea (via the coast road, 10km) It is easiest to take the coast road and not the main east island route. The Old Quarter wall should be followed along Vass Friderikis, or Dimocratias (whichever you prefer, they are the same road), around past the Police Training College, beyond St Athanasius Gate to the junction by St Francis Catholic Church and a derelict petrol station. Turn right along Stefanou Casouli St to where the road divides around a traffic drum or small, circular waist-high roundabout. The right fork heads towards the main east road and the left fork to the coast road, which rejoins the main road at Faliraki. Take the coast road.

AG MARINA (4.½km from Rhodes City) The first tourist spot on the east coast, developed, one feels, to take advantage of the overcrowding in some of the islands more congested holiday resorts. The not-so-smart seaside expansion, almost part of the 'downtown' Rhodes City, East End sprawl, has a slightly tatty milieu. The beach is agreeably sandy, with a 1930s lido building, showers and sun umbrellas.

Between Rhodes City and the Koskinou junction are occasional clumps or outbreaks of gigantic hotel complexes set in not very prepossessing countryside.

THERMEI KALLITHEA The final approach is via a pleasantly well-spread out park, planted with groves of trees terminating in a gravel car park. This is above the spa and a bay with a sandy area dotted with sun umbrellas and separated by rocks from the sea. The North African appearance of the buildings is a result of a whim of the Italians who built the complex, in the 1920s, as a health resort and watering place. The *raison d'etre* lost all relevance once they had departed – 'Built by the Italians, allowed to decay by the Greeks'! The neglect is more noticeable in the surrounding parkland where there are scattered about unused, probably unusable, empty, circular bathing pools.

Steps lead down through formally laid out gardens to a very narrow, pebbly beach complete with a quay mounted shower and sun-beds. Flippers and face masks can be hired from an expatriate American couple who work out of a small shop tucked into one of the buildings. There are also motor boats for rent.

The site is listed in some guide books as being quiet and unpeopled but trip boats and the ubiquitous scooter have changed all that!

Excursion to Petaloudes – the Valley of the Butterflies (25km) Depending on where you are located in Rhodes City, the main, west

coast road can be reached by proceeding along Vas Konstantinou to emerge on Akti Miaouli, towards the northern City; by taking 25th Martiou across Plateia Akadimias (Vas Georgiou) to 28 Octovriou or by heading up Alexandrou Papagou through to Alexandrou Diakou, both of which spill out on to the coast road, lower down on Akti Kanari.

The first part of the road edges a continuation of the Rhodes headland beach but the narrow foreshore is pebbly sand (with a preponderance of pebbles) and row upon row of regimented sun-beds and beach umbrellas. The inland side of the road is a polite, seaside ribbon development mix of tree lined, low-rise, smart hotels, hotels and more hotels – well there is the occasional restaurant and souvenir shop.

KRITIKA (3km from Rhodes City) A straggling, rather sad and pathetic strip of turn-of-the-century, look-alike housing now apparently being uprooted by the bulldozer. Possibly, this now untidy development is in the way of the inevitable march of the hotel. The village was settled by Turkish refugees from Crete, after cessation there in 1898.

From Kritika the quality of the countryside improves even if it is only at the expense of hotel development, commencing with the *Hotel Sirene Beach*.

FANEROMENI (4km from Rhodes City) The site of a small monastery. The road off to the left, towards the interior, bends round via Kandilion village to Monte Smith. Incidentally, the inland surrounds of Rhodes City tend to be littered with small, shanty holdings.

Through Ixia, the coast road approaches:-

TRIANTA (8km from Rhodes City) Almost a town, the settlement has been the subject of some fairly massive hotel construction, but the frontage is attractive with small public gardens edging the beach. This does at least help offset such internationalism as *The Pink Panther Club*, Chinese restaurants and *ad nauseam*. The Church, dedicated to the Assumption of the Holy Mary, has a splendidly carved, 18th century screen.

Alongside the centrally located petrol station there is a turning left to:-

FILERIMOS (13km from Rhodes City) The site of the ancient City State of Ialysos, one of the sponsors, with Kamiros and Lindos, of Rhodes City. The inexorable expansion of the latter ironically reduced Ialysos, once again, to a village by the end of the first century BC. The settlement was positioned on the irregular rectangular flat surface at the top of the thickly wooded hillsides of Mt Filerimos, some 276 metres above sea-level.

The road ends in a car park. The site is open daily between 0800-1900hrs except Sunday when the gates open between 0800-1800hrs. Entrance costs 200drs.

To the left, behind a wall with iron gates as an entrance, is the:-

Church of Our Lady of Filerimos Originally a Knights Church but the subject of much 'putting up and knocking down'. The Knights built it (or at least restored the building), the Turks used it as stables (what did they not?) only for the Italians and Germans to indiscriminately 'rubble' the site. This was during a trifling disagreement between the two countries' soldiers, after Mussolini was forcibly retired. The Church was once again rebuilt, after the Second World War.

In front of the Church, that is between the latter and the car park, lie the remains of:-

The Temple of Athena Poliados & Zeus Polieas Not a lot left apart from a few bits of the original columns. This construction was laid over an earlier, probably Phoenician temple of which there are even less remains, at the top end of the Athena Temple.

In front of the temple site is the:-

Chapel of Ag Georgios A very small, underground Byzantine Church with restored, wall-to-wall 15th century frescoes and a part exposed, earlier Christian cross.

Behind the Church are the cloisters of the:-

Monastery Another substantially restored building. Beyond the cloisters the way leads to a very fine view.

Back at the car park, to the left, from the steps, proceeds to a Doric fountain, on the one hand, and a public lavatory, on the other.

The Doric Fountain Exposed by a landslide, the Italians (inevitably) restored part of this 4th century BC structure.

Straight ahead of the Church of our Lady of Filerimos, steps climb to the Italian inspired Stations of the Cross.

The strategic desirability of the summit and the splendid range and field of vision did not escape the eyes of various commanders through the ages including, reputably, the Genoese, when removing the Byzantines, the Knights when removing the Genoese and Suleiman the Magnificent when removing the Knights – *c'est la vie*.

Back at Trianta the main road continues on to:-

KREMASTI (11km from Rhodes City) Rather overshadowed by the creation of an enormous mausoleum, all right a church, surrounded by acres of marble paving. The village school building is also a curiosity as the costs were met by citizens of Kremasti who had emigrated to North America and decreed that the architectural style should be American neo-colonial....! Well I suppose every expatriate to his own.

A junction heads off past the old civilian airport, which is now a military field, to:-

MARITSA (16km from Rhodes City) A large, pleasant village spread up the hillside and off the tourist beaten track, unless of course the 'little darlings' divert a 'Safari hire car trek' here! A summer-dry river-bed courses the length of the village and the local youth have a disco – maybe I am wrong about being off the holiday-makers ambit! It should be possible, according to most of the island maps, to proceed from Maritsa to Kalamon on the road to Petaloudes but the vivid imagination of the cartographer (referred to in Chapter Five) and the presence of the military have made this particular route a non-starter.

Back on the main coastal road many map makers indulge in perpetuating a myth, as most maps show the Airport as being beyond or alongside the village of Paradissi (Paradision). In actuality the Airport entrance is about 1km prior to the village.

PARADISSI (Paradision – 15km from Rhodes City) Hardly a paradise now, with the extensive airfield intruding, but the village is actually named after a nearby mountain. The road narrows down through this pretty, agricultural settlement but the runway has devoured much of the land that the villagers used to farm.

Some 3km beyond Paradissi, a side road climbs gently, via olive-groves, to Kalamon (5km) and then, after passing a substantial military camp, on to:-

THE PETALOUDES (The Valley of the Butterflies – 25km from Rhodes City) It is common to develop a preconceived idea about how a particular landscape or place will look and this much overworked tourist attraction was a specific instance. I imagined the valley to be wide and spacious with granite rocks dotted about a sparsely vegetated ravine. In actuality the site is an extensively foliaged, steeply climbing, narrow defile down which a stream tumbles in a series of rock pools and waterfalls, very reminiscent of a less savage Black Falls in North Wales. The walk is up a pathway which criss-crosses the stream and pools via rustic bridges and rock steps. The butterflies are dark brown and cream when their wings are folded and red, black, brown and white when in flight. They are difficult to spot whilst at rest but a sharp sound sends clouds of butterflies into the air in a darting, dipping, tumbling flight. Mind you, a very loud, sudden bang would probably send thousands of the tourists, that wend and wind their way up and down the valley, into an aerial display of sorts.

The season for the butterflies, which are not indigenous to the island, is between June and September and it appears these natives of Turkey are attracted by the resinous trees. The valley is open daily between 0900-1800hrs and entrance costs 100drs.

The maps almost all detail a road to Psinthos but.....

Excursion to Psinthsos (30km) Psinthos is best reached from the
east coast road, via Afantou. A spread out, agricultural village with a very large, open square, around which are dotted the mandatory tavernas, the owners of which indulge in some 'schlepping'. Psinthos was the location where the invading Italians finally routed the Turks, in 1912.

ROUTE ONE
To Kattavia via Lindos (91km)
The route involves taking the east coast road, the first part of which, as far as and including Thermei Kallithea, is described under **Excursions to Rhodes City Surrounds**.

FALIRAKI BEACH (15½km from Rhodes City) From Thermei Kallithea the road skirts a long, gently curving, fine shingle and very sandy beach with a number of massive hotel complexes, which include the *Esperides Beach, Blue Sea* and *Rodos Beach*. These are flanked by clear beach either side and all the necessary paraphernalia including sun-beds, sun umbrellas and beach showers. Approaching the far end of the crescent of the bay, the development slides into less international, more 'typically' Greek, a traditional' mix of small hotels, villas and shopping precincts. A number of the villas rented out by various English holiday companies, amongst others, are on the wrong side of the very busy main road. I'm sure no one told the prospective clients! A second, reasonably priced campsite was opened in 1987, *Faliraki Camping* (Tel 85358). The per person charge is 150drs a day, with a tent charged at 300drs.

Another 2km or so along the coast road and a side turning shambles down to:-

CAPE LADIKO (23km from Rhodes City) My notes record that it is rewarding to take the track, which soon becomes unmetalled, where turn left. After a short drive the new, smart *Hotel Ladiko* tops the crest, from whence are revealed views of a small, nearly circular bay set in rocky surrounds at the bottom of a steep slope. The sand is lovely, the water clear, added to which there is a beach shower, beach umbrellas and the *Restaurant Ladiko*. The prices here are reasonable (for Rhodes that is) with a Nes meh ghala costing 58drs, a large Henninger beer 105drs, a plate of macaroni 214drs and a Greek salad 180drs.

A side road off to the left can be negotiated to rejoin the main road where, on the right, is the *Pension Sofi*, almost immediately after which is a turning down to the north end of Afantou Beach. The *Pension Despina* is to the right after which the roadway, for a short distance, becomes a very modern stretch of dual carriageway with a flyover. On the approach to all this gimickery is the *Xenia Hotel* and an 18 hole golf course. Turnings to the right lead to:-

AFANTOU (20km from Rhodes City) Unexceptional, apricots and carpets being at the top of the list of money earners. There are **Rooms**, a petrol station, a travel agent and Post Office. Also on the right, beyond Afantou, is a hillock with the Stations of the Cross winding up a steeply inclined, tarmacadam drive.

To the left of the main road, another 2km advances to the very long, pebbly sand of:-

AFANTOU BEACH (22km from Rhodes City) In recent years some sunbeds and umbrellas as well as a snackbar and beach showers have appeared. The beach is edged by a long, straight, narrow road and at the junction with the access track there is a camouflaged Army lookout post. The inland side of the road is signed as being mined and towards the south end are signs warning those wearing pacemakers to beware due to the presence of possibly damaging radio waves. The road comes to an abrupt dead-end up against the gates of a large radio station and transmitter – *The Voice of America*.

There are some **Rooms** beside the main road, which now passes over a large river-bed. The surrounding countryside has sprouted some plastic green-houses, in addition to the olive groves, all set in low lying land with numerous ceramic factories and warehouses dotted about – that old Spanish ambience.

Prior to reaching Kolympia (Kolibia) there is a right-hand turning towards the interior, which road is probably one of the most beautiful I have passed along. It proceeds through groves of firs and pomegranates followed by a lush, green pine forest without a dwelling, let alone a taverna, in sight. On the way to Archipolis, a lane sheers off to:-

EPTA PIGAI (Seven Springs – 30km from Rhodes City) Well not directly, as it is necessary to turn left again. This advances to a meeting of the waters, as it were, with a man-made lake (Italian actually) fed by seven streams, in addition to a waterfall and the mandatory restaurant. Some of the tables are supported on flat topped rocks in and alongside the water, all set in prolifically wooded countryside. To reach the bright green lake surrounded by heavy foliage, rather similar to a jungle lagoon, it is necessary to walk through a long, narrow, stream running tunnel – an odd and quite exciting sensation. It is safe to swim in the lake but not advisable to get to close to the wall of the dam.

Further along the Archipolis road, still in the lovely, green landscape, is a church set up on the left-hand side. To the front of this is a water fountain, with three sprouts, shaded by a large, hollow plane tree.

The next village is:-

ARCHIPOLIS (34km from Rhodes City) Prior to reaching this unexceptional village, a road to the right heads off towards Psinthos, initially winding through very attractive pine tree clad scenery, which gives way to olive groves.

Straight on, or west from Archipolis leads to Eleousa and other villages on the mountainsides of Mt Profitis Ilias, which are described under **Route Two**.

KOLYMPIA (Kolibia – 26km from Rhodes City) The main road, a wide stretch of highway, rushes past an Italian built series of accommodation blocks, alongside which is a side road to the coast. This turning dodges round the old people's home (for that is what the accommodation buildings are), after which it is an arrow straight, tree lined, majestic, three kilometre avenue. On either side of this road are dotted the occasional 1920s Italian forerunner of a Wimpy home, a standard design villa with external ovens and a number of columns supporting the first floor terrace.

Another unusual feature is the precast, water full, mini irrigation aqueducts which line the length of the road. They are still fed from a waterfall the other side of the main road. This source of irrigation is tied in with the system at Epta Pigai and installed by the Italians to update the agriculture of the area. There are four or five nice looking *Pensions* either side of the avenue down to the coast, where the road divides around the headland of Cape Vagia. There are also two Rent A Moped firms. This area is now being developed and mega hotels are planned for the near future. For instance where the tree lined avenue ends, a huge hotel is being built to the left (*Fsw*), between the road and the *Voice of America* transmitter. A smaller, new hotel is just to the right.

To the right, a track proceeds past a small, circular cove with a childrens' holiday camp in the foreground and table-like, sandstone rock edging the sea and the small sandy shore. Further on is another but much larger and more pleasant bay with fine shingle edging a sandy seashore, complete with beach umbrellas and a 'Surf Centre' operating from the beach. The far end is edged by a towering, rocky promontory. At the approach to the bay, a low, tawdry taverna sprawls over a small, tree shaded hillock. There are outside toilets and old, domed bread ovens to one side of the main building, the latter still being pressed into service. I suppose it would be indelicate to indicate that the toilets were being pressed into service!

To the left of the Cape Vagia headland, the path meanders down to a small caique pier and repair yard flanked by a taverna and, to the left (*Fsw*), a slab rock seashore edged by a small, narrow, fine shingle beach (some sand). A mimosa, some tamarisk trees and a few beach umbrellas edge the clean beach with, in the distance, the radio station end of Afantou Beach. This sea-shore collection of dwellings is possibly on the 'Evening Out.... Traditional Fishing Hamlet' coach party schedule. Certainly a canvas covered patio opposite the taverna is lined with a seemingly disproportionate number of chairs and tables – at the ready as it were.

Back on the main road, and proceeding towards Arhanglos, after about 3km a left turn leads down to:-

TSAMBIKA BEACH (31km from Rhodes City) The 2km access road is now newly paved and descends steeply to a very large, scrub clad plain which backs a long and beautifully sandy beach. There is, as there often is under 'Murphys' well-known law, a snag. This is that despite the average travel guides assurance that the location is 'uncrowded' or 'relatively unfrequented', don't believe it. The scheduled bus service is supplemented by coach tours, trip boats as well as swarms of scooters, motor bikes and hire cars. Further-more the gentle serenity of the spot is 'supported' by rafts, pedaloes, para-scending, 'personal speedboats' for hire, beach umbrellas and sun-beds. The necessities of the inner man are catered for by two *Cantinas* (actually old caravans) to the right (*Fsw*), with a generator buzzing away in the background, and a beach taverna to the left. The taverna has a shower point on the edge of its patio.

This extremely popular, large bay is edged by cliffs with the sand blown high up the almost vertical rock face. Cars and motorbikes are ranked to one side of the sign-bestrewn rock sited at the bottom of the access road. Did I hear beach warden?

As an act of nature it is lovely but....

Tsambika Monastery (31km from Rhodes City) A turning off the Tsambika Beach road takes the intrepid traveller to this white, Byzantine monastery. It is surrounded by stone walls and, being set close by the mountain top, there are splendid views. The Monastery is the site for a religious ceremony, or fertility rite, and on September 8th women wishing to conceive children climb the steep approach on foot and pray that they may give birth.

Three kilometres further along the main road to Arhangelos and a signpost indicates the route down to:-

STEGENA (35km from Rhodes City) A long, wide, paved road descends to this delightful village, set on the near side of a pretty bay. Most travellers are on the look-out for a 'find', a discovery which so often promises but usually eludes. Well, Stegena is one of these spots, rare on an island as heavily exploited as Rhodes. But there are a few beach umbrellas as well as some wind surf boards for hire and a trip boat makes the excursion, so hurry!

Incidentally, on the way down do not take the old road (which is not very clearly signed as being closed), that is unless you are capable of clearing two 10m landslides. The straggling village, made up of adobe style buildings, lines the sea-shore but is mainly bunched at the start of the cove. There is a taverna, a brand new but small block of four apartments for rent and a group of single storey dwellings. The latter are mainly fishermen's shacks, occupied when the fish run, and are followed by moorings for dinghies and outboard engined craft in the mouth of a small river. Beyond this are two more tavernas, side by side, edging the roadway which borders a fine shingle, sandy foreshore. The sand gives way to a small, smooth pebble sea-bed. The track is lined by cultivated land, vegetation and trees, including olives and oranges, and some gardens fringing the beach. A large, irregular, rocky protrusion divides the bay, at the far right-hand end of which is a caique cove. A small, unpretentious restaurant, some *Rooms* to let and beach showers all help to complete this very pleasant location.

Returning from Stegena, it is possible to follow a mosquito infested, swamp of a river-bed all the way to:-

ARHANGELOS (33km from Rhodes City) This very large, sprawling village, which I regard as particularly unlovely, has an 'Old Quarter,' is set in fertile land and is famed for its distinctive leather boots. The winter 'fresh' or flood runs strongly and the river-bed and bridge are substantially constructed. Accommodation includes the modern *Hotel Fivos* and E class *Hotel Archangelos*. Petrol is available. Above the settlement lurks a 15th century Fort, built on the instructions of Knight Grand Master Orsini.

There is a choice of roads from Arhangelos, as the New Road sweetly curves almost parallel to the coastline whilst the Old Road twists and turns through verdant fields, thickly planted with fruit-laden trees and cypresses, all the way to the village of:-

MALONA (39km from Rhodes City) Immediately prior to the village, a left-hand turning crosses the New Road to:-

HARAKI (43km from Rhodes City) A small, comparatively quiet, lovely seaside village with a slender, clean, curving, almost circular pebble beach off to the north side of the headland, against which are tucked some caique moorings. The tree lined Esplanade sweeps round to a sandy, shingly beach to the far left. *Rooms*, beach bungalows and a few tavernas.

Back at Malona the road leads on to:-

MASSARI (41km from Rhodes City) From this village another side road curves down across the New Road and then, by an unmade track, not to a village but a long, gently curving bay edged by the pebbly sand sea-shore of:-

HARAKI BEACH This is overlooked, on the left, by the ruined Castle of Feraclos which is set on a low promontory, the south side of the headland. The fort, used by the Knights as a jailhouse for prisoners of war and their own miscreants, was one of the last castles to fall to the invading Turks. The track emerges on to the beach alongside the almost obligatory, tree shaded, Army camp. The crystal clear sea more than makes up for the pebbly beach.

The Old and New roads merge after the New Highway has crossed a dry, very broad river-bed, which is subject to continual excavation for building materials. Where the roadway has been embanked it cuts across an old, possibly wartime runway that almost spills into the sea.

KALATHOS (50km from Rhodes City) A one-eyed village, sited to the right of the main road, with a surprisingly large hotel, *The Mouratis,* and not one, but two petrol stations.

Some 1½km further on the road forks. To the right proceeds to Lardos and Kattavia and to the left to Lindos. Prior to this a side lane drops down to the splendidly sited *Lindos Beach Hotel*, which towers over a small cove, nestling in a crook of the headland that contains the legendary:-

LINDOS (56km from Rhodes City) (Tel prefix 0244) Although a
breathtakingly beautiful sight from where the road crests the rise and Lindos and its Acropolis comes into view, I feel sure that the overwhelming and unavoidable pre-publicity results in a rather anti-climatic feeling. Certainly, even if the visitor is entranced, the natives will surely ensure that the initial delight is dashed. Many of the inhabitants have become very worldly-wise and bored with the whole money-making treadmill on which the holiday industry has forced the Lindiots. Oh dear me.

The steeply descending road spews out on to the tree shaded, small, almost circular Main Square, Plateia Eleftherias. Only mopeds and taxis can park here, cars having to proceed to a car park above the square or down to the beach. There is a small tourist office edging the Square. An acute left-hand turn plummets down past two discos to Grand Harbour Bay and the fairly small, sandy, crowded beach. The crowding is due to both humans and beach umbrellas.

The old village is entered from the far side of the Square, whence the visitor is absorbed into what appears to be one huge maze of a bazaar. The tiny alleys are too narrow for mechanised traffic, only the clip-clop of donkeys' hooves breaking through the ceaseless babble of human voices. Around the periphery of the village, off the well signposted 'beaten track' to the steps climbing towards the Acropolis, are some winding streets still devoid of commercialism, with hardly a bar or taverna in sight.

Lindos retained its Italian connection, remaining a superior holiday location for many years. John Ebdon in his immensely amusing book *Ebdons Odyssey** relates the distinctly apocryphal story of how, in the recent past, when the wind was in the right direction, the clinking of cocktail glasses could be heard, at the appropriate hour, as far away as Rhodes City. Would that he could see the place now! The cocktail glass has been nudged aside by more egalitarian pursuits and the 'smart set' have ghosted away in the face of the overwhelming tide of popular package holiday clients. Oh well, that's progress isn't it?

The Villa companies have taken over most of the old houses and their plaques proudly declare the official villa name. Traditional food shops and stalls have almost all been displaced by a welter of cocktail bars, fast food establishments, 'pubs' and tourist shops.

On the bright side, one of the distinctive qualities of Lindos has been its ability to survive for so many years, in fact thousands of years. It is referred to in Dorian times, that is prior to 1000 BC, but a one time population of some 17,000 has now dropped to approximately 700 inhabitants. Goodness only knows what the summer-time number reaches.

**Published by Peter Davies Ltd. London.*

THE ACCOMMODATION & EATING OUT
The Accommodation Not a lot, most suitable locations having been block-booked by the holiday companies. That which is available is very

expensive and usually full. Departure, or possible only the death of an incumbent will free a bed! The Eleftherias Square Tourist office will help locate a room.

An important factor for villa holidaymakers to bear in mind is the location of their villa vis-a-vis the donkey route from the Main Square to the Acropolis. The donkey droppings on this well-worn path result in an above normal number of mosquitoes in the vicinity. You have been warned.

A number of visitors sleep on the beach every night.

The Eating Out The only inexpensive offerings are the souvlaki stands. Service, if that is the correct descriptive word for the ministration, generally borders on the brusque and rude. Restaurants range from the expensive to the extremely costly. One particular Lindos 'eating hole' achieved the first *GROC's Candid Guide Award of the Overflowing Rubbish Bin* for serving tinned peas.

THE A TO Z OF USEFUL INFORMATION

BANKS The National Bank is close to the Main Square, off Acropolis St – what is not? Opens Monday to Thursday 0900-1400hrs; Friday 0900-1330hrs and Saturday 0900-1330hrs.

BEACHES Obviously the Grand Harbour as well as the much smaller St Pauls Bay, of which more later.

BICYCLE, SCOOTER & CAR HIRE Lindos Rental is as expensive as elsewhere on the island. The sign for **Pefkos Rent A Car**, at No 247, assures potential clients that they are *A Trusted Friend!*

BREAD SHOPS Yes, next door to the National Bank.

BUSES The Main Square doubles up as the bus terminal.

Bus timetable
Lindos to Rhodes City
Daily   0700, 0730, 0945, 1030, 1130, 1300, 1430, 1500, 1630, 1800hrs.
One-way fare: 300drs.

FERRY-BOATS & FLYING DOLPHINS *See* **Ferry-boats &...., A To Z, Rhodes City**
A scheduled excursion boat departs from Grand Harbour Bay daily at 1430hrs for Rhodes City. One-way fare 1000drs.

LAUNDERETTE Yes, at No. 456, but closes on Sunday. A wash costs some 600drs.

MEDICAL CARE
Chemists & Pharmacies Yes.
Clinic (Tel 31224). To the left of Acropolis St, down the hill opposite the donkey park.

OTE No. 156, behind *Alexis Bar*, on Acropolis St. Open Monday to Friday between 0730-1510hrs.

PLACES OF INTEREST
The Acropolis A splendid situation but around which the Knights plonked down castle walls over and around earlier Byzantine fortifications. Once again the enthusiastic laudation and favourable comparisons with Delphi, that precedes a visit to the site, may well result in some disappointment.

It is possible to travel on a donkey for which it costs 300drs to ascend and 250drs to descend! Even if I had a secret wish to partake of this rather demeaning means of travel, I am probably too heavy for the unfortunate animals. The steep ascent on foot is by narrow, zig-zagging flights of steps, along the route of which are scattered Lindiot women with their weaving and crochet work spread out for sale over convenient rocks.

Once on the flat area edged by cypress trees, immediately beneath the walls of the medieval fortress are some Byzantine cisterns. Then, swinging round almost in a semi-circle, the rock wall on the left reveals the relief of part of a trireme or 2nd century BC warship. Unless I am very much mistaken this is very similar to the one carved into the rock beside the quay road of Simi Town Harbour.

Entrance costs 400drs and the site opens daily at 0800hrs closing at 1730hrs, except Sundays when the gates close at 1630hrs. The ability of the Greeks to employ two people (where one would do) to effect the issue and acceptance of admission tickets is nowhere better illustrated than here. The ticket man sits in his hut whilst the ticket collector lolls on a stool, alongside.

After the climb to the walls the entrance way is through a dungeon, no, no a 'vaulted hall' – the more usual descriptive phrase. Whatever, this vaulted hall resembles a Second World War pill-box and thus should possess that distinctive, dank, animal smell but, surprisingly, does not. The area is a muddle of 4th century BC Acropolis, a 13th century Byzantine church and the surrounding medieval castle walls. It should be no surprise that the site was reconstructed by the once, ever present and energetic Italian archaeologists and, even now, is undergoing even more renovation.

From the aforementioned vaulted hall, beneath the Fort Commanders' rooms, the remains of the Church are on the left. This is followed by a stairway to and through an entrance gate (propylaea) towards the forecourt of the Temple and on to the Temple of Athene Lindia, which dramatically terminates at the perimeter wall edging the cliff which overlooks both the:-

Ancient Theatre Not a lot left, apart from some of the seating and gangways, and:-

St Pauls Bay A small, almost circular bay surrounded by bare rock. This is supposedly the spot where a bolt of lightning and a clap of thunder caused the rock to split asunder. This caused a lagoon to become a harbour, thus enabling a storm tossed boat, in danger of capsizing and bearing St Paul, to reach safety. Well, well! His unexpected arrival in AD 51 is not unnaturally considered to be when Christianity reached the island and has given rise to the annual festival of St Paul on the 28th and 29th June.

Lindos Churches These include the Church of the Assumption of the Madonna (St Mary, Panaghia), sited close to the middle of the main village and the junction of Acropolis and Apostolou Pavlou Sts. Possible older than the inscription of 1484-90, for these dates may refer to a period of rebuilding by the Knights. The external appearance, pure, simple Byzantine with the red tiled, domed, seven sided cupola offsetting the white walls, starkly contrasts with the dark gorgeousness of the interior, the excellent frescoes (originally painted in 1779, but restored in 1927), the wooden screen and the Byzantine icons.

Houses of Lindos Famous for the sheer number that have survived, relatively intact, to the modern day. Some, medieval in age, are notable for the uppermost 'Captains Rooms' which gave a clear view of the Harbour. The interiors of these houses are often distinctive, possessing decorated, lofty wooden ceilings and mosaic floors. Later houses of the 16th and 17th century sport an unusual family bed arrangement wherein this important household feature is raised on a platform, set under an arch, in the main room and reached up a low flight of steps. One other architectural hallmark worthy of note are the individually decorated doors and their accompanying hand knockers. They are so distinctive that there is available, at some of the village tourist shops, a poster illustrating many of the Lindiot doors and costing 250drs. Two other idiosyncracies are the ceiling suspended, angled mirrors (also seen on the island of Simi, as are some of the other features of Lindian houses) and the wall-hung decorated plates, some dating from the 16th century, which probably originated in Persia, but are now definitely of Rhodian manufacture.

Many of the villagers have thrown open their doors but now only to sell ceramics, plates, shawls and quilts.

Tomb of Kleoboulus A tentative connection to a 6th century BC tyrant leader of Lindos, who ruled for 40 years and was one of the Seven Sages of the ancient world. This circular tomb, made of large, cut square stones, is sited on the headland of the Grand Harbour, possibly dating from the 5th or 4th century BC and used as a church in medieval times.

A number of relics from Lindos now reside in Copenhagen Museum, as a result of excavations by the Danes in the early 1900s. Need one say any more?

POST OFFICE Close by the donkey marshalling yard on Acropolis St, close to the Main Square (again what is not?).

POLICE Further along Acropolis St than the Post Office.

TOILETS There is a reasonably clean public lavatory by the Main Square.

TRAVEL AGENTS & TOUR OFFICES Dozens and dozens of offices but the one to note is the:-

Tourist Office, Plateia Eleftherios (the Main Sq). The office opens daily between 0900-1300hrs and 1700-2000hrs.

From Lindos the road to Pefka passes St. Paul's Bay, crosses the brow of a hill and winds across a plain, edged by a glowering bay on one side and menacing cliffs on the other. Surely this must have been a Minoan settlement, an impression reinforced if Gournia (Crete) is recalled. The evening brings about that same brooding atmosphere of anticipation, of ancient overlay and ghostly presence. Whatever, over the rim of the hill edging the plain on the far side and into view hoves the burgeoning:-

PEFKA (58km from Rhodes City) The houses are widely spread out over a small but wide lowland, the low cliffs of which edge a splendid, gently curving bay. Pause to consider that there was only the beach here some eight years ago and that the rambling development now in evidence will no doubt infill, with a vengeance. Those few *Rooms* available and the *Pension* are pre-booked by holiday companies. There is a general shop and a kafeneion. The very sandy, narrow beach, has a sprinkling of beach umbrellas and a small *Cantina* against the cliff face. A number of sailing yachts lie at anchor at the far, east end of the bay.

Instead of forking off to Lindos, the main road passes through:-

PILON (Pilona) (53km from Rhodes City) It may well be worth considering giving Lindos the 'accommodation cold shoulder' to stay here, at the *Hotel Pylona* (Class

D - tel 44247). Double rooms, sharing the bathroom, cost from 1500drs and en suite from 1800drs. Breakfast is charged at 200drs. The hotel has a nice restaurant, added to which they operate a scooter hire business. There is another *Pension* and taverna in the village.

Beyond Pilon the main road now skirts:-

LARDOS (57km from Rhodes City) The village itself is unremarkable though it does host a hotel, a petrol station and the only other campsite on Rhodes, the:-

St George Tourist(Tel 0244 44203).The superb facilities include swimming pool, various sports courts and grounds, a bar, restaurant, shop, disco and TV lounge, to name but a few. There is a camp bus to Lardos village. Mind you the piper must be paid as one person and a tent cost a staggering 750drs per day and two people and a tent 1500drs.

Also in the vicinity are two pleasing spots. The one on the Pefka coast road, has beautiful sand set in a small circular bay, backed by shrub covered dunes, but some rubbish is present. The other is along the Old Road, which almost parallels the New Highway. Beyond the *Lardos Beach Apartments*, a long, fine pebble beach stretches as far as the *Lardos Beach Restaurant*, sited at the end of the bay, and complete with, not only thatched beach umbrellas but a car parking sign alongside the restaurant. Ugh!

Two side roads branch inland, the first to:-

Thari Monastery The turning proceeds initially to Laerma village, which has its own delightful church. Then taking the Laerma to Profilia route, after some 2km a track winds to the Monastery. This ancient building, dating from as long ago as the 9th century, is famous for its outstanding, high quality, 13th century frescoes,

and the second to:-

Ipseni Monastery At the far end of Lardos village, a 4km track leads to the Monastery, in front of which a hill is set out with the Stations of the Cross. The shaded grounds sport a welcome fountain.

The main road, now marked with double white lines, curves sharply around a small, hilly projection after which a most unsightly factory and concrete jetty hove into view. Although the works seem deserted there are the mandatory collection of apparently abandoned machinery, lorries and trucks. Soon after this blot on the landscape a splendid bay is passed on the left.

Keep to the Old Road skirting the coastline and a series of bays of varying length, some sheltered and secluded, some with fine shingle, some of rock which border the road until the route clatters into:-

'A SORT OF SEASIDE SHANTY TOWN' (66km from Rhodes City) No other description will do for this untidy, unnamed, ramshackle settlement of jerry-built chalets with a couple of tavernas and a small, signposted beach.

About ½km on sees the start of a very long, lovely, pebbly beach, almost without an umbrella in sight, which stretches out along the clear sea's edge for some 11km. The few beach umbrellas are in front of the beach tavernas in the area of:-

GENNADION (70km from Rhodes City) Opposite this unpretentious village a track runs down to the beach, to a section where the bottom shelves quite steeply and two tree shaded tavernas edge the foreshore. The right-hand one (*Fsw*) is possibly the better choice and may well hold a tasteful, midday exhibition of Greek dancing. The staff of the left-hand beach taverna are uninterested, the small portion dishes are often served in an incorrect order and the charges are apparently calculated on a different scale to that either ordered or served. This may, only may, be as a result of their being on the coach trip and caique circuit. There you go.

Incidentally, I consider Gennadion marks the eastern coast watershed, the Rhodian cultural dividing line whereover, and south of which, Greek island civilisation commences. The point at which this demarcation rives the west coast is Monolithos.

From here on it is probably best to take to the New Road, which is reasonably well metalled, that is apart from spaced out, irregular and infuriatingly small sections where the road surface has broken up, more especially beyond:-

HOHLAKAS (83km from Rhodes City) In the village, and from the main road, there are signposts indicating the surfaced road down to the small:-

PLIMMIRI BAY On the right is a beach of shingly sand and a pebble sea bottom. The tree shaded *Restaurant Plimmiri* (rather a fine, descriptive term for this shack) is the sole culinary establishment. Requests for a menu will probably result in a client being directed to the kitchen – full of Greek women cooking. To the left is a finger quay with a small caique bay beyond. Unfortunately the location is on the fun-loving, beach buggy 'Safari Run'.

From hereon the landscape is expansive and dished. Prior to reaching Kattavia the road rolls through the rather strange, almost deserted village of:-

AG PAVLOS (88km from Rhodes City) My notes ramble on about 'the spot not seeming to have a *raison d'etre*... scattered farm buildings, one of a monastic appearance and a large, 1930s(?), Italianesque agglomeration of buildings of religious aspect which border the roadside and are now partially filled with hay and farm equipment'.

A turning to the left peters out, after some 2km, into a track that shapes towards Cape Prassonissi, the southernmost point of the island, whereon a lighthouse.

Three kilometres on and the last village of the eastern route is attained, that is:-

KATTAVIA (91km from Rhodes City) The final approach to this sleepy, rural farming community is on an unmetalled slip road that judders into the irregular square at the heart of Kattavia. Reference again to my notes reveals 'Cows and petrol'.

From Kattavia the rough surfaced road to Mesanagros climbs up and on to the spine of the local hills, resulting in some splendid views.

ROUTE TWO
To Kattavia via Kamiros Skala & Monolithos (108km from Rhodes City) The west coast road to Paradissi is covered under Excursions to Rhodes City Surrounds.

At the turning off to Theologos (Tholos) there is a petrol station and 3km further on the main road passes through Soroni village and on to:-

FANES (26km from Rhodes City) At the far end of the village a right-hand track, signposted *Hotel Delfini – Fish Restaurant*, traipses across a windswept stretch of open coastline to a narrow, stony beach. Attractive in a slightly unkempt fashion with a four-head shower (yes a four-head shower, I've dreamt of a ...) and two concrete precast seats. The hotel to the left (*Fsw*) runs a wind surfing school, so there are lots of enthusiasts here.

Back at the village, some 4km along the Eleousa turning inland, a tree lined track trails off to the left past a clearing, complete with a quadruped circuit (yes a... Oh well, it doesn't matter, read on), to:-

Ag Soulas Church The purpose of the Church seems to be to host the annual feast and celebrations held on the 30th July. One of the unusual features of this event is a donkey derby. Reminds one of Watford, doesn't it?

. The Dimilia and Eleousa road is a 12km uphill climb but I have included this description in with that of the inland incursion to the Eleousa, Platania, Apollona and Nani circuit around Mt Profitis Ilias, from:-

KALAVARDA (30km from Rhodes City) The inland turning rises steeply, in a series of loops, to the large village of:-

SALAKOS (38km from Rhodes City) A pleasant, spread out village set around a large, irregular, tree shaded public square with a drinking water fountain, surrounded by cafes and tavernas.

The road soldiers on for some 5km through Kapion to a junction at which the left turning makes a northern loop around:-

Mt Profitis Ilias The 'experts' estimates regarding the height of this pine tree covered mountain vary between 650 and 900m, which if one is short of breath, could have an appreciable effect on a climber's enjoyment of the hike. There is a wooded path from Salakos village to the mountain top which crosses the road close by the *Hotel Elafina Mt* (Class A). The hotel is Swiss in style, set in thick trees into which the occasional goat clambers. Some deer are penned in large, wooded enclosures and there is a childrens' playground. Naturally splendid views.

The descending nine kilometres road is unpaved and rough in places, passing through heavily wooded countryside, in which, at about half-way, is a solitary chapel.

On the final approach to Eleousa is an inexplicably positioned, very large, pleasant, tempting looking spa-type pool with a stone 'funnel' in the middle. The waters host some fish and a couple of ducks. This is a very pleasant and secluded picnic spot prior to:-

ELEOUSA (59km from Rhodes City) An unusual village with a bewildering road layout and in the centre of which is a very large, 'Hacienda' type dwelling complete with an extensive palm tree planted courtyard. This is an Army camp. The confusion in respect of the road directions is how on earth to get out of the place, well more to get to where you really want to go, a desire not helped by two signs 'Eleousa', pointing in opposite directions!

Between Eleousa and Platania the hillsides are denuded of vegetation due to forest fires. On my last but one fact finding visit, the village of Archipolis experienced a serious conflagration. The resultant smoke almost blotted out the sky over most of the northern end of the island, the sun showing through as a diffused, red orb. The wind blown air smelt strongly of charred olive wood. From the Lindos Acropolis it was possible to watch the 'fire engine' aircraft skid on to the water of Kalathos Bay and, once laden with sea-water, rumble on to the fire, drop their load, only to loop back to pick up more sea water. This went on for some three days. Most absorbing.

PLATANIA A very pleasant, unspoilt village, after which the hillsides roll on to:-

APOLLONA A'so, so', not so nice and oh so average village which, for some inexplicable reason, is on the excursion coach circuit. Naturally there are lots of tavernas with signs in English. Which comes first, the coaches or the tavernas? Petrol is available, close by the junction with the road to Laerma.

Between this point and the junction with the main road back to Salakos, the countryside is gentle farmland until a fountain bowery marks a transition, once again, to pine clad hills.

Back at Kalavarda the main road 'grips' the coastline, close to sea-level, until adjacent to the archaeologists' delight of Kamiros. Proximity to the site is marked by three taverna/restaurants positioned on two small, pleasant, adjacent headlands. Trees grow down to the water's edge and there is a pleasant, sandy beach on which are set some beach umbrellas. Two of the tavernas are 'imaginatively' named respectively *Old Kamiros* and *New Kamiros*, beyond which a road, on the left, advances gently up a slope for 1km to:-

ANCIENT KAMIROS (34km from Rhodes City) Open daily between 0800-1900hrs and 0800-1800hrs on Sundays. Entrance costs 200drs. The excavations are hidden from view until a rise is breasted and the Ancient City is revealed to the left, lying in a large, shallow, saucer shaped depression set in the gentle hillside. The site, dating back in part to the 6th century BC, was discovered in 1860 and extensively excavated by the Italians around 1929. Surprisingly there is no evidence or sign of an Acropolis, or other fortifications, and history does not record any invasion. The overwhelming impression, at one or two locations on Rhodes island, of the original presence of the Minoans is lent credence by both legend and conjecture that the first inhabitants of Kamiros were from Crete. No concrete reason has been established for the final abandonment of the City, the remains of which include a very large, 6th century BC water cistern, a restored Stoa, that has unfortunately experienced a collapse, a Temple to Athena as well as drainage pipes and a main street off which radiate various remains, including a Doric temple.

Back in the 20th century, the coastal road, which has recently been resurfaced, is encroached upon by low, landward foothills which advance inexorably towards the sea's edge. In the area of Mandrikon, the coastal strip widens out in to a vaguely lunar, mucky plain. Another Cretan, but modern, influence flaps into view in the shape of some plastic greenhouses. Eminent archaeologists assure me they are not Minoan!

The road climbs around a bluff and drops down again to a large headland and inlet in which nestles the port of:-

KAMIROS SKALA (48km from Rhodes City) (Tel 0246) A fairly pretty location with three tavernas accommodating the tourist business. This is extensive for a number of reasons, more especially as the small fishing port is on the tourist excursion coach trip circuit – *See a Traditional Rhodes Fishing Village*. You will note I write accommodating, not competing, as the tavernas just snuggle there and the tourists swamp over them, resulting in even slower and more costly service than usual. The tavernas serve fish, fish and fish with fish to relieve and extend the menu alternatives!

The *Pension/Taverna* on the roadside has very nice, spacious, tidy double rooms sharing a clean bathroom and costing 1200drs per night.

The *Fish Taverna Arthemenis* (Tel 31303), just to the left of the track down to the shore, has accommodation. A meal here of one chop, a plate of kalamares, a Greek salad, tzatziki, a kortaki retsina and bread costs a rather pricey 1400drs.

Down on the left, close by the small mole and the commercial harbour, is a rather piratical looking taverna, patronised by the definitely piratical looking locals, which serves excellent but expensive fare.

Another reason for Kamiros Skala's busy activity is the 'Chalki connection, that is the:-

Ferry-boats This local service to Chalki is based on Chalki island so it is not possible to make a day trip.

Mid-season the boat departs at 1415hrs on Mondays and Thursdays returning about 0730hrs the following day, BUT this service is subject to variables, such as the weather. At the outset of the 1987 season, the one-way fare cost 500drs, which doubled by June, but after energetic complaints was reduced to 850drs by September. I should think so! *See* **Chalki island, Chapter 13** for further details of this connection.

Beyond Kamiros Skala, the road commences to climb steeply and wind inland whilst to the right Kamiros Castle hoves into view, way across a valley. If the detour is thought worthwhile the ruined fortress, once restored by the Knights, makes a splendid location for a view over the inshore islands that are dotted about off this sector of Rhodes island. They include Strongili, Makri, Tragoussia and Alimnia with Chalki in the distance. The journey skirts the west side of Mt Attaviros (1215m), amply covered with vegetation and trees almost to the summit, which is singularly bare, almost in the style of a monk's tonsure.

After Kritinia a left-hand turning takes an inland, circular route via Ebonas village, famed for lusty and strong women and from whence, with the aid of a guide, the summit of the mountain can be reached. This journey wanders round to the village of Agios Isidoros and back to the main road. In this region tobacco and grapes are agriculturally predominant.

Between Kritina and Sianna an unmetalled track, that plummets to the right, is grandly signposted:-

Glyfada Restaurant & Rooms The five kilometre dirt road loops steeply down through extensively pine forested hills to a small, remote settlement on the edge of the coast. There are two taverna/pensions, the remains of a lookout tower, a strip of large pebble sea-shore and a small caique quay.

The Glyfada Restaurant A taverna really, with rooms, set back some fifty metres from the foreshore, and run by Harry and his wife. Originally from Rhodes they spent most of their life in Australia and consequently have a very marked, Australian accented English.

Their hospitality is straightfoward, the rooms simple, and lit by oil lamps, the shower and lavatories basic and, despite the relative isolation, the company is good. You might be offered a 'special' ouzo about which Harry waxes lyrical, in flowery prose, singing the praises of the amber nectar... In reality I am fairly sure the potent brew is very similar to Cretan raki – a refined but powerful ouzo. On my last visit, when I mentioned that the shower did not work, Harry's wife showed me the alternative, a tap round the back with a piece of hosepipe attached. Simple but effective as long as you have a companion handy to aim the hose. The lack of hot water is a little annoying and the flush of the toilets reverberates throughout the building, especially in the middle of the night. Mind you, any sound is magnified as the walls of the rooms are paper thin. As Harry does not always turn on the generator, he lights paraffin pressure lamps at dusk which, due to the poor quality of the fuel, quite often give out small explosions and plumes of flames with the resultant danger of conflagration. In this connection he hands guests a torch to use during the night. The patio is shared with marauding cats and the bees or wasps that inhabit the vegetation that shelters the terrace.

The meals are, like everything else here, simple but wholesome. Many of the vegetables are freshly picked from the garden. A double room costs 800drs.

Harry is disposed to extol the virtues of the beach. His directions must be followed to the half-metre otherwise you may believe, as I do, that the sandy section he has found, in amongst the enormous pebbles, is yet another Greek myth.

The Paradissi Taverna The building is close by the shoreline and its name was probably why I was under the impression that the beach might be a golden stretch of warm, yielding sand!

For those who wish to escape the all-pervading tourist invasion of Rhodes this spot is a find.

The main road continues high above the now distant coastline through pine clad, Rio Grande type countryside on to the village of:-

SIANNA (75km from Rhodes City) A pretty, working village hanging on to the hillside with many kafeneions and a glorious view down along the distant Apolakkia Bay. The church clock, as elsewhere in the countryside, has painted hands. A number of guide books refer to a path from here to Cape Armenistis but the best way down to the headland is from beyond:-

MONOLITHOS (80km from Rhodes City) The existence of the village almost seems to be to signpost the upper road to Frourion. I did not and cannot quite understand this because I am not sure where Frourion is but the flinty track does lead to a large lay-by overlooking the startingly sited:-

Monolithos Castle (82km from Rhodes City) The fort nestles neatly on the top of a 250m high pillar of rock which rises needle-like out of the plain in the middle distance. There is a vast backcloth of incredibly blue sea in which is set the rocky headland of Armenistis and a small island off the Cape. A magic mix of Aegean Walt Disney seascape and a German Rhineland castle. Access to the Castle is gained by following the stony track down and round to below the far side of the rock on which it is perched. In the Castle confines is the small and unremarkable Chapel of Ag Pantaleonos.

Prior to reaching the viewpoint overlooking Monolithos Castle, a turning off to the right is signposted to Kimisala, Kirameni and Pyrgos but don't bother unless you enjoy bumping over extremely rugged, rocky paths that clatter down through sylvan clad hillsides. Close by Mt Armenistis are the vestiges of a long deserted village some way above the sea, on the edge of a small ravine.

Back at Monolithos village, the wide, mostly unmade and badly rutted roadway gently descends through groves of olives to:-

APOLAKKIA (91km from Rhodes City) The plastic littered approach to the village is generally rather messy with the final run-in over a summer-dry river-bed.

An agricultural settlement with few concessions to other than the locals' pursuits, and why not. But there is a periptero, the *Pension Manolis, Restaurant Manolis*, several tavernas and, a 100m down the unmetalled Kattavia track, the *Hotel Restaurant Skoutas* and *Pension Kosta*. There is also a petrol station but the owner may well require awakening or arousing and it is often necessary to request a local to assist.

On Sunday mornings, during the grape season, a back-of-truck market turns up in the form of an agricultural rotavator pulling a truck from the back of which is suspended a pair of scales.

A road traverses the island all the way to the east coast road at Gennadion (*See* **Route One**) whilst the west coast road turns back towards the coastline. After some 3km signposts indicate Furni, around a headland to the acute right, and Limni, but neither is more than a house or two. Additionally, a track wanders down to a long beach, which is made up of cleanish, large stones. There are sweet-water, if brackish pools close by the sea, and goat herds, rather incongruously, graze their sheep and goats right up to and across the foreshore.

The first stretch of the coast road is edged by rock dunes which are followed by sand dunes, scrub trees and ravines set in the wild countryside. There is some cultivation amongst the low, stumpy hills on the inland side.

After 7km a track to the left sallies forth to:-

Skiada Monastery (102km from Rhodes City) An interesting diversion. The Monastery, in the control of caretakers, is set in perfect island countryside, far from the madding crowds of tourist hordes (to only slightly misquote *Gray's Elegy*), and with magnificent sea views away in the distance. Accommodation, but not food, is sometimes available.

The main track starts to rise into more substantial hills on the last section of this route, curving away from the coastline and after some 9km reaches Kattavia (*See* **Route One**).

13 CHALKI (Chalkis, Khalkia, Khalki, Halki) ***

Dodecanese Islands

FIRST IMPRESSIONS
Arid; quiet; no *Room* signs; 'mass digging up', crumbling away and reconstruction; very, very saline (and cold) water.

SPECIALITIES
Away-from-it-all package tourists.

RELIGIOUS HOLIDAYS & FESTIVITIES
include: 2nd August – Festival Ag Ioannis.

VITAL STATISTICS
Tel prefix 0241. The island has an area of 28sqkm and a population of about 340 people.

HISTORY
Naturally followed the 'hemline' of nearby Rhodes. The Knights of St John built a Castle overlooking the old capital,The Chora.

GENERAL
Chalki may well be a slight disappointment, though it is a little difficult to pinpoint quite why. Given the rave reviews in some tour guides heralding its peace and seclusion, it is rather a shock to find that the island's few *Rooms* and pensions are occupied to capacity by away-from-it-all package tourists, who are very evident at the port's few quayside tavernas in the evenings.

The island is painfully barren, grey and brown, and the tap water so salty that it actually stings the eyes. One might as well go for a dip in the sea, as shower in some pensions.

But all is not lost as the number of tourists is still limited. I suppose it is not so surprising that those present are obvious, considering that the island's total population is under three hundred and fifty people, and most of them are gathered in Chalki's only settlement, Nimborio Port. Fishing is still a more extensive occupation than is the tourist industry, and for those searching for an away-from-it-all package holiday, Chalki must be a very good bet (as well as a more than welcome relief from the hordes on Rhodes). On the other hand, if I were on Rhodes, and contemplating a quieter alternative, I would probably head for Kastellorizo or Tilos, not Chalki.

One perspicacious reader commented that generally the desire to get rich has taken priority over service and friendliness!

NIMBORIO (Emborio, Skala): capital & port (Illustration 16).
The port is charming and very picturesque, but it is undergoing a major 'quarrying'. New pipes are being laid, old houses are frantically being renovated, in order to accommodate even more package holiday-makers, whilst a few ruined dwellings and derelict sites add to the general ambience of confused muddle, though this may be a temporary state of affairs.

The beach, some ten minutes walk away, is sandy but has sprouted beach

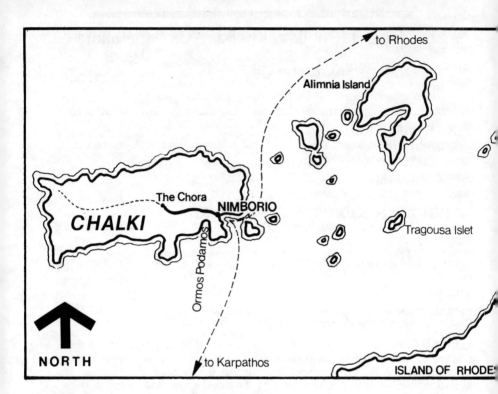

Illustration 15 Chalki island.

umbrellas, a surefire indicator of the presence of an overwhelming number of package tourists.

ARRIVAL BY FERRY

Only the smaller ferries (**FB Panormitis** and the **CF Nireas**)can dock at the centrally situated Ferry-boat Quay (*Tmr* 1C/D3) which, like everything else in the port, is undergoing reconstruction. For this reason, the **CF Golden Vergina** does not call as often as is scheduled. The Tourist office in Rhodes advises that this ferry-boat doe not call at all, whilst the Chalkians maintain it calls once a week! Perhaps matters will improve once the quay is finished? The Kamiros Skala (Rhodes) 'scheduled' caique berths alongside the same Quay (*Tmr* 2C3 & C4/5). Room owners rarely meet the boats, which should set the warning bells ringing!

THE ACCOMMODATION & EATING OUT

The Accommodation An extremely odd, nay, almost unique situation exists on Chalki in respect of the letting of *Rooms*. There is not one single sign advertising either Rooms or a Pension on the entire island. The reason, which soon becomes evident, is that virtually all the available space is taken up by two British package tour companies for the holiday season. So, although the island is relatively uncrowded, it can be difficult, even outside the peak months, to find accommodation. That which is available is overpriced. The already difficult situation is made even worse by the fact that the very large *Hotel Xenontas*, at the far, right-hand end of Emborio Bay (*Fsw*), is often filled with conference visitors and closed to tourists. There is not much left! Incidentally, none of the accommodation inspected displays the official room price card, not even the Pension adjacent to the Police station.

Rooms (*Tmr* 3B5/6)
Directions: To the left (*Sbo*) of the Ferry-boat Quay, in a street one back and parallel to the Esplanade.

Iraklides, the accommodating owner, sometimes wanders down to meet the boats. The house overlooks the bay. The bedrooms, which are fitted with sparse but modern furniture, are pleasant, if expensive at 2000drs for an en suite double room or 1500drs, sharing a bathroom, on the floor below. The two upstairs rooms open onto a balcony with a lovely view of the port. On the other hand they are only separated by an ill-fitting sliding door, so pray that the 'neighbours' are quiet and discreet, as every movement can be heard!

Still this house is a much better bet than the:-

Pension
Directions: A good five minutes walk round the bay in the direction of the *Hotel Xenontas*. Take the steps up from the Ferry-boat Quay, just to the right (*Sbo*) of the Toilet block (*Tmr* 16B/C6), and turn left (*Sbo*) following the path round the bay. Where the houses begin to thin out, a rocky area interspersed with trees is reached, and the path dips slightly to the left. The Pension is to the left of the path, overhanging the sea – a large white building with a grey corrugated metal roof at the back, and no sign.

It is rumoured that '...the owner is a bit of a rogue'. This 'nod' is confirmed when he requests 2000drs for a double room, sharing the bathroom in the basement. Exclamations of shock, horror and ridicule might succeed in reducing this rate by 200drs. The proximity of the adjacent Police station does not appear to cramp the patron's style.

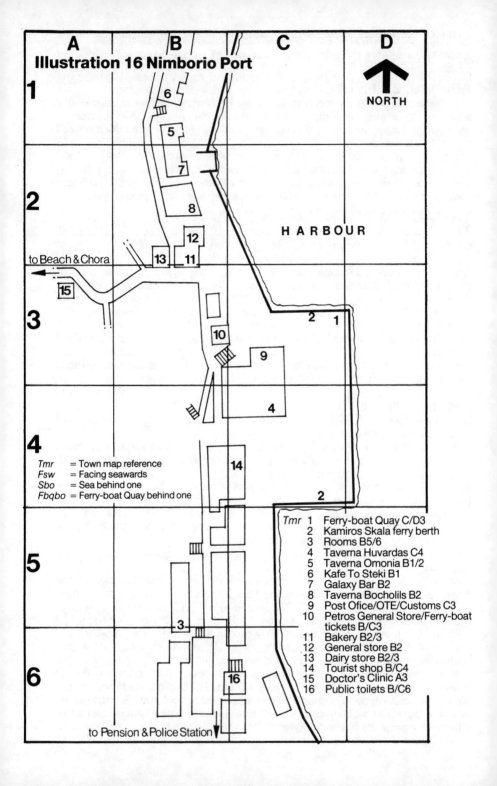

Illustration 16 Nimborio Port

NORTH

HARBOUR

to Beach & Chora

Tmr = Town map reference
Fsw = Facing seawards
Sbo = Sea behind one
Fbqbo = Ferry-boat Quay behind one

Tmr 1 Ferry-boat Quay C/D3
2 Kamiros Skala ferry berth
3 Rooms B5/6
4 Taverna Huvardas C4
5 Taverna Omonia B1/2
6 Kafe To Steki B1
7 Galaxy Bar B2
8 Taverna Bocholils B2
9 Post Ofice/OTE/Customs C3
10 Petros General Store/Ferry-boat tickets B/C3
11 Bakery B2/3
12 General store B2
13 Dairy store B2/3
14 Tourist shop B/C4
15 Doctor's Clinic A3
16 Public toilets B/C6

to Pension & Police Station

Pension Argyrenia
Directions: Take the Podamos Beach road and the *Argyrenia* is a newish, single storey building set out on three terraces behind the School.

There are no single rooms and a double room with modern bathroom and hot water shower are charged at 2000drs.

The Eating Out At least more plentiful than the Accommodation. The tavernas are spread along the waterfront Esplanade with their tables set out in front.

Taverna Huvardas (*Tmr* 4C4).
Directions: This very popular taverna is housed in the same block as the Post Office, right in front of the Ferry-boat Quay.

A good variety at reasonable prices though the chips may be undercooked and the bread taste as though it has been soaked in after shave! A meal for two of octopus (generous helpings), two plates of giant beans, chips, feta, two beers and (inedible) bread costs 1680drs. The resident waitress, a German girl speaking good English, is most pleasant. She is particularly helpful to ferry-boat arrivals looking for rooms, which, under the circumstances, is very considerate of her.

Taverna Omonia (*Tmr*) 5B1/2)
Directions: To the right (*Sbo*) of the Ferry-boat Quay, facing out over the Esplanade.

Less busy and less expensive than the *Huvardas*, added to which the owners are pleasant. A helping of green beans, feta, a beer and (edible) bread costs just 280drs. Proffered payment for an extra soft drink might well be waived aside.

Kafe To Steki (*Tmr* 6B1)
Directions: Further on round the Esplanade to the right (*Sbo*).

A very nice place around which the fisherman sit and mend their nets of a morning. A limon costs 45drs and the friendly owner also serves glasses of unsaline cold water!

Other 'offerings' include the *Taverna Bocholils* (*Tmr* 8B2) which has a slightly well-to-do air and serves lobster.

None of the tavernas appear to serve breakfast, which, considering the preponderance of tourists, is an odd omission.

Costas at the *Cafe/Pastry Shop*, close by the Church steps, remains reasonably priced, continues to give good service and keeps smiling.

THE A TO Z OF USEFUL INFORMATION
BANKS None, but the Post Office (*Tmr* 9C3) transacts foreign exchange, as does nearby Petros General Store (*Tmr* 10B/C3), of which more later. (*See* **Commercial Shopping Area, A To Z**).

BEACHES The Port has no beach so the sun and sand hedonists must make a ten minute walk. Take the main asphalt road (named Boulevard Tarpon Springs!) which leaves the Ferry-boat Quay from beside the Bakery (*Tmr* 11B2/3) and winds gently up the hillside. In 1987 this road was under 'reconstruction' and pedestrians had to pick their way through mounds of cement powder piled alongside a deep ditch into which pipes were being laid. Beyond these perils the road drops over the crest of the hill, past the corrugated metal, island generating station on the left, and down a painfully dry, grey and rocky slope to the fine grey sand of Podamos Beach. Horror of horrors, this narrow beach is lined with sun umbrellas and beds. It must become very crowded in high season as the beach is not very large.

Nikos Taverna, on the backshore, provides food (a souvlakia for 380drs and dolmades 200drs) but the promising looking *Rooms* are filled with package tourists all summer.

For alternative beaches *See* **Excursions to Nimborio Surrounds**.

BICYCLE, SCOOTER & CAR HIRE None.

BREAD SHOPS There is a Bakery (*Tmr* 11B2/3) close to the waterfront, at the bottom of the Chora/beach road.

BUSES None.

COMMERCIAL SHOPPING AREA Not surprisingly, none as such, but there are two well-stocked General Stores (*Tmr* 10B/C3 & 12B2), both on the waterfront. Petros' shop (*Tmr* 10B/C3) serves sliced meat as well as canned foods, and many other supplies. He also changes money and sells tickets for all the ferry-boats. A Shop (*Tmr* 13B2/3) selling dairy products, including yoghurt, and limited fresh fruit and vegetables, is just behind the Bakery, at the outset of the Chora/beach road. There is a Tourist shop (*Tmr* 14B/C4), to the left (*Sbo*)of the Post Office block, which sells sun-tan oil, hats, tea towels (on which is depicted the only island map), T-shirts and other 'vital' items.

Opening hours are the 'small island norm'.

CINEMA & DISCOS None.

FERRY-BOATS Chalki is connected with Rhodes several times a week, and less frequently with Crete. The trusty **Panormitis** makes a weekly call in each direction, as does the less trusty **Nireas** (sister-ship to the infamous **Kyklades**, oh dear!). The **Golden Vergina** is supposed to call in when it can manage to dock. A more frequent, private ferry service connects Chalki with the Rhodes west coast hamlet port of Kamiros Skala.

Ferry-boat timetable (Mid-season)

Day	Departure time	Ferry-boat	Ports/Islands of Call
Tuesday	2300hrs (approx)	Nireas	Diafani(Karpathos),Karpathos,Kasos, Sitia(Crete),Ag Nikolaos(Crete).
Wednesday	2300hrs (approx)	Nireas	Rhodes,Simi,Tilos,Nisiros,Kos, Karpathos,Astipalaia,Piraeus(M).
Friday	1430hrs	Panormitis	Diafani(Karpathos),Karpathos,Kasos.
Saturday	0530hrs	Panormitis	Rhodes.
Saturday*	1800hrs	Golden Vergina	Rhodes.

*It may or may not call!

Chalki to Kamiros Skala(Rhodes) The caique ferry connection to Kamiros Skala is theoretically a regular service, but in practice it is nothing of the kind (surprise, surprise!). The Tourist office in Rhodes City informs that the boats run twice weekly out of the high season months and every day during the months of August and early September. The plan is that the caique should depart Chalki at 0530hrs each morning, returning from Kamiros Skala at 1500hrs. Thus the morning boat should coincide with the early, once a day bus from Kamiros Skala to Rhodes City in the morning, and the 1340hrs bus from Rhodes to Kamiros Skala (not to be confused with the regularly serviced Ancient Kamiros, some 13km north) in time for the afternoon departure. The crossing takes 1½hrs and costs 750drs (or 850drs or 1000drs! – *See* **Kamiros Skala, Rhodes island**). What actually seems to happen is that, although the Rhodes to Chalki boat leaves fairly regularly at the appointed time, the Chalki departures vary tremendously. This is not wholly unconnected with the desires of the tour operators, who wish their clients to depart from and arrive on Chalki at rather more convenient times. So, about twice a week, the boat leaves at 0530hrs, otherwise it may be 1100hrs or even 1500hrs! The only way to find out is to ask the captain the day before a planned departure. Sharp eyed readers will note that the late departures mean there is no bus back to Rhodes City from Kamiros Skala until the following morning, and also that the connection arrives too late for travellers to take a ferry-boat from Rhodes City to anywhere else on the same day. In these circumstances it is necessary to hitch-hike or stay overnight at Kamiros Skala. Unfortunately it is no use appealing to the none-too-helpful representatives of the tour agencies, whose coaches meet the boat to bus their clients back to Rhodes City. They refuse point-blank to carry other passengers, even if the bus is two-thirds empty and a traveller offers to pay (Grrr...). They tell all manner of lies (e.g. 'there's a bus later on' or 'we're full' – ha ha!) to avoid carrying 'excess baggage'.

FERRY-BOAT TICKET OFFICES Petros (*Tmr* 10B/C3), he of the General Store, sells tickets for all connections (except for Kamiros Skala, where you pay on the boat). He can advise the most likely time of arrival of the **Nireas**, up to twelve hours before the event.

MEDICAL CARE There are no pharmacies, just the Doctor's Clinic (*Tmr* 15A3) which is located on the left of beach/Chora road, at a left kink in the street. There isn't a sign but the building is a low, white house with dark brown, newly painted shutters.

NTOG/TOURIST OFFICE None.

OTE The office is situated in the same building as the Post Office (*Tmr* 9C3) and up the external stairs. Opens weekdays only, between 0800-1500hrs.

PLACES OF INTEREST Not many. No museum, no mosque but the pretty Ag Nikolaos Church – to the right along the Quay (*Sbo*) – has a pleasant mosaic pebble courtyard, and claims the tallest campanile in the Dodecanese.

POLICE
Town One door beyond the *Pension* (*See* **The Accommodation**), five minutes walk from the Harbour. The building has no sign but is recognisable from its unusual, red painted, domed roof and peeling, cream painted walls. The island policeman is young, friendly, helpful and very informal.
Port None officially, but the Customs office (*Tmr* 9C3) in the Quay building, beneath the Post Office, fulfils the function.

POST OFFICE (*Tmr* 9C3) Up the external stairs of the Quay edging block. Transacts foreign currency exchange and also houses the OTE. Opens weekdays between 0800-1500hrs.

TELEPHONE NUMBERS & ADDRESSES

Doctor (*Tmr* 15A3)   Tel 57206
Customs (Port police) (*Tmr* 9C3)   Tel 57255
Police, town   Tel 57213

TOILETS (*Tmr* 16B/C6) A reasonably clean, white painted block to the left (*Sbo*) end of the Quay.

EXCURSIONS TO NIMBORIO SURROUNDS

Caiques run trips to various island beaches, including Areta, Kania, Trachia and Yiali. The best beach is on the nearby islet of Alimnia where there is also a ruined castle. But the fare of 1000drs per person for the 1 hour voyage seems rather excessive.

ROUTE ONE

To The Chora About 1½ hours walk from the port, following the road, 'Boulevard Tarpon Springs', out of the Port and beyond the beach, leads to the ruined and now uninhabited mountaintop Chora. The Knights of St John built a Castle here, on the site of an ancient acropolis. Wonderful views over the sea and the island.

A passer by having a drink, Rhodes Old Quarter.

14 KASTELLORIZO (Kastelorizo, Kastellorizon, Kastelloriso, Castelorizo, Megisti, ΚΑΣΤΕΛΛΟΡΙΖΟ) *****

Dodecanese Islands

FIRST IMPRESSIONS
Attractive port; bygone affluence; crumbling houses and ruins; crystal clear seas; inexpensive seafood; fiercely Greek.

SPECIALITIES
Seafood; Stravo and Katimari, two pastry sweets made with honey and nuts.

RELIGIOUS HOLIDAYS & FESTIVALS
include: 24th April – Feast of St George, at the two large churches in Megisti (both named Ag. Georgios) and the Monastery of Ag Georgios in the mountains; 21st May – Ag Konstantinos (the main Church on Horafia Square); 20th July – Festival, Profitias Ilias.

VITAL STATISTICS
Tel prefix 0241. The island is about 6km from top to toe, up to 3km from east to west with a total area of 9sqkm. The population numbers about 250 souls. Kastellorizo is the most easterly of the Greek islands and lies only 2km from the Turkish coastline.

HISTORY
Mentioned by Homer, the island's first named settler was supposed to be a King Meges from Echinada, who may have given the island its alternative name of Megisti. On the other hand, Megesti (or Megiste – the largest) probably relates to the fact that Kastellorizo is the biggest of a small archipelago of some ten or twelve uninhabited islands and islets.

The island sent ships to Troy and has been inhabited since Neolithic times. The Dorians first built a castle where the 'Red Castle' now stands, and they also constructed an ancient acropolis at Paleokastro, the walls of which are still visible.

The island fell under the rule of Rhodes for much of its history, with the Knights of St John reconstructing the Castle in the 1380s. The red rock used in the building of the fort's wall resulted in the island's current name, Kastellorizo (from the Italian Castello Rosso or Red Fortress). In 1440 it was occupied for the first time by the Turks after whom came the King of Naples, in 1450. By 1523 the island was made part of the Ottoman empire, though the Venetians occupied Kastellorizo for two more periods in 1570 and 1659.

Kastellorizo took part in the War of Independence in 1821, being the first Dodecanese island to revolt, but in 1833 the island was given back to the Turks in exchange for the island of Evia. After 1856 the French were nominally in charge. Even so the islanders prospered greatly as shipowners towards the end of the 19th century. This was Kastellorizo's period of supreme affluency, when many of its big houses were built and between 15,000 and 17,000 people lived on the island. The island's merchant navy numbered as many as three hundred ships but, unlike the Kasiots, the shipowners did not understand the revolution that steam was to bring to the world's merchant navies.

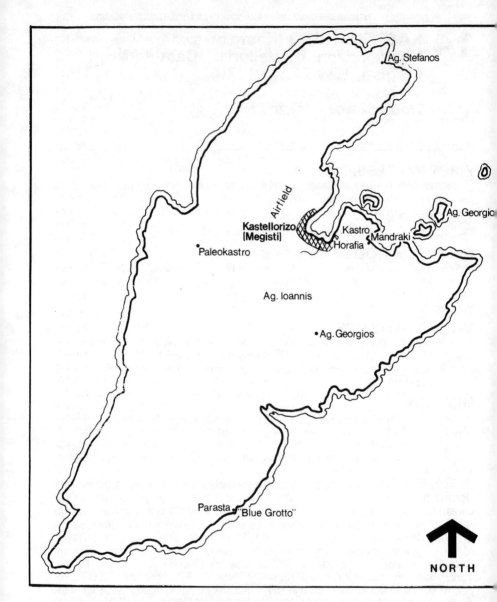

Illustration 17 Kastellorizo island

However, it was the First World War that heralded the outset of the island's modern tragedy. During the hostilities Kastellorizo was bombarded by both the Turks and Germans, which shell fire destroyed many of the port's buildings. With the economic downturn, 'serious' emigration began. In 1927 a great earthquake destroyed many more buildings, despite which, during the 1930s Kastellorizo enjoyed a short autumn of prosperity. In common with a number of other Greek islands, the coming of the sea-plane, combined with Italian suzerainity, resulted in daily flights to the island from a number of Western European capital cities. But it was the events of the Second World War which really finished off the island. The population, already lowered by many thousands, were evacuated to Egypt by the Allies, who occupied the island. Prior to their return, the island had been almost completely destroyed – though there are different 'stories' about how this occurred. One version maintains that the destruction was caused by enemy bombardment. Another account broadcasts that the British themselves carried out the despoilation, either to cover the massive amount of looting their troops had wrought, or on the 'scorched earth' policy – if we can't have it, it will be no use to any one else, so there!

Whatever the reasons, the town and port had been burnt down and ruined beyond recognition. If that were not enough, the few islanders who chose to return at the end of the war had to survive the ship sinking. It is said that the expatriate islanders (of whom most emigrated to Australia, a few to America and others spread throughout Greece) always consider themselves as Kastellorizons first and foremost, and natives of their adopted country second. Furthermore the two hundred and fifty residents left behind are simply caretaking for those temporarily absent!

GENERAL

Despite the historical disasters, tourism, such a despoiler elsewhere, may prove to be the one saving grace. Although as yet in its infancy, the holiday industry has already brought about a revival of interest in the island. However, Kastellorizo is still a very quiet, unspoilt little place and not a moment should be lost in visiting, before it is too late. A recently constructed airport, with reasonably frequent summer connections to Rhodes, has made this a more realistic proposition. Admittedly there are no beaches but there are plenty of quiet, rocky coves for bathing and the seas are fish-filled and amazingly clear. The people, though reportedly 'odd', do not appear so peculiar, although there are a few, very obvious cases of inbreeding. They certainly are most friendly and helpful.

Kastellorizo is a FIND – a great, characterful little island, excellent for exploration with good facilities for food and accommodation.

KASTELLORIZO (Kastellorizon, Megisti): capital town & only port (Illustration 18) The initially attractive appearance of the port and town belies the fact that most of it has been ruined. A wander through the back streets of the areas known as Horafia and Mandraki soon paint a much truer picture.

ARRIVAL BY AIR

The little airfield is situated on top of the island, about a ten minute drive from the Town. There is a waiting room and not much else – apart from the Greek flag. Goats are chased off the runway prior to an aircraft's arrival or departure. A brown minibus bearing the sign *Hotel Megisti* meets the plane and charges 200drs for the journey down to the town (though when questioned they deny all knowledge of the vehicle). Despite the comparatively high fare it is best to pay, otherwise it is a very hot, long walk.

ARRIVAL BY FERRY

The ferry-boats dock at the Quay (*Tmr* 1E4) to the left (*Sbo*) of the deep bay in which the port and town is set. As the ferry calls only twice a week, it is met by most of the population, including owners of accommodation, and general chaos

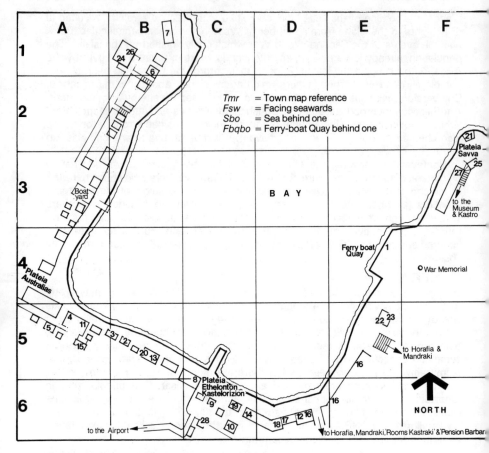

Illustration 18 Kastellorizo Port

Tmr			
1	Ferry-boat Quay E4	15	Baker A5
2	Rooms B5	16	Food stores
3	Kafe Η ΑΠΟΛΑΨΣΗΣ A/B5	17	Fruit & Vegetable shop D6
4	Rooms/General store A5	18	Supermarket D6
5	Rooms Ο ΠΑΡΑΔΕΙΣΟΣ A5	19	Periptero C6
6	'Blue & White' Pension B1/2	20	Tourist shop B5
7	Hotel Megisti B1	21	Disco F2
8	Taverna Lazarakis B/C5/6	22	Doctor E5
9	Restaurant Mavrou C6	23	Olympic office E5
10	Restaurant Oraia Megisti C6	24	Post Office/OTE B1
11	Taverna International A5	25	The Mosque F3
12	Cafe Restaurant ΣΑΜΨΑΚΟΥ D6	26	Town police B1
13	Taverna Little Paris B5	27	Port police F3
14	Snackbar C/D6	28	Public toilets C6

ensues. It is best to locate a **Room** fairly quickly, because the patrons tend only to be on the premises when the ferry has just arrived. At other times a visitor will have to scour the cafes and tavernas for the proprietors.

THE ACCOMMODATION & EATING OUT
The Accommodation Although finding accommodation is usually no problem, mid-July to mid-August can prove rather difficult. Perhaps all those expatriate islanders make the pilgrimage during these height of the season months?

From the Ferry-boat Quay (*Tmr* 1E4) walk along the waterfront towards the back of the bay. A narrow side-street off to the left, just before the fruit and vegetable market (*Tmr* 17D6), is signed *Horafia, Mandraki* and leads down a twisting street between crumbling mansions. After about 150m, at a right bend in the street, is the:-

Rooms Kastraki
Directions: As above and on the left in a tall, angular building.

Well kept, if rather dark bedrooms, share the bathroom. A double room costs from around 1400drs. The owner can be hard to find.

Twenty metres further along and the same, narrow street widens out into a dilapidated Square, to the right of which is the:-

Pension Barbara   Tel 29295
Directions: As above and situated in a three storey building, with the name painted in blue and yellow on the wall outside.

This colour scheme continues indoors, where a rickety blue and yellow staircase connects the wooden landings. Shared bathrooms have a sign *The water is not to be drunk*. The top storey rooms open on to a pleasant, flower laden wooden balcony and there is a communal fridge on each floor. The pension is quite nice, if a bit quirky, though it is difficult to shake off the impression that the place is about to collapse around one's ears! 'Barbara' does not live in the house (does she know something we don't?). Double rooms are charged at 1400drs.

Following the Esplanade around the bay, past the quayside square, Plateia Ethelonton Kastelorizion, leads to **Rooms** (*Tmr* 2B5 - tel 29292), and, in the next block, the *Kafe* Η ΑΠΟΛΑΨΣΗΣ (*Tmr* 3A/B5) also advertises **Rooms**, but as the telephone number is 29295 this presumably refer to *Pension Barbara*.

Two possibilities are to be found on Plateia Australias:-
Rooms (General Store) (*Tmr* 4A5)
Directions: As above.

These are owned by a very large old lady, whose accommodation is decidedly 'provincial', with shared bathrooms, and costing 1200drs for a double room.

Turning left down the narrow side-street, beside the Church, leads to a three storey, blue and white, rather palatial looking building at the end of the street, the:-

Ο ΠΑΡΑΔΕΙΣΟΣ (*Tmr* 5A5)   Tel 29074
Directions: As above.

Double rooms from about 1400drs, but the owners are hard to locate.

'Blue & White' Pension (*Tmr* 6B1/2)
Directions: Facing on to the waterfront quayside, across the 'U' shaped bay from the Ferry-boat Quay. This Pension has no sign but, if not propositioned on disembarking from the ferry, ask at the quayside *Taverna International* (*Tmr* 11A5).

A very nice place to stay, as it is possible to swim immediately in front of the pension, which stands out being painted in pale blue and white. Smallish double rooms cost 1400drs, sharing the bathroom. There is constant, very hot water, a shared fridge and kitchen, with cooking facilities, and a 'back yard' complete with washing lines and pegs. Because of the shape of the bay, music tends to echo all around (well every noise echoes). This is fine as long as the auditory assault is gentle Greek music from the quayside tavernas, but not so good if it emanates from the disco opposite! If you dislike rock music ask for a room at the back, though this is a shame as the front rooms have such super views.

The same advice applies to the modern but tasteful:-

Hotel Megisti (*Tmr* 7B1) (Class C)
Directions: Just beyond the *Blue & White Pension*

Very clean, comfortable and usually occupied by Australian expatriates. A double room with en suite bathroom costs 3000drs a night. The hotel has a broad patio and is a lovely place for an evening drink. These are inexpensive with a lemonade costing 50drs and a Nes meh ghala 60drs.

The Eating Out There are some excellent tavernas but they are not as inexpensive as might be thought. This is because they not only cater for yacht owners, who tend to 'encourage' higher prices, but all supplies have to come from Rhodes now, as distinct from Turkey (*See* **Excursions to Kastellorizo Town Surrounds**). Perversely seafood is comparatively cheap.

Plateia Ethelonton Kastelorizion (*Tmr* C5/6) is the 'Taverna' Square, and the best here (indeed the best on Kastellorizo) is the:-

Taverna Lazarakis (*Tmr* 8B/C5/6)
Directions: As above.

Less showy and expensive than the nearby *Restaurant Mavrou* (*Tmr* 9C6), the Lazarakis has its tables spread out on the square and the small boat jetty. The taverna is run by 'Papa' and his two young and extremely pleasant sons. The latter are among the few youthful islanders to live here all year round, and will talk at length about the future (or lack thereof) of the island. The taverna usually displays a big 'fish of the day' on the waterfront, ready for 'the carving'. A meal for two of 2 excellent swordfish kebabs (400drs each), 2 small retsinas, a Greek salad and bread costs 1260drs.

Restaurant Mavrou (*Tmr* 9C6)
This establishment exhibits one of the cardinal No, No's, a glass case displaying some of the menu alternatives. The cabinets contents include swordfish kebabs (500drs) and octopus (400drs a portion).

Restaurant Oraia Megisti (*Tmr* 10C6)
Directions: At the rear of the same Square as the aforementioned establishments.

Taverna International (*Tmr* 11A5)
Directions: This extremely pleasant taverna is beyond 'Taverna' Square,

towards Plateia Australias, with its tables on the quayside and beneath a cool, shady, vine covered trellis.

Excellent food. Try the delicious kalamari stiffado (squid stew) for 380drs. A meal of 1 moussaka, 1 briam, 1 tzatziki, bread, a small bottle of retsina and a sweet was charged at 1150drs. They serve the traditional local pastries – Stravo (with honey & walnuts) and Katimari. A very pleasant breakfast spot at a cost of about 400drs for two.

Other quayside eating places include the *Cafe Restaurant ΣΑΜΨΑΚΟΥ (Tmr* 12D6) and the *Taverna Little Paris (Tmr* 13B5). There is also a Snackbar (*Tmr* 14C/D6), which offers cheese and spinach pies and pizzas.

For a change from the busy waterfront scenario why not try the:-

Taverna Platania
Directions: This little taverna is up on the hill at Horafia, in what can only be described as a desolate situation on the wide, grand, ruined Horafia Square. All the 'main roads' from the left (*Sbo*) of the waterfront lead here, as this was once the centre of town life, prior to the Second World War 'blitz'. The Square is bordered by two churches, the School, the village hall and several ruined buildings. The usual clientele are a few, old locals. A tasty meal, for two of giant beans, chicken and chips, Greek salad, bread and 3 largers (only the expensive, imported small bottles available) costs 1160drs. A plate of 4 small fish costs 280drs.

THE A TO Z OF USEFUL INFORMATION
AIRLINE OFFICE & TERMINUS (*Tmr* 23E5) In the same building as the Doctor and up a flight of external wooden stairs round the back. A one-man affair, but he does speak English. There isn't an Olympic Airways bus (*See* **Buses, A To Z**).

Aircraft timetable (Mid-season)
Kastellorizo to Rhodes

Tuesday, Thursday	1015hrs
& Sunday	
Return	.
Tuesday, Thursday	0910hrs
& Sunday	

One-way fare: 4420drs, duration 45mins.

BANKS There is no bank, but the owner of the *Taverna International (Tmr* 11A5), Agapitos Benitsis, is the representative for the National Bank of Greece. The Post Office (*Tmr* 24B1) conducts foreign currency exchange.

BEACHES There are no beaches on the island, not 'nowhere'. In July and August fishermen ferry tourists across to the islet of Ag Georgios whereon a chapel, a house, and a few shingle slopes, which nearly qualify as beaches, but not quite.

It is suggested that the owner of a proposed hotel, which it is rumoured is to be built in the barren little bay of Ag Stefanos, is going to 'build a beach' as well ....good luck to him!

BREAD SHOPS There is a bakery (*Tmr* 15A5) beyond the *International Taverna*, and along a narrow alley. He bakes daily in the months of July & August, otherwise two or three times a week.

BUSES The island's only bus is the private minibus which runs to the Airport and back, when a flight is due (*See* **Arrival by Air**). It departs from the quayside about one hour before a flight is due to depart. The fare costs 200drs. Note there is no separate Olympic Airways bus.

CINEMA None.

COMMERCIA SHOPPING AREA There are adequate food shops all around the quayside (*Tmr* 16), a Fruit and Vegetable market (*Tmr* 17D6) as well as a Supermarket (*Tmr* 18D6). The 'Periptero' (not a kiosk here – *Tmr* 19C6). sells cigarettes, postcards, island maps, when available, and old photos of Kastellorizo, as does the 'Tourist Shop' (*Tmr* 20B5). Note that fresh fruit and vegetables are only available when the ferry-boat docks and all will have been sold by the next morning. The same applies to yoghurt which is sold at the Periptero (*Tmr* 19C6), run by a blind man.

Despite strictly observing the siesta, most shops open on Sundays.

DISCO (*Tmr* 21F2) Yes, surprisingly, at the very right-hand end (*Fsw*) of the quay, near the Mosque. Opens sporadically and intrusively blasts the bay with noisy music, but usually closes by 2330 hrs.

FERRY-BOATS The only reliable ferry is the **FB Panormitis**, a small, rugged craft which also brings supplies but doesn't carry vehicles. The journey on this craft takes about seven hours from Rhodes. Kastellorizo is also on the route of the 'mythical' **Kyklades**, but this boat is an occasional, 'if ever' visitor and not to be relied upon. The islanders are informed of this latter craft's imminent arrival by a phone call from the Port police in Rhodes. For some peculiarly Greek reason, the **Kyklades** is scheduled to arrive not only on the same day but at exactly the same time as the **Panormitis** – though in practice this rarely, if ever, occurs.

Ferry-boat timetable (Mid-season)

Day	Departure time	Ferry-boat	Ports/Islands of Call
Wednesday	1730hrs	Panormitis	Rhodes.
Sunday	2400hrs	Panormitis	Rhodes.
	2400hrs	Kyklades	Rhodes.

One-way fare: None; duration 6-7 hours.

FERRY-BOAT TICKET OFFICES None. Ferry-boat travel between Rhodes and Kastellorizo is free all year round.

MEDICAL CARE
Chemists & Pharmacies None.
Doctor (*Tmr* 22E5) There is a surgery at the bottom of the broad, white stairs leading to Horafia. However, the doctor often disappears to Rhodes for long periods, during which time sick people are collected by helicopter – best not to be ill!

NTOG/TOURIST OFFICE None.

OTE (*Tmr* 24B1) In the same building as the Post Office, behind the *Blue & White Pension*. Open weekdays only between 0800-1500hrs. In 1987 the phones were out of order on Kastellorizo for in excess of two months, so there was no contact with the outside world, at all!

PLACES OF INTEREST

The Castle To get to the fortress either follow the path marked Museum from behind the Mosque (*Tmr* 25F3), watching out for the snakes, until immediately prior to the Museum. Then follow a broad, walled, ruined street to the right, which climbs up the hill to the Castle and the old windmill or take the narrow street from the left of Horafia Square (*Facing Mandraki*) which advances through ruined houses to the hilltop.

The Castle was originally built in Doric times. The 'Red Castle', which is believed to have given the island its name, was rebuilt by the Knights of St John around 1380 and the Greek flag still flies proudly from the hilltop tower.

A now white-painted, section of the fort has been renovated and accommodates the island's:-

Museum To find the building follow the signs behind the Mosque (*Tmr* 25F3). Very pleasantly laid out indeed and way above the average 'small island' museum – but then Kastellorizo has a 'way above average' history. Interesting exhibits include clay pottery from a 13th century shipwreck, a one hundred year old sponge diver's suit, with iron shoes and compressor, and old photographs and drawings of the port, town and island in its heyday. The museum is open daily, including weekends, between 0800-1430hrs, but is closed Tuesdays.

The Lycian Tomb Instead of bearing right outside the Museum, up to the Castle, continue straight on beyond the Museum and down the hill, amid ruined dwellings, until is reached a very steep, uneven staircase cut into the rock face, where it is necessary to watch one's footing. The tomb is at the top and to the right, distinguised by a heavy stone entrance beyond which can be seen the burial chamber. It is the only such tomb in modern Greece.

The Mosque (*Tmr* 25F3) The two hundred year old Turkish Mosque, situated on the quayside, is attractive from the outside and used to house the Town Museum. It is now closed to the public.

POLICE

Port (*Tmr* 27F3) The office is sited in a large building, close to the Ferry-boat Quay.

Town (*Tmr* 26B1) The office is to the forefront of the Post Office block. A few soldiers from the Castle also 'hang out' here. A friendly and informal facility.

POST OFFICE (*Tmr* 24B1) *See* **OTE**. Transacts foreign currency exchange.

TAXIS None.

TELEPHONE NUMBERS & ADDRESSES

Doctor (*Tmr* 22E5)	Tel 29067
Olympic Airways (*Tmr* 23E5)	Tel 29880
Police, town (*Tmr* 26B1)	Tel 29068
Town Hall	Tel 29069

TOILETS A fairly clean block (*Tmr* 28C6) on Plateia Ethelonton Kastellorizion, and more on the Horafia Square, near the *Platania Taverna*.

EXCURSIONS TO KASTELLORIZO TOWN SURROUNDS

Caique Trips These are available around the island; to other nearby islets and, most commonly, to the 'Blue Grotto' on the island's east coast. For details of these boat trips look for the signs at various waterfront shops and cafes. However it can be difficult to take advantage of boat trips outside of the very height of season, because the fisherman require at least four passengers, if not five or six, to make the journey worthwhile.

The Blue Grotto is certainly not to be missed, if at all possible. The caiques take about forty minutes to reach the cave, which is almost invisible from outside as the entrance is very low indeed. Inside however, the cave opens out into a vast cavern in which the sunlight reflects off the surface of the sea, making everything a fluorescent blue. There are stalagtites in the cave and a 'resident' pair of seals, who come here to breed. If they are 'at home' their presence can be distinguished by the loud splashing noises. Some of the fishing boat trips allow their passengers a swim inside the cave. A journey to the Blue Grotto, and back, costs between 300drs and 500drs per person, depending on the number of 'punters'.

'Non-Excursion' to Turkey
An official day trip to Turkey used to be on the tourist agenda and is still mentioned in most guide books. In fact, this practice was stopped in 1985 by the Port police who, presumably on Government orders, halted all Kastellorizo trips to Turkey, even the islanders' own sorties. This is much regretted because Turkish foodstuffs and other goods were much cheaper and more convenient than those shipped in from Rhodes.

ROUTE ONE
To Horafia & Mandraki
Taking this short walk over the hill to the left (*Sbo*) from the Port details the full extent of the area's demise. Previously the hill on which the Castle still stands was covered with houses, which were destroyed during the Second World War.

Wide roads, paths, archways and squares still remain however. Taking either the broad, white painted flight of steps from the nameless Plateia (alongside the doctor (*Tmr* 22E5), or the side-street near the fruit market (*Tmr* 17D6), leads to the broad Square bearing the sign Horafia. On one side is the huge and impressive Church of Ag Georgios, to another side the Church of Ag Constantinos, the lower and more modern of the two churches. Next to Ag Constantinos is the School – much too large for the island's present day head count of thirty-five pupils. Behind the childrens' swings is the Town Hall. All these buildings are in good repair but there are ruins to all sides.

Continuing past the *Platania Taverna*, down the main road sloping towards the sea on the other side, heads for the seaside area known as Mandraki where all that now remains are some huge, crumbling mansions, some of which are in good repair, but most of which have fallen down. The road continues beside the shore to the left towards the cemetery which is set down on a promontory. Beyond this is another possible site for a new hotel, but the promising looking continuation of the road merely leads to the town's rubbish tip.

The only other paved road on the island is that which advances to the Airport.

15 KARPATHOS (Scarpanto)
Dodecanese Islands

****

FIRST IMPRESSIONS
Island charm; dwellings dotted about; wealthy villages and returned expatriates; many white chapels; wind tortured trees; poor drinking water, but due to be repiped in 1987, from mountain springs; cats and flies.

SPECIALITIES
None that I can think of.

RELIGIOUS HOLIDAYS & FESTIVALS
include: 28-29th August – St John the Headless, Avlona.

VITAL STATISTICS
Tel prefix 0245. Nearly 50km long, up to 12km wide (and down to 4km narrow) with an area almost as large as the island of Kos but a population of only some 5,500 (compared to the 18,000 of Kos), of which about 1,500 live in the capital, Karpathos (Pighadia).

HISTORY
Overshadowed by its larger and more populous neighbours, the history of Karpathos follows closely in their footsteps. Findings of antiquity are few and far between and even then only small and fragmentary, but there is evidence of a number of important, ancient sites. An idiosyncrasy was that the Knights only stayed two years, handing the island back to the previous overlords, the Venetian Cornaros family. The Turks, in the shape of the pirate Barbarossa, took over in 1538.

GENERAL
The island's charms and attractions are becoming known by self-generating popularity (in addition to the well-meaning efforts of European travel companies), otherwise I might hesitate to extol the virtues of Karpathos. Until recently a lovely, relatively undeveloped island with all the classic ingredients of a 'find'. These include inhabitants who make few concessions, but are very welcoming to visitors, and roads (more third-rate donkey tracks) that tumble their rock strewn, flint surface to this or that destination. Donkey tracks they maybe but they certainly pass through stunning countryside, only to arrive at very little or nothing, and this after heading for a name on the map as large as a house. Another indicator of the to-date lack of tourist exposure is that it is sometimes impossible to purchase a drink at a taverna – the locals beating one to an order by 'putting them in'. The donor is usually indicated by a nod of the proprietor's head. Perhaps another pointer to the 'lack of tourist infiltration' is that only one or two clocks shows any (let alone the correct) time. Mind you, there are a number of 'warning straws' in the wind, the major one of which is the almost frantic and grandiose enlargement of the island's Airport. Additionally the German tourists insist on proclaiming how cheap everything is, which to an alert Greek is as good as a price increase.

The natives advise that travellers should visit the island in the month of May for the flowers and September for the fruit and to swim but between the 15th June and the 15th September the wind blows and blows and blows....

A curious inheritance law, shared with the Dodecanese islands of Leros and Simi, is that the eldest daughter, not the eldest son, is the rightful heir. This anomaly

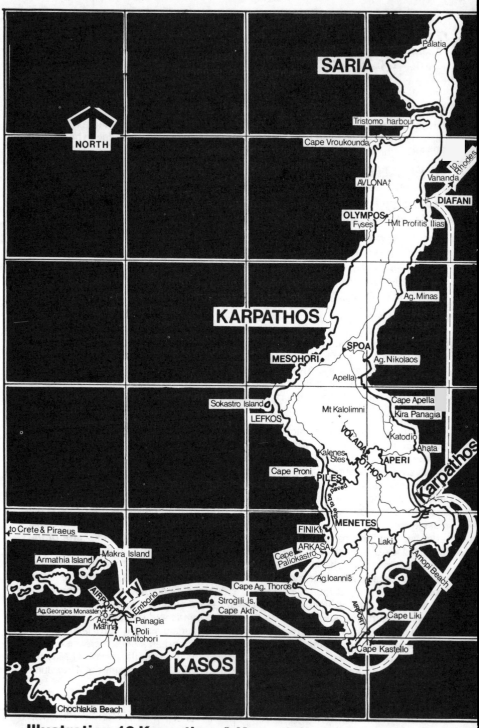

Illustration 19 Karpathos & Kasos islands

has led to hardship, not only for the sons of a family but mother and the other daughters. Reputably this quirk encouraged the males to emigrate in order to make their fortunes elsewhere in the world, but then most islands lost the young men due to lack of work and the glitter of golden opportunities in the New World. Certainly Karpathos is an island where the returning expatriates have resulted in 'North American' being the second language and the seeding of some unusual and unexpected cultural pursuits. Manifestations include *The Video Club* and a remarkably disproportionate incidence of ladies' hairdressers. Tourists' loud-mouthed comments on any subject may well be understood by a wider audience than a circle of fellow holiday-makers. It has to be admitted I'm a fine one to talk...

Karpathos' drinking water was brackish, if not actually saline, but in 1987 a programme was underway to pipe water from mountain springs.

KARPATHOS (Pighadia): capital town & main port (Illustration 20)
The Town and Harbour is set down on the edge of a large and lovely bay flanked by mountainsides to the north, with a small islet plonked down in the middle of the inlet. The Town gives an impression of being comparatively new and some additional development is underway. The layout is a little muddling to start with and rather larger than at first would appear to be the case.

The night time activities of the town's stray cats can keep even a heavy sleeper awake.

ARRIVAL BY AIR
The small, inter-island Skyvan aircraft are look-alikes for propeller powered, early Land Rovers, complete with wallpapered interiors. They land and take off from the airfield, which resembles a 'Mash' unit and is located some 15km from Karpathos Town. The not inconsiderable site is the subject of massive earthwork movement. You notice I eschew the use of the word development because that is not what seems to be under way. The giant earthmovers appear to be shovelling the mother soil and rock haphazardly around the large, saucer-shaped depression in which the civil engineering work is taking place. Half the camouflage painted machinery, occupying a sector surrounded by large caravans and shacks, appears to be undergoing extensive rebuilding and repair. Rumour has it that the work is going to take years and years and...

The airport structure, not a building, is a single storey prefab in which prospective travellers shuffle about. There is a lady serving coffee, a tap for ice cold water and toilets.

It crosses my mind that the chances of getting on an incorrect flight are quite high when several flights arrive and depart on the same day. This is due to the rather detached and disinterested attitude of the officials who, to be fair, become very harassed, to say the least. The Skyvans buzz in and out from the island of Crete, Rhodes and Kasos.

Taxis queue to deliver and pick up passengers, whilst Olympic Airways operates a convenient coach service to Karpathos Town. If in a hurry, visitors are advised to take a taxi as the airport bus has a habit of functioning on an 'accumulation basis' – that is they may wait for the next plane to arrive, which can take up to an hour. Even the locals are not amused! The coach fare costs 120drs whilst the taxis charge in the region of 800drs, but it is commonplace for a number of people to share a cab.

ARRIVAL BY FERRY
The neat, substantial quay (*Tmr* 1C/D1) has been adapted to allow ferries to dock

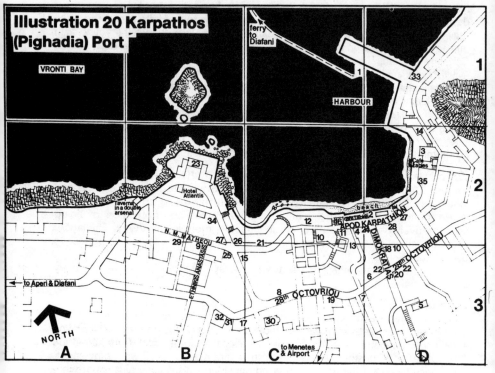

Illustration 20 Karpathos (Pighadia) Port

VRONTI BAY

ferry to Diafani

HARBOUR

Hotel Atlantis

Taverna in a double arsenal

N. M. MATHEOU

ETHNIKIS ANASTASIS

APOD KARPATHION

DIMOKRATIAS

28th OCTOVRIOU

28th OCTOVRIOU

Café Cables

to Aperi & Diafani

NORTH

to Menetes & Airport

Tmr	1.	Ferry-boat Quay C/D1
	2.	Clock Tower C/D2
	3.	Hotel Coral/Restaurant Rendezvous D2
	4.	Hotel Zephyros C/D2/3
	5.	Hotel Karpathos D3
	6.	Hotel Avra C/D3
	7.	Rooms To Rent - Harrys C/D3
	8.	Rooms To Kanaki C3
	9.	Hotel Anessis B2/3
	10.	Rooms To Rent
	11.	Kafeteria Edelweiss C/D2/3
	12.	Kafeneion Halikas C2
	13.	Restaurant Pizza C/D2/3
	14.	Taverna To Kyma D1/2
	15.	Airline office B/C2/3
	16.	Bank/Georgios Taverna C2
	17.	Scooter hire - Francesca B/C3
	18.	Maloftis Car Hire/Karpathos Travel D2/3
	19.	Bread shop C3
	20.	Bus terminal D3

Tmr	= Town map reference
Fsw	= Facing seawards
Sbo	= Sea behind one
Fbqbo	= Ferry-boat Quay behind one

21.	Butcher B/C2/3
22.	Supermarkets
23.	Municipal offices B2
24.	Possi Travel C/D2
25.	OTE B/C2/3
26.	Supermarket/paper shop B/C2/3
27.	Pharmacies
28.	Dental Surgeon D2
29.	Hospital B2/3
30.	Church C3
31.	Post Office B/C3
32.	Police B3
33.	Public toilets D1
34.	Taverna Kassos B2
35.	Zorba's Taverna D2

on all three sides, depending on the direction of the wind. The short Esplanade to the centre of the settlement is quite often littered with the large packing cases of American or Canadian expatriates returning, once and for all, to the island of their birth.

After disembarking walk down the Ferry-boat Quay, turn right along the waterfront and follow the road round to the Clock Tower (*Tmr* 2C/D2) – only five minutes at a brisk pace.

For the best accommodation 'pickings' turn left up the Main Street, Odhos Dimokratias, and then right on 28th Octovriou St.

Note, passengers wishing to disembark at Diafani must check that any particular ferry-boat is scheduled to dock there and not only at Pighadia (or vice versa).

THE ACCOMMODATION & EATING OUT

The Accommodation Unusually there is a deficiency of published and visible room rates, a strange omission, bearing in mind the insistence of the information being available on most islands. At the height of the season *Rooms* can be difficult to find and it is advisable to act quickly to obtain accommodation at one of the limited, but very good places available. These include the:-

Hotel Coral (*Tmr* 3D2) Apod Karpathion.
Directions: The first accommodation encountered.

Possible block booked and owned by a very surly man, who is also proprietor of a pharmacy (*Tmr* 27D2). A double room with en suite bathroom is charged at 1500drs.

Hotel Zephyros (*Tmr* 4C/D2/3) (Class E) Apod Karpathion   Tel 22235
Directions: Straight on past the 'High St' (Odhos Dimokratias) turning and alongside Possi Travel. It is necessary to climb the narrow stairs to find anyone, and when you do it may well not be an overwhelming or enthusiastic reception.

A double room costs about 1200drs.

Odhos Dimokratias connects the Esplanade, Apod Karpathion, and Odhos 28th Octovriou. Almost opposite the junction with 28th Octovriou, and to the left, across a 'bombed vehicle lot', is the:-

Karpathos Hotel (*Tmr* 5D3) (Class D) 25 Vassileos Konstantinou Tel 22347
Directions: As above.

A single room sharing the bathroom is charged at 1100drs, a double room sharing a bathroom 1600drs and en suite 1900drs. Beware, the construction lorries that park hereabouts overnight burst into life rather early in the morning.

A few buildings along Odhos 28th Octovriou, to the right, is the:-

Hotel Avra (*Tmr* 6C/D3) (Class E) No 28, 28th Octovriou   Tel 22388
Directions: As above and a comparatively modern building.

Only double rooms sharing the bathrooms are available which cost 1350drs, rising to 1600drs (1st May-30th Sept).

A further 'pant or two' up the now steeply rising road, and on the left is:-

'Harry's Rooms to Rent' (*Tmr* 7C/D3) 28th Octovriou   Tel 22188
Directions: As above.

A very pleasant choice with clean, well decorated rooms fitted with solid, wooden furniture. Each room has a section of the balcony that runs round the house. The shared modern bathrooms, which are spotlessly clean and tiled, don't have any of the oft present, 'evil shortcomings'. The water is hot all day with soap and towels supplied. The very helpful and nice owners are Harry, who directs operations, and his wife, who spends most of her time cleaning the pension. A single room costs 1015drs, a single person in a double room is charged 1340drs and a double room costs 1670drs.

Hotel Anessis (*Tmr* 9B2/3) (Class D) 2 Ethnikis Anastasis/N & M Matheou
Tel 22100

Directions: Keeping along Apod Karpathion from the Harbour Esplanade leads switchback style to a Square on which is the OTE (*Tmr* 25B/C2/3). Straight across the Square and the Hotel is sited on the far corner of the first turning to the left.

The old couple, who ran the hotel for some twenty years, have, or were about to retire. They plan to hand over to their nephew who is to return from the USA with 'big plans'! He should be in position in 1988. Through the cleaner, who translates for them, they are proud to advise that theirs was the first hotel in Karpathos. Single rooms sharing the bathroom cost 900drs and with an en suite bathroom 1300drs, which rates increase to 950/1500drs (1st June-30th Sept). Double rooms only share bathrooms at a cost of 1200drs, rising to 1350drs.

Rooms To Kanaki (*Tmr* 8C3) 28th Octovriou.
Directions: Continuing west along Odhos 28th Octovriou, beyond the main road turning off to Menetes and the accommodation is on the right.

An en suite double room is expensive at a cost of 2300drs per night.

Rooms 'Menetes Road'   Tel 22477
Directions: From 28th Octovriou turn up the Menetes road for a good ten minutes climb out of town. The building is situated on the left, at the very top of the hill.

Apart from the views over Vronti Bay, the inconvenience of the position is well balanced by the low price for a double room of 1000drs and a triple room of 1400drs, all sharing the bathrooms.

Other rooms can be found in the town (*Tmr* 10) and on the Menetes road out of town. Rooms, pensions and hotels are also sited on the route to Aperi, which skirts Vronti Bay. The *Hotel Panorama* (Class C – tel 22739) has been recommended, with en suite double rooms costing from 3400drs, which includes breakfast.

The Eating Out
Some splendid establishments and a surprising breadth of variety, especially in comparison with, say, Kos which does not have a taverna to rival *To Kyma* (*Tmr* 14D1/2) or *Zorbas Taverna* (*Tmr* 35D2), nor a kafeneion to match *Kafeneion Halikas* (*Tmr* 12C2).

Breakfast, where and when available, betrays Germany and Scandinavian tourist influences – everything with cake, and no souvlakis here. It is essential to 'forage' early for the evening 'troughing', certainly no later than 2000hrs, as the restaurants and tavernas fill up very early.

Kafeteria Edelweiss (*Tmr* 11C/D2/3)
Directions: Sited on the Esplanade road, where it rises away from the seafront, close by the Bank (*Tmr* 16C2), with tables across the roadway, alongside the sea wall.

Mentioned not for the establishment's reasonable prices – no way with a small can of beer costing 100drs, but because it is one of the places open early on in the day and is very pleasantly located. The service is hesitant as the personnel is limited to one harassed and forgetful waiter. Breakfast, costing 300drs, includes coffee, toast and cake (yes cake, I warned you) with butter and jam.

Kafeneion Halikas (*Tmr* 12C2)
Directions: On beyond the *Edelweiss*, to the right, on a rise in the road with the seafront in sight and alongside the roof on an unfinished, unidentifiable community building.

Open breakfast to night-time. A Greek salad with bread, a beer and coffee costs 300drs. The most enjoyable time to visit, if you can find a seat, is in the evening when the locals settle down to the serious drinking. If you are lucky you will bump into the local philosopher, a sparkling eyed professor (well, local schoolmaster), Manolis Kritikos. Conversation is sometimes sketchy as he does have an eye for the (tourist) ladies but his self-taught English is excellent.

Restaurant Pizza (*Tmr* 13C/D2/3)
Directions: In the lane connecting Apod Karpathion and 28th Octovriou.

Mike, the proprietor, who speaks first-rate Canadian, opens in the evening, scattering the restaurant tables and chairs along the roadside across the way from the large establishment. The service is excellent, the value good but collecting a bill is often a lengthy business. A spaghetti bolognese costs 240drs and a pizza 350drs.

Taverna To Kyma (*Tmr* 14D1/2)
Directions: Almost on the Quay Square.

The proprietor is an inspired man who works very hard but gets frightfully flustered as the pressure of orders piles up and the evening bubbles on. To be truthful, the good natured service becomes muddled and chaotic with the owner working at a run. The menu is varied, if a little expensive and perhaps on the greasy side, but may include, apart from the more prosaic offerings, liver, sweetbreads, and fassolakia freska (green beans). A meal for one of stuffed tomatoes, tzatziki, a beer, feta and bread costs 550drs.

Georgios Taverna (*Tmr* 16C2)
Directions: Beneath the Bank, on Odhos Apos Karpathion.

I really am unable to work out how this gentleman stays in business. Over a number of years I, and others, have been unable to buy a meal. Apart from simply not being open at traditional hours and turning clients away with the advice that there is no hot food available (despite there being plenty in evidence), the proprietor has a habit of leaving patrons so long that they are forced to leave, rather than pass away due to starvation! It has to be admitted that the owner is the only waiter, but that is his fault.

Zorbas Taverna (*Tmr* 35D2)   * * * *
Directions: Alongside the Esplanade, on the way round from the Ferry-boat Quay.

This establishment is friendly and inexpensive. The hard working-working owner speaks excellent English, having spent some twenty-five years in Australia. He opens up for customers who tip-off the 0500hr ferry-boat and serves an excellent breakfast. Two Nes meh ghala and toast and marmalade for one costs just 200drs. But the yoghurts are the house speciality. They are simply magnificent being served with piles of honey, walnuts, cherries and a fruity sauce. Yoghurt and honey plus coffee for two costs only 400drs. An evening meal for two of veal stifado, chicken and rice, Greek salad, feta, bread and retsina costs 1000drs.

Restaurant Rendezvous (*Tmr* 3D2)
Directions: Closer to the Ferry-boat Quay than *Zorbas* and in the ground floor of the *Hotel Coral*.

Seemingly run by a consortium of hunky young men, at least one of whom, having returned from the USA, speaks excellent American. Not only good value but one of the few places open after 10pm at night. A meal for two of beans, pasta, tzatziki, chicken, chips and a small bottle of quality red wine costs 940drs.

Taverna Kassos (*Tmr* 34B2)
Directions: Round towards the 'Municipal offices' promontory and rather off the 'tourist track', despite which it is a popular eaterie.

The establishment is bamboo shaded and exotically decorated with a seascape and map of Kasos on two of the walls. This latter is the legacy of a previous owner, the present patron being a larger than life character, if rather cynical. His present overpowering regret is that, having spent nine years in Australia and six in the USA, he returned to Karpathos, sent his daughter to the local school where she met, fell in love with and married the local bus driver. Regret? Well, he had to pay over his accrued American savings as a dowry! A meal for two of moussaka, chicken souvlakia with rice, Greek salad, beetroot salad and a kortaki retsina costs 1250drs. A little on the expensive side – perhaps he is hoping to claw back some of that 'lost' money?

THE A TO Z OF USEFUL INFORMATION

AIRLINE OFFICE & TERMINUS (*Tmr* 15B/C2/3) Now a large office of modern appearance located close to the Matheou and Karpathion Sts crossroads. The two Olympic buses park close by. The office is open weekdays between 0800 and 1400hrs.

Aircraft timetable (Mid-season)
Karpathos to Kasos (& vice versa)

Saturday & Sunday	1015hrs
Return	
Tuesday & Thursday	1200hrs

One-way fare: 1190drs; duration 15mins.

Karpathos to Rhodes

Daily	1010, 1630, 1840hrs
Monday, Wednesday & Friday	1015, 1225hrs
Tuesday & Thursday	0805, 1235hrs
Saturday & Sunday	1240hrs
Return	
Daily	0910, 1530, 1740hrs
Monday, Wednesday & Friday	0915, 1125hrs
Tuesday & Thursday	0705, 0915hrs
Saturday & Sunday	0915hrs

One-way fare: 4510drs; duration 40mins.

Karpathos to Sitia(Crete)

Tuesday & Thursday	1015hrs
Return	
Saturday & Sunday	1145hrs

One-way fare: 4510drs; duration 35mins

Karpathos to Athens
Via Rhodes.

BANKS (*Tmr* 16C2) One on the Esplanade, on the right, almost opposite the *Kafeteria Edelweiss*. As it is the island's only foreign exchange bank the relevant desk does get rather busy.

BEACHES The Town possesses a small, rather littered strip of sandy beach, close by the Town Clock. The seaborne, domestic ducks, whose land base is beneath the tables of an adjacent taverna, often disport themselves on this particular bit of sand.

However the main beach is a dusty fifteen minute trudge in the direction of Aperi and takes in two bays. The first, smaller bay, which makes for a very pleasant bathe, is a sandy shore which climbs steeply, the sand forming a backcloth to the beach and the crest of which is topped off by the ruins of a couple of old houses. To the left (*Fsw*), alongside the outset of some small boulders, is a grove of trees affording welcome shade. Where the north horn of this first bay curves round, bamboo groves screen a taverna that caps the mini-headland. The inshore area hereabouts is swampy. Beyond the taverna, a much larger, curving, sandy foreshore encircles the adjoining bay, petering out by a distant refinery plant. Neither beach is crowded, the furthest being usually almost empty of people.

BICYCLE, SCOOTER & CAR HIRE Prior to hiring transport it is essential to consider the mountainous nature of the island's terrain, the general state of the major roads in the south and the lack of almost any metalled roads in the north. There are no bicycles for hire. Hiring two or four wheeled transport is difficult due to the shortage of conveyances and if a traveller only has a few days it is imperative to get on with it.

Gatoulis (*Tmr* 17B/C3)
Directions: Close to the top end of Odhos 28th Octovriou.

Run by Francesca, a large, cuddly, friendly young lady. The 100cc Vespas are rather worn out but the motorbikes are in reasonable condition. The hire rates are expensive, with a scooter costing 1800drs per day, falling to 1700drs for three days hire. Francesca's English is good but she omits to explain that there is only one petrol station and that there are only some 50km of metalled road. Francesca's 'little failings' also include an irritating habit of not advising prospective hirers that her scooters are fully booked, that is until the actual morning of the intended hire. This can prove quite annoying, to say the least. One thing that is without question is unfailing helpfulness.

There is a second rental firm, at the opposite corner of the crossroads from Gatoulis.

M Maloftis (*Tmr* 18D2/3) Originally only a car hire firm, Maloftis is now a full-blown Travel Agent and operates from Odhos Dimokratias. As elsewhere in Greece, car hire is not inexpensive with his Renault cars costing from 6200drs per day with a refundable damage deposit of 10000drs per day.

BOOKSELLERS (*Tmr* 26B/C2/3) There is a small supermarket 'housing' a foreign language newspaper counter. The usual, two or three day old papers but few British versions available.

BREAD SHOPS (*Tmr* 19C3) Yes, at No 76 on 28th Octovriou St, up the hill and beyond *Harry's Pension*.

BUSES Ah, well yes! The buses lurk at the *ad hoc* terminal (*Tmr* 20D3) on the far corner of the crossroads formed by Odhos Dimokratias and 28th Octovriou. To confuse matters further there is a Bus park behind a prominent church (*Tmr* 30C3).

Information regarding timetables is as difficult to acquire as the proverbial dragons teeth, but here goes.

Bus timetable
Karpathos Town to Piles via Aperi, Volada, Othos.
Monday to Saturday   0745, 1115, 1400, 1700hrs
Return journey
Monday to Saturday   0815, 1200, 1530, 1745hrs

Karpathos Town to Amopi Beach*
Monday to Saturday   0930hrs
Return journey
Monday to Saturday   1600hrs
One-way fare: 150drs
*This service very much depends on demand and the weather!

Karpathos Town to Arkasa via Menetes
Monday to Saturday   1300hrs
Return journey
Monday to Saturday   0700hrs

Karpathos Town to Mesohori via Spoa
Tuesday, Thursday   1500hrs
 & Saturday

The services do not operate on Sundays or holidays. Due to the 'uncertainties' of the bus services, the taxis are very active.

See **Possi Travel, Ferry-boat ticket offices, A To Z**.

COMMERCIAL SHOPPING AREA No market but the usual mix of specialist shops and a number of good value Supermarkets including a large unit on the corner of Dimokratias and 28th Octovriou (*Tmr* 22C/D3) and another alongside the Bus terminal (*Tmr* 20D3).

Fish are sold daily from boxes laid out on the pavement, opposite the Town Clock (*Tmr* 2C/D2), and there is a Butcher (*Tmr* 21B/C2/3). Most shops close by 1930hrs.

DISCO One at least on the Aperi road.

FERRY-BOATS Pull in at the Quay (*Tmr* 1C/D1), at the east end of the Esplanade.

Ferry-boat timetable (Mid-season)

Day	Departure time	Ferry-boat	Ports/Islands of Call
Wednesday	0500hrs	Nireas	Kasos,Sitia(Crete),Ag Nikolaos(Crete).
	1415hrs	Golden Vergina	Rhodes.
	2000hrs	Nireas	Diafani(Karpathos),Chalki,Rhodes,Simi, Tilos,Nisiros,Kos,Kalimnos,Astipalaia, Amorgos,Paros,Piraeus(M).
Thursday	0530hrs	Golden Vergina	Kasos,Sitia(Crete),Ag Nikolaos(Crete), Anafi,Santorini,Piraeus(M).

Friday	2000hrs	Panormitis	Kasos.

Saturday	0100hrs	Panormitis	Diafani(Karpathos),Chalki,Rhodes.
	1300hrs	Golden Vergina	Diafani(Karpathos),Chalki,Rhodes.

Sunday	0530hrs	Golden Vergina	Kasos,Sitia(Crete),Ag Nikolaos(Crete), Anafi,Santorini,Folegandros, Milos,Piraeus(M).

FERRY-BOAT TICKET OFFICES
Possi Travel (*Tmr* 24C/D2), Apod Karpathion   Tel 22235
Directions: Facing the Esplanade.
   The irascible, pebble-spectacled, elderly Greek gentleman is distinctly unhelpful and has a disturbing habit of blocking a prospective client's path at the threshold of his agency. His rejoinders tend to be monosyllabic so perhaps it is fortunate that he is now only agent for the **CF Nireas**.
   There are signs in his windows for bus and caique excursion trips which include:-

Bus excursions
Monday	Kira Panaghia.
Tuesday & Thursday.	Spoa, Mesohori, Lefkos Beach.
Saturday	Arkasa.
Sunday	A coach round-trip to Aperi, Othos, Piles, Finiki, Arkasa, Menetes, Karpathos Town, between 0900-1700hrs and at a cost of 1000drs.

Adelais (ΑΔΕΛΑ) caique
Monday	Apella Beach.
Tuesday	Diafani.
Wednesday	Apella Beach.
Thursday	Diafani.
Friday	Apella Beach.
Saturday	Diafani.
Sunday	Diafani.

This craft berths in the crook of the Ferry-boat Quay (*Tmr* 1C/D1).
   The office opens Monday to Saturday between 0800-1300hrs and additionally on Monday, Tuesday, Thursday and Fridays between 1700-2000hrs.

Maloftis Karpathos Travel (*Tmr* 18 D2/3), Odhos Dimokratias   Tel 22754
Directions: On the left (*Sbo*) of the High St.
   This office is agent for the **CF Golden Vergina**, as well as the:-

Xryso Excursion boat
Tuesday, Thursday, Saturday & Sunday	Diafani, Palatia, Tristomo.
Monday, Wednesday & Friday.	Kira Panaghia, Ag Nikolaos.

Note the trip boats are often very crowded and latecomers can miss the boat (whoops), due to lack of space. For the evening return journey a cardigan or sweater will not go amiss because the sun dips below the mountain range, that runs the length of the island, rather earlier than might be expected.

Taking into account the general state of the roads, for once, trip boat excursions are a meritorious possibility.

HAIRDRESSERS More ladies than mens.

MEDICAL CARE
Chemists & Pharmacies (*Tmr* 27) There are two on the Esplanade and another on the 'OTE' Square.
Dentist There is a Dental Surgeon (*Tmr* 28D2).
Hospital (*Tmr* 29B2/3). Now situated alongside Odhos N & M Matheou.

MUNICIPAL OFFICES (*Tmr* 23B2) Yet another block of Italian inspired public offices, with the town hall clock showing a perpetual five to one.

NTOG None. *See* **Travel Agents & Tour Offices, A To Z.**

OTE (*Tmr* 25B/C2/3) On the dusty Square formed by the crossroads of Apod Karpathion and Matheou Sts. A pleasantly disorganised office, the staff of which are very helpful, cheerful and speak good English. Opens daily between 0730-2100hrs, but closed Sundays and holidays.

PETROL The one and only petrol station is positioned on the Aperi road. Note that there is no petrol available anywhere else on the island, so scooter trips to the north of Karpathos must be planned with great care, after which abandon the idea! For these reasons refer to the various Route descriptions and bear in mind a Vespa tankful is unlikely to suffice. A more positive answer is to negotiate with one of the Excursion boat 'chappies' to bring you and the scooter back. It will cost an extra 500drs or so for the scooter. Two stroke mixture is priced at about 550drs for five litres.

PLACES OF INTEREST Due to the lack of archaeological remains, not a lot which is a change, is it not? Even the Church (*Tmr* 30C3) is modern. The trip boat excursions may fill the void (*See* **Ferry-boat Ticket offices, A To Z**).

POLICE
Town (*Tmr* 32B3) Proceed up Odhos 28th Octovriou and the office is a few buildings along from the Post Office.

POST OFFICE (*Tmr* 31B/C3) As for the Town police, just beyond the Francesca Gatoulis scooter hire establishment.

TAXIS (*Tmr* C/D2) The main, well the one and only rank is in Odhos Dimokratias at the junction with the Esplanade. A recognised method of general travel and a great deal of sharing takes place. This is understandable considering, for example, that the one-way bus fare to Amopi Beach is 150drs, and that 'your friendly' taxi only costs some 400drs. For journeys to Olympos or Diafani a taxi is the only (expensive) alternative to the trip boats, but once a punter has experienced the rigours of the route the high cost will be understood!

TRAVEL AGENTS & TOUR OFFICES *See* **Ferrry-boat Ticket offices, A To Z.**

TOILETS There are a set at the bottom of the Ferry-boat Quay (*Tmr* 33D1), but they are very ethnic, being 'squatties', and jolly smelly.

ROUTE ONE
To the Airport via Laki (15km) The road out of Karpathos Town
is a fairly steep, steady climb.

AMOPI BEACH (8km from Karpathos Town) The turning to Amopi is unsignposted, only being identifiable by a notice board indicating the *Poseidon Restaurant* close by the junction. The road winds down with Laki Beach to one side of the small headland and Amopi to the left. *Rooms* are advertised on both beaches.

The road peters out on the edge of the lovely, sandy beach and small bay, with the *Golden Beach Taverna* to one side. This establishment, the main taverna of three, is to be avoided as unquestioning holiday-makers have allowed the management to slip into 'naughty, naughty ways'. The range of food on offer is limited, the portions small and the prices not inexpensive. The waiter is often surly and only serves drinks when he can be bothered. His sister, also surly, presides over the self-service counter and administers the bills. The rounding up or down is always up. Grandpa acts as potman and would not be out of place on a dustcart, and Grandma perspires profusely, often lying in a wicker chair fanning herself with a flyswat and guzzling water (?) from a plastic container.

A number of small, neat holiday flats have been built on the edge of the foreshore with more under construction.

Houses, and the occasional chapel, are to be found dotted around the landscape on the route to the Airport, the other feature of which is the almost horizontally wind blown, stunted trees scattered about the fairly barren countryside. Once the road commences to wind down through the unforgiving, granite stone littered plain towards the southernmost headland, the view is quite dramatic with curving beaches to the east of Cape Liki, on which is impaled a stranded ship.

The Airport and flights have been discoursed about in the Introduction.

ROUTE TWO
To Finiki via Menetes & Arkasa (20km) The turning at the
main road junction for Laki marks the start of a very steep, winding climb to the hilltop village of:-

MENETES (8km from Karpathos Town) Built on and over the crest of the hillside, this is an unspoilt Greek village, with some 1930s Italian influenced architecture and marvellous view.

The road westward from Menetes is similar to driving over a moorland of granite speckled with green, and one may well be congratulating Karpathos on its lack of bamboo shaded tourist tavernas, beach umbrellas and beds, air conditioned buses, donkey rides when, whoops, into view pops up:-

ARKASA (17km from Karpathos Town) The old town, sited across a ravine and celebrated for the remains of a 5th century church, is rather pleasant, if scruffy with a wedding cake church spire and tavernas spread around the main square. But it has spawned a rather unpleasant suburb, more correctly a new development and not a very lovely one at that. If this were not enough, holiday condominiums and a villa complex have been built close by the seashore. Oh goody! Also close to the seashore are several *Rooms* and the *Restaurant To Dilina*.

To the right, (*Fsw*), the road turns north along the coast. After some 1½km there is a very unlovely village rubbish dump alongside a cemetery, on the unmade track to:-

FINIKI (20km from Karpathos Town) The southwards angled path to the left advances to this unattractive fishing hamlet in which some new, square buildings have been erected. The track into the dusty settlement passes a couple of tavernas and ends by a low monument in which is set a water tap. To the left is a small, dirty, sandy beach and to the right a concrete quay to which moor some quite large fishing vessels, all overlooked by a chapel mounted on the hillock to the right.

The Old Road, a wide track, advances along the coast on an attractive 7km journey to the village of Piles but there is a New Road. This is due to be surfaced by 1988 and runs all the way to Cape Proni, it being necessary to turn right, after 5km, to reach Piles. (*See* **Route Three**).

Back at Arkasa, facing out to sea looks over the headland of Cape Paliokastro. There is a classical and mystical ambience about the setting, which is not surprising as it was the ancient site of Arkesia.

To the left of the main road into Arkasa, a green painted sign, proclaiming *Rooms For Rent*, points along an unmade track, down which, after some 200m, a pension and taverna straddle the tree shaded road. To the right a path leads to a sandy beach on which *Nudism Prohibited*. Proceeding further along the track, the landscape opens out into a beautiful, if barren countryside. The shoreline is mostly rocky with the occasional cove of shingly beach, which are unfortunately littered with sea and wind-blown plastic. The map does indicate an unmetalled track connecting with the main Airport road but the profusion of odd paths, interspersed with deep ravines, will probably defy any but the most determined traveller. A very wide track has been driven through to Cape Ag Thoros on which stands, in solitary isolation, a chapel set in a surround of blue sea with the island of rocky Kasos in the middle distance.

ROUTE THREE
To Piles via Aperi, Volada & Othos (15km) The road runs
parallel to the foreshore of Karpathos Town Bay, nearly all the way round to the small refinery and then starts to climb and wind its way up to:-

APERI (8km from Karpathos Town) This squeaky-clean, up-hill village is the 'Gerrards Cross' of Karpathos, positively reeking of wealth. This opulence is due to money remitted from abroad and the return of well heeled expatriates. The houses even display name plates and dates proclaiming which family funded the building – similar to personalised car number plates? There are few shops and no road signs. Aperi was once the island's capital in the days when the inhabitants had to constantly flee from marauding pirates – instead of intrusive tourists?

Immediately beyond Aperi, and prior to the steep turning off for the eastern route north (signposted to Ag Nikolaos *See* **Route Five**), is a roadside chapel, Cycladean in style.

Still climbing, the road advances to:-

VOLADA (10km from Karpathos Town) A similar village to Aperi and from whence, looking upwards, brings a sight of:-

OTHOS (12km from Karpathos Town) The main road (*sic*) narrows through the village. This is constructed in the form of a crescent around the curved hillside, high above and looking down over Vronti Bay, way down the valley. Immediately beyond Othos a rise is breasted and, with the road starting to slope down to Piles, the island of Kasos slides into view. Further on, by a cemetery, the route overlooks the coastal plain between Arkasa and Cape Ag Thoros, stretched out in a beautiful panorama.

PILES (15km from Karpathos Town) A small, lovely, winding, typically Greek island village. The local cheese is scrumptious and can be purchased in the first general store to the right, on entering the village.

Immediately prior to Piles a road leads off south to join up with Finiki (*See* **Route Two**) and through Piles the New Road continues on to the western coastway north. (*See* **Route Four**).

ROUTE FOUR
To Diafani via Lefkos, Mesohori & Spoa (48km) Take
Route One or **Three** and proceed either along the Old or New Road. The two roads merge just to the north of Cape Proni from whence it is a stunningly beautiful, but poorly surfaced journey, alternately crossing open, sun-scorched countryside and plunging through fir tree bowers, all the while skirting Mt Kalolimni. Some 3km north of Piles, a turning to the left angles back southwards to a lovely, crescent shaped bay, with large slab rock set in a deserted, small, shingle foreshore with only one homestead in view.

Beyond Cape Proni, the wide unmade track falls away to the west, with distant views of Lefkos set in a captivating, small curving bay. After some 24km, a signpost indicates the 2km turning off to Lefkos. Here the absolutely magnificent panorama takes in a small chapel on a natural, encircling cove within the larger bay, south of the island of Sokastro.

LEFKOS (26km from Karpathos Town) The access road is paved and, where it enters the village, bends to the right. A path to the left leads to a beach where is a small, red domed church and a few shed-like buildings standing on the backshore. At the right-hand turn, a hand-painted sign proclaims *Rooms To Rent* but the best is still to come. Beyond a Pension/taverna on the left, the road curves to the left revealing the fantastic view over a long, sandy beach set in a deep bay with a few white, square homesteads scattered about and a chapel on the headland.

The road runs out on a grassy headland, on all sides of which are sandy beaches. The sea is brilliantly blue and clear and this is a superb, five star location with miles of sandy beach and rocky, sea washed islets. At the end of the headland are a couple of tavernas, the first one of which, *Vasilis & Maria Rent Rooms*, has double rooms for 800drs, yes 800drs a night.

There is a sign *Nudist Beach* but as there are only ever a dozen or so people here, apart from the height of the season months of July and August, it would be possible to stage a 'starkers' extravaganza without attracting any attention. The only shadow on this idyllic state of affairs is that Possi Travel run an excursion bus here on Tuesdays and Thursdays. Admittedly it is a very small bus!

Back on the 'main road', after another 4km the wide track rises through the same mix of stunningly beautiful countryside to the junction signposted:-

MESOHORI (29km from Karpathos Town) It is inconceivable that a visitor will not be enchanted by Mesohori village, which hangs on the sloping mountain side, high above the coastline.

The track to Mesohori ends alongside a warehouse of sorts and entrance to the village is via a flight of·steps at the top and on the right of which is a large house being converted into a Pension. These steps lead to a maze of narrow, whitewash edged lanes that wind up and down and in and around the white cubic houses. Deep in the middle of the village is a simple 'upstairs taverna', the directions to which defy description. I only found my way there by asking and being handed on from one villager to another. Once located, you can rely on a simple but super meal. For example a vast Greek salad, a very large plate of kalamares cooked with green beans, tomatoes and onions, two beers, a lemon drink and bread finished off with a plate brimming with grapes costs some 550drs. Beat that. Communication with the few card playing locals is difficult but a knowledge of Italian is a help.

Back at the 'main track', after some 3km and immediately past a ridge on which stands five ruined windmills, the route runs into a spacious, dusty, totally unsignposted junction. It has to be admitted that there are new signs if approaching this junction from either the eastern coast route or from the direction of Diafani. The track to the right is the eastern coast route back to Karpathos Town (See **Route Five**), whilst the left fork leads to another, narrow junction immediately above.:-

SPOA (33km (western route) or 24km (eastern route) from Karpathos Town The path to the right leads to this unexceptional village, beyond which a track descends to the tiny harbour of Ag Nikolaos.

Before and above Spoa, the track climbing the hillside to the left looks to be a minor donkey path, but persevere for this is the Diafani road – no, no a slip of the tongue, certainly not a road. I suppose the route from Spoa to Olympos is one of the worst, spine juddering rides I have ever experienced. The landscape in places is lunar, the area having suffered severe forest fires, with round topped hills shouldering aside ravines and fjord–like sea indents. The track, which undulates violently, often fords small spring-like streams (the mountain side sometimes appears to 'leak'), in places runs along the top of the narrow, mountainous spine of the island, with steepling drops to either side, only to plunge down to the bottom of the sheer sided mountain and then climb steeply out again. After 8km, a turning to the right tumbles down to the beach at Ag Minas. Do ignore the left-hand branch track another 1½km further on along the route.

Prior to attaining the celebrated village of Olympos, and before rounding the slopes of Mt Profitis Ilias, on which the village is built, there is what I can only describe as a 'Deserted Medieval Village', a hauntingly terraced, abandoned habitation, that is apart from one stone built house around which are signs of cultivation. I have also observed one person, a donkey and a pick-up truck.

OLYMPOS (45km (eastern route) from Karpathos Town) The approach is marked by more, very neat terracing, a number of now disused windmills, many small and beautifully painted chapels, sundry round, stone threshing floors and the occasional woman spinning on the threshold of the family house, complete with distaff and spindle. A dead bus 'lurks' to the right whilst the village lies to the left, around and surmounting a hill-top on the side of the mountain. First impressions include the village women attired in their distinctive head-dress and costumes, the many churches, rich soil and a general air of neatness. This latter virtue is encouraged by any number of large, orange litter bins.

The inaccessibility of the village until comparatively recent times has preserved an ancient way of life in a kind of time warp. The houses reputedly retain an affinity with those of Homer's day, the give-away indicators being the sectioning into three, the striking, solid timber doors with wooden keys and locks and the colourfully painted verandas. The house interiors are singular, more especially the front rooms which are dominated by a balcony bed or furniture, including carved dressers which are more often than not laden with gilt photographs, plates, glass and trinkets standing on embroidered, woven coverings and or lacework.

The women, dressed in their traditional costume, bake the village's bread in the outdoor, community ovens which are sited up a stony path to the left. A batch is prepared whenever the village runs out – about once a week. The inhabitants are said to retain a dialect dating back to the Dorians. The womens' unique dress consists of a black headscarf, often embroidered, a white ruffled and buttoned shirt, black waistcoat, a black or grey skirt overlaid with a large apron, thick stockings and boots or sandals, depending on the weather, in addition to which ample jewellery is worn.

There are many simple *Rooms* and small pensions in the village and the average double room rate, sharing a bathroom, is 1000drs per night. A combined pension and taverna is run by one of the partners in the trip boat that runs between Karpathos Town and Diafani – would it be otherwise? At the *Hotel Astra*, on the 'main road' (ho, ho) into the village 'proper', a modern double room, with an en suite bathroom, costs 1600drs and this is the most expensive accommodation in Olympos.

For bus connections *See* **Diafani**. As for the rest of the island, Olympos village should be visited before the airport extension is completed. You have been warned!

A path westward drops steeply towards the tiny port and beach of Fyses.

From Olympos to Diafani, the carriageway resembles a wide, dry river-bed and is a downward tumbling and winding swathe which cuts through the surrounding pine forests. It is rumoured that this length of the route is to be surfaced, after which the road from Spoa will be treated. Oh yes!

A turning off to the left, on a broad, sweeping bend in the track, proceeds to the small, abandoned settlement of:-

AVLONA (50km from Karpathos Town) The area is well watered with springs and possesses a rich soil.

From Avlona paths lead left to Cape Vroukounda and a beach, whereon are littered remains and ruins of an ancient civilisation with chambers cut into the cliff-face. At the site of Ag Ionnis a festival is held every year, on 28/29th August, in remembrance of St John the Headless (Ugh!) around which dates the tracks and byways become quite crowded with locals and expatriates.

A path to the right leads to the ancient harbour of Tristomo, almost at the very north end of the island, the sea entrance to which is difficult, except in calm weather.

To top off Karpathos, a narrow, fairly shallow channel separates the deserted island of Saria, once host to the now abandoned, waterless, 8th century east coast settlement of Palatia.

Back at the main road (what main road?) the boulderous track tumbles down on to a wide, rocky causeway edging the village of:-

DIAFANI (49km from Karpathos Town)

ARRIVAL BY ROAD

The entrance to the port almost has to be divined but pick the largest (short) lane, which is the High St and runs down to the seafront. The village is built on a grid layout and the flavour is similar to that of Olympos, but rather more Turkish. The women, of gypsy appearance, dress in traditional costume, woollen leggings, leather boots and jewellery, including large, gold, dangly ear-rings.

ARRIVAL BY FERRY

The pint-sized finger quay, to the right (*Sbo*) of the *Mayflower Hotel*, is usually draped with fishing nets and can only accommodate the smaller inter-island ferries such as the **FB Panormitis** – as long as the sea's are not rough. The larger boats, when and if they stop, employ a local boat owner to ferry passengers, their goods and chattels to and from the shore at a per head fee of 50drs.

For Ferry-boat connections *See* **Karpathos Town.**

THE ACCOMMODATION & EATING OUT

The Mayflower Hotel (Class B Pension)
Nick Vasiliadis and his wife run this small but pleasant hotel, the six rooms have thirteen beds and the rates for a double room start at 1000drs. His American is excellent and was learnt in Baltimore.

There is also the *Golden Beach Hotel & Restaurant*, the *Pensions Diafani Palace* and *Claros*. The proprietor of the Golden Beach is a partner in the trip boat business and agent for the ferry-boat companies.

The numerous tavernas usually display and proclaim their offerings in English.

The pebble and sand beach stretches to the right of the quay (*Fsw*). Camping is organised at the far end of the cove, which is edged by low cliffs topped off by a church. There is another agreeable beach at Vananda, about ½hr to the north of Diafani.

Diafani does not possess a Bank, OTE (but does have public local telephones), petrol station or a Post Office.

The oft-mentioned trip boat owners and crew are surly and generally rather unhelpful, which is rather significant as they make up a fair percentage of the local population. This attitude may be because they are rather lionised by the Scandinavians and Germans. On the other hand, I have had cause to be very grateful for their assistance in getting back to Karpathos Town on an occasion when I ran out of petrol. They just loaded the scooter on board and carted us back. But the one-way fare from Diafani to Karpathos Town is pricy at 750drs per head and a scooter is charged at about 500drs.

Probably the best way to visit Olympos is to stay at Diafani for a day or two and make use of the local bus, a taxi or walk (well perhaps not). If you must make the two hour trek on foot there is a 'stream accompanied path' through the forest. Close by Olympos this trail criss-crosses the vehicle track but the route indicators can be difficult to spot.

The Diafani bus connects with Olympos weekdays at 0800hrs (for school children who attend the Olympos school), 1100hrs (for ferry-boaters) and 1700hrs.

ROUTE FIVE

To Diafani via the east coast The eastern coast route, connecting north and south of the island, has the advantage of being shorter and comparatively less traumatic than Route Four. Initially follow **Route Three**. The necessary track branches off above the village of Aperi to advance via the lower flanks of Mt Kalolimni. There are side turnings down to Kira Panaghia as well as the lovely and sandy beach of Apella, crowded in by towering cliffs. This passage joins with the western route (*See* **Route Four**), just prior to Spoa, at a rather 'lunar' junction.

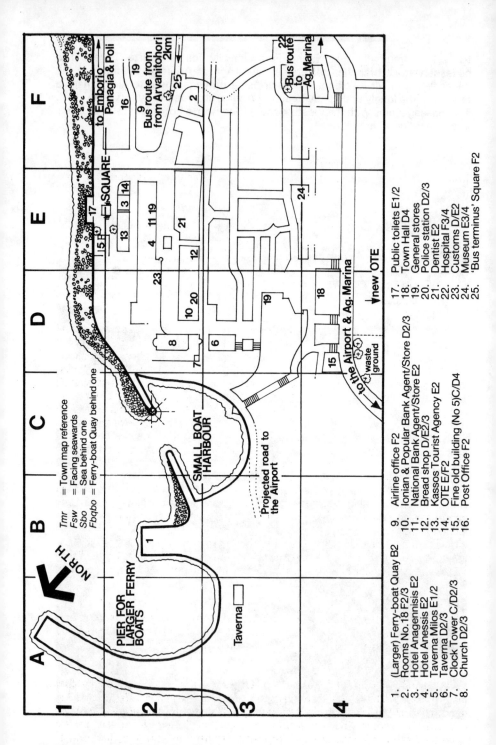

Illustration 21 Fry Port

16 KASOS (Kassos) *

Dodecanese Islands

FIRST IMPRESSIONS
Stones, boulders and more stones...; barren, messy and sad; depopulated; very friendly, welcoming people; chickens everywhere.

SPECIALITIES
Not a lot except for Suez Canal pilots and, of course, the Holocaust.

RELIGIOUS HOLIDAYS & FESTIVALS
include: 6/7th June – Celebrations in memory of the 'Holocaust', Kasos Town.

VITAL STATISTICS
Tel prefix 0245. Length 18km, up to 7km wide and a population of about 1,200.

HISTORY
Being so adjacent, it mirrors the events of Karpathos island, with some notable exceptions. The inhabitants once numbered about 20,000 people, but now only some 1,200 soldier on. Apart from the unattractive nature of the place, depredation of the population was 'helped along' by the Egyptians, then allies of the Turks. They razed the island to the ground, well more to the stone, in a savage assault in 1824, still referred to as the 'Holocaust' (what's new!). Apart from killing the menfolk and firing the villages, the Egyptians carried off 2,000 women and children to slavery. Such are the vagaries of history, that only thirty five years later some 5,000 Kasiot men 'upped and off' to Egypt to assist in the construction of the Suez Canal. This act of navvying, added to the renowned skill of the island sailors, had an interesting spin-off in that many of the islanders became Suez pilots, resulting in a once sizeable Greek community at Port Said. Then, forerunners of their tanker owning countrymen years later, a number of perspicacious citizens used their initiative, saw the advantages of steam, returned to Kasos, presumably hocked the goats and granny and were amongst the first Greeks to opt for and operate steamships in preference to sail.

There are now few tangible remains of the resultant family fortunes (*See* **Panaghia, Route Two**) because they also had the foresight to emigrate again. There is a local saying that if all the Kasiot shipowners were to return to Kasos, then they would circle the island three times.

GENERAL
Nowadays many of the inhabitants commute to North America for months at a time. It is wise counsel, as on Karpathos island, to voice adverse comments in a *sotto voce* – most of the locals have a good understanding of English, more American really.

It is interesting that follow up research only confirms my original proposition that Kasos really is almost without a redeeming feature. Plus points include the unfailing friendliness of the islanders and the thought that Kasos undoubtedly remains untouched by tourism. Thus travellers who wish to see 'Greece in the raw' can do no better than drop in (and quickly 'drop out'). Furthermore, since my first visit to Kasos, I have had the totally unforgettable experience of researching Salaminas

(Mainland islands), after which there can be no doubt that this latter island nudges Kasos up and off the bottom rung of the 'Golden Duffer Ladder' of appalling Greek islands.

FRY (Phry, Fri, Ophrys): capital town & port (Illustration 21)

Whereas some years ago the 'suburb' of Emborio was the only ferry-boat port, a new finger pier has been constructed adjacent to Fry Town, north of the settlement. This and the Airport rather disproves the constant contention, the obsessional grizzle by Mr Manousos (a local worthy of whom more, much more) that the Government simply refuse to promote the touristic 'delights' of Kasos.

ARRIVAL BY AIR

A sweet, neat, little, earth airfield some 15 minutes walk from Fry. The airport is graced with a simple, small shed, which is being extended. At the moment this contains passenger seats and a very clean toilet block. When the extension is complete it is planned to provide a bar serving drinks.

On the last visit, the 'air traffic controller', who presides over a 1952 receiver, had been stationed there for ten months and was very, very keen to get a transfer, but with no luck to date. His complaints were (inevitably) '...stones, no food, stones, no nightlife, stones and no women'! Surely not in that order?

Passengers are expected to walk into town. There are two taxis but one is usually broken down and the remaining driver is pretty busy shuffling locals about. Anybody lucky enough to catch a cab will have to pay 250drs. The bus does not include the Airport on its scheduled route but truck driving locals usually offer a lift.

The present track from the airfield becomes dusty and dirty at the outskirts of Fry. The buildings either side of this road are old and decrepit or simply falling down. My notes record that... *the remains of an old display cabinet rots away on one side of the road, a ramshackle chicken yard and shed fences in some rather scrawny, earth scratching chickens and faces a waste site on which rubbish is littered. Some of the old streets and houses are worthy of note but it is a squalid, incoherent town!*. Need one say more.

ARRIVAL BY FERRY

Arrangements have changed a lot in recent years. The smaller ferry-boats, which include the **Nireas** and **Panormitis**, still dock at Emborio Port whilst the larger ferries, such as the **Golden Vergina**, berth at the new finger pier (*Tmr* 1B2).

Emborio Port (Illustration 22) The port area is also rather squalid and

untidy. The sea leg of the small harbour is closed off by a quite substantial commercial quay. The space left for the ferry-boats is strictly limited and their docking at night is impressive, to say the least, more especially because, as usual, they dock stern-on. The ferries plough into the small neck of the harbour entrance and, using the ship's searchlight to focus the mountainous hillside, perform the tricky manoeuvre with all the panache of a Mini car driver backing into a tight parking space.

The larger fishing boats berth in one crook of the Harbour wall and a thin stretch of beach runs down to the other angle, where the smaller craft are slipped over smooth, flat rocks.

Pretensions to grandeur are evidenced by the small, still projected public garden, the municipal toilet block, which is 'kept' in an indescribable condition, and a rather avant-garde but unused, column mounted port office.

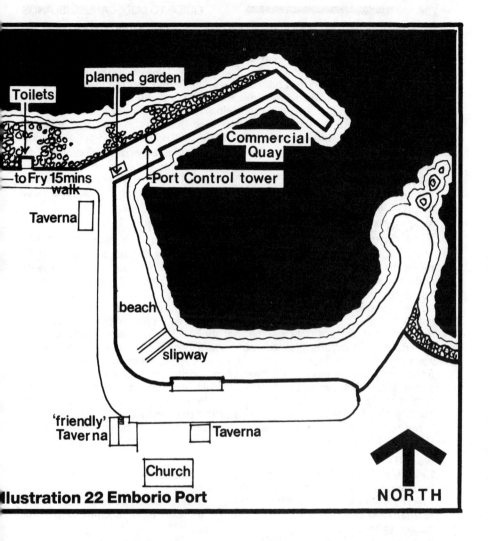

Toilets

planned garden

—to Fry 15mins walk

Taverna

Port Control tower

Commercial Quay

beach

slipway

'friendly' Taverna

Taverna

Church

Illustration 22 Emborio Port

NORTH

Three tavernas vie for the traveller's business and my own favourite is the larger one situated on the angled corner, opposite the slipway berthed boats. The family and various helpers assist in a rather slovenly but engaging fashion and the large patio is pleasant. This taverna is a meeting place for the Kasiot youth. The toilet, or more strictly the area in which to carry out one's ablutions, is reached by climbing the steep bank behind the taverna and stumbling into a ruins bestrewn hayfield. Hey ho! Emmanuel Manousos does chide me (not only about this matter!), pointing out that there is a 'perfectly adequate and unoffensive lavatory a few steps beyond the entrance to the Church courtyard'. Smacked hand Geoffrey!

The large Church to the right of the taverna is worthy of more than a passing glance. An old lady, who lives close by, is the custodian of the key and, with pride, shows visitors the interior, which is suffering from a serious attack of damp. The grandiose, pebble mosaic floor is interesting and harks back to the days of the affluent, now long departed Sea Captains.

As the Airfield is to the west of town, this port is to the east, about 15 minutes walk round the curving coastline. The road passes through a scattering of houses, past the old and new schools, a column-fronted building of grandiose proportions and uncertain antecedents, a windmill and, half-way between port and town, on the right, a fairly modern block with **Rooms**. That the locals do have a heart is nowhere better illustrated than on this walk for, amongst the dusty rubbish and general sleazy state of the roadside, young saplings were planted some years ago, albeit inside rusting, forty gallon oil drums. This was a necessary precaution in order to hinder stray donkeys and goats, who usually eat anything green. There certainly is little enough plant life without any pillaging by animals. Unfortunately these well intentioned efforts have come to naught, as most of the saplings have died.

THE ACCOMMODATON & EATING OUT
The Accommodation At some stage visitors must meet the 'Mr Big' of Kasos, Emmanuel S. Manousos, if only because this hard-working zealot owns the *Hotel Anagennisis*, as well as, in the same block, a travel agency and large store. In actual fact he is a slim, quietly dressed man with thinning hair and a passionate, all-consuming belief in the tourist future of Kasos. He speaks excellent English, having lived in America and been a merchant navy ship's captain. Unfortunately the earnest, but very pleasant Mr Manousos is 'up against it' for not only are the 'delights' of Kasos questionable but local politics and politicians are not four-square behind him. It is rumoured, for instance, that the Mayor, of far Left persuasion, decreed that instead of advertising the pleasures of a particular, sandy beach (a very desirable and incidentally much needed facility for Kasos), the sand would be better used for building purposes. Mr Manousos and his more Right-of-centre colleagues, eagerly, nay fanatically, beating the drum of tourism, were not amused.

But to proceed with the subject in hand, before discussing the few hotels, there are **Rooms** hidden away here and there – not many but they include:-

No. 18 (*Tmr* 2F2/3)
Directions: Beyond the Square formed by the junction of the roads to Arvanitohori and Ag Marina, and on which the bus parks.

A pleasant little house with flower covered facade, run by an ancient 'Grand Mama' who may have to break through the cobwebs to come out of the garden gate.

There is a Pension half-way between the Town and Emborio Port.

Hotel Anagennisis (*Tmr* 3E2) (Class C)   Tel 41323
Directions: Overlooks the Main Square, which edges the sea.

Surprisingly, bearing in mind the owner, Mr Manousos', obsession, nay desperation to increase tourism, he usually first proffers his most expensive, finest double room facing the sea with en suite bathroom facilities. Fine but this 'bridal suite', costs between 1750 and 2190drs. Resist these blandishments, plead poverty, explain you are English and you may well be offered a double room costing from 1500drs to 1625drs (1st July-30th Sept). Admittedly they face the back street but are quite adequate with a hand basin, a reasonably comfortable bed with nice, fat pillows, as well as clean, ironed bedsheets. The shared showers are of the two position variety, cold or 'my goodness that's hot! The lavatory, which is cleaned every day, tends to become very smelly. The prices listed are the official rates. The proprietor has been known to request as much as 1725drs for the least expensive double room and there are reports of his asking as much as 3500drs, but this can only be a rumour!

Hotel Anessis (*Tmr* 4E2) (Class C) 9 G Mavrikaki   Tel 41201
Directions: One block behind tHe *Anagennisis* but, as there is no sign, it might be necessary to ask for final instructions.
     Only double rooms with en suite bathrooms. Prices start from 1750drs rising to 2000drs (1st June-30th Sept).

See **Beaches, A To Z** for an interesting possibility at Ag Georgios Monastery.

The Eating Out My all-round choice, from the small selection, would be the:-

Taverna Milos (*Tmr* 5E1/2)
Directions: On the left flank (*Fsw*) of the Main Square . The barn like building has a large terrace, the wall of which edges the sea lapped boulders a few metres below. Due to the prevailing winds, the north-west side of the patio is protected by woven rush matting.
     The proprietor's father, a Suez pilot for 25 years, helps his son out when necessary and the owner is also assisted by a motley collection of young lads and a fellow of lascar appearance. Reasonably priced offerings which are eaten with the sound of the sea in one ear and, possibly, pop music in the other (ear). The father's second language is French but the son speaks reasonably good English. An excellent Greek salad, loukanika (sausages), a plate of chips, bread and a small beer costs 470drs. The menu includes pizza, chops and interesting mezes. Incidentally the lavatories are adequate.

Another, more 'local' Taverna (*Tmr* 6D2/3) is sited opposite the Church and (its separate) Clock Tower. Incidentally, the clock hands facing seawards are permanently 'set' at 20 to 6, whilst the inland face works, but is 15 minutes fast.
     Various other bars serve meals.

THE A TO Z OF USEFUL INFORMATION

AIRLINE OFFICE & TERMINUS (*Tmr* 9F2) The office is located in a dilapidated building across the street from the Post Office, although last minute information informs me that it has been moved to the 'old' OTE office (*Tmr* 14E/F2). Supposedly opens Monday to Friday between 0700-1400hrs but... There is no airport bus. By the by, ignore the various Olympic ticket signs in Mr Manousos' travel agency. He is not allowed to supply '...because I don't like Mr Papandreou (The Prime Minister) so he has stopped me selling them' – a quote!

Aircraft timetable (Mid-season)
Kasos to Rhodes (& vice versa)

Monday, Wednesday	0805hrs
Friday & Sunday	
Return	
Monday, Wednesday	0705hrs
Friday & Sunday	

One-way fare: 4420drs; duration 40mins.

Kasos to Karpathos*
Tuesday & Thursday   1200hrs
Return
Saturday & Sunday   1015hrs
One-way fare: 1190drs; duration 15mins.
*Note connections can be made at Karpathos with Rhodes bound flights.

Kasos to Sitia(Crete)
Saturday & Sunday   1050hrs
Return
Tuesday & Thursday   1110hrs
One-way fare: 3470drs; duration 35mins.

BANKS None, only agents, one for the Ionian and Popular (*Tmr* 10D2/3) and the other for the National Bank of Greece (*Tmr* 11E2), both run by storekeepers.

BEACHES Yes, well. The Town Beach is a small patch of large pebbles, nestling between large slabs of shelving lava rock covered in a fine down of dead seaweed, some tar and a fair sprinkling of flotsam and plastic. Oh Kasos is every face set against you!
    There is a better prospect, some way beyond the airport strip, west around the headland. This is close to Ag Georgios Monastery where, incidentally, visitors can stay at night for free!
    The 'recognised' beach is sandy and set in pleasant surroundings but is located on the nearby Armathia island, which can only be reached by using the local caique service from the small (and pretty) Town Harbour. Isn't that just Kasos' luck. The sea journey takes 15mins and costs 500drs.

Mr Manousos raves on about the three hour distant Chochlakia Beach, way down at the south-west end of the island. Oh yes!

BICYCLE, SCOOTER & CAR HIRE None.

BREAD SHOPS One (*Tmr* 12D/E2/3), in an easterly direction from the Church and Clock Tower.

BUSES Well one bus actually, the turn round point for which is the Square (*Tmr* 25F2), close by the *KKE* office notice board. The small bus describes a circular route via Ag Marina and Arvanitohori. The driver deserves a medal as the route through the two villages is, in some sections, very, very narrow and winding.
    The bus schedule refers to a 'Kathistres' which is a 'suburb' of Ag Marina. The driver, who speaks English, makes additional sallies to help out passengers who, say, want to go to Panaghia.

Bus timetable
Kasos Town to Ag Marina & Arvanitohori

Daily   0700, 0800 and every hour on the hour until 2000hrs.
One-way fares: Kasos Town to Ag Marina 50drs
                        to Arvanitohori 50drs.

The round trip costs 100drs and the duration is about 45mins.

COMMERCIAL SHOPPING AREA None. In fact due to the necessity for everything to be shipped in, more especially fruit, vegetables, milk, yoghurt and cheese, most items are always out of stock. Poor old Kasos!
    There are a number of General stores (*Tmr* 10D2/3, 11E2 & 19) which open

some or all of the day. Chickens and turkeys are very common, but should this not be dealt with under Flora and Fauna?

DISCOS There isn't even a disco. Probably the local youngsters do not have the energy to club together to make the venture worthwhile.

FERRY-BOATS *See* **Arrival By Ferry.**

Ferry-boat timetable (Mid-season)

Day	Departure time	Ferry-boat	Ports/Islands of Call
Wednesday	0700hrs	Nireas	Sitia(Crete),Ag Nikolaos(Crete).
	1100hrs	Golden Vergina	Karpathos,Rhodes.
	1800hrs	Nireas	Karpathos,Diafani(Karpathos),Chalki, Rhodes,Simi,Tilos,Nisiros,Kos,Kalimnos, Astipalaia,Amorgos,Paros,Piraeus(M).
Thursday	0700hrs	Golden Vergina	Sitia(Crete),Ag Nikolaos(Crete),Anafi, Santorini,Piraeus(M).
Friday	2300hrs	Panormitis	Karpathos,Diafani(Karpathos), Chalki,Rhodes.
Saturday	1100hrs	Golden Vergina	Karpathos,Diafani(Karpathos),Chalki, Rhodes
Sunday	0730hrs	Golden Vergina	Sitia(Crete),Ag Nikolaos(Crete),Anafi, Santorini,Folegandros,Milos,Piraeus(M).

FERRY-BOAT TICKET OFFICE
Kassos Maritime & Tourist Agency (*Tmr* 13E2) The proprietor, Mr Manousos, has waged a constant battle to increase the number of inter-island ferries that call at Kasos, in order to bump up the tourists that visit the island. The office is open six days a week, closing between 1300-1630hrs.

The agent for The Ionian and Popular Bank (*Tmr* 10D2/3) has a notice in his window, drawing ferry-boat travellers' attention to the free, third class tickets available between Kasos and Rhodes (and vice versa) during the months of April, May, September and October. Passengers wishing to travel in a higher class pay the difference. This concession is to encourage out of season passenger traffic to and from Kasos.

MEDICAL CARE
Chemists & Pharmacies None, but the general stores stock this-and-that. The official information leaflet advertises that the town possesses ...*a surgery with oxygen, a sterilisation unit and a doctor* – better than a bricklayer stepping in I suppose!
Dentist (*Tmr* 21E2). Across the street from a general store and situated in a ramshackle little building.
Doctor *See* **Telephone Numbers & Addresses, A To Z**.
Hospital (*Tmr* 22F3/4). Housed in a largish, yellow painted, rather pleasant looking building on the side of the Square from whence the bus heads for Ag Marina.

NTOG No.

OTE (*Tmr* 14E/F2) Very centrally located at the end of the 'Manousos' block and open Monday to Friday between 0730-1510hrs. Another facility is 'under construction' (*Tmr* D4) with the dish receiver in place but, in 1987, not yet open.

PETROL No, but Mr Manousos (who else?) has been trying to remedy this since 1985 – for the life of me, I cannot see why. Unlucky Mr Manousos is up against a Government veto.

PLACES OF INTEREST Not a lot really, although a desultory effort has been made to create a focal point of the rather abject Main Square (*Tmr* E1/2). A central monument, an urn draped with a cloth, is flanked by four small cannons, well three as one has toppled into the Square...

There is a fine but rapidly dilapidating building at No 5 (*Tmr* 15C/D4), opposite the waste ground plot, on the road out to the airfield.

Museum (*Tmr* 24E3/4). Yes...! Even the key holder, the redoubtable Mr Manousos, is unable to recommend this 'forgettable' archaeological backwater. To quote '... there is a Museum, but we are unfortunate in Kasos that most of our ruins are underground'. Well they would be, wouldn't they? The building is not labelled but a couple of tiny, rusty cannons and some broken hunks of column piled outside marks the spot.

POLICE
Town (*Tmr* 20D2/3). In the 'bakery' street and on the right, heading towards the fishing boat harbour.

POST OFFICE (*Tmr* 16F2) Yes (that caught you out!) at No 5, almost opposite a general store. This latter is interestingly owned by one of the islanders who commutes between Kasos and the USA during the year.

TAXIS Yes, but elusive.

TELEPHONE NUMBERS & ADDRESSES
Doctor   Tel 41333

TRAVEL AGENTS & TOUR OFFICES
Kassos Maritime & Tourist Agency (*Tmr* 13E2) *See* **Ferry-boat Ticket office, A To Z**. The 'public spirited' Mr Manousos has produced an island map with a town plan and an imaginative descriptive text.

TOILETS Fry possesses a fairly disgusting facility (*Tmr* 17E1/2), the position of which really does not need identifying as anyone with the remotest olfactory sense should be able to sniff them out. They are built into and below the sea wall, alongside the Main Square.

ROUTE ONE
To Arvanitohori via Ag Marina (4km) From the Bus Square (*Tmr* 25F2), the narrow, badly surfaced tarmacadam road winds through the back streets of Fry, calling for unbelievable judgement on behalf of the bus driver, who is understandably fond of using his horn. The road emerges at the west of town, curving up the heavily terraced but painfully dry foothills, passing the right fork which drops down to the Airport. Incidentally, there are no bus stops, the driver simply pulling up outside peoples houses. The first village reached is:-

AG MARINA (1km from Fry Town) This attractive village straddles the hill overlooking Fry, and is dominated by a pleasantly constructed, cobalt blue and white painted, red domed church, with a separate, wedding cake tiered bell tower.
From Ag Marina the road drops gradually at first but increasingly steeply towards Arvanitohori, demanding more valiant efforts on the part of the driver.

At one point the route crosses a painfully dry river-bed, full of stones and scorched looking, dead trees – which rather seems to sum up Kasos...!

ARVANITOHORI (2km from Fry Town) A straggling settlement with quite a lot of new building taking place amongst the slow ruin of the old. The village name refers to the fact that this was where a nucleus of Albanians settled in a 16th century migration. There are *Rooms* to let.

At Arvanitohori the bus makes a ten-point turn to regain the circular route back to Fry.

ROUTE TWO
To Poli via Panaghia (4km) The turning for the inexorable climb up the ever ascending foothills takes off from the Fry to Emborio Port road. After about one kilometre a narrow road, to the left, branches off to what, at first sight, looks like a new housing estate, at the village of:-

PANAGHIA (1 km from Fry Town) A closer look is well worth while because the way through the newer houses leads to an 'Old Quarter' wherein, unfortunately, the original large houses of the Sea Captains and ship owners have fallen or are falling down. It must have been a substantial and prosperous community once upon a time, but the wealthy emigrated when the Italians appeared on the scene, moving to Syros island and London, never to return. A certain amount of bulldozing appears to be taking place and the Greeks, never ones to waste building materials, have used the once stately wooden doors and window shutters of the mansions to assist in the construction of jerry-built chicken and turkey pens.

Surprise, surprise, there are Cycladean style public toilets up the steps of the path beyond and to one side of the surprisingly large church and clock tower... Men's to one hand and ladies to the other.

The villagers chat and may well profer a hospitable drink.

The main road if one can use such a descriptive word, windingly ascends to:-

POLI (3km from Fry Town) The hike to this neat village takes about one hour. To the left side, a wide track advances to a well kept church and clock tower set in the hillsides, with old terracing climbing up and up and up the flanks of the towering mountain range to the right.

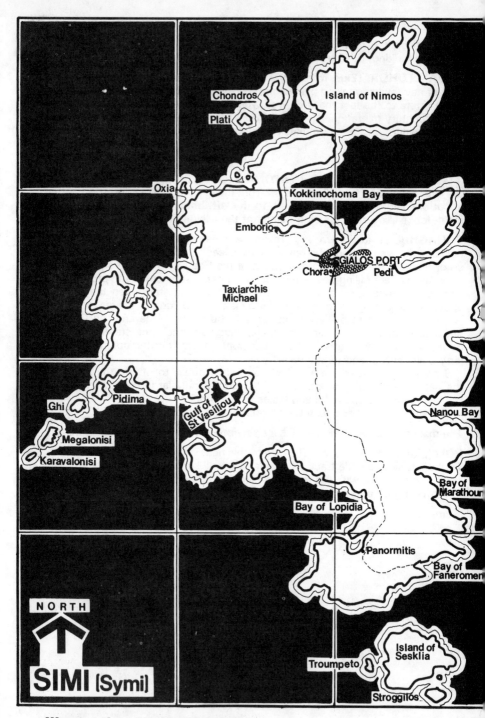

Illustration 23 Simi island

17 SIMI (Symi, Syme)
Dodecanese Islands

Scenically ★★★★
Ambience ★★

FIRST IMPRESSIONS
Breathtakingly beautiful island port; tourist trap and trip boat paradise – overcharging (is there a connection?); shortage of accommodation and water.

SPECIALITIES
Day trips.

RELIGIOUS HOLIDAYS & FESTIVALS
include: 7th-9th November – Panormitis Monastery.

VITAL STATISTICS
Tel prefix 0241. About 12km long and 10km wide with a population of 2,500, most of whom live in or around the main town (Chora) and the port (Gialos).

HISTORY
Much of Simi's history has revolved around their ability as builders of sea-going vessels. The islanders were purported to have supplied battleships as long ago as the Trojan wars when they built and crewed three of the legendary triremes. The Knights of St John and the Turks, during their respective occupations, used the skill of the Symiot boatbuilders who, incidentally, were the first of the Dodecanese islands to rise up against their Turkish overlords during the War of Independence. Another curiosity is that the official surrender of the Dodecanese to the Allies was signed, on the 8th May 1945, in the building half-way along the north side of Gialos Harbour, now the *Pension (& Restaurant) Les Katerinettes* (*Tmr* 5B1/2). Apart from boatbuilding, another lost island skill is that of sponge diving, which is now almost entirely the preserve of the islanders of Kalimnos. That is not to say sponges are not sold here.

The deserted, empty and derelict houses, seen on many Greek islands, are a constant source of bewilderment to overseas visitors. It is possible to identify the root cause as the Greek inheritance laws, in addition to which, quite often, beneficiaries of a will may be a number of children who fail to agree on the best course of action in respect of a particular property. On Simi, in common with one or two other Aegean islands, the legacies pass through the female line, which has resulted in an even greater migration of young males than is usual.

GIALOS/SIMI: the port (as opposed to The Chora, the old town) (Illustration 24) Simply, one of the most strikingly attractive Greek island port's, the first visit to which must remain indelibly engraved on any seaborne caller's memory. But not all that 'glistens is gold...' The lack of the usual Greek social graces forcibly strikes most visitors, as must the inordinate amount of rubbish littering the back streets that climb the surrounding hillsides.

The inter-island ferries steam into the horseshoe bay of Gialos Port, around the steep hillsides of which the buildings rise, amphitheatre-like in the fashion of a Doric set of playing cards. It seems as if each house is piled on the one below. In fact one of the modern-day social engineering problems confronting the citizens is that often the cellar and septic tank of one dwelling is the upper

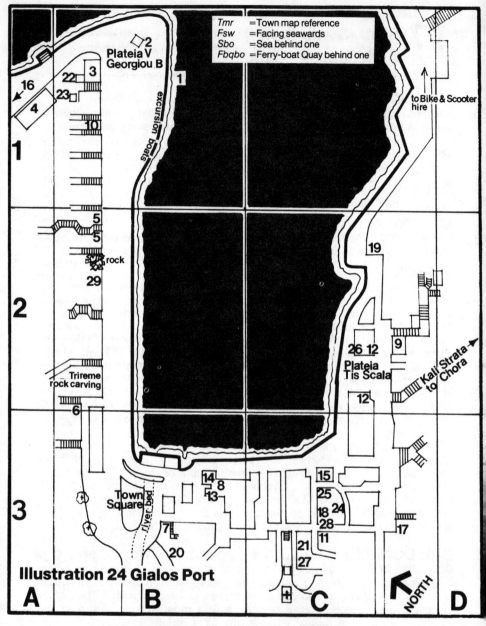

Illustration 24 Gialos Port

Tmr	=Town map reference	
Fsw	=Facing seawards	
Sbo	=Sea behind one	
Fbqbo	=Ferry-boat Quay behind one	

NORTH

Tmr 1. Ferry-boat Quay B1
2. Clock Tower B1
3. Town Police office B1
4. Hotel & 'Kafe' -bar Nireus A1
5. Pension & Restaurant Les Katerinettes B1/2
6. Hotel Panormitis B2/3
7. Hotel Glafkos B3
8. Hotel & Restaurant Zephyrus B3
9. Rooms Agli C2
10. Pastry shop B1
11. Taverna O Merakles C3
12. Taverna Trawler C2/3
13. Souvlaki stall B3
14. Cheese pie shop B3
15. Ionian & Popular Bank C3

16. (To the) Beach
17. Baker C/D3
18. Baker C3
19. Bus park C2
20. OTE B3
21. Pharmacy C3
22. Post Office B1
23. Port police B1
24. Public toilets C3
25. Symi Tours C3
26. Symian Holidays C2
27. Dentist C3
28. National Bank of Greece C3
29. Sunny Land Travel office B2

bedroom wall of the next one down! That and the chronic shortage of drinking water have combined to channel the tourist development of Simi into a day-trip 'paradise'.

It was but a few years ago that the Port only fully opened for the period immediately prior to the arrival of the trip boats, closing on their departure. These factors led to a general attitude of 'take a profit while you can'. It is no coincidence that it is of Simi that the, possibly apocryphal, story is told of the police being forced, on several occasions, to close down every restaurant and taverna in the place for excessive profiteering. There is no doubt that overcharging takes place and that the normal, leisurely Greek nature has been supplemented by a disagreeable and graceless 'take it or leave it' attitude. The locals get very indignant when these unpalatable home truths are presented to them, expostulating 'No, who....?' When advised of a particular instance they cry 'Ah well him, yes we know all about him!' ('Not me guv'!). In defence of the islanders, they are subject to a daily invasion of up to six or seven excursion boats from Rhodes and Kos every day, week in, week out for some seven months – which would be quite enough to try the patience of any saint.

Gialos and its surrounds become extremely hot during the day as the windless bay acts almost like an oven, which makes two reasons for the wise to abandon the port area between the trip boat hours of 1000 and 1600hrs.

Fortunately there is no airport so we only have to discourse about:-

ARRIVAL BY FERRY (*Tmr* 1B1)
The inter-island ferries berth close by the Clock Tower (*Tmr* 2B1), across the quayside from the Greco-Italianesque Police Headquarters (*Tmr* 3B1), at the right-hand (*Sbo*) tip of the Harbour. From here it is a trudge along an unmade and, at night, poorly lit Esplanade to the centre of activity, at the bottom of the Harbour.

The excursion boats from Rhodes and Kos also dock close to the Ferry-boat Quay.

THE ACCOMMODATION & EATING OUT
The Accommodation Difficult to locate and expensive with double rooms costing a minimum of 1300drs per night. Furthermore owners may well insist on a minimum of two or three days room occupation. Those that do find rooms tend to stay put, as there is a steady flow of devoted Simi visitors who stop-over for the duration of their vacation. The standard of accommodation varies between 'simple to primitive'. A graphic illustration is the story told to us by a middle-aged Greek lady regarding a stay she 'enjoyed' at Simi, some few years ago. When she asked to see the bathroom, the elderly owner directed our friend to a very large rain-water butt! Enough to say she beat a hasty retreat.

The situation may be relieved by the still awaited completion of the refurbishment of the *Hotel Nireus*. This latter event is now some four years overdue!

Symi Tours, Symian Holidays and or Sunny Land can assist in the location of accommodation. (*See* **Travel Agents & Tour Offices, A To Z**).

Hotel Kafe-Bar Nireus (*Tmr* 4A/1) (Class B) 2 Plateia Vassileos Georgiou B
Tel 71386
Directions: Along the waterfront to the right (*Sbo*), immediately around the corner from the Police HQ (*Tmr* 3B1).

The reopening of this municipally owned establishment is scheduled for... sometime in the future!

The *Hotel Aliki* (Tel 71655), beyond the *Nireus*, is an A class establishment and probably too 'rich' at 5400drs for a double room, naturally en suite. Unquestionably a lovely set-up, but the quayside here is not wide enough for the hotel's waterfront tables and chairs to be anything but part of the 'ramblas'. As the only local beach is this way....! Another drawback is that this particular section of the bay can be rather smelly.

Along the Esplanade, towards the centre of the port, the next accommodation is the:-

Pension Les Katerinettes (*Tmr* 5B1/2)   Tel 71671
Directions: As above.
   The lady who runs the establishment speaks excellent English. A double room costs 2000drs, but this pension is usually block booked. Easing out a resident to make space is extremely difficult.

Accommodation is also available at the:-

Hotel Panormitis (ΜΑΝΟΡΜΙΤΗΣ) (*Tmr* 6B2/3)
Directions: Two-thirds of the way along the Esplanade. Immediately beyond the rock carving of a trireme, turn up the small side-street and narrow steps to the right-hand side of the square building.

Following the sea wall round to the left and over the bridge leaves the Town Square on the right.

Hotel Glafkos (*Tmr* 7B3)
Directions: Across the road and summer-dry river-bed from the Town Square.
   Old fashioned, 'island provincial' and run by elderly couple. A double room, sharing a bathroom, costs from 1500drs.

The Hotel (& Restaurant) Zephyrus (*Tmr* 8B3)
Directions: Above the *Restaurant Zephyrus*.
   Basic accommodation, sharing the bathrooms, with a double room costing from 1300drs per night.
Further on round the Esplanade, along the other side of the quay and behind the *Trawler Taverna* (*Tmr* 12C2/3), or, more correctly, Plateia Tis Skala, is:-

Rooms Agli (*Tmr* 9C2)
Directions: As above.
   Maria, the Mama who runs this clean pension with the help (or more accurately hindrance) of her disenchanting (sic) daughters, does not live on the premises, but up the steep steps to the left of the accommodation.
   A double room sharing a bathroom costs 1350drs, but she may well insist on a minimum stay of three days. There is a communal fridge on the landing.
   Maria has purchased another house to one side of and beyond the main Town Square. This building is quite interesting as it is, in the main, unspoiled by the conversion to *Rooms*, that is except for the modern bathroom built on the back of the house. Architecturally of note are the wooden shutters, old wooden stairs, the ceiling hinged mirror (reminiscent of Lindos on Rhodes island) and old-fashioned, kitchen dresser. The water is drawn from a well, but now with the aid of a modern, Japanese pump unit.

For more accommodation *See* **The Chora (or Old Town)**.

The Eating Out
The various establishments are on the expensive side, in addition to which much 'schlepping' takes place. Beer is often only obtainable in cans (a pet hate of mine) or, worse still, 'on draught'.

The Pastry Shop (*Tmr* 10B1)
Directions: The first waterfront cafe along from the Clock Tower.
   A good value, friendly place but the service is a little slapdash. It is probably the best location from which to watch the ferry-boats dock.

There are a large number of eating places, but I have chosen to list just a few, including the:-

Taverna (Ο ΜΕΡΑΚΛΘΣ) (*Tmr* 11C3)
Directions: In a street parallel to, and one back from, the waterfront.
   If the proprietor recognises you as a 'stop-over', rather than a day-tripper, he becomes rather more gracious and attentive. Unfortunately the diminutive portions are expensive and there are only large bottles of retsina available.

Taverna Trawler (*Tmr* 12C2/3) Plateia Tis Skala.
Directions: Alongside the 'east' Esplanade.
   The chairs and tables of this excellent establishment occupy most of the Square on which it is located. The owners employ a rather peculiar system of displaying their fish and other wares in a bar on the right-hand (*Sbo*) side of the plateia and cooking the meals in a cellar kitchen and outside grill on the other side of the Square. The prices are reasonable, for Simi that is, and they sell a small bottle of retsina. A plate of giant beans, feta and a large beer cost 400drs. The service becomes a 'little hectic' as the evening wears on.

There is a souvlaki stall (*Tmr* 13B3) behind the shop serving cheese pies (*Tmr* 14B3), both close to the Esplanade.
   Perhaps the fact that I saw a man carving a giro cone of meat using an electric carving knife, not with the traditional sharp blade, sums up 'matters gastronmic'. Even more 'emblematic' of the sheer awfulness is the automatic coffee machine propped on the Square close to the *Cheese Pie Shop* (*Tmr* 14B3). The instructions literally read.... *HOT COFFEE. SUGARED COFFEE, MORE SUGARED COFFEE. MORE SUGARED COFFEE WITH MILK*. Oh dear!

THE A TO Z OF USEFUL INFORMATION
BANKS The Ionian and Popular (*Tmr* 15C3) has a branch, as does the National Bank of Greece (*Tmr* 28C3).

BEACHES The Town Beach involves a walk beyond the Police HQ (*Tmr* 3B1), past the *Hotel Aliki*, skirting the small caique repair yard and beneath the splendid, large, cobalt domed Church. This was built in 1948 to celebrate the reunion with Greece and is reached up a steep flight of steps. Beyond a small bluff beneath the church leads to a beach bar discotheque. It is necessary to wander through this establishment to gain access to the very small, crowded, fine pebble beach located in a lovely setting. There is a certain amount of nude bathing on the rocks beyond.

BICYCLE, SCOOTER & CAR HIRE Despite the official island maps optimistically detailing roads that are simply nothing more than rough tracks, which is most of the island's roadways, there is a rental firm, the:-

Scooter & Bike Hire

Directions: They operate from a 'waterfront warehouse' located beyond the Bus park (*Tmr* 19C2), on the right-hand (*Fsw*) side of Gialos Port Bay.

The hire rates are extremely expensive with a bicycle costing 400drs per day and a scooter 1800drs. As there is no petrol station, fuel is included in the rental.

For car hire refer to the **Travel Agents & Tour Offices, A To Z**.

BREAD SHOPS Well, actually baker's and there are two. One (*Tmr* 17C/D3) is run by a splendid, moustachioed man with every appearance of being a comic opera bandit and the other (*Tmr* 18C3) by a rather ungracious family. The latter, on occasions, exhibit the unfortunate aspect of the Simi shopkeepers pecuniary peculiarities. The bread costs some 50drs but the change often only slowly 'see's the light of one's hand', just in case a client might depart without waiting for the same.

BUSES There are now two 'buslets' or, more accurately, multi-seated vans. One is painted blue, 'The Simi Bus', and the other green. The vehicles have to be small enough to wriggle through the winding, narrow streets of The Chora on the way up and over to the port village of Pedi. There are no other metalled roads, despite the cartographer's imaginative use of red indicating any number of 'roads of motorway standard'. Motorway – donkey maybe! The lay-by in which the buses park (*Tmr* 19C2), is to the right-hand (*Fsw*) side of the Harbour. The two bus drivers are young men of manic persuasion, probably hopeful of achieving a Grand Prix drive. Their lust for speed is relieved by attempting to race against all or any other traffic at the same time as recklessly hurtling along the street.

Bus timetable
The theory is that one bus should depart from Gialos Port at the same time as the other leaves Pedi. The timetable kicks off daily at 0800hrs and thereafter every half-hour until 1830hrs, after which they depart hourly until 2230hrs. Now, that is the theory. The schedule is complicated by the buses pulling up at undesignated places and not halting at official bus stops! Unwitting tourists, naturally enough, queue at the 'proper stops', only to have to chase the receding back of the bus in order to determine the driver's idea of where he will stop. The one-way fare to Pedi costs 40drs.

Trip boats tend to take the place of public transport. *See* **Travel Agents & Tour Offices, A To Z**.

COMMERCIAL SHOPPING AREA None. There are various stores and shops but prices can be very high. Most provisions have to be ferried in and the vegetables offered are generally of poor quality.

There are Peripteros, the liquor store, opposite the Baker (*Tmr* 18/C3), sells bulk ouzo and there is a Butcher close to the *Hotel Glafkos* (*Tmr* 7B3). Small island opening hours with siesta for all but the tourist shops.

DISCOS One located in the old market building AKTAION, beyond the Bus park (*Tmr* 19C2) and aptly named *Waves*.

FERRY-BOATS & FLYING DOLPHINS The inter-island ferries dock at the far, left-hand (*Fsw*) end of the Esplanade (*Tmr* 1B1), alongside the Clock Tower. Stern to berthing may well prove to be a tricky manoeuvre in a strong wind. The quay wall is scattered with old gun barrels fixed vertically to provide mooring bollards, but they are spaced rather close together and the ferry ramp may, in adverse conditions, catch these stout obstacles. The adjacent quayside is often used for the bulk storage of building materials.

The hydrofoils, which pull up alongside the quay half-way down from the Ferry-boat berth, only run if there are sufficient passengers who wish to visit Simi from Rhodes.

Ferry-boat timetable (Mid-season)

Day	Departure time	Ferry-boat	Ports/Islands of Call
Monday	1400hrs	Panormitis	Tilos,Nisiros,Kos,Kalimnos,Leros, Lipsos,Patmos,Arki,Angathonisi, Pythagorion(Samos).
Wednesday	0600hrs	Panormitis	Rhodes.
Thursday	0600hrs	Nireas	Tilos,Nisiros,Kos,Kalimnos,Astipalaia, Amorgos,Piraeus(M).
	1130hrs	Panormitis	Tilos,Nisiros,Kos,Kalimnos.
Friday	0530hrs	Panormitis	Rhodes.

In addition to the above there is local excursion/ferry-boat as follows:-

Daily	1545hrs	FB Simi	Rhodes.
Thursday & Saturday	0545hrs	FB Simi	Rhodes

The **FB Simi** departs from the Excursion boat stretch of the Port, the town side of the Ferry-boat Quay (*Tmr* 1B1).

Flying Dolphin timetable (Mid-season)
Note: Only runs if there are enough Rhodes passengers.

Day	Departure time	Ports/Islands of Call
Monday to Saturday	1600hrs	Rhodes
Sunday	0845hrs	Kos, Rhodes.
	1930hrs	Rhodes.

FERRY-BOAT & FLYING DOLPHIN TICKET OFFICES Inter-island and excursion ferry-boat tickets can be obtained on board.

MEDICAL CARE
Chemists & Pharmacies (*Tmr* 21C3) There is one alongside the rather unusual, rectangular church courtyard.
Dentist (*Tmr* 27C3) Next door to the Pharmacy.
Doctor The island doctor's surgery is in The Chora.

OTE (*Tmr* 20B3) Located in a pleasant, old, stone building to the left (*Sbo*) of the river-bed. The office opens Monday to Friday between 0800-2000hrs.

NTOG None.

PETROL No.

PLACES OF INTEREST Not a lot but the very interesting Chora (the Old Town) possesses a small Museum and, overlooking the Chora, a Castle built by the Knights (well, well), within the walls of which is a church.

The ridge overlooking the Port, and to the left of the Castle, is ringed with 'dead' windmills.

The large, carved portion of rocky hill-side, located half-way down the right-hand side of the bay (*Sbo*), close by the *Hotel Panormitis* (*Tmr* 6B2/3), portrays a trireme. This is similar (at least to my eyes) to the famous sculpture at the entrance to the Lindos (Rhodes) Acropolis, but I can find no mention of it in official literature.

POST OFFICE (*Tmr* 22B1) Up the steps to the side of the Police Station.

POLICE
Port (*Tmr* 23B1) Almost opposite the Post Office.
Town (*Tmr* 3B1).

TAXIS They rank close to the Bus 'terminus' (*Tmr* 19C2) and the drivers include a lady.

TOILETS (*Tmr* 24C3) Yes, in the block behind, and to one side of the Ionian and Popular Bank.

TRAVEL AGENTS & TOUR OFFICES They will advise and assist regarding all and everything. Firms include:-

Symi Tours (*Tmr* 25C3 – tel 71307), who also operate a book-swop scheme,
Symian Holidays (*Tmr* 26C2 – tel 71077)
and:-
Sunny Land (*Tmr* 29B2 – tel 71413).

They also book and or advise in respect of the multitudinous trip boats that encircle most of the island and its inlets, with fares ranging between 500drs and 1200drs per head.

THE CHORA: the old town
The bus makes the trip up to the old town, high on the hill-side above Gialos Port, on the way to Pedi village. The Chora may also be reached by walking, well more scaling the wide, broad flagstone staircase which leads off Plateia Tis Scala (*Tmr* C2). The flight of steps decants on to the Chora Main Square, whereon the *Rainbow Hotel* to the right of some old windmills.

The Chora and Gialos are as different as a quiet old town and a bustling, frenetic port could be. The Chora is a very large village which has evolved in a maze of garishly coloured houses, lanes and alleys that jig up and down and round and about. The chaos of the layout is such that the Museum and Castle, so thoughtfully signposted at the outset, are 'left to their own devices' and have to be hunted down. Why not spend a day or three in this peaceful, high altitude backwater, away from the madding crowds.

ROUTE ONE
To Pedi via The Chora (2km)
It does seem further, much further than two kilometres when walking up to The Chora and down to Pedi. The bus takes to the long, uphill track, that streaks out of the Port from the right-hand (*Fsw*) side of the bay, before winding and 'narrowing' tortuously back into The Chora. The straight, steeply angled, metalled road down to the port and small hamlet, that makes up the village of Pedi, is hemmed in by hills that are almost painfully dry. I do not state 'small' port as the concrete jetty that stretches into the bottle-necked bay is surprisingly large. Quite often, fairly big ships berth alongside for running repairs and painting.

The road makes a T-junction with the waterfront, opposite the main jetty. The 'High Street', or 'Esplanade', hugging the edge of the curving bay to the right (*Fsw*), is simply a track edging the backshore, with very small, stone jetties projecting, here and there, into the water. Prior to the bus pulling up on an unmade square, it charges along the narrow but sandy shore on a track which is indistinguishable from the beach. It certainly makes the sunbathers sit up in a panic... and this happens every thirty minutes. Much of the water's edge is composed of large pebbles whilst the shallow, shelving sea-bed is slimy, algae covered round stones.

Half-way round the semi-circle of the bay is the curious architecture and even more freakish external decoration of the *Sun Beach Cafe Bar*, which does tend to pull one up with a start. The acropolis style upper storey is painted pink and the terraced ground floor, brick red with white lines to simulate brickwork – Oh well, it takes all sorts. This cafe-bar is followed by a taverna and the foreshore finally runs out in the backyard of a private house, plonked down on the water's edge.

The *Pedi Beach Hotel & Restaurant* is now completed but requests 5500drs per night for an en suite double room, which charge does include breakfast...! Meals are also expensive with a plate of stuffed tomatoes costing 350drs and a Greek salad 220drs.

There are unheralded **Rooms** in the village as long as a prospect wants to stay several nights. Enquiries at the few travel offices or of locals will elicit directions, but the accommodation is expensive with a double room costing from 2000drs upwards.

The bay possesses a scattering of spindly trees and a couple of palm trees growing close by the centrally located Church. To the left (*Fsw*), the foreshore curves away without even the semblance of a track. The wide, raised concrete patios and steps of the equally spaced houses are connected in a series of small jetties. This frontage finally runs out on a disorganised, flat, scrubbly plain at the far left-hand end of the bay.

ROUTE TWO
Panormitis Monastery Excursion
The Monastery lies at the south end of the island and one tour company organises a bumpy 'Truck Trip', costing 1300drs. A more genteel, if somewhat crowded voyage can be made by trip boat, at a cost of 1100drs. Bookings should be made at one of the Gialos Port Travel Agents.

The substantial, if rather palace-like, 18th century Monastery Archangel Michael and associated buildings, which incorporate a museum, stretch along the edge of a lovely bay with a small, sandy beach (the island's only 'genuine' sandy beach). Entrance to the Monastery is free but note the 'clothing rules' are strictly applied, and there is none for hire.

It is possible to stay overnight, but the once free hospitality has now been replaced by the (secular?) charge of some 1200drs. There are a couple of pricey restaurants but a pleasant waterfront cafe is not outrageously expensive and the staff are very helpful. The latter establishment sells a very limited range of supplies and if out of bread, for instance, are just as likely to send a client to the very gates of the Monastery

The location is probably more organised than would be expected and is the venue for the extravaganza of a religious festival held between the 7-9th November.

ROUTE THREE
Emborio (Nimporios) Excursion
About two kilometres to the west of Gialos Port, Emborio, historically a commercial port, now doubles up as a summer holiday beach. There are some Byzantine mosaics still visible.

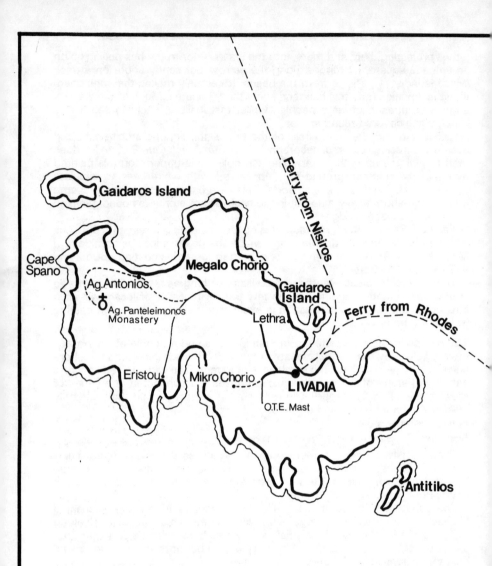

Illustration 25 Tilos island

18 TILOS (Telos, Episkopi)
Dodecanese Islands

****

FIRST IMPRESSIONS
Quiet; remote; undeveloped; few inhabitants; singing crickets; jackdaws; clear seas; stale bread.

SPECIALITIES
Honey.

RELIGIOUS HOLIDAYS & FESTIVALS
include: 15th August – Festival, Panaghia Church, Mikro Chorio; 23rd August – Festival, Panaghia Monastery, Nr Livadia; 27th August – Festival, Ag Panteleimonos Monastery.

VITAL STATISTICS
Tel prefix 0241. The island is some 17½km, north-west to south-east, and 'waists' down to 3km at the narrowest point, with a population of approximately 300.

HISTORY
As for the other Dodecanese islands but one claim to fame is the mastadon skeletons found in caves in the hills, some fifteen years ago.

GENERAL
One occasionally ponders about this and that (what ho Jeeves), and why Tilos remains so unvisited certainly is a mystery. There is a pleasant port; plentiful water (and the Army); an old town, Megalo Chorio; a ruined castle; many beaches, some of very good quality; reasonably frequent ferry-boat connections and some accommodation. So where are the visitors? It has to be admitted that there was little or no island transport and (until 1986) few metalled roads but that has not stopped less attractive, more unpretentious islands with far more 'drawbacks' from attracting swarms of visitors.

LIVADIA (Levadhia): port (Illustration 26) Set in a large, broad, hill surrounded inlet, with the development to the right-hand side (*Sbo*), and a clean, narrow, almost white, pebble and shingle seashore sweeping away to the left round the bay. From a distance the whiteness of the sea's edge gives the appearance of waves breaking on the foreshore.

The small but adequate port facility is inconveniently edged by enormous concrete lamp standards. In the hurly-burly and excitement of a ferry-boat's arrival it is not unknown for one of the island's few lorries to collide with one of them. The *Taverna Blue Sky* (*Tmr* 2A2), conveniently sited on the edge of the quay, sports an *Information Board* and the hillside 'terraces' its way up behind the building.

The seafront and port is prettily planted with tamarisk and cypress trees whilst there is a grove of fruit trees to the east of the attractive, 'standard' Italian municipal building which houses the police and customs offices.

ARRIVAL BY FERRY
This will be at the reasonably large concrete quay (*Tmr* 1A/B1) backed by the *Blue Sky Taverna*. The usual chaos of ferry-boat arrivals is 'enhanced' by the fact that, as there are so relatively few ferry-boat arrivals, all the locals turn out to collect

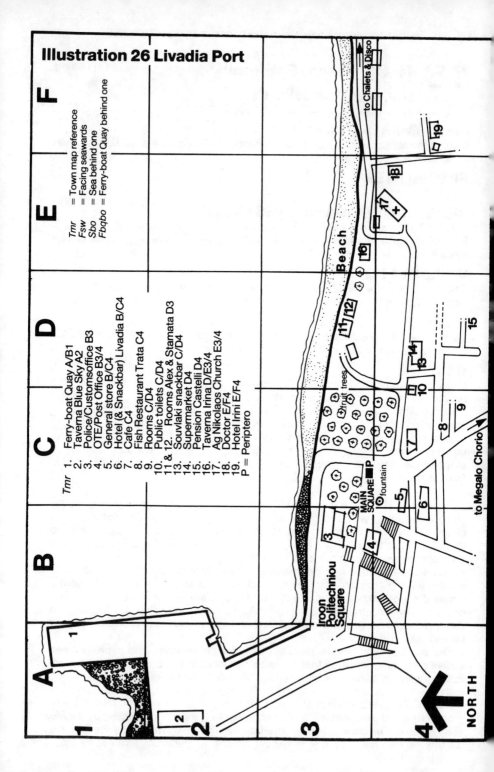

Illustration 26 Livadia Port

Tmr = Town map reference
Fsw = Facing seawards
Sbo = Sea behind one
Fbqbo = Ferry-boat Quay behind one

Tmr
1. Ferry-boat Quay A/B1
2. Taverna Blue Sky A2
3. Police/Customs office B3
4. OTE/Post Office B3/4
5. General store B/C4
6. Hotel (& Snackbar) Livadia B/C4
7. Cafe C4
8. Fish Restaurant Trata C4
9. Rooms C/D4
10. Public toilets C/D4
11 & 12. Rooms Alex & Stamata D3
13. Souvlaki snackbar C/D4
14. Supermarket D4
15. Pension Castelli D4
16. Taverna Irina D/E3/4
17. Ag Nikolaos Church E3/4
18. Doctor E/F4
19. Hotel Irini E/F4
P = Periptero

Iroon Politechniou Square

Beach

MAIN SQUARE P
fountain

fruit trees

to Chalets & Disco

to Megalo Chorio

NORTH

food, bread, mail, relatives and anything else which may have been unloaded. Room owners sometimes meet the ferries, though they are easy to miss amid the general confusion.

THE ACCOMMODATION & EATING OUT
The Accommodation Up until recent years the island had only one hotel, but now the new *Hotel Irini* and another Pension also vie for the business with the few **Rooms** scattered throughout the village. The first hotel in sight is the:-

Hotel Livadia (*Tmr* 6B/C4) (Class E)   Tel 53202
Directions: Above the Main Square.
   Inexpensive, with double rooms sharing a bathroom costing from 900drs and those with an en suite bathroom 1200drs.
   The snackbar in the basement is expensive. A Coke, toasted sandwich and two small bottles of retsina cost 600drs. There is an advertisements in respect of boat trips to distant beaches (though on enquiring the fisherman concerned takes some finding). The hotel also has a minibus used to transport clients and others to various island 'attractions'.

Rooms (*Tmr* 9C/D4)
Directions: Up the hill beyond the *Hotel Livadia* and to the left.
   Overpriced at 1300drs for a double room, which is in fact the family living room in rather shabby disguise.

Better to turn left out of the Main Square (*Sbo*) and then immediately left again to the seafront and:-
Rooms Alex & Stamata (*Tmr* 11 & 12D3)
Directions: As above, close to the beach backshore.
   I have lumped them two together because the two ladies, who run the respective establishments, seem to work in tandem - well, certainly in a co-operative fashion. Additionally their accommodations are very similar, with identical prices. A very pleasant double room, sharing the sparklingly clean bathroom, costs 1060drs although it is possible to negotiate a small discount for more than two nights stay (1000drs a night).
   Both *Alex* and *Stamata* have patios built out over the sea's edge, and Stamata's serves breakfast for 130drs per head, which includes Nes meh ghala, bread, butter and jam. There is also the provision of a shared fridge and washing line. Super accommodation, splendidly situated in a marvellous place at great prices. Can one say more?

Following the road on beyond the lane down to *Rooms Alex and Stamata* leads past the Church (*Tmr* 17E3/4) to the backshore of the beach. Immediately beyond the Church, a lane to the right is signposted to the:-

Hotel Irini (*Tmr* 19E/F4) (Class C)   Tel 53293
Directions: As above and on the left, along a short track.
   Extremely pretty, tasteful and attractive accommodation... at a price. These superb en suite double rooms, with balcony and inclusive of breakfast, cost 2500drs. The hotel owner, a rather 'pushy' young man is nevertheless extremely enthusiastic about tourism on Tilos. His modern, spotless hotel has many thoughtful and useful requirements including a telephone, island maps, a book and magazine-swop scheme as well as a jeep in which he runs his clients around the island, if they so wish. He also gives detailed advice on the

various places of interest. The hotel caters for 'away-from-it-all-package tourists' from *Twelve Islands* but, apart from the height of season months, there is usually 'room at the inn'.

The other place to stay is the:-
Pension Castelli (*Tmr* 15D4)
Directions: Left (*Sbo*) from Square towards the Church, then first right, left, right and left.
　　Modern and reasonably priced with shared bathrooms. A single room costs 600drs and a double room 1200drs.

The Eating Out For a small place, the selection is fair enough, but than you don't really need a vast range when you can find a taverna as nice as the:-

Taverna Irina (*Tmr* 16D/E3/4)
Directions: Proceed to the Church, where swing down towards the beach backshore.
　　Run by Georgi, a very friendly and affable man, who speaks good, self-taught English. Food is reasonably priced, and very tasty. Stuffed courgettes, tzatziki, taramosalata, chips, Greek salad, bread, and a bottle of retsina costs 720drs. His octopus in a sauce is an excellent suggestion when available.

The other establishment well worth patronising is the:-
Taverna Blue Sky (*Tmr* 2A2)
Directions: On the edge of the large Ferry-boat Quay.
　　Yiannis, the very nice taverna owner who is a veritable mine of local information, is helped out by a couple of personable young lads. Good food at reasonable prices. For instance a tasty, filling pizza for two costs 500drs.
Other eating places include the aforementioned, rather overpriced *Livadia Snackbar* (*Tmr* 6B/C4) and, across the road from the *Livadia*, the *Fish Restaurant Trata* (*Tmr* 8C4). This is also expensive with two souvlaki, one portion of fish and one bottle of retsina costing 1500drs.

The A TO Z OF USEFUL INFORMATION
BANKS None. *See* **Post Office, A To Z.**

BEACHES The white pebble beach of Livadia Port stretches for about 2km around the long bay with beautifully clear sea for bathing. This is the best beach in the area. Those who wish to try another location should take the cliff path north from the Port which leads, after an hour's walk, to Lethra, a narrow, white pebble beach.

BICYCLE, SCOOTER & CAR HIRE None in 1987, but there are rumours that, as from 1988, scooters may be available.

BOOKSELLERS No, but the *Hotel Irini* (*Tmr* 19E/F4) sells some paperbacks and operates a book-swop scheme.

BREAD SHOPS The island had no bakery as recently as 1987, though one was being built. Until that is 'up and running', bread is brought in, twice weekly, from Rhodes and sold in the Supermarket (*Tmr* 14D4). Stocks can run low and taverna bread acquires a distinctly 'hard edge' on the second day.

BUSES None but at about 1000hrs daily a brown pick-up truck appears on the Main Square from Megalo Chorio. This acts as a communal taxi for those who want to go elsewhere. *See Hotel Livadia* (*Tmr* 6B/C4) and *Hotel Irini* (*Tmr* 19E/F4) for alternative transport.

CINEMA No.

COMMERCIAL SHOPPING AREA Ha, ha – more a new Supermarket (*Tmr* 14D4) and the old, ubiquitous 'everything' General store (*Tmr* 5B/C4) bordering the Main Square. Although, in days of yore, water abundant Tilos grew many crops, agricultural products have dwindled, along with the population. Nowadays most fruit and vegetables have to be 'shipped' in.

Opening hours are the small island 'norm'.

DISCOS Yes (groan) the **Live Sound Disco** opened in June 1987, about 500m along the beach road. However, it does not seem to 'boom', either in terms of noise or custom!

FERRY-BOATS Ferries drop in five days a week.

Ferry-boat timetable (Mid-season)

Day	Departure time	Ferry-boat	Ports/Islands of Call
Monday	1615hrs	Panormitis	Nisiros,Kos,Kalimnos,Lipsos,Patmos, Arki,Angathonisi,Pythagorion(Samos).
Tuesday	1730hrs	Nireas	Simi,Rhodes.
Wednesday	0300hrs	Panormitis	Simi,Rhodes.
Thursday	0800hrs	Nireas	Nisiros,Kos,Kalimnos,Astipalaia, Amorgos,Paros,Piraeus(M).
	1300hrs	Panormitis	Nisiros,Kos,Kalimnos.
Friday	0300hrs	Panormitis	Simi,Rhodes.

FERRY-BOAT TICKET OFFICES There isn't an office, tickets being purchased on the Ferry-boat Quay, immediately prior to departure, or on board the particular ferry.

MEDICAL CARE
Chemist & Pharmacy/Doctor (*Tmr* 18E/F4). The doctor's surgery, beyond the Church, doubles up as a pharmacy. There is another doctor in Megalo Chorio.

NTOG No.

OTE (*Tmr* 4B3/4) The office is combined with the Post Office on the Main Square. Opens between 0730-1400hrs, weekdays only.

PETROL Not surprisingly, no petrol station and not much petrol to be begged, stolen or borrowed either.

POLICE
Port The Customs officers double up as Port policemen. They are located in the same large, blue and white castellated building on the edge of the seafront Square, Plateia Iroon Politechniou, as the other police force:-
Town (*Tmr* 3B3)

POST OFFICE (*Tmr* 4B3/4) On the Main Square and open weekdays between 0730-1400hrs. Transacts foreign currency exchange.

TAXIS *See* **Buses, A To Z.**

TELEPHONE NUMBERS & ADDRESSES

Doctor (*Tmr* 18E/F4)	Tel 53294
Megalo Chorio	Tel 53210
Police, town (*Tmr* 3B3)	Tel 53222

TOILETS (*Tmr* 10C/D4) To the left (*Sbo*) from the Main Square. A new block but now not very 'invitingly' maintained. Both the toilet block and the Police station 'sport' large, ultra-violet flycatchers!

TRAVEL AGENTS & TOUR OFFICES None.

ROUTE ONE
To Megalo Chorio (9km) (and the beaches of Eristou & Ag Antonios) via Mikro Chorio
Although there is a cement road linking Livadia Port with Megalo Chorio, which continues on to Eristou, transport is difficult to find. There are no buses, no taxis and no scooter or bicycle hire. However, until 1986 even the road between Livadia and Megalo Chorio was not paved. Now this has been completed, rumour has it that, as early as 1988, the island may have a bus, moped hire... and even a petrol station! On the other hand, up to midsummer 1987 there was no sign of any of these 'activities'.

The only means of 'public' transport to date is provided by the brown Datsun pick-up truck, which appears in Livadia's Main Square at 1000hrs daily and transports passengers to Megalo Chorio and or the Monastery, if demand is sufficient.

The road from Livadia towards Megalo Chorio climbs steeply, in a series of hairpin bends, up the hillside behind the Port. After one kilometre the road levels out and another narrow, cement road takes off to the left. This is signed *OTE* and leads either to the transmitter/receiver on top of the mountain or, more interestingly, after a few hundred metres, a rough, narrow track, labelled *Mikpo Xopio* on a hand painted sign, which advances to the hillside village of:-

MIKRO CHORIO This is a weird, quiet, deserted place around which to wander. The pink, red and white, 'edible-looking' village Church is the only building which is still kept in a good state of repair. The key is, or was, kept in a hole up and to the left of the door. The lovely icons are well worth viewing.

The main road continues, on a gentle downward slope, past quarry workings on the right and a narrow valley to the left. After 9km, above the road on the hillside, hoves into view:-

MEGALO CHORIO (9km from Livadia Port) The islands biggest settlement and the only other inhabited village besides the Port, boasting a population of 210 people. A pretty, quiet, whitewashed village, with narrow streets and steps twisting among the houses. A path leads up to the ruined Venetian fortress, on the rock above the village. The Castle, as is the case of other Dodecanese strongholds, was built on and over much earlier fortifications and incorporates some easily noticeable features from the ancient buildings. These include details of the main gateway as well as the marble flights of steps inside the gates.

There are an almost disproportionate number of churches and a small, single story museum that the locals hoped to fill with island archaeological finds as well as the previously referred to extinct elephant bones. But no such luck as any bits and pieces of an intrinsic value were long ago trucked off to Athens and Rhodes... Ho, hum!

Megalo Chorio has *Rooms*. The first, modern-looking cafe on the left, on entering the village, charges just 800drs for a clean and pleasant double room with shared bathroom. There are other **Rooms**, higher up the village, costing 1300drs but with an en suite bathroom. A couple of tavernas, a Post Office and a doctor complete Megalo Chorio's facilities. Those who do not mind some walking might consider this is a good base for exploring the north of the island.

Beyond Megalo Chorio, the paved road divides, the left fork remaining surfaced, and leading, after about 3km, to the superb, long, sandy beach at Eristou. Why Tilos remains such a backwater when it can boast this vast stretch of deserted, golden sand must remain a mystery. Lack of transport has something to do with it, but why haven't the tour companies moved in? On reflection best not to mention Tilos at all, just bless one's luck and visit before it's swamped!
Shade is provided by tamarisk trees that grow along the backshore, which is made up of rough, grainy sand. Near the water's edge, the beach is firm sand. A few fishing boats are pulled up onto the shore which just goes on and on and on.
Accommodation is available at the pleasant, family-run *Taverna Tropicana*, a couple of hundred metres back up the road. A double room, sharing a bathroom, is charged at 1000drs per night.
A track leads across sandy scrub to the left (*Fsw*) and another taverna with rooms at the same price. A Greek salad, chips and large beer costs 295drs. The surrounding area is shaded by trees, but is also fly-infested. Rumour says a big hotel is to be built here soon – so hurry!

Taking the right fork beyond Megalo Chorio, the road becomes a well main-tained but unmetalled track, which eventually divides around the beach at Ag Antonios. To the right, the road leads to a small harbour backed by a taverna, and behind that, the:-

Hotel Australia Tel 53297
It must be a source of never ending amazement that the hard-working. enthusiastic Georgaras brothers chose to build their extremely pleasant hotel here instead of at Eristou, but there you go. A double room, with en suite bathroom, costs 1500drs.
Certainly the location is peaceful and isolated, with reasonable facilities for bathing but the beach is narrow, pebbly and messy. The brothers woefully lamant that it used to be sandy but the sand was used for building. Every so often working parties of soldiers are detailed off to clear the place up, but even they can't manage to widen the beach! It is also a very breezy situation, which Mr Georgaras insists is an advantage because it never gets too hot... I can only comment that when I was last there, a gale was blowing and the breakers were fairly rolling in.

Instead of turning right, towards the hotel, left advances past a ruined windmill. The deteriorating track eventually climbs around Cape Spano to the impressive, well maintained but uninhabited mountainside Monastery of Ag Panteleimonas.

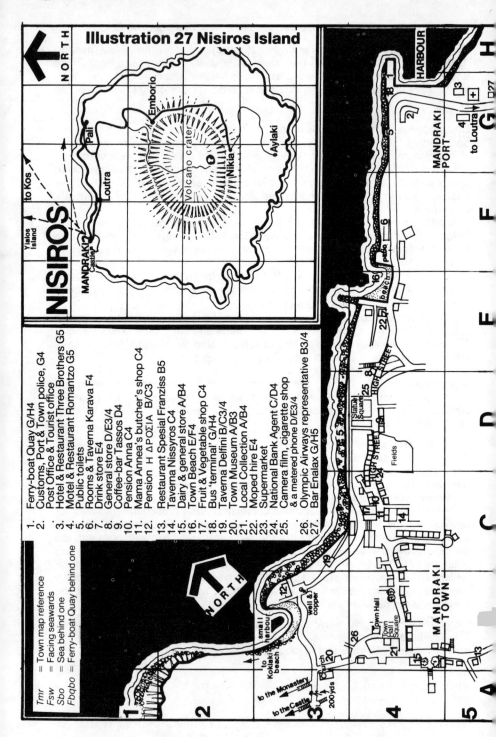

Illustration 27 Nisiros Island

NISIROS

to Kos

Yialos Island

MANDRAKI Castle

Loutra · Pali · Emborio

Volcano crater

· Nikia · Aylaki

Illustration 28 Mandraki Port

NORTH

Tmr = Town map reference
Fsw = Facing seawards
Sbo = Sea behind one
Fbqbo = Ferry-boat Quay behind one

1. Ferry-boat Quay G/H4
2. Customs, Port & Town police, G4
   Post Office & Tourist office
3. Hotel & Restaurant Three Brothers G5
4. Motel & Restaurant Romantzo G5
5. Public toilets
6. Rooms & Taverna Karava F4
7. Drink store E4
8. General store D/E3/4
9. Coffee-bar Tassos D4
10. Pension Anna C4
11. Mama Annea's butcher's shop C4
12. Pension Η ΔΡΟΣΙΑ B/C3
13. Restaurant Spesial Franziss B5
14. Taverna Nissyros C4
15. Dairy & general store A/B4
16. Town Beach E/F4
17. Fruit & Vegetable shop C4
18. Bus 'terminal' G/H4
19. Taverna Delfini B/C3/4
20. Town Museum A/B3
21. Local Collection A/B4
22. Supermarket
23. National Bank Agent C/D4
24. Camera film, cigarette shop
    & a metered phone D/E3/4
25. Olympic Airways representative B3/4
26. Bar Enalax G/H5

HARBOUR

MANDRAKI PORT

to Loutra

beach

HIGH STREET

Statue Square

Fields

MANDRAKI TOWN

Town Hall
Town Square

well & copper

small harbour

to Koklaki beach

Church

to the Monastery

to the Castle

200yds

19 NISIROS (Nisyros, Nissiros) & Yialos
Dodecanese Islands

****

FIRST IMPRESSIONS
Crumbling, Italian built municipal buildings; amazingly diverse town; flies; very friendly inhabitants; pictorial representations of a shops business activity.

SPECIALITIES
Sumada, an almond cordial which is diluted with water to drink, and available in shops, cafes and tavernas.

RELIGIOUS HOLIDAYS & FESTIVALS
include: 20-21st June – Festival of Ag Nikitas, Church close to the Harbour; 15th August – Festival of Panaghia – Monastery of the Lady Virgin of the Rocks.

VITAL STATISTICS
Tel prefix 0242. The island is almost circular, being 10km wide and 8km long. Of the 1300 total population, 800 live in Mandraki Town and Port. The island's central core is a sulphurous, bubbling volcano recessed in a large, circular crater, some 4km across.

HISTORY
As for other islands in the group.

GENERAL
Due to a general lack of facilities, to date Nisiros has remained a day-trip island. The curious partake of excursion boat visits from Kos Town, as well as caique voyages from Kardamena (Kos) to view the volcano and while away the rest of the day. Fortunately there are not sufficient tourist 'attractions', nor is the town of Mandraki such that it can interest, or for that matter handle a large influx of daily visitors. For these reasons Nisiros has not a become a 'bargain basement' Simi and the number of trip boats calling are limited to one or two a day.

Those inquisitive visitors that do make the sea voyage are jammed into one of two buses that marshal on the Harbour quay and then crawl and steeply wind their way up the extensively terraced and very green mountain slopes. Deciduous trees are quite 'thick on the ground' of the countryside bounding the journey to the volcano. The road breasts the rim of the large, cultivated but parched looking sunken plain which edges the core of the volcano. The buses descend on an unmade road in the very large crater, to one side of which is the epicentre of the sulphuric activity. One of the most noticeable things is the total lack of touristabilia, a complete absence of 'T'-shirts and postcards. Good! Once having sniffed the pungent air, viewed the yellow, fissure riven land, taken a short respite at the shack-like cafe-bar, perhaps used the curiously sited, small garden shed of a toilet (spaced some 100 metres to one side of the cafe), and then it's back to Mandraki. Here the inquisitive (and not so inquisitive) loiter away the rest of the day in an apparently lack-lustre, rather bored fashion. As the maze-like town only slowly offers up and reveals its charms and secrets, the committed traveller would do well to spend at least several days here, as Nisiros is a Dodecanese jewel.

MANDRAKI capital village & port (Illustration 28). A strange,

many faceted, strung out locale. The immediate approach from the Harbour is shabby, unprepossessing and dusty and is followed by a narrow lane, toy town milieu.

That sector of the village which climbs the hillside takes on a Greek Welsh village quality (Is there such a thing?). The terraced houses and their small flights of steps edge the very narrow alleys and the women sit on their doorsteps, dressed in traditional costumes, knitting and gossiping. Where are the tumbrils?

Keeping to the left, the Town takes on the character of a vehicle-less,French Dordogne village. The grand Town Hall is followed by, to the left, a tree shaded square edged by cafe-bars, (well more kafeneions really) and, a little further on, a French style restaurant, the *Spesial Franzis*. The owner goes the 'whole hog', wearing a tall chef's hat and striped pinafore.

Without doubt a lovely location.

ARRIVAL BY FERRY

A reasonably irregular inter-island service is backed up by daily caique trip boats from Kardamena (Kos), in addition to excursion craft from Kos Town. Boats dock at the Ferry-boat Quay (*Tmr* 1G/H4).

The quay, which doubles up as a terminal for the island and 'Volcano' buses, is on a bend in the road which connects Mandraki Town to Loutra, Pali and the crater-edge villages of Emborio and Nikia. Opposite the quay, on the same bend, is the crumbling, curved, Italian-Greco neo-municipal administration block (*Tmr* 2G4) that houses the Customs, Port police, Post Office, Town police (in that order) and a Tourist office.

THE ACCOMMODATION & EATING OUT

The Accommodation To the left (*Fbqbo*), up a slight rise, both accommodation and eating out are 'catered' for by the:-

Three Brothers Hotel & Restaurant (*Tmr* 3G5)

Directions: On the left, alongside a church, and a rather smarter place than the original establishment.

Opposite, on the right, is the:-

Romantzo Motel (sic) & Restaurant (*Tmr* 4G5)   Tel 31340

Directions: As above.

Double rooms with en suite bathroom cost 1300drs. If space allows the owners tolerate single use of a double room from 700drs. Nick, the owner, is praised for his friendly help and willingness to defer to clients' wishes.

Both hotels have large terraces and are in reality restaurant/pensions.

Apart from the two aforementioned establishments, it is necessary to make the five or ten minute walk to the town, from the right-hand fork. The sea bordering road leaves one of the town's public lavatories on the right. After some 100 metres, also on the right, is:-

Rooms & Taverna Karava (*Tmr* 6F4)

Directions: As above and recognizable by the awning covered taverna tables and chairs.

Incidentally the owner is the Captain of the **Nisiros Express**, a trip boat that sails daily between Mandraki Port and Kardamena (Kos). The facilities are excellent and the bedrooms have en suite bathrooms but are expensive at a double room charge of 2200drs. Incidentally the taverna is good as well.

Beyond this establishment the road skirts a dirty, sandy beach, edged by a small quay. A few swings have been erected and a children's playground created on the sandy backshore, with a few small caiques lying about.

Beyond the Drink store (*Tmr* 7E4), the road divides. The right-hand, High St turning proceeds on past a statue mounted Square (which edges the sea below), the *Coffee-bar Tassos* (*Tmr* 9D4), a general store and shop, some fields to the left and a few metal shuttered stores on the right. The High St then dives back into a narrow lane hemmed in by buildings, in amongst which are a scattering of shops and the:-

Pension Anna (*Tmr* 10C4)
On the right but doesn't open, if at all, until the height of season months.

A few shops, and a side turning, beyond the *Pension Anna* and, on the left, is:-

Mama Annea's Butchers Shop (*Tmr* 11C4)
Directions: As above and identified by a richly painted cow's head and the a sign on the wall, *Rooms to Rent*.

Mama Annea, a very pleasant and helpful lady, owns the *Pension Drosia* and accompanies visitors to her accommodation. From the shop it is necessary to turn right down the next shallow flight of steps and keep close by the sea wall as far as a very small Square. This circles and is dominated by a large, old fashioned, communal fire warmed copper combined with a well. Almost the Greek equivalent of a 'Twin-Tub', and still used on some washdays. On the far side is the:-

The Pension (ΗΔΡΟΣΙΑ **Drosia**) (*Tmr* 12B/C3)
Directions: As above.

The *Drosia* is very clean, if a touch spartan. The shower water of the shared bathroom is hot all and every day and the location is superb, the narrow balcony looking out over the adjacent sea well. The bedroom furniture is solid, even if there aren't any lampshades, and the room rate includes use of a kitchen complete with cooker and fridge. Oh, yes there is also a clothes line and pegs. What's the catch? None, the double room rate being charged at 800drs (Yes 800drs). It must be the best value in the Greek islands.

The Eating Out A fairly wide variety including, at the far, upper end of town, the:-

The Restaurant Spesial Franzis (*sic*) (*Tmr* 13B5)
Directions: At the 'Town Hall' Square (*Tmr* B4), turn left (*Harbour behind one*) and walk across the next Square. The restaurant is on the left.

The restaurant is slanted towards the day-trippers and the proprietor/cook dresses up as detailed in the Introduction.

My favourite (whose a teacher's pet, then?) is the:-
Taverna Nissyros (*Tmr* 14C4)
Directions: From the direction of the Harbour, in a side-alley to the left of the High St, beyond Mama Annea's butchers shop (*Tmr* 11C4).

Run by a very pleasant Mama and her daughter and frequented equally by the few overnight tourists and locals. The prices are very reasonable and each day a speciality of the day is freshly prepared. A meal of 3 small stick souvlaki, squid, 'fish' (4 small fish, 200drs), tzatziki, tomato salad, an orange drink, 2 bottles of retsina and bread costs 1000drs.

This is one of those islands and one of those tavernas where a fresh bottle may well mysteriously appear at a diner's elbow. Super, but a word of warning. If you can identify the benefactor and return the favour you will only be bought another bottle and so it goes on... and on ... Here's to you, blue eyes!

The Taverna Delfini (*Tmr* 19B/C3/4)
Directions: On the last seafront 'Square' heading towards the *Pension Drosia*.
The owners are an extremely friendly old couple and prices are very reasonable. A 'breakfast' of 2 Nes meh ghala and warm milk cost 300drs. A meal for 4 including a plate of mullet (3 reasonable sized fish 150drs), 3 stick souvlaki (50drs a stick), 2 tzatziki, 1 green beans, 1 squid, a plate of mezes, a Greek salad, 6 bottles of retsina (well, 1 bottle was put by for future consumption) and 4 glasses of *sumada* (the local almond cordial) cost 2060drs. Incredible value and note the plate of 3 mullet only cost 150drs.

THE A TO Z OF USEFUL INFORMATION
BANKS (*Tmr* 24C/D4). Actually an agent for the National Bank, who also has a small shop selling some pharmaceutical products.

BEACHES There is a small Town Beach (*Tmr* 16E/F4), two-thirds of the way to the Harbour, as mentioned in the preamble. It is messy, kelp covered and rather cluttered with 'this and that', the locals treating it as another Town Square. Every so often a bulldozer loads the kelp into lorries to get rid of it.
To the left of Mandraki Town (*Fsw*) is the unusual Koklaki Beach, which is not so much a beach, more a small bay of very large pebbles and stones. To get there it is necessary to climb round the tiny harbour, close by *Pension* ΗΔΡΟΣΙΑ (*Tmr* 12B/C3), and follow the rocky path, scrambling over the volcanic boulders beneath the cliffs. A farmer keeps his pigs in the under-cut of the rock face. The sea is clear and warm but the brownish stones are uncomfortably large.
Two hundred metres to the east, beyond the Ferry-boat Harbour, is a wisp of narrow beach with some sand and a lot of pebbles.

BICYCLE, SCOOTER & CAR HIRE The *Romantzo Motel* (*Tmr* 4G5) hires mopeds and there is another outfit (*Tmr* 22E4) on the High St. Both charge a pricey 1400drs a day, but this does include a tank of fuel as there aren't any fuel stations. Pricey? Yes these are only single seater mopeds, not scooters.

BREAD SHOPS The bread is baked at Pali, transported to Mandraki Town daily and, between 0900hrs and 1030hrs, sold from 'the truck', as it were. The site chosen for this *ad hoc* arrangement is behind a fruit and vegetable shop (*Tmr* 17C4), amongst a pile of discarded vegetable crates, in the sea-skirting alley used by local vehicles to get to this part of the town. At least the islanders do not give in and rely on Kos for supplies.

BUSES Two buses make the round trip, from close by the Harbour quay (*Tmr* 18G/H4), to *Busto Volkano* and back, as well as the school trip early in the morning and midday. There is the blue/orange painted corporation bus, with a lady bus conductor and which makes unscheduled stops, as well as the red coloured, private *Volcano Tour Bus*.
The service is, unquestionably, jolly expensive.

Bus timetable
From Mandraki Harbour

Monday, Wednesday	0700hrs	Loutra,Pali,Emborio,Nikia.
& Friday	1100hrs	Volcano.
	1230hrs	Volcano.
	1300hrs	Loutra,Pali,Emborio,Nikia.
	1445hrs	Volcano.
Tuesday & Thursday	1100,1230,1445hrs	Volcano.
Saturday	0700hrs	Loutra,Pali,Emborio,Nikia.
	1100hrs	Volcano.
	1230hrs	Volcano.
	1445hrs	Volcano.

Return fares:the 'corporation' bus (blue/orange) 250drs
the private bus (red)   300drs
Note there is absolutely no way of predicting which 'colour' of bus will turn up!

COMMERCIAL SHOPPING AREA There isn't a central market but there are a large number of shops spaced throughout the town selling a surprisingly diverse range of items, including electrical goods and at least two shoe repairers. The main consignment of fruit and vegetables are usually shipped in on the 1800hr Monday night ferry-boat.
A most unusual feature is the custom of decorating shops with an oil painted picture representing the activity within. For instance a cow's head advertises the butcher's shop.
Opening hours are the usual small island 'norm'.

DISCO Curiously enough there are two, the **Bar Enalax** (*Tmr* 27G/H5), close to the Harbour, and the **Mira Mare Restaurant Night Club**, half-way to Loutra, well more accurately 1km distant from Mandraki Harbour.

FERRY-BOATS The service is satisfactory, especially if the Kos connections are taken into account.

Ferry-boat timetable (Mid-season)

Day	Departure time	Ferry-boat	Ports/Islands of Call
Monday	1500hrs	Nireas	Tilos,Simi,Rhodes.
	1830hrs	Panormitis	Kos,Kalimnos,Leros,Lipsos,Patmos, Arki,Angathonisi,Pythagorion(Samos).
Tuesday	2400hrs	Panormitis	Tilos,Simi,Rhodes.
Thursday	1000hrs	Nireas	Kos,Kalimnos,Leros,Lipsos,Patmos, Piraeus(M).
	1630hrs	Panormitis	Kos,Kalimnos.
	2400hrs	Panormitis	Tilos,Simi,Rhodes.

Local excursion & trip boats. *See* **Ferry-boats, A To Z, Kos Town & Kardamena, Kos island,** as well as **Excursion to Yialos.**

FERRY-BOAT TICKET OFFICES There are no ferry-boat offices. Tickets are sold by a lady who squats down in the shade of a metal container, to one side of the island map sited on the edge of the Ferry-boat Quay (*Tmr* 1G/H4). She takes up position about one hour prior to a ferry-boat's arrival.

MEDICAL CARE One or two of the shops sell pharmaceutical products including the National Bank agent (*Tmr* 24C/D4). Anybody in need of medical care should get themselves to Kos.

NTOG More a Tourist office (*Tmr* 2G4), located in the same Municipal building as the Police and Post Office. They distribute a Nisiros leaflet as well as answer enquiries in respect of the various timetables. The staff are very pleasant and helpful.

OTE None, but one shop (*Tmr* 25D/E3/4) has a metered phone.

PLACES OF INTEREST
The Monastery of the Lady Virgin of the Rocks* Perched on the cliff-edge hemming the town in at the west or left-hand end (*Fsw*) and reached via a steep, narrow flight of steps that ascend from the 'Welsh Quarter'. A signpost points the way. Unusually the door is often left open. A very lovely, 'standard', rich and dark Byzantine monastery interior.

* Variously and also named Panaghia Spiliani or Virgin of the Cave.

The Castle Dominates the hillside headland to the west of the town and accessed by the next flight of steps up from those to the Monastery. The signs variously label the direction *To the Castle* and *To the Ancient Wall*. Where the steps run out, a medieval, up-hill stone path takes over until a broad swathe cuts across the track. Here turn right up the hill to the ruined, large hewn block fort walls, which are up to three metres thick in places. The views are magnificent.

A local farmer/shepherd has taken advantage of the fortification, using a section of the wall to form one side of his small holding and animal enclosures. Perhaps it is the same enterprising man who keeps the pigs penned, way down at the bottom of the cliff-face of Koklaki Bay.

The Castle can also be reached by a road that spurs off the coastal road to Loutra, beyond the Harbour.

Town Museum (*Tmr* 20A/B3) This is situated in a quaint corner, opposite a Byzantine Church which is undergoing extensive restoration and possesses some splendid wall paintings. The tiny, two storey Dickensian house contains items of local interest and is open daily between 1000-1300hrs and 1800-2000hrs, except Wednesday and Sunday afternoons. Admission is free.

One other collection is in the private house (*Tmr* 21A/B4) of a local historian and archaeologist. He has made some very interesting finds but is, I believe, slowly going blind and has had to severely curtail his activities. Greek is necessary to enjoy a conversation with him.

POLICE
Port & Town (*Tmr* 2G4) Both are located in the 'Municipal' building, close by the Harbour.

POST OFFICE (*Tmr* 2G4) In the same block as the Police.

TELEPHONE NUMBERS & ADDRESSES
Police, town (*Tmr* 2G4)   Tel 31201

TOILETS There are two public toilets. One, close by the Ferry-boat Quay on the road into Town (*Tmr* 5G4), is cleaned regularly and the other (*Tmr* 5D3/4) is near to 'Statue' Square.

Before finishing this discourse of 'matters sanitary', it is important to report that the environs are very well equipped with pedal-operated bins, which (of course) rarely appear to be emptied – more's the pity. The town's rubbish is collected by a very small, three-wheeled cab which can only just squeeze between the buildings edging some of the narrow streets.

TRAVEL AGENTS & TOUR OFFICES *See* **NTOG, A To Z**. There is, for some extraordinary reason, an Olympic Airways representative (*Tmr* 26B3/4) – amazing!

ROUTE ONE
To Nikia (about 10km), via Loutra, Pali & Emborio There
is only one route really.

From Mandraki Town the road turns past the Ferry-boat Harbour and along the side of the seashore.

The *Hotel Harikos*, on the right, has at long last been completed. It was rumoured that the building had to be delayed in order to give the American expatriate backer time enough to save up some more drachmae. Some away-from-it-all package holiday-makers book into the hotel. Let's hope someone else doesn't build onother hotel, resulting in more package tourists, then more hotels followed by, wonder of wonders, an airfield....!

Note the benches bordering the road and pleasantly positioned for weary walkers.

After an ostensibly long trudge, one chances upon the rather strange hamlet of:-

· **LOUTRA (2km from Mandraki Town)** A large, seafront building, partly in ruins, houses a small and rather incongruous taverna. Next door, a very large, warehouse-type building is actually a (government owned) thermal spa. Rooms are available here for patients who bathe in the hot mineral waters collected in the tanks to the inland side of the building.

From Loutra the road climbs and winds up the well vegetated but dusty hillside past the town rubbish dump and old olive groves. Half-way towards the Pali turning, some deserted workings overhang the sea with the usual scattering of abandoned vehicles. A quarry quay and works-buildings sprawl over a bluff, beneath which is a delightful, silver sand beach that benefits from very warm, volcano warmed water. A big, new hotel is under construction at the top of this beach.

High on the hillside, close by a chapel, a side turning branches off to the left, down to:-

PALI (4km from Mandraki Town) Rather than follow the extravagant loops of the road, it is possible to scramble down the slopes, recross the road and wander into the nearside of this very spread out fishing hamlet, close by a church. To the left is a rocky breakwater forming a large caique harbour. Immediately prior to the spacious village square, more an open space really, in the middle of Pali, are *Rooms*, a taverna and a smart hotel, very smart considering the location, despite which a double room only costs 1500drs.

A taverna, which squats on the far side of the square, serves reasonably priced food with a meal of moussaka, a Greek salad and a beer costing 450drs. At the far end of the village, close to a church, is another taverna which has *Rooms*. The owner/cook is pleasant, English speaking and runs a first class outfit. A superb Greek salad, a large plate of chips, a tzatziki, a bottle of water and bread sufficient to feed three, yes three, costs 500drs. A double room, sharing a bathroom, costs 1000drs a night.

From Pali centre, a straight track edges the long, volcanic sand, but rather littered beach to the left. To the right spreads ramshackle, sprawling, dwellings and scatterings of the village's outskirts. The road peters out in a morass at the back of a yet unfinished construction project, alongside a semi-refurbished building, which are both destined to be more thermal baths. It is not so much that the road peters out, more that it was dug up before this project has been completed.

By scrambling over the rubble, the track continues past a Tyrolean caravan (yes a Tyrolean...) of rather bad taste, possibly the property of an expatriate North American, and hideously inscribed *Halcyon Days* (*sic*).

Should a traveller wish to get away from it all, then it is only necessary to continue on the deteriorating path into lovely, wild and deserted countryside.

Back at the main road, the route snakes on up the beautiful mountain sides to a junction. Here the right-hand turning leads to the volcano and the left-hand to the crater edge villages of:-

EMBORIO & NIKIA Emborio is nearly deserted and much of it is in ruins. Nikia is more attractive, alive and closer to the rim of the large, sunken plain of the volcano. Both villages enjoy magnificent views of Nisiros and the adjacent islands of Tilos, Yialos and Kos, as well as the Turkish mainland.

The 'delights' of the volcano trip have been discoursed about in the General Introduction.

EXCURSION TO YIALOS ISLAND (Giali)
Yialos is some twenty minutes boat trip from Nisiros, from whence a return trip costs 600drs.

The odd appearance of the island is due to extensive surface mining for building materials. The excavations are slowly chewing away at the island's 'superstructure', rather similar to one of those 'Pack Man', pub-video games, or in this case 'Island Champing Man'.

Workers commute daily from Nisiros and a lift might be hitched on their boat. Despite the drawback of the noise caused by the quarrying machinery, Yialos has a splendid, sandy beach.

20 KOS, (Cos, ΚΟΣ) & Pserimos
Dodecanese Islands

**

FIRST IMPRESSIONS
Mass tourism; the 'Costa Brava' of the Greek islands; bland, unexceptional but expensive food and eating places; magpies; inadequate signposting; speed limit signs; verdant growth; oleanders and bougainvillea; 'army training ground' look to much of the countryside; marvellous ruins.

SPECIALITIES
Cheap alcoholic spirits and perfumes (as for Rhodes).

RELIGIOUS HOLIDAYS & FESTIVALS
include: 24th June – Fire of St John; 30th July – Festival of St Apostle, Antimachia; August – Festival of, the Re-enactment of the Oath of Hippocrates, Asklepieion; 6th August – Saviours Metamorphosis, Kos; 7th September – Festival of St Virgin of Tsukanon, Kardamena.

VITAL STATISTICS
Tel prefix 0242. The second largest of the islands in this group, being 45km from tip to toe and up to 10½km at the widest point. Due to the irregular shape these figures are subject to diverse interpretation. Of the population of some 18,000, about 8,000 live in the capital. Note that despite being second in size to Rhodes Island, Kos is only about one fifth the area, so it is a poor second.

HISTORY
Naturally, the geographical proximity has resulted in much of the island's history paralleling that of Rhodes. Alexander the Great, occupied Kos in 336 BC. On his death, the Egyptians took over and their rulers, the Ptolemies, visited, as did Cleopatra who is rumoured, for safe-keeping, to have kept some of the family jewels on Kos. The Romans held sway until the Byzantine Empire took over, only for the Saracens, in the 11th century, to sack the place. It took the Knights six years longer to take over Kos than it did to conquer Rhodes, but they lost it to the Turks in the same year as Rhodes.

Earthquakes wrought havoc during the last century BC, early AD and as recently as 1933, Kos Town and Harbour were badly damaged by tremors. Interestingly enough this last, devastating seismic disturbance revealed hitherto unsuspected archaeological finds.

GENERAL
For years Kos was raved about by the travel writers and even as recently as eight to ten years ago it was feasible to escape from the all-pervading hordes of summer visitors. Nowadays that is almost impossible, as the holiday centres are equally spread out throughout this green and pleasant land, from Kos to Kefalos and from Kardamena to Mastichari. In fact, the only areas that the developers have left unsullied are the eastern side of the Mt Dikeos range and the area to the west of Mt Latra, and then only because both are almost inaccessible.

In the few country villages the peasant women still wear the native working day clothes of head-dress, white shawl, black skirt and thick, coarse stockings.

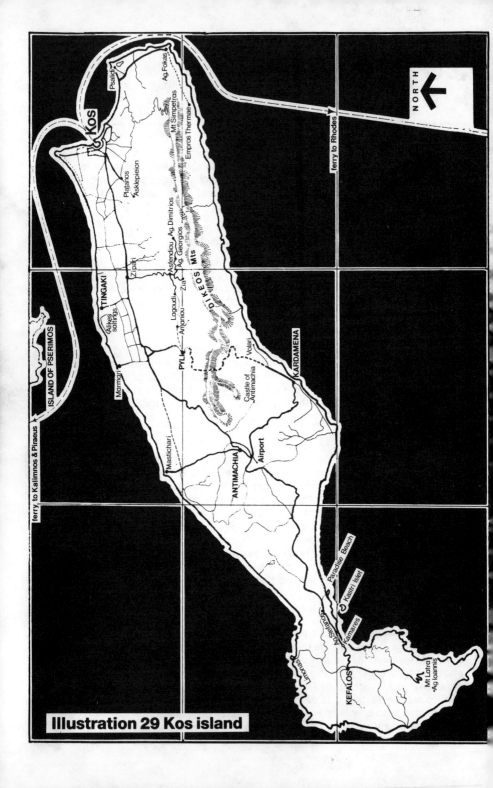

Illustration 29 Kos island

The north and south sides of the island have distinct and different weather characteristics. The northern coast enjoys a constant cooling breeze resulting in small waves breaking on the sea-shore whilst the windless southern shores tend to be hotter and the sea calm.

Similarly to Rhodes, Kos is a duty-free port and alcoholic spirits are remarkably cheap. Incidentally, despite the island's name, there is not a lettuce in sight.

ARRIVAL BY AIR

The airport is located in approximately the centre of the island and arrivals by Olympic Airways can take advantage of the airline bus. Naturally package tourists will be collected by their holiday companies' own transport but freelance travellers will be at the mercy of taxis or can walk to the adjacent village of Antimachia, where a scheduled bus service stops. (*See* **Bus timetables, Buses, A To Z, Kos Town**).

KOS: capital town & main port. (Illustration 30). Unlike Rhodes,

this smaller Harbour is wholly and attractively enveloped by the town. Furthermore the fortress of Kos, a comparatively small affair, romantically borders one edge of the Port.

The quayside and its immediate surrounds are a gathering place for the marina jet-set whilst the inner town, abounding with archaeological ruins, has an almost tropical milieu. This impression is heightened by the huge palm trees that line some of the roads and the giant, colourful, luxuriant bougainvillea, oleander and jasmin that burgeon forth, leaving the air heavy with an almost pungent, aromatic, sweet smelling odour from the profusion of flowers and herbs. The outer town has a quiet, prosperous, suburban ambience.

The authorities, in their great wisdom, have decided to replace the old, blue background, stencilled street signs. These had both Greek and Roman scripted names. The very smart replacements are made of marble but unfortunately only bear a carved Greek version of the street name which are extremely difficult to read – that is difficult to other than Greeks. Fair enough, but the worthy town burghers have also taken it into their heads to alter a number of the street names at the same time, but not necessarily concurrent with replacing the old name plates. Nasty!

Some of the streets of the town have been made one-way to cope with the heavy traffic. Sounds familiar.

ARRIVAL BY FERRY

The ferry-boats dock (*Tmr* 1B/C2/3) alongside the narrow necked access of the almost circular Harbour, close by the Castle of the Knights of St. John (*Tmr* 2C3). To get to the main town it is necessary to walk along the quay, past the large cafeteria (*Tmr* 3C3). This stays open all night and provides a very handy service, especially to those travellers dumped off the inevitable early morning ferry-boat. Incidentally, the convenience of having somewhere to sit comfortably in the early hours has to be balanced against the behaviour of some of the backpackers who find the availability of all-night drinking rather 'tiring'.... It is a strange place, the duty-free liquor shelves rubbing shoulders with a cafe-bar, snacks and hot food counter. At least the lavatories are fairly clean. The staff occasionally bed down for a rest behind the drinks counter.

From this establishment, keep to the narrow quay walk, with the Castle walls to the left and the Harbour to the right, following the waterfront around to the right.

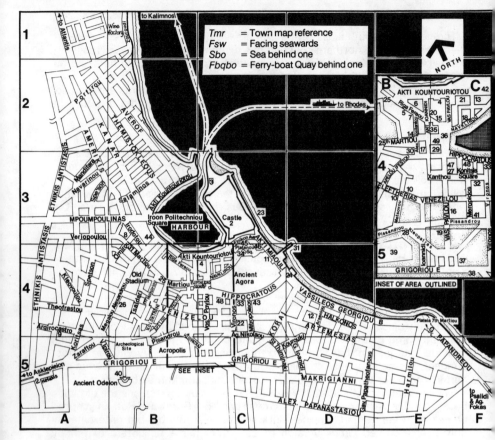

Illustration 30 Kos Port

Tmr
1. Ferry-boat Quay B/C2/3
2. Castle of the Knights of St John C3
3. All-night Cafeteria & toilets C3
4. Tourist office B/C3/4
5. Hotel Kalymnos B4
6. Souvlaki snackbar B/C4
7. Hotel Dodekanisos B4
8. Pension Alexis A/B3/4
9. Pension Andreas Vouliakis A4/5
10. Rooms To Let
11. Hotel Iviscos C/D3/4
12. Hotel Hara D4
13. Restaurant Limnos C4
14. Snackbar Ideal B4
15. Restaurant Neon Faliron B/C4
16. Snackbar Australia Sydney C4
17. Leachis building B/C4
18. Restaurant Drosia C4
19. Airline office & terminus B/C4/5
20. National Bank of Greece B/C4
21. Credit Bank C4
22. Hotel Maratina C4
23. Beaches
24. Police Officers club C/D4
25. Car, scooter & bicycle hire B4
26. Scooter hire A/B4
27. Bread shop B/C4
28. Bus terminal B/C4/5
29. Market B/C4
30. Cinema B4
31. Hydrofoil Quay C/D3/4
32. OTE C4
33. Petrol C4
34. Plateia Platanou/Hatji-Hasan Mosque C3/4
35. Museum B/C4
36. Deftdar Mosque B/C4
37. Temple & Altar of Dionysos C5
38. Casa Romana C5
39. Acropolis B4/5
40. Odeion Theatre A/B5
41. Post Office C4/5
42. Taxi rank C4
43. Hospital C4
44. Public toilets B3/4
45. Public toilets C3/4
46. Government House/Police station C/D3/4
47. The Greek Kitchen Taverna C4
48. Doctor C4
49. Plateia Eleftherias/Main Square B/C4

Fortunately, it is only 500-600m from the point of disembarkation to the Municipal Tourist office (*Tmr* 4B/C3/4) and a couple of hotels overlooking the port. Additionally the ferry-boats are met by the owners of the various pensions or those acting for them.

THE ACCOMMODATION & EATING OUT
The Accommodation

Hotel Kalymnos (*Tmr* 5B4) (Class E) 9 Riga Fereou   Tel 22336
Directions: Along the Esplanade and standing back, where Riga Fereou St runs into the Esplanade, Akti Kountouriotou. Shabby but convenient for those turned off a ferry late at night. Situated in a very noisy location as the marine cafe society does not quieten down till well into the early hours, more especially the *Karis Snackbar* which belts out non-stop pop.

The owner managers are unhelpful and unpleasant. Double rooms only, sharing a bathroom, from about 1500drs a night.

Hotel Dodekanisos (*Tmr* 7B4) (Class D) 2 Alex Ipsilantou   Tel 28460
Directions: Just around the corner from Odhos Riga Fereou.

No less noisy. Single rooms sharing the bathroom cost 1250drs and with an en suite bathroom 1750drs, whilst a double room sharing costs 2000drs, and en suite 2400drs.

Hotel Helena (*Tmr* B3/4) (Class D) 5 Megalou Alexandrou St   Tel 22740
Directions: To the right (*Sbo*), along the Esplanade, Akti Kountouriotou, for some three blocks, as far as the blue barrel that substitutes as a roundabout. Here the main road, Megalou Alexandrou, 'avenues' off, at a right-angle.

Well recommended with vine covered balconies overlooking the road. Prices for a single room, sharing the bathroom, are 1500drs. A double room sharing a bathroom costs 2000drs and 2500drs with an en suite bathroom.

From Megalou Alexandrou to the right, along Odhos Irodotou, leads to Omirou St, the first turning on the left. On the far corner is:-

Pension Alexis (*Tmr* 8A/B3/4) (Class E) 9 Irodotou/Omirou St   Tel 28798
Directions: As above.

A very pleasant, 'provincial digs' with the dark, ground floor double rooms costing 1800drs and the first floor rooms, sharing the pleasant, large terrace, costing 2000drs. Breakfast, served on the patio, can be coffee or a full-blown 'English' affair and, although an extra, the cost (from 170drs) represents good value. As with most similar pensions there is a 'rare' scramble for the bathroom. The neatly bearded Alexis masterminds the operation and has a very smooth line of patter whilst his wife does the work and father helps out. The atmosphere is pleasantly cosmopolitan and off-beat, the international guests come from wide and varied backgrounds and Alexis can be very helpful, if a little patronising.

On the corner, opposite *Alexis*, is a less high-profile pension with well appointed, slightly more expensive rooms. The owners, being older than Alexis, do not possess his command of English (nor his smooth approach) and seem bewildered by his success in filling his rooms. Well worth approaching if Alexis is full or you do not wish to be a 'bit-part' player in his daily 'production'.

Pension Andreas Vouliakis (*Tmr* 9A4/5) 2 Argirocastro St   Tel 28740
Directions: Proceed westwards along Megalou Alexandrou, over El Venizelou, to an open roundabout. Here turn right along Odhos Argirocastro, the second

exit to the right. Possibly rather distant from the centre of the town, being almost on the outskirts, but commensurately quieter.

Well recommended, I have stayed here on a number of occasions. The placid, unobtrusive owner, Andreas, and his wife live on the premises of their good value, clean pension. A nice touch is the communal refrigerator on each floor. The toilets and showers are shared and, as the water is heated by solar energy, it is necessary to be at the head of the race for the 'douche'. A double room costs from 1200drs.

A number of **Rooms** for rent are centred on a stretch of Odhos El Venizelou (*Tmr* B/C4), between the intersection with Vassileos Pavlou and Apelou Sts. These include:- No. 36 El Venizelou (*Tmr* 10B4) and No. 29 El Venizelou/ Metsouvou (*Tmr* 10B4)

For more expensive pastures, from the Harbour Esplanade turn left (*Sbo*) to follow the very pretty, curving, palm-tree-lined Finikon Avenue beneath the Castle access bridge and out on to the carriageway of Akti Miaouli.

Hotel Iviscos (Ibiscus) (*Tmr* 11C/D3/4) (Class C) 2 Akti Miaouli Tel 22214
Directions: As above. The hotel is beyond the large, Government occupied, municipal building on the right.

Only en suite rooms are available with a single commencing at 2000drs and a double room 2600drs. These rates climb respectively to 2400 & 2900drs (1st May-30th June) and then to 2700 & 3400drs (1st July-30th Sept).

Hotel Hara (*Tmr* 12D4) (Class D) 6 Halkonos/2 Arseniou Sts　　Tel 22500
Directions: Beyond the *Hotel Iviscos*, and eastwards along Akti Miaouli, turn right into Arseniou St after which the first street, at right-angles, is Odhos Halkonos.

No single rooms. Double rooms all have en suite bathrooms starting off at 2600drs and rising to 2990drs (1st July-30th Sept).

Keeping to the coast road, in the direction of the eastern island headland, beyond Kos Town, advances, after 2300m, to the campsite of:-

Kos Camping (Class C) PO Box 48, Psalidi　　　　　　　　Tel 23275
Directions: As above and a fair walk.

Kos Camping comes very well recommended. It has to be admitted the site is the wrong side of the road, as it were, but the setting is pleasant with the tents spaced out beneath olive trees and bushes. The facilities are excellent and include a wash room, kitchen, clean toilets and showers (with hot water), international phone, a very well stocked supermarket, a small bar and a kiddies playground. Next door to the campsite is a taverna and the pebble beach is just across the road. The friendly staff speak English and the owners also hire mopeds and bicycles. Daily fees are 300drs per person and 120drs for the tent. Tents can be hired at a cost of 200drs per day.

Don't forget the Tourist office (*Tmr* 4B/C3/4) has extensive lists of accommodation with details of their class and charges *See* **NTOG, A To Z.**

The Eating Out
The town is singularly bereft of even good, let alone outstanding, eating places. Banality and mediocrity are the 'rule of the stomach'. There are any number of snackbars, an example of which is a souvlaki pita counter (*Tmr* 6B/C4) on Odhos Riga Fereou. But a souvlaki here costs 100drs.

The majority of gastronomic establishments are lined out 'table by cloth' along the Castle end of Akti Kountouriotiou. If I had to select one of these run-of-the-mill offerings it would be the:-

Restaurant Limnos (*Tmr* 13C4) Akti Kountouriotiou.
Directions: As above.
Clean, quick, polite and reasonably priced service, that is reasonably priced for Kos Harbour. An average meal for two, with a bottle of retsina, cost 1000drs.

There is a plethora of snackbars including the:-
Ideal (*Tmr* 14B4). Alex Ipsilantou/25th Martiou
Directions: At the far, west side of the Main Sq, Plateia Eleftherias (*Tmr* 49B/C4).
This self-service outfit offers fair value, fast food.

A more traditional taverna is the:-
Restaurant Neon Faliron (*Tmr* 15B/C4)
Directions: At the top, or more literally the upper Main Sq end, of Odhos Riga Fereou (which angles down to the Esplanade).
Mainly caters for Scandinavians so good food at expensive prices. A Greek salad costs 200drs, a tzatziki 190drs, moussaka 300drs, veal chops, roast chicken 'special' 350drs, and shish-kebabs 450drs. To add insult to the 'rip-off' a 20% surcharge is levied during July and August! I hope readers will resist the temptation to patronize the place during these month's!

Proceeding along Vassileos Pavlou from the Main Sq, and on the right, beyond the Market (*Tmr* 29B/C4), is the very pleasant, tree shaded (well, almost tree obliterated), raised square or terrace in the centre of Plateia Xanthou. On the Pavlou edge of this terrace are the tables and chairs of cafe-bars on the opposite side of the road. I used to patronise:-

Anargiros (The Pancake Cafe).
Directions: As above.
Bearing in mind the separation of kitchen from client, overdue delivery of an order (even by Greek standards) may indicate that the waiter has been run over. A pleasant spot but very expensive with a yoghurt and honey costing a princely 200drs. Ouch!
Nowadays I prefer to advocate the nearby:-

Greek Kitchen Taverna (*Tmr* 47C4)
Directions: As above.
The waiters appear to constantly bicker amongst themselves but the food is good and reasonably priced. A meal for two of a plate each of dolmades and stuffed aubergines (*papoutsi*), some feta cheese, 1 beans, 1 tzatziki and 2 beers cost 970drs. A breakfast for two of yoghurt and honey, bread and marmalade as well as 2 Nes meh ghala was charged at 270drs.

Further along Vassileos Pavlou, on the left (*Sbo*), in the block immediately prior to a waste ground Fun-Fair area, is the:-

Australia Sydney (*Tmr* 16C4) 29 Vassileos Pavlou.
Directions: As above.
A somewhat down-at-the-heel snackbar offering good value and variety, which is well patronised by the locals. A meal for two of liver, beans, feta, tzatziki, bread and two beers costs 850drs.

Off Vassileos Pavlou, to the left along El Venizelou and in the second block, next to a Kodak camera shop and opposite the Post Office (*Tmr* 41C4/5), is a splendid *Pie and Sandwich Snackbar*. This is run by a French speaking, Greek lady and her husband.

Further eastwards, El Venizelou runs into a small Square. Turning left along Korai St leads on to the Esplanade, Vassileos Georgiou B. Incidentally, this seafront road could also have been reached by proceeding along the palm-tree lined Finikon Avenue, on to the dual carriageway of Akti Miaouli which runs into Vassileos Georgiou B. The junction of Korai St and Vas Georgiou B is opposite a sea bordering, Greco-Italianesque pile of architecture. Part of this houses the Police officers' mess with, to one side, a public, paved, seaside patio complete with beach shower and sun umbrellas. Vassileos Georgiou B, the tree lined highway out of Kos Town towards Ag Fokas, borders a pebbly, narrow beach (and the sea) to the left and some smart hotels, restaurants and cafe-bars to the right.

Back at the Main Sq (Eleftherias or Freedom Sq) (*Tmr* 49B/C4), two restaurants occupy the ground floor of the distinctive, 1930s Leachis' building (*Tmr* 17B/C4). Their blind covered, pavement based tables and chairs face out over the Square and the Mosque of Deftedar (*Tmr* 36B/C4). The restaurant beneath the tower is fair value and clients can while away an hour or so here in more peaceful surrounds than the waterfront frenzy. One of the more theatrical waiters may well reward a client's custom with a 'matinee' performance.

The opposite side of the Square, beyond the Mosque and across the road from the eastern side of the Museum (*Tmr* 35B/C4), is the bougainvillea covered, medieval gateway, the Portal Forou or 'Gate of the Taxes'. Through this stone arch is a very pleasant, flowering, tree edged terrace, Odhos Navklirou, which curves down to Platanou Square. The vine trellis sheltered pavement, bordering the Ancient Agora on the right, has row upon row of prettily laid out tables and chairs. These belong to the restaurants housed on the left-hand side of the crescent. Close to the arch is the:-

The Restaurant Drosia (*Tmr* 18C4)
Directions: As above.
The menus are varied but, by any standards, are expensive, very expensive.

At the bottom of Odhos Navklirou, beyond the Hatji-Hasan Mosque, is the delightful Plantanou Square (*Tmr* 34C3/4). This is edged by a variety of buildings including the Mosque, a central, Italianesque municipal block, the approach works and stone walkway to the Castle, that bridges Finikon Avenue, and the fabled Plane Tree beneath which Hippocrates is 'legended' to have taught.
Beyond the central building, to one side of the Plane Tree and its surrounds, a Greek Mama runs a small cafe-bar in shaded and quiet surroundings.

A reader recommends *Barba George Taverna*, not far from *Pension Alexis* (*Tmr* 8A/B3/4) but it may prove to be rather expensive.

THE A TO Z OF USEFUL INFORMATION
AIRLINE OFFICE & TERMINUS (*Tmr* 19B/C4/5) Situated on the right-hand side and very nearly at the far end of Vassileos Pavlou. The office ticks over with the usual Greek mixture of studied indifference and chaos. The airline bus operates with a rather nail biting disregard for aircraft departure times.

Aircraft timetable (Mid-season)
Kos to Athens (& vice versa)
Daily   0715, 2000, 2150hrs
Return
Daily   0545, 1830, 2020hrs
One-way fare: 6400drs; duration 50mins

Kos to Leros
Monday, Wednesday   1500hrs
  & Friday
Return
Monday, Wednesday   1415hrs
  & Friday
One-way fare: 2140drs; duration 15mins

Kos to Rhodes
Daily   1430hrs
Return
Daily   1340hrs
One-way fare: 4070drs; duration 30mins

BANKS
The National Bank of Greece (*Tmr* 20B/C4) Located in a large building on the corner of Ant Ioannidi and Riga Fereou. Next door, down the street towards the Harbour, is the bank's exchange office. Despite the very sensible separation of the two disparate functions of normal banking and the frenzy of foreign currency exchange, the office is usually easily identifiable by the long queues that develop. Two English speaking, laconic and nonchalant young Greek gentlemen efficiently marshal the foreign exchange desk. Personal cheques are changed when backed by a Eurocheque card. This facility opens weekdays only between 0815-1400hrs and 1800-2000hrs.

Credit Bank (*Tmr* 21C4) Towards the Castle end of Akti Kountouriotou.
   Another Bank is situated in the ground floor of the *Hotel Maratina* (*Tmr* 22C4) Do not forget the Post Office (*Tmr* 41 C4/5) also conducts exchange transactions.

BEACHES The nearest beach to the Harbour is a narrow, small pebble and sand, rather grubby strip in the shadow of the Castle walls (*Tmr* 23C3). At least it is convenient for a quick dip.
   Another easily reached and convenient spot is the Mini-Lido to the left (*Fsw*) of the seafront building in which is situated the Police officers' club (*Tmr* 24C/D4). Beach umbrellas, beds and a shower.

The Town is flanked by narrow beaches.

To the northern, or left-hand side (*Fsw*), a long, clean, shelving beach of coarse grained sand edges the clear sea. Naturally enough sun-beds and parasols but this area is rather 'downtown' Kos, with a messy admixture of old industrial buildings, homes, hotels, tavernas, restaurants and discos. Mind you the locality beyond the *Hotel Atlantis*, is now flanked by a new road and blessed with a really sandy beach, is pencilled in for development!
   To the south, or right-hand of Kos Town, the tree lined Esplanade edges a narrow pebble beach that stretches all the way to Plateia 7th Martiou, *See* **Excursion to Ag Fokas**.

BICYCLE, SCOOTER & CAR HIRE Due to the suitability of the north coast of the island for cycling, scooter hire remains very inexpensive compared to most other Greek islands. A number of the hire firms are based on El Venizelou St (*Tmr* B/C4), between the junction with Megalou Alexandrou and Vassileos Pavlou.

Stamatis Hire is at the bottom end of Odhos Navklirou and **National Rent-A-Car** is located on El Venizelou, almost opposite the Post Office (*Tmr* 41C4/5). There is a small, rather 'doo-hickey' car, scooter and bicycle hire outfit (*Tmr* 25B4) in the dusty, short extension to Riga Fereou.

My favourite scooter hire outfit (*Tmr* 26A/B4), who has been in business, to my knowledge, for eight or nine years, is located on the left of Megalou Alexandrou, beyond the junction with El Venizelou. His sign simply reads *Rent* and the rates are very, very reasonable with a day's hire starting at 900drs, falling to 1600drs for two days.

Some writers advocate hiring bicycles on the island as, apart from the spine of mountains to the south, the countryside is fairly flat. This is a relative statement and even the ride to the Asklepieion is an uphill climb, and in the heat of the midday sun... Well it's up to you. Masochists may like to know that daily hire rates for bicycles are 200drs and upwards. The German package holiday companies organise conducted 'cycle tours'. They would!

BOOKSELLERS There are a number of foreign language newspaper shops, stocking best-seller paperbacks, ranged up the right-hand (*Sbo*), colonnaded side of Odhos Vassileos Pavlou.

BREAD SHOPS There is one shop (*Tmr* 27B/C4) on the left-hand side of Odhos Vassileos Pavlou, opposite the large, tree shaded terrace of Plateia Xanthou, one block south of the Main Sq (Plateia Eleftherias).

BUSES The Bus terminal (*Tmr* 28B/C4/5) is located on Plateia Pissandrou, an open square in Pissandrou St. This is to the south side of the Olympic office and adjacent to large areas of archaeological remains (which include 'The House of the Abduction of Europe'... sounds risque!). The ticket office is a small, shack sited down a gentle slope from Plateia Pissandrou. Tickets are purchased on the bus.

Bus timetables: Please note these are subject to alteration from year to year, even if it is only fine tuning, and only relate to the summer schedules between May and September. I am rather paranoic about this caveat since receiving one or two 'slap-hand' strictures from not-so-enthusiastic correspondents!

Kos Town to Asfendiou
Monday to Saturday	0700, 1300hrs
Return journey	
Monday to Saturday	0745hrs
Monday to Wednesday	1630hrs
Thursday	1530hrs
Friday	1500hrs
One-way fare: 85drs.	

Kos to Kardamena
Daily	0930, 1300hrs
Monday to Saturday	1630,2030hrs
Sunday	1700hrs
Return journey	
Daily	0745, 1015hrs
Monday to Saturday	1520, 1715hrs
Sunday	1600hrs
One-way fare: 150drs.	

Kos Town to Pyli

Daily	0700, 1300hrs
Monday to Saturday	1030, 2030hrs
Return journey	
Daily	0730hrs
Monday to Saturday	1100hrs
Monday to Wednesday	1645hrs
Thursday to Sunday	1600hrs

One-way fare: 85drs.

Kos Town to Tingaki

Daily	0930, 1300hrs
Monday to Saturday	1030hrs
Monday to Wednesday	1715hrs
Thursday	1615hrs
Friday	1600hrs
Return journey	
Daily	0945hrs
Monday to Saturday	1115hrs
Monday to Wednesday	1530, 1700hrs
Thursday to Sunday	1615hrs

One-way fare: 60drs.

Kos Town to Kefalos via Paradise Beach, Ag Stefanos, Kamares

Daily	0915, 1300hrs
Monday to Saturday	2030hrs
Sunday	1700hrs
Return journey	
Daily	0715, 1015hrs
Monday to Saturday	1500, 1730hrs
Sunday	1530hrs

One-way fare: 210drs.

Kos Town to Antimachia

Daily	1300hrs
Monday to Saturday	2030hrs
Return journey	
Daily	0745hrs
Monday to Saturday	1530, 1745hrs
Sunday	1545hrs

One-way fare: 120drs.

Kos Town to Mastichari

Daily	0930, 1300hrs
Monday to Saturday	1630, 2030hrs
Sunday	1700hrs
Return journey	
Daily	0800, 1000hrs
Monday to Saturday	1730hrs
Sunday	1615hrs

One-way fare: 140drs.

CAMPING *See* The Accommodation

CINEMAS One, the **Orfeas** (*Tmr* 30B4), behind the Main Sq (Plateia Eleftherias) restaurants (*Tmr* 17B/C4), on 25th Martiou. There is another, the **Kentrikon**, on Odhos Pissandrou. Entrance costs about 170drs.

COMMERCIAL SHOPPING AREA

The Market (*Tmr* 29B/C4) This is a fanciful, castellated, square building positioned on the edge of Plateia Eleftherias. Ranged around the periphery, inside a colonnaded passageway, are small shops selling meat, vegetables and groceries. The Market opens early morning to siesta time weekdays and Saturday mornings.

Fish is sold from crates on the Harbour Quay wall and fruit and vegetables from the back of small trucks half-way round the Esplanade, but on the other side of the road.

Ifestou St, which snakes off from the west of Plateia Eleftherias (*Tmr* 49B/C4), has, for some years, contained a 'Plaka-look-alike' mix of tinsmiths and antique shops. Now, no doubt in order to boost tourist earnings, a half-hearted attempt has been made to extend this atmosphere across El Venizelou into and along Apelou St. Need one say any more?

There is a fruit and vegetable shop, which also sells bottled drinks, on 25th Martiou, next door to the *Ideal Snackbar* (*Tmr* 14B4). Open on Sunday mornings, which can prove useful.

DISCOS Numerous, three of which are bunched up in the wine factory area or north end of Kos Town with two on Odhos Zouroudi (*Tmr* B1).

FERRY-BOATS & FLYING DOLPHINS

Ferry-boats 'Pull in' at the pier (*Tmr* 1B/C2/3) beyond the Castle walls. A very comprehensive service but, due to some of the distances travelled and number of islands included in the overall schedules, timetables do tend to slip, by up to several hours.

Flying Dolphins Depart and arrive at the quay (*Tmr* 31D4) projecting into the sea from the Esplanade, between 'County Hall' (*Tmr* 46C/D3/4) and the Police officers' club (*Tmr* 24C/D4).

Ferry-boat timetable (Mid-season)

Day	Departure time	Ferry-boat	Ports/Islands of Call
Monday	1900hrs	Panormitis	Kalimnos,Leros,Lipsos,Patmos,Arki, Angathonisi,Pythagorion(Samos).
Tuesday	0400hrs	Omiros	Rhodes.
	1300hrs	Nireas	Nisiros,Tilos,Simi,Rhodes.
	1600hrs	Kamiros/Ialysos	Kalimnos,Leros,Patmos,Piraeus(M).
	2200hrs	Panormitis	Nisiros,Tilos,Simi,Rhodes.
Wednesday	0300hrs	Kamiros/Ialysos	Rhodes.
	1530hrs	Kamiros/Ialysos	Kalimnos,Leros,Patmos,Piraeus(M).
Thursday	0400hrs	Omiros	Rhodes.
	1300hrs	Nireas	Kalimnos,Astipalaia,Amorgos, Paros,Piraeus(M).
	1530hrs	Omiros	Vathy*(Samos),Chios,Mitilini(Lesbos), Limnos,Kavala(M).
	1830hrs	Panormitis	Kalimnos.
	2200hrs	Panormitis	Nisiros,Tilos,Simi,Rhodes.

*I am fairly sure this craft docks at Vathy and not Pythagorion(Samos) but readers must treble-check.

Friday	0300hrs	Kamiros/Ialysos	Rhodes.
	1530hrs	Kamiros/Ialysos	Kalimnos,Leros,Patmos,Piraeus(M).
Saturday	0300hrs	Kamiros/Ialysos	Rhodes.
	1530hrs	Kamiros/Ialysos	Kalimnos,Leros,Patmos,Piraeus(M).
Sunday	1530hrs	Kamiros/Ialysos	Kalimnos,Leros,Patmos,Piraeus(M).

In addition to the above there are more costly, scheduled excursion craft (that is more costly than the larger ferry-boats):-

Daily	0830hrs	Delfini	Nisiros.
Return fare 1200drs.			
Daily except	0840hrs	Stefamar	Kalimnos.
Tuesdays & Sundays			
Return fare 845drs.			
Tuesday & Sunday	0840hrs	Stefamar	Nisiros.
Daily	0845hrs	Nautilus II	Kalimnos & Pserimos.
Return fare to include 'Pick Nick': 1500drs.			
Daily	0900hrs		Pserimos
Return fare 700drs.			

Also *See* Mastichari Port for a Kalimnos connection and Kardamena for Nisiros excursion boats.

Flying Dolphin timetable (Mid-season)

Day	Departure time	Ports/Islands of Call
Daily	0800hrs	Rhodes.
except Sundays		
Sunday	1800hrs	Simi,Rhodes.
Thursday & Saturday	0930hrs	Patmos.

FERRY-BOAT & FLYING DOLPHIN TICKET OFFICES Mainly centred on the Esplanade road of Akti Kountouriotou (shoulder to shop front with the Tourist office (*Tmr* 4B/C3/4) and Port police) and Odhos Vassileos Pavlou, beneath the colonnaded walkway on the right (*Sbo*), the offices of which are 'jostled' in amongst the newspaper shops.

HAIRDRESSERS You're okay girls, there are some five or six. But is an Aegean island still Greek where ladies' hairdressers are present in this number? Surely Not!

LAUNDERETTE Well at least three dry cleaners, including one (*Tmr* A/B2/3) on Odhos Kanari and El Venizelou Sts. There is a launderette at the outset of Odhos Themistokleous (*Tmr* B3). A wash costs 400drs and the drier 150drs.

MEDICAL CARE
Chemists & Pharmacies Very 'thick underfoot', as are doctors and dentists. I suppose this is natural for the island that nurtured our 'old friend' Hippocrates, but there must be more medical supernumaries per head of population than anywhere else in Greece.
Dentists There is one (*Tmr* B4) on No 38 El Venizelou, at the junction with Metsovou St. Another surgery is also on Metsovou St, next door to *Maxime's Cafe*, at No. 14, a yellow painted house close to the bus terminal.

Doctors Plentiful including Dr E Perdis (*Tmr* 48C4) on Odhos Hippocratous. His surgery is open daily (weekends as well) 0830-1330hrs and 1700-2100hrs. Conveniently there is a large pharmacy next door.

Hospital (*Tmr* 43C4). Appropriately on Odhos Hippocratous.

NTOG (EOT) (*Tmr* 4B/C3/4) The old Tourist police building has been requisitioned (now the Tourist police have decamped to join the Town police) by the Municipal Tourist office. Run by a 'hunky', helpful young man who proffers lists of accommodation, ferry-boat and bus timetables and more. The doors open daily between 0730-2100hrs.

OTE (*Tmr* 32C4) 6 Vironos St. A tatty office with a sign requesting *Please queue up for all telephone boxes*. Despite this simple and straightforward request, certain tourists still persevere in barging through, but I deny that they are all of Teutonic background, even if pressed... The 'Brits', of course, form a queue at the drop of a sun-hat, so we are in the clear.... The office opens Monday to Friday between 0730-2400hrs and Saturday, Sunday and holidays between 0730-1510hrs.

PETROL Apart from the station on the edge of town there is a pair of pumps (*Tmr* 33C4) on Odhos Hippocratous.

PLACES OF INTEREST Seemingly Kos, more than perhaps any other Greek town, has remains littered all over the place. In fact, it is almost impossible not to fall over a Roman this or ancient Greek that...

Ancient Agora & Port Quarter (*Tmr* C4) The most convenient way on to this very large, sprawling site is from Akti Miaouli, opposite the Flying Dolphin Quay, alongside the *Hotel Iviscos* (*Tmr* 11C/D3/4). A number of interesting exhibits, dating as far back as the 4th century BC, lurk in the weed and boulder bestrewn landscape. Interestingly enough, it was the 1933 earthquake that destroyed many medieval buildings and enabled the eager Italian architects to get to work.

Close by the north end of this site is the:-

Square of The Hippocratic Plane Tree (*Tmr* 34C3/4) Lovely Plateia Platanou is dominated by an extremely old and arthritic tree, the branches of which are supported at every possible point by forked crucks (no, no crucks!). Old as the tree may be, and estimates vary widely from 400 to 1000 years, it cannot possibly be between 2,400 and 2,500 years old, which it would have to be for Hippocrates to have taught beneath its foliage. Under the spreading branches a pleasant fountain bubbles into an old sarcophagus. The buildings in and around the Square are of a most diverse and dissimilar architectural milieu. They include:-

The Mosque of the Loggia/Hatji-Hasan Built in the late 1700s by, surprise, surprise, the Turk, Hasan (Hadji-Hatji) Pasha. A pleasant flight of marble steps, a splendid minaret as well as the many coloured stones used in the construction make an impressive sight. The Italians, not to be left out, built, in the 1930s, an ambitious Town Hall (*Tmr* 46C/D3/4), now housing offices of the police, judiciary and administration.

From the Square, a flight of steps leads to a stone bridge spanning Odhos Finikon or, more poetically, the Avenue of the Palms, which gives access to:-

The Castle of the Knights (*Tmr* 2C3) An imposing Crusader Castle, the walls of which are in a surprisingly good state of repair. The fort was built on the ruins of a previous fortification, close by the mouth of the entrance to the Harbour. The

Avenue of Palms/Finikon St was originally a moat. To effect the construction, the Knights of the Order of St John 'borrowed' a great deal of the materials from other, older Greek and Roman remains, especially the Asklepeion. The Castle is now appropriately used to store recently excavated archaeological finds awaiting a final resting place. This site, as well as the Museums and Roman Villa are open: Monday to Saturday between 0900-1500hrs; Sundays and holidays between 0930-1430hrs and closed Tuesdays.

The Main Square (*Tmr* 49B/C4) has a number of interesting features including:-
The Museum (*Tmr* 35B/C4) A rather bland, small, yellow building of Italian construction, with an interesting collection of statues.

Deftedar Mosque (*Tmr* 36B/C4) Makes an island site towards one corner of the Square. Various tourist shops are incongruously let into the base of the building.

Behind the Mosque is the very pretty, if isolated, flower covered 'Gate of the Forum', or 'The Taxes', dating from medieval times.

From Eleftherias Square, westwards along Odhos 25th Martiou, quickly leads to a small archaeological site famed for its mosaics. An interesting way to gain access is to walk along the cul-de-sac extension to Riga Fereou St and turn left between two houses, the one on the right containing a restaurant bar, the *Flamingo Pub*, in front of which stands a very large, re-rooting tree, but I digress. Once on the site the path is a length of ancient road, with the occasional ruin here and there, once again all in amongst the weeds. ·
    Further on along 25th Martiou, which becomes 31st Martiou, gives access to a larger archaeological site, bounded by Odhos Megalou Alexandrou and known as the **Old Stadium**.
    Once again back at Eleftherias Square (*Tmr* 49B/C4), Vassileos Pavlou proceeds to a junction with Grigoriou E, off which are a lot of interesting archaeological 'goodies'.
    To the left (*Harbour behind one*) is the:-

Temple & Altar of Dionysos (*Tmr* 37C5) Dated 3rd century BC, opposite which is the:-
Casa Romana (*Tmr* 38C5) The 3rd century AD remains of a Roman house superimposed on the ruins of a larger Greek mansion, dated between 50-30 BC. The splendidly reconstructed house contains remnants and mosaic floors which are 'column by pediment' with the ruins of some Roman baths. The entrance fee is 200drs and the restored exhibit is well worth a visit.
    West on Odhos Grigoriou E leads past a very large 'L' shaped site on the right (*Tmr* B4/5). This includes an:-

Acropolis (*Tmr* 39B4/5) The old site, with a minaret now in position.

Roman Road A stretch of paved way, with the remains of Roman houses here and there.

House of Europe Further west and famous for its mosaics.
    Hereabouts the site takes a turn to the north which advances to more Roman roadways, or Via Cardo, followed by the ancient remains of: *The Nymphaeum, The Xystos* (gymnasium), baths, (once) sumptuous latrines, taverns and more mosaics.

Across Odhos Grigoriou E is one of my favourite Kos remains, the:-
Ancient Odeion (*Tmr* 40A/B5) A theatre which is approached through and framed

by a deliciously cool avenue of stately cypresses. Although extensively restored it is a beautiful construction, in a lovely setting, and is occasionally used for modern-day productions.

Two other sites deserve a mention and include some Thermae or Baths at the Harbour end of Megalou Alexandrou, bounded by Irodotou and Iroon Politchniou Sq (*Tmr* B3/4). The other site is, or more accurately was, a car park off El Venizelou. This particular location looks suspiciously like one of the British National Car Parks – yellow luminous signs with a hut and other familiar trappings. Here a general, leisurely archaeological excavation is under way.

POST OFFICE (*Tmr* 41C4/5) Eastwards on Odhos Venizelou, beyond the junction with Meropidos St. The doors are open Monday-Friday between 0730-2030hrs.
   Postage stamps are available from some of the Harbour Esplanade peripteros.

POLICE

Port Alongside the Municipal Tourist office (*Tmr* 4B/C3/4).
Town & Tourist (*Tmr* 46C/D3/4) Located in the large municipal block, alongside the quadrangle containing the old Hippocratic plane tree.

SPORTS FACILITIES Not a lot in the Town, unless you wish to play football or basket ball – well, why not?

TAXIS (*Tmr* 42C4) There is a rank alongside the conjunction of the Harbour road, Akti Kountouriotou, and Platanou Sq.

TELEPHONE NUMBERS & ADDRESSES

Hospital (*Tmr* 43C4) 21 Hippocratous St	Tel 22330
Olympic Airways (*Tmr* 19B/C4/5) 22 Vas Pavlou	Tel 2833-2
Taxi rank (*Tmr* 42C4)	Tel 22777/23333
Police (*Tmr* 46C/D3/4)	Tel 22222
Tourist office (*Tmr* 4B/C3/4) 7 Akti Kountouriotou	Tel 28724/24460

TRAVEL AGENTS & TOUR OFFICES A number on Vas Pavlou and Akti Kountiouriotou Sts, as well as on 25th Martiou and El Venizelou.

TOILETS Not as 'potty' conscious as Rhodes. There is one, set in the reverse side of the Market building (*Tmr* 29B/C4), another snuggled away on the junction of Megalou Alexandra with Akti Kountouriotou (*Tmr* 44B3/4) and yet another on Finikon Avenue (*Tmr* 45C3/4) – almost beneath the bridge between Platanou Sq and the Castle.

EXCURSIONS TO KOS TOWN SURROUNDS
Excursion to Asklepieion via Platanos (4km) Leave Kos Town along Odhos Megalou Alexandrou and turn right at the junction with Koritsas and Grigoriou E Sts. About 1km out of town the road forks right for Kefalos and left to Platanos. Take the left turning. Half-way along the slightly rising road to Platanos and on the left is a long, white wall with red stone capping concealing a:-

Turkish Cemetery Possibly rivals the one in Rhodes City, but rather tatty. The wrought iron gate is fastened with a chain and padlock. No worry, they can be slipped over the top of the gate. The gravestones, in excellent condition, are stacked together in piles and the distinctive, carved headpieces show up well.

PLATANOS (2km from Kos Town) A rather scruffy village prior to the Asklepieion, with a number of tourist orientated tavernas 'slugging it' out for the available trade.

The final approach, all uphill, is through a narrow avenue, lined with stately cypress trees. Along this metalled lane continually streams a tide of air-conditioned tour buses, as this remarkable site is very much a part of the tourist merry-go-round, if not the major constituent of the 'circus', no circuit (a natural slip of the pen).

The Asklepieion (4km from Kos Town) The Sanctuary is named after the God of healing and is considered to have been constructed, after the death of Hippocrates, in the 4th century BC on the site of sacred ground. The situation of the first medical school in the world is certainly impressive, if not breath-taking, the various terraces or levels rising up the pine tree clad hillside.

A 6th century AD earthquake 'rubbled' the site, the lazy Knights borrowed much of the stonework to build their castle at Kos Town but the Italians carried out extensive restoration of the archaeological site – where did they not?

From the top level, gained by ascending the large and grand stone staircase, the views are truly magnificent.

Lawrence Durrell in his book *The Greek Islands** writes that to camp in or near the Asklepieion may result in a very disturbed night's sleep, hinting that the ghosts of the ancients still haunt the location.

* *Published by Faber & Faber Ltd.*

I make no apologies for recording a version of the Hippocratic oath as set out below.

'I swear by Apollo Physician, by Esculapius**, by Hygeia***, by Panacea**** and by all the gods and goddesses, making them my witnesses, that I will carry out, according to my ability and judgement, this oath and this indenture. To hold my teacher in this art equal to my own parents; to make him partner in my livelihood; when he is in need of money to share mine with him; to consider his family as my own brothers, and to teach them this art, if they want to learn it, without fee or indenture; to impart precept, oral instruction, and all other instruction to my own sons, the sons of my teacher, and to indentured pupils who have taken the physician's oath, but to nobody else. I will use treatment or help the sick according to my ability and judgement, but never with a view to injury and wrong-doing. Neither will I administer a poison to anybody when asked to do so, nor will I suggest such a course. Similarly I will not give a woman a pessary to cause abortion. But I will keep pure and holy both my life and my art. I will not use the knife, not even, verily, on sufferers from stone, but I will give place to such as are craftsmen therein. Into whatsoever houses I enter, I will enter to help the sick, and I will abstain from all intentional wrong-doing and harm, especially from abusing the bodies of man or woman, bond or free. And whatsoever I shall see or hear in the course of my profession, as well as outside my profession in my intercourse with men, if it be what should not be published abroad, I will never divulge, holding such things to be holy secrets. Now if I carry out this oath, and break it not, may I gain for ever reputation among all men for my life and for my art; but if I transgress it and forswear myself, may the opposite befall me.*

Excursion to Ag Fokas (7km) From Kos Town, Akti Miaouli Avenue

proceeds eastwards past the various grand Italianesque buildings into Vas Georgiou B. This avenue is bordered by the sea and a very narrow, pebbly beach on the left. On the right is a mishmash of hotels, restaurants, housing and flats which slowly degenerate in quality as the avenue proceeds towards

*Son of Zeus (Jupiter) and Leto. **Son of Apollo and a god, amongst other things, of the healing art. ***Daughter of Esculapius, and a goddess of health. ****(Another) daughter of Esculapius.

Plateia 7th Martiou, and then Odhos G Papandreou, in the direction of the hamlets of Psalidi, Ag Fokas and Empros Thermae. On the way, about 400m beyond the *Continental Palace Hotel* and just past the turning down to the *Ramira Beach Hotel*, are the *Restaurant Nea Syntrivani* and the *Restaurant Antonis*. Both establishments are recommended for inexpensive, well cooked, excellent value food, pleasantly served in an atmosphere approaching the 'real' Greek ambience. Can one say more?

The coastal journey skirts the town's rubbish dump, the headland of Psalidi and on to Ag Fokas, where, at a cleft in the road a turning winds down to a snackbar. From this point another 4km of unmade track leads to the hot sulphurous spring at Empros Thermae, which dribbles across the cliff edged, blackish beach into the sea.

ROUTE ONE
To Kefalos via Zipari, Antimachia and Kamares (43km)
This is really the one and only route, with a number of forays off to north and south coasts. The main Kefalos road from Kos Town, on past the Platanos side turning, is the subject of ribbon development with a number of Spanish style villas set in Spanish style, urban sprawl. Thankfully this messy state of affairs peters out and is replaced by the occasional taverna and more widely scattered buildings set in a broad plain bounded, on the left, by the Dikeos mountain range.

ZIPARI (8km from Kos Town) Petrol is available beyond the village.
In Zipari a side turning to the left winds up the mountainside, through lovely, varied tree clad hillsides. The large eucalyptus trees that used to line the road were cut back to stumps following the cold winter of 1987. One wonders if this 'butchery' was to keep the home fires burning?

At a junction in **Asfendiou** village, roads lead off to the right, centre and left. The left turning proceeds to the very pretty, typically Greek villages of:-

AG GEORGIOS (14km from Kos Town) A number of derelict houses nestle in amongst the leisurely village
and on to:-

AG DIMITRIOS (15km from Kos Town) As Ag Georgios, but more so with a rather nice church.

Apart from the commonplace nature of these untidy but pleasing, crumbling villages, their noteworthiness lies in the fact that they are very nearly the only quintessential Greek island villages left on Kos. Need I say more! It is certainly very rewarding to walk through and round them.

Straight on at Asfendiou village leads to Zia, via a very attractive, almost Alpine hillside road, with running stream water all the year round. Below the roadway, on a sharp right-hand bend, is the old communal bath/washing area immediately prior to the village of:-

ZIA (14km from Kos Town) Billed as a 'typical Greek mountain village', that is the one thing it certainly is not with two clean, spruce tavernas, the *Cafe Olympia*, a trim tourist shop and some very smart houses. So what's Greek?

There used to be clean public toilets but they have been closed, much to the chagrin of the owner of the *Cafe Olympia*. He claims his outside toilet is now being used by 'eight or nine' coach loads of people everyday. Of course they don't always leave the place clean – so much so that he rushes in the moment someone comes out! If he finds they have left it in an unsatisfactory state, he hauls the offender back and makes them clean up... Not a pretty sight! Despite these, no doubt hectic moments, the cafe is quite pleasant. The proprietor brews an 'interesting', red coloured cinnamon drink (*kanela*) and a fruity type of ouzo made from grape skins. A Nes meh ghala costs 50drs and there is a limited menu available.

The publicity has resulted in Zia becoming a 'plastic replica', so why not pop round the corner to see Ag Georgios and or Dimitrios before they are dusted down, smartened up and become commuter villages for wealthy, Kos Town business people?

From Asfendiou a now paved road winds across the countryside to **Lagoudi** village, from whence a dusty, unmade, flinty track forks right and then left for **Amaniou** village. The route emerges close by a small, beggarly church on the right-hand side. Left at this T-junction and a surprisingly broad, impressive, metalled road climbs steeply up to... well, nowhere really, petering out in a very attractive cleft, high up on the side of Mt Dikeos. To say nowhere is not strictly true as the track continues to climb to **Old Pyli**, now a deserted village, more a pile of rubble really, but still overlooked by the remains of a Byzantine Castle.

The track from Amaniou to Pyli is practically impassable, not because of the appalling surface or lack of track but because a sentry-guarded, ramshackle military base straddles the road. If an intrepid traveller does get through to Pyli, a left turn at the village advances along a wide, unmetalled, stony donkey track over and round the mountainside, through a rather green but lunar landscape (if that is not a contradiction in terms) and down to a coastal plain. This route proceeds along a straight, tree lined avenue to Kardamena. Ignore those maps that detail the route as being a major or even a minor road, but it is exciting!

Pyli is more usually reached from a turning off the main road, some 4km on from Zipari. For the more conventional route to Kardamena read the route description from Antimachia village.

Assuming all this is too much, back at Zipari, after 1km a side road to the right arrows down to:-

TINGAKI (11km from Kos Town) A very smart, small but very pleasant, if crowded, resort. To the right of the central grove of trees up-market hotels edge the broad, sandy beach, from which projects a metal framed quay. There is some dry kelp in evidence at the water's edge. On the horizon, is Pserimos island which, at its closest, is some 3km distant.

A newspaper shop, postcards, a beach bar or three, two restaurants, a *Cantina*, a beach shower, sun-beds and umbrellas complement the natural qualities of sand and sea. These attributes are necessary as Tingaki is the target of many Kos Town holiday-makers, quite a number of whom cycle out daily. For those resident at Tingaki there is moped and bicycle hire firm — *Mikes For Bikes*: *If you don't like to hike, see Mike for a bike...* Yes!

The side turning from the main road accommodates a disco, several large, smart, Spanish style restaurants (the type of barn-like place that seem empty most of the time) and a couple of houses with **Rooms**. In fact there is a total of seven hotels and pensions with the *Hotel Paxinos* (Class C — tel 29306) weighing in with single rooms, en suite, costing 1800drs and a double room en suite 2250drs.

A track, parallel to the main road and the coast, stretches both east and west. The westward direction edges a large area of saltings (Alikes) as far as the seaside village of:-

MARMARI (15km from Kos Town) Here is the A class *Hotel Caravia*, to which backpackers need not apply, and at 8400drs for a double room, probably would not wish, or be able to afford to so do.

The burgeoning Marmari beach resort is usually reached from the main Kos Town to Kefalos road but, prior to attaining the main side turning to Marmari, there is a fork in the road alongside a cement works and pond. The left-hand turning leads to:-

PYLI (15km from Kos Town) Not an outstanding village even if there is a Byzantine church built over an ancient tomb. Pyli is not to be muddled with Old Pyli which, confusingly, is some 4km away, through Amaniou village.

The main road soldiers on past a small concentration of plastic (greenhouses) and fields containing a noticeable number of grazing cows. After 2km, a cross country road,to the right, cuts off a large corner to join the Antimachia to Mastichari road.

The countryside either side of the main road becomes a cross between moorland heath and army firing range landscape, with the occasional windmill dotted about. A kilometre before the village of Antimachia, a narrow, flinty path to the left switchbacks up and down past a military camp to:-

The Castle of Antimachia Sometimes labelled *Soroko* on the maps, the second-rate donkey track does not quite make the fort's walls. The Castle is a large and impressive structure,with sound battlements,dating back to the Knights. The main gates are around to the left but the fortress can be entered almost directly, by a flight of steps giving access through a small, doorless gateway. The interior is rather messy but there is a small church in the centre of the edifice. Scattered about are remnants of dwellings which, possibly, once housed local inhabitants when they had to flee from the depredations of marauding pirates. The isolation and views are splendid.

ANTIMACHIA (25km from Kos Town) Almost the centre of the island and certainly the epicentre of a convoluted road system with two large round-abouts, a bypass and the Airport close by. Almost sounds like home, doesn't it? Despite the tourist maps usually being wildly inaccurate about this area, the signposting is not too bad around the village. Within Antimachia there are no signs at all. The village is dusty and sprawling with a large, working windmill and was once famed for its melons. There is a petrol station on the bypass.

The first, large roundabout gives access to Antimachia and the road to the coastal fishing port of:-

MASTICHARI (30km from Kos Town) The first part of the road is in a bad state and has been so for some eight or nine years.

My notes once stated that when I visited Kos I would always make directly for this ramshackle, seaside location. That was before the old, two taverna hamlet, beach and headland, with a small wooden pier, became the recipient of a comparatively massive port facility. The right-hand taverna (*Fsw*) has been displaced by the *Mastihari Beach Hotel*. This looks over the man-made port whilst the left-hand taverna, whose patio used to almost 'dip its stone' into the sea, is now on the edge of the large, barrack-like square adjacent to the port and on to which the road decants. But that is progress isn't it...?

The left-hand taverna, the *Kalia Kardia*, now 'sports' waiters, instead of Mama and her two sons casually attending to the punters' requirements, but the prices are still reasonable. An orange drink costs 40drs and meals include moussaka 250drs and *Veal Gulps* (*sic* or sick!) at a cost of 360drs.

To the right (*Fsw*), across the road into the port, is the *Sunset Taverna*, next to which is the *Pizza Taverna* and then a bar.

The broad, sandy beach around the corner to the left is still beguiling with a beach shower close to a scattered grove of trees. A number of beach restaurants have been developed along the backshore and parasols now march across the sandy shore. Some sea-borne kelp dries out on the water's edge.

To the right, beyond the port breakwater, the seafront has not changed much and still runs out on a boulderous foreshore, edged by a small, scrub and stunted-tree headland.

There are numerous **Rooms** to let, as almost every other building advertises beds, and there are three Pensions which include the *Faenareti* (Class D – tel 51395) with double rooms en suite costing 2000drs and the *Hotel Andreas* (Class B – tel 51556), where the double room rate for one night of 2000drs falls to 1400drs for a longer stay.

Scooters are available for hire and no doubt Mastichari will continue to grow and grow and grow (as has Kardamena). The village is already spreading, or backing up the approach road, along which are a number of tour company villas. The Airport is fairly close but Mastichari remains an attractive location.

During the season there are boat trips from the port to Kalimnos and Pserimos islands. The **Apollo** excursion boat connects twice daily to Kalimnos, the journey taking 30mins at a cost of only 250drs. The departure times are 0830hrs and 2200hrs, returning at 2000hrs and 2300hrs. However the *raison d'etre* for this craft is to ferry holiday-makers, who have travelled by Olympic Airways to Kos airport, over to their Kalimnos accommodation. Oh dear! Thus the Apollo only sails when the aircraft-to-bus-to-Mastichari connection is completed, and then only takes on other passengers if there is space. (The boat office telephone number is 28507).

From Mastichari a donkey track can be braved, which proceeds westwards along the coast, past the ruins of Ag Ioannis Church, to an interesting area of rather plastic-littered dunes and a sandy beach. This is absolutely deserted, with not even a beach-bar in sight, but may well be a prime site for the next Kos holiday hotel complex! The donkey track supposedly links round to with Antimachia but....

Back on the main road, the 1¼km bypass progresses to the second, large roundabout, whereon there are turnings to Antimachia village, the main Kefalos road, a spur off to the Airport and the road to:-

KARDAMENA (27km from Kos Town) (Illustration 31) The five
kilometre drive to the village is unexceptional. Those holiday-makers who expect to find a small, attractive fishing community and village, a quiet backwater steeped in a centuries-old way of life, pursuing country crafts, travelling by donkey and caique, each rustic day stretching into another as fisher-folk mend their nets and while away their spare time in the local kafeneion, their wives cleaning out sponges and gutting fish, all as described in various package holiday brochures, will be in for a very big shock. Even the original core of the village is now hard to detect, as 'Costa del Greco' has overlaid the place. Now the hardships of Greek island life have been reduced to deciding which 'happy-

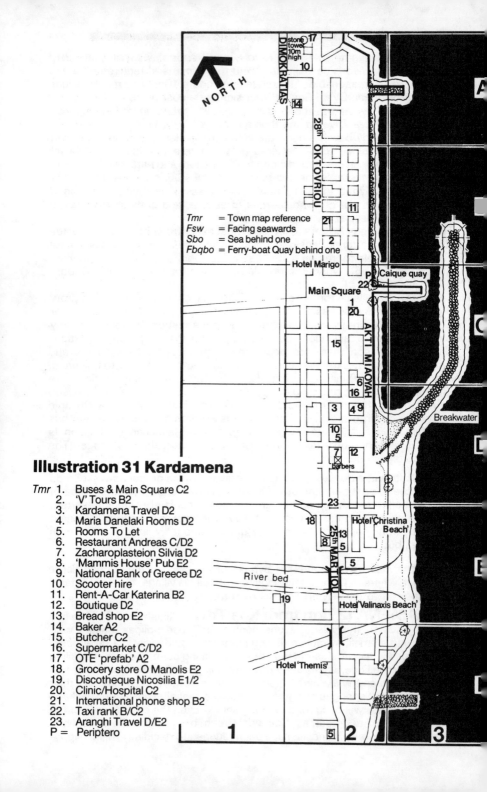

Illustration 31 Kardamena

Tmr 1. Buses & Main Square C2
2. 'V' Tours B2
3. Kardamena Travel D2
4. Maria Danelaki Rooms D2
5. Rooms To Let
6. Restaurant Andreas C/D2
7. Zacharoplasteion Silvia D2
8. 'Mammis House' Pub E2
9. National Bank of Greece D2
10. Scooter hire
11. Rent-A-Car Katerina B2
12. Boutique D2
13. Bread shop E2
14. Baker A2
15. Butcher C2
16. Supermarket C/D2
17. OTE 'prefab' A2
18. Grocery store O Manolis E2
19. Discotheque Nicosilia E1/2
20. Clinic/Hospital C2
21. International phone shop B2
22. Taxi rank B/C2
23. Aranghi Travel D/E2
P = Periptero

hour bar', with half-price cocktails, to frequent, which 'chips with everything' taverna, complete with mock peasant goat trimmings, to 'trough it at', which old English pub, with pressure lager on tap, to drown one's sorrows in. Even the Pension accommodation have tiled bathrooms! Mind you, beauty and sensibilities are in the eye of the beholder. On a visit some years ago, whilst patronizing the Kos Town to Kardamena bus, a young mother from Ruislip declared that Kardamena was nice, yes nice but primitive! I only hope the 'dear girl' never visits the islands of Nisiros or Tilos or spends the night in an old Simi pension!

More, much more is in store as to the far left of the Bay (*Fsw*) an enormous complex – the *Norida Beach* has been constructed and to the far, well not so far, right is a villa development complete with street lights stretching towards Kardamena centre. Yes, street lights!

Not all is lost though. John Ebdon in his book *Ebdon's Odyssey** lovingly details his experiences of Kardamena in the 1970s. His favourite taverna and its owners, Silvia and her husband, are still there.

*Published by Peter Davies Ltd.

Arrival will normally be by road and the buses decant their passengers on the Main Square (*Tmr* 1C2).

THE ACCOMMODATION & EATING OUT

The Accommodation Most of the hotels and pensions are now block booked with wall-to-wall package tourists but, perhaps surprisingly, the buses are still met by owners of accommodation. There are some very pleasant, private rooms including:-

Maria Danelaki (*Tmr* 4D2)   Tel 91474
Directions: To the right (*Fsw*) of the Main Square (*Tmr* IC2), in the street one back and parallel to the Esplanade.

This is a nicely decorated, well appointed house with double rooms sharing a bathroom from 2000drs. Note Maria does not arrive from Athens to open up until mid-June.

There are also **Rooms**, amongst others, at those locations marked *Tmr* 5.

Just to thrust home the point that this is no traditional Greek village fishing port, it is worth noting that there is a 300drs per hour baby-sitting agency. Enough said!

The Eating Out There are a number of reasonably priced snackbars, tavernas and restaurants including:-

Andreas Restaurant (*Tmr* 6C/D2)
Directions: To the right (*Fsw*) from the Main Square, one block before the National Bank of Greece.

Average prices for meals. The beer is reasonably priced, for Kardamena that is, at 90drs for a 500gm bottle of Amstel, compared to 150drs a few doors along.

For breakfast try:-
Zacharoplasteion Silvia (*Tmr* 7D2)
Directions: One street back from the Esplanade, just beyond and the other side of the road to a boutique.

Mama Silvia speaks some English and she and her husband, who doubles up as a barber next door, run a very friendly place with breakfast being served until late in the night. You may well question the breakfast but that is all their licence covers so, as they are in deadly rivalry with the establishment next door, they cannot stray from the culinary 'straight and narrow'. Toast, butter, marmalade and coffee, costs 150drs per head. Still as described in *Ebdon's Odyssey*, referred to previously.

Before leaving the subject of entertainment I am forced to draw attention to *Mammis House Pub* (*Tmr* 8E2). Well need one say anymore!

THE A TO Z OF USEFUL INFORMATION

BANKS Yes, the **National Bank of Greece** (*Tmr* 9D2), as well as a number of travel companies who cash travellers cheques (*See* **Travel Agents & Tour Offices, A To Z**).

BEACHES A beautiful, sandy beach but almost totally covered by beach umbrellas, sun-beds and almost every colour, hue, shade, size and state of human body.

BICYCLE, SCOOTER & CAR HIRE Yes, almost everywhere including at *Tmr* 10A2 and *Tmr* 10D2, as well as **Rent-a-Car Katerina** (*Tmr* 11B2).

BOUTIQUE (*Tmr* 12D2) Kardamena has a boutique. Well it would, wouldn't it!

BREAD SHOP One (*Tmr* 13E2) and a Baker (*Tmr* 14A2), even if it is at the far, north end of town, on a dusty, scruffy little square.

BUSES Turn round on the Main Square (*Tmr* 1C2). *See* **Bus timetable, Buses, A To Z, Kos Town.**

COMMERCIAL SHOPPING AREA No market but a plentiful supply of shops of all shapes and sizes including O Manolis Grocery store (*Tmr* 18E2) and Angys store (next to Kardamena Travel – *Tmr* 3D2), which stocks drink, cigarettes and stamps. There is also a Butcher's (*Tmr* 15C2).

DISCOS Well there would be. They include the **Nicosilia** (*Tmr* 19E1/2) beside the summer-dry river-bed.

FERRY-BOATS No ferry-boats, but there are a couple of excursion craft that connect with Nisiros island including the:-
Chrysoula This is owned by the handsome, slightly piratical looking Capt Gerasimos. He and his 'forceful' wife and pretty daughter run a daily boat trip to Nisiros island, except Sunday when they slide round to 'Bubble Beach'. His caique is a large craft and the round trip to Nisiros costs about 1200drs per head. Why not stop over for a night or two and experience the joys and privations of a truly Greek island? (*See* the relevant chapter). At the height of season, the craft departs at 1000hrs and tickets are available from the bottom of the pier, on the Main Square. Their signboard depicts an imaginative, primitive art version of Nisiros as a vast exploding Volcano surrounded by five mini exploding volcanoes!
Nisiros Express This craft departs for Nisiros on Sunday, Monday, Wednesday, Thursday and Saturday at 0930hrs. The round trip costs 1400drs.

MEDICAL CARE
Chemists & Pharmacies Well not really, but basics are available from the one or two of the supermarkets (*Tmr* 16C/D2).
Clinic/Hospital (*Tmr* 20C2).

OTE There is an OTE 'prefab' (*Tmr* 17A2) close by the stone tower, but it was yet to kick into life as late as mid-1987. The sign on the door is not much help – *Banking Hours* and that was it. There is a metered international phone in a store (*Tmr* 21B2), which is only open shop hours.

SPORTS FACILITIES Naturally enough pedaloes, wind surfing and water skiing abound, as well as para-skiing, this latter having proved deadly at this resort. Certainly a few years ago rumour, only rumour, suggested that certain unlicensed operators had managed to smack one client into a hotel (which did not give way), used another para-skier to cut a swathe through the massed beach umbrellas (with the result that both the participant and a sunbather expired) and one other punter accidentally garroted a passer-by with the tow line. Who would have guessed it could all be so excitingly dangerous?

TAXIS (*Tmr* 22B/C2) Rank on the Main Square.

TRAVEL AGENTS & TOUR OFFICES Numerous, with selected offices acting for the various package holiday companies. These include V Tours (*Tmr* 2B2), Kardamena Travel & Exchange (*Tmr* 3D2), Aranghi Travel and Rent-A-Car & Money Xchange (*Tmr* 23D/E2). Most of these offices offer foreign currency exchange facilities.

Back at the main road, the route to Kefalos from the Airport roundabout is one of the most boring I have ever travelled on any Greek island. The road narrows, initially between poor farmland on the right and heath on the left which then degenerates into scrubbly moorland with the Army ever-present. Occasional clumps of pines, that spasmodically edge the road, exhibit the wind tortured nature of the landscape. Prior to breasting the rise, high above Ag Stefanos, one or two lanes wander off down to:-

PARADISE BEACH (approx 35km from Kos Town) Also called 'Bubble Beach', due to the large amount of bubbles that filter up from the sea-bed. The steep, main track to the beach empties on to an upper and then a lower vehicle park, the choice depending on a traveller's bravery, or perhaps foolhardiness. The final descent is made on foot. For once the descriptive adjective, paradise, does not belie the long, lovely, curving, sandy beach but even here there are some sun umbrellas!

Over a crest on the main road above Ag Stefanos, and one of the most breathtaking and lovely views comes into sight. Mt Latra rears up in the middle distance, Nisiros island crouches darkly on the far horizon, whilst on the immediate left is an incredible *Club Mediterranee* complex. Down below, close to the shore of the long, gently curving, sandy bay, is the islet of Kastri topped off by a diminutive chapel, all set in a sparkling sea sprinkled with wind surfers. The development of this area has been rapid and the area between the one-time hamlets of Ag Stefanos and Kamares is quickly infilling with a rag-bag of hasty developments.

At **Ag Stefanos** there is *Rooms Chrysoula* on the right, where the road enters the village, and behind the *Greek Taverna Kefalos*. Double rooms sharing a bathroom cost 1200drs.

Between **Kamares**, where petrol is available, and the hill-top village of Kefalos, are many *Rooms* to let and a number of hotels. These include the *Hotel Sydney* (Class D – tel 71286) where all rooms have en suite bathrooms with singles costing 1700drs and a double 2300drs.

KEFALOS (40km from Kos Town) From Kamares the village of Kefalos can be seen peeping over the towering hillside and, to the right of the village, a working windmill is conspicuous. The final ascent is very steep and finishes in a tight series of hairpin bends.

Kefalos is a nice village despite having greatly expanded. It is now quite large and spread out with a tight centre and dusty, sprawling surrounds. The recommended *Kali Kardia Taverna*, carnation bedecked and brightly coloured, is to the right of the High St. A snack of 3 souvlaki sticks, chips, feta, Greek salad and a beer costs 600drs.

From the village a number of dirt tracks radiate, including an unmade 4km lane, past the aforementioned windmill, to **Limonas**, a small, man-made harbour with a tiny stretch of sand.

Beyond Kefalos, the 7 or 8km road to Ag Ioannis, and the southern-tip of the island, switchbacks up and up and up and then down, only to go up again, part through a fire devasted area that has left a swathe of blackened, petrified trees marching along the steep hillside. The views are truly amazing with the land falling away, comparatively gently, over a boulderous landscape to the coastline far below.

KOS ISLAND EXCURSION TO PSERIMOS ISLAND The
large inter-island ferries plough past Pserimos but the island is regularly serviced by a number of short haul excursion boats from Kos Town and Mastichari (Kos), as well as Kalimnos island.

The supposed tranquillity of the island is disturbed by the flood and ebb of day-trip tourists but outside these intrusions the sixty or so inhabitants relapse into their placid existence.

The *Pension & Restaurant Tripolitis*, owned by Mr Saroukos, supplies both simple accommodation and sustenance and is beautifully sited, close by the sea's edge. The delightful, sandy beach is also 'serviced' by three other tavernas and there is a general store.

Half an hours walk from the port are two more sandy beaches where 'resident' tourists tend to escape for the day.

Incidentally one correspondent queried if "my wife had tried the Pserimos public toilet – a free standing squatty without even a hole in the ground!"

A popular monastic and religious festival on the 14th and 15th of August overwhelms the island's sparse facilities so don't plan to make a visit either side of these dates.

Backyard beauty, Kefalos, Kos.

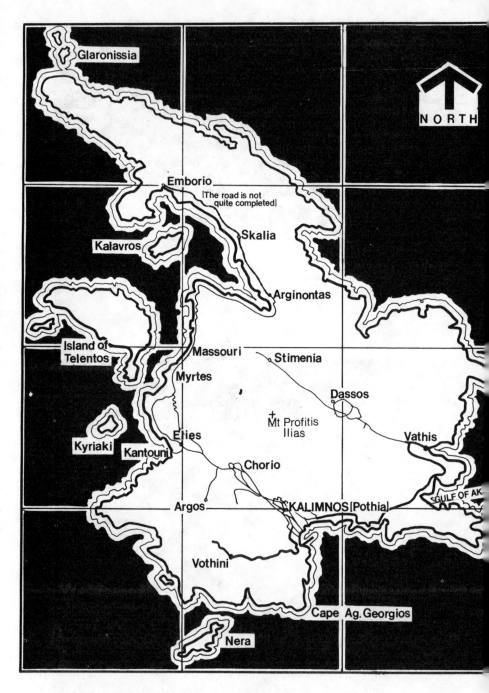

Illustration 32 Kalimnos island

21 KALIMNOS (Kalymnos, Calymnos) ****

Dodecanese Islands

FIRST IMPRESSIONS
Larger and livelier than expected; scooters and motorbikes; a warren of back streets; arid, 'nude' mountains; almost luxuriant valleys; preponderance of men; trees, flowers and fishing boats; stray dogs and cats; gritty, saline taste to the water.

SPECIALITIES
Sponges, divers and honey.

RELIGIOUS HOLIDAYS & FESTIVALS
include: 10-20th April – Blessing the fishing boats – Kalimnos Town; 27th July – Festival Ag Panteleimon.

VITAL STATISTICS
Tel prefix 0243. The island is up to 21km long and 13km wide. Most of the 13,000 or so population live in or around the island capital.

HISTORY
Much as Kos.

GENERAL
Geographically a large island but, due to the mountainous nature and thus inaccessibility of much of the land, it actually masquerades as a small location.

Kalimnos Town particularly, and the island less so, comes as a surprise, if not a shock, for its development as a holiday location has been so rapid that even books up to a few years old chatter on about apparent poverty, the crippling effect of sponge diving, the unpreparedness of the island for tourism, the comparative peace and quiet and more....

The actuality is that any poverty has been hidden under a blanket of recent wealth attributable to the rise in Greek affluence, in general, and tourism, pertaining to Kalimnos, in particular. Forget peace and quiet as the capital town absolutely hums and the air is rent by the scream of seemingly thousands of high powered, explosively noisy motorbikes, which are absolutely everywhere. No side-street can be considered safe from their intrusion and that is at any time of day or night, although there is supposed to be a ban on the night-time auditory assault.

Personally I find the hills too bare to be beautiful, except during the spring explosion of flowers, but individual areas are outstandingly lovely. It is said that during the Italian occupation, the inhabitants painted their houses in the blue and white colours of the Greek flag, thus keeping alive their nationalistic aspiration and at the same time infuriating their unwanted overlords. Even today a few houses can still be seen with this colour scheme, as they can on the island of Karpathos.

Stelios must be the saint's name for the island, as is Spiros on Corfu island.

KALIMNOS (Pothia): capital town and port (Illustration 33)
Much larger and livelier than would be imagined from reading the average travel book. The quayside absolutely throbs at night but, despite the overlay of tourism, much of old Kalimnos still remains, as will become apparent.

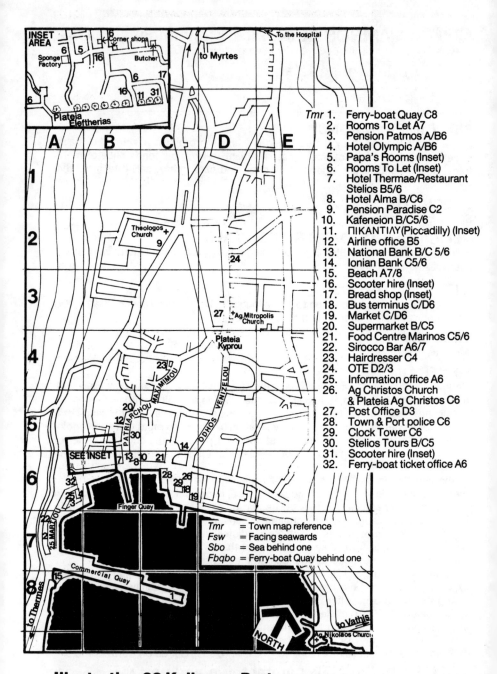

Tmr 1. Ferry-boat Quay C8
2. Rooms To Let A7
3. Pension Patmos A/B6
4. Hotel Olympic A/B6
5. Papa's Rooms (Inset)
6. Rooms To Let (Inset)
7. Hotel Thermae/Restaurant Stelios B5/6
8. Hotel Alma B/C6
9. Pension Paradise C2
10. Kafeneion B/C5/6
11. ΠΙΚΑΝΤΙΛΥ (Piccadilly) (Inset)
12. Airline office B5
13. National Bank B/C 5/6
14. Ionian Bank C5/6
15. Beach A7/8
16. Scooter hire (Inset)
17. Bread shop (Inset)
18. Bus terminus C/D6
19. Market C/D6
20. Supermarket B/C5
21. Food Centre Marinos C5/6
22. Sirocco Bar A6/7
23. Hairdresser C4
24. OTE D2/3
25. Information office A6
26. Ag Christos Church & Plateia Ag Christos C6
27. Post Office D3
28. Town & Port police C6
29. Clock Tower C6
30. Stelios Tours B/C5
31. Scooter hire (Inset)
32. Ferry-boat ticket office A6

Tmr = Town map reference
Fsw = Facing seawards
Sbo = Sea behind one
Fbqbo = Ferry-boat Quay behind one

Illustration 33 Kalimnos Port

ARRIVAL BY FERRY

Ferry-boats berth at the far end of the large quay (*Tmr* 1C8) and arrivals have to walk down the long pier before turning right towards the Town.

THE ACCOMMODATION & EATING OUT

The Accommodation The ferries are met by room owners, which is a good thing as the private accommodation is mainly grouped in a small, maze-like area behind Plateia Eleftherias. The Esplanade hotels tend to be hidden behind the profuse cover of the roadside trees and, as their signs are poorly illuminated, it is necessary to keep a sharp eye open for their whereabouts.

The first *Rooms* available from the bottom of the Ferry-boat Quay are almost immediately across 25th Martiou, behind the central row of small garden plots dividing the road, and to the right:-

Rooms (*Tmr* 2A7)
Directions: As above and situated three buildings south of the *Sirocco Bar* (*Tmr* 22A6/7).

The name of the establishment has been obliterated by weather and time, but the board is still attached to the modern verandah. The building is painted in an unattractive, matt brown wash.

There are also *Rooms* next door to the above accommodation, that is the fourth building south of the *Sirocco Bar*.

Hotel Olympic (*Tmr* 4A/B6) (Class C) Ag Nikolaos/Plateia Eleftherias
Tel 28801
Directions: Along the Esplanade road and on the corner, opposite the pleasure boat part of the quay.

If you can afford to stay here, all well and good, but the hotel is fairly full of 'off-the-beaten-track' package tourists. A double room, with an en suite bathroom costs from 3200drs a night. A useful service is that the manager will, for a small commission, disdainfully change traveller's cheques on a Sunday. In fact the management are generally disdainful.

Beyond the *Hotel Olympic*, the quay turns sharp right at Plateia Eleftherias. In the area behind the Esplanade is a tangle of side-streets rich in accommodation. These include:-

Papas (*Tmr* 5 Inset)
Directions: See the plan!

Rudimentary accommodation, in a pleasant area, costing about 1500drs for a double room with shared bathroom. Papa is a hawk-eyed fellow who appears silently at, or close to, your elbow (in the style of Jeeves of Wodehouse fame). Some years ago an Australian Greek girl friend was given a downstairs single room and had to sleep with her head (literally) in the oven. Fortunately it was an electric unit (the room had been a kitchen)! I seem to remember she also locked herself out one fun-filled night. There are small, narrow ground and first floor terraces, on which clients can take a cramped breakfast.

Other *Rooms* 'lurk' in the surrounding area (*Tmr* 6 Inset). These edge very noisy, busy streets, because, although they appear to be narrow back lanes, they are in actuality main routes off and on the Esplanade.

Hotel Thermae (*Tmr* 7B5/6) (Class C) Tel 29425
Directions: Above *Stelios Restaurant*, half-way along the Esplanade towards

the finger quay and statue. The upper floor, and therefore the sign, is hidden behind the lovely trees that edge the waterfront road.

Quite clean, double rooms, with an en suite bathroom, cost from 2200drs.

Hotel Alma (*Tmr* 8B/C6) (Class D) Patriarchou Maximou   Tel 28969
Directions: Further along the Esplanade, beyond the *Hotel Thermae* and alongside the National Bank. The entrance is a few yards down the side-street, not on the front.

Pleasant and a good choice. A double room, sharing a bathroom, is charged at 1200drs and with an en suite bathroom at 1500drs.

Pansion Ο Παραδεφσοσ **(Paradise)** (*Tmr* 9C2)
Directions: Alongside Theologos Church, this accommodation is in an old building of pleasing appearance.

Pension Patmos (*Tmr* 3A/B6)   Tel 29219
Directions: Situated behind the *Hotel Olympic*.

Very nice rooms but, as the owners are usually absent, it is necessary to telephone in order to raise anyone.

The Eating Out There are cafe-bars almost everywhere, the most noticeable of which is the very large, cavernous:-

Kafeneion (*Tmr* 10B/C5/6)
Directions: To one side of the *Hotel Alma*. This grand building must have been designed with another purpose in mind, possibly the Town Hall?

Between the Kafeneion and the *Hotel Alma* (*Tmr* 8B/C6) is the *Cafe* H ΑΙΓΑΗ where a coke and fresh orange juice costs 105drs.

We must each have our own favourite watering hole and mine is the:-
ΠΙΚΑΝΤΙΛΥ (Piccadilly) (*Tmr* 11 Inset)
Directions: Close by the town statue, bordering Plateia Eleftherias.

Situated in a large terrace edging the pavement and Esplanade, and a splendid location at which to while away part of the day over a coffee or two for 150drs. The management does not hustle so it is also a reasonably priced meeting place.

Generally, there is a wide, if uninspiring, choice of restaurants and tavernas including the establishments that prosper 'table by chair' on the stretch of Esplanade between the corner of Plateia Eleftherias and the *Hotel Alma*. In this location is:-

Stelios Restaurant (*Tmr* 7B5/6)
Directions: As above and situated in the ground floor of the *Hotel Thermae*.

They advertise their gastronomic choice in three languages and serve a variety of dishes at prices to suit most pockets. This international service is prompt, if a little casual. A meal for two of a plate of mincemeat and rice, 1 kalimares, a Greek salad, bread, a lager, a Coke and bottled water costs 1000drs.

Other offerings line the eastern end of the Esplanade, beyond the Market (*Tmr* 19C/D6), which include *Diomidis Taverna*, the *Greek Tavern* and *Black Beards*. Typical of the establishments hereabouts is that obtainable at the split-cane covered patio of the Esplanade taverna. This is located close by the telephone box and an ultra-violet light insect killing machine suspended over the pavement. The old man, round and perspiring, seems an excellent chef with an interesting menu. This includes, for instance, dolmades in a lemon sauce and tzatziki in a batter, as well as a wide variety of fish dishes. Unfortunately the choice belies the service and standards. The young waiter is extremely casual, the orders often being served incorrectly, in addition to which he tends to add tax to a tax-priced-meal. This is difficult to check because, quite often, individual items are not priced on the menu.

THE A TO Z OF USEFUL INFORMATION

AIRLINE OFFICE (*Tmr* 12B5) Yes, despite there being no Airport.

BANKS Several including the:-
National Bank (*Tmr* 13B/C5/6) situated on the Esplanade and the **Ionian Bank** (*Tmr* 14C5/6), Odhos Venizelou.
See Hotel Olympic (*Tmr* 4A/B6), **The Accommodation** for weekend/emergency cashing of traveller's cheques.

BEACHES It may now be necessary to travel as the latest reports rumour that the small, triangulated Town Beach (*Tmr* 15A7/8), once tucked away in the angle formed by the Ferry-boat Quay and the road to Thermes, has been engulfed by new dock works. A one and a half kilometre walk south from the Harbour, along the Thermes road, leads to the (dead?) *Hotel Thermae*, alongside which is a small pebbly beach.

BICYCLE, SCOOTER & CAR HIRE There are a number of scooter hire establishments scattered around the side-streets, in the area behind Plateia Eleftherias (*Tmr* 16 Insert), as well as on the Esplanade road between the finger quay and the Clock Tower (*Tmr* 29C6). These Esplanade proprietors, typified by the chap next door to The Marinos Food Centre (*Tmr* 21C5/6 – yes a food centre, of which more later), tend to be a little sharp and have a habit of quoting one rate and attempting to charge another. The average day rate is 1000drs but for two days this can be squeezed down. Another sleight-of-hand is for the firm's newest units to be put on show but the hirer to be given an older, clapped out version.

Scooter Hire (*Tmr* 31 Inset)
Directions: On the Esplanade.
   This gentleman must hire the least expensive Vespa's anywhere in the Greek islands, with a daily rate of 800drs a day.
   On Kalimnos it is not unusual to see families of up to five astride a Vespa. One gentleman hunter, seen on a similar bike, had not only four dogs paired in overhanging pillion saddle boxes, a lady on the pillion but, additionally, a dog draped across his lap and another lying in the footwell. On the last trip a chap was seen steering his Vespa with one hand whilst pulling a shopping trolley with the other!

BREAD SHOPS One, ΑΡΤΟΠΙΕΙΟΝ, in the side-street alongside and prior to the Ionian Bank (*Tmr* 14C5/6) and another (*Tmr* 17) in the maze of streets detailed in the 'Inset'.

BUSES The bus service has been extended in the last few years and the 'terminus' (*Tmr* 18C/D6) moved to a white painted outline on the road between the Ag Christos Church (*Tmr* 26C6) and the Market (*Tmr* 19C/D6). The timetable is pinned to the nearby wall.

Bus timetable (Mid-season)
Kalimnos Town to Massouri
Daily   0700, 0830, 1000, 1100, 1300, 1430, 1600, 1730, 1930, 2100hrs
Return journey
Daily   0730, 0900, 1030, 1200, 1330, 1500, 1630, 1800, 1930, 2200hrs

Kalimnos Town to Emborio*
Monday, Wednesday   0820, 1600hrs
  & Friday

*The road into Emborio, not being completed (1987), the bus presently stops at Arginontas. The bus driver is of the opinion that it will not be completed for another couple of years (Jonah!).

Kalimnos Town to Vathis
Daily   0800, 1300hrs
Return journey
Daily   1300hrs

CINEMAS Yes.

COMMERCIAL SHOPPING AREA (*Tmr* 19C/D6) Labelled the 'City Hall' on the official map (well actually *Hity Hall*), but the building is almost entirely taken up by the Market. The stalls inside sell fruit, vegetables and meat. Outside, on the first section of the Esplanade, in an easterly direction, both sides of the street are lined with trucks and stalls selling fish and flowers in addition to other offerings. Fruit is very plentiful.

At the other end of town (and the spectrum), towards Plateia Eleftherias, there is a frail old man, with his bicycle wheeled trolley, selling sunflower seeds. This reminds me that it is a practice, on this island, for men and boys to wander round the bars, tavernas and restaurants selling bags of (overpriced) peanuts.

The streets are liberally lined with shops, especially in the area bounded by Plateia Ag Christos and The Ionian Bank on Odhos Venizelou. There are two Supermarkets in the same street as the Olympic office, one at No. 2, **The Right Price** and another (*Tmr* 20B/C5) beyond the airline office. On the Esplanade is a most unusual store, the **Marinos Food Centre** (*Tmr* 21C5/6), a deep, narrow fronted shop with apparently everything on offer, including honey and yoghurt.

DISCOS The **Disco UFO Flying Saucer** is located above the cafe next door to 'The Right Price Supermarket', at No 2, Odhos Patriarchou Maximou and referred to above.

FERRY-BOATS They dock at the top of the large, rather messy, commercial quay (*Tmr* 1C8). This is also used by local, incredibly antiquated cargo boats which unload building materials and sand with obsolete deck-operated cranes.

Ferry-boat timetable (Mid-season)

Day	Departure time	Ferry-boat	Ports/Islands of Call
Monday	2300hrs	Panormitis	Leros,Lipsos,Patmos,Arki, Angathonisi,Pythagorion(Samos).
Tuesday	0130hrs	Ialysos/Kamiros	Kos,Rhodes.
	0600hrs	Kyklades	Kos,Rhodes.
	1130hrs	Nireas	Kos,Nisiros,Tilos,Simi,Rhodes, Karpathos,Kasos,Sitia(Crete), Ag Nikolaos(Crete).
	1700hrs	Ialysos/Kamiros	Leros,Patmos,Piraeus(M).

	2000hrs	Panormitis	Kos,Nisiros,Tilos,Simi,Rhodes.
Wednesday	0130hrs	Ialysos/Kamiros	Kos,Rhodes.
	1700hrs	Ialysos/Kamiros	Leros,Patmos,Piraeus(M).
Thursday	0130hrs	Ialysos/Kamiros	Kos,Rhodes.
	1500hrs	Nireas	Astipalaia,Amorgos,Paros, Piraeus(M).
	2000hrs	Panormitis	Kos,Nisiros,Tilos,Simi,Rhodes.
	2030hrs	Kyklades	Kos,Nisiros,Tilos,Simi,Rhodes. Karpathos,Kasos.
Friday	0130hrs	Ialysos/Kamiros	Kos,Rhodes.
	1700hrs	Ialysos/Kamiros	Leros,Patmos,Piraeus(M).
Saturday	0130hrs	Ialysos/Kamiros	Kos,Rhodes.
	1700hrs	Ialysos/Kamiros	Leros,Patmos,Piraeus(M).
Sunday	1700hrs	Ialysos/Kamiros	Leros,Patmos,Piraeus(M).

See **Travel Agents & Tour Offices, A To Z.**

FERRY-BOAT TICKET OFFICES The most reliable information is dispensed by the NTOG office (*Tmr* 25A6). There is a ticket office, one along from the *Sirocco Bar* (*Tmr* 22A6/7). This office is supposedly open in the mornings as well as the evenings from 1800hrs for an hour or so. But the elderly proprietor's night-time attendance is often restricted to opening the office, leaving the door open, wandering off up the street and then abruptly closing down, and all this prior to 1800hrs! There is another ferry-boat ticket office (*Tmr* 32A6), bordering Plateia Eleftherias.

HAIRDRESSERS One (*Tmr* 23C4) on the street that snakes between Kyprou Square and the Esplanade, where it emerges alongside the National Bank (*Tmr* 13B/C5/6).

LUGGAGE STORE See **NTOG, A To Z**.

MEDICAL CARE
Chemists & Pharmacies Plenty with three or four grouped together on Odhos Venizelou, in the area of the Ionian Bank (*Tmr* 14C5/6).
Dentist One in the same building as Marinos Food Centre (*Tmr* 21 C5/6)
Doctors There is a doctor close to Plateia Kyprou (*Tmr* D3/4).
Hospital A large facility on the Elies/Myrtes road, just off the Town plan (*See* **Route One**).

NTOG (*Tmr* 25A6) Not so much a Greek Tourist Board office, more a Town Information office. This is located in a tiny, chapel-like building, at the end of a neat path set in a very small park, alongside the *Hotel Olympic*. On the edge of this particular garden there is a statue of a 'seated fellow' holding a trident.
    The girl speaks good English and is very keen to help. She has all the schedules and timetables, as well as the more usual hand-outs. The office opens daily between 0830-1300hrs and 1500-2000hrs. There is free luggage storage here.

OTE (*Tmr* 24D2/3) North from Plateia Kyprou, beyond Ag Mitropolis Church. Open Monday to Friday between 0730-2200hrs.

PETROL There are stations here and there including one to the east of the Market (*Tmr* 19C/D6), one alongside Plateia Kyprou (*Tmr* D3/4) and another on the road to Myrtes, on the outskirts of Kalimnos Town. The island is not that large that it becomes a problem from one tank fill to the next.

PLACES OF INTEREST
Ag Christos Church (*Tmr* 26C6) Sited on the imposing Main Square which is edged by a long municipal building, occupied by the Police and Customs offices, and a Clock Tower. Whilst mentioning the latter it is interesting to note that most, if not nearly all, Kalimnos timepieces are working and remarkably accurate – as distinct from those of say Karpathos and Kasos.

This large Church is not only strikingly beautiful but has attracted the interest of native and expatriate Greeks, mainly originating from Kalimnos, who have given of their time to redecorate and refurbish the internal decorations and icons.

POLICE
Port Located in the same building as the:-
Town (*Tmr* 28C6) Not to be bothered with tourist activity and enquiries.

POST OFFICE (*Tmr* 27D3) Ignore the Town Map as the office is positioned opposite Ag Mitropolis Church. Opening hours are weekdays between 0730-1600hrs.

SPONGE DIVERS The tourists are treated to a charade in which a diver dons some fairly tatty looking diving gear whilst standing on a stage, or more correctly the stern of a boat. This performance is similar to that enacted by airline stewards showing disinterested passengers the 'life-jacket routine'. In days of yore, in fact well into the 20th century, the divers achieved the depths necessary to harvest the crop, by tucking flat stones beneath their arms. Although most island men became divers, the profession was hazardous and often resulted in premature ageing and crippling injuries.

The sponges, before treatment, are living multi-cellular aquatic animals feeding by filtering sea-water through their many pores. Originally they could be picked up in the shallows but over hundreds of years the sponge divers were driven deeper and deeper as well as further and further afield. Eventually it became commonplace for the fleet to depart for the North African coast, towards the end of April, not to return until late in the summer. Naturally enough this routine led to feast days marking the departure and return of the fleet, a tradition which remains rooted in the festival celebrations still held today and absorbed into the yearly pattern of life. It may well be that the trade resulted in the disproportionate number of males, young and old, that are apparent in Kalimnos Town. There is a sponge treatment factory (*See* the town map Inset), behind Plateia Eleftherias.

TAXIS Taxis double up as small minibuses and stop off and pick up passengers as required. There is a rank on the corner of the quay, almost opposite the *Hotel Olympic* (*Tmr* 4A/B6), and another, the main one, on Plateia Kyprou (*Tmr* D3/4). This latter has a taxi rank office and published fare schedule (for taxi-buses) as follows:-
per person: Elies 50drs; Kantouni 60drs; Myrtes 70drs and Massouri 80drs.

TELEPHONE NUMBERS & ADDRESSES
Hospital	Tel 28851
Taxi rank	Tel 28989
Tourist office	Tel 29310

TRAVEL AGENTS & TOUR OFFICES There are some gathered together in the *Olympic Hotel* area of Plateia Eleftherias as well as **Stelios Tours** (*Tmr* 30B/C5) in Odhos Patriarchou Maximou.

TRIP BOAT EXCURSIONS There are caique trips to every upturned stone around the Kalimnos coastline, as well as excursion boats to Kos, Patmos and

Turkey. Kalimnos is on the Kos Town and Mastichari(Kos) trip boat schedules. Quite honestly it is best to hop off somewhere, that is anywhere other than Kalimnos Town, before 1000hrs when the first of the Kos boats hoves into sight.

ROUTE ONE
To Emborio (20½km) via Elies, Myrtes & Massouri The
one-way systems to the north-west, that thread their way in and out of Kalimnos Town, finally join together beyond the Hospital. To the left, on a small hill set against the background of a much taller mountain, is the ruined Castle Chrissocherias (or Castle of the Knights) and three windmills. Within the castle walls are two very small churches. The location of the fort is typical of the medieval practice of making a secure place, a little inland from the coast, as a refuge from pillaging pirates.

Further on leads to:-

CHORIO (2.8km from Kalimnos Town) This once capital town is overlooked, to the right, by the dank, glowering ruins of another castle and fortifications amongst which are set a number of tiny churches. Two of these are painted white all over and still kept in good order. The backcloth is Mt Profitis Ilias.

This route is very lovely and tree lined with fir trees almost all the way to:-

ELIES (5.4km from Kalimnos Town) From here, to the crest overlooking the sea, the pines give way to stately gum trees.

The *Marinos Taverna*, opposite a kafeneion, is worthy of a visit as the proprietor serves stuffed lamb, the traditional Easter 'goody', on Wednesdays, Fridays, Saturdays and Sundays throughout the year. This is one of the only restaurants, here or anywhere else to my knowledge, that does so outside the Easter period.:-

To the left, two turnings, one in Elies, the other more clearly identifiable half-way to Myrtes, drop slowly down to:-

KANTOUNI (6.5km from Kalimnos Town) This village is almost entirely a Greek holiday resort. An unexpectedly long, sandy beach with only one or two restaurants, cafe-bars and the *Hotel Drossos*, set back. The road runs out on the southern extremity of the foreshore.

Unless I forget, surely the *Casa Irene Restaurant* and mini-golf deserve a mention! More seriously a double room with an en suite bathroom and balcony, within 5 minutes of the beach, costs about 1300drs a night. The *Dionysus Taverna* is 'mentioned in dispatches' and the *Sun and Sand Taverna*, just off the beach, is highly recommended. The latter serves excellent soup and fish dishes at acceptable prices.

Apart from the road round, the impressive beach heads off northwards, past two chapels, to a concrete path that skirts the land side of an enormous rock set down firmly on the surrounding terrain. On the way up, over and around this rock, the path passes *The Cantina-The Pub By The Rock*, with a 'Happy Hour' between 8-9pm (well if you must you will) and a chapel butted on to the side of a house prior to spilling on to the small Plateia Linaria set above the sea. The sandy beach below is much smaller but rather overrun with seaweed at the south rock end. The Square is more an irregular rhomboid, on the right of which are some very pleasant **Rooms** in a comparatively large house, followed by a store and, across a small, steep lane, a block of apartments. The path curves away from the Square down to beach level and a terrace, whereon a small cafe-bar at the end of the bay. Meals here are rather expensive with a souvlakia costing 470drs but squid only 250drs.

A dirt path wanders on round past a tiny, rectangular, benzina harbour to a small, boulderous bay.

From Elies village the road drops steeply to:-
MYRTES (7.5km from Kalimnos Town) This seaside village marks an outbreak of pure, package holiday tourism. The pretty, tree lined avenue is spanned by various establishments including the *Hotel Themis* (B class), the *Pension Le Petiti Parias*, *Pub Kalidna*, *Hotels Myrtios* (D class), *Atlantis*, *Delfini* (C class), as well as many more and **Rooms** to rent. Naturally there is scooter and vehicle hire.

A narrow side road to the left descends to a small fishing boat quay. On the immediate right (*Fsw*), edging the grey, pebbly but clean, steeply shelving beach is the *Restaurant Myrthies*. The proprietor, whose establishment is extensively used by the guests of the local hotels, speaks good English and will answer a few questions in respect of this and that. On the left is an eye catching shop selling sponges. The sign reads as follows:-

Sponge's House
if you are inderested for correct
manufacturing for natural sponges
visit with out obligation our factory
You going to be surprise...!
Yes, well.

There is a public toilet.

Apart from various excursion boat trips, which schedules include a twice daily connection to Xerokampos, Leros, there are caiques which make the short crossing of fifteen minutes or so to:-

TELENTOS (Telendos) island More truly a sunken mountain than an island, it was probably connected to the main island until an earthquake rent the two apart. There is almost certainly the remains of a submerged village in the channel. On the shore of Telentos, facing Kalimnos, is a small settlement with a population of about 100. A couple of beaches, tavernas, accommodation at two pensions, Roman remains and a medieval castle make this an almost ideal get-away location.

The mountain is supposed to resemble a royal lady, forever looking out to sea for her long departed, regal lover. I can never achieve the state of mind required to conjure up this fanciful suggestion. Perhaps another bottle of retsina would help?

The caique that sails between Telentos island and Myrtes, every twenty minutes, acts as a (water) taxi and locals use the service extensively. The one-way fare costs 50drs.

The road from Myrtes passes a house with **Rooms**, *Niki's Guest House* and the *Why Not Pub* – Why not indeed!

MASSOURI (8.5km from Kalimnos Town) A more 'developed', if neater location than Myrtes with two 'pubs', a number of villas, hotels, tavernas, moped hire and the Narcissus Disco.

On a visit some four years ago it was rumoured, only rumoured you understand, that a bevy of Danish beauties ran riot and, in a bacchanalian orgy, even shocked the local lads. Well it's a change from the stories involving British 'bovver' boys.

The beach, grey sand with a pebbly sea edge, can only be 'got at' down a steep flight of steps and is equipped with a beach bar, squatty toilet, wind surfers and sun-beds.

From Massouri, the oleander edged road skirts the coast, the surrounding countryside getting wilder and more dramatic, until the route runs down and alongside the fjord-like bay of:-

ARGINONTAS (12km from Kalimnos Town) This is more a two or three 'donkey droppings' hamlet than a village, spread in and around the olive grove edging the small, gently curving, pebbly, tree lined beach at the end of the bay. There are three tavernas, one at each end of the beach and one set back.

Between Arginontas and Skalia are a number of cave-like depressions at the bottom of the hillside, hosting small, shady, sandy beaches which are a favourite with the locals for swimming.

The road, which is under reconstruction, winds on through hillsides, dotted with beehives, to:-

SKALIA (17km from Kalimnos Town)
and on to:-

EMBORIO (20½km from Kalimnos Town) The village is clean, ethnic, old Greek, spaciously laid out with a central, small T-shaped quay. This is set in a fairly long, shallow, clean, sweeping pebble beach with a little sand and prettily shaded by mature trees. There are chickens and turkeys wandering about on the foreshore and a taverna close to the quay, where the road runs on to the beach. Here a frail old lady, with a shawl wrapped round here head, becomes confused if her son is away and may burst into tears if an order gets too large. Two limon cordials cost 100drs.

There are **Rooms** in the village but, as they are not signed, it is necessary to ask at one of the village's three tavernas. The beach taverna owner plans to construct two rooms alongside his building, which should be 'up and running' in time for the 1988 season.

A lovely location and well worth the journey. Do not be tempted to try to connect with Stimenia village, thus saving retracing one's footsteps, unless walking as the indicated track is no more than a footpath.

ROUTE TWO
To Vathis (8km) The initial stage of this route is remarkable only for its
unattractiveness, passing as it does the island's generating station (in the shadow of which is a full-blown boat repair yard, complete with a number of slipways), two small refineries and the town's rubbish dump. Beyond these, the road clings half-way up (or down, depending on your viewpoint) the side of arid and barren hills, the coast side of which slides boulderously into the sea far below. A couple of small, indented, sandy bays are visible and the Gulf of Aktis makes a very pleasant vista, even if the sea does seem impenetrably black. The island of Saronnisi is in the foreground, with Pserimos island in the middle-distance set against the backdrop of the Turkish mainland.

The road winds down to the plain whereon massed groves of oranges are enclosed in whitewashed, walled enclosures through which the road slowly meanders to:-

VATHIS (8km from Kalimnos Town) A small port stripped of all the non essentials. There are a number of kafeneions, two tavernas and the new *Hotel Galini*. The sea surges into the fjord-like inlet which terminates at the narrow, squared-off harbour. A small caique repair yard flanks the left-hand side (*Fsw*) of the little settlement and, on the right, a track edges the sea for eighty metres or so, with a few small boats moored end on to the bank. This path terminates alongside some large steps and an abandoned building, grandly built for a now long forgotten purpose.

The lanes of the attractive valley behind Vathis, being very narrow, are sorted out into a one-way system. In view of the arrival of the internal combustion engine, which has almost entirely superseded 'donkey power', this is an eminently sensible solution. The locals cannot always resist the temptation to take a short cut the wrong way down one or other of these lanes, which can prove exciting!

I have been advised that a Greek expatriate bought the first orange tree plants back from Palestine, but no one has been able to explain why the walls of the groves are almost substantial enough to be fortifications.

Half-way to Dassos village is a small hamlet complete with a kafeneion and a petrol station.

Mandraki waterfront. Nisiros.

LEROS (ΛΕΡΟΣ)
Dodecanese Islands

****

FIRST IMPRESSIONS
Faded, 1930s Italianesque buildings; palm trees; fencing and barbed wire; green beehives; little agriculture; flocks of goats, sheep and cows; comparatively flat; dust.

SPECIALITIES
None, unless one takes account of the three mental hospitals, for which the island is famed throughout Greece. Leros is also known as a place of exile.

RELIGIOUS HOLIDAYS & FESTIVALS
include: Sunday before the Shrove Monday – Carnival; 26th September – Second World War commemoration, Lakki.

It is widely regarded that, at carnival times, the islanders behave and dress in a manner dating back to ancient, pagan festivities.

VITAL STATISTICS
Tel prefix 0247. The population of some 8,500 live on an island so savagely indented by the sea that it resembles an ink blot. Leros is about 15km long and between 11½km and 1¼km wide.

HISTORY
A Homeric island, much of its history is shared with the rest of the Dodecanese, apart from one or two notable exceptions. For instance it is one of two or three islands in the group where inheritances pass through the female line.

During the Second World War the island was the scene of a very bloody campaign in which some 5,000 British troops were cut down during German parachute assults. The Italians, overmasters since 1912, had capitulated and the Allies filled the vacuum but, unfortunately, failed to take Rhodes, from whence the Germans launched their devastating attack on November 12th 1943. To help reinforce our troops, at the height of the most ferocious fighting, British Headquarters sent some 'chaps' from Samos who arrived too late and were themselves wiped out. The moving testament to this little known campaign is a beautifully kept, very moving war cemetery, close to Alinda village, containing the graves of one hundred and seventy nine British, two Canadian and two South African servicemen.

In almost comic contrast, annually, on the 26th September, the Greeks honour thirty of their Greek sailors, who also died during the Second World War. The day-long ceremony includes the attendance of as many naval ships as can be mustered, a military band, almost the whole of the senior servicemen and church leaders in the region, TV cameras, radio crews and the entire island population, plus many visitors. The centre of the jamboree is a commemorative stone mounted on a stone patio along the broad park-like Esplanade of Lakki Port. It appears that, during the war, the only operational Greek warship left in action slipped into the bay, under the impression that fraternal forces were in occupation. This was a major misjudgement as the crew found themselves staring down the gun barrels of distinctly unfriendly and efficient German shore based weapons. Whoops! A tourist may well be regaled with convoluted variations on this theme or, usually,

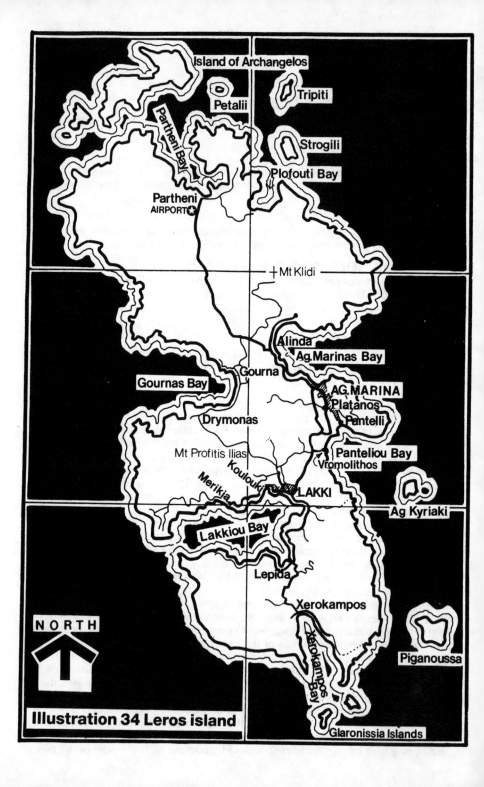

Illustration 34 Leros island

more high-flown and romantic tales, but the above appears to be the gist of the matter. Certainly travellers should arrive several days before the event as there is little or no room at the inn during the festival.

Not to lose the sense of military occasion, the Colonels' junta of 1967-1974 erected a bleak internment camp at Partheni, still in evidence and now used by the military, but for more conventional purposes.

GENERAL
I first glimpsed Leros, many years ago, from the deck of an inter-island ferry, and was then rather mystified and curious about the strange, huge bay and port of Lakki. This impression does not dim over the years, even after closer familiarity but don't be repelled – disembark and head for the other settlements.

The island and the islanders have not yet been overwhelmed by package tourism. Leros is more a holiday resort of the *cognoscenti* than the mob, but development is taking place at the seaside villages of Alinda and Xerokampos.

LAKKI: main port (Illustration 35) At first it comes as a surprise that
Lakki is not the capital. This is not so extraordinary when it is realised that the Italians were almost wholly responsible for the port's development, in conjunction with the massive port facilities across the bay. The islanders simply do not like the place, which is not surprising taking into account the architecture and layout. They are as dissimilar to traditional Greek town development as any mix of '1930s Italian Municipal' and a 'Spaghetti-Western' Hollywood film set could possibly be.

Lakki is a horribly magnificent, if faded and crumbling concrete monument to the Mussolini inspired, Italian dream of a Mediterranean Empire – a latter day Roman Kingdom with grandiose buildings for the then necessary functionaries.

Despite the 1930s look, this is no drink-crazed, prohibition, speak-easy town; in fact it is difficult to find a lively taverna, let alone any semblance of night-life. Anne, who carried out follow-up research, is of the opinion that I should 'come clean' and inform readers not to be put off Leros by Lakki, but to head for Pantelli, or elsewhere – anywhere else but this most odd location.

ARRIVAL BY AIR
It is only in recent years that the oft-threatened completion of this rather bleak strip, close by the northern village of Partheni, has resulted in an adequate service.

ARRIVAL BY FERRY
The truly enormous Ferry-boat Quay (*Tmr* 1A2) is sited at the furthermost section of an equally wide access road,towards the far, or west, end of Lakki.

Arrivals will probably be offered accommodation on disembarking, whatever time of night the ferry arrives (and it is usually late or in the middle of the night). If not, it will be necessary to trudge along the expansive Esplanade, past small parks and open spaces to the centre of the development. A last resort is the narrow, long, tin and glass prefabricated waiting room plonked down at the top end of the quay, a structure which resembles a wartime bus shelter. In 1987 the quay was undergoing extensive repairs and or construction work.

THE ACCOMMODATION & EATING OUT
The Accommodation The generally accepted code of behaviour is that travellers, arriving very late, should wander up to the hotel or pension of their choice, grab a key, and sort the matter out with the proprietor on the morrow.

Considering Lakki's position it is surprising that there are so few hotels, pensions or **Rooms**. On the other hand, taking into account the lack of enthusiasm for and about the place, perhaps it is to be expected.

Hotel Leros Palace (*Tmr* 2B2) (Class C)   Tel 22940
Directions: On the Esplanade, in a major block.

These C class amenities represent very good value with a double room, sharing a bathroom, costing from 1300drs, and with an en suite bathroom, from 1500drs.

Hotel Miramare (*Tmr* 3B1/2) (Class D)   Tel 22053
Directions: Two blocks back from the *Leros Palace* and two blocks towards the Ferry-boat Quay. Visible from the waterfront across some undeveloped land.

Outwardly smarter looking than the *Leros Palace*, but similarly furnished. All rooms have en suite bathrooms. Single rooms start off at 900drs, rising to 1100drs (1st April-30th June) and 1300drs (1st July-30th Sept). Double rooms cost respectively 1450drs, 1650 and 1900drs.

Hotel Katerina (*Tmr* 4B/C1/2) (Class E) 7th MARTIOU (Maptoiy) Tel 22460
Directions: Two blocks back from the Esplanade and within sight of the Platanos main road 'out of town'.

Very clean rooms with small en suite bathrooms. A single costs about 1000drs and a double room 1500drs. Some of the bathrooms are tiny and the water, which is hot 24 hours a day, tends to dribble from the shower head.

Hotel Artemis (*Tmr* 5B1) (Class C)   Tel 22416
Directions: Alongside Letec Travel, some five blocks back from the Esplanade (along the street that runs down from the 'dead' Cinema).

All rooms have en suite bathrooms with a single room charged at 1400drs and a double room 2000drs. These rates rise, respectively, to 1500 and 2100drs. Management tend to request at least 200drs over the official prices, goodness knows why as the place is not overly attractive.

The *Hotel Panteli* (*Tmr* 6C2), once close by the junction of the Esplanade and the Platanos main road, has now closed but the ground floor cafe-bar, a convenient rendezvous, is still there and has the only metered telephone in the Port. Mark you, telephone connections from Lakki, even to Athens, are difficult and international calls are a near impossibility.

Should accommodation be desperately short, and finances permit, there is the:-

Hotel Xenon Argelou (*Tmr* 7C1) (Class B)   Tel 22514
Directions: To the right of the main Platanos road and along a turning off, immediately prior to the Town football ground. Approached down a gravel path through an arched gateway.

In fact classified as a Pension with a double room, sharing a bathroom, costing 2250drs and with an en suite bathroom 2800drs.

The Eating Out Printed menus are, all over the island, generally noticeable by their absence. If Lakki lacks breadth of accommodation, then eating places are almost non-existent. One of the more prominent is the:-

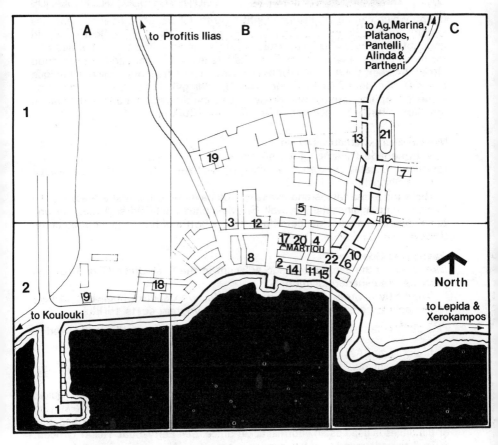

Illustration 35 Lakki Port

Tmr	= Town map reference
Fsw	= Facing seawards
Sbo	= Sea behind one
Fbqbo	= Ferry-boat Quay behind one

Tmr
1. Ferry-boat Quay A2
2. Hotel Leros Palace B2
3. Hotel Mira Mare B1/2
4. Hotel Katerina B/C1/2
5. Hotel Artemis B1
6. Cafe-bar C2
7. Hotel Xenon Argelou C1
8. Restaurant Pizzeria B2
9. Cafe-bar A2
10. National Bank C2
11. Rent-A-Car Leros B2
12. Scooter hire B1/2
13. Bread shop C1
14. ('Dead') Cinema B2
15. Kastis Travel & Shipping B/C2
16. Petrol station C1/2
17. Post Office B2
18. Port police A/B2
19. Hospital B1
20. Public toilets B2
21. Football ground C1
22. Foreign newspapers B/C2

Restaurant Pizzeria (*Tmr* 8B2)
Directions: At the far west or left-hand end (*Sbo*) of a semi-derelict Italianesque block edging the Esplanade.

A barn-like, 'greasy spoon' with rotting, steel framed windows and a television set usually blaring away. The proprietor, a large, thick-set but jolly man with a greasy apron, serves passable food and stays open until the early hours, which can be vital to late night ferry travellers. Mine host presents his kitchen with a flourish, although I am not sure why. Mrs Beaton would undoubtedly have suffered an attack of the vapours at the state of affairs but, for those who still wish to eat here, the fare is not too bad, and not too good either. A Greek salad, a plate of beans (large, white haricots, which are unique to the Dodecanese islands), a moussaka (puddingy), 1 'pot' beef and rice with a cheese topping (stodgy and greasy, but served piping hot and could suffice for two), 1 bottle of retsina and bread costs 1000drs.

More pleasant alternatives include:-
The 'Esplanade Taverna' (It has no name)
Directions: Located between the office of Rent-A-Car (*Tmr*) 11B2) and Kastis Travel & Shipping (*Tmr* 15B/C2).

There are a few tables and chairs on the pavement, the rest are across the Esplanade up against the sea wall. Souvlaki pitas cost 70drs. A meal for one of red beans in a spicy sauce, feta, bread, a bottle of beer and a coffee costs 390drs.

Taverna O Sostos
Directions: In the same block and adjacent to the Post Office (*Tmr* 17B2). A pleasant, tree shaded location.

Owned by a Greek and his Swedish wife, who speaks English, and very reasonably priced. Two Nes meh ghala and a yoghurt costs 150drs.

One other establishment of importance to the ferry-boat traveller is the seedy:-

Cafe-bar (*Tmr* 9A2)
Directions: Situated almost opposite the bottom of the wide track to the Ferry-boat Quay.

The piratical proprietor is a jolly (nosey) extrovert with a propensity for the quick, toothless chat up in his three words of pidgin English. Apart from the cafe staying open all hours, well at least until the relevant ferry-boat or boats have berthed, one of the tables is used as an informal ticket office. *See* **Ferry-Boat Ticket Offices, A To Z** to understand why this service is essential. Why wait? It is simply that it is very difficult to find a ticket office open, anytime anywhere in Lakki.

THE A TO Z OF USEFUL INFORMATION
AIRLINE OFFICE & TERMINUS As yet there is no central Olympic office. *See* **Central Travel Agent & Spiros Tours & Olympic, Platanos**.

Aircraft timetable (Mid-season)
Leros to Athens (& vice versa).

Monday, Tuesday & Saturday	0800hrs
Wednesday & Friday	1535hrs
Return	
Monday, Tuesday & Saturday	0635hrs
Wednesday & Friday	1250hrs

One-way fare: 8620drs; duration 1hr 5mins.

Leros to Kos ·

Wednesday & Friday	1415hrs
Return	
Wednesday & Friday	1500hrs

One-way fare: 2140drs; duration time 15mins.

BANKS The National Bank of Greece (*Tmr* 10C2) is on the right (*Sbo*) of the Platanos main road, close to the junction with the Esplanade.

BEACHES None in the Port. It is necessary to walk westward past the Ferry-boat Quay and up and around the bluff above Lakki. This pleasantly wooded track proceeds, after 1km, to a tiny, tree lined lido at Koulouki. There is a snackbar and a very small, narrow strip of sandy beach. A further 1½km along the same stony track leads to Merikia, a rather strange but pleasant area by the sea's edge, set amongst a grove of trees in which are a number of large, ruined buildings. The beach is narrow and covered in kelp.

BICYCLE, SCOOTER & CAR HIRE The most easily located is the:-

Rent-A-Car Leros (*Tmr* 11B2) On the Esplanade, close to the junction with the Platanos road. Bikes and scooters are available in quantity, if not quality. Papa, despite having only one hand, still manages to start and ride his scooters, whilst his daughter, who has a smattering of English, and her brother help out. The general condition of the conveyances tends to leave something to be desired. Bicycles cost 150drs a day and scooters from 900drs, but this does include a full tank of fuel. This seems strange as there are a number of petrol stations conveniently dotted about, added to which I am sure the fuel Papa uses is dirty, so causing quite a few mechanical problems! Despite these reasonable charges, cars cost the usual high rates. Papa has a habit of pronouncing 'Special' when proffering a scooter, any scooter.

There is another hire outfit (*Tmr* 12B1/2) in the block prior to the *Hotel Miramare*.

BOOKSELLERS (*Tmr* 22 B/C2) More a foreign language newspaper shop.

BREAD SHOPS In short supply, but there is one (*Tmr* 13C1) opposite the football ground, a few metres or more up the Platanos road.

BUSES The service is one that hides its light under a gum tree! There is a rumour, only a rumour, that the island buses stop for a 'rest' outside the jewellers, immediately beyond the National Bank (*Tmr* 10C2) on the Platanos road. A further rumour credits the service with the fact that a bus traverses the island once an hour on the hour but... The taxis, as on Kalimnos, act as community minibuses.

Bus timetable
Lakki Port to Xerokampos
Daily	0800, 1200, 1600hrs.
Return journey	
Daily	0830, 1230, 1630hrs.
One-way fare: 75drs.	

Lakki Port to Partheni via Vromolithos, Platanos, Ag Marina, Alinda, Partheni.
Daily	0900, 1300, 1700hrs.
Return journey	
Daily	1100, 1500, 1900hrs.

CINEMAS A magnificent art deco building (*Tmr* 14B2), alongside the *Hotel Leros Palace*, but it might or might not be closed!

COMMERCIAL SHOPPING AREA None. In fact the range of shops is strictly limited. There are no peripteros on the island and cigarettes are usually sold from small kiosks.

FERRY-BOATS The ships dock at the large quay at the west end of the town (*Tmr* 1A2).

Ferry-boat timetables (Mid-season)

Day	Departure time	Ferry-boat	Ports/Islands of Call
Tuesday	0100hrs	Panormitis	Lipsos,Patmos,Arki,Angathonisi, Pythagorion(Samos).
	1800hrs	Panormitis	Kalimnos,Kos,Nisiros,Tilos,Simi,Rhodes.
	1830hrs	Ialysos/Kamiros	Patmos,Piraeus(M).
	2345hrs	Ialysos/Kamiros	Kalimnos,Kos,Rhodes.
Wednesday	1830hrs	Ialysos/Kamiros	Patmos, Piraeus(M).
	2345hrs	Ialysos/Kamiros	Kalimnos,Kos,Rhodes.
Thursday	2345hrs	Ialysos/Kamiros	Kalimnos,Kos,Rhodes.
Friday	1830hrs	Ialysos/Kamiros	Patmos,Piraeus(M).
	2345hrs	Ialysos/Kamiros	Kalimnos,Kos,Rhodes.
Saturday	1830hrs	Ialysos/Kamiros	Patmos,Piraeus(M).
	2345hrs	Ialysos/Kamiros	Kalimnos,Kos,Rhodes.
Sunday	1830hrs	Ialysos/Kamiros	Patmos,Piraeus(M).

At this point in the schedules ferries can quite often be up to two hours late.

FERRY-BOAT TICKET OFFICES
Kastis Travel & Shipping (*Tmr* 15B/C2)
Directions: On the corner of the Esplanade and Platanos roads. They are agents for the **FB Panormitis**, **CF Ialysos** and **CF Kamiros**.

The opening hours of all the island's ticket offices are so unpredictable that it is probably best to purchase tickets from the 'chaps' who set up camp, an hour or so before the quoted departure time, at the Esplanade *Cafe-bar* (*Tmr* 9A2) *See* **The Eating Out**, yes Eating Out.

MEDICAL CARE
Chemists & Pharmacies Plentiful, even if nothing else is.
Hospital (*Tmr* 19B1).

NTOG None, 'not nowhere'.

OTE None in Lakki. (*See* **Ag Marina** – *Tmr* 9B3). Mark you, a number of scribes advise of the presence of an office in Lakki. On the other hand the *Hotel Leros Palace* (*Tmr* 2B2) and the *Cafe-bar* (*Tmr* 6C2) have metered telephones.

PETROL Two petrol stations, both on the Platanos road, one to the right (*Tmr* 16 C1/2) before the football ground, the other on the left, half-way up the gradually rising road.

PLACES OF INTEREST Not a lot in Lakki.

POST OFFICE (*Tmr* 17B2) A large building facing on to the wide thoroughfare that branches off the Esplanade, opposite the small finger pier and on the corner with Odhos 7th Martiou.

POLICE
Port (*Tmr* 18A/B2).

TAXIS The main rank is at the conjunction of the Esplanade and the Platanos road. A very friendly bunch, many speaking Australian, perhaps more accurately 'grine' – that is Greek 'strine', as Leros is an Australian expatriate island. A typical fare from Lakki to Alinda is 350drs.

TELEPHONE NUMBERS & ADDRESSES

Hospital (*Tmr* 19B1)	Tel 22251
Olympic Airways (*See* **Platanos**)	Tel 23502
Taxi rank	Tel 22550

TOILETS There is a public convenience (*Tmr* 20B2) at the right-hand side (*Sbo*), that is east end, of the block in which the Post Office is situated.

Whilst 'moseying' about in this area, the circular semi-derelict arcade, a perfect example of 1930s Italian Aegean architecture, is worth a look over.

TRAVEL AGENTS & TOUR OFFICES

Kastis Travel & Shipping (*Tmr* 15B/C2). This office offers the following schedule of tours and excursions which all depart from Ag Marina:-

Monday:	to Lipsos. 0845hrs departure, cost 2150drs per person including lunch.
Tuesday:	to Archangelos islet (at the northern tip of Leros), cost 1850drs per person.
Wednesday:	to Patmos, cost 2700drs per person.
Thursday:	to Marati Archeous (where??), cost 2100drs per person.
Friday:	to Angathonisi, cost 2700drs per person.
Saturday & Sunday	the boat is available for charter to wherever clients wish.

A problem is that this office is almost always closed.

Letec Travel

Directions: Situated alongside the *Hotel Artemis* (*Tmr* 5B1).

Peddles tours and excursions.

EXCURSION TO LAKKI PORT SURROUNDS

Excursion to Platanos, Ag Marina & Pantelli (about 4km) Leros road signs, usually an angled arrow, can be confusing, because they are as often as not placed after the relevant turning!

From Lakki Port, the main road winds through the hillsides to the hub of the island's activity, a collection of three villages, Platanos, Pantelli and Ag Marina. These straddle the ridge to Mt Apeliki, which separates the north and south bays.

At a major fork in the main road, the left-hand turning leads directly over and down to the coast. This route emerges by a whacking great, leafy tree in the middle of the road, a little to the west of Ag Marina, where to the left advances to Alinda and Partheni and to the right to Ag Marina. Back at the fork, the right-hand turning by-passes the road to Pantelli, way down below, and winds along the ridge past the small *Hotel To Rodon* (Class E – tel 22075). This hotel has double rooms with en suite bathrooms which cost 1850drs, rising to 2220drs (15th June-15th Sept).

Beyond the *To Rodon* is:-

PLATANOS VILLAGE: capital (3.5km from Lakki Port) (Illustration 36) This village is built on and over the crest of a ridge. To the north the ground falls away sharply towards the port of Ag Marina and to the south towards the fishing hamlet of Pantelli.

Platanos village is dominated by a Castle, originally Byzantine, in the shadow of which the pretty, small Main Square radiates out round a central plane tree. The large, almost disproportionately large, Town Hall occupies one side of the Square

(*Tmr* 1B3/4). The rest of the Plateia is edged by bustling businesses, shops and stalls and is jammed with taxis that 'rank' on the Square.

To the left of the Square (*Town Hall behind one*) is a largish cafe-bar, half-left a collection of fruit and vegetables shops followed by a poky, but busy *Kafeneion*. This latter establishment is deservedly popular and serves a super souvlaki, with an egg mixed in, for 60drs. It also possesses a metered telephone and there are **Rooms** above, although they must be rather noisy. The only drawback is that it shuts at rather odd times, such as Saturday lunchtime, though it is open from 1100hrs through to 0200hrs! On the right-hand interior wall is an old, panoramic photograph *Panorama di Lero* detailing the Castle, Ag Marina, Platanos and Pantelli. The proprietor explains that much of the old housing on the upper castle slopes was destroyed by bombing during the Second World War.

If found closed, the rather more modern and expensive *Cafe-bar* next door, going towards the 'toothpaste squeezed' extension to the Main Square, also serves a good souvlaki. Two souvlakis and a small bottle of beer costs 240drs here, but sitting outside can be rather dusty in a breeze.

On the right of the Square, almost on the edge of the Pantelli/Lakki road is the smart *Restaurant/Cafe-bar* ΠΤΘΑΡΙ. The engaging proprietor, if of a rather sharp appearance, runs a clean, 'tight' establishment and serves enjoyable kalamares.

Straight ahead and up the hill is an extension to the Main Square, as if squeezed out of a toothpaste tube. Half-left is a steep cul-de-sac on the left side of which is the large, stately office of Central Travel (*Tmr* 2B/C3) which represents Olympic Airways, but owns up to declining to sell ferry-boat tickets. For those who require a vendor of boat tickets, there is an office on the side of the Lakki road (*Tmr* 26A/B4). Opposite Central Travel is a Dry Cleaners. Half-right a narrow lane winds away, on the left of which is a vendor of cigarettes who sits in a small, bare room, furnished only with a deal table. Also off this smaller Square is a cigarette wholesaler, a butcher and a shop belonging to the proprietor of the *Pension Chrysoulla*, a recommended pension at Alinda.

To the left side of the Town Hall (*Tmr* 1B3/4) is a narrow lane, on which is a newspaper shop (*Tmr* 10B3), on the right, selling English magazines and ancient newspapers. This alley wanders about and off which a right turn leads to a public lavatory block – squatties (*Tmr* 3B3). In all the small side-streets there are a wide variety of shops selling almost everything.

On the corner of the Main Square and the Lakki road, to the left, is a National Bank (*Tmr* 4B3/4), the *Hotel Rosangelika* (*Tmr* 6B4) and a baker (*Tmr* 5B4). Just past the hotel, a lane to the left descends down the valley to Pantelli, of which more later. On the other side of the road to the *Hotel Rosangelika*, across the narrow, pavementless main road, is a doctor (*Tmr* 27B3/4), a *Pension* (*Tmr* 8B4), the office of Spiros Tours and Olympic (*Tmr* 7A/B4), and, on the corner of the road to Lakki, another *Pension* (*Tmr* 18A/B4 – tel 22317) in a large, yellow painted buildings.

The Kastro (Castle) The fortress can be reached on wheels by taking the narrow lane leading half-right from the small Square off Platanos Main Square. This breaks into a rough track which loops round behind the Castle and at one stage runs on a very narrow, contour ridge, which falls sharply and frighteningly away either side of the path. For those on foot, and again from the small Square, a signpost indicates the steps that ascend half-left through the piled up houses followed by open hillside to the Castle.

The view is remarkable but due to the presence of the Army, taking photographs is forbidden. Originally a Byzantine fort it was taken over by the Knights. The church inside the entrance is being rebuilt and a private section, complete with TV aerial, is gated off. The Castle is open daily between 0700-1900hrs.

Back at Platanos, from the Main Square, a road to the left (*Town Hall behind one*), or north, hurtles down to the port of Ag Marina. About half-way is a block on the right which houses the OTE and Post Office (*Tmr* 9B3). The OTE is open weekdays only, between 0730-2200hrs and the Post Office weekdays only, between 0800-1500hrs. The Post Office carries out foreign change transactions. This is convenient as the only bank in Ag Marina is the Agricultural Bank, adjacent to the junction of the Platanos road and Ag Marina Esplanade, close to the Police station. The Agricultural Banks are only structured to deal with, surprise, surprise, farming matters.

A parallel lane off the smaller Platanos Square also steeply descends towards the port and two-thirds of the way down the two join up, prior to:-

AG MARINA: port (Illustration 36) The original harbour of the island. Fortunately the relevant authorities have decided to preserve the tree lined port, which is a perfect example of its genre. Despite which there is now a rather abandoned atmosphere to the place. Is it possible that the departure of the hydrofoil service 'knocked the stuffing out of Ag Marina? Whatever, there is no comparison with the lively ambience of Alinda, or for that matter Pantelli, and Ag Marina seems rather outworn.

Ag Marina does not any more host ferry-boats or Flying Dolphins but is the excursion boat port (*See* **Travel Agents & Tour Offices, A To Z, Lakki**).

From the right to left (*Fsw*), the quay is at the far right or east end of the village, followed by the venerable, stately, but now disused Post Office. The Square, around which are scattered a baker, three tavernas, and their respective tables and chairs, and two tour offices, is one side of the Platanos turning.

The DRM travel office is situated between the Agricultural Bank and the Police station (*Tmr* 11B2) and is 'devoted' to *Thompson's* package tourists. The rival Letec Tours is *Twelve Islands* 'user friendly' and is located on the quayside, the opposite, Main Square side of the Platanos road junction, next door to the *Italian Taverna*. I have nicknamed the latter, which is recognizable by its red chairs, because the proprietor/cook is married to an Italian lady. The nice staff serve good food, particularly fish and Italian dishes, from a clean, modern kitchen. The taverna gets so busy later in the evening that it is often impossible to order more than the main course.

To the west, or left, out of the port and on the right, at the far end, is the Police station (*Tmr* 11B2). There is a baker (*Tmr* 12A/B2) in a terraced row on the right, opposite which is a supermarket (*Tmr* 13A) and another two supermarkets (*Tmr* 13A1/2), almost side by side.

The new road climbs gently upwards. To the right, a narrow, pretty, little lane, which passes a ruined windmill (*Tmr* 14A1) on a promontory, edges the sea and a small beach to one hand and quite grand houses on the other hand. The lane rejoins the new road, which then makes a junction with the main Lakki to Alinda route.

Back at Platanos village, a turning to the left off the Lakki road, beyond the *Hotel Rosangelika*, runs down the right-hand side of the valley. This road passes much waste ground, half-way down a doctor's on the left, the *Taverna Ostria* (*Tmr* 19B5,) the Disco Diana (*Tmr* 15B5) to the right, the surprisingly alpine and twee looking, block booked *Hotel Lavirinthos* (*Tmr* 16B5) to the left, the 'VIP Pub' (yes the 'VIP Pub') (*Tmr* 17B5) to the right and on down to:-

PANTELLI: fishing hamlet (Illustration 36) This lovely little resort reminds me very much of a Greek Polperro. But travellers intending to visit should be quick as package tourists are present and may well be about to 'multiply'! Furthermore popular months and weekends are now generally rather too crowded.

At the bottom, the lane curves sharply left along the fine shingle, sandy but limited, narrow beach which edges the roadside with a few trees fighting for survival. The sea is crystal clear. Straight ahead, and around which the road bends, is a small but long rectangular block, in which are **Rooms** (*Tmr* 24B/C5) over a small taverna, alongside another taverna. These tavernas, set in a row, edge the steeply shelving foreshore. The second taverna serves a restricted but reasonable choice with a meal for two of 2 tzatziki, 2 plates of beans, bread and water costing 840drs.

Beyond the aforementioned tavernas are the manifestations of the village's more serious activity, the working caiques moored haphazardly, but tidily, to the ramshackle finger piers which jut out from the ragged waterfront.

One block back from the waterfront, *The Lotus* advises all and sundry that the restaurant (offers) *reasonable variety at reasonable prices*.

Following the bay round leads to the old fishing quarter of the village with, on the right, the waterside of the houses and their patios 'falling' into the sea. This is a lovely spot, right in the middle of the fishing village activity. On the left are the *Pasion Jrosa* (*sic*) (*Tmr* 20C5) and *Pension Kavas* (*Tmr* 21C5). The Mama who owns the *Jrosa* has opened a lovely little, bamboo shaded, taverna, beautifully situated between two waterside buildings and fishing boat jetties. Prices are very reasonable. The *Pension Kavas* has a superb, almost A class accommodation. A double room, sharing a bathroom, costs 1000drs and with a large, tiled en suite bathroom, 1500drs per night.

A lane climbs up the middle of the valley towards Platanos village. After 100m this road passes a very large, modern hotel with cafeteria to the right followed by two houses with **Rooms**, also on the right (*Tmr* 23 & 25B/C4/5). The second is *Rooms Aphroditi* (Tel 22103). The lane then bends right to run out on a number of flights of steps which connect with either a street back to the south end of Platanos or the lane from Platanos to the Castle. There is no way through for wheeled transport but of course should you have a donkey...

ROUTE ONE
To Xerokampos via Lepida (5km) The road from Lakki skirts the
enormous Bay of Lakkiou, through the tatty outskirts of the settlement followed by pretty, tree lined countryside to:-

LEPIDA (1½km from Lakki Port) Once the Italian naval ordnance and repair yard. The area bordering the road is profusely tree planted and resembles a pre-war holiday camp. The Greeks have taken over part of the site but have left most of the enormous shoreside installations mouldering.

The left-hand fork leads over the hillside to the well spaced out development of:-

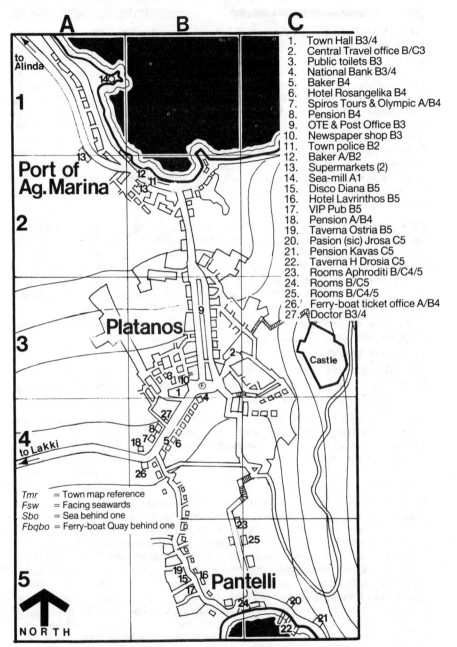

Illustration 36 Platanos, Ag Marina & Pantelli

1. Town Hall B3/4
2. Central Travel office B/C3
3. Public toilets B3
4. National Bank B3/4
5. Baker B4
6. Hotel Rosangelika B4
7. Spiros Tours & Olympic A/B4
8. Pension B4
9. OTE & Post Office B3
10. Newspaper shop B3
11. Town police B2
12. Baker A/B2
13. Supermarkets (2)
14. Sea-mill A1
15. Disco Diana B5
16. Hotel Lavrinthos B5
17. VIP Pub B5
18. Pension A/B4
19. Taverna Ostria B5
20. Pasion (sic) Jrosa C5
21. Pension Kavas C5
22. Taverna H Drosia C5
23. Rooms Aphroditi B/C4/5
24. Rooms B/C5
25. Rooms B/C4/5
26. Ferry-boat ticket office A/B4
27. Doctor B3/4

to Alinda

Port of
Ag. Marina

Platanos

Castle

to Lakki

Tmr   = Town map reference
Fsw   = Facing seawards
Sbo   = Sea behind one
Fbqbo = Ferry-boat Quay behind one

Pantelli

NORTH

XEROKAMPOS (4½km from Lakki Port) The village spreads its way down to a sleepy, quiet and lovely bay with a pebbly beach stretching either side of a rustic taverna. A number of fishing caiques are moored to the small pier in front of the taverna as well as to the right, with domestic ducks bobbing about amongst their hulls. The beach to the left (*Fsw*) is slightly oily, kelpy and the water muddy. There are *Rooms* near the beach and two more cafe-tavernas. The cafe on the left, just before the right turn to the beach, has a metered phone. The 'small pier' taverna serves good, basic food including meatballs and pork cutlets.

An added attraction are the arrival and departure of various caique/trip boats including a 'popular month's' caique connection to Myrtes, Leros island. Departures for this latter service take place at 1200hrs and 1400hrs.

To the right of the village, as it is entered, or a ten minute walk up from the beach, on the ridge of a hill, is:-

Camping Leros (Tel 23372). This is a quiet, shady site run by a Belgian woman, who speaks perfect English. The facilities are fairly basic but include showers, toilets, electricity points, cooking and washing rooms, as well as a breakfast room and a BBQ. They organize a diving club, but people must have a certificate as no training is given. The club boat transports clients to Cape Kryfos. Per night charges at the campsite are:- Adults 250drs, children 150drs, a small tent 150drs, a large tent 220drs and tent rental 350drs.

The offshore Glaronissia islands make it appear that the Bay is no more than an enormous lake.

ROUTE TWO
To Alinda via Vromolithos (7km) From the main Lakki to Alinda road, a very sharp turning to the right, which gives the impression of being about to leap into space, very steeply inclines down to:-

VROMOLITHOS (2km from Lakki Port) This foreshore hamlet spreads along a pretty, sheltered, curved bay with a tree edged and shaded stony foreshore. This is narrow to the right but pleasantly opening out and shingled to the left with a few benzinas moored to the shore. There is a hotel, some *Rooms*, a taverna and a coffee bar. This bay gets busy over the weekends with family groups.

On the tree lined main road that by-passes Platanos village there are some *Rooms*. At the bottom of the hillside junction with the Ag Marina road, the route to Alinda leads off to the left, around the large, centrally mounted tree.

The road undulates and edges the pretty coastline in a series of small bays. About two hundred metres prior to the *Hotel Athena* is the *Taverna El Patio*, which has a very large downstairs room, bordering the beach at the rear of the building. Despite the painfully slow service, that is slow even by Greek standards, there is a variety of nicely cooked, reasonably priced dishes that can be followed by ice-cream or a local gateau. Opposite the *Hotel Athena* is the *Restaurant Esperithes*. This latter establishment, behind a wall and up a flight of steps, serves an unusual, if comparatively expensive, menu (for Greece that is) at about 600drs per head, plus, plus (of course). The offerings include lamb fricasse, beef marengo, prawns, fresh fish and so on.

A broad sweep of road, still adjacent to the water's edge, sweeps past an old kafeneion, and a hillock, whereon a small chapel. Back at sea-level, on the left, is the peaceful, evocative, throat-catching, well-kept British War Cemetery

– no ouzos or Greek salad for these chaps. Do read the War Graves Commission book stowed away in one of the entrance gate piers. In complete and mind bending contrast, the next building that attracts attention is the Disco Diano (Ugh).

The junction of the Partheni and Alinda roads is rather unexpected, with the route to Partheni a sharp turning off to the left. Straight on, beside the pretty, tree lined, narrow, pebbly beach, from which wind surfers are hired, the road proceeds towards the spaced out development that comprises:-

ALINDA (7km from Lakki Port) Still a pleasant location but, even out of the height of the season months, the very narrow beach is busy. The bay is made up of numerous, small, fine shingle and sandy beaches edging the clear water, with an admixture of spread out kafeneions, pensions, hotels and houses. The area may well become 'villa country' but, at the moment, is very, very pleasing, with a lovely view across the bay.

The narrow road passes, variously, the *Pension Cosmopolitan*, and the *Hotel Alinda* with little snackbar alongside the entrance gate. Further on is the quaintly named 'Villa Betty' (can anybody give that name to their house – obviously yes), after which is an eye-catching, seemingly deserted, Italianesque 1930s castle or, more accurately, castellated mansion, set in fairly large grounds. Between a foreign newspaper shop and the dusty shed of a scooter hire outfit, a narrow lane leads back to the *Hotel Carina,*beyond which are the *Pensions Garis* and *Papafotis* and the *Hotel Maleas Beach*. It may sound as if the bay is already undergoing 'Costa' development but the expanse of slowly curving, clear water coastline is well able to cope with the present number of spaced out buildings.

North of the *Hotel Alinda* are two very good, inexpensive waterside tavernas. It may well be necessary to cross the road to actually place the order. A lunchtime meal for two of a cheese omelette, a plate of stuffed tomatoes, 2 plates of feta, 2 lemonades, a small bottle of wine and 2 Nes meh ghala costs 900drs. Close by the tavernas is a quaint, old-fashioned mini-market, run by an elderly gentleman, which exudes the atmosphere of a yester-year grocer.

Almost at the end of the bay, a small track drives to the left up the hillside, and keeping to the right, leads to the:-

Pension Chrysoulla Excellent accommodation in a splendid setting over-looking the bay, with the Castle and villages of Platanos and Ag Marina forming a distant backdrop, and, to the rear, the dramatic slopes of Mt Klidi. The proprietor is Mr Koumbaros who also owns the *Hotel Katerina* in Lakki Port. He and his family live in the ground floor of the pension,which was built by him and his Australian based brother-in-law in the space of three months. Initial impressions that this very smart villa may well prove the exception to the rule are 'happily unfounded'. It was the bathroom that came to our rescue. The sink plug did not and the shower soakaway was positioned in such a manner as to ensure that the water not only didn't drain away, but lay in a puddle so that when sitting on the lavatory it was obligatory to paddle. The lavatory seat would not, nay could not, stay in an upright position and the toilet door wouldn't shut (nor did our room door). The shower's hot water was heralded by much gurgling and spitting prior to the final emission, a scalding stream. I was delighted! A double room costs 2000drs a night, but this does include transport to and from Lakki Port at the beginning and end of a visitor's stay. One particular moan is that the patron's rooster tends to loosely interpret the dawn and can break into a cock-crowing routine at any hour of the day or night.

A general word of warning is that Alinda is prone to mosquitoes.

Before leaving this village, the seafront road continues on past a taverna and skeletal building, perhaps a hotel to-be, and boats moored to the quayside. An unmade track proceeds beyond a very small bay, with a shingly beach, a chapel, an Army outpost only to switchback past a second bay, larger than the first, and a fabulous looking house on the left. The track hereabouts peters out at the site of a small rubbish dump, degenerating into a goat path. This wanders down to a third, small, narrow but lovely bay with a grove of trees in the area of some deserted dwellings and an old warehouse containing large wooden casks and stone troughs. This unofficial nudist beach is made up of shingly sand.

The donkeys tethered in the hills hereabouts have red tassels attached to their headbands, the first time I've seen this.

ROUTE THREE
To Partheni via Alinda (12km) From the Alinda junction, the first
half of the Partheni concrete road is littered with new dwellings being erected all over the place and the occasional, old agricultural shack and homestead, still set in a morass of domestic animals.

A good example of the unusually positioned Leros signposts, conveniently sited well beyond the road to be taken, was that to:-

GOURNA (10km from Lakki Port) The signpost has now disappeared! The hamlet spreads round the mainly rocky but pretty bay. There is a small stretch of narrow, pebbly beach and a chapel, idyllically set on an islet, close by the shore. There are no facilities.

The second turning towards Gourna leads through far more homely (all right, downright scrubbly) countryside edged by 'hill billy' dwellings, all the way down to a swampy looking rubbish tip.

The main concrete road slopes gently down past the airfield, for details of which *See* **Arrival by Air, Lakki Port**. From here it is only a donkey trot along a very unattractive approach to:-

PARTHENI (12km from Lakki Port) Set in an inlet of the Bay of Partheni (surprise, surprise), the edge of which is somewhat marshy. The main *raison d'etre* for the location is the large, business-like Army base, once a concentration camp for the political prisoners of the Colonels' Junta.

Keeping to the right leads to the lovely, clear water bay of:-
PLOFOUTI The unfortunately boulderous, weedy and fine shingle seashore is edged by one lack-lustre, army personnel infested taverna, with an indifferent owner, and a few small caiques.

The situation seems to evoke a slightly foreboding atmosphere of quiet emptiness, a chilling evocation of the ghostly presence of spirits past. Were the Minoans here also?

Dodecanese Islands

FIRST IMPRESSIONS
Cruise ships; tourists; a neat farming-country island; donkeys.

SPECIALITIES
Religion.

RELIGIOUS HOLIDAYS & FESTIVALS
include: 6th March – Festival in memory of the death of the Blessed Christodoulos, The Monastery; 21st May – Saint's day, The Monastery; 15th August – Festival of the Panaghia Church; 21st October – Festival to celebrate the return of the bones of the Blessed Christodoulos from Evia (Euboea). The Monastery also celebrates the national holidays and religious festivals, in very grand style, including the Orthodox Easter and the 'Washing of the Feet', on Maundy Thursday.

VITAL STATISTICS
Tel prefix 0247. The extremely indented island is 14km long and up to 8km wide. In excess of 2,000 of the total population of 3,500 live in Skala Port and The Chora.

HISTORY
Unusually for the Dodecanese, the history of Patmos does not mirror that of the other islands. The reason lies in the Romans exiling St John the Divine to Patmos, in about AD 95. He experienced a revelation which, at the time, caused a 'bit of a stir' around the world. Some hundreds of years later one of St John's admirers transcribed his 'memories' of the Saint, but pirates kept the island clear of pilgrims. That is until 1088, when the Blessed Christodoulos received the sanction of the Orthodox Church to build a monastery on Patmos, in honour of St John. The fame of the religious order protected the fortified Monastery, if not always the island, from the worst depredations of the various overlords. These included the Venetians, a Pope, the Turks, the Venetians briefly again, only for the Turks to take the island back once more. They lost possession for a number of years, after the 1821 War of Independence, took it back to be followed, in turn, by the Italians and Germans. One of the reasons for the Monastery's continued wealth and prosperity was that it owned a fleet of ships even whilst, ostensibly, under the rule of the Turks. The Captains of the ships were in the habit of commissioning stylised, pendant jewellery symbolising their sailing vessels, with baubles hanging down to represent the keels. Some of these renowned pieces are displayed in the Monastery Museum, or Treasury, which is more than can be said for the once great collection of books. Unfortunately the Monastery Library has, over the centuries, been plundered by the learned, including British scholars.

GENERAL
Most guide books ramble on about the Monastery's influence over the island's way of life, particularly in respect of moral standards. You know the sort of thing, a bit kill-joy, no loud music or drunkenness after 'lights out', no discos and a general milieu of spirituality. This may well have been the case in the past but is simply not so any more. Not even the most committed of religious cadres could

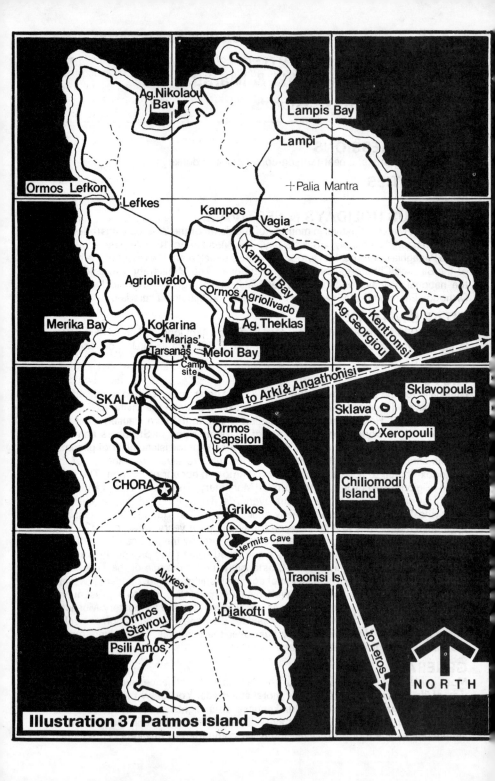

Illustration 37 Patmos island

have held back the merciless, pitiless progress of the cruise ships and their cargo of hedonistic passengers. For instance, on the edge of the Skala Esplanade there is the Meltemi Bar (*Tmr* 18C1), a leisure haunt for cocktail swigging swingers to imbibe to the heavy beat of rock music. The influence of the cruise liners is such that the traditional 'English breakfast', here is styled 'American'. It has to be admitted that on Meloi beach is a sign *On the Holy island of Patmos, there is no camping, and nuding (sic) is not allowed*. This must refer to 'wild' camping, as the board is hard by the campsite!

The countryside is neat, busy and pretty. The heavily indented coastline has resulted in a disproportionately large number of bays for an island as small as this. Unfortunately few are outstanding and the cruise ships now dominate the island's economy. The culture has coped by mutating, so instead of brandishing either native Greek or the alternative tourist countenances, the islanders have developed a third mien, the 'cruise ship persona'. This last, top layer peels away with the departure of the liners and their fun loving, quaintly clothed clientele that decant from and re-enter the mother ship in the fashion of giant flocks of starlings at dawn and dusk. After the ships have 'upped' anchor, the more usual tourist face is revealed but here, on Patmos, a harder, more unyielding layer, which is, I suppose, to be expected. It cannot come as a surprise to reveal that it is rare to plumb the islanders' true personality.

First the good news. If you are lucky and lodge in the environs of, say, Skala Port then you can still meet bona fide natives. The bad news is that, at the height of the season, the liners literally queue to get into the port. On the other hand by accepting the situation, there are hours and hours of enjoyment to be had by simply sitting and watching the antics and inspecting the apparel of the hordes of passengers who disgorge from the giant floating palaces that serenely glide in and out of the bay.

Incidentally, no doubt due to the overpowering monastic presence, the good citizens of Patmos do not appear to indulge so whole-heartedly in the universal destruction and killing of almost anything that moves. There are, therefore, notice-ably more birds in evidence.

SKALA: port (Illustration 38) The only port, with the main body of the harbour village spilling off the enormous quay that dominates the south side. It almost appears that the locals have widened the alleys, lanes and waterfront, as well as pushed back the buildings, in order to allow the passage of even greater throngs to make their foot-dragging way through the streets, but this cannot be so, can it?

The port, if not the island, is overpriced, almost entirely as a result of the incidence of the cruise liners, in addition to waves of trip boats from, for instance, Kos and Samos. Almost everything costs more than on the other islands in the group.

Skala is also a popular port of call for private yachts.

ARRIVAL BY FERRY (*Tmr* 1B/C3/4)
The ferries (and cruise ships for that matter) berth towards the south end of the large, uneven sweep of concrete on which are dotted about crash barriers.

The boats are met by a swarm of people, many offering **Rooms**.

THE ACCOMMODATION & EATING OUT
The Accommodation The referred to human multitude that engulfs the ferry-boat travellers includes an almost frantic group of room owners, who wildly compete for business in an anxiety to fill their accommodation.

It really depends on one's susceptibilities, but I prefer staying in private houses and Patmos is blessed with one of the best I have every stayed in:-

'Marias' Tel 31480

Directions: Mrs Maria Papadatou's house is a fairly long walk from the quay. If a traveller is fortunate, her pretty schoolgirl daughter will 'possess' one, on disembarking, and lead the way to mother's. The daughter's English is very good and she gaily chatters all the way home.

The fifteen minute hike north of Skala Port skirts a small bay, proceeds past the generator station and a small boatyard to the tiny 'suburb' of Tarsanas. At the shallow end of this bay, follow the main road which turns and rises sharply to the left to commence the climb from the small plain towards Kampos. Where the road comes close to west coast Ormos Merika, in the environs called Kokarina, a narrow, unmade road tumbles off to the right and Marias is on the right, set in a comparatively large, low-walled garden. If that sounds complicated why not telephone?

An extremely pleasant double room in this very nice, almost squeaky-clean house costs 1730drs per night. The shared bathroom is excellent and use of the well equipped kitchen is part of the deal. As and when the few rooms are occupied, Maria and her daughters retire into a long, single storey shed at the bottom of the garden. In 1987 Maria acquired the house next door which should be ready for 1988. When her accommodation is all taken, she directs people to her niece, Olga Vassilaki, just down the road.

Maria, whose English is almost non-existent, is a lovely, if rather excitable hostess and nothing is too much trouble for her. When guests arrive, leave or when convenient, she will serve "Coffee, no charge". Another small but essential service that Maria renders is to telephone her contacts on Leros, if that island is your next port of call.

On the way round to Tarsanas, beyond the generator station, a narrow lane to the left climbs a short distance to the:-

Australis Pension

Directions: As above.

A good looking establishment with rooms and en suite bathrooms.
A few yards further on past the *Australis* are some more **Rooms**.

By keeping to the shore hugging road, beyond the Kampos turning, and alongside a petrol station, slightly set back, is the:-

Hotel Hellinis Tel 31275

Directions: As above.

All rooms have en suite bathrooms with a single room costing 1600drs and a double room 2100drs, which rates increase, respectively, to 1800drs and 2300drs (16th June-15th Sept).

Beyond the hotel, the concrete road climbs over the neck of the hillside and down to lovely Ormos Meloi. The sandy beach, with some kelp in the shallow water, is edged by trees. Apart from the water skiing, wind surfing and the moored caiques there are:-

Taverna (& Rooms) Meloi

Directions: As above, in a wonderful setting overlooking the beautiful and tranquil bay.

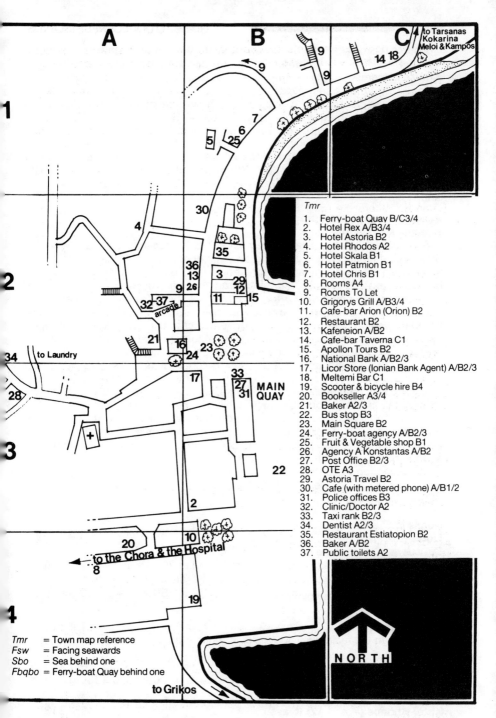

Tmr
1. Ferry-boat Quay B/C3/4
2. Hotel Rex A/B3/4
3. Hotel Astoria B2
4. Hotel Rhodos A2
5. Hotel Skala B1
6. Hotel Patmion B1
7. Hotel Chris B1
8. Rooms A4
9. Rooms To Let
10. Grigorys Grill A/B3/4
11. Cafe-bar Arion (Orion) B2
12. Restaurant B2
13. Kafeneion A/B2
14. Cafe-bar Taverna C1
15. Apollon Tours B2
16. National Bank A/B2/3
17. Licor Store (Ionian Bank Agent) A/B2/3
18. Meltemi Bar C1
19. Scooter & bicycle hire B4
20. Bookseller A3/4
21. Baker A2/3
22. Bus stop B3
23. Main Square B2
24. Ferry-boat agency A/B2/3
25. Fruit & Vegetable shop B1
26. Agency A Konstantas A/B2
27. Post Office B2/3
28. OTE A3
29. Astoria Travel B2
30. Cafe (with metered phone) A/B1/2
31. Police offices B3
32. Clinic/Doctor A2
33. Taxi rank B2/3
34. Dentist A2/3
35. Restaurant Estiatopion B2
36. Baker A/B2
37. Public toilets A2

Tmr   = Town map reference
Fsw   = Facing seawards
Sbo   = Sea behind one
Fbqbo = Ferry-boat Quay behind one

Illustration 38 Skala Port

Double rooms share the bathroom at average rates which start at 1500drs. But it is not for the accommodation that this establishment is listed, oh no! The management's philosophy is to cater (sorry) for the pockets of the campers, not cruise liner passengers, who are hardly likely to make it this far. Whatever the establishment's objectives, this is quite possibly the best taverna on the island. Admittedly the menu choice is not extensive but the food is delicious and the waiters very pleasant. A meal for two of dolmades (meat filled), rice mixed with vegetables, cheese, two bottles of retsina and bread costs 670drs. A meal for one of green beans, chips, feta cheese, bread and a kortaki retsina was charged at 350drs. One of the waiters may, just may, be fishing from the nearby jetty for supplies. Well, there you go.
and:-

Patmos Flowers Camping   Tel 31821
Directions: As above.

An excellent, pretty, pleasant campsite. The enthusiastic and hard-working owner, Stefanos, lovingly presides over the operation, which is situated over a small rise from the sea-lapped foreshore. The flower-filled, well laid out site has room for 200 people. The plots are subdivided by welcome screens of tall bamboo and one area is afforded additional shade from the sun beneath a matt covered framework. The reception building has a mini-market, which is not very well stocked. Additionally there is a cafe-bar, an inexpensive bar, a very clean, well equipped toilet block, with solar heated hot water showers, toilets, washbasins and, outside, clothes washing facilities.

The bar stays open until 0300hrs, serves light snacks and stocks cigarettes to facilitate late night/early morning ferry-boat arrivals. A breakfast of yoghurt, bread and Nes meh ghala, costing 100drs, is cheaper here, as are most items, than prices in Skala Port. The only quibbles, the minutest blemishes in this panegeric must include a mention that the hot water doesn't last very long in the evenings (but where and when does it when solar heated?), that, on occasions, the water supply to some sinks and showers runs out completely and the paucity of the mini-markets' supplies.

The reception is adorned with an old fashioned trumpet gramophone, and the site is open between the 15th May and the 15th October. Rates start at 350drs for an adult.

Hotels in Skala Port include the:-
Hotel Rex (*Tmr* 2A/B3/4) (Class D)   Tel 31242
Directions: Close to the outset of the Chora road.

A single room, sharing a bathroom, starts off at 900drs and with an en suite bathroom 1200drs and a double room with an en suite bathroom costs 1600drs. These rates rise, respectively, to 1000/1500drs and 2000drs (1st July-30th Sept).

Hotel Astoria (*Tmr* 3B2) (Class C)   Tel 31205
Directions: In the main quayside building, opposite the trip boat section of the waterfront.

All rooms have en suite bathrooms, with single rooms costing 1350drs and a double room 1900drs, which rates increase to 1800drs and 2250drs (16th June-15th Sept).

Hotel Rhodos (*Tmr* 4A2) (Class D)   Tel 31371
Directions: Behind the *Estiatopion Restaurant* (*Tmr* 35B2), a lane proceeds westwards and the hotel is on the right.

A single room, sharing a bathroom, is charged at 1100drs, a double room sharing costs 1450drs, and with an en suite bathroom, 1700drs. These charges increase, respectively, to 1350drs and 1700/2200drs (1st June-30th Sept).

Hotel Skala (*Tmr* 5B1) (Class B)   Tel 31343
Directions: Through an archway off the Esplanade.
All rooms have en suite bathrooms with a single room priced at 1780drs and a double room 2670drs, which charges increase to 2320drs and 3740drs (16th June-15th Sept).

Hotel Patmion (*Tmr* 6B1) (Class B) 34 Emm Xenou   Tel 31313
Directions: Almost next door to the *Hotel Skala*. This building follows the curve of the waterfront.
Actually classed as a Pension. Double rooms only. Those sharing a bathroom cost 1300drs and those with an en suite bathroom are charged at 1900drs. These prices increase to 1500/2250drs (16th June-15th Sept).

Hotel Castelli (*Tmr* A1) (Class B)   Tel 31361
Directions: North from the Ferry-boat Quay, a turning left beyond the *Hotel Chris* (*Tmr* 7B1) angles up and round the back of the *Hotels Chris* and *Skala*. The *Castelli* is behind the *Skala* (*Tmr* 5B1).
Another Pension. All rooms have en suite bathrooms with a single room priced at 1300drs and a double room 1750drs, rising to 1800drs for a single and 2250drs for a double room (16th June-15th Sept).

Hotel Chris (*Tmr* 7B1) (Class C)   Tel 31001
Directions: To the north of the Port, alongside the unkempt grounds of an imposing house which used to exhibit a 'For Sale' sign.
All rooms have en suite bathrooms. A single room costs 1300drs and a double room 1900drs. These charges rise to 1500drs and 2300drs (16th June-15th Sept).

Rooms (*Tmr* 8A4)   Tel 31369
Directions: On the left of the Chora road.
Average rates.

About 200-300m further up the Chora road there are **Rooms** and apartments available.

There are other **Rooms** spread throughout Skala Port (*Tmr* 9) including three individual houses on the road from the Esplanade towards the *Hotel Castelli* (described above). Also recommended is the *Pension Sydney*, which has capacious, modern rooms, complete with en suite bathroom and large terrace balcony overlooking the hills, at a cost of 1500drs per night.

The Eating Out For possibly the best taverna 'in town', *See* **Taverna (& Rooms) Meloi, The Accommodation**. Generally prices have been affected by the popularity of the island and cruise line passengers. The presence of the latter makes it necessary to occupy a table early in the evening, as spaces fill up quickly.
As with the accommodation, I have radiated out from the left (*Sbo*). Standing towards the south end of the Ferry-boat Quay, the main Chora road is almost immediately to the fore. A few metres along this road, on the right, is a very smart cafeteria that serves filter coffee, close to the Bookshop (*Tmr* 20A3/4).

At the outset of the Chora road is:-
Grigorys Grill (*Tmr* 10A/B3/4)
Directions: As above.
A varied menu at comparatively reasonable prices. An English lady is the female of the partnership but the atmosphere is rather 'Costa Brava', rather than Greek Taverna.

Arion (Orion)Cafe-bar (*Tmr* 11B2)
Directions: In the main, waterfront block to the right (*Sbo*) of the Main Square.
At night the Arion is the nearest equivalent 'in town' to a smart, singles bar with mood and rock music 'pumping out'. During the day the worn edges show.

To the right and next door is a:-
Restaurant (*Tmr* 12B2)
Directions: As above.
Probably the best value in the Port, after ('well after') the *Taverna Meloi*. A meal for one of moussaka, a Greek salad, bread and a bottle of retsina costs 750drs.

Kafeneion (*Tmr* 13A/B2)
Directions: In the street behind the *Restaurant* (*Tmr* 12B2) described above.
This establishment represents fair value.

Another worthwhile cafe-bar, hiding away almost at the far or north end of the port, is the:-
Cafe-bar Taverna (*Tmr* 14C1)
Directions: Proceeding northwards along the Esplanade and beyond the *White Horse* cocktail cafeteria.
Pleasantly situated, with tables and chairs edging the beach and shaded by a large awning. Satisfactory portions from a limited menu, with a Greek salad costing 150drs and a kortaki retsina 80drs. Omelettes are available.

THE A TO Z OF USEFUL INFORMATION
AIRLINE OFFICE The agent for Olympic Airways is **Apollon Tours** (*Tmr* 15B2). *See* **Ferry-boat ticket offices, A To Z.**

BANKS
National Bank of Greece (*Tmr* 16A/B2/3) In the Main Square but do not enter the bank. Lowly tourists must stand outside, up against a grill on the right-hand side of the building.
The Ionian Bank Represented by the smart Licor Store (*Tmr* 17A/B2/3) on the left (*Sbo*) of the Main Square. The cashier is a thin, disinterested, very white skinned, aristocratic old man. There is more chance of being served here during banking hours.

BEACHES There is one edging the tree lined Esplanade, stretching from the *Hotel Chris* (*Tmr* 7B1) round to the *Meltemi Bar* (*Tmr* 18C1). This sandy and narrow beach, with a steeply shelving sea bottom, runs out on a small bluff across from a sharp bend in the Esplanade, alongside an incongruous, railed-off tomb.

BICYCLE, SCOOTER & CAR HIRE There is a hard-working bike and scooter outfit (*Tmr* 19B4) on the left (*Sbo*) of the Ferry-boat Quay, towards the road to Grikos. A Vespa costs 1200drs a day or 2200drs for two days, from a professional outfit.
There are 'vestiges' of car hire, also alongside the Grikos road.

BOOKSELLERS An interesting shop (*Tmr* 20A3/4) is located thirty or so metres along the Chora road, on the right. The importance of this bookshop is that it has a selection of second-hand, English language books.

BREAD SHOPS A Baker (*Tmr* 21A2/3) is situated behind the National Bank and another (*Tmr* 36A/B2) in the street behind the *Restaurant Estiatopion*. Patmos bread is of the four hour variety.

BUSES The bus terminal (*Tmr* 22B3), well more a pull-up, is on the Ferry-boat Quay. An up-to-date timetable is pinned on a notice board across the way, on the wall of the Police offices (*Tmr* 31B3).

Bus timetable
Skala Port to the Chora/Monastery
Daily	0740, 0930, 1130, 1330, 1530, 1730, 1930hrs
Return journey	
Daily	0800, 1000, 1200, 1345, 1600, 1700, 1800, 2000hrs
One-way fare: 55drs.	

Skala Port to Kampos
Daily	0815, 1030, 1830hrs
Return journey	
Daily	0840, 1100, 1900hrs
One-way fare: 70drs.	

Skala Port to Grikos
Daily	1330, 1630hrs
Return journey	
Daily	1400, 1645hrs
One-way fare: 55drs.	

Chora to Grikos
Daily	1345hrs
Return journey	
There isn't one...!	
One-way fare: 65drs.	

COMMERCIAL SHOPPING AREA None. The various stores and shops radiate out from, are on or in the environs of the Main Square and include a grocery, butcher/dairy and a 'Fruits and Vegetables' room – yes a room (*Tmr* 25B1), alongside the *Hotel Patmion*.

DISCO Not so much a disco, more the *Meltemi Bar* (*Tmr* 18C1).

FERRY-BOATS & FLYING DOLPHINS Both dock on the large quayside (*Tmr* 1B/C3/4). The Port policeman (*Tmr* 31B3) is very helpful, even if his memory is of the 'one day' variety in respect of timetables.

Ferry-boat timetable (Mid-season)
Day	Departure time	Ferry-boat	Ports/Islands of Call
Tuesday	0530hrs	Panormitis	Arki,Angathonisi,Pythagorion(Samos).
	1530hrs	Panormitis	Lipsos,Leros,Kalimnos,Kos,Nisiros, Tilos,Simi,Rhodes.
	2000hrs	Ialysos/Kamiros	Piraeus(M).

	2230hrs	Ialysos/Kamiros	Leros,Kalimnos,Kos,Rhodes.
Wednesday	2000hrs	Orient Express*	Katakolon for Olympia (Peloponnese), Venice(Italy).
	2030hrs	Kamiros	Piraeus(M).
Thursday	1700hrs	Alcaeos/Omiros	Vathy(Samos),Chios,Mitilini(Lesbos), Limnos,Kavala(M).
	2230hrs	Ialysos/Kamiros	Leros,Kalimnos,Kos,Rhodes.
Friday	2030hrs	Ialysos/Kamiros	Piraeus(M).
	2230hrs	Ialysos/Kamiros	Leros,Kalimnos,Kos,Rhodes.
Saturday	2030hrs	Ialysos/Kamiros	Piraeus(M).
	2230hrs	Ialysos/Kamiros	Leros,Kalimnos,Kos,Rhodes.
Sunday	2030hrs		Piraeus(M).

*The Orient Express is a 'scheduled cruise liner'.

Flying Dolphin timetable (Mid-season). The Port police are completely unable to give any information in respect of the hydrofoils and send enquirers to Apollon Tours (*Tmr* 15B2). And why not, they are the Flying Dolphin agents and, as such, sell the tickets. Unfortunately they are also unable to dispense any information! They will guarantee the following:-

Flying Dolphin timetable (Mid-season)

Day	Departure time	Ports/Islands of Call
Wednesday	1600hrs	Kos,Rhodes.

FERRY-BOATS & FLYING DOLPHIN TICKET OFFICES There is an unnamed office (*Tmr* 24 A/B2/3), in the same block as the National Bank, who act as agents for the **FB Alcaeos, Omiros** and **Sapho.**

Agency A Konstantas (*Tmr* 26A/B2)
Directions: In the street behind the *Restaurant Estiatopion.*
  Agents for the **FB Ialysos** and **Kamiros.**

Apollon Tours (*Tmr* 15B2)
Directions: Just to the north side of the Ferry-boat Quay.
  Agents for the hydrofoils, when they travel, as well as the **MV Orient Express,** but primarily a trip boat office. *See* **Travel Agents & Tour Offices, A To Z.**

Astoria Travel (*Tmr* 29B2)
Directions: A few doors along from Apollon Tours, in the main waterfront building.
  Not so much a ferry-boat ticket office, more a trip boat outfit. *See* **Travel Agents & Tour Offices, A To Z.**

LAUNDRY There is a well-signposted launderette, eight minutes walk up the twisting, stepped street which is the last right-hand (*Sbo*) turning prior to the OTE office (*Tmr* 28A3).

LUGGAGE STORE *See* **NTOG, A To Z.**

MEDICAL CARE
Chemists & Pharmacies Numerous.
Clinic *See* **Doctor.**
Dentist (*Tmr* 34A2/3). Further along the 'OTE road'.
Doctor (*Tmr* 32A2). A Medical office, with a doctor in attendance. This clinic is up a flight of stairs, off an arcade alley.
Hospital Two kilometres up the main Chora road.

OTE (*Tmr* 28A3) Open weekdays between 0730-2200hrs. Closed Saturday and Sunday. There is a cafe (*Tmr* 30A/B1/2) with a metered telephone.

NTOG None, but the Police (*Tmr* 31B3) are very helpful and one officer speaks excellent English. The various timetables, including the bus schedules, are displayed on the outside wall of this office, situated in (yet another) Italianesque block. A further, very useful service is that travellers can leave their cases and backpacks beneath the external stairs of the police station.

PETROL There is a station alongside the *Hotel Hellinis*, on the outskirts of Skala, close by the junction with the Kampos road from the Port and opposite a driving school.

PLACES OF INTEREST *See* **The Chora and Monastery, Route One.**

POLICE The Port and Town police offices (*Tmr* 31B3) are combined in the one building. *See* **NTOG, A To Z.**

POST OFFICE (*Tmr* 27B2/3) In the same building as the Police offices and open Monday to Friday between 0800-1430hrs.

TAXIS They rank (*Tmr* 33B2/3) alongside the Police offices, on the Main Square.

TELEPHONE NUMBERS & ADDRESSES

Clinic (*Tmr* 32A2)	Tel 31211/31577
Olympic Airways (*Tmr* 15B2)	Tel 31356
Police, port (*Tmr* 31B3)	Tel 31231
Police, town (*Tmr* 31B3)	Tel 31303
Taxi rank (*Tmr* 33B2/3)	Tel 31225

TOILETS There is a public convenience (*Tmr* 37A2) at the end of the narrow alley off the street, one back and parallel to the Esplanade, behind the main waterfront block.

TRAVEL AGENTS & TOUR OFFICES In the main, these offices are engaged in the excursion and trip boat 'circus'. Fares are considerably more expensive than the scheduled ferry-boats.

Apollon Tours (*Tmr* 15B2). This office offers the following:-

Patmos to Kos	Monday, Tuesday, Wednesday and Friday at 1615hrs, duration 2hrs.
Patmos to Samos	Monday (1620hrs), Wednesday (0900, 1620hrs), Thursday (0900hrs), Friday (1620hrs), Saturday (1620hrs) and Sunday (0900hrs).
Patmos to Lipsos	Daily at 1000hrs.
Patmos to Leros	Wednesday at 1000hrs.
Patmos to Ikaria	Wednesday (0530hrs), Friday and Sunday (0600hrs).

Astoria Travel (*Tmr* 29B2) This office offers the following:-

Patmos to Ikaria & Paros	Monday (0800hrs), Wednesday (0530hrs) and Friday (0600hrs).
Patmos to Samos	Monday (1620hrs), Tuesday (0900hrs), Wednesday (0900, 1620hrs), Thursday (0900hrs), Friday (1620hrs), Saturday (1620hrs) and Sunday (0900hrs).
Patmos to Kos	Monday, Tuesday, Wednesday and Friday at 1620hrs.
Patmos to Kalimnos	Tuesday at 1600hrs.
Patmos to Lipsos	Daily at 1000hrs.
Patmos to Leros	Wednesday, Friday and Sunday at 1000hrs.

The day trip to Lipsos from either of the above offices costs 1200drs return. A less expensive option is offered by the :-

Anna Express This express craft makes the voyage to Lipsos in 45 minutes, at a cost of 1000drs for the return journey. Interestingly enough the boat is named after the girlfriend of the proprietor of the boat. Anna is from Nottingham and has lived the last three years on Lipsos.

Note that these local, private enterprise inter-island routes are not only much more costly but are subject to more 'variation', all right alteration and cancellation, than the scheduled ferries. Furthermore they are contingent upon large-scale, year to year alterations and amendments and are severely curtailed out of season – but what isn't?

ROUTE ONE
To Psili Amos & Diakofti via Chora, the capital, & the Monastery of St John the Divine (some 6km) As the crow
flies, the first section of the journey to the Chora is some two kilometres but by the winding, tree shaded road the distance travelled measures about three kilometres. The route passes the Monastery of the Apocalypse, now a theological college, the Hospital and the Grotto of the Apocalypse, where St John experienced the Revelation. At first the trees which line the road are pines but these are replaced by tall, elegant gum trees, until the last kilometre which is made across boulderous, granite terrain.

The Monastery of St John the Divine The fortified monastery dominates the old capital town and is a five star, 'fully operational' establishment. The final approach is a quiet, upwards cobbled slope hedged in by stalls conducting a fairly low-key 'tourist sell'. At the main gate a 'kindly' soul demands 150drs entrance fee and, when necessary 'loans out' pairs of trousers and or wrap round skirts (not to one and the same person you understand) for 70drs each. This reminds me to reiterate that it is not only good manners but is obligatory to dress with some decorum for a monastery visit. Every day a number of tourists seem determined to ignore this reasonable dictum. So trousers and shirts or skirts and blouses are the order of the day, please.

Contrary to another popular Patmos myth, perpetrated and constantly repeated by some guide books, the Monastery is not the only source of production and sale of postcards and island maps. Certainly the Monastery does sell cards but they are no different than are now available elsewhere.

The Monastery is an attractive and imposing building with magnificent views, not only out over Patmos but as far as and including Samos to the north, Naxos to the west, Kos in the south and, of course, Turkey to the east. Much restoration is under way and, whilst that includes the library, not a lot of the Monastery is open to tourists but the Museum is extremely interesting. The renovation includes the installation of under-floor, blown air central heating! Are the monks getting soft? The opening hours are: Monday closed; Tuesday 1500-1800hrs; Wednesday 1730-1900hrs; Thursday 1400-1800hrs; Friday and Saturday closed; Sunday 1500-1800hrs. But a notice board reads *The above programme is liable to change due to unscheduled visits of ships.* So even the monks bow to the whims and caprices of cruise liners!

THE CHORA (Illustration 39) The old town, or Chora, is a clean, rather antiseptic, whitewashed version of almost any pretty, Cyclades Old Quarter. The Chora tends to remind me of one of those deserted, Mexican villages in the 'Dirty Dozen' type of film, all expectancy but no inhabitants, dogs or even birds – but you know they are there. There are a number of tavernas and kafeneions and two signposts indicate totally conflicting directions to the Main Square, and why not?

The main road skirts the elevated town and continues on to Grikos, for which refer to **Route Two**. About ½km from the Chora, a turning to the right, along an unmade, wide track (and keeping left) lurches to a rather unique, monastic, old stone road. This bends down the gentle hillside, leaving the hamlet of **Alykes** way below, on the right. The laid stone pathway runs out and breaks into track again. The large, pebble beach to the south of Alykes is set in a beautiful bay but the shore edge is piled high with kelp and is rather rubbish littered.

At the far end of the curved bay of Ormos Stavrou is the absolutely lovely, sandy and tree edged beach of **Psili Amos**. A 'dashed' long walk which can sensibly be avoided by taking a boat trip from Skala Port.

A short walk over the neck of land to the east coast leads to the hamlet of **Diakofti** on the Bay of Diakofti. The pleasant, large pebble foreshore is clean and almost deserted, with one lone fisherman's cottage edging the beach,but the sea-bed is rather slimy.

ROUTE TWO
To Grikos (3km) This 'standard', Aegean island road takes in Ormos Sapsilon, hardly a sunbathing bay but there is a clean, narrow, pebbly foreshore.

GRIKOS (3km from Skala Port) A pleasant location but appears rather 'dead'. That is not to say that Grikos is not nice and quiet but there is an 'empty feeling', despite the ample tourist facilities.

The settlement is set in a large, curving cove and the road runs out on the backshore. On the immediate left is a restaurant and 30 paces to the right is another, as well as a small quay. There are a number of ramshackle finger piers to which boats and caiques are moored. The beach to the left and the first section to the right is rather dirty and very seaweedy, but, further to the right, the fine shingle beach becomes clean with wind surf boards for hire.

The *Hotel Grikos*, actually a B class pension (Tel 31167), has single rooms, with en suite bathrooms, at a cost of 1500drs and double rooms, with en suite bathrooms, from 2200drs, which rates increase to 1750drs and 2700drs (1st July-10th Sept). This hotel is one block back from the shore and to the left, as are the *Panorama* furnished apartments and *Hotel Xenia* (Class B – tel 31219). The latter's single rooms, complete with en suite bathrooms, cost 2100drs and double rooms 3000drs, increasing, respectively, to 2500drs and 3600drs (1st July-15th Sept). The management reduces these prices, when desperate for custom – and so they should. There is, at the other end of the scale, the *Hotel Flisvos* (Class D – tel 31380) with double rooms, sharing the bathroom, costing from 1400drs.

In the middle distance an island blots out the view and seems to join with the narrow necked isthmus in the foreground, which ends in a blob of rock.

This is difficult to scale but has a hermit's cave facing seawards, a deep well, some wall carvings and is supposedly always provisioned for any weary traveller who gains access. The view from the top is worth the climb.

ROUTE THREE
To Kampos (5km) & other points north Close by Maria's house (*See* **The Accommodation, Skala Port**), at Kokarina, a track to the left leads down to a narrow, small, weedy beach. An old man has built a shack on the sea's edge, at the far left of the very small bay.

Another two kilometres along the main route and a road to the right ends up fifty metres short of the beach at:-

ORMOS AGRIOLIVADO (4km from Skala Port) The last few steps must be made on foot. The first section of the beach is boulderous with earth spoil forming small swamps. The rest of the beach is shingly sand with signs that include *No Camping, no nudism, The Police Station* and *Please keep the place clean.*
   The foreshore is edged by tamarisk trees with whitewashed trunks. The building on the left (*Fsw*) is now a small beach bar and has a toilet. The house further to the left bears a sign reading *No trespassing*. Surely a lot of signs for a little place...

About ½km further along the main road, a rough track to the left, resembling a summer-dry river-bed, tumbles down to the Bay of Lefkon and terminates on the foreshore. The horrid, shingly beach is covered with thick seaweed and edged by tamarisk trees. To the far left a small craft jetty is overlooked by an imposing, but rather incongruous, house, possibly of Italian design, set back on the hillside.

KAMPOS (5km from Skala Port) Clean and sporting a sign proclaiming the settlement's name. The hilltop village has a cobbled square edged by a church. There is a general store and a taverna. A helpful sign indicates the direction for the beaches. To the left a very steep concrete track runs out in Upper Kampos, from where there are some splendid views over the north-west part of the island.

Back at the main village, the road forks down the hillside to the right, along the waterfront of the small bay of:-

ORMOS KAMPOU A pleasant, shingle beach with quite a few caiques drawn up, three tavernas and some pedaloes and one-man sailing boats for hire. Facing the bay, the caiques/fishing boats are to the right, sunbathing benches (*sic*) and parasols to the left, as is a ski boat run and wind surf board hire. Oh well, it is still a very pleasant location.

At the end of the bay, off to the right, a very steep gravel track, up the hump of the hillside and down the other side, leads to the coastal hamlet of:-

VAGIA A small, shingly beach with fishing boats anchored. A sign nailed to the bottom of a telegraph pole on the crest of the approach proclaims *ROOMS FOR REND*. Vagia is a very nice and peaceful beach, as are a number of the other beaches on this route.

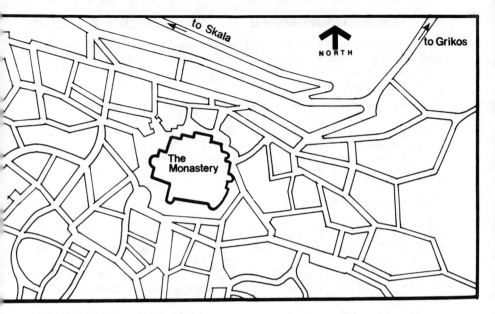

Illustration 39 The Chora

The main road winds on up and around the small mountain of Palia Mantra, through a pleasant landscape, on to a steep, unmade track down to the right-hand end of Ormos Lampis and the beach of the tiny hamlet of:-

LAMPI (9km from Skala Port) Renowned for the coloured stones of this very clean, shingle beach but there are blobs of tar on the foreshore. There is some sand adjacent to the far *Dolphin Taverna*, beyond the small jetty.

The nearside, rather basic taverna has a few single storey changing rooms, some simple double rooms for rent at 1500drs (which price falls to 1000drs for two nights or more) and serves a reasonably priced, if limited menu.

Close inshore, a number of large, workmanlike fishing boats anchor in the bay.

EXCURSIONS TO ARKI & MARATHI (Marathos, Maranthi) ISLANDS

(Illustration 40) The island known as Arki is in fact made up of a total of fourteen islets, islands, and large rocks. Arki itself is really only accessible on the weekly **FB Panormitis**. The trip boats from Patmos (despite advertising trips to 'Arki, Marathi') only run to the islet of Marathi, where there is a sandy beach and a taverna with *Rooms*. To get from Marathi to the beachless, but more interesting, Arki it is necessary to bribe, or at least 'encourage', one of the local caique owners.

MARATHI This low-lying, little islet boasts one permanent resident a family, who live here in the summer to run the taverna. The enterprising owner is originally from Arki, but speaks excellent 'Australian', as do his wife and sons, who also spent most of their lives in Australia. Such is their enthusiasm, that they have installed an electricity generator. The taverna and rooms are clean and very modern and an en suite double room costs 1700drs. The fish meals are excellent, if expensive as usual.

Marathi is a super place to stay for those who desire peace, comfort, good food and a long, sand and shingle beach with very clear sea in which to swim. The natural harbour hosts fishing craft from nearby, bigger islands and is also popular as a stopping off place for private yachts.

Day-trip passengers from Patmos on the Chrysoula caique, should note that the journey in this craft takes well over an hour. If the wind is blowing it can prove an 'interesting' voyage, as the boat is very small and the waves can be very, very large. Passengers may be forced to spend the entire voyage with their heads buried in towels, and still get extremely wet! In these conditions the captain exudes utter confidence and manages the passage with aplomb.

For a more villagey, unique island atmosphere it is necessary to visit:-

ARKI A gentle, hilly little island, covered with greenish scrub, but few trees. There is only one remaining settlement, a cluster of primitive, stone-built dwellings around the inlet which makes up the island's harbour, Port Augusta. Here, forty inhabitants struggle to keep their homes alive.

Fishing is the sole source of income, and fish, eggs, goats milk and cheese are the only self-produced commodities. Everything else, including drinking water, has to be shipped in.

Ferry connections are provided by the 'old trooper', the **FB Panormitis**, which stops off on its weekly trip to Samos. A new quay is being built (yes, really!) but the locals claim it is never likely to be finished! Up to publication, even the pint-sized Panormitis has to drop anchor in the bay so that the caiques can motor out to collect the passengers, supplies and mail, as well as dispatch the 'island produce'.

Ferry times are:-
Tuesday: FB Panormitis 0630hrs to Angathonisi, Samos.
Tuesday: FB Panormitis 1330hrs to Patmos, Lipsos, Leros, Kalimnos, Kos, Nisiros, Tilos, Simi, Rhodes.

Accommodation is available on Arki, but not in private homes, as most houses only have two rooms anyway. There are a few bungalows for rent, owned by the man who runs the Restaurant Taverna to the left (*Sbo*) of the tiny village square. A bungalow sleeping six costs 2000drs per night, but rates are negotiable for fewer occupants.

If this sounds rather like Paradise, so it should. Visitors who stay can pretty well guarantee to be the only resident tourists but perhaps a list of facilities lacking, as opposed to the other way around, will not go amiss. There is no beach (although of course bathing from rocks and rocky coves is possible), no electricity (only oil lamps), no drinking water 'on tap', no Post Office, no shops or a bakery, only one telephone (which is usually broken), no transport, no police station and no policeman (not even the army – shhh!) and the island doesn't even have a priest!

The locals are very kind and hospitable, and to those staying in the taverna-owner's rooms, the proprietor volunteers to supply any needs required. However it is best to arrive prepared, – and take along a phrase book and mosquito repellent!

A track from the village takes off up the hill to a cluster of tumble-down buildings which surround the blue and white church on top. This is Panaghia, where another family still live on.

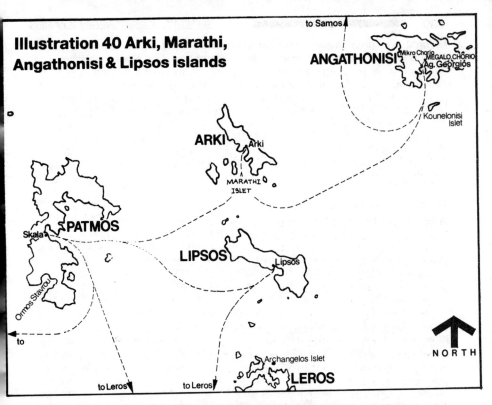

Illustration 40 Arki, Marathi, Angathonisi & Lipsos islands

ANGATHONISI
Mikro Chorio
MEGALO CHORIO
Ag. Georgiós
to Samos
Kounelonisi Islet

ARKI
Arki
MARATHI ISLET

PATMOS
Skala
Ormos Stavrou
to

LIPSOS
Lipsos

to Leros
to Leros
Archangelos Islet
LEROS

NORTH

EXCURSION TO ANGATHONISI (Angathonissi, Agathonisi, Gaidaros, Gaidharos) (Illustration 40) A hundred

and thirty one inhabitants populate this, the most northerly and remote of the Dodecanese islands. The true lover of Greece simply must visit. Despite its small size, the island community is vibrant and surprisingly healthy. Angathonisi does not emit quite the same sense of doom as, for example, nearby Arki. This fortitude can be related to the fact that the population has remained relatively stable over the past twenty years.

There are three settlements on the island – Ag Georgios, the port, and the two villages of Megalo Chorio and Mikro Chorio. Megalo Chorio is on the mountainside to the right (*Sbo*) of the port, and Mikro Chorio, with only a dozen or so inhabitants, is to the left. Both villages are linked to the harbour by a narrow concrete road. This is just wide enough to take the island's two 'trucks' – three wheelers which transport everything, including livestock, people and the mail up and down the hillsides. There is a track that connects these two roads.

Angathonisi can be reached once a week by – you guessed it – the **FB Panormitis** the schedule of which is:-
Tuesday: 0740hrs to Pythagorion(Samos).
Tuesday: 1240hrs to Arki, Patmos, Lipsos, Leros, Kalimnos, Kos, Nisiros, Tilos, Simi, Rhodes.

There are also twice weekly caiques from Samos, to the north, and rumours of a weekly trip boat from Leros, of all places! Only in the very high season do trip boats connect with the island of Patmos.

Accommodation is mainly to be found in the port, Ag Georgios where there are two pensions with five rooms each, as well as a few *Rooms* in private houses. Official pension rates for a double room are 1500drs, with an en suite bathroom, but 'negotiations' will result in lower charges.

There are three tavernas catering mainly for the visitors from private yachts, as other tourists are very few and far between. The cafe near the new, concrete Ferry-boat Quay is a good bet for breakfast. This is especially so when the ferry docks, as most of the island's inhabitants attend this exciting weekly event, and the usual harbourside fishing activity is much enlivened by chaotic quayside scenes. The Port also possesses an excellent, white shingle beach, with clean, clear seas and is, all in all, a great place to stay.

Just above Ag Georgios, at the beginning of the road to Megalo Chorio, is the island's Police station which doubles up as an 'Army camp', housing three soldiers. The young, friendly and very pleasant policeman 'trebles up' as the port policeman and customs official. As he boasts some broken English, he is a useful person for visitors to acquaint themselves with on arrival. Further up the same road is the island's generating station.

Although the pensions and tavernas are down in the bay, most bona fida village life takes place in Megalo Chorio. Here are the island school, the doctor's surgery (which doubles as a pharmacy), the main church, and the island's two general stores, which stock a limited, but very necessary variety of foodstuffs.

There are no banks nor a Post Office and nearly all supplies, including bread, have to be shipped in. The island's wells are no good for drinking water so, when the collected rainwater is used up, water has to be brought in from elsewhere. Goats and cows are grazed; there are wild rabbits and pigeons and figs are grown. Despite this rather basic lifestyle, one does not get the impression that life is unbearably tough on the islanders, who are friendly, helpful, hospitable and always eager to show off their island's delights. As an island map is difficult to acquire, it is fortuitous that the locals are only too happy to point enquirers in the right direction for walks to nearby beaches or ruined settlements. A few words of Greek are a great help.

The Chora, Patmos.

24 LIPSOS (Lipsi, Lipso, Lipsoi) **** Dodecanese Islands

FIRST IMPRESSIONS
Quiet; fishy; blue and white churches; sparklingly vivid town.

SPECIALITIES
Hand woven carpets.

RELIGIOUS HOLIDAYS & FESTIVALS
include: 24th August – Festival of the Madonna of Charos Chapel (when all the dried flowers in the building are supposed to spring to life).

VITAL STATISTICS
Tel prefix 0247. The island is about 9km long, and at the narrowest point, only 1km wide. The year-round population numbers about 650.

HISTORY
Inextricably linked to Patmos, the Monastery of which island owned Lipsos for some six hundred years from Byzantine times.

Some sources link the island with Calypso, seducer of Odysseus in the Odyssey, and the name certainly echoes the enchantress' name. On the other hand the experts plump for Gozo, adjacent to Malta – sorry Lipsos.

GENERAL
Lipsos is usually lumped in with the islets of Arki and Angathonisi as a day-trip possibility, at the end of a chapter on Patmos. In fact, although still very quiet from a tourist point of view, Lipsos is much more set on the road to development than either of the other two, and should be visited quickly if the recently increasing tourist activity is anything to go by.

LIPSOS (Lipsoi, Lipsi, Lipso): port & village (Illustration 42)
This small fishing town is really the only settlement on the island. It is very attractive on first sight, with a Cycladean type, large, blue domed church dominating the scene.

ARRIVAL BY FERRY
Arrival by ferry or trip boat will probably be at the Quay (*Tmr* 1B3) to the left (*Sbo*) of the village. The boats are met by a motley collection of jeeps and Datsun trucks, with wooden boards on top indicating the name of the beach to which they will ferry a passenger. Before leaping in, it is wise to note that only Katsadia Beach has any kind of facility (a taverna with **Rooms**). These vehicles form the island's only transport system.

The previous quay used for ferry-boats was the disproportionately large fishing boat quayside, further to the west. One really does wonder at the provision of street lighting and formal flower beds.

THE ACCOMMODATION & EATING OUT Lipsos has one hotel, the *Calypso* (Class D – tel 41242) (*Tmr* 2A/B2/3) which is very modern and pleasant, with en suite double rooms costing from 1500drs. There are a few 'away from it all' package tourists here but it isn't usually full, except in very high season. Well recommended and transacts foreign exchange.

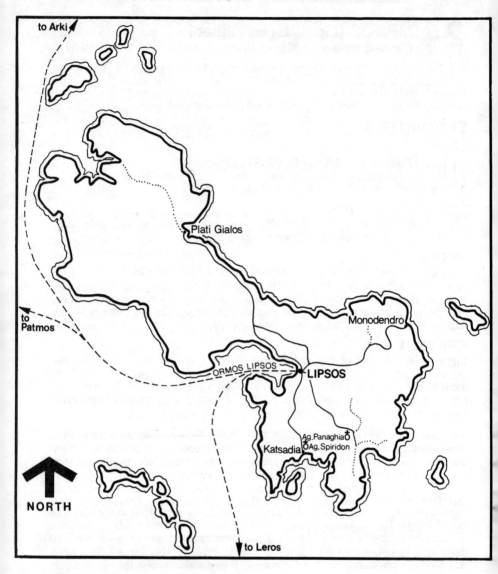

Illustration 41 Lipsos island

Less expensive, but more basic, accommodation is available at the *Pension* (*Tmr* 3A1/2), behind the *Calypso* or the excellently situated *Pension Flisvos* (*Tmr* 14D6) around the bay, as well as **Rooms** in one or two private homes.

A small selection of tavernas include the *Restaurant* in the ground floor of the *Hotel Calypso*, opposite the Ferry-boat Quay, a second *Taverna* (*Tmr* 5C/D2) and the *Fish Taverna* (*Tmr* 15D6), beside the *Pension Flisvos*. The latter two are only open during the height of season months. A more likely looking, reasonably priced establishment, *The Restoran* (*sic*), is to be located on the quayside road west from the *Hotel/Restaurant Calypso*, in the direction of the beach.

THE A TO Z OF USEFUL INFORMATION
BANKS None. *See* **Post Office, A To Z.**

BEACHES
Lendou Beach The nearest beach to the village is a five minute walk to the west of the *Hotel Calypso*. Follow the quayside as far as the *Restoran*, then cut across the dirt path to the track which runs parallel and one street back from the quay. This drops immediately to the beach. A large building proclaims *Rooms and Taverna*, but for some years, including 1987, it has provided neither!

Other island beaches include that at Monodendro, a forty minute walk north-east of the village, and the unofficial nudist beach; the beach at Katsadia (*See* **Route One**) and another at Plati Gialos. This latter is a good hour's walk away, but is long and sandy. The aforementioned Datsun trucks 'ferry' tourists about the island for reasonably good prices. (eg 200drs to Plati Gialos).

BICYCLE, SCOOTER & CAR HIRE None.

BREAD SHOPS None.

COMMERCIAL SHOPPING AREA None but there is one General Store (*Tmr* 12D4) where basic supplies can be purchased – and very little else.

FERRY-BOATS Similarly to Arki and Angathonisi, Lipsos has a very infrequent ferry service. The once weekly **FB Panormitis** is theoretically complemented by the **CF Kyklades**, but it is unwise to rely on this craft. However, the island is also linked, in summer, by at least two, if not three, daily excursion boats to and from Patmos. The **Anna Express** is the cheapest and fastest of these boats, taking approximately forty-five minutes, and costing 1000drs return. Other boats cost 1200drs. The girlfriend of the boat owner, Anna, comes from Nottingham and has spent the last three years on Lipsos.

Ferry-boat timetable (Mid-season)

Day	Departure time	Ferry-boat	Ports/Islands of Call
Tuesday	0430hrs	Panormitis	Patmos,Arki,Angathonisi, Pythagorion(Samos).
	1630hrs	Panormitis	Leros,Kalimnos,Kos,Nisiros, Tilos,Simi,Rhodes.

FERRY-BOAT TICKET OFFICES None, the tickets being purchased on the particular craft.

MEDICAL CARE The island doctor has a Clinic (*Tmr* 10E4), which doubles as a pharmacy, opposite the Church.

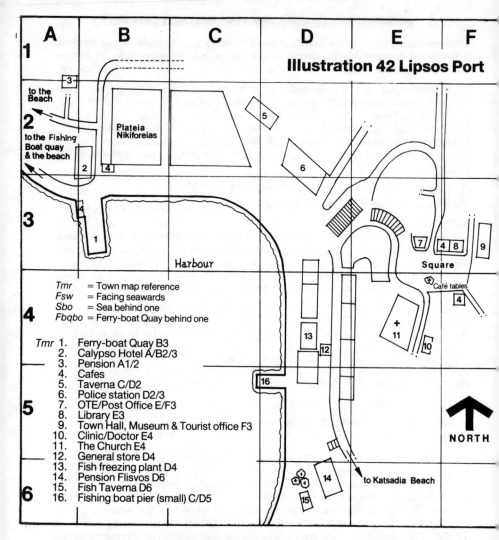

Illustration 42 Lipsos Port

to the Beach

to the Fishing Boat quay & the beach

Plateia Nikiforeias

Harbour

Square

Café tables

NORTH

to Katsadia Beach

Tmr = Town map reference
Fsw = Facing seawards
Sbo = Sea behind one
Fbqbo = Ferry-boat Quay behind one

Tmr 1. Ferry-boat Quay B3
2. Calypso Hotel A/B2/3
3. Pension A1/2
4. Cafes
5. Taverna C/D2
6. Police station D2/3
7. OTE/Post Office E/F3
8. Library E3
9. Town Hall, Museum & Tourist office F3
10. Clinic/Doctor E4
11. The Church E4
12. General store D4
13. Fish freezing plant D4
14. Pension Flisvos D6
15. Fish Taverna D6
16. Fishing boat pier (small) C/D5

NTOG There is an office giving out very limited information, which is run by the municipality and is housed in the ground floor of the Town Hall (*Tmr* 9F3), in the local Museum. Should the Museum and Tourist office be closed, pop up the external stairs to the Town Hall and demand attention!

OTE (*Tmr* 7E/F3). The office is housed in the same building as the Post Office. There are two international, metered telephones and the facility is open between 0800-1500hrs, weekdays only.

PLACES OF INTEREST

Museum This displays local finds from the ocean floor (encrusted vases and the like) and a rather odd collection of jars of water from various 'religious' locations (eg the Mount Athos peninsula) brought together by the village priest. Costumes from Lipsos and other nearby islands are also on show.

POLICE (*Tmr* 6D2/3) The Police station is a large square building at the bottom of the steps leading up to the Village Square. The one policeman is particularly unfriendly, unhelpful and unwilling to give away any kind of information. One has the impression that he dislikes all visitors, on sight. Best to head for the Town Hall (*Tmr* 9F3).

POST OFFICE (*Tmr* 7E/F3) On the edge of the Village Square. Transacts foreign exchange and is open weekdays between 0800-1500hrs.

TAXIS – *See* **Arrival by Ferry.**

TELEPHONE NUMBERS & ADDRESSES
Police (*Tmr* 6D2/3)   Tel 41222/41209

TOILETS There is a public toilet in the ground floor of the Town Hall (*Tmr* 9F3)

Excursion to Katsadia Beach
Rather than bump to Katsadia in a pick-up truck, it is much more rewarding to make the journey on foot. This is about a twenty-five minute walk through fertile countryside and over a hill, from whence the track drops down to the wide, picturesque bay with a narrow, golden sandy beach.

Rooms and food are provided by the extremely primitive *Antoni Gabieri's Rooms and Taverna*. This is run by a bumbling old man and his scolding, grumpy wife. Accommodation costs just 500drs for a double room, but there is no electricity and clients must draw their own water from the well. Food is tasty and inexpensive. A meal for one of pea soup, a beer, feta and a limon cost 340drs, including bread.

This is a pretty, idyllic little spot, but you won't be the only foreigners here as quite a few Greek island aficionados have already sought out Lipsos. Besides the jeeps, caiques run round here from the port in mid-summer.

The waterfront,
Pantelli, Leros.

INDEX

Artwork by:Jonathan Duval & Geoffrey O'Connell
Plans & maps by:Graham Bishop & Geoffrey O'Connell
Typeset by:Disc preparation by Willowbridge Publishers
Output by Unwin Bros.

Contents

Pronunciation

This section is designed to make you familiar with the sounds of Spanish using our simplified phonetic transcription. You'll find the pronunciation of the Spanish letters and sounds explained below, together with their "imitated" equivalents. This system is used throughout the phrase book: simply read the pronunciation as if it were English, noting any special rules below.

The Spanish language

There are almost 350 million speakers of Spanish worldwide – it is the third most widely spoken language after Chinese and English. These are the countries where you can expect to hear Spanish spoken (figures are approximate):

España Spain
Spanish is spoken by almost the entire population (40 million). Other languages: Catalan in north-eastern Spain (6m), Galician in northwestern Spain (3m) and Basque (almost 1m).

México Mexico
Spanish is spoken by most of the 98 million population. Other languages: 6 million speak Indian languages, esp. Nahuatl (1.5 m), Maya (1m) in Yucatán.

América del Sur South America
Spanish is spoken by the great majority in **Argentina** (34 million); **Bolivia** (less than half the 7.5m population), other languages: Quechua (2m), Aymara (1.5m); **Colombia** (35m), other: Arawak, Carib; **Ecuador** (11m), other: Quechua (0.5m); **Paraguay** - three quarters of the 5.5m population, other: Guarani (3m); **Peru** (24m) other: Quechua (5m), Aymara (0.5m); **Uruguay** (3.5m); **Venezuela** (22m), other: Arawak, Carib.

América Central Central America
Spanish is spoken in **Costa Rica** (3.5 million), **Cuba** (11m), **Dominican Republic** (8m); **Puerto Rico** (4m); **El Salvador** (6m); **Guatemala** (10m), other: Quiché (1m), Cakchiquel (0.5m); **Honduras** (5.5m), other: Lenca, Carib; **Nicaragua** (4m); **Panama** (3m).

Estados Unidos United States
Spanish is spoken by approx. 18 million people, especially in Texas, New Mexico, Arizona, California, southern Florida and New York City.

África Africa
Spanish is the official language of **Equatorial Guinea** (4.5m), other: Fang. Spanish is also spoken in the Spanish zone of **Morocco**.

The Spanish alphabet is the same as English, with the addition of the tilde on the letter **ñ**. The acute accent (´) indicates stress, not a change in sound.

Some Spanish words have been incorporated into English, for example **bonanza, canyon, patio, plaza, siesta**.

Until recently in Spanish, **ch** and **ll** were treated as separate letters, alphabetically ordered after **c** and **l** respectively. Look out for this when looking up old telephone directories or dictionaries.

There are some differences in vocabulary and pronunciation between the Spanish spoken in Spain and that in the Americas - although each is easily understood by the other. The *Berlitz Latin-American Spanish Phrase Book and Dictionary* is specifically geared to travelers in Spanish-speaking Americas.

Consonants

Letter	Approximate pronunciation	Symbol	Example	Pronunciation
f, k, l, m, n, p, t, x, y	as in English			
b	1. as in English	*b*	**bueno**	*bweno*
	2. between vowels as in English, but softer	*b*	**bebida**	be*bee*da
c	1. before **e** and **i**, like *th* in *thin*	*th*	**centro**	*thentro*
	2. otherwise like *k* in *kit*	*k*	**como**	*komo*
ch	as in English	*ch*	**mucho**	*moocho*
d	1. as in English *dog*, but less decisive	*d*	**donde**	*dondeh*
	2. between vowels and at the end of a word, like *th* in *this*	*th*	**usted**	oos*teth*
g	1. before **e** and **i**, like *ch* in Scottish lo*ch*	*kh*	**urgente**	oor*khenteh*
	2. otherwise, like *g* in get	*g*	**ninguno**	neen*goo*no
h	always silent		**hombre**	*ombreh*
j	like *ch* in Scottish lo*ch*	*kh*	**bajo**	*bakho*
ll	like *lli* in million	*l-y*	**lleno**	*l-yeno*
ñ	like *ni* in onion	*ñ*	**señor**	*señor*
qu	like *k* in kick	*k*	**quince**	*keentheh*
r	more strongly trilled (like a Scottish *r*), especially at the beginning of a word	*r*	**río**	*reeo*

7

Consonants (cont.)

rr	strongly trilled	*rr*	**arriba**	<u>*arr</u>eeba*
s	1. like *s* in *s*ame			
	2. before **b, d, g, l, m, n,**	*s*	**vista**	<u>*vees</u>ta*
	like *s* in ro*s*e	*z*	**mismo**	*mee<u>z</u>mo*
v	like *b* in *b*ad, but softer	*b*	**viejo**	*vee<u>y</u>ekho*
z	like *th* in *th*in	*th*	**brazo**	<u>*bra</u>tho*

Vowels

Letter	Approximate pronunciation	Symbol	Example	Pronunciation
a	in length, between *a* in English p*a*t, and *a* in English b*a*r	*a*	**gracias**	*gr<u>a</u>theeyas*
e	1. like *e* in g*e*t	*e*	**puedo**	*pw<u>e</u>do*
	2. in a syllable ending in a vowel like *e* in th*ey*	*eh*	**me**	*meh*
i	like *ee* in f*ee*t	*ee*	**sí**	*see*
o	like *o* in g*o*t	*o*	**dos**	*dos*
u	1. like *oo* in f*oo*d	*oo*	**una**	*oona*
	2. silent after **g** in words like **guerra, guiso,** except where marked **ü,** as in **antigüedad**			
y	only a vowel when alone or at the end of a word, like *ee* in f*ee*t	*ee*	**y**	*ee*

Note: to aid pronunciation the phonetic transcription uses **y** where applicable between groups of vowels to indicate the sound value of *y* in *y*es.

Stress

Stress has been indicated in the phonetic transcription:
<u>underlined</u> letters should be pronounced with more stress
(i.e. louder) than the others.

In words ending with a vowel, **-n** or **-s**, the next to last syllable
is stressed, e.g. **mañana** (*mañana*); in words ending in a consonant, the
last syllable is stressed, e.g. **señor** (*señor*); the acute accent (´) is used in
Spanish to indicate a syllable is stressed, e.g. **río** (*reeo*).

Some Spanish words have more than one meaning; the accent mark is
employed to distinguish between them, e.g.: **él** (he) and **el** (the); **sí** (yes)
and **si** (if); **tú** (you) and **tu** (your).

Pronunciation of the Spanish alphabet

A	*ah*		**Ñ**	*<u>en</u>yeh*
B	*beh*		**O**	*oh*
C	*theh*		**P**	*peh*
D	*deh*		**Q**	*koo*
E	*eh*		**R**	*<u>err</u>eh*
F	*<u>ehf</u>eh*		**S**	*<u>ehs</u>eh*
G	*kheh*		**T**	*teh*
H	*<u>ach</u>eh*		**U**	*oo*
I	*ee*		**V**	*<u>oob</u>eh*
J	*<u>khot</u>a*		**W**	*<u>dobl</u>eh beh*
K	*ka*		**X**	*<u>ekee</u>s*
L	*<u>ehl</u>eh*		**Y**	*ee gree<u>ye</u>ga*
M	*<u>em</u>eh*		**Z**	*<u>thet</u>a*
N	*<u>ayn</u>neh*			

Basic Expressions

ESSENTIAL

Yes./No.	**Sí.** *see* / **No.** *no*
Okay.	**De acuerdo.** *deh akwehrdo*
Please.	**Por favor.** *por fabor*
Thank you (very much).	**(Muchas) gracias.** *(moochas) gratheeyas*

Greetings/Apologies Saludos y disculpas

Hello./Hi!	**¡Hola!** *ola*
Good morning.	**Buenos días.** *bwenos deeyas*
Good afternoon/evening.	**Buenas tardes.** *bwenas tardes*
Good night.	**Buenas noches.** *bwenas noches*
Good-bye.	**Adiós.** *adyos*
Excuse me! (getting attention)	**¡Disculpe!** *deeskulpeh*
Excuse me. (may I get past?)	**Disculpe.** *deeskulpay*
Excuse me!/Sorry!	**¡Perdón!/¡Lo siento!** *perdon/lo seeyento*
It was an accident.	**Fue un accidente.** *fweh oon aktheedenteh*
Don't mention it.	**No hay de qué.** *no eye deh keh*
Never mind.	**No tiene importancia.** *no tyeneh eemportantheeya*

Communication difficulties
Dificultades a la hora de comunicarse

English	Spanish	Pronunciation
Do you speak English?	**¿Habla inglés?**	_abla eengles_
Does anyone here speak English?	**¿Hay alguien que hable inglés?**	_eye algeeyen keh ableh eengles_
I don't speak (much) Spanish.	**No hablo (mucho) español.**	_no ablo (moocho) español_
Could you speak more slowly?	**¿Podría hablar más despacio?**	_podreeya ablar mas despatheeyo_
Could you repeat that?	**¿Podría repetir eso?**	_podreeya repeteer eso_
Pardon?/Sorry, I didn't catch that.	**¿Cómo?/Lo siento, no entendí eso.**	_komo/lo seeyento, no entendee eso_
What was that?	**¿Qué ha dicho?**	_keh a deecho_
Could you spell it?	**¿Podría deletrearlo?**	_podreeya deletrayarlo_
Please write it down.	**Escríbamelo, por favor.**	_eskreebamelo por fabor_
Can you translate this for me?	**¿Podría traducirme esto?**	_podreeya tradootheermeh esto_
What does this/that mean?	**¿Qué significa esto/eso?**	_keh seegneefeeka esto/eso_
How do you pronounce that?	**¿Cómo se pronuncia eso?**	_komo se pronoontheeya eso_
Please point to the phrase in the book.	**Por favor señáleme la frase en el libro.**	_por fabor señalemeh la fraseh en el leebro_
I understand.	**Entiendo.**	_enteeyendo_
I don't understand.	**No entiendo.**	_no enteeyendo_
Do you understand?	**¿Entiende?**	_enteeyendeh_

> – Son ciento treinta y cinco pesetas.
> – No entiendo.
> – Son ciento treinta y cinco pesetas.
> – Escríbamelo, por favor...Ah.
> "One hundred and thirty five pesetas"
> ...Aquí tiene.

11

Questions Preguntas

GRAMMAR

Questions can be formed in Spanish:
1. by a questioning intonation; often the personal pronoun is left out, both in affirmative sentences and in questions:

Hablo español.	I speak Spanish.
¿Habla español?	Do you speak Spanish?

2. by using a question word (➤12-17) + the inverted order:

¿Cuándo llega el tren?	When does the train arrive?

Where? ¿Dónde?

Where is it?	**¿Dónde está?** _dondeh esta_
Where are you going?	**¿Dónde vas?** _dondeh bas_
at the meeting place/point	**en el punto de encuentro** en el _poonto_ deh en_kwentro_
away from me	**lejos de mí** _lekhos_ deh mee
from the U.S.	**de los Estados Unidos** deh los es_tados_ oo_nidos_
here	**aquí** a_kee_
in the car	**en el coche** en el _kocheh_
in Spain	**en España** en es_paña_
inside	**dentro** _dentro_
near the bank	**cerca del banco** _therka_ del _banko_
next to the apples	**al lado de las manzanas** al _lado_ deh las man_thanas_
opposite the market	**enfrente del mercado** en_frenteh_ del mer_kado_
there	**allí** al-_yee_
to the hotel	**al hotel** al o_tel_
on the left/right	**a la izquierda/derecha** a la eeth_keeyerda_/de_recha_
on the pavement	**en la acera** en la a_thera_
outside the café	**a la salida del café** a la sa_leeda_ del _kafeh_
up to the traffic lights	**hasta el semáforo** _asta_ el se_maforo_

When? ¿Cuándo?

When does the museum open?	**¿Cuándo abre el museo?** _kwando abray el moosayo_
When does the train arrive?	**¿Cuándo llega el tren?** _kwando l-yega el tren_
10 minutes ago	**hace diez minutos** _athay deeyeth meenootos_
after lunch	**después de comer** _despwes deh komer_
always	**siempre** _seeyempreh_
around midnight	**a eso de las doce de la noche** _a eso deh las dotheh deh la nocheh_
at 7 o'clock	**a las siete en punto** _a las seeyeteh en poonto_
before Friday	**antes del viernes** _antes del beeyernes_
by tomorrow	**para mañana** _para mañana_
every week	**todas las semanas/cada semana** _todas las semanas/kada semana_
for 2 hours	**durante dos horas** _dooranteh dos oras_
from 9 a.m. to 6 p.m.	**de nueve de la mañana a seis de la tarde** _deh nwebeh deh la mañana a says deh la tardeh_
in 20 minutes	**dentro de veinte minutos** _dentro deh beynteh meenootos_
never	**nunca** _noonka_
not yet	**todavía no** _todabeeya no_
now	**ahora** _a-ora_
often	**a menudo** _a menoodo_
on March 8	**el ocho de marzo** _el ocho de martho_
on weekdays	**durante la semana** _dooranteh la semana_
sometimes	**a veces** _a bethes_
soon	**pronto** _pronto_
then	**entonces/luego** _entonthes/looego_
within 2 days	**dentro de dos días** _dentroa deh dos deeyas_

What sort of …? ¿Qué tipo de …?

I'd like something …	**Quiero algo …** _keeyero algo_
It's …	**Es …** _es_
beautiful/ugly	**bonito/feo** _boneeto/fayo_
better/worse	**mejor/peor** _mekhor/peyor_
big/small	**grande/pequeño** _grandeh/pekeño_
cheap/expensive	**barato/caro** _barato/karo_
clean/dirty	**limpio/sucio** _leempeeo/sootheeo_
dark/light	**oscuro/claro** _oskooro/klaro_
delicious/revolting	**delicioso/asqueroso** _deleetheeyoso/askeroso_
early/late	**temprano/tarde** _temprano/tardeh_
easy/difficult	**fácil/difícil** _fatheel/deefeetheel_
empty/full	**vacío/lleno** _batheeyo/l-yeno_
good/bad	**bueno/malo** _bweno/malo_
heavy/light	**pesado/ligero** _pesado/likhehro_
hot, warm/cold	**caliente/frío** _kaleeyenteh/freeyo_
modern/old-fashioned	**moderno/antiguo** _moderno/anteegwoa_
narrow/wide	**estrecho/ancho** _estrecho/ancho_
next/last	**próximo/último** _prokseemo/oolteemo_
old/new	**viejo/nuevo** _beeyekho/nwebo_
open/shut	**abierto/cerrado** _abeeyerto/therrado_
pleasant, nice/unpleasant	**agradable/desagradable** _agradableh/desagradableh_
quick/slow	**rápido/lento** _rrapeedo/lento_
quiet/noisy	**silencioso/ruidoso** _seelentheeyoso/rrooeeydoso_
right/wrong	**bien/mal** _beeyen/mal_
tall/short	**alto/bajo** _alto/bakho_
thick/thin	**grueso/fino** _grooeso/feeno_
vacant/occupied	**libre/ocupado** _leebreh/okoopado_
young/old	**joven/viejo** _khoben/beeyekho_

Nouns in Spanish are either masculine or feminine and the adjectival endings change accordingly. See page 169 for more explanation.

How much/many? ¿Cuánto/Cuántos?

How much is that?	**¿Cuánto es?** _kwanto es_
How many are there?	**¿Cuántos hay?** _kwantos eye_
1/2/3	**uno/dos/tres** _oono/dos/tres_
4/5	**cuatro/cinco** _kwatro/theenko_
none	**ninguno** _neengoono_
about 100 pesetas	**unas 100 pesetas** _oonas theeyen pesetas_
a little	**un poco** _oon poko_
a lot of traffic	**mucho tráfico** _moocho trafeeko_
enough	**bastante** _bastanteh_
few/a few of them	**pocos(-as)** _pokos(-as)_
a few of them	**unos(-as) pocos(-as)** _oonos(-as) pokos(-as)_
many people	**mucha gente** _moocha khenteh_
more than that	**más que eso** _mas keh eso_
less than that	**menos que eso** _menos keh eso_
much more	**mucho más** _moocho mas_
nothing else	**nada más** _nada mas_
too much	**demasiado** _demaseeyado_

Why? ¿Por qué?

Why is that?	**¿Por qué?** _por keh_
Why not?	**¿Por qué no?** _por keh no_
because of the weather	**por el tiempo** _por el teeyempo_
because I'm in a hurry	**porque tengo prisa** _porkeh tengo preesa_
I don't know why	**No sé por qué** _no seh por keh_

Who?/Which? ¿Quién?/¿Cuál?

Which one do you want?	¿Cuál quiere? *kwal keeyereh*
Who is it for?	¿Para quién es? *para keeyen es*
either … or …	o … o … *o… o …*
her/him	ella/él *el-ya/el*
me	mí *mee*
you	ti *tee*
them	ellos *el-yos*
none	ninguno *neengoono*
no one	nadie *nadeeay*
not that one	ése no *eseh no*
one like that	uno como ése *oono komo eseh*
someone/something	alguien/algo *algeeyen/algo*
that one/this one	ése/éste *eseh/esteh*

Whose? ¿De quién(es)?

Whose is that?	¿De quién es eso? *deh keeyehn es eso*
It's … mine/ours	Es … mío/nuestro *es meeyo/nwestro*
yours	suyo/tuyo/vuestro *sooyo/tooyo/bwestro*
his/hers/theirs	suyo *sooyo*
It's … turn.	Es … turno. *es …toorno*
my/our	mi/nuestro *mee/nwestro*
your	su/tu/vuestro *soo/too/bwestro*
his/her/their	su *soo*

GRAMMAR

Possessive adjectives agree in number and gender with the noun they modify, i.e. with the thing possessed and not the possessor.

	singular	*plural*
my	mi	mis
your (fam. sing.)	tu	tus
your (polite form)	su	sus
his/hers/its	su	sus
our	nuestro(-a)	nuestros(-as)
your (fam. plur.)	vuestro(-a)	vuestros(-as)
their	su	sus

How? ¿Cómo?

How would you like to pay?	**¿Cómo le gustaría pagar?** *komo le goostareeya pagar*
How are you getting here?	**¿Cómo va a venir aquí?** *komo ba a beneer akee*
by car	**en coche** *en kocheh*
by credit card	**con tarjeta de crédito** *kon tarkheta deh kredeeto*
by chance	**por casualidad** *por kasooalidath*
equally	**igualmente** *eegwalmenteh*
extremely	**sumamente** *soomamenteh*
on foot	**a pie** *a peeyeh*
quickly	**rápidamente** *rapeedamenteh*
slowly	**despacio** *despatheeyo*
too fast	**demasiado deprisa** *demaseeyado depreesa*
totally	**totalmente** *totalmenteh*
very	**muy** *mwee*
with a friend	**con un(a) amigo/a** *kon un(a) ameego/a*
without a passport	**sin pasaporte** *seen pasaporteh*

Is it ...?/Are there ...? ¿Es/está?/¿Hay ...?

Is it ...?	**¿Es/está ...?** *es/esta*
Is it free? (of charge)	**¿Es gratis?** *es gratees*
It isn't ready.	**No está listo.** *no esta leesto*
Is/are there ...?	**¿Hay ...?** *eye*
Is there a bus into town?	**¿Hay un autobús para ir a la ciudad?** *eye oon aootoboos para eer a la theeoodath*
There are showers in the rooms.	**Hay duchas en las habitaciones.** *eye doochas en las abeetatheeyones*
Here it is/they are.	**Aquí tiene/los tiene.** *akee teeyeneh/los teeyeneh*
There it is/they are.	**Ahí está/están.** *ahee esta/estan*

Can/May? ¿Puedo?

Can I have …?	**¿Puedo tomar …?** *pwedo tomar*
Can we have …?	**¿Podemos tomar …?** *podemos tomar*
Can you show me …?	**¿Puede enseñarme …?** *pwedeh enseñarmeh*
Can you tell me?	**¿Puede decirme?** *pwedeh detheermeh*
Can you help me?	**¿Puede ayudarme?** *pwedeh ayoodarmeh*
Can I help you?	**¿Puedo ayudarle?** *pwedo ayoodarleh*
Can you direct me to …?	**¿Puede indicarme cómo ir a …?** *pwede eendeekarmeh komo eer a*
I can't.	**No puedo.** *no pwedo*

What do you want? ¿Qué quiere?

I'd like …	**Quiero …** *keeyero*
Could I have …?	**¿Podría tomar …?** *podreeya tomar*
We'd like …	**Queremos …** *keremos*
Give me …	**Déme …** *demeh*
I'm looking for …	**Estoy buscando …** *estoy booskando*
I need to …	**Necesito …** *netheseeto*
go …	**ir …** *eer*
find …	**encontrar . . .** *enkontrar*
see …	**ver …** *behr*
speak to …	**hablar …** *ablar*

– Disculpe.
– ¿Sí?
– ¿Puedo?
– Sí, por supuesto.
– Gracias.
– De nada.

Other useful words
Otras palabras útiles

fortunately	**afortunadamente** *afortoonada<u>men</u>teh*
hopefully	**con algo de suerte** *kon <u>al</u>go deh <u>swer</u>teh*
of course	**por supuesto** *por soo<u>pwes</u>to*
perhaps	**quizá** *kee<u>tha</u>*
unfortunately	**desgraciadamente** *desgratheeyada<u>men</u>teh*
also	**también** *tambee<u>yen</u>*
and	**y** *ee*
but	**pero** *<u>pero</u>*
or	**o** *o*

Exclamations Exclamaciones

And so on.	**Etcétera, etcétera.** *et<u>the</u>tera et<u>the</u>tera*
At last!	**¡Por fin!** *por feen*
Carry on.	**Continúa.** *kontee<u>noo</u>a*
Nonsense.	**Tonterías.** *tonte<u>ree</u>yas*
Quite right too!	**¡Puedes estar seguro(-a)!** *<u>pwe</u>des es<u>tar</u> se<u>goo</u>ro(-a)*
You're joking!	**¡No me digas!** *no meh <u>dee</u>gas*
How are things?	**¿Cómo te va?** *<u>ko</u>mo teh ba*
great/brilliant	**estupendamente** *estoopenda<u>men</u>teh*
great	**muy bien** *mwee bee<u>yen</u>*
fine/okay	**bien** *bee<u>yen</u>*
not bad	**no demasiado mal** *no dema<u>seeya</u>do mal*
not good	**no muy bien** *no mwee bee<u>yen</u>*
fairly bad	**bastante mal** *bas<u>tan</u>teh mal*
terrible	**fatal** *fa<u>tal</u>*

Accommodations

All types of accommodation, from hotels to campsites, can be found through the tourist information center (**Oficina de turismo**).

Early reservation is essential in most major tourist centers, especially during high season or special events. If you haven't booked, you're more likely to find accommodations available outside towns and city centers.

Hotel *otel*
There are five official categories of hotels: luxury, first class A, first class B, second class and third class. There may be price variations within any given category, depending on the location and the facilities offered. There are also, of course, plenty of unclassified hotels where you will find clean, simple accommodations and good food.

Refugio *refookhyo*
Small inns in remote and mountainous regions. They are often closed in winter.

Albergue de juventud *albergeh deh khoobentooth*
Youth hostel. There is usually no age limit; become a member and your **carnet de alberguista** will entitle you to a discount. There isn't an extensive network in Spain, but **casas de huéspedes (CH)** and **fondas (F)** provide budget-conscious alternatives.

Apartamento amueblado *apartamento amweblado*
A furnished apartment (flat) mainly in resorts. Available from specialized travel agents or directly from the landlord (look for the sign **se alquila** – to let, for rent).

Hostal *ostal*
Modest hotels, often family concerns, graded one to three stars; denoted by the sign **Hs**.

Parador *parador*
Palaces, country houses or castles that have been converted into hotels and are under government supervision. Their aim is to provide the chance to experience "the real Spain." The central reservation agency is **Paradores de España** ☎ 435 97 00.

Pensión *pensyon*
Boardinghouses, graded one to three stars; denoted by the sign **P**.

Reservations/Booking Reservas

In advance Con antelación

Can you recommend a
hotel in …?

**¿Puede recomendarme un
hotel en …?** _pwede
rekomen<u>dar</u> (meh/nos) oon o<u>tel</u> en

Is it near the center (of town)?

¿Está cerca del centro (de la ciudad)?
esta <u>ther</u>ka del <u>then</u>tro (deh la theeyoo<u>dath</u>)

How much is it per night?

¿Cuánto cuesta por noche?
<u>kwan</u>to <u>kwes</u>ta por <u>no</u>cheh

Is there anything cheaper?

¿Hay algo más barato?
eye <u>al</u>go mas ba<u>ra</u>to

Could you reserve/book me a
room there, please?

**¿Podría reservarme una habitación allí
por favor?** po<u>dree</u>a reser<u>bar</u>meh <u>oo</u>na
abeetatheeyon al-<u>yee</u> por fa<u>bor</u>

How do I get there?

¿Cómo llego allí? <u>ko</u>mo l-<u>yego</u> al-<u>yee</u>

At the hotel En el hotel

Do you have any vacancies?

¿Tienen habitaciones libres?
teeyenen abeetatheeyones <u>lee</u>bres

I'm sorry, we're full.

Lo siento, está todo ocupado.
lo see<u>yen</u>to, esta <u>to</u>do oku<u>pa</u>do

Is there another hotel nearby?

¿Hay otro hotel por aquí cerca?
eye <u>o</u>tro otel por a<u>kee</u> <u>ther</u>ka

I'd like a single/double room.

Quiero una habitación individual/doble.
kee<u>yero</u> <u>oo</u>na abeetatheeyon
eendeebeedoo<u>al</u>/<u>do</u>bleh

A room with …

Una habitación con …
<u>oo</u>na abeetatheeyon kon …

twin beds

dos camas dos <u>ka</u>mas

a double bed

una cama de matrimonio
<u>oo</u>na <u>ka</u>ma deh matree<u>mo</u>neeyo

a bath/shower

un baño/una ducha
oon <u>ba</u>ño/<u>oo</u>na <u>doo</u>cha

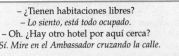

– ¿Tienen habitaciones libres?
– Lo siento, está todo ocupado.
– Oh. ¿Hay otro hotel por aquí cerca?
– Sí. Mire en el Ambassador cruzando la calle.

Reception Recepción

I have a reservation. **Tengo una reserva. Me llamo ...**
My name is ... *tengo oona reserba. meh l-yamo*

We've reserved a **Hemos reservado una habitación doble**
double and a single **y una individual.**
room. *emos reserbado oona abeetatheeyon dobleh ee oona eendeebeedooal*

I confirmed my reservation **Confirmé mi reserva por carta.**
by mail. *konfeermeh mee reserba por karta*

Could we have adjoining **¿Nos podrían dar habitaciones**
rooms? **conjuntas?** *nos podreeyan dar abeetatheeyones konkhoontas*

Amenities and facilities Diversión e instalaciones

Is there ... in the room? **¿Hay ... en la habitación?**
eye ... en la abeetatheeyon

air conditioning **aire acondicionado** *ayray akondeethyonado*
TV/telephone **televisión/teléfono** *telebeeseeyon/telefono*
Does the hotel have (a)...? **¿Tiene el hotel ...?**
teeyeneh el otel

fax facilities **fax** *fax*
laundry service **servicio de lavandería**
serbeetheeyo deh labandereeya

satellite TV **antena parabólica**
antena paraboleeka

sauna **sauna** *saoona*
swimming pool **piscina** *peestheena*
Could you put ... in the room? **¿Podrían poner ... en la habitación?**
podreean poner ... en la abeetatheeyon

an extra bed **otra cama** *otra kama*
a crib/child's cot **una cuna** *oona koona*
Do you have facilities for **¿Tienen instalaciones para los**
the disabled? **minusválidos?**
teeyenen eenstalatheeyones para los meenusbaleedos

children **los niños** *los neeños*

22

How long ...? ¿Cuánto tiempo ...?

We'll be staying ...	**Nos quedaremos ...** *nos kedaremos ...*
overnight only	**sólo esta noche** *solo esta nocheh*
a few days	**unos días** *oonos deeyas*
a week (at least)	**una semana (por lo menos)** *oona semana (por lo menos)*
I'd like to stay an extra night.	**Quiero quedarme una noche más.** *keeyero kedarmeh oona nocheh mas*

– Tengo una reserva. Me llamo John Newton.
– Ah, hola Sr. Newton. Vamos a ver. Una habitación individual.
    – ¿Cuánto tiempo se queda?
– He reservado para dos noches,
    pero quiero quedarme otra noche.
– Muy bien. Firme aquí, por favor ...
    y aquí tiene la llave de su habitación.

¿Puedo ver su pasaporte, por favor?	May I see your passport, please?
Rellene este formulario/ firme aquí, por favor.	Please fill in this form/ sign here.
¿Cuál es su número de matrícula?	What is your car registration number?

DESAYUNO INCLUIDO	breakfast included
SE DAN COMIDAS	meals available
SÓLO LA HABITACIÓN ... PESETAS	room only ... pesetas
NOMBRE	name/first name
DOMICILIO/CALLE/NÚMERO	home address/ street/number
NACIONALIDAD/PROFESIÓN	nationality/profession
FECHA/LUGAR DE NACIMIENTO	date/place of birth
NÚMERO DE PASAPORTE	passport number
NÚMERO DE MATRÍCULA	car registration number
LUGAR/FECHA	place/date
FIRMA	signature

23

Price Precio

How much is it …?	**¿Cuánto es …?** *kwanto es*
per night/week	**por noche/semana** *por nocheh/semana*
for bed and breakfast	**por desayuno y habitación** *por desayoono ee abeetatheeyon*
excluding meals	**excluyendo las comidas** *exklooyendo las komeedas*
for full board (American Plan [A.P.])	**por pensión completa** *por penseeyon kompleta*
for half board (Modified American Plan [M.A.P.])	**por media pensión** *por medeeya penseeyon*
Does the price include …?	**¿Incluye el precio …?** *eenklooyeh el pretheeo*
breakfast	**el desayuno** *el desayoono*
service	**el servicio** *el serbeetheeo*
VAT	**IVA** *eeba*
Do I have to pay a deposit?	**¿Tengo que pagar una señal/una fianza?** *tengo keh pagar oona señal/oona feeantha*
Is there a discount for children?	**¿Hay un descuento para los niños?** *eye oon deskwento para los neeños*

Decision La decisión

May I see the room?	**¿Puedo ver la habitación?** *pwedo behr la abeetatheeyon*
That's fine. I'll take it.	**Está bien. Me la quedo.** *esta beeyen. meh la kedo*
It's too …	**Es demasiado …** *es demaseeyado*
dark/small	**oscura/pequeña** *oskoora/pekeña*
noisy	**ruidosa** *rooeedosa*
Do you have anything …?	**¿Tiene algo …?** *teeyeneh algo*
bigger/cheaper	**más grande/más barato** *mas grandeh/mas barato*
quieter/warmer	**más tranquilo/menos frío** *mas trankeelo/menos freeyo*
No, I won't take it.	**No, no me quedo con ella.** *no, no meh kedo kon el-ya*

Problems Problemas

The ... doesn't work.	**... no funciona.** *no foontheeyona*
air conditioning	**el aire acondicionado** *el ayreh akondeetheeyonado*
fan	**el ventilador** *el benteelador*
heating	**la calefacción** *la kalefaktheeyon*
light	**la luz** *la looth*
I can't turn the heat/ heating on/off.	**No puedo encender/apagar la calefacción.** *no pwedo enthender/ apagar la kalefaktheeyon*
There is no hot water/ toilet paper.	**No hay agua caliente/papel higiénico.** *no eye agwa kaleeyenteh/papel eekheeyeneeko*
The faucet/tap is dripping.	**El grifo gotea.** *el greefo goteya*
The sink/toilet is blocked.	**El lavabo/wáter está atascado.** *el lababo/bater esta ataskado*
The window/door is jammed.	**La ventana/puerta está atascada.** *la bentana/pwerta esta ataskada*
My room has not been made up.	**No han hecho la habitación.** *no an echo la abeetatheeyon*
The ... is broken.	**... está roto(-a).** *... esta roto(-a)*
blind/shutter	**la persiana** *la perseeyana*
lamp	**la lámpara** *la lampara*
lock	**el pestillo** *el pesteel-yo*
There are insects in our room.	**Hay insectos en nuestra habitación.** *eye eensektos en nwestra abeetatheeyon*

Action Acción

Could you have that seen to?	**¿Podrían encargarse de eso?** *podreeyan enkargarseh deh eso*
I'd like to move to another room.	**Quiero mudarme a otra habitación.** *keeyero moodarmeh a otra abeetatheeyon*
I'd like to speak to the manager.	**Quiero hablar con el administrador.** *keeyero ablar kon el admeeneestrador*

Requirements Exigencias

The 220-volt, 50-cycle AC is the norm throughout Spain. If you bring your own electrical appliances, buy a Continental adapter plug (round pins, not square) before leaving home. You may also need a transformer appropriate to the wattage of the appliance.

About the hotel Sobre el hotel

Where's the …?	**¿Dónde está …?** _dondeh esta_
bar	**el bar** _el bar_
bathroom	**el cuarto de baño** _el kwarto deh baño_
bathroom/toilet	**el servicio** _el serbeetheeyo_
dining room	**el comedor** _el komedor_
elevator	**el ascensor** _el asthensor_
parking lot/car park	**el aparcamiento** _el aparkameeyento_
shower	**la ducha** _la doocha_
swimming pool	**la piscina** _la peestheena_
tour operator's bulletin board	**el tablón de anuncios del operador turístico** _el tablon deh anoontheeyos del operador tooreesteeko_
Does the hotel have a garage?	**¿Tiene garaje el hotel?** _teeyeneh garakheh el otel_
Can I use this adaptor here?	**¿Puedo utilizar este adaptador aquí?** _pwedo ooteeleethar esteh adaptador akee_

MARQUE …	dial …
PARA HABLAR CON RECEPCIÓN	for reception
MARQUE …	dial …
PARA UNA LÍNEA EXTERIOR	for an outside line
NO MOLESTAR	do not disturb
PROHIBIDO COMER EN LA HABITACIÓN	no food in the room
PUERTA DE INCENDIOS	fire door
SALIDA DE EMERGENCIA	emergency exit
SÓLO PARA UTILIZAR MÁQUINAS DE AFEITAR	shavers only

Personal needs Necesidades personales

The key to room …, please.	**La llave de la habitación …, por favor.** *la l-yabeh dehla abeetatheeyon … por fabor*
I've lost my key.	**He perdido la llave.** *eh perdeedo la l-yabeh*
I've locked myself out of my room.	**No puedo entrar en mi habitación.** *no pwedo entrar en mee abeetatheeyon*
Could you wake me at …?	**¿Podría despertarme a las/la …?** *podreeya despertarmeh a las/la …*
I'd like breakfast in my room.	**Quiero que me traigan el desayuno a la habitación.** *keeyero keh meh traygan el desayoono a la abeetatheeyon*
Can I leave this in the safe?	**¿Puedo dejar esto en la caja fuerte?** *pwedo dekhar esto en la kakha fwerteh*
Could I have my things from the safe?	**¿Podría darme mis cosas de la caja fuerte?** *podreeya darme mees kosas de la kakha fwerteh*
Where can I find …?	**¿Dónde puedo encontrar a …?** *dondeh pwedo enkontrar a…*
maid	**la chica del servicio** *la cheeka del serbeethyo*
our tour representative	**nuestro representante turístico** *nwestro representanteh tooreestiko*
May I have …?	**¿Pueden darme …?** *pweden darmeh*
bath towel	**una toalla de baño** *oona toayl-ya deh baño*
blanket	**la manta** *la manta*
hangers	**perchas** *perchas*
pillow	**almohada** *almoada*
soap	**jabón** *khabon*
May I have …? (to drink/eat)	**¿Puedo tomar …?** *pwedo tomar …*
Is there any mail for me?	**¿Hay correo para mí?** *eye korreho para mee*
Are there any messages for me?	**¿Hay algún mensaje para mí?** *eye algoon mensakheh para mee*

BREAKFAST ➤ 43; CHANGING MONEY ➤ 138

Renting
Alquilar

We've reserved an apartment.	**Hemos reservado un apartamento.** _emos reserbado oon apartamento_
in the name of …	**a nombre de …** _a nombreh deh_
Where do we pick up the keys?	**¿Dónde recogemos las llaves?** _dondeh rekokhemos las l-yabes_
Where is the…?	**¿Dónde está …?** _dondeh esta_
electricity meter	**el contador de la luz** _el kontador deh la looth_
fuse box	**la caja de fusibles** _la kakha deh fooseebles_
valve	**la llave de paso** _la l-yabeh deh paso_
water heater	**el calentador** _el kalentador_
Are there any spare …?	**¿Hay … de repuesto …?** _eye … deh repwesto_
gas bottles/fuses	**bombonas de gas butano/fusibles** _bombonas deh gas bootano/fooseebles_
sheets	**sábanas** _sabanas_
Which day does the cleaner come?	**¿Qué día viene la limpiadora?** _keh deeya beeyeneh la leempeeadora_
When do I put out the trash/rubbish?	**¿Cuándo hay que sacar la basura?** _kwando eye keh sakar la basoora_

Problems? ¿Algún problema?

Where can I contact you?	**¿Dónde me puedo poner en contacto con usted?** _dondeh meh pwedo poner en kontakto kon oosteth_
How does the stove/cooker/ water heater work?	**¿Cómo funciona la cocina/el calentador?** _komo foontheeyona la kotheena/el kalentador_
The … is/are dirty.	**… está/están sucios.** _esta/estan sootheeyos_
The … has broken down.	**… se ha estropeado.** _seh a estropeyado_
We have accidentally broken/lost …	**Hemos roto/perdido … sin querer.** _emos roto/perdeedo … seen kerer_
That was already damaged when we arrived.	**Eso ya estaba estropeado cuando llegamos.** _eso ya estaba estropeado kwando l-yegamos_

Useful terms Expresiones útiles

boiler
el calentador/la caldera
el kalentador/la kaldehra

crockery
la vajilla *la bakheel-ya*

cutlery
los cubiertos *los koobeeyertos*

freezer
el congelador *el konkhelador*

frying pan
la sartén *la sarten*

kettle
la hervidora eléctrica *la erbeedora elektreeka*

lamp
la lámpara *la lampara*

refrigerator
el frigorífico *el freegoreefeeko*

saucepan
el cazo *el katho*

stove/cooker
la cocina *la kotheena*

washing machine
la lavadora *la labadora*

Rooms Habitaciones

balcony
el balcón *el balkon*

bathroom
el cuarto de baño *el kwarto deh baño*

bedroom
el dormitorio *el dormeetoreeyo*

dining room
el comedor *el komedor*

kitchen
la cocina *la kotheena*

living room
el salón/la sala de estar
el salon/la sala deh estar

toilet
el servicio *el serbeetheeyo*

Youth hostel El albergue juvenil

Youth hostels in Spain are few and far between, though a list is available from the Spanish National Tourist Office.

Do you have any places left for tonight?
¿Tiene alguna habitación libre para esta noche? *teeyeneh algoona abeetatheeyon leebreh para esta nocheh*

Do you rent/hire out bedding?
¿Alquilan ropa de cama? *alkeelan ropa deh kama*

What time are the doors locked?
¿A qué hora cierran las puertas? *a keh ora theeyeran las pwertas*

I have an International Student Card.
Tengo el carnet internacional de estudiante. *tengo el karnet eenternatheeyonal deh estoodeeanteh*

REQUIREMENTS ➤ 26; *CAMPING* ➤ 30

Camping De acampada

Spanish campgrounds are categorized luxury, 1st, 2nd or 3rd class. Facilities vary, but all have toilets, showers, drinking water and 24-hour surveillance. For a complete list of camp sites, facilities and rates contact any Spanish National Tourist Office.

Reservations Reservas

Is there a camp site near here?	**¿Hay un cámping cerca de aquí?** eye oon _kampeen_ _therka_ deh a_kee_
Do you have space for a tent/trailer/caravan?	**¿Tienen una parcela para una tienda/ roulotte?** tee_ye_nen _oona_ par_the_la _para_ _oona_ tee_ye_nda/roo_lot_
What is the charge ...?	**¿Cuánto cobran ...?** _kwan_to _kob_ran
per day/week	**por día/semana** por _dee_ya/se_ma_na
for a tent/a car	**por tienda/por coche** por tee_ye_nda/por _ko_cheh
for a trailer/caravan	**por roulotte** por roo_lot_

Facilities Instalaciones

Are there cooking facilities on site?	**¿Tienen instalaciones para cocinar en el recinto?** tee_ye_nen eenstalatee_ye_ones _para_ ko_thee_nar en el re_theen_to
Are there any electric outlets/ power points?	**¿Hay tomas de tierra?** eye _to_mas deh tee_ye_rra
Where is/are the ...?	**¿Dónde está/están ...?** _don_deh esta/es_tan_
drinking water	**el agua potable** el _ag_wa po_ta_bleh
trash cans	**las papeleras** las pape_le_ras
laundry facilities	**el servicio de lavandería** el ser_bee_theeyo deh laband_ere_eya
showers	**las duchas** las _doo_chas
Where can I get some butane gas?	**¿Dónde puedo comprar gas butano?** _don_deh _pwe_do kom_prar_ gas boo_ta_no

AGUA POTABLE	drinking water
PROHIBIDO ACAMPAR	no camping
PROHIBIDO HACER HOGUERAS/ BARBACOAS	no fires/barbecues

Complaints Quejas

It's too sunny here.
Hay demasiado sol aquí.
eye demaseeyado sol akee

It's too shady/crowded here.
Hay demasiada sombra/ gente aquí. *eye demaseeyada sombra/khenteh akee*

The ground's too hard/uneven.
El suelo está demasiado duro/ desnivelado. *el swelo esta demaseeyado dooro/desneebelado*

Do you have a more level spot?
¿Tiene una parcela más nivelada? *teeyeneh oona parthela mas neebelada*

You can't camp here.
No puede acampar aquí. *no pwedeh akampar akee*

Camping equipment Equipo de acampada

butane gas	**el gas butano** *el gas bootano*
campbed	**la cama de cámping** *la kama deh kampeen*
charcoal	**el carbón** *el karbon*
flashlight	**la linterna** *la leenterna*
groundcloth	**el aislante para el suelo** *el ayslanteh para el swelo*
rope	**la cuerda tensora** *la kwerda tensora*
hammer	**el martillo** *el marteel-yo*
mallet	**el mazo** *el matho*
matches	**las cerillas** *las thereel-yas*
(air) mattress	**el colchón (inflable)** *el kolchon (eenflableh)*
paraffin	**la parafina** *la parafeena*
kerosene stove	**el hornillo de queroseno** *el orneel-yo deh keroseno*
knapsack	**la mochila** *la mocheela*
sleeping bag	**el saco de dormir** *el sako deh dormeer*
tent	**la tienda** *la teeyenda*
tent pegs	**las estacas** *las estakas*
tent pole	**el mástil** *el masteel*

Checking out Salida

What time do we need to vacate the room?	**¿A qué hora tenemos que desocupar la habitación?** *a keh ora tenemos keh desokoopar la abeetatheeyon*
Could we leave our baggage/luggage here until …?	**¿Podríamos dejar nuestro equipaje aquí hasta las …?** *podreeyamos dekhar nwestro ekeepakheh akee asta las …*
I'm leaving now.	**Me voy ahora.** *meh boy a-ora*
Could you order me a taxi, please?	**¿Me podría pedir un taxi, por favor?** *meh podreeya pedeer oon taksee por fabor*
I/We've had a very enjoyable stay.	**He/Hemos disfrutado mucho nuestra estancia.** *eh/emos deesfrootado moocho nwestra estantheeya*

Paying Pagar

May I have my bill, please?	**¿Me da la cuenta, por favor?** *meh da la kwenta, por fabor*
How much is my telephone bill?	**¿Cuánto es la cuenta de teléfono?** *kwanto es la kwenta deh telefono*
I think there's a mistake in this bill.	**Creo que hay un error en esta cuenta.** *krayo keh eye oon error en esta kwenta*
I've made … telephone calls.	**He hecho … llamadas.** *eh echo … l-yamadas*
I've taken … from the mini-bar.	**He tomado … del minibar.** *eh tomado … del meeneebar*
Can I have an itemized bill?	**¿Pueden darme una cuenta detallada?** *pweden darmeh oona kwenta detal-yada*
Could I have a receipt?	**¿Podría darme un recibo?** *podreeya darmeh oon retheebo*

Tipping: a service charge is generally included in hotel and restaurant bills. However, if the service has been particularly good, you may want to leave an extra tip. The following chart is a guide:

	Suggested tip
Porter	100 Ptas.
Hotel maid, for extra services	100-200 Ptas.
Waiter	10% up to 1000 Ptas. then 5%

Eating Out

Restaurants

Bar *bar*
Bar; drinks and tapas served, sometimes hot beverages too.

Café *kafeh*
Cafés can be found on virtually every street corner. An indispensable part of everyday life, the café is where people get together for a chat over a coffee, soft drink or glass of wine.

Cafetería *kafetereeya*
Coffee shop; there's counter service or – for a few pesetas more – you can choose – a table. Fast food is generally served and the set menu is often very good.

Casa de comidas *kassa deh komeedass*
Simple inn serving cheap meals.

Heladería *eladereeya*
Ice-cream parlor

Merendero *merendero*
Cheap open-air bar; you can usually eat outdoors.

Parador *parador*
A government-supervised establishment located in a historic castle, palace or former monastery. A parador is usually noted for excellent regional dishes served in a dining room with handsome Spanish decor.

Venta *benta*
Restaurant; often specializing in regional cooking.

Pastelería/Confitería *pastelereeya/konfeetereeya*
Pastry shop; some serve coffee, tea and drinks.

Posada *possada*
A humble version of a fonda; the food is usually simple but good.

Refugio *refookhyo*
Mountain lodge serving simple meals.

Restaurante *restowranteh*
Restaurant; these are classified by the government but the official rating has more to do with the decor than with the quality of cooking.

Salón de té *salon deh teh*
Tearoom; an upmarket cafeteria.

Taberna *taberna*
Similar to an English pub or American tavern in atmosphere; always a variety of tapas on hand as well as other snacks.

Tasca *taska*
Similar to a bar; drinks and tapas are served at the counter; standing only.

Meal times Horas de comida

el desayuno *el dessayoono*
Breakfast: generally served from 7 to 10 a.m.. Traditionally just toast or a roll and coffee; hotels are now offering more filling fare for tourists, serving a buffet breakfast ➤43.

el almuerzo *el almwertho*
Lunch is generally served from around 2 or 3 p.m. The Spaniards like to linger over a meal, so service may seem on the leisurely side. In a hurry, go for fast-food outlets, pizzerias or cafés ➤40.

la cena *la theyna*
Dinner is usually served far later than at home, from 8.30 p.m. (10 p.m. in Madrid) to 11 p.m. However, in tourist areas you can get a meal at most places just about any time of day.

Spanish cuisine Cocina española

The variety of Spanish cuisine comes from Celtic, Roman, Arab and New World influences, together with the profusion of Atlantic and Mediterranean seafood.

Most restaurants will offer a good value daily special (**menú del día**) – usually a three-course meal with house wine at a set price. Service and taxes are always included in the price.

A table for ..., please.	**Una mesa para ..., por favor.**
	oona mesa para ..., por fabor
1/2/3/4	**uno/dos/tres/cuatro**
	oono/dos/tres/kwatro
Thank you.	**Gracias.** *gratheeyas*
I'd like to pay.	**Quiero pagar.** *keeyero pagar*

Finding a place to eat
Encontrar un sitio para comer

Can you recommend a good restaurant?	**¿Puede recomendarme un buen restaurante?** *pwedeh rekomendarmeh oon bwen restawranteh*
Is there ... near here?	**¿Hay ... cerca de aquí?** *eye ... therka deh akee*
a traditional local restaurant	**un restaurante típico** *oon restawranteh teepeeko*
Chinese restaurant	**un restaurante chino** *oon restawranteh cheeno*
Greek restaurant	**un restaurante griego** *oon restawranteh greeyego*
Italian restaurant	**un restaurante italiano** *oon restawranteh eetaleeyano*
inexpensive restaurant	**un restaurante barato** *oon restawranteh barato*
vegetarian restaurant	**un restaurante vegetariano** *oon restawranteh bekhetareeyano*
Where can I find a(n) ...?	**¿Dónde puedo encontrar ...?** *dondeh pwedo enkontrar*
burger stand	**una hamburguesería** *oona amboorgesereeya*
café/restaurant with a garden	**una cafetería/un restaurante con jardín** *oona kafetereeya/oon restawranteh kon khardeen*
fast food restaurant	**un restaurante de comida rápida** *oon restawranteh deh komeeda rapeeda*
ice-cream café	**una heladería** *oona eladereeya*
pizzeria	**una pizzería** *oona peethereeya*
steak house	**una churrasquería** *oona choorraskereeya*

Reservations Reservas

I'd like to reserve
a table for 2
this evening at …

Quiero reservar una mesa para dos para esta noche a las …
keeyero reserbar oona mesa para dos para esta nocheh a las

We'll come at 8:00.

Llegaremos a las 8:00.
l-yegaremos a las ocho

A table for 2, please.

Una mesa para dos, por favor.
oona mesa para dos por fabor

We have a reservation.

Tenemos una reserva. *tenemos oona reserba*

¿A nombre de quién, por favor?	What's the name, please?
Lo siento. Tenemos mucha gente/ está completo.	I'm sorry. We're very busy/full.
Tendremos una mesa libre dentro de … minutos.	We'll have a free table in … minutes.
Tendrá que volver dentro de … minutos.	You'll have to come back in … minutes.

Where to sit Dónde sentarse

Could we sit …?

¿Podríamos sentarnos …?
podreeyamos sentarnos

over there

allí *al-yee*

outside

fuera *fwera*

in a non-smoking area

en una zona de no fumadores
en oona thona deh no foomadores

by the window

al lado de la ventana
al lado deh la bentana

Smoking or non-smoking?

¿Fumador o no fumador?
foomador o no foomador

> – Quiero reservar una mesa para esta noche.
> – *¿Para cuánta gente?*
> – Para cuatro.
> – *¿Para qué hora?*
> – Para las ocho.
> – *¿A nombre de quién, por favor?*
> – A nombre de Smith.
> – *Muy bien. Hasta entonces.*

Ordering Pedir

Waiter/Waitress!	**¡Camarero/Camarera!** *kamarero/kamarera*
May I see the wine list, please?	**¿Puedo ver la carta de vinos?** *pwedo behr la karta deh beenos*
Do you have a set menu?	**¿Tienen un menú del día?** *teeyenen oon menoo del deeya*
Can you recommend some typical local dishes?	**¿Puede recomendarme algunos platos típicos de la zona?** *pwedeh rekomendarmeh algoonos platos teepeekos deh la thona*
Could you tell me what … is?	**¿Podría decirme lo que … es?** *podreeya detheermeh lo keh … es*
What is in it?	**¿Qué lleva?** *keh l-yeba*
What kind of … do you have?	**¿Qué clase de … tiene?** *keh klaseh deh … teeyeneh*
I'll have …	**Tomaré …** *tomareh*
a bottle/glass/carafe of …	**una botella/un vaso/una garrafa de …** *oona botel-ya/oon baso/oona garrafa deh*
… as a starter/main course/ side order	**… de primero/segundo/guarnición** *deh preemero/segoondo/gwarneetheeyon*

¿Van a pedir ya?	Are you ready to order?
¿Qué va a tomar?	What would you like?
¿Quieren beber algo primero?	Would you like to order drinks first?
Le recomiendo …	I recommend …
No tenemos …	We haven't got …
Eso tardara … minutos.	That will take … minutes.
Que aproveche.	Enjoy your meal.

– *¿Van a pedir ya?*
– *¿Puede recomendarnos algo típicamente español?*
– *Sí, le recomiendo el/la …*
– *Vale, tomaré eso con guarnición de ensalada, por favor.*
– *No faltaba más. ¿Y qué quiere de beber?*
– *Una garrafa de vino, por favor.*

DRINKS ➤ 49; MENU READER ➤ 52

Side dishes/Accompaniments
Platos de acompañamiento

Could I have ... without ...?
¿Podrían servirme ... sin ...?
podreeyan serbeermeh ... seen

With a side order of ...
De guarnición ... _deh gwarneetheeyon_

Could I have salad instead of vegetables, please?
¿Podría tomar ensalada en lugar de verduras, por favor? _podreeya tomar ensalada en loogar de berdooras por fabor_

Does the meal come with vegetables/potatoes?
¿Viene la comida con verduras/patatas? _beeyeneh la komeeda kon berdooras/patatas_

Do you have any sauces?
¿Tienen salsas? _teeyenen salsas_

Would you like ... with that?
¿Quiere ... con eso? _keeyereh ...kon eso_

vegetables/salad
verduras/ensalada _berdooras/ensalada_

potatoes/fries
patatas/patatas fritas _patatas/patatas freetas_

sauce
salsa _salsa_

ice
hielo _eeyelo_

May I have some ...?
¿Me puede traer ...? _me pwedeh trayer_

bread
pan _pan_

butter
mantequilla _mantekeel-ya_

lemon
limón _leemon_

mustard
mostaza _mostatha_

pepper
pimienta _peemeeyenta_

salt
sal _sal_

seasoning
aderezo _aderetho_

sugar
azúcar _athookar_

artificial sweetener
edulcorante artificial _edoolkorante arteefeetheeyal_

blue cheese dressing
salsa de queso azul _salsa deh keso athool_

vinaigrette/French dressing
vinagreta/vinagreta francesa _beenagreta/beenagreta franthesa_

MENU READER ➤ 52

General questions
Preguntas generales

Could I/we have a(n) (clean) ..., please?
¿Podría traerme ... (limpio/a), por favor?
podreeya trayerme ... (leempeeyo/a) por fabor

ashtray
un cenicero *oon theneethero*

cup/glass
una taza/un vaso *oona tatha/oon baso*

fork/knife
un tenedor/cuchillo *oon tenedor/koocheel-yo*

napkin
una servilleta *oona serbeel-yeta*

plate/spoon
una plato/una cuchara *oona plato/oona koochara*

I'd like some more ..., please.
Quiero más ..., por favor. *keeyero mas ... por fabor*

Nothing more, thanks.
Nada más, gracias. *nada mas gratheeyas*

Where are the bathrooms/ toilets?
¿Dónde están los servicios? *dondeh estan los serbeetheeyos*

Special requirements Peticiones especiales

I mustn't eat food containing ...
No debo comer comida que tenga ... *no debo komer komeeda keh tenga*

salt/sugar
sal/azúcar *sal/athookar*

Do you have meals/ drinks for diabetics?
¿Tienen comidas/bebidas para diabéticos? *teeyenen komeedas/bebeedas para deeya beteekos*

Do you have vegetarian meals?
¿Tienen comidas vegetarianas? *teeyenen komeedas bekhetareeyanas*

For the children Para los niños

Do you do children's portions?
¿Hacen porciones para niños? *athen portheeyones para neeños*

Could we have a child's seat, please?
¿Podrían ponernos una silla para niños? *podreeyan ponernos oona seel-ya para neeños*

Where can I feed/ change the baby?
¿Dónde puedo darle de comer/cambiar al niño? *dondeh pwedo darleh deh komer/kambeeyar al neeño*

CHILDREN ➤ 113

Fast food/Café
Restaurante de comida rápida

Something to drink Algo para beber

I'd like …	**Quiero …** _kee<u>ye</u>ro_
beer	**una cerveza** _<u>oo</u>na ther<u>be</u>tha_
(hot) chocolate	**un chocolate (a la taza)** _oon choko<u>la</u>teh (a la <u>ta</u>tha)_
tea/coffee	**un té/un café** _oon teh/oon ka<u>feh</u>_
black/with milk	**solo/con leche** _<u>so</u>lo/kon <u>le</u>cheh_
fruit juice	**un zumo de fruta** _oon <u>thoo</u>mo deh <u>froo</u>ta_
mineral water	**un agua mineral** _<u>oo</u>n <u>a</u>gwa meene<u>ral</u>_
red/white wine	**un vino tinto/blanco** _oon <u>bee</u>no <u>teen</u>to/<u>blan</u>ko_

And to eat … Y de comer …

A piece of …, please.	**Un trozo de …, por favor.** _oon <u>tro</u>tho deh … por fa<u>bor</u>_
I'd like two of those.	**Quiero dos de ésos.** _kee<u>ye</u>ro dos deh <u>e</u>sos_
burger	**una hamburguesa** _<u>oo</u>na amboor<u>ge</u>sa_
cake (small/large)	**un dulce/una tarta** _oon <u>dool</u>theh/<u>oo</u>na <u>tar</u>ta_
fries/omelet/sandwich	**patatas fritas/una tortilla francesa/** **un bocadillo** _pa<u>ta</u>tas <u>free</u>tas/<u>oo</u>na tor<u>teel</u>-ya fran<u>the</u>sa/oon boka<u>deel</u>-yo_
A … ice cream, please.	**Un helado de …, por favor.** _oon e<u>la</u>do deh … por fa<u>bor</u>_
chocolate/strawberry/vanilla	**chocolate/fresa/vainilla** _choko<u>la</u>teh /<u>fre</u>sa/bayneel'-ya_
A … portion, please.	**Una porción …, por favor.** _<u>oo</u>na porthee<u>yon</u> … por fa<u>bor</u>_
small/medium/large	**pequeña/mediana/grande** _pe<u>ke</u>ña/medee<u>ya</u>na/<u>gran</u>deh_
It's to take out/away.	**Para llevar.** _<u>pa</u>ra l-ye<u>bar</u>_
That's all, thanks.	**Eso es todo, gracias.** _<u>e</u>so es <u>to</u>do, <u>gra</u>theeyas_

– ¿Qué va/van a tomar?
– Dos cafés, por favor.
– ¿Solos o con leche?
– Con leche, por favor.
– ¿Algo más?
– Eso es todo, gracias.

Complaints Quejas

I have no knife/fork/spoon.
No tengo cuchillo/tenedor/cuchara.
no tengo koocheel-yo/tenedor/koochara

There must be some mistake.
Debe de haber un error.
debeh deh aber oon error

That's not what I ordered.
Eso no es lo que pedí.
eso no es lo keh pedee

I asked for …
Pedí … *pedee*

I can't eat this.
No puedo comerme esto.
no pwedo komermeh esto

The meat is …
La carne está … *la karneh esta*

overdone
demasiado hecha *demaseeyado echa*

underdone
cruda *krooda*

too tough
demasiado dura *demaseeyado doora*

This is too …
Esto está demasiado …
esto esta demaseeyado

bitter/sour
amargo/ácido *amargo/atheedo*

The food is cold.
La comida está fría.
la komeeda esta freeya

This isn't fresh.
Esto no está fresco. *esto no esta fresko*

How much longer will
our food be?
¿Cuánto más tardará la comida?
kwanto mas tardara la komeeda

We can't wait any longer.
We're leaving.
No podemos esperar más. Nos vamos.
no podemos esperar mas. nos bamos

Have you forgotten our drinks?
¿Se le han olvidado las bebidas?
seh leh an olbeedado las bebeedas

This isn't clean.
Esto no está limpio.
esto no esta leempeeyo

I'd like to speak to the
head waiter/manager.
Quiero hablar con el metre/encargado.
keeyero ablar kon el metreh/enkargado

41

Paying Pagar

Tipping: Service is generally included in the bill, but if you are happy with the service, a personal tip of 100 pesetas per person up to 10% for the waiter is appropriate and appreciated.

I'd like to pay.	**Quiero pagar.** *keeyero pagar*
We'd like to pay separately.	**Queremos pagar por separado.** *keremos pagar por separado*
It's all together, please.	**Póngalo todo junto, por favor.** *pongalo todo khoonto por fabor*
I think there's a mistake in this bill.	**Creo que hay un error en esta cuenta.** *kreyo keh eye oon error en esta kwenta*
What is this amount for?	**¿De qué es esta cantidad?** *deh keh es esta kanteedath*
I didn't have that. I had …	**Yo no tomé eso. Yo tomé …** *yo no tomeh eso. yo tomeh*
Is service included?	**¿Está el servicio incluido?** *esta el serbeetheeyo eenklooweedo*
Can I pay with this credit card?	**¿Puedo pagar con esta tarjeta de crédito?** *pwedo pagar kon esta tarkheta deh kredeeto*
I've forgotten my wallet.	**Me he olvidado la cartera.** *meh eh olbeedado la kartera*
I haven't got enough money.	**No tengo dinero suficiente.** *no tengo deenero soofeetheeyenteh*
Could I have a VAT receipt, please?	**¿Podría darme un recibo con el IVA, por favor?** *podreeya darmeh oon retheebo kon el eeba por fabor*
Can I have an itemized bill, please?	**¿Podría darme una cuenta detallada?** *podreeya darmeh oona kwenta detal-yada*
That was a very good meal.	**La comida estuvo muy buena.** *la komeeda estoobo mwee bwena*

> – ¡Camarero! ¿Me puede traer la cuenta, por favor?
> – Por supuesto. Aquí tiene.
> – ¿Está el servicio incluido?
> – Sí.
> – ¿Puedo pagar esto con tarjeta de crédito?
> – Por supuesto…
> – Gracias. La comida estuvo muy buena.

Course by course Platos

No trip to Spain would be complete without sampling some of the wonderful **tapas** on offer.

Breakfast Desayuno

I'd like …	**Quiero …** *keeyero*
bread	**pan** *pan*
butter	**mantequilla** *mante<u>keel</u>-ya*
fried eggs	**huevos fritos** <u>*weboss freetoss*</u>
scrambled eggs	**huevos revueltos** <u>*weboss rebweltoss*</u>
fruit juice	**un zumo de fruta** *oon <u>thoo</u>mo deh <u>froo</u>ta*
jam	**mermelada** *mermel<u>a</u>da*
milk	**leche** *<u>le</u>cheh*
roll	**panecillo** *pene<u>theel</u>-yo*

Appetizers/Starters Entremeses

croquetas *kro<u>ke</u>tass*
Croquettes made with ham, fish, egg or a wide variety of other fillings.

ensaladilla rusa *ensala<u>deel</u>-ya <u>rr</u>oossa*
Potatoes with peas, tuna, boiled eggs and olives mixed with mayonnaise.

champiñones al ajillo *champee<u>ño</u>nes ahl a<u>kheel</u>-yo*
Mushrooms fried in olive oil with garlic.

tapas *<u>ta</u>pass*
A huge variety of snacks served in cafés and tapa bars, ranging from meat balls, cheese, smoked ham, mushrooms, fried fish plus sauces and exotic-looking specialties of the house. **Una tapa** is a mouthful, **una ración** half a plateful, and **una porción** a generous amount.

aceitunas (rellenas)	*athe<u>too</u>nass (rel-ye<u>n</u>ass)*	(stuffed) olives
albóndigas	*al<u>bon</u>dee-ass*	spiced meatballs
almejas	*al<u>me</u>khass*	clams
calamares	*kala<u>ma</u>ress*	squid
callos	*<u>kal</u>-yoss*	tripe (in hot paprika sauce)
caracoles	*kara<u>ko</u>less*	snails
chorizo	*cho<u>ree</u>tho*	spicy sausage
gambas	*<u>gam</u>bass*	prawns (shrimps)
jamón	*kha<u>mon</u>*	ham
mejillones	*mekheel-<u>yo</u>ness*	mussels
pimientos	*peem<u>yen</u>toss*	peppers
pinchos	*<u>peen</u>choss*	grilled skewered meat

Soups Sopas

caldo gallego	_kaldo gal-yego_	meat and vegetable broth
consomé al jerez	_konsomeh al khereth_	chicken broth with sherry
sopa de ajo	_sopa deh akho_	garlic soup
sopa de cebolla	_sopa deh thebol-ya_	onion soup
sopa de fideos	_sopa deh feedeyoss_	noodle soup
sopa de mariscos	_sopa deh mareeskoss_	seafood soup
sopa de verduras	_sopa deh berdoorass_	vegetable soup

ajo blanco _akho blanko_
cold garlic and almond soup garnished with grapes (_Andalucia_)

gazpacho _gathpacho_
a cold tomato soup with cucumber, green pepper, bread, onion and garlic

sopa castellana _sopa kasteel-yana_
baked garlic soup with chunks of ham and a poached egg

sopa de cocido _sopa deh kotheedo_
a kind of broth, with beef, ham, sausage, chickpeas, cabbage, turnip, onion, garlic, potatoes

Egg dishes Huevos

huevos a la flamenca _weboss a la flamenka_
eggs baked with tomato, onion and diced ham; often garnished with asparagus tips, red peppers or slices of spicy pork sausage (_Andalucia_)

huevos al nido _weboss al needo_
"eggs in the nest"; egg yolks set in small soft rolls; fried and then covered in egg white

huevos rellenos _weboss rrel-yenos_
boiled eggs filled with tuna fish and dressed with mayonnaise

tortilla _torteel-ya_
round Spanish omelet; popular varieties include: ~ **de patatas** (potato with onions), ~ **de jamón** (ham), ~ **paisana** (potatoes, peas, prawns or ham), ~ **de queso** (cheese), ~ **de setas** (mushroom)

Fish and seafood Pescado y mariscos

atún	*atoon*	tuna
bacalao	*bakalao*	cod
boquerones	*bokeroness*	herring/whitebait
caballa	*kabal-ya*	mackerel
chipirones	*cheepeeroness*	baby squid
cigalas	*theegalass*	sea crayfish (prawns)
langosta	*langosta*	spiny lobster
mero	*mero*	sea bass
pez espada	*peth espada*	swordfish
pulpo	*poolpo*	octopus
trucha	*troocha*	trout

bacalao a la catalana *bakalao a la katalana*
salt cod in ratatouille sauce, with onions, eggplant, zucchini courgettes, tomatoes and pepper (Catalonian specialty)

calamares a la romana *kalamaress al la rromana*
squid rings deep-fried in batter

pulpo a la gallega *poolpo a la gal-yega*
octopus dressed with olive oil and paprika

lenguado a la vasca *lengwado a la baska*
baked sole with sliced potatoes in a mushroom, red pepper and tomato sauce

trucha a la navarra *troocha a la nabarra*
grilled trout stuffed with ham

Paella Paella

Paella – an immensely popular dish. Basically, paella is made of golden saffron rice garnished with meat, fish, seafood and/or vegetables. Here are four of the most popular ways of preparing paella (*pa-el-ya*):

de verduras *de berdoorass*
artichokes, peas, broad beans, cauliflower, garlic, peppers, tomato

de marisco *de mareesko*
fish and seafood only

valenciana *balenthyana*
chicken, shrimp, mussels, prawn, squid, peas, tomato, chili pepper, garlic – the classic paella

zamorana *thamorana*
ham, pork loin, pig's feet, chili pepper

Meat Carne

carne de buey	*karneh deh bwehee*	beef
carne de cerdo	*karneh deh therdo*	pork
carne de cordero	*karneh deh kordero*	lamb
carne de ternera	*karneh deh ternera*	veal
chuletas	*chooletass*	chops
conejo	*konekho*	rabbit
faisán	*faissan*	pheasant
filete	*feeleteh*	steak
hígado	*eegado*	liver
jamón	*khamon*	ham
pato	*pato*	duck
pavo	*pavo*	turkey
pollo	*pol-yo*	chicken
muslo de pollo	*mooslo deh pol-yo*	chicken leg
pechuga de pollo	*pechooga deh pol-yo*	breast of chicken
riñones	*reeñoness*	kidneys
salchichas	*salcheechass*	sausages
tocino	*totheeno*	bacon

Specialties Especialidades

asado de cordero *assado deh kordero*
roast lamb with garlic and wine

cochinillo asado *kocheeneel-yo assado*
crispy roasted suckling pig

cocido madrileño *kotheedo madreeleño*
hotpot, stew

empanada gallega *empanada gal-yega*
pork and onion pie

estofado de ternera *estofado deh ternera*
veal stew with wine, carrots, onions and potatoes

lomo de cerdo al jerez *lomo deh therdo al khereth*
roast loin of pork with sherry

pollo en pepitoria *pol-yo en pepeetoreeya*
chicken in egg and almond sauce

riñones al jerez *rreeñoness al khereth*
lamb kidneys in an onion and sherry sauce

Vegetables Verduras

arroz	*arroth*	rice
berenjena	*berekhena*	eggplant
cebolla	*thebol-ya*	onion
champiñones	*champeeñoness*	button mushrooms
guisantes	*qeessantes*	peas
judías verdes	*khoodeeass verdess*	green beans
lechuga	*lechooga*	lettuce
patatas	*patatas*	potatoes
pimientos morrones	*peemyentoss morroness*	sweet red peppers
repollo	*repol-yo*	cabbage
setas	*setass*	mushrooms
tomates	*tomatess*	tomatoes
zanahorias	*thana-oryass*	carrots

ensalada *ensalada*
salad; typical varieties to look out for: ~ **de atún** (tuna),~ **de lechuga** (green); ~ **de pepino** (cucumber), ~ **del tiempo** (seasonal), ~ **valenciana** (with green peppers, lettuce and oranges)

lentejas estofadas *lentekhass estofadass*
green lentils with onions, tomatoes, carrots and garlic

pisto *peesto*
a stew of green peppers, onions, tomatoes and zucchini/courgettes; you might also see it referred to as **frito de verduras**

Fruit Fruta

cerezas	*therethass*	cherries
ciruelas	*theerwelass*	plums
frambuesas	*frambwesass*	raspberries
fresas	*fresass*	strawberries
granadas	*granadas*	pomegranates
manzana	*manthana*	apple
melocotón	*melokoton*	peach
naranja	*narankha*	orange
plátano	*platano*	banana
pomelo	*pomelo*	grapefruit
uvas	*oovass*	grapes

Cheese Queso

Burgos _boorgos_
A soft, creamy cheese named after the province from which it originates.

Cabrales _kabrales_
A tangy, veined goat cheese; its flavor varies, depending upon the mountain region in which it was produced.

Manchego _manchego_
Produced from ewe's milk, this hard cheese from **La Mancha** can vary from milky white to golden yellow. The best manchego is said to come from **Ciudad Real.**

Perilla _pereel-ya_
A firm, bland cheese made from cow's milk; sometimes known as **teta**.

Roncal _rronkal_
A sharp ewe's milk cheese from northern Spain; hand-pressed, salted and smoked with leathery rind.

blue	**tipo roquefort** _teepo rrokefort_
cream	**cremoso** _kremosso_
hard	**duro** _dooro_
mild	**suave** _swabeh_
ripe	**curado** _kurado_
soft	**blando** _blando_
strong	**fuerte** _fwerteh_

Dessert Postre

bizcocho	_beethkocho_	sponge cake
brazo de gitano	_bratho deh geetano_	rum cream roll
canutillos	_kanooteel-yos_	custard horns with cinnamon
crema catalana	_krema katalana_	caramel pudding
flan	_flan_	creme caramel
fritos	_freetos_	fritters
galletas	_gal-yetas_	cookies/biscuits
mantecado	_mantekado_	rich almond ice cream
pastel de queso	_pastel deh keso_	cheesecake
tarta de manzana	_tarta deh manthana_	apple tart
tortitas	_torteetas_	waffles

helado _elado_
Ice cream; popular flavors include: ~ **de chocolate** (chocolate), ~ **de fresa** (strawberry), **de limón** (lemon), ~ **de moka** (mocha), ~ **de vainilla** (vanilla).

Drinks Bebidas
Aperitifs Aperitivos

For most Spaniards, a before-dinner drink of vermouth or sherry is as important as our cocktail or highball. Vermouth (**vermut**) is rarely drunk neat but usually on the rocks or with seltzer water. Some Spaniards content themselves with a glass of local wine. You'll probably be given a dish of olives or nuts to nibble on. Or in a bar specializing in tapas, you can order various snacks.

Sherry (**jerez** *khereth*) is Spain's most renowned drink. It has alcohol or brandy added to "fortify" it during the fermentation process. Sherry was the first fortified wine to become popular in England – "sherry" derives from the English spelling of the town **Jerez**, where the wine originated.

Major sherry producers include Lustau, Osborne, Pedro Domecq, Antonio Barbadillo, Gonzalez Byass, Bobadilla, House of Sandeman, Valdespino, John Harvey & Sons.

Sherry can be divided into two groups:

fino *feeno*
These are the pale, dry sherries that make good aperitifs. The Spaniards themselves are especially fond of **amontillado** and **manzanilla**. Some of the best **finos** are Tío Pepe and La Ina.

Oloroso *olorosso*
These are the heavier, darker sherries that are sweetened before being bottled. They're fine after-dinner drinks. One exception is amoroso which is medium dry. Brown and cream sherries are full bodied and slightly less fragrant than **finos**.

Beer Cerveza

Spanish beer, generally served cool, is good and relatively inexpensive. Try **Águila especial** or **San Miguel especial**.

A beer, please.	**Una cerveza, por favor.** *oona therbetha por fabor*
light beer	**cerveza rubia** *therbetha roobya*
dark beer	**cerveza negra** *therbetha negra*
foreign beer	**cerveza extranjera** *therbetha ekstrankhera*
small/large beer	**cerveza pequeña/grande** *therbetha pekeña/grandeh*

Wine Vino

Spain has the largest area under vine in the world and is the third largest producer and exporter.

Spain's best wine comes from **Rioja**, a region of Old Castile of which **Logroño** is the center. Wine makers there add **garantía de origen** to wine they feel is of above average quality.

The **Penedés** region near Barcelona is a major source of the world's best selling white sparkling wine, **cava**.

Traditionally, white wine goes well with fish, fowl and light meats, while dark meats call for a red wine. A good rosé or dry sparkling **Cava** goes well with almost anything.

Ask for the patron's own wine "**el vino de la casa**" you should receive a good wine, corresponding to the quality of the establishment.

I want a bottle of white/red wine.	**Quiero una botella de vino blanco/tinto.** _kyero oona botel-ya deh beeno blanko/teento_
a carafe	**una garrafa** _oona garrafa_
half bottle	**una media botella** _oona medya botel-ya_
a glass	**un vaso** _oon basso_
a small glass	**un chato** _oon chato_
a liter	**un litro** _oon leetro_
a jar	**una jarra** _oona kharra_

Reading the label

añejo mature	**joven** young
blanco white	**liviano** light
bodegas cellar	**moscatel** sweet dessert wine
cava white, sparkling wine	**muy seco** very dry
de cuerpo full bodied	**reserva** aged over 3 years
DO (Denominación de Origen) regulated quality	**rosado** rosé
DOCa superior wine (Rioja only)	**seco** dry
dulce sweet	**tinto** red
embotellado en bottled in	**vino de calidad** quality wine
espumoso sparkling	**vino de cosecha** vintage wine
gran reserva aged 3 years in a barrel then 3 years in the bottle (exceptional years only)	**vino de crianza** aged in oak barrels for minimum of 6 months

Wine regions Regiones vinícolas

Aragón Campo de Borja, Calatayud, Cariñena, Navarra, Rioja (Alta, Alavesa, Baja), Somotano

Basque Chacolí de Guetaria, Rioja Alavesa

Castilla y León Bierzo, Cigales, Ribera del Duero, Rueda, Toro

Cataluña Alella, Ampurdán-Costa Brava, Conca de Barberà, Costers del Segre, Penedès (center of the Cava sparkling wine region), Priorato, Tarragona, Terra Alta

Galicia Rías Baixas, Ribeiro, Valdeorras

Central Spain Alicante, Almansa, Bullas, Jumilla, La Mancha, Levante, Méntrida, Utiel-Requena, Valdepeñas, Valencia, Vinos de Madrid, Yecla

Southern Spain Condado de Huelva, Jerez, Málaga, Manzanilla-Sanlúcar de Barrameda, Montilla-Moriles

Islands Binissalem (Balearic), Tacoronte-Acentejo (Canaries)

Sangría *san<u>gree</u>a*

wine punch/cup made with red wine, fruit juice, brandy, slices of fruit, diluted with soda and ice; ideal for hot weather

Spirits and liqueurs Licores

You'll recognize: **ginebra** (gin), **ron** (rum), **oporto** (port wine), **vermut**, **vodka**, **whisky**.

double (a double shot)	**doble** *<u>dob</u>leh*
straight/neat	**solo** *<u>so</u>lo*
on the rocks	**con hielo** *kon <u>ye</u>lo*
with soda/tonic	**con soda/tónica** *kon <u>so</u>da/<u>to</u>neeka*

Non-alcoholic drinks Bebidas sin alcohol

I'd like a cup of coffee.	**Quiero una taza de café.** *<u>kye</u>ro <u>oo</u>na <u>ta</u>tha deh ka<u>feh</u>*
(hot) chocolate	**un chocolate (caliente)** *oon choko<u>la</u>teh (kali<u>yen</u>teh)*
iced fruit juice	**un granizado** *oon granee<u>tha</u>do*
lemonade	**una limonada** *<u>oo</u>na leemo<u>na</u>da*
milk	**leche** *<u>le</u>cheh*
milk shake	**un batido** *oon ba<u>tee</u>do*
orangeade	**una naranjada** *<u>oo</u>na naran<u>kha</u>da*
soda water	**una soda** *<u>oo</u>na <u>so</u>da*
(iced/mineral) water	**agua (helada/mineral)** *<u>a</u>gwa (e<u>la</u>da/meene<u>ral</u>)*

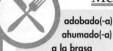

Menu Reader

adobado(-a)	ado*bado*(-a)	marinated
ahumado(-a)	aho*omado*	smoked
a la brasa	a la *brasa*	braised
al grill	al *greel*	grilled
al horno	al *orno*	baked
al vapor	al *bapor*	steamed
asado(-a)	a*sado*	roasted
con especias	kon espe*theeyas*	spicy
con nata	kon *nata*	creamed
cortado en taquitos	kor*tado* en ta*keetos*	diced
dorado(-a) al horno	do*rado*(-a) al *orno*	oven browned
empanado(-a)	empa*nado*(-a)	breaded
escaldado(-a)	eskal*dado*(-a)	poached
frito(-a)	*freeto*(-a)	fried
guisado(-a)	gee*sado*(-a)	stewed
hervido(-a)	er*beedo*	boiled
refrito(-a)	re*freeto*(-a)	sautéed
relleno(-a)	rel-*yeno*(-a)	stuffed
muy poco hecho(-a)	mwee *poko echo*(-a)	rare/underdone
poco hecho(-a)	*poko echo*	medium rare
medio hecho(-a)	me*deeyo echo*	medium
bien hecho(-a)	*beeyen echo*	well-done

A a la parrilla grilled/broiled
a la romana deep-fried
a punto medium (done)
abocado sherry made from sweet
and dry wine
acedera sorrel
aceitunas (rellenas) (stuffed) olives
achicoria chicory
agua water; ~ caliente hot ~; ~
helada iced ~; ~ mineral mineral ~
aguacate avocado

aguardiente spirits (eau-de-vie)
ahumado smoked
ajo garlic; ~ blanco garlic soup ➤ 43
ajoaceite garlic mayonnaise
al adobo marinated
al ajillo in garlic and oil
al horno baked
albahaca basil
albaricoques apricots
albóndigas spiced meatballs
alcachofas artichokes

alcaparra caper
alioli garlic mayonnaise
aliñado seasoned
almejas clams; **~ a la marinera** cooked in hot, pimento sauce
almendra almond; **~ garrapiñada** sugared
almuerzo lunch
almíbar syrup
alubia bean
Amontillado medium-dry sherry with nutty taste
anchoas anchovies
añejo mature
anguila ahumada smoked eel
angula baby eel
Angélica Basque herb liqueur
anisado aniseed-based soft drink
anticucho beef heart grilled on skewer with green peppers
Anís del Mono anisette
aperitivos aperitifs
apio celery
arándanos blueberries
arenque (ahumado) (smoked) herring
arepa flapjack made of corn (maize)
arroz rice; **~ a la cubana** boiled rice served with tomato sauce and a fried egg; **~ a la valenciana** with vegetables, chicken, shellfish; **~ blanco** boiled, steamed; **~ negro** with seafood and squid ink; **~ primavera** with spring vegetables; **~ con costra** with pork meatballs (Val.); **~ con leche** rice pudding

asado roast
asturias strong, fermented cheese
atún tuna
avellanas hazelnuts
aves poultry
azafrán saffron
azúcar sugar

B **bacalao** cod
banderillas gherkins, chile peppers and olives on a skewer
batata sweet potato, yam
batido milk shake
bebidas drinks ➤ 49-51
bebidas sin alcohol non-alcoholic drinks ➤ 51
becada woodcock
berberecho cockle
berenjena eggplant/aubergine
berraza parsnip
berro cress
berza cabbage
besugo (sea) bream
bien hecho well done
biftec beef steak
bizcocho sponge cake; **~ borracho** steeped in rum and syrup
bizcotela glazed cookie/biscuit
blanco white
blando soft; medium (egg)
Bobadilla Gran Reserva wine-distilled brandy
bocadillo sandwich
bocadillo de jamón ham sandwich
bollos cake

bonito tuna
boquerones herring/whitebait
botella bottle
brevas blue figs
(en) brocheta (on a) skewer
budín blancmange, custard
buey ox
burgos soft, creamy cheese ➤ 48
buñuelitos small fritters

C **caballa** mackerel
cabeza headcheese/brawn
cabra goat
cabrales tangy goat cheese ➤ 48
cabrito kid
cacahuetes peanuts
café coffee ➤ 51
calabacín zucchini/courgette
calabaza pumpkin
calamares squid; ~ **a la romana** fried in batter ➤ 45
caldereta de cabrito kid stew
caldillo de congrio conger-eel soup with tomatoes and potatoes
caldo consommé
caldo gallego meat and vegetable broth ➤ 44
caliente hot
Calisay quinine-flavored liqueur
callos tripe; ~ **a la madrileña** tripe in piquant sauce with spicy pork sausage and tomatoes
camarón shrimp
canela cinnamon
cangrejo (de mar/de río) crab/crayfish

cantarela chanterelle mushroom
capón capon
caracoles snails
caramelos candy; sweets
Carlos I wine-distilled brandy
carne meat ➤ 46
carne a la parrilla charcoal-grilled steak
carne de buey beef
carne de cangrejo crabmeat
carne de cerdo pork
carne de cordero lamb
carne de ternera veal
carne molida chopped/minced beef
carne picada chopped/minced meat
carnero mutton
carta menu; **a la ~** a la carte
casero homemade
castanola sea perch
castañas chestnuts
catalana spicy pork sausages ➤ 44
caza game
(a la) cazadora with mushrooms, spring onions, herbs in wine
Cazalla aniseed liqueur
cazuela de cordero lamb stew with vegetables
cebollas onions
cebolleta spring onion
cebollino chive
cebrero blue-veined cheese
cena dinner, supper
centolla spider-crab, served cold
cerdo pork
cereales cereal

cerezas cherries

cerveza beer ➤ 49

chalote shallot

champiñón button mushroom

chancho adobado pork braised with sweet potatoes, orange and lemon juice

chanfaina goat's liver and kidney stew, served in a thick sauce

chanquete herring/whitebait

chato a small glass

chile chili pepper

chilindrón sauce of tomatoes, peppers, garlic, ham and wine (*Pyr.*)

chimichurri hot parsley sauce

Chinchón aniseed liqueur

chipirones baby squid

chirivías parsnips

chocolate (caliente) (hot) chocolate

chopa type of sea bream

chorizo spicy sausage made of pork, garlic and paprika

chuletas chops

chupe de mariscos scallops served with creamy sauce and gratinéed with cheese

churro sugared tubular fritter

cigalas sea crayfish (Dublin Bay prawns)

cincho hard sheep-milk cheese

ciruelas plums; **~ pasas** prunes

clavo clove

cochifrito de cordero highly seasoned stew of lamb or kid

cochinillo asado crispy roasted Castilian suckling pig

cocido boiled; beef stew with ham, fowl, chickpeas and potatoes

cocido al vapor steamed

coco coconut

codorniz quail

cohombrillos pickles/gherkins

cola de mono blend of coffee, milk, rum and pisco

coles de bruselas Brussels sprouts

coliflor cauliflower

comida meal

comino caraway

compota stewed fruit

con hielo on the rocks

con leche with milk

con limón with lemon

condimentos herbs

coñac brandy ➤ 51

conejo rabbit; **~ al ajillo** rabbit with garlic; **~ de monte** wild rabbit

confitura jam

congrio conger eel

consomé al jerez chicken broth with sherry

copa nuria egg yolk and egg white, whipped and served with jam

corazonada heart stewed in sauce

corazón heart

cordero lamb

Cordoníu brand of Catalonian sparkling wine

cortadillo small pancake with lemon

corto strong coffee

corzo deer

costilla chop
crema soup; **~ batida** whipped cream; **~ catalana** caramel pudding; **~ española** dessert of milk, eggs, fruit jelly; **~ nieve** frothy egg yolk, sugar, rum
cremoso cream
criadillas sweetbreads
(a la) criolla with green peppers, spices and tomatoes
croqueta croquette, fish or meat cake
crudo raw
Cuarenta y Tres egg liqueur
Cuba libre rum coke
cubierto cover charge
cuenta bill, check
curanto dish of seafood, vegetables and suckling pig in an earthen well

D **damasco** variety of apricot
dátiles dates
de cordero lamb's
de cuerpo full-bodied
de lechuga green; lettuce
de ternera calf's
del tiempo in season
desayuno breakfast
descafeinado decaffeinated
doble double (a double shot)
dulce dessert wine; sweet
dulce de naranja marmelade
durazno peach
duro hard (egg)

E **edulcorante** sweetener
embuchado stuffed with meat
embutido spicy sausage
empanada pie or tart with meat or fish filling; **~ de horno** filled with minced meat; **~ gallega** tenderloin of pork, onions and chili peppers in a pie
empanadillas small savory pastries stuffed with meat or fish
empanado breaded
emperador swordfish
en dulce boiled
en escabeche marinated
en salazón cured
en salsa braised in casserole
en su jugo pot roasted
enchilada tortilla stuffed and served with vegetable garnish and sauce
encurtido pickled
endibia endive (chicory)
eneldo dill
ensalada salad ➤ 47; **~ rusa** diced cold vegetables with mayonnaise
entremeses (variados) (assorted) appetizers
escabeche de gallina chicken marinated in vinegar and bay leaves
escarcho roach
escarola escarole
espaguetis spaghetti
espalda shoulder
(a la) española with tomatoes

especialidades de la casa specialties of the house

especialidades locales local specialties

especias spices

espinacas spinach

espumoso sparkling

espárragos (puntas de) asparagus (tips)

esqueixado *(Cat.)* mixed fish salad

(al) estilo de in the style of

estofado braised; stewed

estragón tarragon

 fabada (asturiana) stew of pork, beans, bacon and sausage

faisán pheasant

fiambres cold cuts

fideo thin noodle

filete steak; **~ de lenguado empanado** breaded fillet of sole; **~ de lomo** fillet steak (tenderloin); **~ de res** beef steak

fino pale, dry sherry ➤ 49

firto de patata deep-fried potato croquette

(a la) flamenca with onions, peas, green peppers, tomatoes and spiced sausage

flan caramel pudding

frambuesas raspberries

(a la) francesa sautéed in butter

fresas strawberries

fresco fresh, chilled

fresón large strawberry

fricandó veal bird, thin slice of

meat rolled in bacon and braised

frijoles beans; **~ refritos** fried mashed beans

frito fried

fritos fritters

fritura mixta meat, fish or vegetables deep-fried in batter

fruta fruit ➤ 48; **~ escarchada** candied fruit

frío cold

fuerte strong

Fundador wine-distilled brandy

G **galletas** cookies/biscuits; **~ de nata** cream cookies/biscuits; **~ saladas** crackers

gallina hen

gallo cockerel

gambas (grandes) shrimps/prawns; **~ a la plancha** grilled; **~ al ajillo** with garlic

ganso goose

garbanzos chickpeas

garrafa carafe

gaseosa carbonated/fizzy

gazpacho cold tomato soup ➤ 44

ginebra gin; **~ con limón** gin-fizz; **~ con tónica** gin and tonic

(a la) gitanilla with garlic

gordo fatty, rich

granadas pomegranates

granadina pomegranate syrup mixed with wine or brandy

granizados iced drinks

gratinado gratinéed

grelo turnip greens
grosellas espinosas gooseberry
grosellas negras black currants
grosellas rojas red currants
guacamole avocado purée
guarnición garnish, trimming
guayaba guava (fruit)
guinda sour cherry
guindilla chili pepper
guisado stewed
guisantes peas

H **habas** broad beans
habichuela verde French/green beans
hamburguesa hamburger
hayaca central cornmeal pancake, usually with minced-meat filling
helado ice cream ➤ 48
hervido boiled; poached
hielo ice
hierbas herbs; **~ finas** mixture of herbs
higaditos de pollo chicken liver
hígado liver
higos figs
hinojo fennel
hoja de laurel bay leaf
hongo mushroom
horchata de almendra/chufa ground almond drink ➤ 51
(al) horno baked
hortaliza greens
hueso bone

huevos egg; **~ a la española** stuffed with tomatoes and served with cheese sauce; **~ a la flamenca** baked with tomato, onion and diced ham; **~ al nido** "eggs in the nest" ; **~ al trote** with tuna ; **~ cocidos** boiled; **~ duros** hard-boiled eggs; **~ escalfados a la española** poached egg on onions, tomatoes, peppers and zucchini; **~ fritos** fried eggs; **~ revueltos** scrambled eggs
humita boiled corn with tomatoes, green peppers, onions and cheese

I **(a la) inglesa** underdone; boiled; served with boiled vegetables

J **jabalí** wild boar
jalea jelly
jamón ham; **~ en dulce** boiled and served cold; **~ y huevos** ham and eggs
(a la) jardinera with carrots, peas and other vegetables
jengibre ginger
jerez sherry ➤ 49
judías blancas white beans
judías verdes green beans
jugo fresh juice; gravy, meat juice; **~ de fruta** fruit juice
jurel type of mackerel

L **lacón** shoulder of pork
lampreas lamprey
langosta spiny lobster; **~ con pollo** with chicken

langostinos shrimps (prawns)

lavanco wild duck

leche milk

lechón suckling pig

lechuga lettuce

legumbres pulses

lengua tongue

lenguado sole; ~ **a la vasca** baked with potatoes ➤ 45

lentejas lentils ➤ 45

licor liqueur ➤ 50

liebre hare; ~ **estofada** jugged

lima lime

limonada lemonade

limón lemon

lista de platos menu

lista de vinos wine list

litro a liter

liviano light

lobarro type of bass

lombarda red cabbage

lomo loin

loncha slice of meat

longaniza long, highly seasoned sausage

lubina bass

M **macedonia de frutas** mixed fruit salad

(a la) madrileña with *chorizo* sausage, tomatoes and paprika

magras al estilo de Aragón cured ham in tomato sauce

Mahón type of goat cheese ➤ 48

(a la) mallorquina highly seasoned (fish and shellfish)

maíz sweet corn

manchego ewe's milk cheese ➤ 48

mandarina tangerine

mantecado rich almond ice cream

mantequilla butter

manzana apple

Manzanilla dry, pale sherry

maní peanut

marinera fish and seafood only

(a la) marinera with mussels, onions, tomatoes, herbs and wine

mariscos seafood ➤ 45

matambre rolled beef stuffed with vegetables

mazapán marzipan

media botella half bottle

medio pollo asado half a roasted chicken

mejillones mussels

melaza treacle, molasses

melocotón peach; ~ **en almíbar** in syrup

melón melon

membrillo quince paste

menestra green vegetable soup; ~ **de pollo** casserole of chicken and vegetables

menta mint

menudillos giblets

merengue meringue

merienda afternoon snack

merluza hake

mermelada jam; ~ **amarga de naranjas** marmalade

mero sea bass

miel honey

(a la) milanese with cheese, generally baked

minuta menu

mojo picón piquant red sauce *(Can.)*

mojo verde green herb sauce served with fish *(Cat.)*

mole poblano chicken served with sauce of chili peppers, spices and chocolate

molleja sweetbread

mora mulberry

morcilla blood sausage (black pudding)

morilla morel mushroom

moros y cristianos rice and black beans with diced ham, garlic, green peppers and herbs

mostaza mustard

mújol mullet

muslo de pollo chicken leg

muy hecho well done

muy seco very dry

N **nabo** turnip

naranja orange

naranjada orangeade

nata cream; **~ batida** whipped

natillas custard

níspola medlar (fruit)

nopalito young cactus leaf served with salad dressing

nueces walnuts

nueces variadas assorted nuts

nuez moscada nutmeg

O **olla** stew; **~ gitana** vegetable stew; **~ podrida** stew made of vegetables, meat, fowl and ham

oloroso dark sherry ➤ 49

oporto port

ostras oysters

oveja ewe

P **pa amb tomàquet** bread with tomato and salt *(Cat.)*

pabellón criollo beef in tomato sauce, garnished with beans, rice and bananas

paella paella

paletilla shank

palitos skewered appetizer **~ de queso** cheese sticks/straws

palmito palm heart

palta avocado

pan bread; **~ de pueblo** plain white bread

panecillos rolls

papas potatoes; **~ a la huancaína** with cheese and green peppers; **~ arrugadas** new potatoes baked and rolled in rock salt *(Can.)*

parrillada grill; **~ mixta** mixed

pasado done, cooked; **~ por agua** soft *(egg)*

pasas raisins

pastas cookies/biscuits; pastas

pastel cake; **~ de choclo** corn/ maize with minced beef, chicken, raisins and olives; **~ de queso** cheesecake

pastelería pastries

pasteles cake; pastry

patatas potatoes; **~ (a la) leonesa** potatoes with onions; **~ fritas ~** French fries/chips; **~ nuevas** new potatoes

pato duck/duckling

paté pâté

pavo turkey

pechuga de pollo breast of chicken

pepinillos pickles/gherkins

pepino cucumber

(en) pepitoria stewed with onions, green peppers and tomatoes

pera pear

perca perch

percebes goose barnacles

perdiz partridge; **~ en escabeche** cooked in oil with vinegar, onions, parsley, carrots and green pepper; served cold; **~ estofada** served in a white-wine sauce

perejil parsley

perifollo chervil

perilla firm cheese ➤ 48

pescadilla whiting

pescado fish ➤ 45; **~ frito** fried

pez espada swordfish

picadillo minced meat, hash

picado minced

picante sharp, spicy, highly seasoned

picatoste deep-fried slice of bread

pichón pigeon

pierna leg

pimentón paprika

pimienta pepper

pimientos a la riojana sweet peppers stuffed with minced meat

pimientos morrones sweet red pepers

piña pineapple

pincho moruno grilled meat on a skewer

pintada guinea fowl

pisco grape brandy

pisto green pepper stew ➤ 47

(a la) plancha grilled on a griddle

plato plate, dish, portion; **~ del día** dish of the day

platos fríos cold dishes

platos típicos specialties

plátano banana

poco hecho rare/underdone

pollito spring chicken

pollo chicken; **~ a la brasa** grilled; **~ asado** roast; **~ pibil** simmered in fruit juice and spices

polvorón almond cookie/biscuit

pomelo grapefruit

ponche crema eggnog liquor

porción small helping of tapas

postre dessert ➤ 48

potaje vegetable soup

puchero stew

puerros leeks

pulpitos baby octopus

pulpo octopus

punto de nieve dessert of whipped cream with beaten egg whites

puré purée; **~ de patatas** mash potatoes

Q **queso** cheese ▸ 48

quisquillas common shrimps (prawns)

R **rábano** radish; ~ **picante** horseradish

rabo de buey oxtail

ración large helping

raja slice, portion

rallado grated

rape monkfish

raya ray, skate

rebanada slice

rebozado breaded, fried in batter

recomendamos we recommend

refrescos cold drinks

regular medium

rehogada sautéed

relleno stuffed

remolacha beet (beetroot)

repollo cabbage

requesón fresh-curd cheese

riñones kidneys; ~ **al jerez** braised in sherry

róbalo haddock

rodaballo turbot

(a la) romana dipped in batter and fried

romero rosemary

romesco sauce of nuts, chili, tomatoes, garlic and breadcrumbs (Cat.)

ron rum

roncal sharp ewe's milk cheese ▸ 48

ropa vieja cooked, leftover meat and vegetables, covered with tomatoes and green peppers

rosado rosé

rosbif roast beef

rosquilla doughnut

rubio red mullet

ruibarbo rhubarb

S **sal** salt

salado salted, salty

salchichas sausages

salchichón salami

salmonetes red mullet

salmón salmon; ~ **ahumado** smoked salmon

salsa sauce

salsa a la catalana sauce of tomato and green peppers

salsa a la vasca parsley, peas, garlic; a delicate green dressing for fish in the Basque country

salsa alioli garlic sauce

salsa de tomate ketchup

salsa en escabeche sweet and sour sauce

salsa española brown sauce with herbs, spices and wine

salsa mayordoma butter and parsley sauce

salsa picante hot pepper sauce

salsa romana bacon or ham, egg cream sauce

salsa romesco green peppers, pimentos, garlic; popular chilled dressing for fish on the east coast around Tarragona

salsa verde parsley sauce

salteado sautéed

salvia sage

sandía watermelon

sangrita tequila with tomato, orange and lime juices

sangría wine punch ➤ 50

sardinas sardines

seco dry

sencillo plain

sepia cuttlefish

serrano cured

sesos brains

setas mushrooms

sidra cider

sobrasada salami

soda soda water

sol y sombra blend of wine-distilled brandy and aniseed liqueur

solo black (coffee); straight/neat

solomillo de cerdo tenderloin of pork

sopa soup ➤ 44; **~ de buey** oxtail; **~ de ajo** garlic; **~ de arroz** rice; **~ de camarones** shrimp; **~ de cangrejos** crayfish; **~ castellana** baked garlic; **~ de cebolla** onion; **~ de cocido** a kind of broth; **~ de espárragos** asparagus; **~ de fideos** noodle; **~ de mariscos** seafood; **~ de patatas** potato; **~ de pescado** fish; **~ de tomate** tomato; **~ de verduras** vegetable; **~ juliana** bouillon of finely shredded vegetables; **~ sevillana** highly spiced fish soup

sorbete (iced) fruit drink

suave mild

suizo bun

suplemento sobre ... ...extra

surtido assorted

T **taco** wheat or cornflour pancake, usually with meat filling and garnished with spicy sauce

tajada slice

tallarín noodle

tamal pastry dough of coarsely ground cornmeal with meat or fuit filling, steamed in corn-husks

tapas snacks ➤ 43

tarta de almendras almond tart

tarta de manzana apple tart

tarta de moka mocha cake

tarta helada ice-cream cake

tartaletas small open tarts filled with fish, meat, vegetables or cheese

taza de café cup of coffee

té tea ➤ 51

ternera veal

tinto red

Tío Pepe brand of sherry

tipo roquefort blue

tocino bacon

tocino de cielo dessert of whipped egg yolks and sugar

tojunto rabbit stew

tomates tomatoes

tomillo thyme

tónica tonic water

tordo thrush
toronja type of grapefruit
tortilla omelet; **~ al ron** rum; **~ de alcachofa** artichoke; **~ de cebolla** onion; **~ de espárragos** asparagus; **~ de jamón** ham; **~ de patatas** potato; **~ de queso** cheese; **~ de setas** mushroom; **~ gallega** potato omelet with ham, chili; **~ paisana** with potatoes, peas, prawns or ham
tortitas pancakes/waffles
tostadas toast
tripas tripe
Triple Seco orange liqueur
trucha trout; **~ a la navarra** stuffed with ham; **~ frita a la asturiana** floured and fried in butter, garnished with lemon
trufas truffles
tumbet ratatouille and potato-type casserole with meat or fish (*Maj.*)
turrón nougat

U **ulloa** soft cheese from Galicia
uvas grapes; **~ blancas** green; **~ negras** black
uvas pasas raisins

V **vaca salada** corned beef
vainilla vanilla
valenciana classic *paella* ➤ 44
variado varied, assorted
varios sundries
vaso glass

venado venison
veneras scallops
verduras vegetables ➤ 47
vermut vermouth
vieira scallop
villalón mild cheese ➤ 48
vinagreta piquant vinegar dressing
vino wine ➤ 50; **~ de mesa** table wine; **~ del país** local wine
(a la) vizcaína with green peppers, tomatoes, garlic and paprika

WX YZ **whisky** whisky; **~ americano** bourbon; **~ con soda** whisky and soda; **~ escocés** Scotch
xampañ Catalonian sparkling wine
xató olive and endive salad (*Cat.*)
yema egg yolk
yemas dessert of whipped egg yolks and sugar
yogur yogurt
zamorana ham, pork loin, pig's feet/trotters, chili pepper
zanahorias carrots
zarzamoras blackberries
zarzuela savory stew of assorted fish and shellfish (*Cat.*); **~ de pescado** selection of fish with highly seasoned sauce
zumo fresh juice; **~ de fruta** fruit juice

Travel

ESSENTIAL

A ticket to ...	**Un billete para ...** *oon beel-yeteh para*
How much ...?	**¿Cuánto ...?** *kwanto*
When?	**¿Cuándo ...?** *kwando*
When will ... arrive/leave?	**¿Cuándo llega/sale ...?** *kwando l-yega/saleh*

Spain has a fairly well-developed transport system, so you should be able to enjoy trouble-free traveling. The rail network radiates out from Madrid.

Safety Seguridad

Spain is a relatively safe country and violent crimes against tourists are rare; but if you do feel insecure, the phrases below may help.

Would you accompany me to the bus stop?	**¿Me acompaña a la parada de autobús?** *meh akompaña a la parada deh aootoboos*
I don't want to ... on my own.	**No quiero ... solo(-a)** *no keeyero ...solo(-a)*
stay here	**quedarme aquí** *kedarmeh akee*
walk home	**ir a casa andando** *eer a kasa andando*
I don't feel safe here.	**No me siento seguro(-a) aquí.** *no meh seeyento segooro akee*

Arrival A la llegada

Most visitors, including citizens of all EU countries, the US, Canada, Eire, Australia and New Zealand, require only a valid passport for entry to Spain.

Import restrictions between EU countries have been relaxed on items for personal use or consumption which are bought duty-paid within the EU. Suggested maximum: 90L. wine or 60L. sparkling wine; 20L. fortified wine, 10L. spirits and 110L. beer.

Duty Free Into:	Cigarettes	Cigars	Tobacco	Spirits	Wine
Spain	200	50	250g	1L	2L
Canada	200 and	50 and	400g	1L or	1L
UK	200 or	50 or	250g	1L and	2L
U.S.	200 and	100 and	discretionary	1L or	1L

Passport control Control de pasaportes

Can I see your passport, please?	**¿Puedo ver su pasaporte, por favor?** _pwedo behr soo pasaporteh por fabor_
We have a joint passport.	**Tenemos un pasaporte conjunto.** _tenemos oon pasaporteh konkhoonto_
The children are on this passport.	**Los niños están en este pasaporte.** _los neeños estan en esteh pasaporteh_
What's the purpose of your visit?	**¿Cuál es el propósito de su visita?** _kwal es el proposeeto deh soo beeseeta_
I'm here on vacation/ on business.	**Estoy aquí de vacaciones/en viaje de negocios.** _estoy akee deh bakathyones/ en beeyakheh deh negothyoss_
I'm just passing through.	**Estoy de paso ...** _estoy deh paso_
I'm going to ...	**Voy a ...** _boy a_
I won't be working here.	**No voy a trabajar aquí.** _no boy a trabakhar akee_
Who are you here with?	**¿Con quién viaja?** _kon keeyen beeyakha_
I'm ...	**Viajo...** _beeyakho_
on my own	**solo(-a)** _solo(-a)_
with my family	**con mi familia** _kon mee fameeleeya_
with a group	**con un grupo** _kon oon groopo_

WHO ARE YOU WITH? ➤ 120

Customs Aduana

I have only the
normal allowances.

Sólo lo normal.
solo lo normal

It's a gift/for my personal use.

Es un regalo/para uso personal.
es oon regalo/para ooso personal

¿Tiene algo que declarar?	Do you have anything to declare?
Tiene que pagar impuestos por esto.	You must pay duty on this.
¿Cuándo compró esto?	Where did you buy this?
Abra esta bolsa por favor.	Please open this bag.
¿Tiene más equipaje?	Do you have any more luggage?

I would like to declare ... **Quiero declarar ...** *keeyero deklarar*

I don't understand. **No entiendo.** *no enteeyendo*

Does anyone here speak English? **¿Hay alguien aquí que hable inglés?**
eye algeeyen akee keh ableh eengles

ADUANAS	customs
ARTÍCULOS LIBRES DE IMPUESTOS	duty-free goods
ARTÍCULOS QUE DECLARAR	goods to declare
CONTROL DE PASAPORTES	passport control
NADA QUE DECLARAR	nothing to declare
POLICÍA	police
PASO DE LA FRONTERA	border crossing

Duty-free shopping
Comprar artículos libres de impuestos

What currency is this in? **¿En qué moneda/divisa está esto?**
en keh moneda/deebeesa esta esto

Can I pay in ...? **¿Puedo pagar en ...?**
pwedo pagar en

dollars/pesetas/pounds **dólares/pesetas/libras**
dolares/pesetas/leebras

Plane El avión

A number of private airlines, such as Air Europa and Aviaco, offer competitive prices across the internal air network and selected international flights.

Tickets and reservations Billetes y reservas

When is the … flight to Madrid?	**¿Cuándo sale el vuelo … a Madrid?** _kwando saleh el bwelo … a madreeth_
first/next/last	**primer/próximo/último** _preemer/prokseemo/oolteemo_
I'd like 2 … tickets to …	**Quiero dos billetes … a …** _keeyero dos beel-yetehs … a_
one-way/single	**de ida** _deh eeda_
round-trip/return	**de ida y vuelta** _deh eeda ee bwelta_
first class	**de primera clase** _deh preemera klaseh_
business class	**de clase preferente** _deh klaseh preferenteh_
economy class	**económico** _ekonomeeko_
How much is a flight to …?	**¿Cuánto cuesta un vuelo a …?** _kwanto kwesta oon bwelo a_
Are there any supplements/reductions?	**¿Tiene algún suplemento/descuento?** _teeyeneh algoon sooplemento/deskwento_
I'd like to … my reservation for flight number …	**Quiero … mi reserva del vuelo número …** _keeyero … mee reserba del bwelo noomero_
cancel	**cancelar** _kanthelar_
change	**cambiar** _kambeeyar_
confirm	**confirmar** _konfeermar_

Inquiries about the flight Preguntas sobre el vuelo

How long is the flight?	**¿Cuánto dura el vuelo?** _kwanto doora el bwelo_
What time does the plane leave?	**¿A qué hora sale el avión?** _a keh ora saleh el abeeyon_
What time will we arrive?	**¿A qué hora llegamos?** _a keh ora l-yegamos_
What time do I have to check in?	**¿A qué hora tengo que facturar?** _a keh ora tengo keh faktoorar_

NUMBERS ➤ 216; TIME ➤ 220

Checking in Facturación

Where is the check-in
desk for flight …?

¿Dónde está el mostrador
de facturación del vuelo …?
_dondeh esta el mostrador
deh faktooratheeyon del bwelo_

I have …
3 cases to check in

Tengo … _tengo_
tres maletas para facturar
tres maletas para faktoorar

2 pieces of hand luggage
How much baggage is
allowed free?

dos bultos de mano _dos booltos deh mano_
**¿Cuánto equipaje está permitido sin
pagar?** _kwanto ekeepakeh esta
permeeteedo seen pagar_

Su billete/pasaporte por favor.	Your ticket/passport please.
¿Quiere un asiento que dé a la ventana o al pasillo?	Would you like a window or an aisle seat?
¿Fumador o no fumador?	Smoking or non-smoking?
Por favor, pase a la sala de embarque.	Please go through to the departure lounge.
¿Cuántos bultos de equipaje tiene?	How many pieces of baggage do you have?
Lleva exceso de equipaje.	You have excess baggage.
Tendrá que pagar un suplemento de … pesetas por kilo de equipaje en exceso.	You'll have to pay a supplement of . . . pesetas per kilo of excess baggage.
Eso pesa demasiado/eso es demasiado grande para pasar como equipaje de mano.	That's too heavy/large for hand baggage.
¿Hizo las maletas usted?	Did you pack these bags yourself?
¿Contienen algún artículo punzante o eléctrico?	Do they contain any sharp or electrical items?

LLEGADAS	arrivals
NO DEJE SU EQUIPAJE DESATENDIDO	do not leave bags unattended
REVISIÓN DE SEGURIDAD	security check
SALIDAS	departures

LUGGAGE/BAGGAGE ➤ 71

Information Información

Is there any delay on flight …?	**¿Lleva retraso el vuelo …?** *l-yeba retraso el bwelo*
How late will it be?	**¿Cuánto tiempo lleva de retraso?** *kwanto teeyempo l-yeba deh retraso*
Has the flight from … landed?	**¿Ha aterrizado el vuelo procedente de …?** *a aterreethado el bwelo prothedenteh deh*
Which gate does flight … leave from?	**¿De qué puerta sale el vuelo …?** *deh keh pwerta saleh el bwelo*

Boarding/In-flight Embarque/Durante el vuelo

Your boarding card, please.	**Su tarjeta de embarque, por favor.** *soo tarkheta deh embarkeh por fabor*
Could I have a drink/ something to eat please?	**¿Podría tomar algo de beber/comer, por favor?** *podreeya tomar algo deh beber/komer por fabor*
Please wake me for the meal.	**Por favor, despiérteme para la comida.** *por fabor despeeyertemeh para la komeeda*
What time will we arrive?	**¿A qué hora llegaremos?** *a keh ora l-yegaremos*
A vomit/sick bag please.	**Una bolsa para el mareo por favor.** *oona bolsa para el mareyo por fabor*

Arrival Llegada

Where is/are …?	**¿Dónde está/están …?** *dondeh esta/estan*
currency exchange	**la ventanilla de cambio** *la bentaneel-ya deh kambeeyo*
buses	**los autobuses** *los aootobooses*
car rental/hire	**el alquiler de coches** *el alkeeler deh koches*
exit	**la salida** *la saleeda*
taxis	**los taxis** *los taksees*
telephone	**los teléfonos** *los telefonos*
Is there a bus into town?	**¿Hay un autobús que va a la ciudad?** *eye oon aootoboos keh ba a la theeyoodath*
How do I get to the … Hotel?	**¿Cómo se va al Hotel? …** *komo seh ba al otel …*

Baggage/Luggage Equipaje

Tipping: The official rates are 100 Ptas. per bag.

Porter! Excuse me!	**¡Mozo! ¡Disculpe!**
	motho. dees<u>kool</u>peh
Could you take my	**¿Podría llevar mi equipaje a …?**
luggage to …?	*po<u>dree</u>ya l-ye<u>bar</u> mee ekee<u>pa</u>keh a*
a taxi/bus	**un taxi/autobús** *oon <u>tak</u>see/aooto<u>boos</u>*
Where is/are …?	**¿Dónde está/están …?** *<u>don</u>deh es<u>ta</u>/es<u>tan</u>*
luggage carts	**los carritos para el equipaje**
	los ka<u>rree</u>tos <u>pa</u>ra el ekee<u>pa</u>keh
luggage lockers	**las taquillas** *las ta<u>keel</u>-yas*
luggage check	**la consigna** *la kon<u>seeg</u>na*
Where is the luggage	**¿Dónde está el equipaje del vuelo …?**
from flight …?	*<u>don</u>deh es<u>ta</u> el ekee<u>pa</u>keh del <u>bwe</u>lo*

Loss, damage and theft
Equipaje perdido/estropeado/robado

My luggage has been lost/	**Han perdido/robado mi equipaje.**
stolen.	*an per<u>dee</u>do/rro<u>ba</u>do mee ekee<u>pa</u>keh*
My suitcase was damaged	**Mi maleta se ha estropeado en el tránsito.**
in transit.	*mee ma<u>le</u>ta seh a estrope<u>ya</u>do en el*
	<u>tran</u>seeto
Our luggage has not arrived.	**Nuestro equipaje no ha llegado.**
	<u>nwes</u>tro ekee<u>pa</u>keh no a l-ye<u>ga</u>do
Do you have claims forms?	**¿Tienen formularios para reclamaciones?**
	tee<u>ye</u>nen formoo<u>la</u>reeoss para
	rreklama<u>thee</u>oness

¿Puede describir su equipaje?	What does your luggage look like?
¿Tiene la etiqueta de recogida?	Do you have the claim check/ reclaim tag?
Su equipaje …	Your luggage …
puede que lo hayan mandado a …	may have been sent to …
puede que llegue hoy	may arrive later today
Vuelva usted mañana, por favor.	Please come back tomorrow.
Llame a este número para comprobar que su equipaje ha llegado.	Call this number to check if your luggage has arrived.

POLICE ➤ 152; COLORS ➤ 143

Train Tren

On Spain's rail network **RENFE (Red Nacional de los Ferrocarriles Españoles)** children under 4 travel free; aged 4–12 pay half fares.

Check out the various discounts/reductions and travel cards available. Rates are cheaper on "off days" (**días azules**). Some travel cards can also be used for local buses and subway. Another way is to buy tickets in a "checkbook" form at travel agents. These can be exchanged for train tickets at special rates on "off days".

Tickets can be purchased and reservations made in travel agencies or at railway stations. The purchase of a ticket usually means that you are allocated a seat. You can reserve/book seats in advance. For longer journeys there is a smoking car, otherwise the train is non-smoking.

AVE _abeh_
High-speed train (**alta velocidad española**), operating between Madrid and Seville in just two hours.

EuroCity _e-oorotheetee_
International express, first and second classes.

Talgo, Electrotren, TER _talgo, elektrotren, tehr_
Luxury diesel, first and second classes; supplementary charges over the regular fare; seats should be reserved/booked in advance. Similar services are provided by **Intercity** and **Tren Estrella**.

Expreso, Rápido _ekspresso, rrapeedo_
Long-distance expresses; stopping at all main towns.

Omnibus, Tranvía, Automotor _omneeboos, tranbeea, awtomotor_
Local train; making frequent stops.

Auto Expreso _awto ekspresso_
Car train allows you to load your car and travel in a sleeper; discounts available on the car freight if more than one berth reserved/booked.

Coche cama _kocheh kama_
Sleeping car; compartments with wash basins and 1 or 2 berths. A cheaper way of sleeping during your journey is to buy a **litera,** one of the berths in a compartment of six.

Coche comedor _kocheh komedor_
Dining car; generally included on overnight journeys. Otherwise, there may be a buffet car; lunch served at your seats on certain trains; or simply a sandwich and drinks car on shorter trips.

Furgón de equipajes _foorgon deh ekeepakhess_
Baggage car/luggage van; only registered luggage permitted.

To the station A la estación

How do I get to the rail station?	**¿Cómo se llega a la estación de trenes ?** _komo seh l-yega a la estatheeyon deh trenes_
Do trains to León leave from ... Station?	**¿Salen de la estación ... los trenes a León?** _salen deh la estatheeyon ... los trenes a leyon_
How far is it?	**¿A qué distancia está?** _a keh deestantheeya esta_
Can I leave my car there?	**¿Puedo dejar mi coche allí?** _pwedo dekhar mee kocheh al-yee_

At the station En la estación

Where is/are ...?	**¿Dónde está/están ...?** _dondeh esta/estan_
currency-exchange office	**la oficina de cambio de moneda** _la ofeetheena deh kambeeyo deh moneda_
information desk	**la ventanilla de información** _la bentaneel-ya deh eenformatheeyon_
baggage check	**la consigna** _la konseegna_
lost-and-found office/ lost property	**la oficina de objetos perdidos** _la ofeetheena deh obkhetos perdeedos_
luggage lockers	**las taquillas** _las takeel-yas_
platforms	**los andenes** _los andenes_
snack bar	**el bar** _el bar_
ticket office	**el despacho de billetes** _el despacho deh beel-yetes_
waiting room	**la sala de espera** _la sala deh espera_

A LOS ANDENES	to the platforms
ENTRADA	entrance
INFORMACIÓN	information
LLEGADAS	arrivals
RESERVAS	reservations
SALIDA	exit
SALIDAS	departures

DIRECTIONS ➤ _94_

73

Tickets Billetes

I'd like a … ticket to Todelo.	**Quiero un … billete a Toledo.** keeyero oon … beel-yeteh a toledo
one-way/single	**de ida** deh eeda
round-trip/return	**de ida y vuelta** deh eeda ee bwelta
first/second class	**de primera/segunda clase** deh preemera/segoonda klaseh
concessionary	**con descuento** kon deskwento
I'd like to reserve a seat …	**Quiero reservar una plaza …** keeyero reserbar oona platha
aisle seat	**un asiento que dé al pasillo** oon aseeyento keh deh al paseel-yo
window seat	**un asiento que dé a la ventana** oon aseeyento keh deh a la bentana
berth	**una litera** oona leetera
Is there a sleeper/sleeping car?	**¿Hay coche cama?** eye kocheh kama
I'd like a … berth.	**Quiero una … litera.** keeyero oona … leetera
upper/lower	**de arriba/abajo** deh arreeba/abakho
Can I buy a ticket on board?	**¿Puedo comprar un billete dentro del tren?** pwedo komprar oon beel-yeteh dentro del tren

Price Precio

How much is that?	**¿Cuánto es?** kwanto es
Is there a discount for …?	**¿Hacen descuento a …?** athen deskwento a
children/families	**los niños/las familias** los neeños/las fameeleeyas
senior citizens	**los pensionistas** los penseeyoneestas
students	**los estudiantes** los estoodeeyantes
Do you offer a cheap same-day return/round-trip?	**¿Tienen una oferta por un billete de ida y vuelta en el mismo día?** teeyenen oona oferta por oon beel-yeteh deh eeda ee bwelta en el meesmo deeya
There is a supplement of …	**Hay que pagar un suplemento de …** eye keh pagar oon sooplemento deh

Queries Preguntas

Do I have to change trains?

¿Tengo que cambiar de trenes? _tengo keh kambeeyar deh trenes_

It's a direct train.

Es un tren directo. _es oon tren deerekto_

You have to change at …

Tiene que cambiar en … _teeyeneh keh kambeeyar en_

How long is this ticket valid for?

¿Para cuánto tiempo vale este billete? _para kwanto teeyempo baleh esteh beel-yeteh_

Can I take my bicycle on to the train?

¿Puedo llevar mi bicicleta en el tren? _pwedo l-yebar mee beetheekleta en el tren_

Can I return on the same ticket?

¿Puedo volver con el mismo billete? _pwedo bolber kon el meesmo beel-yeteh_

In which car/coach is my seat?

¿En qué compartimento está mi asiento? _en keh komparteemento esta mee aseeyento_

Is there a dining car on the train?

¿Hay coche restaurante en el tren? _eye kocheh restawranteh en el tren_

– Quiero un billete a Madrid, por favor.
  – ¿De ida o ida y vuelta?
– De ida y vuelta, por favor.
  – Son diez mil pesetas.
– ¿Tengo que cambiar de trenes?
  – Sí, tiene que cambiar en Córdoba.
– Gracias. Adiós.

Train times Horario de trenes

Could I have a timetable please?

¿Podría darme un horario (de trenes), por favor? _podreeya darmeh oon orareeyo (deh trenes) por fabor_

When is the … train to Vigo?

¿Cuándo sale el … tren a Vigo? _kwando saleh el …tren a beego_

first/next/last

primer/próximo/último _preemer/prokseemo/oolteemo_

There's a train to … at …

Hay un tren a … a las … _eye oon tren a … a las …_

| How frequent are the trains to…? | ¿Con qué frecuencia salen los trenes a …? |
| | kon keh frekwentheeya salen los trenes a |

| once/twice a day | una/dos veces al día |
| | oona/dos bethes al deeya |

| 5 times a day | cinco veces al día |
| | theenko bethes al deeya |

every hour | **cada hora** _kada ora_

What time do they leave? | **¿A qué hora salen?** _a keh ora salen_

on the hour | **a la hora en punto** _a la ora en poonto_

20 minutes past the hour | **a las y veinte** _a las ee baynteh_

What time does the train stop/ arrive in …? | **¿A qué hora para/llega el tren a …?** _a keh ora para/l-yega el tren a_

How long is the trip/journey? | **¿Cuánto dura el viaje?** _kwanto doora el beeyakheh_

Is the train on time? | **¿Llega puntual el tren?** _l-yega poontoowal el tren_

Departures Salidas

Which platform does the train to … leave from? | **¿De qué andén sale el tren a …?** _deh keh anden saleh el tren a_

Where is platform 4? | **¿Dónde está el andén número cuatro?** _dondeh esta el anden noomero kwatro_

over there | **allí** _al-yee_

on the left/right | **a la izquierda/derecha** _a la eethkeeyerda/derecha_

under the underpass | **debajo del pasaje subterráneo** _debakho del pasakheh soobterraneyo_

Where do I change for …? | **¿Dónde tengo que cambiar para …?** _dondeh tengo keh kambeeyar para_

How long will I have to wait for a connection? | **¿Cuánto tiempo tengo que esperar para un enlace?** _kwanto teeyempo tengo keh esperar para oon enlatheh_

Boarding Montarse en el tren

Is this the right platform
for the train to …?

¿Es éste el andén para el
tren a …? *es esteh el
anden para el tren a*

Is this the train to …?

¿Es éste el tren a …?
es esteh el tren a

Is this seat taken?

¿Está ocupado este asiento?
esta okoopado esteh aseeyento

I think that's my seat.

Creo que ése es mi asiento.
kreyo keh eseh es mee aseeyento

Here's my reservation.

Aquí tengo la reserva.
akee tengo la rreserba

Are there any seats/berths
available?

¿Hay asientos/literas libres?
eye aseeyentos/leeteras leebres

Do you mind …?

¿Le importa …? *leh eemporta*

if I sit here

si me siento aquí *see meh seeyento akee*

if I open the window

si abro la ventana *see abro la bentana*

On the journey En el viaje

How long are we
stopping here for?

¿Cuánto tiempo paramos?
kwanto teeyempo paramos

When do we get to …?

¿Cuándo llegamos a …?
kwando l-yegamos a

Have we passed …?

¿Hemos pasado …? *emos pasado*

Where is the dining/
sleeping car?

¿Dónde está el coche restaurante/cama?
*dondeh esta el kocheh restawranteh/
kama*

Where is my berth?

¿Dónde está mi litera?
dondeh esta mee leetera

I've lost my ticket.

He perdido el billete.
eh perdeedo el beel-yeteh

FRENO DE EMERGENCIA   emergency brake
PUERTAS AUTOMÁTICAS   automatic doors

Long-distance bus/Coach Autobús

Travel by coach is good if you want to visit out-of-the-way places. Most buses only serve towns and villages within a region or provinces. From larger cities you can book cross country and international lines – information is available from the local central bus station (**estación de autobuses**).

Where is the bus/ coach station?	**¿Dónde está la estación de autobuses?** _dondeh esta_ la _estatheeyon_ deh _awtobooses_
When's the next bus/ coach to …?	**¿Cuándo sale el próximo autobús a …?** _kwando saleh_ el _prokseemo awtoboos_ a
Which terminal does it leave from?	**¿De qué andén sale?** _deh keh anden saleh_
Where are the bus stops/ coach bays?	**¿Dónde están los andenes?** _dondeh estan_ los _andenes_
Does the bus/coach stop at …?	**¿Para el autobús en …?** _para_ el _awtoboos_ en
How long does the trip/ journey take?	**¿Cuánto dura el viaje?** _kwanto doora_ el _beeyakheh_

Bus Autobús

In most buses you pay as you enter. For larger cities with fixed fares, a 10-journey pass (**un bonobús**) is cheapest – but remember to use the cancelling machine by the driver for each trip. These tickets are sold at newspaper stands in Madrid; in Barcelona at banks, lottery-ticket shops and metro stations.

Where is the bus station/terminal?	**¿Dónde está la estación de autobuses?** _dondeh esta_ la _estatheeyon_ deh _awtobooses_
Where can I get a bus to …?	**¿Dónde se coge un autobús a …?** _dondeh se kokheh oon awtoboos_ a …

Tiene esa parada de allí/ al bajar la calle.	You need that stop over there/down the road.
Tiene que tomar el autobús número …	You need bus number …
Tiene que cambiar de autobús en …	You must change buses at …

PARADA DE AUTOBUSES	bus stop
PARADA SOLICITADA	request stop
PROHIBIDO FUMAR	no smoking
SALIDA DE EMERGENCIA	(emergency) exit

78

DIRECTIONS ➤ 94; TIME ➤ 220

Buying tickets Comprar billetes

Where can I buy tickets?	**¿Dónde se puede comprar billetes?** _dondeh seh pwedeh komprar beel-yetes_
A ... ticket to the beach, please.	**Un billete ... para la playa, por favor.** _oon beel-yeteh ... para la playa por fabor_
one-way/single	**de ida** _deh eeda_
round-trip/return	**de ida y vuelta** _deh eeda ee bwelta_
multiple journey	**bonobús** _bonoboos_
day/weekly/monthly	**para todo el día/la semana/el mes** _para todo el deeya/la semana/el mes_
How much is the fare to ...?	**¿Cuánto cuesta el billete a ...?** _kwanto kwesta el beel-yeteh a_

Traveling De viaje

Is this the right bus/tram to ...?	**¿Es éste el autobús a ...?** _es este el awtoboos a_
Could you tell me when to get off?	**¿Podría decirme cuándo me tengo que bajar?** _podreeya detheermeh kwando meh tengo keh bakhar_
Do I have to change buses?	**¿Tengo que hacer transbordo?** _tengo keh ather transbordo_
How many stops are there to ...?	**¿Cuántas paradas hay hasta ...?** _kwantas paradas eye asta_
Next stop please!	**¡Próxima parada, por favor!** _prokseema parada por fabor_

> **AL PICAR SU BILLETE**   validate your ticket

– Disculpe. ¿Es éste el autobús que va al ayuntamiento?
   – No. Tiene que tomar/coger el número ocho. Allí está...
   – Un billete para el ayuntamiento, por favor.
      – Son cien pesetas, por favor.
   – ¿Podría decirme cuándo tengo que bajarme?
      – Queda a cuatro paradas de aquí.

NUMBERS ➤ 216; DIRECTIONS ➤ 94

Subway/Metro **Metro**

There are extensive subway/underground systems in Madrid and Barcelona, with a striking new system in Bilbao. Big maps outside each station make the systems easy to use. Cheaper ten-ride tickets (**billete de diez viajes**) are available.

Barcelona offers un bon-bus T1, which allows travel on both metro and the bus network.

Most metro systems close at 11 p.m.. on weekdays and at 1 a.m. on Saturdays.

General Inquiries **Preguntas generales**

Where's the nearest subway/ metro station?	**¿Dónde está la próxima estación de metro?** _dondeh esta la prokseema estatheeyon deh metro_
Where do I buy a ticket?	**¿Dónde se compran los billetes?** _dondeh seh kompran los beel-yetes_
Could I have a map of the subway/metro?	**¿Podría darme un mapa del metro?** _podreeya darmeh oon mapa del metro_

Traveling **De viaje**

Which line should I take for …?	**¿Qué línea tengo que coger para …?** _keh leenaya tengo keh kokher para_
Is this the right train for …?	**¿Es éste el tren para …?** _es esteh el tren para_
Which stop is it for …?	**¿Qué parada es la de …?** _keh parada es la deh_
How many stops is it to …?	**¿Cuántas paradas quedan para …?** _kwantas paradas kedan para_
It's the next stop.	**Es la próxima parada.** _es la prokseema parada_
Is the next stop …?	**¿Es … la próxima parada?** _es … la prokseema parada_
Where are we?	**¿Dónde estamos?** _dondeh estamos_
Where do I change for …?	**¿Dónde tengo que hacer transbordo para …?** _dondeh tengo keh ather transbordo para_

A OTRAS LÍNEAS/ CORRESPONDENCIA	to other lines/ transfer

NUMBERS ➤ 216; BUYING TICKETS ➤ 74, 79

Ferry El Ferry

Ferry companies operating services from the UK to Spain include Brittany Ferries (Portsmouth–Santander, Plymouth–Santander) and P&O (Portsmouth–Bilbao).

Regular ferry services are run to the Balearic Islands (from Valencia) and Canary Islands (by **Compañía Transmediterránea SA**).

Why not spend the day in Africa? A ferry trip to Tangiers (Morocco) and Ceuta (Spanish territory) operates from Algeciras.

When is the car ferry to …?	**¿Cuándo sale el ferry a …?**
	kwando saleh el ferree a
first/next/last	**primer/próximo/último**
	preemer/prokseemo/oolteemo
hovercraft/ship	**el aerodeslizador/el barco**
	el aeyrodesleethador/el barko
A round-trip/return	**Un billete de vuelta para …**
ticket for …	*oon beel-yeteh deh bwelta para*
1 car and 1 trailer/caravan	**un coche y una roulotte**
	oon kocheh ee oona rooloteh
2 adults and 3 children	**dos adultos y tres niños**
	dos adooltos ee tres neeños
I want to reserve a … cabin.	**Quiero reservar un camarote …**
	keeyero reserbar oon kamaroteh
single/double	**individual/doble**
	eendeebeedoowal/dobleh

BOTE SALVAVIDAS	life boat
FLOTADOR	life preserver/life belt
PUNTO DE REUNIÓN	muster station
PROHIDO EL ACCESO	no access

Boat trips Excursiones en barco

Is there a …?	**¿Hay …?** *eye*
boat trip	**una excursión en barco**
	oona ekskoorseeyon en barko
river cruise	**un crucero por el río**
	oon kroothero por el reeyo
What time does it leave/return?	**¿A qué hora sale/vuelve?**
	a keh ora saleh/bwelveh
Where can we buy tickets?	**¿Dónde se compran los billetes?**
	dondeh seh kompran los beel-yetes

TIME ➤ 220; BUYING TICKETS ➤ 74, 79

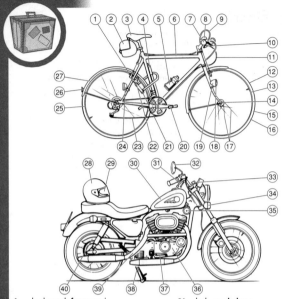

1	brake pad **frenos** mpl	21	lock **candado** m
2	bicycle bag **cesta** f	22	generator/dynamo **dinamo** m
3	saddle **sillin** m	23	chain **cadena** f
4	pump **bomba** f	24	rear light **luz** f **trasera**
5	water bottle **botella** f **para el agua**	25	rim **llanta** f
6	frame **cuadro** m	26	reflectors **reflectores** mpl
7	handlebars **manillar** m	27	fender/mudguard **guardabarros** mpl
8	bell **timbre** m	28	helmet **casco** m
9	brake cable **cable** m **de los frenos**	29	visor **visor** m
10	gear shift/lever **palanca** f **para cambiar de marcha**	30	fuel tank **depósito** m **del combustible**
11	gear/control cable **cable** m **de las marchas/de control**	31	clutch lever **palanca** f **del embrague**
		32	mirror **espejo** m
12	inner tube **cámara** f	33	ignition switch **interruptor** m **de arranque**
13	front/back wheel **rueda** f **delantera/trasera**	34	turn indicator/switch **intermitente** m
14	axle **eje** m	35	horn **cláxon** m
15	tire/tyre **neumático** m	36	engine **motor** m
16	wheel **rueda** f	37	gear shift/stick **palanca** f **para las marchas**
17	spokes **radio** m	38	kick/main stand **pie** m
18	bulb **luz** f	39	exhaust pipe **tubo** m **de escape**
19	headlamp **luz** f **delantera**	40	chain guard **protector** m **de la cadena**
20	pedal **pedal** m		

82

Bicycle/motorbike Bicicleta/moto

I'd like to rent a …

Quiero alquilar …
keeyero alkeelar

3-/10-gear bicycle

una bicicleta de tres/diez marchas *oona beetheekleta deh tres/deeyeth marchas*

mountain bike

una bicicleta de montaña *oona beetheekleta deh montaña*

moped

un ciclomotor *oon theeklomotor*

motorbike

una moto *oona moto*

How much does it cost per day/week?

¿Cuánto cuesta por día/semana? *kwanto kwesta por deeya/semana*

Do you require a deposit?

¿Hay que pagar una señal? *eye keh pagar oona señal*

The brakes don't work.

Los frenos no funcionan. *los frenos no foontheeyonan*

There is/are no … lights.

No hay … luces. *no eye … loothes*

The front/rear tire has a flat.

El neumático delantero/trasero está pinchado. *el neyoomateeko delantero/ trasero esta peenchado*

Hitchhiking Hacer autostop

Where are you heading?

¿Adónde se dirige? *adondeh seh deereekheh*

I'm heading for …

Me dirijo a … *meh deereekho a*

Can you give me/us a lift?

¿Me/nos puede llevar? *meh/nos pwedeh l-yebar*

Is that on the way to …?

¿Está de camino a …? *esta deh kameeno a*

Could you drop me off …?

¿Me podría dejar …? *meh podreeya dekhar*

here

aquí *akee*

at the … exit

a la salida … *a la saleeda*

in the center

en el centro *en el thentro*

Thanks for the lift.

Gracias por traernos. *gratheeyas por trayernos*

Taxi/Cab Taxi

Taxis are marked SP (**servicio público**) and a green sign indicates **libre** when free; in tourist areas they are often unmetered, though fares to most destinations are fixed and displayed at the main taxi rank.

Tipping suggestions: 10% for the taxi driver.

Where can I get a taxi?	**¿Dónde puedo coger un taxi?** _dondeh pwedo kokher oon taksee_
Do you have the number for a taxi?	**¿Tiene el número de un radio taxi?** _teeyeneh el noomero deh oon radeeyo taksee_
I'd like a taxi …	**Quiero un taxi …** _keeyero oon taksee_
now	**ahora** _a-ora_
in an hour	**dentro de una hora** _dentro deh oona ora_
for tomorrow at 9:00	**para mañana a las nueve** _para mañana a las nwebeh_
The pick-up address is …, going to …	**La dirección es … y me dirijo a …** _la deerektheeyon es … ee meh deereekho a_

○━━━━━━━━━ **LIBRE** ━━━━━━━━━━━ for hire ━━━━━━━○

Please take me to …	**Por favor, lléveme a …** _por fabor l-yebemeh a_
airport	**el aeropuerto** _el ayropwerto_
rail station	**la estación de trenes** _la estatheeyon deh trenes_
this address	**esta dirección** _esta deerektheeyon_
How much will it cost?	**¿Cuánto costará?** _kwanto kostara_
How much is that?	**¿Cuánto es?** _kwanto es_
You said … pesetas.	**Dijo … pesetas.** _deekho … pesetas_
Keep the change.	**Quédese con el cambio.** _kedeseh kon el kambeeyo_

> – ¿Podría llevarme a la estación, por favor?
> – Por supuesto.
> – Gracias. ¿Cuánto es?
> – Cuatrocientas pesetas, por favor.
> – Quédese con el cambio.

Car/Automobile El coche

While driving, the following documents must be carried at all times: valid full driver's license/licence, vehicle registration document and insurance documentation. If you don't hold an EC format license, an International Driving Permit is also required. Insurance for minimum Third Party risks is compulsory in Europe. It is recommended that you take out International motor insurance (for a **"Green Card"**) through your insurer.

The most common crime against tourists in Spain is theft from rental/ hire cars. Always look for secure parking areas overnight and never leave valuables in your car at any time.

Conversion Chart

km	1	10	20	30	40	50	60	70	80	90	100	110	120	130
miles	0.62	6	12	19	25	31	37	44	50	56	62	68	74	81

Road network

A (**autopistas**) – toll expressway/motorway (blue sign) and (**autovías**) – free expressway/motorway (green sign); N (**nacional**) – main road; C (**comarcal**) – secondary road (white sign); V (**vecinal**) – local road (prefixed by letter denoting province)

Speed limits kmph (mph)	Residential areas	Built-up area	Outside built-up area	Expressway/motorway
Cars	20 (12)	50 (31)	90-100 (56-62)	120 (74)
Cars towing trailer/caravan			70 (44)	80 (50)

Minimum driving age: 18. Essential equipment: warning triangle, nationality plate and a set of spare head- and rear-lamp bulbs; wearing seat belts is compulsory. Children under 10 must travel in the rear.

Traffic on main roads has priority; where 2 roads of equal importance merge, traffic from the right has priority. Tolls are payable on certain roads, they can be high.

Traffic police can give on-the-spot fines up to 50,000 Ptas. (ask for a receipt). A **boletín de denuncia** is issued, specifying the offense; guidelines in English for an appeal appear on the back.

The use of horns is prohibited in built-up areas except for emergencies. Alcohol limit in blood: max. 80mg/100ml. Note that any alcohol may impair concentration.

Gas/Petrol (Octane)	Leaded	Unleaded	Diesel
	Normal (92)	Sin plomo (95),	Gasóleo 'A' (98)

Car rental Alquiler de coches

Third-party insurance is included in the basic charge, usually with a Collision Damage Waiver.

The minimum age varies from 21 if paying by credit card, 23 if paying by cash. In the latter case, a large deposit will be charged.

Where can I rent a car?	**¿Dónde puedo alquilar un coche?** *dondeh pwedo alkeelar oon kocheh*
I'd like to rent a car.	**Quiero alquilar un coche.** *keeyero alkeelar oon kocheh*
2-/4-door car	**un coche de dos/cuatro puertas.** *oon kocheh deh dos/kwatro pwertas*
an automatic	**un coche automático** *oon kocheh aootomateeko*
with 4-wheel drive	**con tracción a las cuatro ruedas** *kon traktheeyon a las kwatro roowedas*
with air conditioning	**con aire acondicionado** *kon ayreh akondeetheeyonado*
I'd like it for a day/a week.	**Lo quiero para un día/una semana.** *lo keeyero para oon deeya/oona semana*
How much does it cost per day/week?	**¿Cuánto cuesta por día/semana?** *kwanto kwesta por deeya/semana*
Is mileage/insurance included?	**¿Va el kilometraje/seguro incluido?** *ba el keelometrakheh/segooro eenklooweedo*
Are there special weekend rates?	**¿Tienen precios especiales de fin de semana?** *teeyenen pretheeyos espetheeyales deh feen deh semana*
Can I leave the car at …?	**¿Puedo dejar el coche en …?** *pwedo dekhar el kocheh en*
What sort of fuel does it take?	**¿Qué tipo de combustible gasta?** *keh teepo deh komboosteebleh gasta*
Where is high/full/low/ dipped beam ?	**¿Dónde están las largas/cortas?** *dondeh estan las largas/kortas*
Could I have full insurance please?	**¿Podría hacerme un seguro a todo riesgo?** *podreeya athermeh oon segooro a todo rreeyesgo*

Gas station Estación de servicio

Where's the next filling station, please?	**¿Dónde está la próxima gasolinera, por favor?** _dondeh esta la prokseema gasoleenera por fabor_
Is it self-service?	**¿Es de autoservicio?** _es deh owtoserbeetheeyo_
Fill it up, please.	**Lleno, por favor.** _l-yeno por fabor_
… liters of gasoline, please.	**… litros de gasolina, por favor.** _… leetros deh gasoleena por fabor_
premium/super/regular	**súper/normal** _sooper/normal_
unleaded/diesel	**sin plomo/diesel** _seen plomo/dee-ehsel_
Where is the air pump/water?	**¿Dónde está el aire/agua?** _dondeh esta el ayreh/agwa_

PRECIO POR LITRO   price per liter

Parking Aparcamiento

Metered parking is common in most towns; some take credit cards as well as coins. In certain zones of Madrid, prepaid slips **(tarjeta de aparcamiento)** are required, available from tobacconists.

It is an offense to park facing against the traffic.

Vehicles that are illegally parked may be towed away **(grúa)**; you will find a yellow triangle with your registration number and address of the car-pound.

Is there a parking lot/ car park nearby?	**¿Hay un aparcamiento cerca?** _eye oon aparkameeyento therka_
What's the charge per hour/per day?	**¿Cuánto cobran por hora/día?** _kwanto kobran por ora/deeya_
Do you have some change for the parking meter?	**¿Tienen cambio para el parquímetro?** _teeyenen kambeeyo para el parkeemetro_
My car has been booted/ clamped. Who do I call?	**A mi coche le han puesto el cepo.** **¿A quién llamo?** _a mee kocheh leh an pwesto el thepo. a keeyen l-yamo_

Breakdown Asistencia en carretera

For help in the event of a breakdown:
refer to your breakdown assistance documents; or
contact the breakdown service: Spain: ☎ (91) 742 1213.

Where is the nearest garage?	**¿Dónde está el taller más cercano?** *dondeh esta el tal-yer mas therkano*
I've had a breakdown.	**He tenido una avería.** *eh teneedo oona abereeya*
Can you send a mechanic/ tow truck?	**¿Puede mandar a un mecánico/una grúa?** *pwedeh mandar a oon mekaneeko/oona groowa*
I belong to … recovery service.	**Soy del servicio de grúa …** *soy del serbeetheeyo deh groowa …*
My registration number is …	**Mi número de matrícula es …** *mee noomero deh matreekoola es*
The car is …	**El coche está …** *el kocheh esta*
on the freeway/motorway	**en la autopista** *en la aootopeesta*
2 km from …	**a dos kilómetros de …** *a dos keelometros deh*
How long will you be?	**¿Cuánto tiempo tardará?** *kwanto teeyempo tardara*

What is wrong? ¿Qué le pasa?

I don't know what's wrong.	**No sé qué le pasa.** *no seh ke leh pasa*
My car won't start.	**Mi coche no arranca.** *mee kocheh no arranka*
The battery is dead.	**La batería no funciona.** *la batereeya no foontheeyona*
I've run out of gas.	**Se me ha acabado la gasolina.** *seh meh a akabado la gasoleena*
I have a flat.	**Tengo un pinchazo.** *tengo oon peenchatho*
There is something wrong with …	**Algo va mal en …** *algo ba mal en*
I've locked the keys in the car.	**Me he dejado las llaves en el coche.** *meh eh dekhado las l-yabes en el kocheh*

Repairs Reparaciones

Do you do repairs?	**¿Hacen reparaciones?** *athen reparatheeyones*
Could you have a look at my car?	**¿Podrían echarle un vistazo al coche?** *podreeyan echarleh oon beestatho al kocheh*
Can you repair it (temporarily)?	**¿Puede hacerle una reparación (provisional)?** *pwedeh atherle oona reparatheeyon (probeeseeyonal)*
Please make only essential repairs.	**Por favor, hágale reparaciones básicas solamente.** *por fabor agaleh reparatheeyones baseekas solamenteh*
Can I wait for it?	**¿Puedo esperar?** *pwedo esperar*
Can you repair it today?	**¿Puede arreglarlo hoy?** *pwedeh arreglarlo oy*
When will it be ready?	**¿Cuándo estará listo?** *kwando estara leesto*
How much will it cost?	**¿Cuánto costará?** *kwanto kostara*
That's outrageous!	**¡Eso es un escándalo!** *eso es oon eskandalo*
Can I have a receipt for the insurance?	**¿Pueden darme un recibo para el seguro?** *pweden darmeh oon retheebo para el segooro*

El/la ... no funciona.	The ... isn't working.
No tengo las piezas necesarias.	I don't have the necessary parts.
Tendré que mandar a pedir las piezas.	I will have to order the parts.
Sólo puedo repararlo provisionalmente.	I can only repair it temporarily.
Su coche no tiene arreglo.	Your car is a write-off.
No se puede arreglar/reparar.	It can't be repaired.
Estará listo ...	It will be ready ...
hoy mismo	later today
mañana	tomorrow
dentro de ... días	in ... days

DAYS OF THE WEEK ➤ 218; NUMBERS ➤ 216

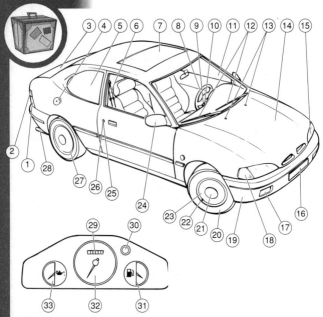

1 tail lights/back lights
   las luces traseras
2 brakelights **las luces de los frenos**
3 trunk/boot **el maletero**
4 gas tank door/petrol cap
   la tapa del depósito de gasolina
5 window **la ventana**
6 seat belt **el cinturón de seguridad**
7 sunroof **el techo solar**
8 steering wheel **el volante**
9 starter/ignition **el encendido**
10 ignition key **la llave (de encendido)**
11 windshield **el parabrisas**
12 windshield/windscreen wipers
   las escobillas
13 windshield/windscreen washer
   el limpiaparabrisas
14 hood/bonnet **el capó**
15 headlights **los faros**

16 registration plate **las placas**
17 fog lamp **el faro antiniebla**
18 turn signals/indicators
   las intermitentes
19 bumper **el parachoques**
20 tires/tyres **las llantas**
21 hubcap/wheel cover **el tapacubos**
22 valve **la válvula**
23 wheels **las ruedas**
24 outside/wing mirror
   el espejo lateral
25 central locking **el cierre centralizado**
26 lock **el seguro (la cerradura)**
27 wheel rim **el rin de la rueda**
28 exhaust pipe **el tubo de escape**
29 odometer/milometer
   el cuentakilómetros
30 warning light
   la luz de advertencia

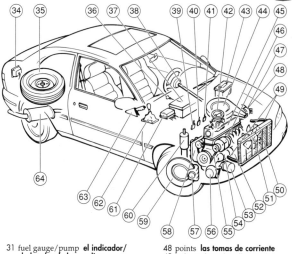

31 fuel gauge/pump **el indicador/ la bomba de la gasolina**
32 speedometer **el velocímetro**
33 oil gauge **el indicador del nivel de aceite**
34 backup/reversing lights **las luces de marcha atrás**
35 spare wheel **la rueda de repuesto**
36 choke **el estárter**
37 heater **la calefacción**
38 steering column **la columna de dirección**
39 accelerator **el acelerador**
40 pedal **el pedal**
41 clutch **el embrague**
42 carburetor **el carburador**
43 battery **la batería**
44 alternator **el alternador**
45 camshaft **el árbol de levas**
46 air filter **el filtro de agua**
47 distributor **el distribuidor**

48 points **las tomas de corriente**
49 radiator hose (top/bottom) **la manguera del radiador (arriba/abajo)**
50 radiator **el radiador**
51 fan **el ventilador**
52 engine **el motor**
53 oil filter **el filtro de aceite**
54 starter motor **el motor de arranque**
55 fan belt **la correa del ventilador**
56 horn **la bocina [el pito]**
57 brake pads **las pastillas de los frenos**
58 transmission/gearbox **la caja de cambio**
59 brakes **los frenos**
60 shock absorbers **los amortiguadores**
61 fuses **los fusibles**
62 gear shift/lever **la palanca de cambios**
63 handbrake **el freno de mano**
64 muffler **el silenciador**

Accidents Accidentes

In the event of an accident:

1. put your red warning triangle about 100 meters behind your car;

2. report the accident to the police (compulsory if there is personal injury); don't leave before they arrive;

3. show your driver's license/licence and green card;

4. give your name, address, insurance company to the other party;

5. report to the appropriate insurance bureaus of the third party and your own company;

6. don't make any written statement without advice of a lawyer or automobile club official;

7. note all relevant details of the other party, any independent witnesses and the accident.

There has been an accident.	**Ha habido un accidente.** *a abeedo oon aktheedenteh*
It's …	**Ha ocurrido …** *a okoorreedo*
on the highway/motorway	**en la autopista** *en la aootopeesta*
near …	**cerca de …** *therka deh*
Where's the nearest telephone?	**¿Dónde está el teléfono más cercano?** *dondeh esta el telefono mas therkano*
Call …	**Llame a …** *l-yameh a*
the police	**la policía** *la poleetheeya*
an ambulance	**una ambulancia** *oona amboolantheeya*
a doctor	**un médico** *oon medeeko*
Can you help me, please?	**¿Puede ayudarme, por favor?** *pwedeh ayoodarmeh por fabor*

Injuries Lesiones

There are people injured.	**Hay gente herida.** *eye khenteh ereeda*
He is seriously injured/bleeding.	**Está gravemente herido/sangrando.** *esta grabementeh ereedo/sangrando*
She's unconscious.	**Está inconsciente.** *esta eenkonstheeyenteh*
He can't breathe/move.	**No puede respirar/moverse.** *no pwedeh respeerar/moberseh*
Don't move him.	**No lo mueva.** *no lo mweba*

Legal matters Asuntos legales

What's your insurance company? **¿Cuál es su compañía de seguros?** *kwal es soo kompañeeya deh segooros*

What's your name and address? **¿Cuál es su nombre y su dirección?** *kwal es soo nombreh ee soo deerektheeyon*

He ran into me. **Chocó conmigo.** *choko konmeego*

She was driving too fast/ too close. **Conducía demasiado rápido/cerca.** *kondootheeya demaseeyado rapeedo/therka*

I had right of way. **Yo tenía derecho de paso.** *yo teneeya derecho deh paso*

I was (only) driving at … km/h. **Sólo conducía a … kilómetros por hora.** *solo kondootheeya a … keelometros por ora*

I'd like an interpreter. **Quiero un intérprete.** *keeyero oon eenterpreteh*

I didn't see the sign. **No vi la señal.** *no bee la señal*

He/She saw it happen. **El/Ella lo vio.** *el/el-ya lo beeyo*

The registration number was … **El número de matrícula era …** *el noomero deh matreekoola era*

¿Puedo ver su … por favor?	Can I see your … please?
carnet/permiso de conducir	driver's license/licence
certificado del seguro	insurance certificate
documento del registro del coche	vehicle registration document
¿A qué hora ocurrió?	What time did it happen?
¿Dónde ocurrió?	Where did it happen?
¿Hay alguien más involucrado?	Was anyone else involved?
¿Hay testigos?	Are there any witnesses?
Se pasó del límite de velocidad.	You were speeding.
Sus faros no funcionan.	Your lights aren't working.
Tendrá que pagar una multa (en el sitio).	You'll have to pay a fine (on the spot).
Tenemos que tomar su declaración en la comisaría.	We need you to make a statement at the station.

TIME ➤ 220

93

Asking directions
Preguntar el camino

Excuse me please.	**Disculpe, por favor.**	*dees<u>kool</u>peh por fa<u>bor</u>*
How do I get to …?	**¿Cómo se va a …?**	<u>ko</u>mo seh ba a
Where is …?	**¿Dónde está …?**	<u>don</u>deh es<u>ta</u>
Can you show me on the map where I am?	**¿Puede indicarme dónde estoy en el mapa?**	*<u>pwe</u>deh eendee<u>kar</u>meh <u>don</u>deh es<u>toy</u> en el <u>mapa</u>*
I've lost my way.	**Me he perdido.**	*meh eh per<u>dee</u>do*
Can you repeat that please?	**¿Puede repetir eso, por favor?**	*<u>pwe</u>deh repe<u>teer</u> eso por fa<u>bor</u>*
More slowly, please.	**Más despacio, por favor.**	*mas des<u>pa</u>theeyo por fa<u>bor</u>*
Thanks for your help.	**Gracias por su ayuda.**	*<u>gra</u>theeyas por soo a<u>yoo</u>da*

Traveling by car Viajar en coche

Is this the right road for …?	**¿Es ésta la carretera para …?**	*es <u>esta</u> la karre<u>te</u>ra <u>pa</u>ra*
How far is it to … from here?	**¿A qué distancia está … de aquí?**	*a keh dees<u>tan</u>theeya <u>esta</u>… deh a<u>kee</u>*
Where does this road lead?	**¿Adónde va esta carretera?**	*a<u>don</u>deh ba <u>esta</u> karre<u>te</u>ra*
How do I get onto the highway/motorway?	**¿Cómo se va a la autopista?**	*<u>ko</u>mo seh ba a la aooto<u>pees</u>ta*
What's the next town called?	**¿Cómo se llama el próximo pueblo?**	*<u>ko</u>mo seh l-<u>ya</u>ma el <u>prok</u>seemo <u>pwe</u>blo*
How long does it take by car?	**¿Cuánto tiempo se tarda en coche?**	*<u>kwan</u>to tee<u>yem</u>po seh <u>tar</u>da en <u>ko</u>cheh*

– Disculpe, por favor. ¿Cómo se va a estación de trenes?
– Coja el tercer desvío a la izquierda y después todo recto.
– Tercera a la izquierda. ¿Está lejos?
– Está a cinco minutos andando.
– Gracias por su ayuda.
– De nada.

Location Situación

Está ...	It's ...
todo recto	straight ahead
a la izquierda	on the left
a la derecha	on the right
al otro lado de la calle	on the other side of the street
en la esquina	on the corner
doblando la esquina	round the corner
yendo hacia ...	in the direction of ...
frente a .../detrás de ...	opposite .../behind ...
al lado de .../después de ...	next to .../after ...
Baje por ...	Go down the ...
bocacalle/calle principal	side street/main street
Cruce ...	Cross the ...
plaza/puente	square/bridge
Tome/Coja ...	Take the ...
el tercer desvío a la derecha	third turning to the right
Tuerza a la izquierda.	Turn left.
después del primer semáforo	after the first traffic lights
en el segundo cruce	at the second intersection/crossroad

By car En coche

Está ... de aquí.	It's ... of here.
al norte/sur	north/south
al este/oeste	east/west
Tome/coja la carretera para ...	Take the road for ...
Se ha equivocado de carretera.	You're on the wrong road.
Tendrá que volver a ...	You'll have to go back to ...
Siga las señales para ...	Follow the signs for ...

How far? ¿A qué distancia?

Está ...	It's ...
cerca/no está lejos/bastante lejos	close/not far/a long way
a cinco minutos a pie	5 minutes on foot
a diez minutos en coche	10 minutes by car
aproximadamente a cien metros bajando la calle	about 100 meters from the end of the street

TIME ➤ *220; NUMBERS* ➤ *216*

Road signs Señales de tráfico

ACCESO SÓLO	access only
CALLE DE SENTIDO ÚNICO	one-way street
CARRETERA CERRADA	road closed
CEDA EL PASO	yield/give way
DESVÍO	detour/diversion
ESCUELA/COLEGIO	school
PÓNGASE EN EL CARRIL	stay in lane/get in lane
PUENTE BAJO	low bridge
RUTA ALTERNATIVA	alternative route
UTILICE LOS FAROS	use headlights

Town plans Mapas de la ciudad

aeropuerto	airport
aparcamiento	parking lot
aseos	toilets
calle mayor	main street
campo de actividades deportivas	playing field/ sports ground
casco antiguo	old town
cine	movie theater/cinema
comisaría de policía	police station
correos (oficina de)	post office
edificio público	public building
estación	station
estación de metro	subway/metro station
estadio	stadium
iglesia	church
oficina de información	information office
parada de autobús	bus stop
parada de taxis	taxi rank
parque	park
pasaje subterráneo	underpass
paso de peatones	pedestrian crossing
ruta de autobús	bus route
servicios	toilets
teatro	theater
usted está aquí	you are here
zona peatonal	pedestrian zone/ precinct

Sightseeing

Tourist information office
Oficina de Información Turística

Tourist information offices are often situated in the town center; look for **Oficina de turismo** or **Información**.

There are numerous local festivals to look out for: e.g. **Las Fallas de Valencia** (March), **La Feria de Sevilla** (April), **San Isidro** (Madrid on May 15), **Los Sanfermines de Pamplona** (July), **La Merc** (Barcelona on 23 Sept.).

Where's the tourist office?	**¿Dónde está la oficina de turismo?** _dondeh esta la ofeetheena deh tooreesmo_
What are the main points of interest?	**¿Cuáles son los sitios de interés?** _kwales son los seeteeyos deh interes_
We're here for …	**Nos quedaremos aquí …** _nos kedaremos akee_
only a few hours	**sólo unas horas** _solo oonas oras_
a day	**un día** _oon deeya_
a week	**una semana** _oona semana_
Can you recommend …?	**¿Puede recomendarme …?** _pwedeh rekomendarmeh_
a sightseeing tour	**un recorrido por los sitios de interés** _oon rekorreedo por los seeteeyos deh eenteres_
an excursion	**una excursión** _oona ekskoorseeyon_
a boat trip	**una excursión en barco** _oona eskoorseeyon en barko_
Are these leaflets free?	**¿Son gratis estos folletos?** _son gratees estos fol-yetos_
Do you have any information on …?	**¿Tiene alguna información sobre …?** _teeyeneh algoona eenformatheeyon sobreh_
Are there any trips to …?	**¿Hay excursiones a …?** _eye ekskoorseeyones a_

DAYS OF THE WEEK ➤ 218; DIRECTIONS ➤ 94

97

Excursions Excursiones

How much does the tour cost?	**¿Cuánto cuesta la visita?** _kwanto kwesta la beeseeta_
Is lunch included?	**¿Va incluida la comida?** _ba eenklooeeda la komeeda_
Where do we leave from?	**¿De dónde se sale?** _deh dondeh seh saleh_
What time does the tour start?	**¿A qué hora comienza la visita?** _a keh ora komeeyentha la beeseeta_
What time do we get back?	**¿A qué hora volvemos?** _a keh ora bolbemos_
Do we have free time in …?	**¿Tenemos tiempo libre en …?** _tenemos teeyempo leebreh en…_
Is there an English-speaking guide?	**¿Hay un guía que hable inglés?** _eye oon geeya keh ableh eengles_

On tour Durante la visita

Are we going to see …?	**¿Vamos a ver …?** _bamos a behr_
We'd like to have a look at …	**Queremos echar un vistazo a …** _keremos echar oon beestatho a_
Can we stop here …?	**¿Podemos parar aquí …?** _podemos parar akee_
to take photographs	**para hacer fotos** _para ather fotos_
to buy souvenirs	**para comprar recuerdos** _para komprar rekwerdos_
for the bathrooms/toilets	**para ir al servicio** _para eer al serbeetheeyo_
Would you take a photo of us, please?	**¿Podría sacarnos una foto, por favor?** _podreeya sakarnos oona foto por fabor_
How long do we have here/in …?	**¿Cuánto tiempo tenemos para estar aquí/en …?** _kwanto teeyempo tenemos para estar akee/en_
Wait! … isn't back yet.	**¡Esperen! … todavía no ha vuelto.** _esperen … todabeeya no a bwelto_
Stop the bus, my child is feeling sick.	**Pare el autobús - mi hijo(-a) se marea.** _pareh el aootoboos. mee eekho(-a) se mareya_

98

Sights Lugares de interés

Town maps are on display in city centers, train, tram and many bus stations, and at tourist information offices.
Many tourist offices will give you a free folding map of the town with useful tourist information.

Where is the …	**¿Dónde está …?** _dondeh esta_
abbey	**la abadía** _la abadeeya_
art gallery	**la galería de arte** _la galereeya deh arteh_
battle site	**el lugar de la batalla** _el loogar deh la batal-ya_
botanical garden	**el jardín botánico** _el khardeen botaneeko_
castle	**el castillo** _el kasteel-yo_
cathedral	**la catedral** _la katedral_
church	**la iglesia** _la eegleseeya_
downtown area	**el centro** _el thentro_
fountain	**la fuente** _la fwenteh_
library	**la biblioteca** _la beebleeyoteka_
market	**el mercado** _el merkado_
(war) memorial	**el monumento** _el monoomento_
monastery	**el monasterio** _el monastereeyo_
museum	**el museo** _el mooseyo_
old town	**el casco antiguo** _el kasko anteegwo_
opera house	**el teatro de la ópera** _el teyatro deh la opera_
palace	**el palacio** _el palatheeyo_
park	**el parque** _el parkheh_
parliament building	**el palacio de las cortes** _el palatheeyo deh las kortes_
ruin	**la ruina** _la rooeena_
shopping area	**la zona de tiendas** _la thona deh teeyendas_
statue	**la estatua** _la estatooa_
theater	**el teatro** _el teyatro_
tower	**la torre** _la torreh_
town hall	**el ayuntamiento** _el ayoontameeyento_
viewpoint	**el mirador** _el meerador_
Can you show me on the map?	**¿Puede indicarme en el mapa?** _pwedeh eendeekarmeh en el mapa_

DIRECTIONS ➤ 94

Admission Entrada

Museums are usually closed on Mondays, important holidays and over siesta (2 p.m. to 4 p.m.). Usual opening hours are: 10 a.m. – 1 or 2 p.m., 4 p.m. – 6 or 7 p.m.

Is the … open to the public?	**¿Está … abierto(-a) al público?** *esta …abeeyerto al poobleeko*
Can we look around?	**¿Podemos echarle un vistazo a los alrededores?** *podemos echarleh oon beestatho a los alrrededores*
What are the opening hours?	**¿A qué hora abre?** *a keh ora abreh*
When does it close?	**¿A qué hora cierra?** *a keh ora theeyerra*
Is it open on Sundays?	**¿Está abierto los domingos?** *esta abeeyerto los domeengos*
When's the next guided tour?	**¿Cuándo es la próxima visita con guía?** *kwando es la prokseema beeseeta kon geeya*
Have you a guide book (in English)?	**¿Tiene una guía (en inglés)?** *teeyeneh oona geeya (en eengles)*
Can I take photos?	**¿Puedo hacer fotos?** *pwedo ather fotos*
Is there access for the disabled?	**¿Tiene acceso para minusválidos?** *teeyeneh aktheso para meenoosbaleedos*
Is there an audio-guide in English?	**¿Tienen auriculares para seguir la visita en inglés?** *teeyenen aooreekoolares para segeer la beeseeta en eengles*

Paying/Tickets Pagar/Entradas

How much is the entrance fee?	**¿Cuánto cuesta la entrada?** *kwanto kwesta la entrada*
Are there any discounts for …?	**¿Hacen descuento a …?** *athen deskwento a*
children	**los niños** *los neeños*
disabled	**los minusválidos** *los meenoosbaleedos*
groups	**los grupos** *los groopos*
senior citizens	**los pensionistas** *los penseeyoneestas*
students	**los estudiantes** *los estoodeeyantes*
1 adult and 2 children, please.	**un adulto y dos niños, por favor.** *oon adoolto ee dos neeños por fabor*
I've lost my ticket.	**He perdido la entrada.** *eh perdeedo la entrada*

- Cinco entradas, por favor.
¿Hacen descuentos?
- *Sí. Los niños y los pensionistas
pagan 200 pesetas.*
- Dos adultos y tres niños, por favor.
- *Son mil seiscientas pesetas, por favor.*

ABIERTO	open
CERRADO	closed
ENTRADA GRATUITA	admission free
HORARIO DE VISITAS	visiting hours
LA PRÓXIMA VISITA ES A LA/LAS ...	next tour at ...
PROHIBIDA LA ENTRADA	no entry
PROHIBIDO UTILIZAR EL FLASH	no flash photography
TIENDA DE RECUERDOS	gift shop
ÚLTIMA VISTA A LAS 17H	Latest entry at 5 p.m.

Impressions Impresiones

It's ...	**Es ...** *es*
amazing	**increíble** *eenkrayeebleh*
beautiful	**bonito** *boneeto*
bizarre	**extraño** *ekstraño*
boring	**aburrido** *aboorreedo*
breathtaking	**impresionante** *impreseeyonanteh*
brilliant	**maravilloso** *marabeel-yoso*
interesting	**interesante** *eenteresanteh*
magnificent	**magnífico** *magneefeeko*
romantic	**romántico** *romanteeko*
strange	**extraño** *ekstraño*
stunning	**precioso** *pretheeoso*
superb	**espléndido** *esplendeedo*
terrible	**terrible** *terreebleh*
ugly	**feo** *feyo*
It's good value.	**Está muy bien de precio.**
	esta mwee beeyen deh pretheeyo
It's a rip-off.	**Es un timo.** *es oon teemo*
I like it.	**Me gusta.** *meh goosta*
I don't like it.	**No me gusta.** *no meh goosta*

a escala uno cien scale 1:100

acuarela watercolor

aguja spire

al estilo (de) in the style of

ala wing (of building)

almena battlement

antigüedades antiques

aposentos apartments (royal)

arma weapon

armadura armory

artesanía crafts

baños baths

biblioteca library

boceto sketch

bóveda vault

cementerio churchyard

cenotafio cenotaph

cerámica pottery

conferencia lecture

construido(-a) en built in

contrafuerte buttress

corona crown

cripta crypt

cuadro painting

cúpula dome

decorado(-a) por decorated by

descubierto(-a) en discovered in

destruido(-a) por destroyed by

detalle detail

dibujo drawing

diseñado(-a) por designed by

diseño design

donado(-a) por donated by

dorado(-a) gilded

dorado(-a) gold(en)

edificio building

emperador emperor

emperatriz empress

empezado(-a) en started in

entrada doorway

eregido(-a) en erected in

escalera staircase

escenario stage

escuela de school of

escultor sculptor

escultura sculpture

exposición exhibit

exposición exhibition

exposición temporal temporary exhibit

fachada facade

foso moat

friso frieze

fundado(-a) en founded in	**placa** plaque
gárgola gargoyle	**plata** silver
grabado engraving	**plata** silverware
grabado etching	**por** by (person)
jardín de diseño formal formal garden	**prestado(-a) a** on loan to
joyas jewelry	**primer piso** level 1
lápida headstone	**puerta** gate
lienzo canvas	**reconstruido (-a) en** rebuilt in
mandado(-a) por commissioned by	**reina** queen
mármol marble	**reino** reign
la maqueta model	**reloj** clock
moneda coin	**restaurado(-a) en** restored in
muebles furniture	**retablo** tableau
muestra display	**retrato** portrait
murió en died in	**rey** king
muro (outside) wall	**salón para grandes recepciones** stateroom
nacido(-a) en born in	**siglo** century
obra maestra masterpiece	**silla del coro** choir (stall)
óleos oils	**talla** carving
pabellón pavilion	**talla de cera** waxwork
paisaje landscape (painting)	**tapiz** tapestry
pared (inside) wall	**terminado(-a) en** completed in
patio courtyard	**torre** tower
piedra stone	**traje** costume
piedra semipreciosa gemstone	**tumba** grave
pila bautismal font	**tumba** tomb
pintado(-a) por painted by	**vestíbulo** foyer
pintor/pintora painter	**vidriera** stained-glass window
	vivió lived

103

Who/What/When?
¿Quién/Qué/Cuándo?

What's that building?	**¿Qué es ese edificio?** *keh es <u>eh</u>seh edee<u>fee</u>thee<u>ey</u>o*
Who was the ...?	**¿Quién fue ...?** *kee<u>yen</u> fweh*
architect/artist/painter	**el arquitecto/el artista/el pintor** *el arkee<u>tek</u>to/el ar<u>tees</u>ta/el peen<u>tor</u>*
When was it built/painted?	**¿Cuándo se construyó/pintó?** *<u>kwan</u>do seh konstroo<u>yo</u>/peen<u>to</u>*
What style is that?	**¿De qué estilo es eso?** *deh keh es<u>tee</u>lo es eso*

realizaciones romanas   200 b.c.–500 a.d.
Ruins from the Roman civilization are commonplace in Spain esp. the aqueduct at Segovia, the bridge at Córdoba, the triumphal arch in Tarragona, the Theatre in Mérida.

arte árabe   ca. 8–end 15
Moorish architecture and art had a huge influence in Spain; esp. ornamental brickwork, fretted woodwork, mosaics, calligraphy, carved plaster work. Three great periods can be identified: arte califal (ca. 8-9th, esp. horseshoe-shaped arch of mosque in Córdoba), arte almohade (ca. 10-1250, esp. Giralda tower in Seville), arte granadino (1250-1492, esp. stucco and ceramics in the Alhambra, Granada).

gótico   ca. 13–end 15
Very complex architectural forms, using pointed arches, rib vaults and elaborate stone ornamentation (Isabelline); esp. cathedrals of Burgos, León, Toledo, Seville. This evolved into Plateresque – a lacelike carving of intricate facades; esp. Patio de las Escuelas, Salamanca.

renacimiento   ca. 15–16
The Renaissance left many monuments in Spain; esp. El Escorial near Madrid, the palace of Charles V at Alhambra.

barroco   ca. 17–18
Exuberant architectural style, esp. convent of San Esteban in Salamanca, Palacio del Marqués de Dos Aguas in Valencia.

siglo de Oro   ca.17
The Golden Century saw a flourishing of the arts; esp. artists: **El Greco, Velázquez, Zurbarán, Murillo;** writers: **Miguel de Cervantes, Fray Luis de León, Santa Teresa.**

modernismo   late ca. 19–ca. 20
A period of crisis in national self-confidence saw world-renowned cultural figures; esp. artists: **Picasso, Miró, Dalí;** architects: **Gaudí;** writers: **Unamuno, Lorca.**

Rulers Gobernantes

What period is that? **¿De qué época es eso?**
deh keh epoka es eso

romana   **206 b.c.– 410 a.d.**
The Romans occupied Spain on defeating the Carthaginians in
the Second Punic War. 600 years of rule brought a road network,
seaports and skills in mining, agriculture and trade. On the collapse of the
Roman Empire, Spain was invaded and dominated by the Visigoths.

árabe   **711–1492**
The first Moorish invasion from North Africa defeated the Visigoths. For
almost 800 years Moorish control of Spain fluctuated as the Christian
Reconquest expanded. Ferdinand and Isabella complete the expulsion of
the Moors in 1492.

reyes católicos   **1474–1516**
National unity under Isabel of Castile and Fernando of Aragón saw the
Spanish Inquisition (**Inquisición**) set up in 1478 and Columbus claim newly
discovered lands for Spain (1492).

la casa de Asturias   **1516–1700**
The Habsburgs House, financed by plundered wealth from the New
World, extended its influence: Charles V (**Carlos I**) made claims on Bur-
gundy, the Netherlands and Italy.

los Borbones   **1700–1923**
A period of continued military and cultural decline under the Bourbons.
The invasion by Napoleon in 1808 forced the abdication of **Carlos IV**. The
19th century saw the loss of most of Spain's territories in Central and
South America.

dictadura del General Franco   **1939–75**
In a bloody Civil War (**guerra civil Española**) **General Franco**'s fascist forces
overthrow the Republic and declare a dictatorship that lasts until his death.

la democracia   **1975–**
Juan Carlos I becomes a constitutional monarch. 1992 saw EXPO '92 in Seville,
the Olympics in Barcelona and Madrid the Cultural Capital of Europe.

Churches Iglesias

Predominantly Roman Catholic, Spain is rich in cathedrals and churches
worth visiting. Although large churches are normally open to the public
during the day, services should be respected and most churches request
that bare shoulders are covered before entering.

Catholic/Protestant church   **la Iglesia católica/protestante**
          la eegleseeya katoleeka/protestanteh

mosque   **la mezquita** *la methkeeta*

synagogue   **la sinagoga** *la seenagoga*

mass/the service   **la misa/el servicio** *la meesa/el serveetheeyo*

In the countryside En el campo

I'd like a map of …	**Quiero un mapa de …** keey<u>e</u>ro oon <u>ma</u>pa deh
this region	**esta región** <u>es</u>ta rekhee<u>yon</u>
walking routes	**las rutas de senderismo** las <u>roo</u>tas deh sender<u>ee</u>smo
bicycle routes	**las rutas para bicicletas** las <u>roo</u>tas <u>pa</u>ra beethee<u>kle</u>tas
How far is it to …?	**¿A qué distancia está …?** a keh dees<u>tan</u>theeya es<u>ta</u>
Is there a right of way?	**¿Hay derecho de paso?** eye de<u>re</u>cho deh <u>pa</u>so
Is there a scenic route to …?	**¿Hay una carretera panorámica a …?** eye <u>oo</u>na karre<u>te</u>ra panor<u>a</u>meeka a
Can you show me on the map?	**¿Puede indicármelo en el mapa?** <u>pwe</u>deh eendee<u>kar</u>melo en el <u>ma</u>pa
I'm lost.	**Me he perdido.** meh eh per<u>dee</u>do

Organized walks/hikes El senderismo organizado

When does the guided walk/hike start?	**¿Cuándo empieza el paseo/la excursión a pie?** <u>kwan</u>do empee<u>ye</u>tha el pa<u>se</u>yo/la ekskoorsee<u>yon</u> a pee<u>yeh</u>
When will we return?	**¿Cuándo volveremos?** <u>kwan</u>do bolbe<u>re</u>mos
What is the walk/hike like?	**¿Cómo es el paseo/la excursión a pie?** <u>ko</u>mo es el pa<u>se</u>yo/la ekskoorsee<u>yon</u> a pee<u>yeh</u>
gentle/medium/ tough	**fácil/regular/duro** <u>fa</u>theel/regoo<u>lar</u>/<u>doo</u>ro
Where do we meet?	**¿Dónde nos encontramos?** <u>don</u>deh nos enkon<u>tra</u>mos
I'm exhausted.	**Estoy exhausto(-a).** es<u>toy</u> eks<u>aw</u>sto(-a)
How high is that mountain?	**¿Qué altura tiene esa montaña?** keh al<u>too</u>ra tee<u>ye</u>neh <u>e</u>sa mon<u>ta</u>ña
What kind of … is that?	**¿Qué clase de … es ése(-a)?** keh <u>kla</u>seh deh … es <u>e</u>se(-a)
animal/bird	**animal/pájaro** anee<u>mal</u>/<u>pa</u>kharo
flower/tree	**flor/árbol** flor/<u>ar</u>bol

HIKING GEAR ➤ 145

Geographic features
Características geográficas

bridge	**el puente** *el pwenteh*
cave	**la cueva** *la kweba*
cliff	**el acantilado** *el akanteelado*
farm	**la granja** *la grankha*
field	**el campo** *el kampo*
footpath	**el sendero** *el sendero*
forest	**el bosque** *el boskeh*
hill	**la colina** *la koleena*
lake	**el lago** *el lago*
mountain	**la montaña** *la montaña*
mountain pass	**el paso de montaña** *el paso deh montaña*
mountain range	**la cordillera** *la kordeel-yera*
nature reserve	**la reserva natural** *la reserba natooral*
panorama	**el panorama** *el panorama*
park	**el parque** *el parkeh*
pass	**el paso** *el paso*
path	**el camino** *el kameeno*
peak	**el pico** *el peeko*
picnic area	**la zona para picnics** *la thona para peekneeks*
pond	**el estanque** *el estankeh*
rapids	**los rápidos** *los rapeedos*
ravine	**el barranco** *el barranko*
river	**el río** *el reeyo*
sea	**el mar** *el mar*
spa (place to stay)	**el balneario** *el balneareeyo*
stream	**el arroyo** *el arroyo*
valley	**el valle** *el bal-yeh*
viewing point	**el mirador** *el meerador*
village	**el pueblo** *el pweblo*
vineyard/winery	**el viñedo** *el beeñedo*
waterfall	**la catarata** *la katarata*
wood	**el bosque** *el boskeh*

Leisure

What's on? ¿Qué espectáculos hay?

Local papers and, in large cities, weekly entertainment guides (such as **Guía del Ocio**) will tell you what's on.

Do you have a program of events?	**¿Tiene un programa de espectáculos?** *teeyeneh oon programa deh espektakoolos*
Can you recommend a good …?	**¿Puede recomendarme un(a) buen(a) …?** *pwedeh rekomendarmeh oon(a) bwen(a)*
Is there a … on somewhere?	**¿Hay … en algún sitio?** *eye … en algoon seeteeyo*
ballet/concert	**un ballet/un concierto** *oon bal-yet/oon kontheeyerto*
movie/film	**una película** *oona peleekoola*
opera	**una ópera** *oona opera*
When does it start/end?	**¿A qué hora empieza/termina?** *a keh ora empeeyetha/termeena*

Tickets for concerts, theater, and other cultural events are on sale at special ticket agencies. In small towns these may be in kiosks, book or music stores: ask at the local tourist office.

Availability Disponibilidad

Where can I get tickets?	**¿Dónde se pueden comprar las entradas?** *dondeh seh pweden komprar las entradas*
Are there any seats for tonight?	**¿Hay entradas para esta noche?** *eye entradas para esta nocheh*
I'm sorry, we're sold out.	**Lo siento, no quedan entradas.** *lo seeyento, no kedan entradas*
There are … of us.	**Somos …** *somos*

Tickets Entradas

How much are the seats?

¿Cuánto cuestan estas localidades? _kwanto kwestan estas lokaleedades_

Do you have anything cheaper?

¿Tiene algo más barato? _teeyeneh algo mas barato_

I'd like to reserve …

Quiero reservar … _keeyero reserbar_

3 for Sunday evening

tres para el domingo por la noche _tres para el domeengo por la nocheh_

1 for Friday matinée

una para la matiné del viernes _oona para la mateeneh del beeyernes_

¿Cuál es … de su tarjeta de crédito?	What's your credit card …?
el número	number
la fecha de caducidad	expiration/expiry date
Por favor, recoja las entradas …	Please pick up the tickets …
antes de las … de la tarde	by … p.m.
en el mostrador de reservas	at the reservations desk

May I have a program please?

¿Puede darme un programa, por favor? _pwedeh darmeh oon programa por fabor_

Where's the coat room?

¿Dónde está el guardarropa? _dondeh esta el gwardarropa_

- Teatro Nacional, dígame.
- Buenos días, quiero reservar dos entradas para la función de "El Mercader de Venecia" de esta noche, por favor.
- Por supuesto. ¿Puede darme el número de su tarjeta de crédito, por favor?
- Sí, es el 050- 365 7874.
- ¿Qué tipo de tarjeta es?
- Es una VISA, ¿Aceptan VISA?
- Sí, por supuesto. ¿Cuál es la fecha de caducidad, por favor?
- El siete del noventa y siete.
- Gracias, por favor, recoja las entradas en el mostrador de reservas.

AGOTADO	Sold out
ENTRADAS PARA HOY	Tickets for today
RESERVAS POR ADELANTADO	Advance reservations

NUMBERS ➤ 216

109

Movies/Cinema Cine/Películas

Foreign films are usually dubbed into Spanish, but some movies/cinemas show films in the original version (**V.O.**).

Spain has a developing film industry of its own, with world-famous directors such as Almodóvar and Buñuel.

Is there a multiplex cinema near here?	**¿Hay un multicine cerca de aquí?** *eye oon moolteetheeneh therka deh akee*
What's playing at the movies? (What's on at the cinema tonight?)	**¿Qué ponen en el cine esta noche?** *keh ponen en el theeneh esta nocheh*
Is the film dubbed/subtitled?	**¿Está doblada/subtitulada la película?** *esta doblada/soobteetoolada la peleekoola*
Is the film in the original English?	**¿Está la película en el inglés original?** *esta la peleekoola en el eengles oreekheenal*
Who's the main actor/actress?	**¿Quién es el actor/la actriz principal?** *keeyen es el aktor/la aktreeth preentheepal*
A ..., please.	**..., por favor** *por fabor*
box/carton of popcorn	**un cucurucho de palomitas** *oon kookooroocho deh palomeetas*
chocolate ice cream	**un polo de chocolate** *oon polo deh chokolateh*
hot dog	**un perrito caliente** *oon perreeto kaleeyenteh*
soft drink/soda	**un refresco** *oon refresko*
small/regular/large	**pequeño/de tamaño normal/grande** *pekeño/deh tamaño normal/grandeh*

Theater Teatro

What's playing at the ... Theater?	**¿Qué función ponen en el teatro ...?** *keh foontheeyon ponen en el teyatro*
Who's the playwright?	**¿Quién es el autor?** *keeyen es el aootor*
Do you think I'd enjoy it? I don't know much Spanish.	**¿Cree que me gustará? No sé mucho español.** *kreyeh keh meh goostara. no seh moocho español*

Opera/Ballet/Dance
Ópera/Ballet/Dance

Who's the composer/soloist? **¿Quién es el/la compositor(a)/solista?**
keeyen es el/la komposeetor(a)/soleesta

Is formal dress expected? **¿Hay que vestirse de etiqueta?**
eye keh besteerseh deh eteeketa

Where's the opera house? **¿Dónde está el teatro de la ópera?**
dondeh esta el teyatro deh la opera

Who's dancing? **¿Quién baila?** *keeyen bayla*

I'm interested in contemporary dance. **Me interesa la danza contemporánea.**
meh eenteresa la dantha kontemporaneya

Music/Concerts Música/Conciertos

Where's the concert hall? **¿Dónde está la sala de conciertos?**
dondeh esta la sala deh kontheeyertos

Which orchestra/band is playing? **¿Qué orquesta/grupo toca?**
keh orkesta/groopo toka

What are they playing? **¿Qué van a tocar?** *keh ban a tokar*

Who is the conductor/soloist? **¿Quién es el/la director(a)/solista?**
keeyen es el/la deerektor(a)/soleesta

Who is the support band? **¿Quiénes son los teloneros?**
keeyenes son los teloneros

I really like … **Me gusta mucho …** *meh goosta moocho*

country music **la música country** *la mooseeka kaoontree*

folk music **la música folk** *la mooseeka folk*

jazz **el jazz** *el jazz*

music of the 60s **la música de los sesenta**
la mooseeka deh los sesenta

pop **la música pop** *la mooseeka pop*

rock music **el rock** *el rok*

soul music **el soul** *el "sowl"*

Have you ever heard of her/him? **¿Ha oído hablar de ella/él?**
a oyeedo ablar deh el-ya/el

Are they popular? **¿Son famosos?** *son famosos*

Nightlife Vida nocturna

What is there to do in the evenings?
¿Qué se puede hacer por las noches?
keh seh pwedeh ather por las noches

Can you recommend a good …?
¿Puede recomendarme un buen …?
pwedeh rekomendarmeh oon bwen

Is there a … in town?
¿Hay … en esta ciudad?
eye … en esta theeyoodath

bar **un bar** *oon bar*
casino **un casino** *oon kaseeno*
discotheque **una discoteca** *oona deeskoteka*
gay club **una discoteca gay** *oona deeskoteka gay*
nightclub **un club nocturno** *oon kloob noktoorno*
restaurant **un restaurante** *oon restawranteh*

Is there a floor show/cabaret?
¿Hay un espectáculo de cabaret?
eye oon espektakoolo deh kabaret

What type of music do they play?
¿Qué tipo de música tocan?
keh teepo deh mooseeka tokan

How do I get there?
¿Cómo se va allí? *komo seh ba al-yee*

Admission Entrada

What time does the show start?
¿A qué hora empieza el espectáculo?
a keh ora empeeyetha el espektakoolo

Is evening dress required?
¿Hay que ir con traje de noche?
eye keh eer kon trakheh deh nocheh

Is there a cover charge?
¿Hay una consumición mínima?
eye oona konsoomeetheeyon meeneema

Is a reservation necessary?
¿Hay que hacer una reserva?
eye keh ather oona reserba

Do we need to be members?
¿Hay que ser socios? *eye keh sehr sotheeyos*

How long will we have to stand in line?
¿Cuánto tiempo tendremos que hacer cola?
kwanto teeyempo tendremos keh ather kola

I'd like a good table.
Quiero una buena mesa.
keeyero oona bwena mesa

INCLUYE UNA CONSUMICIÓN GRATIS

includes one complimentary drink

112

Children Niños

Can you recommend something for the children?	**¿Puede recomendarme algo para los niños?** _pwedeh rekomendarmeh algo para los neeños_
Are there changing facilities here for babies?	**¿Tienen instalaciones para cambiar al bebé?** _teeyenen eenstalatheeyones para kambeeyar al bebeh_
Where are the bathrooms/toilets?	**¿Dónde están los servicios?** _dondeh estan los serveetheeyos_
amusement/game arcade	**el salón recreativo** _el salon rekreateebo_
fairground	**la feria** _la fereeya_
kiddie/paddling pool	**la piscina infantil** _la peestheena eenfanteel_
playground	**el patio de juegos** _el pateeyo deh khwegos_
play group	**el club infantil** _el kloob eefanteel_
zoo	**el zoológico** _el thoo-o-lokheeko_

Baby-sitting Cuidado de los niños

Can you recommend a reliable baby-sitter?	**¿Puede recomendarme una canguro de confianza?** _pwedeh rekomendarmeh oona kangooro deh konfeeyantha_
Is there constant supervision?	**¿Supervisan a los niños constantemente?** _sooperbeesan a los neeños konstantementeh_
Are the helpers properly trained?	**¿Están cualificados los empleados?** _estan kwaleefeekados los empleados_
When can I drop them off?	**¿Cuándo puedo dejarlos?** _kwando pwedo dekharlos_
I'll pick them up at …	**Los recogeré a las …** _los rekokhereh a las_
We'll be back by …	**Volveremos antes de las …** _bolberemos antes deh las_
What age is he/she?	**¿Qué edad tiene?** _keh edath teeyeneh_
She's 3 and he's 18 months.	**La niña tiene tres años y el niño dieciocho meses.** _la neeña teeyeneh tres años ee el neeño deeyetheeocho meses_

Sports Deportes

Whether you are a fan or a participant, Spain has the weather and facilities to satisfy most sports enthusiasts. Soccer (**fútbol**) is the most popular sport, inspiring fierce devotion – particularly in Madrid and Barcelona. Spain is famous for its golf courses, especially on the Costa del Sol. Tennis, horse riding and hill climbing are also popular. And look out for **pelota** (**jai alai** in the Basque country and Latin America) – a furiously fast ball game involving curved wicker-basket gloves.

Spectating Como espectador

Is there a soccer/football game (match) this Saturday?	**¿Hay un partido de fútbol este sábado?** *eye oon parteedo deh footbol esteh sabado*
Which teams are playing?	**¿Qué equipos juegan?** *keh ekeepos khwegan*
Can you get me a ticket?	**¿Puede conseguirme una entrada?** *pwedeh konsegeermeh oona entrada*
What's the admission charge?	**¿Cuánto cobran por entrar?** *kwanto kobran por entrar*
Where's the racetrack/racecourse?	**¿Dónde está el hipódromo?** *dondeh esta el eepodromo*
Where can I place a bet?	**¿Dónde puedo hacer una apuesta?** *dondeh pwedo ather oona apwesta*
What are the odds on ...?	**¿A cómo están las apuestas para ...?** *a komo estan las apwestas para*
athletics	**atletismo** *atleteesmo*
basketball	**baloncesto** *balonthesto*
cycling	**ciclismo** *theekleesmo*
golf	**golf** *golf*
horse racing	**carreras de caballos** *karreras deh kabal-yos*
soccer/football	**fútbol** *footbol*
swimming	**natación** *natatheeyon*
tennis	**tenis** *tenees*
volleyball	**voleybol** *boleebol*

Playing Como participante

Where's the nearest …?	**¿Dónde está … más cercano?** _dondeh esta … mas therkano_
golf course	**el campo de golf** _el kampo deh golf_
sports club	**el polideportivo** _el poleedeporteebo_
Where are the tennis courts?	**¿Dónde están las pistas de tenis?** _dondeh estan las peestas deh tenees_
What's the charge per …?	**¿Cuánto cuesta por …?** _kwanto kwesta por_
day/ hour	**día /hora** _deeya/ora_
game/round (golf)	**partido/juego** _parteedo/khwego_
Do I need to be a member?	**¿Hay que ser socio?** _eye keh sehr sotheeyo_
Where can I rent …?	**¿Dónde puedo alquilar …?** _dondeh pwedo alkeelar_
boots	**unas botas** _oonas botas_
clubs	**unos palos de golf** _oonos palos deh golf_
equipment	**el equipo** _el ekeepo_
a racket	**una raqueta** _oona raketa_
Can I get lessons?	**¿Me pueden dar clases?** _meh pweden dar klases_
Is there an aerobic class?	**¿Hay clases de aerobic?** _eye klases deh ayrobeek_
Do you have a fitness room?	**¿Tienen un gimnasio?** _teeyenen oon khimnaseeyo_
Can I join in?	**¿Puedo hacerme socio?** _pwedo atherme sotheeyo_

Lo siento, no quedan plazas.	I'm sorry, we're booked up.
Hay que pagar una señal/fianza de …	There is a deposit of …
¿Qué talla tiene?	What size are you?
Necesita una foto tamaño carnet.	You need a passport size photo.

PROHIBIDO PESCAR	no fishing
SÓLO PARA LOS TENEDORES DE LICENCIA	permit holders only
VESTUARIOS	changing

At the beach En la playa

Spain offers hundreds of miles of beaches for every taste. The most developed offer a full range of facilities for water sports; nor is it too difficult to locate near-deserted coves for a quieter time.

Is the beach …?	**¿Es la playa …?** *es la playa*
pebbly/sandy	**de guijarros/de arena** *deh geekharros/deh arena*
Is there a … here?	**¿Hay … aquí?** *eye … akee*
children's pool	**una piscina para niños** *oona peestheena para neeños*
swimming pool	**una piscina** *oona peestheena*
indoor/outdoor	**cubierta/al aire libre** *koobeeyerta/al ayreh leebreh*
Is it safe to swim/dive here?	**¿Es seguro nadar/tirarse de cabeza aquí?** *es segooro nadar/teerarse deh kabetha akee*
Is it safe for children?	**¿Es seguro(-a) para los niños?** *es segooro(-a) para los neeños*
Is there a lifeguard?	**¿Hay socorrista?** *eye sokorreesta*
I want to rent …	**Quiero alquilar …** *keeyero alkeelar*
deck chair	**una tumbona** *oona toombona*
jet ski	**una moto acuática** *oona moto akwateeka*
motorboat	**una motora** *oona motora*
row boat	**una barca de remos** *oona barka deh remos*
sail boat	**un velero** *oon belero*
diving equipment	**un equipo de buceo** *oon ekeepo deh boothayo*
umbrella/sunshade	**una sombrilla** *oona sombreel-ya*
surfboard	**una tabla de surf** *oona tabla deh soorf*
water skis	**unos esquís acuáticos** *oonos eskees akwateekos*
windsurfer	**una tabla de windsurf** *oona tabla deh weensoorf*
For … hours.	**Por … horas.** *por … oras*

Skiing Esquiar

Spain's 27 ski resorts attract an increasing number of devotees. Most are situated in the Pyrenees (e.g. **Baqueira-Beret, La Molina, Pas de la Casa, Cerler**), while the Andalusian **Sierra Nevada** offers Europe's sunniest skiing.

I'd like to rent …	**Quiero alquilar …** *keeyero alkeelar*
poles	**unos bastones** *oonos bastones*
skates	**unos patines** *oonos pateenes*
ski boots/skis	**unas botas de esquiar/unos esquís** *oonas botas deh eskeeyar/oonos eskees*
These are too …	**Éstos(-as) son demasiado …** *estos(as) son demaseeyado*
big/small	**grandes/pequeños** *grandes/pekeños*
These are too loose/tight.	**Están demasiado sueltos/apretados.** *estan demaseeyado sweltos/apretados*
A lift pass for a day/ 5 days, please.	**Un pase de teleférico para un día/cinco días, por favor.** *oon paseh deh telefereeko para oon deeya/theenko deeyas por fabor*
I'd like to join the ski school.	**Quiero dar clases de esquí.** *keeyero dar klases deh eskee*
I'm a beginner.	**Soy principiante.** *soy preentheepeeyanteh*
I'm experienced.	**Tengo experiencia.** *tengo ekspereeyentheeya*

ARRASTRE	drag lift
TELEFÉRICO/CABINA	cable car/gondola
TELESILLA	chair lift

Bullfight La corrida

The bullfight (**la corrida**) may fascinate or appall you. To a Spaniard, a bullfight is not a choice of life and death for the bull. It is simply an opportunity for it to die heroically. First the matador goads the bull with a large cape (**capote**). Then the **picador** weakens the bull by lancing its neck. **Banderilleros** on foot thrust three barbed sticks between its shoulder blades. The matador returns to taunt the bull with a small red cape (**muleta**), leading up to the final climax of the kill. The bullfighting season lasts from March to October.

I'd like to see a bullfight.	**Quiero ver una corrida.** *keeyero behr oona korreeda*

117

Making Friends

Introductions Presentaciones

Greetings vary according to how well you know someone. The following is a guide:

It's polite to shake hands, both when you meet and say good-bye; it is considered impolite not to.

Begin any conversation, whether with a friend, shop assistant or police-men, with a "**buenos días**." Speak to them using the formal form of "you" (**Usted**) until you are asked to use the familiar form (**Tú**).

In Spanish, there are three forms for "you" (taking different verb forms): **tú** (singular) and **vosotros** (plural) are used when talking to relatives, close friends and children (and between young people); **usted** (singular) and **ustedes** (plural) – often abbreviated to **Vd./Vds**. – are used in all other cases. If in doubt; use usted/ustedes.

Hello, we haven't met.	**Hola, no nos conocemos.** *ola no nos konothemos*
My name is …	**Me llamo …** *meh l-yamo*
May I introduce …?	**Quiero presentarle a …** *keeyero presentarleh a*
John, this is …	**John, éste(-a) es …** *jon esteh(-a) es*
Pleased to meet you.	**Encantado(-a) de conocerle(-la).** *enkantado(-a) deh konotherle(-la)*
What's your name?	**¿Cómo se llama?** *komo seh l-yama*
How are you?	**¿Cómo está?** *komo esta*
Fine, thanks. And you?	**Bien, gracias. ¿Y usted?** *beeyen gratheeyas. ee oosteth*

> – Hola, ¿Cómo está?
> – Muy bien, gracias. ¿Y usted?
> – Bien, gracias.

Where are you from?
¿De dónde es usted?

Where do you come from?	**¿De dónde es usted?** _deh dondeh es oosteth_
Where were you born?	**¿Dónde nació?** _dondeh natheeyo_
I'm from …	**Soy de …** _soy deh_
Australia	**Australia** _awoostraleeya_
Britain	**Gran Bretaña** _gran bretaña_
Canada	**Canadá** _kanada_
England	**Inglaterra** _eenglaterra_
Ireland	**Irlanda** _eerlanda_
Scotland	**Escocia** _eskotheeya_
U.S.	**Estados Unidos** _estados ooneedos_
Wales	**Gales** _gales_
Where do you live?	**¿Dónde vive?** _dondeh beebeh_
What part of … are you from?	**¿De qué parte de … es usted?** _deh keh parteh deh … es oosteth_
Spain	**España** _españa_
Argentina	**Argentina** _arkhenteena_
México	**Méjico** _mekheeko_
We come here every year.	**Venimos todos los años.** _beneemos todos los años_
It's my/our first visit.	**Es mi/nuestra primera visita.** _es mee/nwestra preemera beeseeta_
Have you ever been …?	**¿Ha estado alguna vez …?** _a estado algoona beth_
to Britain/the U.S.	**en Gran Bretaña/Estados Unidos** _en gran bretaña/estados ooneedos_
Do you like it here?	**¿Le gusta esto?** _leh goosta esto_
What do you think of the …?	**¿Qué le parece …?** _keh le paretheh_
I love the … here.	**Me encanta … de aquí.** _meh enkanta … deh akee_
I don't care for the … here.	**No me gusta demasiado … de aquí.** _no meh goosta demaseeyado …deh akee_
food/people	**la cocina/la gente** _la kotheena/ la khenteh_

119

Who are you with?
¿Con quién ha venido?

Who are you with?	**¿Con quién ha venido?** *kon keeyen a beneedo*
I'm on my own.	**He venido solo(-a).** *eh beneedo solo(-a)*
I'm with a friend.	**He venido con un(a) amigo(-a).** *eh beneedo kon oon(a) ameego(-a)*
I'm with my …	**He venido con** *eh beneedo kon*
wife	**mi mujer** *mee mookher*
husband	**mi marido** *mee mareedo*
family	**mi familia** *mee fameeleeya*
children	**mis hijos** *mees eekhos*
parents	**mis padres** *mees padres*
boyfriend/girlfriend	**mi novio(-a)** *mee nobeeyo(-a)*
my father/mother	**mi padre/mi madre** *mee padreh/mee madreh*
my son/daughter	**mi hijo/mi hija** *mee eekho/mee eekha*
my brother/sister	**mi hermano/mi hermana** *mee ermano/mee ermana*
my uncle/aunt	**mi tío/mi tía** *mee teeyo/mee teeya*
What's your son's/wife's name?	**¿Cómo se llama su hijo/mujer?** *komo seh l-yama soo eekho/mookher*
Are you married?	**¿Está casado(-a)?** *esta kasado(-a)*
I'm …	**Estoy …** *estoy*
married/single	**casado(-a)/soltero(-a)** *kasado(-a)/soltero(-a)*
divorced/separated	**divorciado(-a)/separado(-a)** *deebortheeyado(-a)/separado(-a)*
engaged	**prometido(-a)** *prometeedo*
We live together.	**Vivimos juntos.** *beebeemos khoontos*
Do you have any children?	**¿Tiene hijos?** *teeyeneh eekhos*
2 boys and a girl.	**Dos niños y una niña.** *dos neeños ee oona neeña*
How old are they?	**¿Qué edad tienen?** *keh edath teeyenen*
They're ten and twelve.	**Tienen diez y doce años respectivamente.** *teeyenen deeyeth ee dotheh años respekteebamenteh*

What do you do?
¿A qué se dedica?

What do you do?	**¿A qué se dedica?** *a keh seh dedeeka*
What are you studying?	**¿Qué estudia?** *keh estoodeeya*
I'm studying …	**Estudio …** *estoodeeyo*
I'm in …	**Me dedico a …** *meh dedeeko a*
business	**asuntos comerciales** *asoontos komertheeyales*
retail	**la venta al por menor** *la benta al por menor*
sales	**las ventas** *las bentas*
I'm in engineering.	**Trabajo de ingeniero.** *trabakho deh eenkhenyero*
Who do you work for?	**¿Para quién trabaja?** *para keeyen trabakha*
I work for …	**Trabajo para …** *trabakho para*
I'm a/an …	**Soy …** *soy*
accountant	**contable** *kontableh*
housewife	**ama de casa** *ama deh kasa*
student	**estudiante** *estoodeeyanteh*
I'm …	**Estoy …** *estoy*
retired	**jubilado(-a)** *khoobeelado(-a)*
between jobs	**entre un trabajo y otro** *entreh oon trabakho ee otro*
I'm self-employed.	**Trabajo por mi cuenta.** *trabakho por mee kwenta*
What are your interests/hobbies?	**¿Cuáles son sus pasatiempos/hobbies?** *kwales son soos pasateeyempos/hobees*
I like …	**Me gusta(n) …** *me goosta(n)*
music	**la música** *la mooseeka*
reading	**leer** *leh-er*
sports	**los deportes** *los deportes*
I play … (game)	**Juego a …** *khwego a*
Would you like to play …?	**¿Quieres jugar a …?** *keeyeres khoogar a*
cards	**las cartas** *las kartas*
chess	**al ajedrez** *al akhedreth*

What weather! ¡Vaya tiempo!

What a lovely day!	¡Qué día tan bonito! *keh deeya tan boneeto*
What awful weather!	¡Qué tiempo más feo! *keh teeyempo mas feyo*
Isn't it cold/hot today!	¡Vaya frío/calor que hace hoy! *baya freeyo/kalor keh atheh oy*
Is it usually as warm as this?	¿Hace normalmente tanto calor como ahora? *atheh normalmenteh tanto kalor komo a-ora*
Do you think it's going to … tomorrow?	¿Cree usted que mañana va a …? *kreyeh oosteth keh mañana ba a*
be a nice day	hacer buen tiempo *ather bwen teeyempo*
rain	llover *l-yobehr*
snow	nevar *nebar*
What is the weather forecast?	¿Cuál es el pronóstico del tiempo? *kwal es el pronosteeko del teeyempo*
It's …	Está … *esta*
cloudy	nublado *nooblado*
rainy	lluvioso *l-yoobeeyoso*
thundery	tronando *tronando*
It's foggy.	Hay niebla. *eye neeyebla*
It's frosty.	Hay heladas. *eye eladas*
It's icy.	Hay hielo. *eye eeyelo*
It's snowy.	Hay nieve. *eye neeyebeh*
It's windy.	Hace viento. *atheh beeyento*
Has the weather been like this for long?	¿Lleva mucho así el tiempo? *l-yeba moocho asee el teeyempo*
What's the pollen count?	¿Cuál es el índice de polen? *kwal es el eendeetheh deh polen*
high/medium/low	alto/regular/bajo *alto/regoolar/bakho*
What's the forecast for skiing?	¿Qué tiempo hace para esquiar? *keh teeyempo atheh para eskeeyar*

PRONÓSTICO DEL TIEMPO   weather forecast

Enjoying your trip?
¿Se lo está pasando bien?

¿Está de vacaciones?	Are you on vacation?
¿Cómo ha venido aquí?	How did you get here?
¿Qué tal el viaje?	How was the journey?
¿Dónde se aloja?	Where are you staying?
¿Cuánto tiempo lleva aquí?	How long have you been here?
¿Cuánto tiempo va a quedarse?	How long are you staying?
¿Qué ha hecho hasta ahora?	What have you done so far?
¿Qué es lo próximo que va a hacer?	Where are you going next?
¿Está pasando unas buenas vacaciones?	Are you enjoying your vacation?

I'm here on …	**Estoy aquí …** _estoy akee_
a business trip	**en viaje de negocios** _en beeyakheh deh negotheeyos_
vacation	**de vacaciones** _deh bakatheeyones_
We came by …	**Vinimos en …** _beeneemos en_
train/bus/plane	**tren/autobús/avión** _tren/aootoboos/abeeyon_
car/ferry	**coche/ferry** _kocheh/ferree_
I have a rental car.	**He alquilado un coche.** _eh alkeelado oon kocheh_
We're staying in …	**Nos alojamos en …** _nos alokhamos en_
an apartment	**un apartamento** _oon apartamento_
a hotel/campsite	**un hotel/un cámping** _oon otel/ oon kampeen_
with friends	**con unos amigos** _kon oonos ameegos_
Can you suggest …?	**¿Puede sugerirme …?** _pwedeh sookhereermeh_
things to do	**algo que hacer** _algo keh ather_
places to eat/visit	**algunos sitios para comer/ver** _algoonos seeteeyos para komer/behr_
We're having a great/awful time.	**Lo estamos pasando muy bien/mal.** _lo estamos pasando mwee beeyen/mal_

Invitations Invitaciones

Would you like to have dinner with us on …?	**¿Quiere cenar con nosotros el …?** *keeyereh thenar kon nosotros el*
May I invite you to lunch?	**¿Puedo invitarle(-la) a comer?** *pwedo eenbeetarle(-la) a komer*
Can you come for a drink this evening?	**¿Puede venir a tomarse algo esta noche?** *pwede beneer a tomarseh algo esta nocheh*
We are having a party. Can you come?	**Vamos a dar una fiesta. ¿Puede venir?** *bamos a dar oona feeyesta. pwede beneer*
May we join you?	**¿Podemos ir con ustedes?** *podemos eer kon oostedes*
Would you like to join us?	**¿Quiere(n) venir con nosotros?** *keeyereh(n) beneer kon nosotros*

Going out Salir

What are your plans for …?	**¿Qué planes tiene(n) para …?** *ke planes teeyeneh(n) para*
today/tonight	**hoy/esta noche** *oy/esta nocheh*
tomorrow	**mañana** *mañana*
Are you free this evening?	**¿Está libre esta noche?** *esta leebreh esta nocheh*
Would you like to …?	**¿Quiere …?** *keeyereh*
go dancing	**ir a bailar** *eer a baylar*
go for a drink/meal	**ir a tomar una copa/a cenar** *eer a tomar oona kopa/a thenar*
go for a walk	**dar un paseo** *dar oon paseyo*
go shopping	**ir de compras** *eer deh kompras*
Where would you like to go?	**¿Adónde le gustaría ir?** *adondeh leh goostareeya eer*
I'd like to go to …	**Quiero ir a …** *keeyero eer a*
I'd like to see …	**Quiero ver …** *keeyero behr*
Do you enjoy …?	**¿Le gusta …?** *leh goosta*

Accepting/Declining
Aceptar/Rehusar

Great. I'd love to.
Estupendo. Me encantaría.
estoopendo. meh enkantareeya

Thank you, but I'm busy.
Gracias, pero estoy ocupado(-a)
gratheeyas pero estoy okoopado(-a)

May I bring a friend?
¿Puedo llevar a un amigo?
pwedo l-yebar a oon ameego

Where shall we meet?
¿Dónde quedamos? *dondeh kedamos*

I'll meet you …
Quedamos … *kedamos*

in the bar
en el bar *en el bar*

in front of your hotel
en frente de su hotel
en frenteh deh soo otel

I'll come by at 8.
Pasaré a recogerle a las ocho.
pasare a rrekokherle a las ocho

Could we make it
a bit later/earlier?
**¿Podríamos quedar un poco antes/
más tarde?**
*podreeyamos kedar oon poko
antes/mas tardeh*

How about another day?
¿Qué le parece otro día?
keh leh paretheh otro deeya

That will be fine.
Muy bien. *mwee beeyen*

Dining out/in Cenar fuera/en casa

If you are invited home for a meal, always take a gift – a bottle of wine,
sparkling wine, chocolates or flowers.

Let me buy you a drink.
Permítame que le/la invite a una copa.
*permeetameh keh leh/la eenbeeteh a
oona kopa*

Do you like …?
¿Le gusta …? *leh goosta*

What are you going to have?
¿Qué va a tomar?
keh ba a tomar

That was a lovely meal.
Fue una comida estupenda.
fweh oona komeeda estoopenda

Encounters Citas

Are you waiting for someone?	**¿Espera a alguien?** *espera a algeeyen*
Do you mind if I …?	**¿Le importa si …?** *leh eemporta see*
sit here/smoke	**me siento aquí/fumo** *meh seeyento akee/foomo*
Can I get you a drink?	**¿Puedo invitarle(-la) a una copa?** *pwedo eenbeetarleh(-la) a oona kopa*
I'd love to have some company.	**Me encantaría estar acompañado(-a).** *meh enkantareeya estar akompañado(-a)*
Why are you laughing?	**¿Por qué se ríe?** *por keh seh reeyeh*
Is my Spanish that bad?	**¿Hablo español tan mal?** *ablo español tan mal*
Shall we go somewhere quieter?	**¿Vamos a otro sitio más tranquilo?** *bamos a otro seeteeyo mas trankeelo*
Leave me alone, please!	**¡Déjeme en paz, por favor!** *dekhemeh en path por fabor*
You look great!	**¡Estás guapísimo(-a)!** *estas gwapeeseemo(-a)*
May I kiss you?	**¿Puedo besarte?** *pwedo besarteh*
I'm not ready for that.	**No estoy preparado(-a) para eso.** *no estoy preparado(-a) para eso*
I'm afraid we've got to leave now.	**Me temo que tenemos que irnos ahora.** *meh temo keh tenemos keh eernos a-ora*
Thanks for the evening.	**Gracias por la velada.** *gratheeyas por la belada*
Can I see you again tomorrow?	**¿Puedo volver a verle(-la) mañana?** *pwedo bolber a berleh(-la) mañana*
See you soon.	**Hasta luego.** *asta loowego*
Can I have your address?	**¿Puede darme su dirección?** *pwedeh darmeh soo deerektheeyon*

SAFETY ➤ 65

Telephoning Llamar por teléfono

Public telephone booths/boxes take either coins only (marked with a green T), or coins and phonecards (with a blue T sign). Phonecards (**tarjeta telefónica**) are available from post offices and tobacconists. Few phones accept credit cards.

Most public cafés and bars have public phones – feel free to enter and ask for the telephone.

To phone home from Spain, dial 07 followed by: Australia 61; Canada 1; Ireland 353; New Zealand 64; South Africa 27; UK 44; U.S. 1. Note that you will usually have to omit the initial 0 of the area code.

Can I have your telephone number?	**¿Me da su número de teléfono?** *meh da soo noomero deh telefono*
Here's my number.	**Aquí tiene mi número.** *akee teeyeneh mee noomero*
Please call me.	**Llámeme, por favor.** *l-yamemeh por fabor*
I'll give you a call.	**Le/La llamaré.** *leh/la l-yamareh*
Where's the nearest telephone booth?	**¿Dónde está la cabina más cercana?** *dondeh esta la kabeena mas therkana*
May I use your phone?	**¿Puedo usar su teléfono?** *pwedo oosar soo telefono*
It's an emergency.	**Es urgente.** *es oorkhenteh*
I'd like to call someone in England.	**Quiero llamar a alguien en Inglaterra.** *keeyero l-yamar a algeeyen en eenglaterra*
What's the area/ dialing code for ...?	**¿Cuál es el prefijo de ...?** *kwal es el prefeekho deh*
I'd like a phone card, please.	**Quiero una tarjeta para llamar por teléfono, por favor.** *keeyero oona tarkheta para l-yamar por telefono por fabor*
What's the number for Information/Directory Enquiries?	**¿Cuál es el número de información?** *kwal es el noomero deh eenformatheeyon*
I'd like the number for ...	**Quiero que me consiga el número de teléfono de ...** *keeyero keh meh konseega el noomero deh telefono deh*
I'd like to reverse the charges/call collect.	**Quiero llamar a cobro revertido.** *keeyero l-yamar a kobro reberteedo*

Speaking Al hablar por teléfono

Hello. This is …	**Hola. Soy …** _ola. soy_
I'd like to speak to …	**Quiero hablar con …** _keeyero ablar kon_
Extension …	**Extensión …** _ekstenseeyon_
Speak louder/more slowly, please.	**Hable más alto/despacio, por favor.** _ableh mas alto/despatheeyo por fabor_
Could you repeat that, please.	**¿Puede repetir eso, por favor?** _pwedeh repeteer eso por fabor_
I'm afraid he/she's not in.	**Me temo que no está.** _meh temo keh no esta_
You've got the wrong number.	**Se ha equivocado de número.** _seh a ekeebokado deh noomero_
Just a moment.	**Un momento.** _oon momento_
Hold on, please.	**Espere, por favor.** _espereh por fabor_
When will he/she be back?	**¿Cuándo volverá?** _kwando bolbera_
Will you tell him/her that I called?	**¿Puede decirle que he llamado?** _pwedeh detheerleh keh eh l-yamado_
My name is …	**Me llamo …** _meh l-yamo_
Would you ask him/her to phone me?	**¿Puede decirle que me llame?** _pwedeh detheerleh keh meh l-yameh_
Would you take a message, please?	**¿Puede darle un recado, por favor?** _pwedeh darleh oon rekado por fabor_
I must go now.	**Tengo que irme.** _tengo keh eermeh_
Nice to speak to you.	**Me encantó hablar con usted.** _meh enkanto ablar kon oosteth_
I'll be in touch.	**Nos mantendremos en contacto.** _nos mantendremos en kontakto_
Bye.	**Adiós.** _adeeyos_

Stores & Services

For a view of what Spaniards are buying, take a look in the big department stores El Corte Inglés and Galerías Preciados, which have branches in most sizeable towns. Although chain stores are becoming popular, most shops are still individually owned and each is individual in character. Many smaller shops are still to be found outside of the main town centers.

ESSENTIAL

I'd like …	**Quiero …** _keeyero_
Do you have …?	**¿Tiene(n) …?** _teeyeneh(n)_
How much is that?	**¿Cuánto cuesta eso?** _kwanto kwesta eso_
Thank you.	**Gracias**. _gratheeyas_

ABIERTO	open
CERRADO	closed
REBAJAS	sale
LIQUIDACIÓN POR CIERRE	closing down

Stores and services
Tiendas y servicios

Where is …? ¿Dónde está …?

Where's the nearest …?	**¿Dónde está … más cercano(-a)?** _dondeh esta … mas therkano(-a)_
Where's there a good …?	**¿Dónde hay un(a) buen(a) …?** _dondeh eye oon(a) bwen(a)_
Where's the main shopping mall/centre?	**¿Dónde está el centro comercial principal?** _dondeh esta el thentro komertheeyal preentheepal_
Is it far from here?	**¿Está lejos de aquí?** _esta lekhos deh akee_
How do I get there?	**¿Cómo se llega hasta allí?** _komo seh l-yega asta al-yee_

Stores Tiendas

antique shop	**la tienda de antigüedades** _la teeyenda deh anteegwedades_
bakery	**la panadería** _la panadereeya_
bank	**el banco** _el banko_
bookshop	**la librería** _la leebrereeya_
butcher shop	**la carnicería** _la karneethereeya_
camera shop	**la tienda de fotografía** _la teeyenda deh fotografeeya_
pharmacy/chemist's	**la farmacia** _la farmatheeya_
clothing store/clothes shop	**la tienda de ropa** _la teeyenda deh rropa_
delicatessen	**la charcutería** _la charkootereeya_
department store	**los grandes almacenes** _loss grandes almathenes_
drugstore	**la farmacia** _la farmatheeya_
fish store/fishmonger	**la pescadería** _la peskadereeya_
florist's	**la floristería** _la floreestereeya_
gift shop	**la tienda de regalos/bazar** _la teeyenda deh rregalos/bathar_
greengrocer	**la verdulería** _la berdoolereeya_
produce store	**la tienda de alimentación** _la teeyenda deh aleementatheeyon_

health food shop	**la tienda de alimentos naturales** *la teeyenda deh aleementos natoorales*
jewelry store/jeweler's	**la joyería** *la khoyereeya*
market	**el mercado** *el merkado*
pastry shop	**la pastelería** *la pastelereeya*
record/music shop	**la tienda de discos** *la teeyenda deh deeskos*
shoe store/shop	**la zapatería** *la thapatereeya*
shopping mall/centre	**el centro comercial** *el thentro komertheeyal*
souvenir shop	**la tienda de recuerdos** *la teeyenda deh rekwerdos*
sports shop	**la tienda de deportes** *la teeyenda deh deportes*
supermarket	**el supermercado** *el soopermerkado*
cigarette kiosk/tobacconist's	**el estanco** *el estanko*
toy and game store/shop	**la juguetería** *la khoogetereeya*
liquor store/wine and spirit merchant's	**la tienda de bebidas alcohólicas** *la teeyenda deh bebeedas alko-oleekas*

Services Servicios

clinic	**el ambulatorio** *el amboolatoreeo*
dentist	**el dentista** *el denteesta*
doctor	**el médico/doctor** *el medeeko/doktor*
dry cleaner's	**la tintorería** *la teentorereeya*
hairdresser's (ladies/men)	**la peluquería de señoras/caballeros** *la pelookereeya deh señoras/kabal-yeros*
hospital	**el hospital** *el ospeetal*
laundromat	**la lavandería** *la labandereeya*
library	**la biblioteca** *la beebleeoteka*
optician	**el óptico** *el opteeko*
police station	**la comisaría de policía** *la komeesareeya deh poleetheeya*
post office	**correos** *korreos*
travel agency	**la agencia de viajes** *la akhentheeya deh beeyakhes*

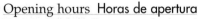

Opening hours Horas de apertura

In tourist resorts, shops generally are open on Sunday and
holidays and stay open until late. In larger towns, local
markets are open in the morning daily and in the afternoon on
Fridays only; in smaller towns, they operate on one morning a week.

When does the … open/shut?	**¿A qué hora abre/cierra …?** *a keh ora abreh/theeyerra*
Are you open in the evening?	**¿Abren por la noche?** *abren por la nocheh*
Do you close for lunch?	**¿Cierran a la hora de comer?** *theeyerran a la ora deh komer*
Where is the …	**¿Dónde está …?** *dondeh esta*
cashier/cash desk	**la caja** *la kakha*
escalator	**la escalera mecánica** *la eskalera mekaneeka*
elevator/lift	**el ascensor** *el asthensor*
store guide	**el directorio de la tienda** *el deerektoreeyo deh la teeyenda*
It's in the basement.	**Está en el sótano.** *esta en el sotano*
It's on the ground floor.	**Está en la planta baja** *esta en la planta bakha*
first floor	**primer piso** *preemer peeso*
Where's the … department?	**¿Dónde está la sección de …?** *dondeh esta la sektheeyon deh*

ABIERTO TODO EL DÍA	open all day
CERRADO A LA HORA DEL ALMUERZO	closed for lunch
HORAS DE TRABAJO	business hours
ENTRADA	entrance
ESCALERAS	stairs
SALIDA	exit
SALIDA DE EMERGENCIA	(emergency) exit
SALIDA DE INCENDIOS	fire exit

Service Servicio

Can you help me?

¿Puede ayudarme?
pwedeh ayoo<u>dar</u>meh

I'm looking for …

Estoy buscando …
es<u>toy</u> boos<u>kan</u>do

I'm just browsing.

Sólo estoy mirando.
<u>so</u>lo es<u>toy</u> meer<u>an</u>do

It's my turn.

Me toca a mí. _meh <u>to</u>ka a mee_

Do you have any …?

¿Tienen …? _tee<u>ye</u>nen_

I'd like to buy …

Quiero comprar … _kee<u>ye</u>ro kom<u>prar</u>_

Could you show me …?

¿Podría enseñarme …?
pod<u>ree</u>ya ense<u>ñar</u>meh

How much is this/that?

¿Cuánto cuesta esto/eso?
<u>kwan</u>to <u>kwes</u>ta <u>es</u>to/<u>e</u>so

That's all, thanks.

Eso es todo, gracias.
<u>e</u>so es <u>to</u>do <u>gra</u>theeyas

Buenos días/Buenas tardes señora/señor.	Good morning/afternoon madam/sir.
¿Le atienden?	Are you being served?
¿Qué desea?	What would you like?
Ahora mismo voy a comprobarlo.	I'll just check that for you.
¿Eso es todo?	Is that everything?
¿Algo más?	Anything else?

– _¿Necesita ayuda?_
– No, gracias, sólo estoy mirando.
– _Bien._
– Disculpe.
– _Sí, ¿en qué puedo ayudarle?_
– ¿Cuánto cuesta eso?
– _Um, voy a comprobarlo …Cuesta mil pesetas_

AUTOSERVICIO	self-service
CAJA CENTRAL	customer service
OFERTA ESPECIAL	special offer

133

Preference Preferencia

I want something …	**Quiero algo …** *keeyero algo*
It must be …	**Debe ser …** *debeh sehr*
big/small	**grande/pequeño(-a)** *grandeh/pekeño(-a)*
cheap/expensive	**barato(-a)/caro(-a)** *barato(-a)/karo*
dark/light	**oscuro(-a)/claro(-a)** *oskooro(-a)/klaro(-a)*
light/heavy	**ligero(-a)/pesado(-a)** *leekhero(-a)/pesado(-a)*
oval/round/square	**ovalado(-a)/redondo(-a)/cuadrado(-a)** *obalado(-a)/redondo(-a)/kwadrado(-a)*
genuine/imitation	**auténtico(-a)/de imitación** *aootenteeko(-a)/deh eemeetatheeyon*
I don't want anything too expensive.	**No quiero nada demasiado caro.** *no keeyero nada demaseeyado karo*
In the region of … pesetas.	**Alrededor de las … pesetas.** *alrrededor deh las … pesetas*

¿Qué … quiere?	What … would you like?
color/forma	color/shape
calidad/cantidad	quality/quantity
¿De qué clase quiere?	What sort would you like?
¿Qué precio está dispuesto a pagar aproximadamente?	What price range are you thinking of?

Do you have anything …?	**¿Tiene(n) algo …?** *teeyeneh(n) algo*
larger	**más grande** *mas grandeh*
better quality	**de mejor calidad** *deh mekhor kaleedath*
cheaper	**más barato** *mas barato*
smaller	**más pequeño** *mas pekeño*
Can you show me …?	**¿Puede enseñarme …?** *pwedeh enseñarmeh*
that/this one	**ése-aquél/éste** *eseh-akel/esteh*
these/those ones	**éstos/ésos-aquéllos** *estos/esos-akel-yos*
the one in the window/ display case	**el de la ventana/la vitrina** *el deh la bentana/la beetreena*
some others	**otros** *otros*

Conditions of purchase
Condiciones de compra

Is there a guarantee?	**¿Tiene garantía?** *teeyeneh garanteeya*
Are there any instructions with it?	**¿Lleva instrucciones?** *l-yeba eenstrooktheeyones*

Out of stock Agotado

Lo siento, no nos quedan.	I'm sorry, we haven't any.
Se nos ha(n) agotado.	We're out of stock.
¿Puedo enseñarle algo más/otra clase?	Can I show you something else/ a different sort?
¿Se lo mandamos a pedir?	Shall we order it for you?

Can you order it for me?	**¿Me lo puede mandar a pedir?** *meh lo pwedeh mandar a pedeer*
How long will it take?	**¿Cuánto tiempo tardará?** *kwanto teeyempo tardara*
Where else might I get …?	**¿En qué otro sitio puedo conseguir …?** *en keh otro seeteeyo pwedo konsegeer*

Decision La decisión

That's not quite what I want.	**Eso no es realmente lo que quiero.** *eso no es reyalmenteh lo keh keeyero*
No, I don't like it.	**No, no me gusta.** *no no meh goosta*
That's too expensive.	**Es demasiado caro.** *es demaseeyado karo*
I'd like to think about it.	**Quiero pensármelo.** *keeyero pensarmelo*
I'll take it.	**Me lo quedo.** *meh lo kedo*

> – *Buenos días. Quisiera una sudadera.*
> – *¿De qué clase?*
> – *Naranja, por favor. Y quiero algo grande.*
> – *Ahí tiene. Ésa vale 2.500 pesetas.*
> – *Umm. Eso no es realmente lo que quiero.*
> *Gracias. Adiós.*

Paying Pagar

Small businesses may not accept credit cards; however, large stores, restaurants and hotels accept major credit cards, traveler's checks/cheques and Eurocheques – look for the signs on the door.

Tax can be reclaimed on larger purchases when returning home (outside the EU).

Where do I pay?	**¿Dónde pago?** _dondeh pago_
How much is that?	**¿Cuánto cuesta eso?** _kwanto kwesta eso_
Could you write it down, please?	**¿Podría escribirlo?** _podreeya eskreebeerlo_
Do you accept …?	**¿Aceptan …?** _atheptan_
traveler's checks/cheques	**cheques de viaje** _chekehs deh beeyakheh_
I'll pay …	**Pago …** _pago_
by cash	**en metálico** _en metaleeko_
by credit card	**con tarjeta de crédito** _kon tarkheta deh kredeeto_
I don't have any smaller change.	**No tengo monedas más pequeñas.** _no tengo monedas mas pekeñas_
Sorry, I don't have enough money.	**Lo siento, no tengo suficiente dinero.** _lo seeyento no tengo soofeetheeyenteh deenero_

¿Cómo va a pagar?	How are you paying?
La máquina no acepta la operación.	This transaction has not been approved/accepted.
Esta tarjeta no es válida.	This card is not valid.
¿Me puede enseñar otra prueba de identificación?	May I have further identification?
¿No tiene billetes más pequeños?	Have you got any smaller change?

Could I have a receipt please?	**¿Podría darme un recibo?** _podreeya darmeh oon rretheebo_
I think you've given me the wrong change.	**Creo que me ha dado el cambio equivocado.** _kreyo keh meh a dado el kambeeyo ekeebokado_

POR PAVOR PAGUE AQUÍ	please pay here
SE DETENDRÁ A	shoplifters will be
LOS CLEPTÓMANOS	prosecuted

136

Complaints Reclamaciones

This doesn't work.	**Esto no funciona.**
	esto no foontheeyona
Where can I make a complaint?	**¿Dónde puedo hacer una**
	reclamación? *dondeh pwehdo*
	ather oona rreklamatheeyon
Can you exchange this, please?	**¿Puede cambiarme esto, por favor?**
	pwedeh kambeeyarmeh esto por fabor
I'd like a refund.	**Quiero que me devuelvan el dinero.**
	keeyero keh meh debwelban el deenero
Here's the receipt.	**Aquí tiene el recibo.**
	akee teeyeneh el rretheebo
I don't have the receipt.	**No tengo el recibo.** *no tengo el rretheebo*
I'd like to see the manager.	**Quiero ver al encargado.**
	keeyero behr al enkargado

Repairs/Cleaning Reparaciones/Limpieza

This is broken. Can you repair it?	**Esto está roto. ¿Me lo puede arreglar?**
	esto esta rroto. meh lo pwedeh arreglar
Do you have … for this?	**¿Tiene(n) …para esto?** *teeyeneh(n) para esto*
a battery	**una pila** *oona peela*
replacement parts	**piezas de recambio**
	peeyethas deh rrekambeeyo
There's something wrong with …	**Hay algo que no funciona en …**
	eye algo keh no foontheeyona en
Can you … this?	**¿Puede … esto?** *pwedeh esto*
clean	**limpiar** *leempeeyar*
press	**planchar** *planchar*
patch	**remendar** *rremendar*
alter	**hacerle un arreglo a**
	atherleh oon arrehglo a
When will it (they) be ready?	**¿Cuándo estará(n) listo(s)?**
	kwando estara(n) leesto(s)
This isn't mine.	**Esto no es mío.** *esto no es meeyo*
There's … missing.	**Falta …** *falta*

Bank/Bureau de Change
Banco/Oficina de cambio

At some banks, cash can be obtained from ATMs/dispensers with Visa, Eurocard, American Express and many other international cards. Instructions are often given in English.

You can also change money at travel agencies and hotels, but the rate will not be as good.

Remember your passport when you want to change money.

Where's the nearest …?	**¿Dónde está … más cercano?** _dondeh esta … mas therkano_
bank	**el banco** _el banko_
currency exchange office/ bureau de change	**el despacho de cambio** _el despacho deh kambeeyo_

CAJEROS	cash machines
EMPUJAR/TIRAR/APRETAR	push/pull/press
TODAS LAS OPERACIONES	all transactions

Changing money Cambiando dinero

Can I exchange foreign currency here?	**¿Puedo cambiar divisas extranjeras aquí?** _pwedo kambeeyar deebeesas ekstrankheras akee_
I'd like to change some dollars/pounds into pesetas.	**Quiero cambiar dólares/libras a pesetas.** _keeyero kambeeyar dolares/leebras a pesetas_
I want to cash some traveler's checks/cheques/Eurocheques.	**Quiero cobrar cheques de viaje/ eurocheques.** _keeyero kobrar chekes deh beeyakheh/eurochekes_
What's the exchange rate?	**¿A cuánto está el cambio?** _a kwanto esta el kambeeyo_
How much commission do you charge?	**¿Cuánto se llevan de comisión?** _kwanto seh l-yeban deh komeeseeyon_
I've lost my traveler's checks. These are the numbers.	**He perdido los cheques de viaje. Aquí tiene los números.** _eh perdeedo los chekes deh beeyakheh. akee teeyeneh los noomeros_

Security Seguridad

¿Podría ver ...?	Could I see ...?
su pasaporte	your passport
alguna forma de identificación	some identification
su tarjeta	your bank card
¿Cuál es su dirección?	What's your address?
¿Dónde se aloja(n)?	Where are you staying?
Rellene este impreso, por favor.	Fill in this form, please.
Firme aquí, por favor.	Please sign here.

Cash machines/ATMs
Cajeros (automáticos)

Can I withdraw money on my credit card here?

¿Puedo sacar dinero aquí con mi tarjeta de crédito?
pwedo sakar deenero akee kon mee tarkheta deh kredeeto

Where are the ATMs/cash machines?

¿Dónde están los cajeros (automáticos)?
dondeh estan los kakheros (aootomateekos)

Can I use my ... card in the cash machine?

¿Puedo usar la tarjeta ... en el cajero (automático)?
pwedo oosar la tarkheta ... en el kakhero (aootomateeko)

The cash machine has eaten my card.

El cajero (automático) se ha tragado la tarjeta.
el kakhero (aootomateeko) seh a tragado la tarkheta

COMISIÓN DEL BANCO	bank charges
DIVISA EXTRANJERA	foreign currency
CAJERO AUTOMÁTICO	automated teller/ cash machine

Currency	**Peseta (pta.)**
	Coins: 1, 5, 10, 25, 50, 100, 200, 500
	Notes: **1000, 2000, 5000, 10000**

Pharmacy Farmacia

Pharmacies are easily recognized by their sign: a green or red cross, usually lit up.

If you are looking for a pharmacy at night, on Sundays or holidays, you'll find the address of duty pharmacies (**famacia de guardia**) listed in the newspaper or displayed in all pharmacy windows.

Where's the nearest (all-night) pharmacy?	**¿Dónde está la farmacia (de guardia) más próxima?** _dondeh esta la farmatheeya (deh gwardeeya) mas prokseema_
What time does the pharmacy open/close?	**¿A qué hora abre/cierra la farmacia?** _a keh ora abreh/theeyerra la farmatheeya_
Can you make up this prescription for me?	**¿Puede darme el medicamento de esta receta?** _pwedeh darmeh el medeekamento deh esta rretheta_
Shall I wait?	**¿Me espero?** _meh espero_
I'll come back for it.	**Volveré a recogerlo.** _bolbereh a rrekokherlo_

Dosage instructions
Instrucciones para la dosificación

How much should I take?	**¿Cuánto tengo que tomar?** _kwanto tengo keh tomar_
How often should I take it?	**¿Cada cuánto tiempo lo tomo?** _kada kwanto teeyempo lo tomo_
Is it suitable for children?	**¿Lo pueden tomar los niños?** _lo pweden tomar los neeños_

Tómese ... comprimidos/ cucharaditas ...	Take ... tablets/teaspoons ...
antes/después de cada comida	before/after meals
con agua	with water
enteros(-as)	whole
por la mañana/noche	in the morning/at night
durante ... días	for ... days

DOCTOR ➤ 151

Asking advice Pidiendo consejo

What would you recommend for …?	**¿Qué recomienda usted para …?** *keh rrekomeeyenda oosteth para*
a cold	**el resfriado** *el rresfreeyado*
a cough	**la tos** *la tos*
diarrhea/diarrhoea	**la diarrea** *la deeyarreya*
a hangover	**la resaca** *la rresaka*
hay fever	**la fiebre del heno** *la feeyebreh del eno*
insect bites	**las picaduras de insectos** *las peekadooras deh eensektos*
a sore throat	**el dolor de garganta** *el dolor deh garganta*
sunburn	**las quemaduras producidas por el sol** *las kemadooras prodootheedas por el sol*
travel sickness	**el mareo** *el mareyo*
an upset stomach	**el dolor de estómago** *el dolor deh estomago*
Can I get it without a prescription?	**¿Puedo comprarlo sin receta?** *pwedo komprarlo seen rretheta*

Over-the-counter treatment En la farmacia

Can I have …?	**¿Puede darme …?** *pwedeh darmeh*
antiseptic cream	**una crema antiséptica** *oona krema anteesepteeka*
(soluble) aspirin	**aspirinas (solubles)** *aspeereenas (soloobles)*
bandage	**vendas** *bendas*
condoms	**condones** *kondones*
cotton/cotton wool	**algodón** *algodon*
insect repellent/spray	**repelente/espray para insectos** *repelenteh/espray para eensektos*
pain killers	**analgésicos** *analkheseekos*
vitamin tablets	**vitaminas en comprimidos** *beetameenas en kompreemeedos*

141

Toiletries
Artículos para la higiene personal

I'd like …	**Quiero …** *keeyero*
after shave	**aftershave** *"aftershabe"*
after-sun lotion	**aftersun** *aftersoon*
deodorant	**desodorante** *desodoranteh*
razor blades	**cuchillas de afeitar** *koocheel-yas deh afeyeetar*
sanitary napkins/towels	**compresas** *kompresas*
soap	**jabón** *khabon*
suntan cream/lotion	**crema bronceadora** *krema brontheyadora*
tampons	**tampones** *tampones*
tissues	**pañuelos de papel** *pañwelos deh papel*
toilet paper	**papel higiénico** *papel eekheeyeneeko*
toothpaste	**pasta de dientes** *pasta deh deeyentes*

Haircare Cuidado del pelo

comb	**un peine** *oon peyneh*
conditioner	**suavizante** *swabeethanteh*
hair brush	**un cepillo** *oon thepeel-yo*
hair mousse	**espuma para el pelo** *espooma para el pelo*
hair spray	**espray fijador** *espray feekhador*
shampoo	**champú** *champoo*

For the baby Para el bebé

baby food	**comida para bebés** *komeeda para bebes*
baby wipes	**toallitas** *toal-yeetas*
diapers/nappies	**pañales** *pañales*
sterilizing solution	**solución esterilizante** *solootheeyon estereeleethanteh*

Clothing Ropa

You'll find that airport boutiques offering tax-free shopping may have cheaper prices but less selection.

General Expresiones generales

I'd like ...   **Quiero ...** *keeyero*
Do you have any ...?   **¿Tiene(n) ...?** *teeyeneh(n)*

ROPA DE CABALLERO	menswear
ROPA DE NIÑOS	childrens wear
ROPA DE SEÑORA	ladies wear

Color/Colour Color

I'm looking for something in ...   **Estoy buscando algo ...**
estoy booskando algo

beige	**beige**	*beich*
black	**negro**	*negro*
blue	**azul**	*athool*
brown	**marrón**	*marron*
green	**verde**	*berdeh*
gray/grey	**gris**	*grees*
orange	**naranja**	*narankha*
pink	**rosa**	*rrosa*
purple	**morado**	*morado*
red	**rojo**	*rrokho*
white	**blanco**	*blanko*
yellow	**amarillo**	*amareel-yo*
light ...	**... claro**	*klaro*
dark ...	**... oscuro**	*oskooro*

I want a darker/lighter shade.   **Quiero un tono más oscuro/claro.**
keeyero oon tono mas oskooro/klaro

Do you have the same in ...?   **¿Lo tiene igual en ...?**
lo teeyeneh eegwal en

Clothes and accessories
Ropa y accesorios

belt	**cinturón** *theentooron*
bikini	**bikini** *beekeenee*
blouse	**blusa** *bloosa*
bra	**sujetador/sostén** *sookhetador/sosten*
briefs	**calzoncillos** *kalthontheel-yos*
coat	**abrigo** *abreego*
dress	**vestido** *besteedo*
handbag	**bolso** *bolso*
hat	**sombrero** *sombrero*
jacket	**chaqueta** *chaketa*
jeans	**vaqueros** *bakeros*
leggings	**mallas** *mal-yas*
pants (U.S.)	**pantalones** *pantalones*
panty hose/tights	**medias** *medeeyas*
pullover	**jersey** *khersay*
raincoat	**impermeable** *eempermeableh*
scarf	**bufanda** *boofanda*
shirt	**camisa** *kameesa*
shorts	**pantalones cortos** *pantalones kortos*
skirt	**falda** *falda*
socks	**calcetines** *kaltheteenehs*
stocking	**media** *medeeya*
suit	**traje de chaqueta** *trakheh deh chaketa*
sunglasses	**gafas de sol** *gafas deh sol*
sweatshirt	**sudadera** *soodadera*
swimming trunks/swimsuit	**bañador (de hombre/de mujer)** *bañador (deh ombreh/deh mookher)*
T-shirt	**camiseta** *kameeseta*
tie	**corbata** *korbata*
trousers	**pantalones** *pantalones*
underpants	**calzoncillos** *kalthontheel-yos*
with long/short sleeves	**de manga larga/corta** *deh manga larga/korta*
with V-/round neck	**con cuello de pico/a la caja** *kon kwel-yo deh peeko/a la kakha*

Shoes Zapatos

a pair of ...   **un par de ...**
                       oon par deh

boots   **botas** *botas*
flip-flops   **chancletas** *chankletas*
running/training shoes **zapatillas de deporte**
                       thapateel-yas deh deporteh

sandals   **sandalias** *sandaleeyas*
shoes   **zapatos** *thapatos*
slippers   **zapatillas** *thapateel-yas*

Walking/hiking gear equipo de senderismo

knapsack   **mochila** *mocheela*
walking boots   **botas de montaña** *botas deh montaña*
waterproof jacket   **chaquetón impermeable**
                       chaketon eempermehable
windbreaker/cagoule   **chubasquero** *choobaskero*

Fabric Tela

I want something in ... **Quiero algo de ...** *keeyero algo deh*
cotton   **algodón** *algodon*
denim   **tela vaquera** *tela bakera*
lace   **encaje** *enkakheh*
leather   **cuero** *kwero*
linen   **lino** *leeno*
wool   **lana** *lana*
Is this ...?   **¿Es esto ...?** *es esto*
pure cotton   **puro algodón** *pooro algodon*
synthetic   **sintético** *seenteteeko*
Is it hand washable/   **¿Se puede lavar a mano/a máquina?**
machine washable?   *seh pwedeh labar a mano/a makeena*

LAVAR A MANO	handwash only
LIMPIAR EN SECO	dry clean only
NO DESTIÑE	colorfast
NO PLANCHAR	do not iron

Does it fit? ¿Le está bien?

Can I try this on?	**¿Puedo probarme esto?**	
	pwedo probarmeh esto	
Where's the fitting room?	**¿Dónde está el probador?**	
	dondeh esta el probador	
It fits well. I'll take it.	**Me está bien. Me lo quedo.**	
	meh esta beeyen. meh lo kedo	
It doesn't fit.	**No me está bien.** *no meh esta beeyen*	
It's too...	**Es demasiado ...** *es demaseeyado*	
short/long	**corto(-a)/largo(-a)** *korto(-a)/largo(-a)*	
tight/loose	**estrecho(-a)/ancho(-a)**	
	estrecho(-a)/ancho(-a)	
Do you have this in size ...?	**¿Tienen esto en la talla ...?**	
	teeyenen esto en la tal-ya	
What size is this?	**¿De qué talla es?**	
	deh keh tal-ya es	
Could you measure me, please?	**¿Podría tomarme las medidas, por favor?**	
	podreeya tomarmeh las medeedas por fabor	
I don't know Spanish sizes.	**No conozco las tallas españolas.**	
	no konothko las tal-yas españolas	

Size Talla

	Dresses/Suits						Women's shoes			
American	8	10	12	14	16	18	6	7	8	9
British	10	12	14	16	18	20	$8^{1/2}$	$5^{1/2}$	$6^{1/2}$	$7^{1/2}$
Continental	36	38	40	42	44	46	37	38	40	41

	Shirts				Men's shoes							
American) British)	15	16	17	18	5	6	7	8	$8^{1/2}$ 9	$9^{1/2}$ 10	11	
Continental	38	41	43	45	38	39	41	42	43	43 44	44	45

XL	extra large (XL)
GRANDE	large (L)
MEDIANA	medium (M)
PEQUEÑA	small (S)

1 centimeter (cm.) = 0.30 in.   1 inch = 2.54 cm.
1 meter (m.) = 39.37 in.   1 foot = 30.5 cm.
10 meters = 32.81 ft.   1 yard = 0.91 m.

Health and beauty
Salud y belleza

I'd like a …	**Quiero que me …** *keeyero keh meh*
facial	**haga una limpieza de cutis/cara** *aga oona leempeeyetha deh kootees/kara*
manicure	**haga la manicura** *aga la maneekoora*
massage	**dé un masaje** *deh oon masakheh*
waxing	**haga la cera** *aga la thera*

Hairdresser/Hairstylist Peluquería

Tipping: 5-10% is normal.

I'd like to make an appointment for …	**Quiero pedir hora para …** *keeyero pedeer ora para*
Can you make it a bit earlier/later?	**¿Puede venir un poco más tarde/ temprano?** *pwedeh beneer oon poko mas tardeh/temprano*
I'd like a …	**Quiero …** *keeyero*
cut and blow-dry	**que me corte el pelo y me lo seque** *keh meh korteh el pelo ee meh lo sekeh*
shampoo and set	**un lavado y marcado** *oon labado ee markado*
trim	**que me corte las puntas** *keh meh korteh las poontas*
I'd like my hair …	**Quiero que me …** *keeyero keh meh*
colored/tinted	**tiña el pelo** *teeña el pelo*
highlighted	**haga mechas** *aga mechas*
permed	**haga la permanente** *aga la permanenteh*
Don't cut it too short.	**No me lo corte demasiado.** *no meh lo korteh demaseeyado*
A little more off the …	**Un poquito más por …** *oon pokeeto mas por …*
back/front	**detrás/delante** *detras/delanteh*
neck/sides	**el cuello/por los lados** *el kwel-yo/por los lados*
top	**arriba** *arreeba*
That's fine, thanks.	**Está muy bien, gracias.** *esta mwee beeyen gratheeyas*

147

Household articles
Artículos del hogar

I'd like a(n)/some …	**Quiero …** *keeyero*
adapter	**un adaptador** *oon adaptador*
aluminum foil	**papel de aluminio** *papel deh aloomeeneeyo*
bottle opener	**un abrebotellas** *oon abrebotel-yas*
can/tin opener	**un abrelatas** *oon abrelatas*
candles	**velas** *belas*
clothes pegs/pins	**pinzas de la ropa** *peenthas deh la rropa*
corkscrew	**un sacacorchos** *oon sakakorchos*
lightbulb	**una bombilla** *oona bombeel-ya*
matches	**cerillas** *thereel-yas*
paper napkins	**servilletas de papel** *serbeel-yetas deh papel*
plastic wrap/cling film	**film transparente** *feelm transparente*
plug	**un enchufe** *oon enchoofeh*
scissors	**tijeras** *teekheras*
screwdriver	**un destornillador** *oon destorneel-yador*

Cleaning items Artículos de limpieza

bleach	**lejía** *lekheeya*
dish cloth	**balleta** *bal-yeta*
dishwashing detergent	**lavavajillas** *lababakheel-yas*
garbage/refuse bags	**bolsa de basura** *bolsa deh basoora*
laundry soap/washing powder	**detergente de lavadora** *deterkhenteh deh labadora*

Crockery/Cutlery Vajilla/Cubertería

cups	**tazas** *tathas*
forks	**tenedores** *tenedores*
glasses	**vasos/copas** *basos/kopas*
knives	**cuchillos** *koocheel-yos*
mugs	**tazas** *tathas*
plates	**platos** *platos*
spoons	**cucharas** *koocharas*
teaspoons	**cucharillas** *koochareel-yas*

Jeweler's/Jeweller's Joyería

Regional specialties that may catch your eye, include artificial pearls (**perlas majóricas**) from Majorca and damascene (**damasquino**) from Toledo – steel inlaid with intricate gold designs.

Could I see …?	**¿Podría ver …?** _podreeya behr_
this/that	**esto/eso** _esto/eso_
It's in the window/ display cabinet.	**Está en el escaparate/en la vitrina.** _esta en el eskaparateh/en la beetreena_
I'd like a(n)/some …	**Quiero …** _keeyero_
battery	**una pila** _oona peela_
bracelet	**una pulsera** _oona poolsera_
brooch	**un broche** _oon brocheh_
chain	**una cadena** _oona kadena_
clock	**un reloj de pared** _oon relokh deh pareth_
earrings	**unos pendientes** _oonos pendeeyentes_
necklace	**un collar** _oon kol-yar_
ring	**un anillo** _oon aneel-yo_
watch	**un reloj de pulsera** _oon relokh deh poolsera_

Materials Materiales

Is this real silver/gold?	**¿Es esto plata/oro de ley?** _es esto plata/oro deh ley_
Is there any certification for it?	**¿Tiene el sello?** _teeyeneh el sel-yo_
Do you have anything in …?	**¿Tiene(n) algo …?** _teeyeneh(n) algo_
copper	**de cobre** _deh kobreh_
crystal	**de vidrio** _deh beedreeyo_
cut glass	**de vidrio tallado** _deh beedreeyo tal-yado_
diamond	**de diamantes** _deh deeyamantes_
enamel	**esmaltado** _esmaltado_
gold	**de oro** _deh oro_
gold plate	**chapado en oro** _chapado en oro_
pearl	**de perlas** _deh perlas_
pewter	**de peltre** _deh peltreh_
platinum	**de platino** _deh plateeno_
silver	**de plata** _deh plata_
silver plate	**chapado en plata** _chapado en plata_
stainless steel	**de acero inoxidable** _deh athero eenokseedableh_

Newsstand/Newsagent/Tobacconist
Kiosko de prensa/Estanco

Foreign newspapers can usually be found at rail stations or airports, or on newsstands in major cities.

Cigarettes can be bought from specialist tobacco shops, vending machines, restaurants and supermarkets.

Spanish cigarettes are strong (**negro**) or light (**rubio**). Cigars from the Canary Islands and Cuba are widely available in Spain.

Do you sell English-language books/newspapers?	**¿Venden libros/periódicos en inglés?** _benden leebros/pereeyodeekos en eengles_
I'd like …	**Quiero …** _keeyero_
book	**un libro** _oon leebro_
candy/sweets	**caramelos** _karamelos_
chewing gum	**chicles** _cheekles_
chocolate bar	**una barra de chocolate** _oona barra deh chokolateh_
cigarettes (packet of)	**un paquete de tabaco** _oon paketeh deh tabako_
cigars	**unos puros** _oonos pooros_
dictionary	**un diccionario** _oon deektheeyonareeyo_
English-Spanish	**de inglés-español** _deh eengles español_
guidebook of …	**una guía de …** _oona geeya deh_
lighter	**un encendedor** _oon enthendedor_
magazine	**una revista** _oona rebeesta_
map of the town	**un plano de la ciudad** _oon plano deh la theeyoodath_
road map of …	**un mapa de carreteras de …** _oon mapa deh karreteras deh_
matches	**unos cerillas** _oonos thereel-yas_
newspaper	**un periódico** _oon pereeyodeeko_
American/English	**americano/inglés** _amereekano/eengles_
paper	**papel** _papel_
pen	**un bolígrafo** _oon boleegrafo_
postcard	**una postal** _oona postal_
stamps	**unos sellos** _oonos sel-yos_
tobacco	**tabaco** _tabako_
writing pad	**un cuaderno** _oon kwaderno_

Photography Fotografía

I'm looking for a ... camera	**Busco una cámara ...**
	boosko oona kamara ...
automatic	**automática** *aootomateeka*
compact	**compacta** *kompakta*
disposable	**de usar y tirar**
	deh oosar ee teerar
SLR	**cámara reflex**
	kamara refleks
I'd like ...	**Quiero ...** *keeyero*
battery	**una pila** *oona peela*
camera case	**una funda para la cámara**
	oona foonda para la kamara
(electronic) flash	**un flash (electrónico)**
	oon flash (elektroneeko)
filter	**un filtro** *oon feeltro*
lens	**una lente** *oona lenteh*
lens cap	**una tapa para la lente**
	oona tapa para la lenteh

Film/Processing Carretes/Revelado

I'd like a ... film for this camera.	**Quiero un carrete ... para esta cámara.**
	keeyero oon karreteh ... para esta kamara
black and white	**en blanco y negro**
	en blanko ee negro
color/colour	**de color** *deh kolor*
I'd like this film developed.	**Quiero que me revelen este carrete, por favor.** *keeyero keh meh rebelen esteh karreteh*
Would you enlarge this?	**¿Podrían ampliarme esto?**
	podreeyan ampleeyarmeh esto
How much do ... exposures cost?	**¿Cuánto cuesta revelar ... fotos?**
	kwanto kwesta rebelar ...fotos
When will the photos be ready?	**¿Cuándo estarán listas las fotos?**
	kwando estaran leestas las fotos
I'd like to collect my photos. Here's the receipt.	**Vengo a recoger mis fotos. Aquí tiene el recibo.** *bengo a rekokher mees fotos.akee teeyeneh el retheebo*

Police Policía

There are 3 police forces in Spain. In rural areas and smaller towns, any crime or road accident has to be reported to the **Cuartel de la Guardia Civil**. In larger towns, responsibilities are divided between the local police (**Policía Municipal**) for traffic control, lost property, commerce etc. and the national police (**Cuerpo Nacional de Policía**) for all aspects of personal protection, crime, theft, injuries and immigration.

Beware of pickpockets, particularly in crowded places. Report all thefts to the local police within 24 hours for your own insurance purposes.

To get the police in an emergency, ☎ 091to report a crime in a main town, ☎ 092 for medical assistance.

Where's the nearest police station?	**¿Dónde está la comisaría (de policía) más cercana?** _dondeh esta la komeesareeya (deh poleetheeya) mas therkana_
Does anyone here speak English?	**¿Hay alguien aquí que hable inglés?** _eye algeeyen akee keh ableh eengles_
I want to report …	**Quiero denunciar …** _keeyero denoontheeyar_
accident/attack	**un accidente/asalto** _oon aktheedenteh/asalto_
My child is missing.	**Mi hijo(-a) ha desaparecido.** _mee eekho(-a) a desaparetheedo_
Here's a photo of him/her.	**Aquí tiene una foto de él/ella.** _akee teeyeneh oona foto deh el/el-ya_
I need an English-speaking lawyer.	**Necesito un abogado que hable inglés.** _netheseeto oon abogado keh ableh eengles_
I need to make a phone call.	**Tengo que hacer una llamada.** _tengo keh ather oona l-yamada_
I need to contact the … (American/British) Consulate.	**Tengo que ponerme en contacto con el consulado … (americano/británico)** _tengo keh ponermeh en kontakto kon el konsoolado (amereekano/breetaneeko)_

¿Puede describirle/la?	Can you describe him/her?
hombre/mujer	male/female
rubio(-a)/castaño(-a)	blonde/brunette
pelirrojo(-a)/canoso(-a)	red-headed/gray/grey
con el pelo largo/corto/con entradas	long/short hair/balding
altura aproximada …	approximate height …
edad aproximada …	aged (approximately) …
vestía/llevaba puesto …	he/she was wearing …

CLOTHES ➤ 144; COLORS ➤ 143

Lost property/Theft
Objetos perdidos/Robo

I want to report
a theft/break-in.

Quiero denunciar un robo.
*keeyero denoontheeyar oon
rrobo*

My car's been broken into.

Me han forzado el coche.
meh an forthado el kocheh

I've been robbed/mugged.

Me han robado/atracado.
meh an rrobado/atrakado

I've lost my ...
My ... has been stolen.

He perdido mi ... *eh perdeedo mee*
Me han robado ... *meh an rrobado*

bicycle

la bicicleta *la beetheekleta*

camera

la cámara *la kamara*

(rental) car

el coche (alquilado) *el kocheh (alkeelado)*

credit cards

las tarjetas de crédito
las tarkhetas deh kredeeto

handbag

el bolso *el bolso*

money

el dinero *el deenero*

passport

el pasaporte *el pasaporteh*

purse

el monedero *el monedero*

wallet

la billetera *la beel-yetera*

watch

el reloj (de pulsera)
el relokh (deh poolsera)

What shall I do?

¿Qué hago? *keh ago*

I need a police certificate/form
for my insurance claim.

**Necesito un certificado de la policía para
el seguro.** *netheseeto oon therteefeekado
deh la poleetheeya para el segooro*

¿Qué falta?	What's missing?
¿Cuándo lo robaron?	When was it stolen?
¿Cuándo ocurrió?	When did it happen?
¿Dónde se hospeda?	Where are you staying?
¿De dónde lo cogieron?	Where was it taken from?
¿Dónde estaba usted entonces?	Where were you at the time?
Le vamos a conseguir un intérprete.	We're getting an interpreter for you.
Investigaremos el asunto.	We'll look into the matter.
Por favor, rellene este impreso/ formulario.	Please fill in this form.

Post Office (Oficina de) Correos

Spanish post offices are recognized by the red hunting horn
on a bright yellow background. Mail boxes are yellow and red.

Stamps can be bought from tobacconists, as well as from
the Post Office.

General queries Preguntas generales

Where is the main/
nearest post office?

**¿Dónde está la oficina de correos
principal/más cercana?** *dondeh esta la
ofeetheena de korreyos preentheepal/mas
therkana*

What time does the post office
open/close?

**¿A qué hora abre/cierra la oficina de
correos?** *a keh ora abreh/theeyera la
ofeetheena deh korreyos*

Does it close for lunch?

¿A qué hora se cierra para comer?
a keh ora seh theeyerra para komer

Where's the mailbox/postbox?

¿Dónde está el buzón?
dondeh esta el boothon

Is there any mail for me?
My name is …

¿Hay correo para mí? Me llamo …
eye korreyo para mee. meh l-yamo

Buying stamps Comprando sellos

A stamp for this postcard/
letter, please.
A … pesetas stamp, please.

Un sello para esta postal/carta, por favor.
oon selyo para esta postal/karta por fabor
Un sello de … pesetas, por favor.
oon sel-yo deh … pesetas por fabor

What's the postage for
a postcard/letter to …?

**¿Cuántos sellos se necesitan para una
postal/carta a …?** *kwantos sel-yos seh
netheseetan para oona postal/karta a*

Is there a stamp machine here?

**¿Hay una máquina expendedora de sellos
aquí?** *eye oona makeena expendedora
deh sel-yos akee*

- Hola, quiero mandar estas postales
a los Estados Unidos.
- *¿Cuántas?*
- Cinco, por favor.
- *Son cien pesetas cada una …
quinientas pesetas, por favor.*

Sending parcels Mandando paquetes

I want to send this parcel/package by …	**Quiero mandar este paquete por …** _keeyero mandar esteh paketeh por_
airmail	**correo aéreo** _korreyo ayreyo_
special delivery (express)	**correo urgente** _korreyo oorkhenteh_
registered mail	**correo certificado** _korreyo therteefeekado_
It contains …	**Contiene …** _konteeyeneh_

Por favor, rellene la declaración para la aduana.	Please fill in the customs declaration.
¿Qué valor tienen los objetos?	What is the value?
¿Qué hay dentro?	What's inside?

Other services Otros servicios

I'd like a phonecard, please.	**Quiero una tarjeta para llamar por teléfono.** _keeyero oona tarkheta para l-yamar por telefono_
10/20/50 units.	**De diez/veinte/cincuenta unidades.** _deh deeyeth/beynteh/theenkwenta ooneedades_
Do you have a photocopier here?	**¿Tienen una fotocopiadora aquí?** _teeyenen oona fotokopeeyadora akee_
I'd like to send a message by fax/E-mail.	**Quiero mandar un fax/un mensaje por correo electrónico.** _keeyero mandar oon faks/mensakheh por korreyo elektroneeko_
What's your E-mail address?	**¿Cuál es tu dirección de correo electrónico?** _kwal es too deerektheeyon deh korreyo elektroneeko_
Can I access the Internet here?	**¿Puedo acceder a Internet desde aquí?** _pwedo aktheder ah eenternet desdeh akee_
What are the charges per hour?	**¿Cuánto cuesta por hora?** _kwanto kwesta por ora_
How do I log on?	**¿Cómo entro?** _komo entro_

PAQUETES	parcels
PRÓXIMA RECOGIDA ….	next collection …
RECOGIDA DE CORREO	general delivery/poste restante
SELLOS	stamps
TELEGRAMAS	telegrams

Souvenirs Recuerdos

You'll find no shortage of gift ideas from the Spanish souvenir industry:

Bullfight poster (**el cartel de toros**), bullfighter's cap (**la montera**), bullfighter dolls (**los muñecos de torero**), bullfighter sword (**la espada de torero**), cape (**la capa**), castanets (**las castañuelas**), fan (**el abanico**), guitar (**la guitarra**), mantilla (**la mantilla**), pitcher (**el botijo**), poncho (**el poncho**), reproduction painting (**la reproducción de un cuadro**), tambourine (**la pandereta**).

You will also find a wide selection of fine hand-crafted articles, particularly in special outlets called **artesanía** or the government-sponsored **Artespaña**: carpets (**las alfombras**), ceramics (**objetos de cerámica**), copperware (**objetos de cobre**), earthenware (**la loza de barro**), embossed leather (**el cuero repujado**), embroidery (**el bordado**), fashion (**la moda**), jewelry/jewellery (**las joyas**), lace (**los encajes**), leather goods (**artículos de piel**), Valencian porcelain (**la cerámica de Valencia**), wood carving (**la talla en madera**).

Gifts Regalos

bottle of wine	**una botella de vino** _oo_na bo_tel_-ya deh _bee_no
box of chocolates	**una caja de bombones** _oo_na _kakha_ deh bom_bon_es
calendar	**un calendario** oon kalen_dar_eeyo
key ring	**un llavero** oon l-ya_be_ro
postcard	**una postal** _oo_na pos_tal_
souvenir guide	**un catálogo de recuerdos** oon ka_ta_lago deh re_kwer_dos
tea towel	**un paño de cocina** oon _pa_ño de ko_thee_na
T-shirt	**una camiseta** _oo_na kamee_se_ta

Music Música

I'd like a … **Quiero …** *keeyero*

cassette **una cinta/cassette**
oona theenta/kaseteh

compact disc **un compact disc** *oon "compact disc"*

record **un disco** *oon deesko*

videocassette **una cinta de vídeo**
oona theenta deh beedeyo

Who are the popular native singers/bands? **¿Quiénes son los cantantes/grupos populares de aquí?** *keeyenes son los kantantes/groopos popoolares deh akee*

Toys and games Juguetes y juegos

I'd like a toy/game … **Quiero un juguete/juego …**
keeyero oon khoogeteh/khwego

for a boy **para un niño** *para oon neeño*

for a 5-year-old girl **para una niña de cinco años**
para oona neeña deh theenko años

pail and shovel/bucket and spade **un cubo y una pala** *oon koobo ee oona pala*

chess set **un juego de ajedrez**
oon khwego deh akhedreth

doll **una muñeca** *oona mooñeka*

electronic game **un juego electrónico**
oon khwego elektroneeko

teddy bear **un osito** *oon oseeto*

Antiques Antigüedades

How old is this? **¿Qué antigüedad tiene esto?**
keh anteegwedath teeyeneh esto

Do you have anything of the … era? **¿Tiene algo del periodo …?**
teeyeneh algo del pereeyodo

Can you send it to me? **¿Puede mandármelo?**
pwedeh mandarmelo

Will I have problems with customs? **¿Tendré problemas en la aduana?**
tendreh problemas en la adwana

Is there a certificate of authenticity? **¿Tiene certificado de autenticidad?**
teeyeneh therteefeekado deh aootenteetheedath

ARTISTIC PERIODS ➤ 104

Supermarket/Minimart
Supermercado/Galería commercial

Supermarkets such as **Dia** and **Spar** can be found in town centers; **Alcampo**, **Caprabo**, **Jumbo** and **Pryca** are hypermarket chains situated around larger cities. You will also encounter minimarts (**galería commercial**) and modern substitutes for the tradtional market (**galería de alimentación**).

Opening times for these stores are generally 9:30 a.m. until 1:30 p.m., 4 p.m. to 8 p.m., and Saturdays from 9:30 to 1.30 p.m. with a few open in the afternoon.

At the supermarket En el supermercado

Excuse me. Where can I find …?	**Disculpe. ¿Dónde puedo encontrar …?** _dees__koolpeh_ _dondeh_ _pwedo_ enkon_trar_
Do I pay for this here or at the checkout?	**¿Pago esto aquí o en la caja?** _pago_ _esto_ a_kee_ o en la _kakha_
Where are the baskets/carts?	**¿Dónde están los carritos/las cestas?** _dondeh_ es_tan_ los kar_reetos_/las _thestas_
Is there a … here?	**¿Hay … aquí?** eye … a_kee_
delicatessen	**una charcutería** _oona_ charkootere_eya_
pharmacy	**una farmacia** _oona_ farma_theeya_

ARTÍCULOS PARA EL HOGAR	household goods
CARNE DE AVE	poultry
CARNE FRESCA	fresh meat
CONGELADOS	frozen foods
FRUTA/VERDURA EN CONSERVA	canned fruit/vegetables
PAN Y PASTELES	bread and cakes
PESCADO FRESCO	fresh fish
PRODUCTOS DE LIMPIEZA	cleaning products
FRUTAS Y VERDURAS	fresh produce
PRODUCTOS LÁCTEOS	dairy products
VINOS Y LICORES	wines and spirits

Weights and measures

- **1 kilogram** or **kilo (kg.)** = 1000 grams (g.); **100 g.** = 3.5 oz.; **1 kg.** = 2.2 lb 1 oz. = **28.35 g.**; 1 lb. = **453.60 g.**
- **1 liter (l.)** = 0.88 imp. quart or 1.06 U.S. quart 1 imp. quart = **1.14 l.** 1 U.S. quart = **0.951 l.** 1 imp. gallon = **4.55 l.** 1 U.S. gallon = **3.8 l.**

Food hygiene Higiene de los alimentos

APROPIADO PARA MICROONDAS	microwaveable
APROPIADO PARA VEGETARIANOS	suitable for vegetarians
CADUCA EL ...	sell by ...
CALENTAR ANTES DE CONSUMIR	reheat before eating
CONSUMIR A LOS ... DÍAS DE ABRIR	eat within ... days of opening
MANTENER REFRIGERADO	keep refrigerated

At the minimart En el autoservicio

I'd like some of that/those.	**Quiero un poco de eso/unos cuantos de esos.** _keeyero oon poko deh eso/oonos kwantos deh esos_
this one/these	**éste/éstos** _este/estos_
to the left/right	**a la izquierda/derecha** _al la eethkeeyerda/dehrecha_
over there/here	**ahí/allí** _aee/al-yee_
Which one/ones?	**¿Cuál/cuáles?** _kwal/kwales_
I'd like ...	**Quiero ...** _keeyero_
kilo/half-kilo of apples	**un kilo/medio kilo de manzanas** _oon keelo/medeeyo keelo deh manthanas_
100 grams of cheese	**cien gramos de queso** _theeyen gramos deh keso_
liter/litre of milk	**un litro de leche** _oon leetro deh lecheh_
half-dozen eggs	**media docena de huevos** _medeeya dothena deh webos_
... slices of ham	**... rodajas de jamón** _rrodakhas deh khamon_
piece of cake	**un trozo de pastel/tarta** _oon trotho deh pastel/tarta_
bottle of wine	**una botella de vino** _oona botel-ya deh beeno_
carton of milk	**un cartón de leche** _oon karton deh lecheh_
jar of jam	**un bote de mermelada** _oon boteh deh mermelada_
packet of potato chips/crisps	**una bolsa de patatas** _oona bolsa deh patatas_

– Quiero medio kilo de
ese queso, por favor.
– *Éste.*
– Sí, el Manchego por favor.
– *No faltaba más/Por supuesto.*
– Y cuatro trozos de tarta, por favor.
– *Aquí tiene.*

Provisions/Picnic   Provisiones/Picnic

cookies/biscuits	**unas galletas** _oo_nas gal_yeh_tas
butter	**mantequilla** manteh_kee_lya
cheese	**queso** _keh_so
French fries/chips	**patatas fritas** pa_ta_tas _free_tas
cold meats	**unos fiambres** _oo_nos fee_yam_brehs
potato chips/crisps	**patatas fritas (de bolsa)** pa_ta_tas _free_tas (deh _bol_sa)
eggs	**unos huevos** _oo_nos _weh_bos
grapes	**unas uvas** _oo_nas _oo_bas
ice cream	**helado** eh_la_do
instant coffee	**café soluble** ka_feh_ so_loo_ble
loaf of bread	**una barra de pan** _oo_na _barra_ deh pan
margarine	**margarina** marga_ree_na
milk	**leche** _le_cheh
rolls	**unos panecillos** _oo_nos pane_theel_-yos
sausages	**unas salchichas** _oo_nas sal_chee_chas
six-pack of beer	**seis latas de cerveza** says _la_tas deh thehr_beh_tha
soft drink/soda	**un refresco** oon reh_freh_sko
winebox	**una caja de botellas de vino** _oo_na _ka_kha deh bo_te_lyas deh _bee_no

una barra de pan _oo_na _barra_ deh pan
similar to a French bread stick; other types of bread include **colines** (bread-sticks), **rosquillas** (ring-shaped), **pan integral** (wholemeal bread)
empanadillas empana_deel_-yas
pasties, usually with a meat or tuna filling
una tarta/un pastel _oo_na _tarta_/oon pas_tel
a cake/small cakes; other types include **roscón** (ring-shaped cake, often flavored), **bizcocho** (sponge cake), **magdalenas** (small sponge cakes)

Health

Insurance and payment (➤ 168 for phrases)
Before you leave, make sure your health insurance policy covers any illness
or accident while on vacation/holiday. If not, ask your insurance representative, automobile association or travel agent for details of special health
insurance. A special Spanish health and accident insurance is available
from tourist boards (**ASTES**), covering doctor's fees and clinical care. In
Spain, EU citizens with a Form E111 are eligible for free medical treatment.
However, this only applies to clinics that belong, or are connected, to the
Seguridad Social (national health service). Dental care in this scheme is
limited to extractions.

Getting treatment
A list of English-speaking doctors is available at local tourist offices. There
are hospitals in all principal towns and a first aid station (**casa de socorro**)
in smaller places.

Doctor/General Médico/General

Where can I find a doctor/dentist?	**¿Dónde puedo encontrar un médico/dentista?** <u>don</u>deh <u>pwe</u>do enkon<u>trar</u> oon me<u>dee</u>ko/den<u>tees</u>ta
Where's there a doctor who speaks English?	**¿Dónde hay un médico que hable inglés?** <u>don</u>deh eye oon <u>me</u>deeko keh <u>a</u>bleh een<u>gles</u>
What are the office/ surgery hours?	**¿Cuáles son las horas de consulta?** <u>kwa</u>les son las <u>o</u>ras deh kon<u>sool</u>ta
Could the doctor come to see me here?	**¿Podría venir a verme el médico?** pod<u>ree</u>ya be<u>neer</u> a <u>ber</u>meh el <u>me</u>deeko
Can I make an appointment for ...?	**¿Puede darme una cita para ...?** <u>pwe</u>deh <u>dar</u>meh <u>oo</u>na <u>thee</u>ta <u>pa</u>ra
today/tomorrow	**hoy/mañana** oy/ma<u>ña</u>na
as soon as possible	**lo antes posible** lo <u>an</u>tes po<u>see</u>bleh
It's urgent.	**Es urgente.** es oor<u>khen</u>teh
I've got an appointment with Doctor ...	**Tengo una cita con el /la doctor(a) ...** <u>ten</u>go <u>oo</u>na <u>thee</u>ta kon el/la dok<u>tor</u>(a)

– ¿Pueden darme una cita lo antes posible?
– Está todo completo. ¿Es urgente?
– Sí.
– Bien, podemos darle a las diez y cuarto, con el doctor Sanchez-Royano.
– Diez y cuarto. Muchas gracias.

Accident and injury Accidentes y lesiones

My ... is hurt/injured.	**Mi ... está herido(-a).** *mee ... esta ereedo(-a)*
husband/wife	**marido/mujer** *mareedo/mookher*
son/daughter	**hijo/hija** *eekho/eekha*
friend	**amigo(-a)** *ameego(-a)*
baby	**bebé** *bebeh*
He/She is ...	**El/Ella está ...** *el/el-ya esta*
unconscious	**inconsciente** *eenkonstheeyenteh*
bleeding (heavily)	**sangrando (mucho)** *sangrando (moocho)*
(seriously) injured	**gravemente herido(-a)** *grabementeh ereedo(-a)*
I've got a/an ...	**Tengo ...** *tengo*
blister	**una ampolla** *oona ampol-ya*
boil	**un forúnculo** *oon foroonkoolo*
bruise	**un cardenal** *oon kardenal*
burn	**una quemadura** *oona kemadoora*
cut	**un corte** *oon korteh*
graze	**un rasguño** *oon rasgooño*
insect bite	**una picadura** *oona peekadoora*
lump	**un bulto** *oon boolto*
rash	**un sarpullido** *oon sarpool-yeedo*
sting	**un ardor** *oon ardor*
strained muscle	**un esguince** *oon esgeentheh*
swelling	**una hinchazón** *oona eenchathon*
wound	**una herida** *oona ereeda*
My ... hurts.	**Me duele el/la ...** *meh dweleh el/la*

Short-term symptoms
Síntomas immediatos

I've been feeling ill for … days.	**Llevo … días sintiéndome enfermo.** _l-yebo …deeyas seenteeyen_domeh en_fermo_
I feel faint.	**Estoy mareado(-a).** es_toy_ ma_rea_do(-a)
I'm feverish.	**Tengo fiebre.** _tengo feeyebreh_
I've been vomiting.	**He estado vomitando.** eh es_tado_ bomee_tando_
I've got diarrhea.	**Tengo diarrea.** _tengo deeyarreya_
It hurts here.	**Me duele aquí.** meh _dweleh akee_
I've have (a/an) …	**Tengo …** _tengo_
backache	**dolor de espalda** _dolor_ deh es_palda_
cold	**un resfriado** oon resfree_yado_
cramps	**retortijones** rretorteek_hones_
earache	**dolor de oídos** _dolor_ deh o_yeedos_
headache	**dolor de cabeza** _dolor_ deh ka_betha_
stomachache	**dolor de estómago** _dolor_ deh es_tomago_
I have a sore throat.	**Me duele la garganta.** meh _dweleh_ la gar_ganta_
I have sunstroke.	**Tengo una insolación.** _tengo oona_ eensolathee_yon_

Health conditions Enfermedades

I am …	**Soy …** soy
asthmatic	**asmático(-a)** as_mateeko_(-a)
deaf	**sordo(-a)** _sordo_(-a)
diabetic	**diabético(-a)** deeya_beteeko_(-a)
epileptic	**epiléptico(-a)** epee_lepteeko_(-a)
handicapped	**minusválido(-a)** meenoos_baleedo_(-a)
I'm arthritic.	**Tengo artritis.** _tengo_ ar_treetees_
I'm (… months) pregnant.	**Estoy embarazada (de … meses).** es_toy_ embara_thada_ (deh … _meses_)
I have a heart condition/ high blood pressure.	**Padezco del corazón/de tensión alta.** pa_dethko_ del kora_thon_/deh tensee_yon_ _alta_
I had a heart attack … years ago.	**Me dio un infarto hace … años.** meh _deeyo_ oon een_farto_ _atheh_ … _años_

Doctor's inquiries Preguntas del médico

¿Cuánto tiempo lleva sintiéndose así?	How long have you been feeling like this?
¿Es ésta la primera vez que le pasa?	Is this the first time you've had this?
¿Está tomando otros medicamentos?	Are you taking any other medicines?
¿Es alérgico(a) a algo?	Are you allergic to anything?
¿Lo/la han vacunado contra el tétano?	Have you been vaccinated against tetanus?
¿Ha perdido el apetito?	Have you lost your appetite?

Examination Reconocimiento

Le tomaré la temperatura/ tensión.	I'll take your temperature/ blood pressure.
Súbase la manga, por favor.	Roll up your sleeve, please.
Desvístase de cintura para arriba, por favor.	Please undress to the waist.
Túmbese, por favor.	Please lie down.
Abra la boca.	Open your mouth.
Respire profundamente.	Breathe deeply.
Tosa, por favor.	Cough please.
¿Dónde le duele?	Where does it hurt?
¿Le duele aquí?	Does it hurt here?

Diagnosis Diagnosis

Quiero que le hagan una radiografía.	I want you to have an x-ray.
Necesito una muestra de sangre/heces/orina.	I want a specimen of your blood/stools/urine.
Quiero que vea a un especialista.	I want you to see a specialist.
Quiero mandarlo al hospital.	I want you to go to the hospital.
Está roto(-a)/tiene un esguince.	It's broken/sprained.
Está dislocado(a)/desgarrado(a).	It's dislocated/torn.

Tiene ...	You've got (a/an) ...
apendicitis	appendicitis
cistitis	cystitis
gripe	flu
intoxicación	food poisoning
una fractura	fracture
gastritis	gastritis
una hernia	hernia
una inflamación de ...	inflammation of ...
la varicela	measles
neumonía	pneumonia
ciática	sciatica
amigdalitis	tonsilitis
un tumor	tumor
una enfermedad venérea	venereal disease
Está infectado(-a).	It's infected.
Es contagioso(a).	It's contagious.

Treatment Tratamiento

Le daré ...	I'll give you ...
un antiséptico	an antiseptic
un analgésico	a pain killer
Voy a recetarle ...	I'm going to prescribe ...
un tratamiento de antibióticos	a course of antibiotics
unos supositorios	some suppositories
¿Es usted alérgico(a) a algún medicamento?	Are you allergic to any medicines?
Tome una pastilla ...	Take one pill ...
cada ... horas	every ... hours
... veces al día	... times a day
antes de las comidas	before meals
Consulte a un médico cuando vuelva a casa.	Consult a doctor when you get home.

Parts of the body Partes del cuerpo

appendix	**el apéndice**	*el apendeetheh*
arm	**el brazo**	*el bratho*
back	**la espalda**	*la espalda*
bladder	**la vejiga**	*la bekheega*
bone	**el hueso**	*el weso*
breast	**el pecho**	*el pecho*
chest	**el pecho**	*el pecho*
ear	**el oído**	*el oyeedo*
eye	**el ojo**	*el okho*
face	**la cara**	*la kara*
finger	**el dedo**	*el dedo*
foot	**el pie**	*el peeyeh*
gland	**el ganglio/la glándula**	*el gangleeyo/la glandoola*
hand	**la mano**	*la mano*
head	**la cabeza**	*la kabetha*
heart	**el corazón**	*el korathon*
jaw	**la mandíbula**	*la mandeeboola*
joint	**la articulación**	*la arteekoolatheeyon*
kidney	**el riñón**	*el reeñon*
knee	**la rodilla**	*la rrodeel-ya*
leg	**la pierna**	*la peeyerna*
lip	**el labio**	*el labeeyo*
liver	**el hígado**	*el eegado*
mouth	**la boca**	*la boka*
muscle	**el músculo**	*el mooskoolo*
neck	**el cuello**	*el kwel-yo*
nose	**la nariz**	*la nareeth*
rib	**la costilla**	*la kosteel-ya*
shoulder	**el hombro**	*el ombro*
skin	**la piel**	*la peeyel*
spine	**la columna vertebral**	*la koloomna bertebral*
stomach	**el estómago**	*el estomago*
thigh	**la cadera**	*la kadera*
throat	**la garganta**	*la garganta*
thumb	**el pulgar**	*el poolgar*
toe	**el dedo del pie**	*el dedo del peeyeh*
tongue	**la lengua**	*la lengwa*
tonsils	**las amígdalas**	*las ameegdalas*
vein	**la vena**	*la bena*

166

Gynecologist
En el ginecólogo

I have …

Tengo … _tengo_

abdominal pains

dolores abdominales _dolores abdomeenales_

period pains

molestias del periodo _molesteeyas del pereeyodo_

a vaginal infection

una infección vaginal _oona eenfektheeyon bakheenal_

I haven't had my period for … months.

No me ha venido el periodo desde hace … meses. _no meh a beneedo el pereeyodo desdeh atheh … meses_

I'm on the Pill.

Estoy tomando la píldora. _estoy tomando la peeldora_

Hospital En el hospital

Please notify my family.

Por favor, notifíqueselo a mi familia. _por fabor noteefeekeselo a mee fameeleeya_

What are the visiting hours?

¿Qué horas de visita tienen? _keh oras deh beeseeta teeyenen_

I'm in pain.

Tengo dolores. _tengo dolores_

I can't eat/sleep.

No puedo comer/dormir. _no pwedo komer/dormeer_

When will the doctor come?

¿Cuándo viene el médico? _kwando beeyeneh el medeeko_

Which ward is … in?

¿En qué sala está … ? _en keh sala esta_

I'm visiting …

Vengo a hacer una visita a … _bengo a ather oona beeseeta a …_

Optician En la consulta del oculista

I'm nearsighted/farsighted.

Soy miope/hipermétrope. _soy meeyopeh/eepermetropeh_

I've lost …

He perdido … _eh perdeedo_

one of my contact lenses

una lentilla _oona lenteel-ya_

my glasses

mis gafas _mees gafas_

a lens

una lente _oona lenteh_

Could you give me a replacement?

¿Podría darme otro(-a)? _podreeya darme otro(-a)_

Dentist En el dentista

I have toothache.	**Tengo dolor de muelas.**
	tengo dolor deh mwelas
This tooth hurts.	**Este diente me duele.**
	esteh deeyenteh meh dweleh
I've lost a filling/a tooth.	**Se me ha caído un empaste/un diente.**
	seh meh a kaeedo oon empasteh/
	oon deeyenteh
Can you repair this denture?	**¿Puede arreglar esta dentadura postiza?**
	pwedeh arreglar esta dentadoora posteetha
I don't want it extracted.	**No quiero que me lo saque.**
	no keeyero keh me lo sakeh

Voy a ponerle una inyección/ anestesia local.	I'm going to give you an injection/ a local anesthetic/anaesthetic.
Le hace falta un empaste/ una funda/una corona.	You need a filling/cap/crown.
Tendré que sacárselo.	I'll have to take it out.
Sólo puedo arreglárselo provisionalmente.	I can only fix it temporarily.
Vuelva dentro de ... días.	Come back in ... days.
No coma nada durante ... horas.	Don't eat anything for ... hours.

Payment and insurance Pagos y seguros

How much do I owe you?	**¿Cuánto le debo?** _kwanto leh debo_
I have insurance.	**Tengo un seguro.** _tengo oon segooro_
Can I have a receipt for my health insurance?	**¿Puede darme un recibo para mi seguro médico?**
	pwede darmeh oon rretheebo para mee segooro medeeko
Would you fill in this health insurance form, please?	**¿Me rellena este formulario para el seguro médico, por favor?**
	meh rrel-yena esteh formoolareeyo para el segooro medeeko por fabor
Do you have ...?	**¿Tiene ...?** _teeyeneh_
Form E111/health insurance	**impreso E111/seguro médico**
	empreso ehtheeyento onthe/ segooro medeeko

Dictionary
English - Spanish

To enable correct usage, most terms in this dictionary are either followed by an expression or cross-referenced to pages where the word appears in a phrase. The notes below provide some basic grammar guidelines.

Nouns

Nouns are either masculine (m) or feminine (f). Normally, nouns that end in a vowel add **-s** to form the plural (pl); nouns ending in a consonant add **-es**. The articles they take (a, an, the, some) depend on their gender:

masculine	**el tren**	the train	*feminine*	**la casa**	the house
	un tren	a train		**una casa**	a house
	los trenes	the trains		**las casas**	the houses
	unos trenes	some trains		**unas casas**	some houses

Adjectives

Adjectives agree in gender and number with the noun they are describing. In this dictionary the feminine form (where it differs from the masculine) is shown in brackets, e.g.

pequeño(-a) small = feminine form: **pequeña**

If the masculine form ends in **-e** or with a consonant, the feminine usually keeps the same form:

el mar/la flor azul the blue sea/flower

Most adjectives form their plurals in the same way as nouns:

un coche inglés/dos coches ingleses an English car/two English cars

Verbs

Verbs are generally shown in the infinitive (to say, to eat, etc.). Although there isn't space here to show how every verb declines, here are three of the main categories of regular verbs in the present tense:

	hablar (to speak)	**comer** (to eat)	**reír** (to laugh)
	ends in **-ar**	ends in **-er**	ends in **-ir**
yo	hablo	como	río
tú	hablas	comes	ríes
usted	habla	come	ríe
él/ella	habla	come	ríe
nosostros(-as)	hablamos	comemos	reímos
vosostros(-as)	habláis	coméis	reís
ustedes	hablan	comen	ríen
ellos(-as)	hablan	comen	ríen

Negatives are generally formed by putting **no** before the verb:

Es nuevo. It's new.   **No es nuevo.** It's not new.

A

a few unos(-as)
pocos(-as) 15
a little un poco 15
a lot mucho 15
a.m. de la mañana
able, to be (also ➤ can, could)
poder/ser capaz de
about *(approximately)*
aproximadamente 15
above *(place)* encima de/por encima
de
abroad el extranjero m
abscess abceso m
accept, to aceptar 136; **do you
accept...?** ¿aceptan...?
access *(n)* acceso m 100
accessories accesorios mpl 144
accident accidente m 152; *(road)* 92
accidentally sin querer 28
accommodation alojamiento m
accompany to acompañar 65
accountant contable m/f
ace *(cards)* as m
acne acné m
across cruzando; al otro lado de
acrylic acrílico(-a)
action film película f de acción
actor/actress actor m/actriz f 110
adaptor adaptador m 148
address dirección f 84, 93, 126
adjoining room
habitación f conjunta 22
admission charge precio f
de la entrda
adult adulto m 81, 100
advance, in *(booking)* con antelación;
(paying) por adelantado
aerial *(car/TV)* antena f
after *(time)* después de 13; *(place)*
después de 95
after shave loción f para después del
afeitado; aftershave m 142
after-sun lotion aftersun m 142
afternoon, in the por la tarde 221
age: what age? ¿qué edad? 113
ago hace 13
agree: I agree estoy de acuerdo
air conditioning aire m acondicionado
22, 25

air mattress colchón m inflable 31
airplane avión m
air pump bomba f de aire 87
airline compañía f aérea
airmail correo m aéreo 155
airport aeropuerto m 96
air-steward/hostess azafata(-a) m/f
alcoholic *(drink)* alcohólico(-a)
all todo
all-night pharmacy farmacia f de
guardia 140
allergic, to be ser alérgico(-a) 164
allergy alergia f
allowance permitido m 67
allowed: is it allowed? ¿está permitido?
almost casi
alone solo(-a)
already ya; todavía
also también
alter, to hacer un arreglo 137
alternative route ruta f alternativa 96
always siempre 13
am: I am soy, estoy
ambassador embajador(a) m/f
ambulance ambulancia f 92
American *(adj)* americano(-a) 150, 152;
(person) americano(-a) m/f
American football fútbol americano m
amount cantidad f 42
amusement arcade salón m recreativo
113
anchor, to echar el ancla
and y
anesthetic anestesia f
angling ángulo m
animal animal m 106
anorak anorak m
another otro(-a) 21, 125
antibiotics antibióticos mpl
antifreeze anticongelante m
antique antigüedad f 157
antique shop tienda f de antigüedades
130
antiseptic cream crema f antiséptica 141
any alguno(-a); ninguno(-a) 93
anyone alguien
anyone else alguien más 93
anything cheaper algo más barato 21
anything else? ¿algo más?
apartment apartamento m 28

apologize: I apologize pido perdón; me disculpo

apple manzana f

appointment cita f 161

approximately aproximadamente 152

April abril m 218

archery tiro m con arco

architect arquitecto m 104

are you…? ¿está/es usted…?

Argentina Argentina 119

Argentine *(person)* argentino(-a)

arm brazo m 166

armbands *(swimming)* manguitos mpl

around *(place)* alrededor de; *(time)* a eso de 13

arrange: can you arrange it? ¿puede organizarlo?

arrest, to be under estar detenido(-a)

arrive to llegar 68, 70, 71, 76

art; ~ gallery arte m; galería f de arte 99

artery arteria f

arthritic, to be tener artritis 163

articulated truck camión m articulado

artificial sweetener edulcorante m artificial 38

artist artista m/f 104

as soon as possible lo más pronto; lo antes posible

ashtray cenicero m 39

ask, to pedir; **I asked for…** pedí… 41

asleep, to be estar dormido(-a)

aspirin aspirina f 141

asthmatic, to be ser asmático(a) 163

at *(place)* en 12; *(time)* a 13

at least por lo menos 23

attack asalto 152; *(medical)* ataque m

attendant asistente m/f

attractive atractivo(-a)

August agosto m 218

aunt tía f 120

Australia Australia 119

Australian *(person)* australiano(-a) m/f

authenticity autenticidad f 157

automatic (car, camera) automático(-a) 86, 151

automobile coche m 81, 85-9, 153

autumn otoño m 219

avalanche avalancha f

away lejos 12

awful horrible

B baby bebé m 113, 162; **~ food** comida f para bebés 142; **~ seat** asiento m para bebés; **~ wipes** toallitas fpl 142

baby's bottle biberón m

baby-sitter canguro f 113

back espalda f 166

backache dolor m de espalda 163

backpacking ir de mochilero

baggage equipaje f 32; **~ allowance** peso m máximo; **~ check** facturación f de equipajes 69, 71, 73

baggage reclaim recogida f de equipajes

bakery panadería f 130

balcony balcón 29

ball pelota f

ballet ballet m 108, 111

banana plátano m

band *(musical group)* grupo m 111, 157

bandage vendas fpl 141

bank banco m 130, 138; **~ account** cuenta de banco f; **~ card** tarjeta f de banco 139; **~ loan** préstamo m

bar bar m 26, 112

barbecue barbacoa f; parrilla f

barber barbería f

basement sótano m 132

basin palangana f

basket cesta f 158

bath: to take a darse un baño

bath towel toalla f de baño 27

bathing hut *(cabana)* caseta f

bathroom cuarto m de baño 26, 29

battery pila f 151; *(car)* batería f 88

be, to *(also ➤ am, are)* ser/estar 17; **I am** soy/estoy; **we are** somos/estamos

beach playa f 116

beard barba f

beautiful bonito(-a) 14, 101

because porque 15

because of por 15

bed cama f 21; **I'm going to ~** me voy a la cama

bed and breakfast desayuno y habitación 24

bedroom dormitorio m 29

beer cerveza f 40

before (time) antes de 13, 221

begin, to (also ➤start) empezar/comenzar

beginner principiante m/f 117

beginning principio m; comienzo m

beige beige m 143

belt cinturón m 144

beneath debajo de

berth litera f 74, 77

best el/la mejor; los/las mejores

better mejor 14

between entre

bib babero m

bicycle bicicleta f 75, 83, 153; ~ **hire** alquiler m de bicicletas 83

bidet bidet m

big grande 24, 117, 134

bikini bikini m 144

bill cuenta f 32; factura f; **put it on the bill** póngalo en la cuenta

binoculars prismáticos mpl

bird pájaro m 106

birthday cumpleaños m 219

bishop (chess) alfil m

bite (insect) picadura f

bitten: I've been bitten by a dog me ha mordido un perro

bitter amargo(-a) 41

black negro m 143; ~ **and white film** (camera) carrete m en blanco y negro 151

blanket manta f 27

blind (window) persiana f 25

blister ampolla f 162

blocked, to be estar atascado(-a) 25; **the road is blocked** la carretera está cortada

blood sangre f 164; ~ **group** grupo m sanguíneo; ~ **pressure** tensión f 163, 164;

blouse blusa f 144

blow-dry secado m de pelo

blue azul m 143

blusher (rouge) colorete m

boarding embarque m; ~ **card** tarjeta f de embarque 70

boat bote m 81

boat trip excursión f en barco 81

body: parts of the body partes fpl del cuerpo 166

boil forúnculo m 162

boiler calentador m 29

bone hueso m 166

book libro m 150

book, to reservar 21, 74, 81; hacer una reserva

booking reserva f 22, 36; ~ **office** oficina f de reservas

booklet of tickets taco m de papeletas

bookshop (bookstore) librería f 130

boots botas fpl 145; (for sport) 115

border (country) frontera f

boring aburrido(-a) 101

born: I was born in nací en

borrow: may I borrow your...? ¿puedo coger prestado(-a) su...?

botanical garden jardín m botánico 99

bottle botella f 37, 159; ~ **bank** contenedor m de vidrio

bow (ship) proa f

bowel intestino m

box of chocolates caja f de bombones 156

box office taquilla f

boxing boxeo m

boy niño m 120, 157

boyfriend novio m 120

bra sujetador m 144

bread pan m 38

break, to romper; partir

break-in robo m (con intrusión) 153

breakage avería f

breakdown avería f 88; **to have a ~** tener una avería 88

breakfast desayuno m 26, 27

breast pecho m 166

breathe, to respirar 92, 164

breathtaking impresionante 101

bridge puente m 107

briefcase maleta f

briefs calzoncillos mpl 144

brilliant maravilloso(-a) 101

bring, to traer; llevar

Britain Gran Bretaña 119

British *(adj)* británico(-a) 152; *(person)* británico(-a) m/f

brochure folleto m

broken, to be estar roto(-a) 25, 137; *(bone)* 164

bronchitis bronquitis f

bronze *(adj)* de bronce

brother hermano m 120

brown marrón m 143

browse, to mirar 133

bruise cardenal m 162

brush cepillo m

bucket *(pail)* cubo m 157

buffet car coche m restaurante

build, to construir

building edificio m

built construido(-a) 104

bureau de change despacho m de cambio; oficina f de cambio 138; ventanilla f de cambio 70

burger hamburguesa f 40

burger stand hamburguesería f 35

burglary *(also ➤ theft)* robo m

burn quemadura f 162

burnt, to be *(food)* está quemado(-a)

bus autobús m 70, 78, 79

bus route ruta f de autobús 96

bus station estación f de autobuses 78

bus stop parada f de autobús 96

business: on ~ en viaje de negocios 66; **~ class** clase f preferente 68; **~ trip** viaje m de negocios 123; **~man** hombre m de negocios; **~woman** mujer m de negocios

busy, to be estar ocupado(-a) 125

but pero

butane gas gas butano m 30, 31

butcher shop carnicería f 130

butter mantequilla f 38, 160

button botón m

buy, to comprar 67, 80

by *(time)* para 13, 86; antes de; **~ car** en coche 17; **~ credit card** con tarjeta de crédito 17

bye! ¡adiós!

bypass operación f de bypass

C

cabaret cabaret m 112

cabin camarote m 81

cable car teleférico m

café cafetería f 35

cake *(small)* dulce m; *(big)* pastel m; tarta f 40

cake shop pastelería f

calendar calendario m 156

call, to *(phone)* llamar (por teléfono) 92, 127; **~ for s.o.** llamar a alguien; **~ the police!** ¡llame a la policía! 92; **I'll call back** volveré a llamar

call collect, to llamar a cobro revertido 127

camcorder cámara f de video

camel hair pelo m de camello

camera cámara f 151, 153; **~ case** funda de/para la cámara f 151; **~ shop/store** tienda f de fotografía 130

camp, to acampar

campbed cama f de cámping f 31

camping acampada f 30; **~ equipment** equipo m de cámping 31

campsite cámping m 30

can lata f 159

can I? ¿puedo? 18; **~ I have?** ¿puedo tomar? 18

can you help me? ¿puede ayudarme? 18

can you recommend…? ¿puede recomendar(me/nos)…? 97, 112

can opener abrelatas m

Canada Canadá 119

Canadian *(person)* canadiense m/f

canal canal m

cancel to cancelar 68

candy dulce m 150

canoe canoa f

canoeing piragüismo m

canyon cañón m

cap *(clothing)* gorra f; *(dental)* funda f 168

capital city capital f

car coche m 81, 86-96, 153; **by ~** en coche 95; **~ alarm** alarma f *(del coche)*; **~ ferry** ferry transportador m de coches; **~ hire** alquiler de coches 70, 86; **~ park** *(parking lot)* aparcamiento m 26,

87, 96; **~ parts** 90-91; **~ pound** depósito m de coches; **~ repairs** reparaciones fpl de coches 89; **~ wash** lavado m de coches

carafe garrafa f 37

caravan *(trailer)* roulotte f 30, 81; **~ site** *(trailer park)* cámping m para roulottes

cardphone teléfono m a tarjeta

cards cartas fpl 121

careful: be careful! ¡tenga(n) cuidado!

carpet *(rug)* alfombra f; *(fitted)* moqueta f

carrier bag bolsa f

carton cartón m 159

car wash lavado m de coches

cash, to cobrar 138

cash dinero m en metálico 136; **~ card** tarjeta m del cajero automático 139; **~ desk** caja f 132; **~ machine** *(atm/cash dispenser)* cajero m automático 139

casino casino m 112

cassette cinta f; cassette f 157

castle castillo m 99

casualty dept. (servicio m de) urgencias

cat gato(-a) m/f

catch, to *(bus)* coger

cathedral catedral f 99

cause, to causar

cave cueva f 107

CD CD m

CD-player aparato m de compact (disc)

central heating calefacción central f

center of town centro m de la ciudad 21

ceramics cerámica f

certificate certificado m 157

chair silla f

chair-lift telesilla m 117

change *(coins)* cambio m 87; suelto m; **keep the ~** quédese con el cambio/la vuelta 84

change, to *(money)* cambiar 138; *(ticket)* cambiar 68; *(bus)* cambiar de/hacer trasbordo 79; *(train)* 80; *(clothes)* cambiarse

change: where can I change the baby? ¿dónde puedo cambiar al bebé?

change clothes, to cambiarse de ropa

change lanes, to cambiar de carril

changing facilities instalaciones para cambiar al bebé fpl 113

changing rooms vestuarios mpl

channel *(sea)* canal m

charcoal carbón m 31

charge precio m

charter flight vuelo chárter m

cheap barato(-a) 14, 134

cheaper más barato(-a) 21, 24, 109, 134

check cuenta f 32 [factura f]

check/cheque book talonario m de cheques

check: please check the... por favor, compruebe...

check/cheque guarantee card tarjeta f de crédito/débito

check in, to facturar 68, 69

check-in desk mostrador de facturación m 69

checked *(patterned)* de cuadros

checkers damas fpl

check out, to *(hotel)* salir

checkout caja f 158

cheers! ¡salud!

cheese queso m 160

chess ajedrez m 121; **~ set** juego de ajedrez m 157

chest pecho m 166

chewing chicle m 150

chickenpox sarampión m

child niño(-a) m/f; hijo(-a) 152

child's seat silla f para niños 39; *(in car)* asiento m para niños

children niños mpl 24, 39, 74, 81, 100, 113; hijos mpl 120

children's meals comidas fpl para niños

Chinese *(cuisine)* chino(-a) 35

chips *(UK)* patatas fritas fpl 160

chips *(U.S.)* patatas fritas fpl de bolsa 159, 160

chocolate chocolate m 160; *(flavour)* (de) chocolate 40; **~ bar** barra f de chocolate 150; **box of ~** caja f de bombones

chocolate ice cream polo de chocolate m 110

chop *(meat)* chuleta f

Christmas Navidad f 219

church iglesia f 96, 99, 105

cigarettes, pack of paquete de tabaco m 150

cigars puros mpl 150

cinema *(movie theater)* cine m 96, 110

circle *(balcony)* anfiteatro m

city wall muralla f de la ciudad

clean *(adj)* limpio(-a) 14, 39, 41

clean, to limpiar 137

cleaned: I'd like my shoes cleaned quiero que me limpien los zapatos

cleaner limpiador(a) m/f 28;

cleaning limpieza f 137; **~ utensils** artículos de limpieza mpl 148; **~ lotion** loción limpiadora f; **~ solution (for lenses)** solución limpiadora f

close *(near)* cerca 95

close, to cerrar 100, 132, 140

clothes ropa f 144; **~ line** tendedero m

clothing store/clothes shop tienda de ropa f 130

cloudy, to be estar nublado 122

clown payaso m

clubs *(golf)* palos mpl 115

coach autobús m 78; *(train compartment)* compartimento m 75; **~ bay** andén m 78; **~ station** estación f de autobuses 78

coast costa f

coat abrigo m 144

coathanger percha f

cockroach cucaracha f

code *(area/dialling)* prefijo m

coffee café m 40

coin moneda f

cold *(adj)* frío(-a) 14, 41; *(flu)* resfriado m 141, 163

cold meats fiambres mpl 160

collapse: he's collapsed se ha desmayado

collect, to recoger 151

college universidad f 120

color color m 134, 143; **~ film** carrete m de color 151

comb peine m 142

come back , to volver 36, 140

comedy comedia f

commission comisión f 138

communion comunión f

compact camera cámara f compacta 151

compact disc/disk compact disc m 157

company *(companionship)* compañía f; *(business)* empresa f

compartment *(train)* compartimento m

compass brújula f

complaint queja fpl; **to make a ~** hacer una reclamación 137

computer ordenador m

concert concierto m 108, 111; **~ hall** sala f de conciertos 111

concession descuento m 100

concussion, to have sufrir una conmoción cerebral

conditioner suavizante/acondicionador m 142

condoms condones mpl 141

conductor director(a) m/f 111

confirm, to confirmar 22, 68

confirmation confirmación f

congratulations! ¡felicidades!

connection *(transport)* enlace m

conscious, to be estar consciente

constipation estreñimiento m

Consulate consulado m 152

consult, to consultar 165

consultant *(medical)* asesor(a) m/f médico(-a)

contact lenses lentillas fpl 167

contact, to ponerse en contacto con

contact-lens fluid líquido m para las lentillas

contagious, to be ser contagioso(-a) 165

contain, to llevar/tener; contener 69, 155

contemporary dance danza f contemporánea 111

contraceptive anticonceptivo m

convenient conveniente

cook cocinero(-a) m/f

cook, to cocinar

cooker cocina f 28, 29

cookie galleta f 160

cooking *(cuisine)* cocina f

copper cobre m 149

copy copia f

corked *(wine)* con sabor a corcho 41

A-Z

A-Z

corner esquina f 95
correct correcto(-a)
cosmetics cosméticos mpl
cot cuna f 22
cottage casita f
cotton algodón m; ~ wool (absorbent cotton) algodón m 141
cough tos f 141; ~ syrup jarabe m para la tos
cough, to toser 164
could I have…? ¿puedo tomar…? 18
counter mostrador m
country (nation) país m
country music música f country 111
countryside campo m
couple (pair) pareja f
courier (guide) guía m/f
course (meal) plato m
cousin primo(-a) m/f
cover (lid) tapa f
cover charge (nightclub) consumición f mínima; (restaurant) cubierto m 112
craft shop tienda f de artesanía
cramps retortijones mpl 163
crash: I've had a crash he tenido un accidente
creaks: the bed creaks la cama cruje
crèche guardería f
credit card tarjeta f de crédito 42, 136, 153; ~ number número m de tarjeta de crédito 109
credit status estado m de cuentas
credit, in saldo m positivo
crockery vajilla f 29, 148
cross (crucifix) cruz f
cross, to (road) cruzar
cross-country skiing track pista f de esquí de montaña
crossing (boat) travesía f
crossroad cruce m 95
crowded abarrotado
crown (dental) corona f 168
cruise crucero m
crutches muletas fpl
crystal vidrio m 149
cuisine cocina f 119
cup taza f 39
cupboard armario m
curlers rulos mpl
currency moneda/divisa f 67, 138

currency-exchange office oficina f de cambio 73
curtains cortinas fpl
cushion cojín m
customs aduana f 67, 157; ~ declaration declaración f para la aduana 155
cut corte m 162
cut and blow-dry (sign) cortar y secar 147
cut and style (sign) cortar y peinar
cut glass vidrio tallado m 149
cutlery cubiertos mpl 29; cubertería f
cycle helmet casco m para bicicletas
cycle path carril m para bicicletas
cycle route ruta f para bicicletas 106
cycling ciclismo m 114
cyclist ciclista m/f
cystitis cistitis f 165

D

daily diariamente
damaged, to be estar estropeado(-a) 28, 71
damp (noun) humedad; (adj.) húmedo (-a), mojado(-a)
dance (performance) baile m 111
dancing, to go ir a bailar 124
dangerous peligroso(-a)
dark oscuro(-a) 14, 24, 134, 143
daughter hija f 120, 162
dawn amanecer m 221
day día m 97; ~ ticket tarjeta f para un día 79; ~ trip excursión f
dead muerto(-a); (battery) descargado(-a)
deaf, to be ser sordo(-a) 163
dear (greeting) querido(-a)
December diciembre m 218
decide: we haven't decided yet no nos hemos decidido todavía
deck (ship) cubierta f
deck chair tumbona f 116
declare, to declarar 67
deduct, to (money) deducir
deep hondo(-a), profundo(-a)
deep-freeze congelar
defrost, to descongelar
degrees (temperature) grados mpl
delay retraso m 70
delicate delicado(-a)
delicatessen charcutería f 130, 158

delicious *(food)* delicioso(-a)
deliver, to repartir
denim tela vaquera f
dental floss hilo m dental
dentist dentista m/f 131, 168
dentures dentadura postiza f 168
deodorant desodorante m 142
depart, to *(train, bus)* salir
department *(in store)* sección f 132; ~ **store** grandes almacenes mpl 130
departure *(train)* salida f 76; ~ **lounge** sala de embarque f
depend: it depends on depende de
deposit señal f; fianza f 24, 83,115
describe, to describir 152
design *(dress)* diseño m
designer diseñador(a) m/f
destination destino m
detergent detergente m
develop, to *(photos)* revelar 151
diabetes diabetes f
diabetic diabético(-a; **to be ~** ser diabético(a) 39, 163
diagnosis diagnosis f 164
dialing (area) code prefijo m 127
diamond diamante m 149
diamonds *(cards)* diamantes mpl
diapers pañales mpl 142
diarrhea diarrea f 141; **to have ~** tener diarrea 163
dice dado m
dictionary diccionario m 150
diesel diesel 87
diet, I'm on a estoy a régimen
different, something algo diferente
dine, to cenar
dinghy lancha hinchable f
dining car coche restaurante m 75, 77
dining room comedor m 26, 29
dinner jacket chaqueta f de esmóking
dinner, to have cenar 124
direct directo(-a)
direct, to indicar 18
direct-dial telephone teléfono m de llamada directa
direction dirección f; **in the ~ of** de camino a 95
director *(film, company)* director(a) m/f
directory *(telephone)* guía f telefónica
Directory Enquiries Información f 127
dirty sucio(-a) 14, 28

disabled *(n)* minusválido(-a) 22, 100
disco discoteca f 112
discount descuento m; **can you offer me a ~** ¿puede hacerme un descuento?; **is there a ~ for children?** ¿hacen descuento a los niños?
disgusting asqueroso(-a)
dish *(meal)* plato 37
dish cloth balleta f 148
dishwashing detergent lavavajillas m 148
disk film disquete m
dislocated, to be estar dislocado(a) 164
display cabinet/case vitrina f 134, 149
disposable camera cámara de usar y tirar f 151
distilled water agua destilada f
district distrito m
disturb: don't disturb no molestar; no moleste
dive, to tirarse de cabeza 116
diversion desvío m 96
divorced, to be estar divorciado(-a) 120
dizzy, to feel estar mareado 163
do you accept…? ¿aceptan…? 136
do you have…? ¿tiene…? 37
do: things to do cosas que hacer 123
dock muelle m
doctor médico(-a)/doctor(a) m/f 131, 161
Does anyone here speak English? ¿Hay alguien que hable inglés? 67
dog perro m
doll muñeca f 157
door puerta f 25, 29
dosage dosificación f 140
double doble 81
double bed cama f de matrimonio 21
double room habitación f doble 21
down abajo
downstairs abajo; en el piso de abajo 12
downtown area centro m 99
dozen docena f 159, 217
draft *(wind)* corriente f
drama drama m
draughts damas fpl
dress vestido m 144
drink copa f 124, 125, 126; bebida f 40

drinking water agua potable f 30
drip: the tap (faucet) drips el grifo gotea
drive, to conducir 93
driver conductor(a) m/f
driver's license *(driving license)* carnet/permiso de conducir m
drop off, to *(someone)* dejar 83, 113
drowning: someone is drowning alguien se está ahogando
drugstore droguería f
drunk borracho(-a)
dry cleaner's tintorería f 131
dry clothes, to secar la ropa
dry-clean, to limpiar en seco
dubbed, to be estar doblado(-a) 110
dummy chupete m
during durante 13
dusty polvoriento(-a)
duty-free goods artículos mpl libres de impuestos
duty-free shopping compra f de artículos libres de impuestos 67
duvet edredón m nórdico

E **each: how much each?** ¿a cuánto cada uno(-a)?
ear *(internal)* oído m; *(external)* oreja f 166
ear drops gotas para el oído fpl
earache dolor m de oídos 163
earlier antes 125
early temprano
east este m 95
Easter Pascua f
eat, to comer 41, 167; **places ~** sitios para comer 123
economical económico(-a)
economy class clase f turista 68
eggs huevos mpl 160
eight ocho 216
eighteen dieciocho 216
eighty ochenta 216
either... or o... o... 16
elastic *(adj)* elástico(-a)
electric shaver máquina f de afeitar eléctrica
electrician electricista m
electricity electricidad f

electricity meter contador m de la luz 28
elevator ascensor m 26, 132; **~ pass** pase m de teleférico/telesilla 117
eleven once 216
else, something algo más
embark, to *(boat)* embarcar
embarkation point punto m de embarque
embassy embajada f
emerald esmeralda f
emergency emergencia f; **it's an ~** es una emergencia; **~ exit** salida f de emergencia
enamel esmalte m 149
end, to terminar
end: at the end al final
engaged, to be estar prometido(-a) 120
engine motor m
engineer ingeniero m/f
England Inglaterra 119
English *(person)* inglés(a) m/f; *(language)* inglés m 11, 67, 110, 150, 152, 161
English-speaking que hable inglés 98, 152
enjoy, to gustar 110; disfrutar 121; pasarlo bien 123
enlarge, to *(photos)* ampliar 151
enough bastante 15
enquiry desk ventanilla f de información
ensuite bathroom cuarto de baño dentro de la habitación m
entertainment: what entertainment is there? ¿qué espectáculos hay?
entirely completamente
entrance fee precio m de entrada 100
entry visa visado m de entrada
envelope sobre m
epileptic epiléptico(-a) 163
equally igualmente 17
equipment *(sports)* equipo m
error error m
escalator escalera f mecánica 132
essential fundamental, básico(-a) 89
estate agent agente m/f inmobiliario(-a)
EU UE f
Eurocheque eurocheque m 138
evening dress traje m de noche 112

evening, in the por la noche 221
events espectáculos mpl 108
every day todos los días
every week todas las semanas 13
examination *(medical)* reconocimiento
m
example, for por ejemplo
except excepto
excess baggage exceso m de equipaje
69
exchange rate tasa f de cambio 138
exchange, to cambiar 138
excursion excursión 97
excuse me disculpe 10, 94
exhausted, to be estar exhausto(-a) 106
exhibition exposición f
exit salida f 70
expected, to be suponerse
expensive caro(-a) 14, 134
expire: when does it expire? ¿cuándo
caduca?
expiry date fecha de caducidad f 109
exposure *(photos)* fotos fpl 151
express *(special delivery)* exprés,
urgente 155
extension extensión f 128
extension lead alargador m
extra *(additional)* más
extremely sumamente 17
eye ojo m 166
eyeglasses gafas fpl
eyeliner delineador m de ojos
eyeshadow sombra f de ojos

F **fabric** *(material)* tela f
face cara f 166
facial limpieza f de cutis/cara 147
facilities instalaciones fpl 22, 30
factor factor m
factory outlet almacén m 130
faint, to feel sentirse desfallecer
fairground feria f 113
fall otoño m 219
fall: he's had a fall se ha caído
family familia f 66, 74, 120, 167
famous famoso(-a)
fan ventilador m 25
fan: I'm a fan of soy un
fan/admirador(a)
far lejos 12; **how ~ is it?** ¿a qué
distancia está? 73

fare tarifa f
farm granja f 107
farsighted hipermétrope
167
fashionable, to be estar
de moda
fast rápido(-a) 93
fast food comida f rápida 40; **~
restaurant** restaurante m de comida
rápida 35
fast, to be *(clock)* estar adelantado 221
fast: you were driving too fast
conducías demasiado deprisa
fat grasa f
father padre m 120
faucet grifo m
fault: it's my/your fault es culpa
mía/vuestra
faulty defectuoso(-a)
favorite favorito(-a)
fax *(facilities, machine)* fax m 22, 155
fax bureau papelería f
con servicio de fax
February febrero m 218
feed, to dar de comer
feeding bottle biberón m
feel ill, to sentise enfermo(a) 163
feel sick, to marearse 98
female mujer, hembra 152
fence valla f
ferry ferry, transbordador m 81
festival festival m
fetch help! ¡vaya a buscar ayuda! 92
feverish, to feel tener fiebre 163
few pocos(as) 15
fiancé(e) prometido(-a) m/f
field campo m 107
fifteen quince 216
fifth quinto(a)
fifty cincuenta
fight *(brawl)* pelea f
fill in, to rellenar 155
filling *(dental)* empaste m 168; *(in
sandwich)* relleno m
filling station gasolinera f 87
film *(movie)* película f 108, 110; *(camera)*
carrete m 151; **~ speed** velocidad f del
carrete

A-Z

filter filtro m 151;
  ~ paper *(for coffee)* papel
  m de filtro
fine *(penalty)* multa f 93;
  (well) bien 118
  finger dedo m 166
fire: there's a fire! ¡hay un
incendio!; **~ alarm** alarma f contra
incendios; **~ brigade** bomberos mpl; **~**
escape salida f de incendios; **~**
extinguisher extintor m; **~lighters**
pastillas para encender fuegos fpl;
~place chimenea f; **~wood** leña f
first *(adj.)* primer(a) 68, 75, 81, 217;
  (pron.) primero(-a)
first class (de) primera clase 68, 74
first floor *(UK)* primera f planta
first floor *(U.S.)* planta f baja
first-aid kit botiquín m
fishing rod caña f de pescar
fishing, to go ir de pesca/a pescar
fishmonger's pescadería f 130
fit, to *(clothes)* estar/quedar bien 146
fitting room probador m 146
five cinco 216
fix: can you fix it? ¿puede arreglarlo?
flag bandera f
flannel *(face)* manopla f ; *(material)*
  franela f
flash *(camera)* flash m 151
flashlight linterna f 31
flat pinchazo m 83, 88
flavor: what flavors do you have? ¿qué
sabores tiene?
flea pulga f; **~ market** mercadillo m
flight vuelo m 70; **~ number** número m
de vuelo 68
flip-flops chancletas fpl 145
flood inundación f
floor *(story)* piso m; planta f 132
floor mop fregona f
floor show espectáculo m de cabaret
112
florist's floristería f 130
flour harina f
flower flor f 106
flu gripe f 165
fluent: to speak fluent Spanish hablar
español fluido
fly *(insect)* mosca f
fly, to volar

foggy, to be haber niebla 122
folk art arte m popular
folk music música f folk 111
follow, to seguir 95
food comida f 39, 41; **~ poisoning**
intoxicación f 165
foot pie m 166
football *(soccer)* fútbol m 114
footpath sendero 107
for a day por un día 86
for a week por una semana 86
forecast pronóstico m 122
foreign extranjero(-a); **~ currency**
divisa/moneda f extranjera 138
forest bosque m 107
forget, to olvidar 41, 42
fork tenedor m 39, 41; *(in the road)*
bifurcación f
form impreso m, formulario m
23, 153, 168
formal dress vestido m de etiqueta 111
fortnight dos semanas, medio mes
fortunately afortunadamente 19
forty cuarenta 217
foundation *(makeup)* base f
fountain fuente f 99
four cuatro 216
four-door car coche m de cuatro
puertas 86
four-wheel drive tracción f a las cuatro
ruedas 86
fourteen catorce 216
fourth cuarto(-a) 217
foyer *(hotel/theater)* vestíbulo m
frame *(glasses)* montura f
France Francia
free *(available)* libre 36, 77, 124; *(of
charge)* gratis, sin pagar 69
freezer congelador m 29
frequent: how frequent? ¿con qué
frecuencia? 76
frequently con frecuencia
fresh fresco(-a) 41
Friday viernes m 218
fried frito(-a)
friend amigo(a) m/f 162
friendly amistoso(-a)
fries patatas fpl fritas 38, 40
frightened, to be estar aterrorizado(-a)
fringe flequillo m
from de 12; **~... to...** *(time)* de... a... 13

front door puerta f principal; **~ key** llave f de la puerta principal

frosty, to be haber helado 122

frozen congelado(-a)

fruit juice zumo m de fruta 40

frying pan sartén f 29

fuel *(gasoline)* combustible m 86

full board *(A.P.)* pensión f completa 24

full insurance seguro m a todo riesgo 86

fun, to have divertirse

funny *(amusing)* divertido(-a); *(odd)* raro(-a)

furniture muebles mpl

further: how much further to Madrid? ¿cuánto falta para llegar a Madrid?

fuse fusible m; **~ box** caja f de fusibles 28; **~ wire** cable m de fusible

G gallon galón m (U.S. = 3.78 liters)

game *(toy)* juego m 157

garage garaje m 26

garbage bags bolsas fpl de basura 148

garden jardín m

gardening jardinería f

gas: I smell gas! ¡huelo a gas!; **~ bottle** bombona f de butano 28

gas permeable lenses lentes fpl permeables

gas station gasolinera f 87

gasoline gasolina f 87 **~ can (gas can)** lata de gasolina f

gastritis gastritis f 165

gate *(airport)* puerta f 70

gay club discoteca f gay 112

general delivery reparto general m 155

genuine auténtico(-a) 134, 157

geology geología f

get, to: ~ by pasar; **~ off** *(transport)* bajarse (de) 79; **~ out** *(of vehicle)* salir; **~ to** llegar a 77; **how do I get to…?** ¿cómo se llega a…? 73; ¿cómo se va a…? 94

gift regalo m 67, 156; **~ shop** tienda f de regalos, bazar f 130

girl niña f 120, 157

girlfriend novia f 120

give, to dar

give way, to *(on the road)* dejar/ceder paso 93

glass *(wine)* vaso m, copa f 37, 39; *(optical)* gafas fpl 167

gliding vuelo m sin motor

glossy finish *(photos)* acabado m con brillo

go, to ir; **let's go!** ¡vamos!; **go away!** ¡váyase!; **~ back** *(turn around)* volver 95; **~ for a walk** ir de paseo 124; **~ out** *(in evening)* salir; **~ shopping** ir de compras 124; **where does this bus ~?** ¿a dónde va este autobús?

goggles gafas fpl de bucear

gold oro m 149; **~-plate** baño m de oro

golf golf m 114; **~ course** campo m de golf 115

good *(adj)* bueno(-a), 42; **~ afternoon** buenas tardes 10; **~ evening** buenas tardes 10; **~ morning** buenos días 10; **~ night** buenas noches 10

good value, to be estar muy bien de precio 101

good-bye adiós 10

gorge garganta f

got: have you got any…? ¿tiene(n)…?

grade *(fuel)* grado m

gram gramo m 159

grammar gramática f

grandparents abuelos mpl

grapes uvas fpl 160

grass hierba f

gratuity propina f

gray gris m 143

greasy *(hair)* graso(-a)

green verde m 143

greengrocer's verdulería f 130

greetings saludos mpl 10

grey gris m 143

grilled a la parrilla

grocer's/grocery store tienda f de alimentación 130

ground *(camping)* suelo m 30

groundcloth aislante m para el suelo 31

ground floor planta f baja

group grupo m 66, 100

guarantee garantía f 135

guarantee: is it guaranteed? ¿tiene garantía?

guide *(person)* guía m/f turístico(-a) 98

A-Z

guide book guía f 100, 150
guided tour visita f con guía 100
guitar guitarra f
gum *(mouth)* encía f
gynecologist ginecólogo(a) m/f 167

H **hair** pelo/cabello m 147; **~ brush** cepillo m (para el pelo) 142; **~ dryer** secador m; **~ gel** gel fijador m; **~ mousse** espuma (para el pelo) f 142; **~ slide** pasador m; **~ spray** espray (para el pelo) m 142
haircut corte m de pelo 147
hairdresser/stylist peluquero(a) m/f 147
hairdresser's (ladies/men) peluquería f de señoras/caballeros 131
half, a la mitad 217
half board *(M.A.P.)* media pensión f 24
half fare tarifa reducida f
half past *(time)* y media 220
hammer martillo m 31
hand mano f 166; **~ cream** crema f para las manos; **~ luggage** equipaje m de mano 69; **~ towel** toalla f de las manos
hand washable se puede lavar a mano
handbag bolso m 144, 153
handicap *(golf)* hándicap m
handicapped, to be ser minusválido(-a) 163
handicrafts trabajos mpl de artesanía
handkerchief pañuelo m
handle *(cup)* asa f ; *(drawer, door)* tirador m
hang-gliding vuelo m con ala delta
hanger percha f 27
hangover *(n)* resaca f 141
happen: what happened? ¿qué ocurrió? 93
happy: I'm not happy with the service no estoy contento(-a) con el servicio
harbor/harbour bahía f 99
hard shoulder *(road)* arcén m
hat sombrero m 144
hatchback coche m con tres/cinco puertas

have, to tener; *(hold stock of)* 133; *(drink, food)* tomar 18
have to, to *(must)* tener que 79
hayfever fiebre f del heno; alergia f primaveral 141
head cabeza f 166
head, to *(travel)* dirigirse 83
head waiter metre m 41
headache dolor m de cabeza 163
headband cinta f del pelo
health food shop/store tienda f de alimentos naturales
health insurance seguro m médico 168
hear, to oír
hearing aid sonotone® m
heart corazón m 166; **~ attack** infarto m 163
hearts *(cards)* corazones mpl
heater calentador m
heating calefacción f 25
heavy pesado(-a) 134
height altura f 152
helicopter helicóptero m
hello hola 10, 118
help, to ayudar 18, 94; **can you help me?** ¿puede ayudarme? 92
hemorrhoids hemorroides fpl
her *(adj.)* su 16; *(pron.)* ella 16
here aquí 12
hernia hernia f 165
hers suyo(-a) 16; **it's ~** es suyo(-a), es de ella
high alto(-a)
high (main) street calle f mayor 96
high tide marea f alta
highlight, to *(hair)* hacer mechas 147
hike *(walk)* paseo m 106
hiking senderismo m
hill colina f 107
him él 16
his suyo(-a) 16; su 16
history historia f
hitchhike, to hacer autostop
hitchhiking autostop m 83
HIV-positive seropositivo(-a)
hobby (pastime) hobby m 121
hockey hockey m
hold, to *(contain)* contener
hold on, to esperar 128
hole *(in clothes)* agujero m
home, to go ir a casa

homosexual *(adj.)* homosexual
honeymoon, to be on
estar de luna de miel
horse caballo m
horse racing carreras fpl
de caballos 114
horseback trip excursión f a caballo
hospital hospital m 131, 164, 167
hot caliente 14, 24
hot dog perrito m caliente 110
hot spring fuente f termal
hot water agua f caliente 25; **~ bottle**
bolsa f de agua caliente
hotel hotel m 21; **~ booking** reservas de
hotel 21
hour hora f 97; **in an ~** dentro de una
hora 84
hours *(open)* horas fpl 161
house casa f
housewife ama f de casa 121
hovercraft aerodeslizador m 81
how are you? ¿cómo está? 118
how far? ¿a qué distancia? 94, 106
how long? ¿cuánto tiempo? 23, 75, 76,
88, 94, 98, 135
how many? ¿cuántos(-as)? 15, 80
how much? ¿cuánto? 15, 21, 69, 84, 109
how often? ¿cada cuánto tiempo? 140
how old? ¿qué edad? 120
how? ¿cómo? 17
however sin embargo
hundred cien
hungry, to be tener hambre
hurry, to be in a tener prisa
hurt, to be estar herido(-a) 92, 162;
it hurts duele 162
husband marido m 120, 162

I **I'd like…** quiero… 18, 36, 40
I'll have… tomaré… 37
I've lost… he perdido… 153
ice hielo m 38; **~ dispenser** máquina f
de hielo m; **~ pack** bolsa de hielo f; **~
rink** pista f de hielo
ice cream helado m 40, 160; **~ café**
heladería f 35; **~ cone** cucurucho m de
helado
icy, to be haber hielo 122
identification identificación f 136
ill, to be estar enfermo(-a)
illegal, to be ser ilegal

illness enfermedad f
imitation de imitación
134
immediately
inmediatamente
impressive impresionante
in *(place)* en 12; *(time)* dentro
de 13
in-law: mother-~ suegra f; **father-~**
suegro m
included: is… included? ¿va…
incluido(-a)? 86, 98
Indian *(cuisine)* indio(-a)
indicate, to indicar
indigestion indigestión f
indoor cubierto(-a); **~ pool** piscina f
cubierta 116
inexpensive no muy caro(-a)
infected, to be estar infectado(-a) 165
infection infección f 167
inflammation inflamación f 165
informal *(dress)* informal
information información f 97; **~ desk**
ventanilla f de información 73; **~ office**
oficina f de información 96
injection inyección f 168
injured, to be estar herido(-a) 92, 162;
(athletes) estar lesionado(-a)
insect insecto m 25; **~ bite** picadura f
141, 162; **~ repellent/spray** repelente
para insectos/espray m 141
inside dentro 12
insist: I insist insisto
insomnia insomnio m
instant coffee café instantáneo m
instead of en lugar de
instructions instrucciones fpl 135
instructor instructor(a) m/f
insulin insulina f
insurance seguro m 86, 89, 93, 168; **~
certificate** certificado del seguro m 93;
~ claim reclamación del seguro f; **~
company** compañía de seguros f 93
interest *(hobby)* pasatiempo m 121
interesting interesante 101
international internacional
International Student Card Carnet m
Internacional de Estudiante 29
interpreter intérprete m/f 93, 153
intersection cruce m
interval intervalo m

A-Z

into dentro, en
introduce oneself, to presentarse 118
invitation invitación f 124
invite, to invitar 124
involved, to be estar involucrado(-a) 93
Ireland Irlanda 119
Irish (*person*) irlandés(a) m/f
iron (*for clothes*) plancha f
iron, to planchar
is there...? ¿hay...? 17
island isla f
it is... es... 17
Italian (*adj.*) italiano(-a) 35
itch: it itches pica
itemized bill cuenta f detallada 32, 42

J

jack (*cards*) sota f
jacket chaqueta f 144
jam mermelada f
jammed, to be estar atascado(-a) 25
January enero m 218
jar frasco m; tarro m 159
jaw mandíbula f 166
jeans vaqueros mpl 144
jellyfish medusa f
jet lag, I have estoy sufriendo el cambio de horario
jet ski moto acuática f 116
jeweler's (*jewelry store*) joyería f 149
Jewish (*adj*) judío(-a)
job: what's your job? ¿en qué trabaja?
jogging, to go ir a hacer footing
join: may we join you ¿podemos ir con ustedes? 124
joint articulación f 166; (*meat*) pierna f
joint passport pasaporte m conjunto 66
joke chiste m
journey viaje m 76, 78, 123
jug (*of water*) jarra f
July julio m 218
jumper jersey m 144
junction (*exit*) salida f; (*intersection*) cruce m
June junio m 218

K

kaolin caolín m
keep: keep the change quédese con el cambio/la vuelta

kerosene queroseno m
kerosene stove hornillo m de queroseno 31
ketchup ketchup m
kettle hervidor m 29
key llave f 28, 88; **~ ring** llavero m 156
kidney riñón m 166
kilo(gram) kilo m 69, 159
kilometer kilómetro
kind (*pleasant*) amable
kind: what kind of... ¿qué tipo/clase de...?
king (*cards, chess*) rey m
kiosk quiosco m
kiss, to besar
kitchen cocina f 29
kitchen paper rollo m de cocina
knee rodilla f 166
knickers bragas fpl
knife cuchillo m 39, 41
knight (*chess*) caballo m
know: I don't know no sé
kosher kosher

L

label etiqueta f
lace encaje m
ladies (*toilet*) servicio/aseo m de señoras
lake lago m 107
lamp lámpara f 25, 29
landing (*house*) descansillo m
landlord/landlady casero(-a) m/f
language course curso m de idiomas
large grande 40, 110
last último(-a) 14, 75, 81
last, to (*time*) durar
late tarde 221; (*delayed*) con retraso 70
later más tarde 125, 147
laugh, to reírse
laundromat lavandería f 131
laundry service servicio m de lavandería 22
laundry soap detergente m en polvo 148
lavatory baño m
lawyer abogado(-a) m/f 152
laxative laxante m/f
lead, to (*road*) dirigirse; ir
lead-free (*gas*) sin plomo 87
leader (*of group*) líder m/f
leaflet folleto m 97

leak, to *(roof/pipe)* gotear
learn, to *(language)* aprender
leather cuero m
leave, to *(depart)* salir 76, 78, 81, 98; *(place)* irse, marcharse 126; *(abandon)* dejar 71, 73, 86; **leave me alone!** ¡déjeme en paz!; **I've left my bag in…** me he dejado el bolso en…; **are there any left?** ¿quedan algunos/algunas?
lecturer *(at conference)* conferenciante m/f; *(occupation)* profesor(a) m/f
left, on the a la izquierda 76, 95
left-hand side en el lado izquierdo
left-handed zurdo(-a)
leg pierna f 166
legal, to be ser legal
leggings mallas fpl 144
lemon limón m 38
lemonade *(soda)* gaseosa f; *(real lemons)* limonada f
lend, to: could you lend me…? ¿podría prestarme…?
length longitud f
lens *(camera)* objetivo m; *(glasses)* lente m/f 167; *(contact)* lentilla f 167
lens cap tapa f del objetivo/de la lente 151
lesbian club bar m de lesbianas; discoteca f de lesbianas
less menos 15
lesson clase f
let, to: please let me know por favor, hágamelo saber
letter carta f 154; **by ~** por carta 22
level nivel m 30
library biblioteca f 99, 131
lie down, to echarse/tumbarse
lifebelt flotador m
lifeboat bote m salvavidas
lifeguard socorrista m/f 116
lifejacket chaleco m salvavidas
light *(color)* claro(-a) 14, 134, 143; *(cigarette)* fuego m; *(electric)* luz f 25, 83; *(not heavy)* ligero(-a) 134; **~ bulb** bombilla f
lighter encendedor m, mechero m 150
lighthouse faro m
like: I like it me gusta 101; **I don't like it** no me gusta 101; **I'd like…** quiero…

like this *(similar to)* así
limousine limusina f
line *(metro)* línea f; *(profession)* campo m 121
linen lino m
lip labio m 166
lipsalve protector m de labios
lipstick barra f de labios
liqueur licor m
liter litro m 87, 159
little *(small)* pequeño(-a); **a ~** un poco
live, to vivir; **~ together** vivir juntos 120
liver hígado m 166
living room salón m/sala f de estar 29
lobby *(theater/hotel)* vestíbulo m; hall m
local local; **~ anesthetic** anestesia m local 168; **~ road** carretera f comarcal
lock candado m; *(canal)* exclusa f
locked, to be estar cerrado(-a) (con llave)
locker taquilla f
lollipop chupachup m
long *(clothing)* largo(-a) 146; *(time)* mucho (tiempo); **how long?** ¿cuánto tiempo? 164; **how much longer?** ¿cuánto tiempo más? 41
long-distance bus autobús m de largo recorrido
long-distance call conferencia f
look, to mirar; **~ for** buscar 18; **I'm looking forward to it** me hace mucha ilusión; **I'm just looking** *(browsing)* sólo estoy mirando; **please look after my case for a minute** por favor, cuídeme la maleta un momento
look, to have a *(check)* echarle un vistazo 89;
loose ancho(-a), suelto(-a), 146
lose, to perder 28, 153; **I've lost…** he perdido… 71
loss pérdida f 71
lost, to be perderse; **I've lost…** he perdido…
lost-and-found (lost property office) oficina de objetos perdidos f 73

A-Z

lotion loción f
lots muchos(-as)
loud: it's too ~ *(noise)* es demasiado alto(-a)
louder más alto 128
love: I love you te quiero/amo
low-fat de bajo contenido graso
lower berth litera f de abajo 74
luck: good luck buena suerte 219
luggage *(baggage)* equipaje m 32, 67, 69, 71; ~ allowance límite m de equipaje permitido; ~ locker taquilla f 71, 73; ~ tag etiqueta f de equipaje; ~ ticket recibo m (de consigna); carts carritos mpl para el equipaje 71
lumpy *(mattress)* con bultos
lunch almuerzo m, comida f 98
lung pulmón m
luxury lujo m

M machine washable se puede lavar a máquina
madam señora f
made of, what is it ¿de qué está hecho?
magazine revista f 150
maid chica f de servicio 27
maiden name nombre m de soltera
mail correo m; ~ office oficina f de correos, correos m 96, 131, 154
mail, to mandar por correo 27
mailbox buzón m 154
main principal 130; ~ course segundo m plato 37; ~ rail station estación f de tren central 73; ~ street calle principal f 95
mains *(services)* red f
make *(brand)* marca f
makeup maquillaje m
make: to make tea/coffee hacer té/café
male hombre m, varón m 152
mallet mazo m 31
man hombre m
manager *(company)* director(a) m/f 25; *(shop)* gerente m/f
manicure manicura f 147
manual *(car)* coche m con cambio de marchas manual

many muchos(-as) 15
map mapa m 94, 106, 150
March marzo m 218
margarine margarina f 160
market mercado m 99,131; ~ day día m de mercado
married, to be estar casado(-a) 120
mascara rímel m
mask *(diving)* gafas fpl de bucear
mass misa f 105
massage masaje m 147
match *(game)* partido m 114
matches cerillas fpl 31, 150
material material m ; *(fabric)* tela f
matinée matiné f 109
mat/matt finish *(photos)* acabado m mate
matter: it doesn't matter no importa; what's the matter? ¿qué pasa?
mattress colchón m 31
May mayo m 218
may I...? ¿puedo...? 18, 37
maybe quizás
me mí 16
meal comida f 38, 42, 125
mean, to significar 11
measles varicela f 165
measure, to medir 146
measurement medida f
meat carne f 41
medical certificate certificado m médico
medicine medicina f; medicamento m 164, 165
medium
medium/regular *(adj)* mediano(-a), de tamaño regular; *(steak)* medio hecho(-a)
meet, to quedar 125; encontrarse 106; pleased to meet you encantado(-a) de conocerle(-a) 118
meeting place lugar m de encuentro
member *(of club)* socio(-a) m/f 112
men *(toilets)* servicio/aseo m de caballeros
mend, to arreglar 137
menu menú m
message recado m 128
metal metal m

meter *(taxi)* taxímetro m
methylated spirits alcohol m de quemar
metro *(subway)* metro m 80; **~ station** estación f de metro 80
Mexican *(person)* mejicano(-a)
Mexico Méjico 119
microwave (oven) microondas m
midday medio día m
midnight doce fpl de la noche 220
might: I might not puede que no
migraine jaqueca f; migraña f
mileage kilometraje m 86
milk leche f 160; **with ~** con leche 40; **~ of magnesia** leche de magnesia f
million un millón 216
mind: do you mind? ¿le importa? 77, 126; **I've changed my mind** he cambiado de opinión
mine mío(-a), míos(as) 16; **it's ~** es mío(-a)
mineral water agua f mineral 40
minibar minibar m 32
minibus microbús m
minimart autoservicio m
minimum *(n)* mínimo m
minister pastor m
minor road carretera f secundaria
minute minuto m 221
mirror espejo m
miss, to *(train/bus)* perder; *(stop)* pasarse de
missing, to be faltar 137; desaparecer 152
mistake error m 32, 41, 42
mittens mitones mpl
mobile home caravana f fija, casa rodante f
modern moderno(-a) 14; **~ art** arte m moderno
moisturizing cream crema f hidratante
monastery monasterio m 99
Monday lunes m 218
money dinero m 42, 139, 153
money order giro m postal
money-belt cinturón-monedero m
month mes m 218
monthly ticket tarjeta f para un mes 79
monument monumento m 99

moor, to atracar
moped ciclomotor m 83
more más 15, 67; **I'd like some more** quiero un poco más (de) 39
morning, in the por la mañana 218, 221
Morocco Marruecos
moslem *(adj)* musulmán(a)
mosquito mosquito m; **~ bite** picadura f de mosquito
mother madre f 120
motorbike moto f 83
motorboat motora f 116
motorway *(expressway)* autopista f 94
mountain montaña f 107; **~ bike** bicicleta f de montaña; **~ pass** paso m de montaña 107; **~ range** cordillera f 107
mountaineering montañismo m
moustache bigote m
mouth boca f 166; **~ ulcer** llaga f
move, to *(house)* mudarse de 25; *(car)* cambiar de sitio; **don't move him!** ¡no lo muevan! 92
movie theater cine m
Mr. sr. (señor)
Mrs. sra. (señora)
much mucho 15
mugging atraco m
multiple journey *(ticket)* bonobús m 79
multiplex cinema multicine m 110
mumps paperas fpl
muscle músculo m 166
museum museo m 99
music música f 111; **~ box** caja f de música
musical *(n)* musical m
musician músico(-a) m/f
Muslim *(person)* musulmán(a) m/f
must: I must debo
mustard mostaza f 38
my mi, mis 16
myself: I'll do it myself lo haré yo mismo

 nail polish esmalte m de uñas
nail scissors tijeras fpl para las uñas

name nombre m 36, 93;
my ~ is... me llamo… 118;
what's your ~?
¿cómo se llama? 118
napkin *(serviette)* servilleta
f 39
narrow estrecho(-a) 14
national nacional
national health seguridad f social 161
nationality nacionalidad f
nature reserve reserva f natural 107
nausea náuseas fpl
navy blue azul m marino
near cerca de 12
nearby cerca, por aquí 21, 87
nearest el más cercano, la más cercana
88, 130; el próximo, la próxima
nearsighted miope 167
necessary necesario(-a) 89
neck cuello m 166
need: I need to... necesito… 18
needle aguja f
negative *(photo)* negativo m
neighbor vecino(-a) m/f
nephew sobrino m
nerve nervio m 166
nervous system sistema m nervioso
never nunca 13
never mind no tiene importancia 10
new year año m nuevo 219
New Zealand Nueva Zelanda
newsagent's *(newsdealer)* tienda f de
prensa 150
newspaper periódico m 150
newsstand kiosko m de prensa; puesto
m de periódicos
next próximo(-a) 14, 68, 75, 78, 80, 81,
87; **~ stop!** ¡próxima parada! 79
next to al lado de 12, 95
nice agradable, bonito(-a) 14
niece sobrina f
night noche f; **at ~** por la noche, 221;
per ~ por noche; **~ porter** portero m de
noche
nightclub club nocturno m 112
nightgown camisón m de noche
nine nueve 216
nineteen diecinueve 216
ninety noventa 216
no no 10

no one nadie 16
noisy ruidoso(-a) 14, 24
non-alcoholic sin alcohol
non-smoking *(adj)* para no fumador;
~ area zona de no-fumadores f
none ninguno(-a) 15, 16
noon mediodía m;
doce de la mañana 220
normal normal 67
north norte m 95
Northern Ireland Irlanda del Norte
nose nariz f 166
not that one ese(-a) no 16
not yet todavía no 13
note billete m
notebook cuaderno m 150
nothing to declare nada que declarar
nothing else nada más 15
notice board tablón m de anuncios 26
notify, to notificar 167
November noviembre m 218
now ahora 13, 84
nudist beach playa f nudista
number número m 216; *(telephone)*
número de teléfono; **sorry, wrong ~** lo
siento, se ha equivocado de número
number plate *(registration plate)*
matrícula f
nurse enfermero(-a) m/f
nut *(for bolt)* tuerca f

o'clock, it's... son las… en
punto 220
occasionally de vez en cuando
occupied ocupado(-a)
October octubre m 218
of de
of course por supuesto 19
off-peak fuera de temporada
off-road vehicle vehículo m
todoterreno
office oficina f
often a menudo 13
oil aceite m; **~ lamp** lámpara f de aceite
okay de acuerdo 10
old viejo(-a) 14
old fashioned antiguo(-a) 14
old town casco m antiguo 96 , 99
olive oil aceite de oliva m

omelet (omelette) tortilla f francesa 40
on *(day, date)* el, en 13; *(place)* en/encima de
on board *(ship, plane)* a bordo
on foot a pie 17
on the left a la izquierda 12
on the other side al otro lado 95
on the right a la derecha 12
on, to be *(showing)* estar en cartel
on/off switch interruptor m
on: this round's on me esta ronda la pago yo
once una vez 217; **~ a week** una vez a la semana
one uno 216
one like that uno(-a) como ése(-a) 16
open abierto(-a); **~ to the public** abierto(-a) al público 100; **~ to traffic** abierto(-a) al tráfico
open, to abrir 132, 140
opening hours horas fpl de apertura
opera ópera f 108, 111; **~ house** teatro m de la ópera 99, 111
operation operación f
opposite enfrente de/frente a 12
optician óptico(-a) m/f; oculista m/f 131, 167
or o 19
orange naranja f 143
orchestra orquesta f 111
order, to pedir 32, 37, 41; encargar
organized walk/hike paseo organizado m 106
others otros(-as)
our nuestro(-a) 16
ours nuestro(-a), nuestros(as) 16
out: he's out ha salido
outdoor al aire libre
outdoor pool piscina f al aire libre 116
outside a la salida de, afuera 12; fuera 36
outside lane carril m de adelantamiento
oval ovalado(-a) 134
oven horno m
over there allí 76
overcharged, I've been me han cobrado de más
overdone *(adj)* demasiado hecho(-a) 41
overdraft descubierto m
overheat sobrecalentamiento m

overnight service revelado m en un día
owe: how much do I owe you? ¿cuánto le debo?
own: on my own solo(-a) 65
owner propietario(-a) m/f

P pacifier chupete m
pack of cards baraja f de cartas
pack, to hacer las maletas 69
package paquete m
packed lunch bocadillo m
packet paquete m; **~ of cigarettes** paquete m de tabaco 150
padlock candado m
pain, to be in tener dolores 167
painkiller analgésico m 141, 165
paint, to pintar
painted pintado(-a)
painter pintor(a) m/f 104
painting cuadro m
pair (of) par m (de) 217
pajamas pijama m
palace palacio m 99
palpitations taquicardia f
panorama panorama m 107
pants pantalones mpl
panty hose medias fpl 144
paper papel m 150
paracetamol paracetamol m
paraffin parafina f 31
paralysis parálisis f
parcel *(package)* paquete m 155
pardon? ¿cómo? 11
parents padres mpl 120
park parque m 96, 99, 107
park, to aparcar
parking aparcamiento m 87; **~ disk** ficha f para el aparcamiento; **~ meter** parquímetro m 87
parliament building palacio m de las cortes 99
parting raya f
partner *(boyfriend/girlfriend)* pareja m/f
parts *(components)* piezas fpl 89
party *(social)* fiesta f 124
pass paso m 107
pass, to pasar por; **~ through** estar de paso 66

passenger pasajero(-a) m/f

passport pasaporte m 66, 69, 153; ~ **control** m de pasaportes 66

pastry shop/store pastelería f 131

patch, to remendar 137

path camino m 107

patient paciente m/f

pavement, on the en la acera

pay, to pagar 32, 42, 136; ~ **a fine** pagar una multa 93; ~ **by credit card** pagar con tarjeta de crédito

pay phone teléfono público m

payment pago m

pearl perla f 149

pebbly *(beach)* de guijarros 116

pedestrian crossing paso m de peatones 96

pedestrian zone/precinct zona f peatonal f 96

pedicure pedicura f

pen pluma estilográfica f 150; *(ballpen)* bolígrafo

pencil lápiz m 150

penicillin penicilina f

penknife navaja f

penpal amigo(-a) m/f por correspondencia

pensioner pensionistas mpl 100

people gente f 92, 119

pepper *(spice)* pimienta f 38; *(vegetable)* pimiento m

per day por día 30, 83, 86, 87, 115

per hour por hora 87, 115

per night por noche 21

per week por semana 83

performance función f

perhaps quizá 19

period época f 105; *(menstrual)* periodo m 167; ~ **pains** molestias fpl del periodo 167

perm permanente f

perm, to hacer la permanente 147

permit permiso m

personal stereo equipo m de música personal

peseta peseta f 67

pet animal m de compañía

pharmacy farmacia f 130, 140, 158

phone, to llamar por teléfono

phone call llamada f telefónica 152

phone card tarjeta para llamar por teléfono f 127

photo, to take a hacer una foto

photocopier fotocopiadora f 155

photographer fotógrafo(-a) m/f

photography fotografía f 151

phrase frase 11; ~ **book** libro m de frases 11

piano piano m

pick up, to recoger 28, 113

pickup truck camión de reparto m

picnic picnic m; ~ **area** zona f para picnics 107

piece trozo/pedazo m; porción f 159

pill *(contraceptive)* píldora f 167

pillow almohada f 27; ~ **case** funda f de almohada

pilot light piloto m

pink rosa m 143

pint pinta f

pipe *(smoking)* pipa f; *(tube)* cañería f

pipe cleaners limpiapipas m

pipe tobacco tabaco m de pipa

pitch *(camping)* parcela m; ~ **charge** tarifa f de acampada

pity: it's a pity es una lástima

pizzeria pizzería f 35

place sitio m

place a bet, to hacer una apuesta 114

plain *(not patterned)* sencillo(-a)

plane avión m 68

plans planes mpl 124

plant planta f

plastic bags bolsas fpl de plástico

plate plato m 39

platform andén m 73, 76, 77

platinum platino m 149

play, to *(sport)* jugar; 121; *(instrument)* tocar; *(drama)* representar 110

playground patio m de juegos 113

playgroup sala f de juegos 113

playing cards cartas fpl

playwright escritor(a) m/f 110

pleasant agradable 14

please por favor 10

pliers alicates mpl

plug enchufe m

plumber fontanero m

p.m. de la tarde/noche

pneumonia neumonía f 165
point of interest punto m de interés
point to, to señalar a 11
poison veneno m
poisonous venenoso(-a)
poker (cards) póker m
police policía f 92, 152; **~ certificate** certificado m de la policía 153; **~ station** comisaría f de policía 96, 131, 152
pollen count índice m de polen 122
polyclinic policlínico m 131
polyester polyester m
pond estanque m
pony ride vuelta f en pony
pop music música f pop
popcorn palomitas fpl 110
popular popular
port (harbor) puerto m
porter mozo m, botones m 71
portion porción f 39, 41
Portugal Portugal
possible: as soon as possible lo antes/más pronto posible
possibly posiblemente
post, to (mail) mandar por correo 27
post (mail) correo m; **~ office** oficina f de correos, correos m 150, 154
postcard postal f 150, 154, 156
poster póster m
postman cartero m
potatoes patatas fpl 38
pottery cerámica f
pound (sterling) libra (esterlina) f 67, 138
power cut corte m de luz
power point toma f de corriente
pregnant, to be estar embarazada 163
premium (gas/petrol) súper 87
prescribe, to recetar 165
prescription receta f 140
present (gift) regalo m
press, to planchar 137
pretty bonito(-a)
priest sacerdote m 105
prison cárcel f
probably probablemente 19
program programa m 109; **~ of events** programa de espectáculos m 108

prohibited: is it prohibited? ¿está prohibido?
pronounce, to pronunciar 11
properly correctamente
pub bar m
public holiday fiesta f nacional 219
pullover jersey m 144
pump bomba f; (gas/petrol) surtidor m
puppet show marionetas fpl
purple morado m 143
purpose propósito m 66
purse monedero m 153
put, to poner; **where can I put…?** ¿dónde puedo poner…?; **~ by** (in shop) comprar 135; **can you put me up for the night?** ¿puede alojarnos en su casa esta noche?
putting course pista f de putting golf

Q **quality** calidad f 134
quantity cantidad f 134
quarantine cuarentena f
quarter cuarto m 217; **~ past/after** y cuarto 220; **~ to/before** menos cuarto 220
quay muelle m
queen (cards, chess) reina f
question pregunta f
quick rápido(-a) 14
quickest: what's the quickest way to… ¿cuál es la forma más rápida de llegar a…?
quickly rápidamente 17
quiet silencioso(-a) 14
quieter más tranquilo(-a) 24

R **rabbi** rabino m
race (cars, horses) carrera f; **~ course** pista f de carreras 114
racket (tennis, squash) raqueta f 115
radio radio m 25
rail station estación f de trenes/ferrocarriles f 73
railroad (railway) ferrocarril m
rain, to llover 122

A-Z

raincoat impermeable m, chubasquero m 144
rape violación f 152
rapids rápidos m 107
rare *(steak)* poco hecho(-a); *(unusual)* raro(-a)
rarely rara vez 13
rash sarpullido m 162
rather bastante 17
ravine barranco m 107
razor maquinilla f de afeitar
razor blades cuchillas fpl de afeitar 142
re-enter, to volver a entrar
reading *(interest)* lectura f; ~ **glasses** gafas de leer fpl
ready, to be estar listo (a) 89, 151, 137
real *(genuine)* auténtico(-a) 149
receipt recibo m 32, 136, 137, 151
reception *(desk)* recepción f
receptionist recepcionista m/f 27
reclaim check/tag etiqueta f de reclamación 71
reclaim, to reclamar
recommend, to recomendar 21, 35, 141; **can you recommend…** ¿puede recomendar(me/nos)…? 97; **what do you recommend?** ¿qué me/nos recomienda? 37
record *(LP)* disco m 157
record/music shop/store tienda f de discos 131
red rojo m 143; ~ **wine** vino m tinto 40
reduction descuento m 24, 68, 74, 100
refreshments bebidas fpl
refrigerator frigorífico m 29
refund devolución f del dinero 137
refuse tip basurero m
regard to… saludos a…
region región f
registered mail correo m certificado
registration form formulario m de registro 23
registration number número m de matrícula 88, 93
regular *(gas/petrol)* normal 87; *(size of drink)* de tamaño normal 110
regulations: I didn't know the regulations no conocía las normas
religion religión f
remember: I don't remember no me acuerdo

rent, to alquilar 83, 86, 115, 116, 117; **for rent** de alquiler; *(in notices)* se alquila
rental car coche m alquilado 153
repair, to arreglar 89, 137, 168
repairs reparaciones fpl 89, 137
repeat to repetir 94, 128; **please repeat that** por favor, repítalo 11
replacement part pieza f de recambio 137
report, to denunciar 152
representative representante m/f 27
required, to be requerirse 112
reservation reserva f 22, 68, 77
reservations desk despacho m de reservas 109
reserve, to reservar 36,109
rest, to descansar
restaurant restaurante m 26, 35
retired, to be estar jubilado(-a) 121
return, to *(travel)* volver 74, 75, 81, 98
return ticket billete m de ida y vuelta 68, 74, 79
reverse the charges, to llamar a cobro revertido 127
rheumatism reumatismo/reuma m
rib costilla f 166
right *(correct)* correcto(-a) 14
right of way derecho m de paso 93, 106
right, on the a la derecha 76, 95
right handed diestro(-a)
rip-off *(n)* timo m 101
river río m 107, 116; ~ **cruise** crucero m por el río 81
road carretera f 94; *(street)* calle f 95; ~ **accident** accidente m de carretera; ~ **assistance** asistencia f en carretera 88; ~ **map** mapa m de carreteras 150; ~ **signs** señales fpl de tráfico 96
roast chicken pollo m asado 35
roasted asado(-a)
robbery robo m
rock climbing escalada f en roca
rock concert concierto m de rock
rocks rocas fpl
roller blades ruedas fpl de patín
rolls bollos mpl 160
romance *(film)* película f romántica
romantic romántico(-a)
roof *(house/car)* techo m
roof-rack baca f
rook *(chess)* torre f

room habitación f 21; **~ service** servicio m de habitaciones 26

rope cuerda f

round redondo(-a) 134

round *(of golf)* juego m 115

round-trip ticket billete m de ida y vuelta 68, 74, 79

roundabout rotonda f

route camino m; ruta f 106

rowing remo m; **~ boat** barca f de remos 116

rubbish *(trash)* basura f 28

rucksack mochila f 31, 145

rude, to be ser grosero(-a)

rugby rugby m

ruins ruinas fpl 99

run into, to *(crash)* chocar con 93

run out, to *(fuel)* quedarse sin

rush hour horas fpl punta

S **safe** *(lock box)* caja fuerte f 27;
(not dangerous) seguro(-a) 116; **to feel ~** sentirse seguro(-a) 65

safety 65

safety pins imperdibles mpl

sag: the bed sags la cama se hunde

sailboard tabla f de windsurf

sailboarding windsurfing m

sailboat velero m 116

salad ensalada f

sales rep representante m/f

salt sal f 38, 39

same mismo(-a) 75; **the ~ again please** lo mismo otra vez, por favor

sand arena f

sandals sandalias fpl 145

sandwich bocadillo m

sandy *(beach)* de arena 116

sanitary napkins compresas fpl 142

satellite TV televisión f por satélite; antena f parabólica 22

satin raso/satén m

satisfied: I'm not satisfied with this no estoy satisfecho(-a) con esto

Saturday sábado m 218

sauce salsa f 38

saucepan cazo m 29

sauna sauna f 22

sausage salchicha f, 160

say, to decir;
how do you ~…? ¿cómo se dice…?; **what did he ~?** ¿qué dijo…?

scarf *(wool)* bufanda f; *(silk)* pañuelo m 144

scenic route carretera f panorámica 106

scheduled flight vuelo m regular

school colegio m; escuela f

sciatica ciática f 165

scientist científico(-a) m/f

scooter Vespa/Vespino f/m

Scotland Escocia 119

Scottish *(adj/n)* escocés(a) m/f

scouring pad estropajo m

screw tornillo m

sea mar m 107

seafront paseo m marítimo

seasick, I feel me mareo

season ticket abono m de temporada

seasoning aderezo m 38

seat *(movies)* asiento m 77; *(plane, train)* plaza f

second segundo(-a)

second class de segunda clase 74

second floor *(U.S.)* primera planta f 74

secondhand de segunda mano; **~ shop** tienda f de segunda mano

secretary secretario(-a) m/f

security guard guardia m/f de seguridad

sedative sedante m

see, to ver 24, 37, 93; **~ someone again** volver a ver a alguien

self-employed, to be trabajar por cuenta propia 121

self-service autoservicio m 87

sell, to vender

send, to *(help)* mandar 88, 155

senior citizen pensionista m/f 74

separated, to be estar separado(-a) 120

separately por separado 42

September septiembre m 218

septic tank pozo m séptico

serious grave

served, to be *(meal)* servirse

service servicio m 42;
~ charge servicio m

service station *(gas station)* estación f de servicio 87

services servicios mpl 131
set menu menú del día m
seven siete 216
seventeen diecisiete 216
seventy setenta 217
sex *(act)* acto m sexual
shade tono m 143
shallow poco hondo(-a), profundo(-a) 116
shampoo champú m 142; **~ for dry/oily hair** champú para cabello seco/graso m
shape forma f 134
share, to *(room)* compartir
sharp *(object)* afilado(-a)
shatter, to *(glass)* romperse
shaver máquina f de afeitar; **~ socket** enchufe m para la máquina de afeitar
shaving brush brocha f de afeitar
shaving cream espuma f de afeitar
she ella
sheet *(bedding)* sábana f 28
shelf estante m
ship barco m 81
shirt camisa f 144
shock *(electric)* calambre m
shoe laces cordones mpl de zapatos
shoe polish betún m
shoe repair zapatero m
shoe shop/store zapatería f 131; *(in signs)* calzados f
shoemaker zapatero m
shoes zapatos mpl 145
shop *(store)* tienda f 130
shop assistant dependiente(a) m/f
shopping: ~ area zona f de tiendas 99;**~ basket** cesta f de la compra; **~ center/mall** centro m comercial 130; **~ list** lista f de la compra; **~ cart** carrito m de la compra 158; **to go ~** ir de compras/a comprar
shore *(sea/lake)* orilla f
short corto(-a) 146
shorts pantalones fpl cortos 144
shoulder hombro m 166
show, to enseñar 18, 133; **can you ~ me?** ¿puede indicarme? 94, 106
shower gel gel m de ducha
showers duchas fpl 30;
shut: when do you shut? ¿a qué hora cierran?

shutter persiana f
shy tímido(-a)
sick, to feel sentirse mal; **I'm going to be sick** voy a devolver/vomitar
sickbay *(ship)* enfermería f
side *(of road)* lado m 95
side order guarnición f 37, 38
side street bocacalle f 95
sights lugares mpl de interés
sightseeing tour recorrido por los lugares de interés m 97
sightseeing, to go ir a visitar lugares de interés
sign señal f 93, 95
signpost señal f
silk seda f
silver plata f 149
silver plate baño m de plata
similar, to be parecerse
since *(time)* desde
singer cantante m/f 157
single individual 81; **~ (one-way) ticket** billete m de ida 68, 74, 79; **~ room** habitación f individual 21; **to be ~** estar soltero(-a) 120
sink fregadero m
sister hermana f 120
sit, to sentarse; **sit down, please** siéntese, por favor
six seis 216
sixteen dieciséis 216
sixty sesenta 217
size talla f 146
size tamaño m
skates patines mpl 117
skating rink pista f de patinaje
skis esquí m 117; **~ boots** botas fpl de esquí 117; **~ instructor** instructor(a) m/f de esquí; **~ poles** bastones mpl de esquí 117; **~ suit** traje m de esquí; **~ trousers** pantalones mpl de esquí; **~ wax** cera f para los esquíes
ski lift teleférico m
ski school academia de esquí
skid: we skidded resbalamos/patinamos
skiing esquiar 117
skin piel f 166
skin-diving equipment equipo m de buceo
skirt falda f 144

sleep, to dormir 167

sleeping bag saco m de dormir 31

sleeping car coche-cama m 77

sleeping pill somnífero m; pastilla f para dormir f

sleeve manga f 144

slice rodaja f; loncha f 159

slide film diapositiva f; filmina f

slope *(ski)* cuesta f

slot machine máquina f tragaperras

slow lento(-a) 14

slow down! ¡vaya más despacio!

slow, to be *(clock)* estar atrasado 221

slowly despacio 11, 17, 94, 128

SLR SRL m 151

small pequeño(-a) 14, 24, 40, 110, 117, 134

small change calderilla f; suelto m

smell: there's a bad smell huele mal

smoke, to fumar; **I don't smoke** no fumo

smoking *(adj)* para fumador;**~ area** zona f de fumadores

smoky: it's too smoky hay demasiado humo

snack bar bar m 73

snacks aperitivos mpl 40

sneakers zapatillas fpl de deporte

snooker snooker m

snorkel esnórkel m

snow nieve f

snow, to nevar

soaking solution *(contact lenses)* solución f para lentillas/lentes de contacto

soap jabón m 142

soap powder detergente m en polvo

socket enchufe m

socks calcetines mpl 144

sofa sofá m

sofa-bed sofá-cama m

soft drink *(soda)* refresco m 110, 160

sole *(shoes)* suela f

soluble aspirin aspirinas fpl solubles 141

some algunos(-as); algo de

someone alguien 16

something algo 14, 16

sometimes a veces 13

son hijo m 120, 162

soon pronto 13; **as ~ as possible** tan pronto como sea posible 161

sorry! ¡lo siento! 10

sort clase f; tipo m 134; **a ~ of** una especie de

sour ácido(-a) 41

south sur m 95

South Africa Sudáfrica

South African *(person)* sudafricano(-a)

souvenir recuerdo m 98, 156; **~ guide** catálogo m de recuerdos 156; **~ store/shop** tienda f de recuerdos 131

spa *(spring)* manantial m; *(place to stay)* balneario m

space espacio m; *(in campsite)* parcela f 30

spade *(shovel)* pala f

spades *(cards)* picas fpl

Spain España 119

Spaniard español(a) m/f

Spanish *(language)* español m 11, 126

spare *(extra)* de sobra; *(piece, wheel)* de repuesto

speak, to hablar 11, 41, 67, 128; **do you speak English?** ¿habla inglés? 11

special rate tarifa f especial 86

special requirements peticiones fpl especiales 39

specialist especialista m/f 164

specimen muestra f 164

speed limit límite m de velocidad 93

speed, to llevar exceso de velocidad

spell, to deletrear 11

spend, to *(money)* gastar; *(time)* pasar

spicy *(containing spices)* con especias; *(taste)* a especias

spin-dryer secadora f

spine columna f vertebral 166

sponge esponja f

spoon cuchara f 39, 41

sport deporte m 114

sports club club m deportivo

sports ground campo m de actividades deportivas 96

sports store/shop tienda f de deportes 131

sprained, to be tener un esguince 164

spring manantial m; *(season)* primavera f 219

square cuadrado(-a) 134
stadium estadio m 96
stain mancha f
stairs escaleras fpl
stall: the engine stalls el motor se ha calado
stalls (*orchestra*) patio f de butacas
stamp sello m 150, 154; **~ machine** máquina f expendedora de sellos 154
stand in line, to permanecer en la cola 112
standby ticket billete m de standby
start (*n*) comienzo m
start, to empezar 98, 112; (*car*) arrancar 88
starter primer plato m 37
stately home casa f solariega
statement (*legal*) declaración f 93
station estación f 73, 96
stationer's papelería f
statue estatua f 99
stay, to quedarse 23, 65
steak house churrasquería f 35
stereo equipo m estéreo
sterilizing solution solución f esterilizante 142
stern (*ship*) popa f
stiff neck tortícolis f
still: I'm still waiting todavía estoy esperando
sting ardor m 162
stocking media f 144
stomach estómago m 166; **~ ache** dolor de estómago m 163; **~ cramps** retortijones mpl
stools (*feces*) heces fpl 164
stop (*bus, tram, metro*) parada f 79, 80
stop, to parar 76 98; **please stop here** pare aquí, por favor 84
stopover parada f, escala f
store tienda f 130; **~ detective** detective m/f de una tienda; **~ guide** directorio m 132
straight ahead todo recto 95
straw (*drinking*) pajita f
strawberry (*flavor*) (de) fresa 40
stream arroyo m 107
string cuerda f
striped (*patterned*) a/de rayas

strong (*potent*) fuerte
stuck: the key's stuck la llave se ha atascado
student estudiante m/f 74, 100
study, to estudiar
style estilo m 104
styling mousse espuma f moldeadora
subtitled, to be estar subtitulado(-a) 110
subway pasaje m subterráneo 96
sugar azúcar m 38, 39
suggest, to sugerir 123
suit traje m de chaqueta 144
suitable for apropiado(-a) para
summer verano m 219
sun block filtro m solar
sun lounger tumbona f
suntan cream/lotion crema f bronceadora 142
sunbathe, to tomar el sol
suncare protección f contra el sol 142
Sunday domingo m 218
sunglasses gafas fpl de sol
sunshade (*umbrella*) sombrilla f 116
sunstroke insolación f 163
super (*gas*) súper 87
superb espléndido(-a) 101
supermarket supermercado m 131, 158
supplement suplemento m 68,69, 74
suppositories supositorios mpl 165
sure: are you sure? ¿estás seguro(-a)?
surfboard tabla de surf f 116
surgery (*doctor's office*) consulta f 161
surname apellido m
sweatshirt sudadera f 144
sweet (*taste*) dulce
sweets (*candy*) caramelos mpl, dulces mpl 150
swelling hinchazón f 162
swim, to nadar 116
swimming natación f 114; **~ pool** piscina f 22, 26, 116; **~ trunks** bañador (de hombre) m 144
swimsuit bañador (de mujer) m 144
switch interruptor m
switch on/off, to encender/apagar
swollen, to be estar hinchado(-a)
symptoms síntomas mpl 163
synagogue sinagoga f
synthetic sintético(-a)

T-shirt camiseta f 144, 156
table mesa f 36;
~ **cloth** mantel m
table tennis ping-pong m
tablet comprimido m 140
take, to tomar; *(medicine)* tomar 140,
165; *(carry)* llevar 71; *(time)* tardar; **I'll
take it** *(purchase)* me lo quedo 135
take away, to llevar 40
take photographs, to
hacer fotografías 98, 100
take someone home, to
llevar a alguien a casa
taken *(occupied)* cogido(-a) ocupado(-a)
talcum powder polvos mpl de talco
talk, to hablar
tall alto(-a) 14
tampons tampones mpl
tan moreno m
tap *(faucet)* grifo m 25
taste sabor m
taxi taxi m 70, 71, 84; ~ **driver** taxista
m/f; ~ **rank** parada f de taxis 96
tea té m 40; ~ **bags** bolsitas fpl de té
tea towel paño m de cocina 156
teacher profesor(a) m/f
team equipo m 114
teddy bear osito m 157
teenager adolescente m/f
telephone teléfono m 22, 70, 92, 127;~
bill cuenta f del teléfono 32; ~ **booth**
cabina f telefónica 127; ~ **calls**
llamadas fpl (telefónicas) 32; ~ **kiosk**
cabina f; ~ **number** número m de
teléfono 127
telephone, to llamar por teléfono
television televisión m
telex télex m
tell, to decir 18, 79; **tell me** dígame
temperature temperatura f 164
temporarily provisionalmente 89
ten diez 216
tendon tendón m
tennis tenis m 114; ~ **ball** pelota f de
tenis; ~ **court** pista/cancha f de tenis
115
tent tienda f 30, 31; ~ **pegs** estacas fpl
31; ~ **pole** mástil m 31
terminus terminal f
tetanus tétano m 164

thank you gracias
10, 94
that eso(-a), aquello(-a);
~ **one** ése(-a) 16, 134;
that's all eso es todo 133
theater teatro m 96, 99, 110
theft robo m 153
their su 16
theirs suyo(-a) 16
them ellos 16; **to/for them** a/para
ellos(-as)
theme park parque temático m
then *(time)* entonces, luego 13
there allí 12, 17; ~ **is...** hay... 17
thermometer termómetro m
thermos termo m
these estos(-as) 134
they ellos(-as)
thick grueso(-a) 14
thief ladrón(a) m/f
thigh cadera f 166
thin fino(-a), delgado(-a) 14
think: I think creo 42, 77
think about it, to pensár(se)lo 135
third tercero(-a) 217; **a ~** un tercio 217
thirsty, I am tengo sed
thirteen trece 216
thirty treinta 217
this one éste(-a) 16, 134
those esos(-as), aquel(lla) 134
thousand mil 217
thread hilo m 27
three tres 216
throat garganta f 166
throat lozenges pastillas fpl para la
garganta
through a través de/por
thumb pulgar m 166
thundery, to be tronar 122
Thursday jueves m 218
ticket billete m 68, 69, 74, 75, 77, 79;
entrada f 114; ~ **agency** agencia f de
venta de entradas; ~ **office** despacho m
de billetes 73
tie corbata f 144;
tight estrecho(-a), ajustado(-a) 146;
(clothing) apretado(-a) 117
tights medias fpl 144
till receipt recibo m de caja
time hora f 76, 220; **on ~** puntual 76;
free ~ tiempo m libre 98

timetable horario m 75
tin lata f
tin foil papel m de aluminio
tint, to teñir 147
tinted (glass/lens) con un tinte
tip propina f 32
tipping dar propina 42, 71
tire neumático m 83, 88
tired, to be estar cansado(-a)
tissues pañuelos mpl de papel 142
to (place) a 12
toaster tostador m
tobacco tabaco m 150
tobacco store/tobacconist's estanco m 131
today hoy 68, 124, 218
toe dedo del pie 166
together junto(-a) 42
toilet servicio m 26, 29, 87
toilet paper papel m higiénico 25, 29, 142
toilets servicios mpl 98, 132; aseos mpl
tomorrow mañana 84, 124, 218
tongue lengua f 166
tonic water tónica f
tonight esta noche 110, 124; **for ~** para esta noche 108
tonsillitis amigdalitis f
tonsils amígdala f 166
too demasiado 15, 17, 93; (also) también 19
tooth diente m 168; **~ache** dolor m de muelas
toothbrush cepillo m de dientes
toothpaste pasta f de dientes 142
top (of mountain) cima f
top floor planta f/piso m de arriba
torn, to be (muscle) estar desgarrado(-a) 164
totally totalmente 17
tote totalizador m
tough (food) duro(-a) 41
tour visita f turística, 97; **~ guide** guía m/f turístico(-a); **~ operator** operador(a) turístico(-a) m/f 26; **~ representative** representante m/f turístico(-a) 27
tourist turista m/f

tourist office oficina f de turismo 97
tow rope cuerda f de remolque
tow, to remolcar
tow truck camión m de reparto 88
toward hacia 12
towel toalla f
toweling felpa f
tower torre f 99
town (small) pueblo m; (large) ciudad f 70, 94
town hall ayuntamiento m 99
toy juguete m 157
toy and game shop/store juguetería f 131
track sendero m
tracksuit chándal m
traditional tradicional
traffic tráfico m
traffic jam atasco m (de tráfico)
traffic violation/offense violación/infracción f del código de circulación
tragedy tragedia f
trail sendero m
train tren m 75, 76, 77
train times horarios mpl de trenes 75
training shoes zapatillas fpl de deporte 145
tram tranvía m
transfer (bank) transferencia f; (transport) trasbordo m
transit, in en tránsito
translate, to traducir 11
translation traducción f
translator traductor(a) m/f
travel agency agencia f de viajes 131
travel iron plancha f (de viaje)
travel sickness mareo m 141
travel, to viajar 74
traveler's check cheque m de viaje 136, 138
tray bandeja f
tree árbol m 106
tremendous (good) formidable 101
trip (excursion) excursión f; (journey) viaje m 97
trouble: I'm having trouble with tengo problemas con
trousers pantalones mpl 144
true: that's not true eso no es verdad
try on, to probarse 146

Tuesday martes m 218
tumor tumor m 165
tunnel túnel m
turn, to torcer; **~ down** *(volume, heat)* bajar; **~ off** apagar 25; **~ on** encender 25; **~ up** *(volume, heat)* subir
turning desvío m 95
TV televisión f 22; **~ room** sala f de la televisión
TV-listing *(magazine)* guía f de televisión
twelve doce 216
twenty veinte 216
twice dos veces 217
twin bed dos f pl camas 21
twist: I've twisted my ankle me he torcido el tobillo
two dos 216
type tipo m 112
typical típico(-a) 37

U **ugly** feo(-a) 14, 101
UK (United Kingdom) Reino Unido
umbrella paraguas m
uncle tío m 120
unconscious, to be estar inconsciente 92, 162
under *(place)* debajo de
underdone *(adj)* crudo(-a) 41
underpants calzoncillos m pl 144
underpass pasaje m subterráneo 76
understand, to entender 11; **do you understand?** ¿entiende? 11; **I don't understand** no entiendo 11, 67
undress, to desvestirse 164
unfortunately desgraciadamente 19
uniform uniforme m
unit unidad f
United States Estados Unidos
unleaded gasoline gasolina f sin plomo
unlimited mileage kilometraje m ilimitado
unlock, to abrir
until hasta 221
upper berth litera f de arriba 74
upset stomach dolor m de estómago 141
upstairs arriba, en el piso de arriba
up to hasta 12

urgent urgente 161
us: for/with us para/con nosotros(-as)
U.S. Estados Unidos 119
use, to usar 139
useful útil

V **vacancy** habitación/plaza f libre 21
vacant libre 14
vacation vacaciones f pl 66, 123
vaccination vacuna f
vaginal infection infección f vaginal 167
valet service servicio m de planchado
valid válido(-a)
validate, to *(ticket)* picar 79
valley valle m 107
valuable de valor
value valor m 155
valve llave f de paso 28
vanilla (flavor) (de) vainilla 40
VAT *(sales tax)* IVA m 24; **~ receipt** recibo m con el IVA 42
vegan, to be ser vegetariano(-a) estricto(-a); **suitable for ~** apropiado(-a) para vegetarianos estrictos; **~ dishes** platos para vegetarianos estrictos m pl
vegetable store verdulería f
vegetables verduras f pl 38
vegetarian *(adj/n)* vegetariano(-a) m/f 35; **to be ~** ser vegetariano(-a)
vehicle vehículo m; **~ registration document** documento de registro del vehículo m 93
vein vena f 166
very muy 17
vest chaleco m
video vídeo m; **~ game** videojuego m; **~ recorder** aparato de vídeo m
view: with a view of the sea con vistas al mar
viewpoint/viewing point mirador m 99, 107
village pueblo m 107
vineyard/winery viñedo m 107
visa visa f
visit, to ver 123; visitar; *(hospital)* hacer una visitar a

A-Z

visiting hours horas fpl de visita 167

vitamin tablets vitaminas fpl en comprimidos 141

voice voz f

vomit, to vomitar

W wait (for), to esperar (a) 41, 76, 89, 126, 140; **wait!** ¡espere(n)! 98

waiter! ¡camarero! 37

waiting room sala f de espera 73

waitress! ¡camarera! 37

wake, to *(self)* despertarse; *(s.o. else)* despertar a 27

wake-up call llamada-despertador f

Wales Gales 119

walk, to go for a ir de paseo

walking boots botas fpl de montaña 106, 145

walking/hiking gear equipo m de senderismo 145

wallet cartera f 42; billetera f 153

want, to querer 18

ward *(hospital)* sala f 167

warm caliente 14; *(weather)* caluroso(-a)

warm, to calentar

wash, to lavar

washbasin lavabo m

washer *(for tap/faucet)* junta f

washing machine lavadora f 29

watch reloj m (de pulsera) 153

watch TV, to ver la televisión

water agua f; **~ bottle** bolsa de agua caliente; **~ carrier** garrafa para el agua f; **~ heater** calentador m 28

water-skis esquís acuáticos mpl 116

waterfall catarata f 107

waterproof impermeable; **~ jacket** chubasquero m 145

waterskiing esquí m acuático

wave ola f

waxing depilación f a la cera 147

way *(direction)* camino m; **I've lost my ~** me he perdido 94; **on the ~** de camino 83

we nosotros(-as)

weak *(coffee)* poco cargado

wear, to vestir/llevar puesto(-a)

weather tiempo m 122; **~ forecast** pronóstico m del tiempo 122

wedding boda f; **~ ring** anillo m de boda

Wednesday miércoles m 218

week semana f 23, 97, 218

weekend fin de semana m; **~ rate** tarifa f de fin de semana 86; **at the ~** el fin de semana 218

weekly (ticket) tarjeta f para una semana 79

weight: my weight is... peso…

welcome to... bienvenido(-a) a…

well-done *(steak)* bien hecho(-a)

Welsh *(adj)* galés(a); *(person)* galés(a) m/f

west oeste m 95

wetsuit traje m de neopremo

what? ¿qué? 18

what kind/sort of...? ¿qué clase de…? 37, 106

what time? ¿a qué hora? 68, 76, 81

what's the time? ¿qué hora es? 220

wheelchair silla f de ruedas

when? 13

where? ¿dónde? 12; **~ are you from?** ¿de dónde es? 119; **~ is...?** ¿dónde está...? 99; **~ can we...?** ¿dónde podemos…?

which? ¿cuál? 16; **~ stop?** ¿qué parada? 80

while mientras

white blanco(-a) 143; **~ wine** vino m blanco 40

who? ¿quién? 16

whole: the whole day el día entero

whose? ¿de quién(es) ? 16

why? ¿por qué? 16

wide ancho(-a) 14

wife mujer f 120, 162

wildlife flora f y fauna f

windbreaker chubasquero m 145

window ventana f 25,77; *(shop)* escaparate m 134, 149; **window seat** asiento m de ventanilla 69, 74

windshield parabrisas m

windy, to be hacer viento 122

wine vino m 40

wine list carta f de vinos 37

winter invierno m 219

wishes: best wishes to... saludos a…

with con 17

with long/short sleeves de manga larga/corta 144

with v-/round neck de cuello de pico/a la caja 144

without sin 17

witness testigo m/f 93

wood *(forest)* bosque m 107; *(material)* madera f

wool lana f

work, to trabajar 121; *(function)* funcionar 28, 83, 89; **it doesn't ~** no funciona 25

worry: I'm worried estoy preocupado(-a)

worse peor 14; **it's got/gotten ~** ha empeorado(-a)

worst peor

worth: is it worth seeing? ¿merece la pena guardarlo?

wound herida f 162

write down, to escribir 136

write escribir; **~ soon!** ¡escriba pronto!

writing pad cuaderno m 150

wrong incorrecto(-a); equivocado(-a) 136; **~ number** número m equivocado

128; **there's something ~ with...** hay algo que está mal en...; **what's ~?** ¿qué pasa? 89

x-ray radiografía f 164

yacht yate m

year año m 218

yellow amarillo m 143

yes sí 10

yesterday ayer 218

yogurt yogurt m

you usted(es)/tú/vosotros(-as) 118

young joven 14

your su/tu/vuestro(-a) 16

yours suyo(-a)/tuyo(-a)/vuestro(-a) 16

youth hostel albergue m juvenil 29

zebra crossing paso m de cebra

zero cero m

zip(per) cremallera f

zone zona f

zoo zoológico m 113

zoology zoología f

Dictionary
Spanish - English

This Spanish-English Dictionary covers all the areas where you may need to decode written Spanish: hotels, public buildings, restaurants, shops, ticket offices and on transport. It will also help with understanding forms, maps, product labels, road signs and operating instuctions (for telephones, parking meters, etc.).

If you can't locate the exact sign, you may find key words or terms listed separately.

A **a descontar de su próxima compra** … off your next purchase
a estrenar brand new
a la carte a la carte
a la … … style
a la tarjeta de crédito charge your credit card
a su elección at your choice
abierto open
abierto de … a … y de … a … opening hours
abril April
abrir aquí cut here; open here
abróchense los cinturones fasten your seat belt
acantilado cliff
acceso al garaje prohibido durante la travesía no access to car decks during crossing
accesorios de baño bathroom accessories
accesorios de cocina kitchen equipment
aceite oil (cooking)
acero steel
acto event
actuación gig
actualizado updated
acueducto aqueduct
administración de lotería lottery
admisiones admissions
adultos adults
aerodeslizador hydrofoil
aeropuerto airport
agencia de viajes travel agent's

agencia inmobiliaria estate agent's
agítese bien antes de usar shake well before use
agosto August
agua potable drinking water
al aire libre open-air; outdoor
al recibir respuesta introduzca las monedas on reply, insert coins
albergue de carretera motel
alerta L storm warning
algo que declarar goods to declare
algodón cotton
alimentos dietéticos health foods
almacén de muebles furniture warehouse
almacenes de música music store/shop
almacenes generales general store
alpinismo mountaineering
alquiler de coches car rental
alta tensión high voltage
altitud altitude
altura máxima headroom; maximum height
altura sobre el nivel del mar height above sea level
aluminio aluminum
amarre prohibido no anchorage
andén platform
andenes to the platforms
anfiteatro circle
animales de compañía pet store/shop
antes de entrar, dejen salir let passengers off first
antes de las comidas before meals
anticuario antique store/shop
antigüedades antiques
Año Nuevo ➤ New Year's Day

202

SPANISH ➤ ENGLISH

apague el motor turn off engine
aparcamiento parking lot/car park
aparcamiento autorizado parking permitted
aparcamiento clientes customer car park
aparcamiento de residentes residents only
aparcamiento gratuito free parking
aparcamiento no vigilado parking at your own risk
apartadero wayside/layby
apellido name
apellido de la esposa wife's name
aperitivo aperitif
apto para cocción en horno microondas microwaveable
apto para regímenes vegetarianos suitable for vegetarians/vegans
apuestas deportivas betting shop/bookmaker's
arca de agua water tower
arcén blando soft shoulders
arcén duro hard-shoulder
área de servicio service area
arenas movedizas quick sand
aroma flavoring
arroyo stream
arte art
artículos de regalo gifts
ascensor elevator/lift
asiento de pasillo aisle seat
asiento de ventanilla window seat
asiento número seat no.
asiento reservado para personas que merecen especial atención please give up this seat to the old or infirm
atención al cliente customer service
atletismo athletics
atracción para turistas tourist feature
auténtico genuine
auto-servicio self-service
autobús bus
autocar coach
autocine drive-in
autopista motorway/freeway
autoservicio self-service
autovía dual carriageway; expressway
avenida avenue
avión plane

avisamos grúa/cepo unauthorized vehicles will be clamped/towed away
aviso warning
aviso de tempestad gale warning
ayuntamiento town hall
azúcar sugar

B **bahía** bay
bailador dancer
baile dance
bajar to go down
bajo su responsabilidad at your own risk
baloncesto basketball
balonmano handball
balonvolea volley ball
banco bank
banda magnética abajo a la derecha magnetic strip on underside and to the right
baños baths
barbacoa barbecue
barca de remos rowing boat
barco ship; steamer
bebidas incluidas drinks included
bebidas sin alcohol soft drinks
béisbol baseball
bicicleta bicycle
bienvenido welcome!
billar snooker
billete de abono season ticket
bodega vineyard/winery
bolera bowling
bomberos fire brigade; fire station
bosque forest; wood
botas de esquí ski boots
botes salvavidas lifeboats
botiquín medicine box
bufet self-service
bulevar boulevard
butaca stalls

C **caballeros** gentlemen (toilets)
cada ... horas every ... hours
caduca el ... valid until ...
café coffee
caja checkout

A-Z

caja de ahorros savings bank
caja rápida express checkout
cajero automático cash-dispenser/auto-teller
cajero fuera de servicio teller out of order
cajeros cashiers
cala creek
calcio calcium
calle road; street
calle cortada closed road
calle de sentido único one-way street
calle mayor main/high street
calle sin salida no throughway; closed road
callejón lane
callejón sin salida cul-de-sac
calorías calories
calzada en mal estado poor road surface
camarotes cabins
cambie (a otra línea de metro) change (to other metro lines)
cambie en ... change at ...
camino nature trail
camión truck
cámping con hierba grass camping site
cámping piso de arena sand camping site
cámping piso de piedra stone camping site
campo common/green/park; field
campo de batalla battle site
campo de deporte(s) park/sports ground
campo para meriendas picnic area
camposanto churchyard
cancelado cancelled
canoa canoe
canónigo canon
caña de pescar fishing rod
caño de agua water tap
cañón canyon
capilla chapel
cápsulas capsules
caravana trailer/caravan
carga máxima load limit
carnaval carnival
carne meat

carnicería butcher's
carretera de peaje toll road
carretera en construcción road under construction
carretera estrecha narrow road
carretera helada icy road
carretera secundaria secondary road
carretera sin pavimentar unpaved road
carretillas carts/trolleys
carril bici bicycle path/lane
carril bus bus lane
carta menu
casa house
casa de huéspedes guest house
casa solariega stately home
cascada waterfall
casco protector crash helmet
caseta de baño bathing cabana/hut
castillo castle
cata de vinos wine tasting
catedral cathedral
ceda el paso yield/give way
cementerio cemetery
centrifugar dry spin
centro antiguo old town
centro ciudad downtown area
centro comercial business distict; shopping mall/arcade
centro de jardinería garden center
cepo en rueda wheel clamping/booting
cerrado al tráfico road closed
cerrado closed
cerrado hasta el ... closed until ...
cerrado por descanso semanal day off/closed
cerrado por reformas closed for repairs
cerramos a mediodía closed for lunch
cerveza beer
chaleco salvavidas lifejackets
charcutería delicatessen
ciclismo cycling
cierren la puerta close the door
cine movie theater/cinema
circo circus
circuito de carrera racing track
circulación en ambos sentidos two-way traffic
circulación prohibida closed to traffic
circulen por la derecha/izquierda keep to the right/left
circunvalación bypass

ciudad city
ciudades de vacaciones vacation village
clasificación parental guidance (film classification)
clínica de salud health clinic
clínica oftalmológica eye infirmary
clínica pediátrica pediatric ward
club de campo country club
coche car; coach
cocina cookery
cocinar sin descongelar cook from frozen
colina hill
coloque el tíquet detrás del parabrisas place ticket on windshield
colores sólidos colorfast
comedia comedy
comedor dining room
comedor para desayunos breakfast room
comestibles grocer's
comida para llevar take-out
comienza a las ... (de la mañana/tarde) commencing/begins at ...
comisaría de policía police station
compact disc CD
competición contest
completo full up
compra-venta de ... we buy and sell ...
comprimido tablets
con baño with ensuite bathroom
con cocina self-catering
con las comidas with meals
con plomo leaded
con recargo extra charge/supplement
con suplemento extra charge/supplement
con vistas al mar with sea view
concierto de música pop pop-concert
confección propia homemade
confitería confectioner's
congelado frozen
congelados frozen foods
congestión delays likely
conservantes preservatives
conservar en lugar fresco keep in a cool place
conservar en refrigerador keep refrigerated
conservas preserves

conserve su billete please retain your ticket
consigna left-luggage office
consulta del doctor doctor's surgery
consulte con su médico antes de usar consult your doctor before use
consultorio consulting room
consumir antes de ... best before ...
contador de luz (electricidad) electricity meter
contenedor para botellas bottle bank
contorno contour
control de aduana customs control
control de inmigración immigration control
control de pasaportes passport control
convento convent
correduría de seguros insurance agent's
correos post office
costa coast
cristal reciclado recycled glass
cruce crossing; junction/interchange
cruce de autopista freeway/motorway junction
cruce de ganado cattle-grid
cruceros cruises
cruceros en barco steam cruises
cruceros en el río river trips
cubierta cabin decks
cubierta de sol sun deck
cubierta superior upper deck
cuero leather
cuidado con el perro beware of the dog
cuidados intensivos intensive care
cumbre peak
curvas peligrosas dangerous bend

D **dársena** docks
de etiqueta formal wear
de fácil acceso al mar within easy reach of the sea
de gira on tour
de la mañana/madrugada a.m.
de la tarde/noche p.m.
de ... a ... horas from ... to ...
deje su coche con la 1ª marcha leave your car in first gear

dejen libre la ... keep clear
dejen sus bolsos aquí please leave your bags here
deporte sport
deportes sports store/shop
derecho straight on
derecha right
desayuno breakfast
desconectado disconnected
descuentos reductions
deshechable disposable
desierto desert
desprendimientos falling rocks
después de las comidas after meals
destinación destination
desvío alternative route; detour/diversion
desvío para camiones alternative truck/lorry route
devolución del depósito refund
devuelve cambio returns change
día festivo national holiday
día y noche 24-hour service
diciembre December
diócesis diocese
dirección manager
directo direct; direct service
director (de orquesta) conductor
distancia entre tren y andén mind the gap (metro)
disuélvase en agua dissolve in water
divisas compra currency bought at
divisas venta currency sold at
doblada dubbed
domicilio habitual home address
domingo Sunday
Domingo de Ramos Palm Sunday
Domingo de Resurrección Easter Sunday
dosis dose
droguería drugstore/chemist's
duchas showers
duna dune
durante ... días for ... days

E **edificio público** public building
el chef recomienda ... the chef suggests ...
electricidad/electrodomésticos electrical shop/store/appliances

embajada embassy
embarque boarding now
emergencia emergency (services)
embutidos sausages
empieza a las ... commencing ...
empujad/empujar push
en ayunas on an empty stomach
en caso de avería llamar al ... in case of breakdown, phone/contact ...
en caso de emergencia rompa el cristal break glass in case of emergency
en construcción under construction/proposed
en el acto while you wait
en proyecto under construction/proposed
en sala indoor
en temporada in season
encienda luces de carretera switch on headlights
enero January
enfermería sickbay
enfermos de ambulatorio outpatients
ensanche para adelantar passing bay
entrada entrance; way in
entrada de autopista highway/motorway entrance
entrada libre admission free
entrada por la puerta delantera enter by the front door
entrada sólo para residentes residents only
entradas tickets
equipo de buceo scuba diving equipment
escalera mecánica escalator
escarpa escarpment
escuela school
especialidad de la casa/del chef speciality of the house
espectáculo floor show
espectadores spectators
espera de ... mins. wait: approx ... mins.
espere aquí (detrás de este punto) stand behind this point
espere detrás de la valla please wait behind barrier
espere la luz verde wait for green light
espere respuesta wait for a reply
espere su turno please wait your turn
espere tono wait for tone

esquí de fondo cross-country skiing
esquí naútico waterskiing
esquiar skiing
esquís skis
esta máquina no da cambio
  no change given
está prohibido forbidden
esta tarde this evening
estación de ferrocarril rail station
estación de servicio service station
estación de metro
  subway/underground station
estadio stadium
estanco tobacconist's
estatua statue
estreno first night/premiere
extintor fire extinguisher

F **fábrica** factory
  factor 8 (de protección solar)
  factor 8 (sunlotion)
farmacia pharmacy/chemist
faro lighthouse
febrero February
**fecha de caducidad de la tarjeta de
  crédito** credit card expiration date
fecha de nacimiento date of birth
feria fair
ferrocarril railroad/railway
festival festival
fibra artificial manmade
ficción fiction
fila row/tier
fin de autopista end of
  expressway/motorway regulation
fin de desvío end of diversion
fin de obras end of roadworks
fin del trayecto/servicio terminus
firma signature
firme en mal estado uneven road
  surface
flash prohibido no flash
floristería florist's
flotador rubber ring
fotocopias copying
fotografía photographic shop/store;
  photography
frágil ... cristal fragile ... glass
franquicia de equipaje luggage
  allowance
freno emergencia emergency brake

fresco fresh
frontera border crossing
frutas fruit
frutos secos nuts; snacks
fuegos artificiales
  fireworks
fuente fountain
fuera de servicio out of order
fuerte fortress
fumadores smoking
funicular cable car
funicular aéreo cable car/gondola
fútbol soccer/football
fútbol americano American football

G **gabinete dental** dentist
  galería shopping mall/arcade
  galería de arte art gallery; art
store/shop
galería superior balcony
galletas cookies
ganga bargain
garaje garage; car deck
garaje subterráneo underground
  garage
garganta gorge
gasa de seda chiffon
gasolina gas
gasolina normal two-star
gasolina sin plomo unleaded
gasolinera gas station
gastos bancarios bank charges
giro postal postal orders
giros money orders
giros y transferencias drafts and
  transfers
glutamato monosódico monosodium
  glutamate
gorro de baño obligatorio bathing
  caps must be worn
gotas drops
grada tier
gragea pills
grandes almacenes department store
granja farm
gratis free
gravilla loose gravel
grifo faucet/tap
grúa breakdown services
grupos bienvenidos parties welcome
gruta cave
guardarropa coatroom

A-Z

A-Z

H habitaciones bed (breakfast not usually included)

habitaciones libres rooms to let; vacancies

hacer la habitación this room needs making up

hasta 8 artículos 8 items or less

hay refrescos refreshments available

hecho a medida made to measure

herido casualty

hielo ice; black ice

hierro iron

hilo linen

hípica horse riding

hipódromo racecourse

hockey sobre hielo ice hockey

homeopático homeopath

horario de invierno winter timetable

horario de verano summer timetable

horario de visitas visiting hours

horarios timetables

horas de oficina business hours

horas de recogida times of collection

horas de visita visiting hours

hospicio hospice

hostal de juventud youth hostel

hoy today

I ida sólo single/one way

ida y vuelta return/round-trip ticket

idiomas language

iglesia church

importe exacto exact change; exact fare

imprenta printing

impresionante spectacular (n)

impuestos VAT/sales tax

incluido included in the price; inclusive

incluye primera consumición includes one complimentary drink

inflamable inflammable

información directory enquiries

información al cliente customer information

información nutricional nutritional information

ingredientes ingredients

inserte monedas y pulse botón del producto elegido insert coins, then push bottom of selected item

intersección intersection

introduzca su tarjeta insert your credit card

introduzca una moneda insert coin

introduzca una tarjeta de crédito insert credit card

invierno winter

Islas Baleares Balearic Islands

Islas Canarias Canary Islands

I.V.A. (incluido) VAT/sales tax (included)

izquierda left

J jardín common/green/park; garden

jardines botánicos botanical garden

joyería jeweler's

jueves Thursday

juguetería toystore/shop

julio July

junio June

juzgado courthouse

K kiosko newsagent's

L la dirección declina toda responsabilidad en caso de robo o daños the owners can accept no responsibility for any damage or theft

laborables weekdays (only)

lago lake

lana wool

lavabos restrooms/toilets

lavadero washing facilities

lavado car wash

lavandería laundry/laundrette

lavar a máquina machine washable

leche milk

lechería dairy

legumbres vegetables

lentamente slow

levante el auricular lift receiver

libre for hire; vacant

librería bookshop/store; library
lino linen
lite diet
literas sleeper (train)
liquidación por cierre closing down sale
llamada gratuita toll free number
llame al timbre please ring the bell
llegadas arrivals
lluvia rain
lo mismo servido con … the same served with …
local equipado con sistemas de vigilancia surveillance system in operation
luces lights
lugar site, venue
lugar de nacimiento place of birth
lunes Monday
Lunes de Pascua Easter Monday
luz de carretera use headlights

M **madera** wood
manantial spring
manténgase congelado keep frozen
mantener fuera del alcance de los niños keep out of reach of children
mantenga esta puerta cerrada keep gate shut
mantequería dairy
mañana tomorrow
mar sea
marisma swamp
marque el número dial the number
marque … para obtener línea dial … for an outside line
marque … para recepción dial … for reception
martes Tuesday
marzo March
materia grasa fat content
maternidad maternity
matrícula car registration number
mayo May
mayores de … no children under …
media pensión half board
mejorado(-a) improved
memorial memorial
menú del día set menu
menú turístico tourist menu
mercado market

mercado cubierto covered market
mercancía libre de impuestos duty-free goods
merendero picnic site
mermeladas jams and marmelades
mesas arriba seats upstairs
metro metro/underground
miércoles Wednesday
mina mine
mínimo … minimum …
mirador viewpoint
modo de empleo instructions for use
molino mill
molino de viento windmill
monasterio abbey; monastery
moneda extranjera foreign currency
montaña mountain
montañismo rock climbing
monumento monument
monumento histórico ancient monument
mostrador (para registrarse) check-in counter
mostrador de información information desk
moto de agua jetski
mountain bike mountain bike
muebles furniture
multi cine multiplex cinema
muralla wall
murallas de la ciudad city wall
museo museum
música clásica classical music
música de baile dance music
música de órgano organ music
música en directo live music
música ligera easy-listening music
música regional folk music
muy despacio dead slow

N **nacionalidad** nationality
nada que declarar nothing to declare
natación swimming
navegar sailing
Navidad Christmas
nieve snow
niebla fog

nieve helada icy snow
nieve húmeda wet snow
nieve pesada heavy snow
nieve polvo powdery snow
nilón nylon
niños children
niños sólo acompañados por un adulto no unaccompanied children
no abandone su equipaje do not leave baggage unattended
no acercarse keep clear
no administrar por vía oral not to be taken orally
no aparcar - (vado) (salida de emergencia) do not block entrance
no aparcar no parking
no apoyarse sobre la puerta do not lean against door
no asomarse a la ventana do not lean out of windows
no adelantar no overtaking
no contiene azúcar sugar-free
no da cambio no change given
no daña películas film safe
no dejar desperdicios: multa de ... no littering: fine ...
no deje objetos de valor en el coche do not leave valuables in your car
no devuelve monedas no coins returns
no echar basura don't dump rubbish
no fumadores non-smoking
no hay descuentos no discounts
no hay entradas sold out
no hay entreactos no intervals
no incluido exclusive
no ingerir not for internal consumption
no introducir monedas hasta obtener respuesta do not insert money until answer received
no molestar do not disturb
no pega non-stick
no pisar el césped keep off the grass
no planchar do not iron
no retornable non-returnable
no se aceptan cambios goods cannot be exchanged
no se aceptan devoluciones no refunds
no se aceptan talones no checks
no se aceptan tarjetas de crédito no credit cards
no se admite durante las misas no entry during services (mass)

no se deforma will not lose its shape
no se permite la entrada una vez iniciada la función no entry once the performance has begun
no se permiten alimentos en la habitación no food in the room
no tirar al fuego do not burn
no tirar basura do not litter
no tocar do not touch
no verter escombros no dumping
no-retornable non-returnable
noche night
Nochebuena Christmas Eve
Nochevieja New Year's Eve
noviembre November
nuevas normas de circulación new traffic system in operation
número de la cartilla de la seguridad social social security number
número de la tarjeta de crédito credit card number
número de vuelo flight number
número del pasaporte passport number

O

obispo bishop
objetos perdidos lost property
obra de teatro play
obras a ... mts roadworks ahead
obsequio free gift
octubre October
ocupado occupied/engaged
odontólogo dentist
oferta especial special offer
oficina de cambio (de moneda) currency exchange office, bureau de change
oficina de información information office
oficinas de cambio bureau de change
ojo con los rateros beware pickpockets
ojo con los ladrones thieves about
operadora operator
óptica optician's
oraciones prayers
orilla river bank
oro gold
orquesta sinfónica symphony orchestra
ortodoncista orthodontist
osteópata osteopath
otoño fall/autumn
otros pasaportes non-EU citizens

P

pabellón pavilion
páginas amarillas yellow pages
pagos deposits
pagos y cobros deposits and withdrawals
pague 2 lleve 3 buy 2 get 1 free
pague antes de repostar please pay for gas/petrol before filling car
pague aquí please pay here
palacio palace
palcos boxes
palos de esquí ski poles/sticks
pan bread
panadería baker's/bakery
panorama panorama
pantano bog/marsh; reservoir
pantomima pantomime
papel reciclado recycled paper
papelería stationer's
paquetes parcels
para cabello graso for greasy hair
para cabello normal for normal hair
para cabello seco for dry hair
para dos personas for two
paracaidismo parachuting
parada de ambulancias ambulance station
parada de autobús bus stop
parada de taxi(s) taxi rank/stand
parada discrecional request stop
parada solicitada bus stopping
paraíso superior balcony
pare el motor turn off your engine
pared wall
parlamento parliament building
parque common/green/park
parque de atracciones amusement park
parque nacional country park; national park
parque reserva nature reserve
parque temático theme park
párroco fr. (Father)
parroquia parish
particular private
partido match
pasaje alley
paseo walk
paseo peatonal walkway
paso units

paso a nivel railroad/level crossing
paso de peatones pedestrian crossing
paso exclusivo para peatones pedestrians only
paso subterráneo underground passage
pastelería cake store/shop
patín pedallo
patinage sobre hielo ice skating
patines skates
peaje toll
peatón pedestrians
peligro danger
peligro de avalancha avalanche danger
peligroso dangerous
peluquería hairdresser's/stylist's; barber
multa por viajar sin billete penalty for traveling without a ticket
pendiente gradient
pendiente peligrosa dangerous slope
pensión completa full board
permiso de circulación y ficha técnica registration papers
pesca con caña angling
pesca con licencia obligatoria fishing by permit only
pesca prohibida no fishing
pescadería fish store/fishmonger's
PGC guardia civil highway police
piel leather
píldora pill
piragüismo canoeing
piscina swimming pool
piscina para salto de trampolín diving pool
piso en alquiler apartment to let
pista cerrada piste closed
pista de bicicletas cycle track
pista para principiantes for beginners (piste)
pista track
planeo gliding
plata silver
platea orchestra
plato del día dish of the day
plato regional local specialties
platos preparados precooked meals
playa beach

A-Z

playa de nudistas nudist beach
plaza square
plaza redonda roundabout
podólogo chiropodist
policía police
policía de tráfico traffic police
polideportivo sports center
poliéster polyester
pomada ointment
porcelana china
portero de noche night porter
postres desserts
pozo (water) well
precaución drive carefully; caution
precio de la habitación room rate
precio por litro price per liter
precipicio cliff
prefijo territorial area code
prepare importe exacto please have exact change ready
presa dam
presente en estante hasta ... sell by ...
primavera spring
primer piso first floor (U.S. second floor)
primera clase first class
principal dress circle
privado staff only
probador(es) fitting room(s)
prohibida la entrada keep out; no entry
prohibido a menores de 18 años under-18s not allowed
prohibido a vehículos pesados closed to heavy vehicles
prohibido acampar no camping
prohibido adelantar no overtaking/passing
prohibido bañarse no swimming/bathing
prohibido consumir alimentos adquiridos en el exterior no food purchased elsewhere allowed on the premises
prohibido correr no running
prohibido detenerse entre ... y ... no stopping (between ... and ...)
prohibido esquiar fuera de las pistas no off-piste skiing
prohibido estacionar no waiting
prohibido fotografiar no photography
prohibido fumar en el garaje no smoking on car decks

prohibido hablar al conductor do not talk to the driver
prohibido encender fuego no fires/barbeques
prohibido juegos de pelota no ball games
prohibido la entrada/el paso no entry
prohibido la salida/el paso no exit
prohibido usar el claxon use of horn prohibited
prohibido viajar de pie no standing
protéjase de la luz do not expose to sunlight
próxima visita a las ... next tour at ...
psiquiatra psychiatrist
pueblo village
puente bajo low bridge
puente bridge
puente inferior lower deck
puente levadizo drawbridge
puerta (de embarque) (boarding) gate
puerta corta-fuegos fire door
puerta door; gate
puertas automáticas automatic doors
puerto cerrado (mountain) pass closed
puerto deportivo marina
puerto docks; harbor/harbour; pass
puesto de pescado fishstall
pujar to go up
punto de embarque embarkation point
punto de encuentro meeting point

Q queso cheese
quien rompe, paga all breakages must be paid for
quirófano operating room, (theater)

R radiología x-ray
rambla avenue on covered riverbed
rampa ramp
rápido express train
rápidos rapids
raqueta racket/raquet
rasgar aquí tear here
rayos X x-ray
rebajado bargain
rebajas sale; clearance sale
recambios y accesorios del automóvil car accessory/spares shop/store
recepción reception

recibimos paid
recién pintado wet paint
recital de poesías poetry reading
recogida de equipajes baggage reclaim
recogidas a … next collection at …
reduzca la velocidad slow down
referencia reference
regalos gifts
remitente sender
remo rowing
reparación del calzado shoe repairs
reserva de entradas/plazas ticket reservation
reservada reserved
respete su carril get in lane
respeten este lugar de culto please respect this place of worship
retirar dinero withdrawals
retire el billete take ticket
retornable returnable
retraso/retrasado delayed
revisado(-a) revised
revista review; variety show
revistas magazines
rezos prayers
río river
ronda ring-road
ropa de caballero menswear
ropa de niños children's wear
ropa de señoras ladies wear
ropa interior femenina lingerie
rugby rugby
ruinas ruins
ruta de autobús bus route
ruta del ferry ferry route
ruta opcional alternative route
ruta turística scenic route

S sábado Saturday
sal salt
sala ward
sala de conciertos concert hall
sala de conferencias conference room
sala de curas treatment room
sala de espera passenger lounge; waiting room
sala de juegos games room
sala de máquinas fitness room
salida exit; way out
salida de autopista highway/motorway exit
salida de camiones truck exit
salida de emergencia emergency exit; fire door/exit
salida de incendio(s) fire exit
salida por la puerta trasera exit by the rear door
salidas departures
salón lounge
salón de convenciones convention hall
salón de televisor television room
salsas sauces
salvavidas lifebelt
se aceptan tarjetas de crédito we accept credit cards
se alquila for rent
se envían fax faxes sent
se habla inglés English spoken
se procederá contra el hurto shoplifting will be prosecuted
se procederá contra los intrusos trespassers will be prosecuted
se requiere un documento de identidad proof of identity required
se ruega mostrar su bolso a la salida please show your bags before leaving
se ruega pagar en caja please pay at counter
se ruega un donativo please make a contribution
secador de pelo hairdryer
sector para familias family section
seda silk
según mercado subject to availability
segunda clase second class
segundo piso third floor
seguridad security
selecciones destino select destination/zone
sellos de correo stamps
semáforo provisional temporary traffic lights
Semana Santa Easter
sendero footpath; path
sentido único one-way street
señas address
señoras ladies (toilets)
septiembre/setiembre September
sepultura grave
servicio service charge

A-Z

A-Z

servicio de ampliación enlargement service
servicio de habitaciones room service
servicio incluido service included
servicio no incluido service not included
servicio nocturno night service
servicios toilets/restrooms
sesión continua continuous performance
sesión de noche evening performance
sesión de tarde matinée
si es correcto pulse continuar if correct press "continuar" (continue)
si no pulse cancelar otherwise press "cancelar" (cancel)
si no queda satisfecho de su compra le devolvemos su dinero satisfaction or your money back (money-back guarantee)
si persisten los síntomas, consulte su médico if symptoms persist, consult your doctor
sierra mountain range
silencio durante las oraciones quiet, service in progress
sin grasa fat-free
sin salida para peatones no thoroughfare for pedestrians
sírvase frío served chilled
sobre pedido made to order
solicite parada stopping service
solicite vendedor please ask for assistance
sólo abonados permit-holders/ ticket holders only
sólo bus buses only
sólo domingos Sundays only
sólo en efectivo cash only
sólo entrada access only
sólo hombres men only
sólo laborables weekdays only
sólo lavado a mano hand wash only
sólo mercancías freight only
sólo mujeres women only
sólo para máquina de afeitar shavers only
sólo para uso externo for external use only
sólo personal de la empresa staff only

sólo residentes residents only
sólo vehículos autorizados unauthorized parking prohibited
sombrilla sunshade
sopas soups
subtitulada subtitled
submarinismo deep water diving
sugerencias para servir serving suggestion
súper four-star gasoline
surtidor pump

T

tabla de surf surfboard
tabla de windsurf sailboard
tableta tablet
talla única one size fits all
taller mecánico car repairs
taquilla box office; ticket office
tarifa rate
tarjeta de embarque embarkation card
tarjeta mensual monthly ticket
tarjeta semanal weekly ticket
tarjetas de teléfono phone cards
té tea
teatro theater
teclee su número personal type in your PIN number
teleférico cable car/gondola
teléfono con tarjeta card phone
teléfono de emergencia emergency telephone
teléfono público public telephone
telesilla chairlift
templo chapel; church (non-Catholic)
tenis de mesa table tennis
termine el tratamiento finish the course
terraplén embankment
terraza balcony
tienda de regalos gift shop
tienda libre de impuestos duty-free shop
tintorería dry-cleaner's
tipo de cambio exchange rate
tirad/tirar pull
tire de la palanca pull the handle
todos con guarnición de ... all the above are served with ...
tolerada universal (film classification)
torre tower
tráfico de frente traffic from the opposite direction

tráfico lento slow traffic
tragar entera swallow whole
traje de calle informal wear
tranvía tram; tramway
transbordador ferry
transbordador de pasajeros passenger ferry
tren railroad/railway
tren con literas sleeper (train)
tren de cercanías local train
tribuna para espectadores viewing gallery
tribuna stand/grandstand
trolebús trolleybus
tumba tomb
tumbona deck-chair
túnel tunnel
TV (por satélite) en todas las habitaciones with (satellite) TV in every room

U **última entrada a las …** last entry at …
última gasolinera antes de autopista last gas/petrol station before the highway/motorway
universidad university
urgencias accident and emergency
uso obligatorio de cadenas o neumáticos de nieve use chains or snow tires

V **vagón de (no)-fumadores** (non)smoking compartment
vagón restaurante dining car
válido para zonas … valid for zones …
valle valley
vapor steamer
Vd. está aquí you are here
veces al día … times a day
vehículo pesado heavy vehicles
vehículos lentos slow vehicles
velero sailboat
velocidad máxima maximum speed
velódromo cycle track
veneno poison; poisonous
venta anticipada advance bookings

venta de billetes ticket office
venta inmediata tickets for today
verano summer
verdulería greengrocer's
verduras a elegir choice of vegetables
verduras vegetables
vereda lay-by
verificación de pasaportes passport check/control
verifique su cambio please check your change
vestuario changing rooms
vía preferente main road/principal highway
vía segundaria minor road
viaje travel
viernes Friday
vino wine
vinos y licores wines & spirits
visitas con guía guided tours
vísperas evensong
vista panorámica panoramic view
viveros garden center
vuelos internacionales international flights
vuelos nacionales domestic flights

WX YZ **yate** yacht
yogure yogurt
zapatería shoe store
zapatillas de deporte obligatorias white soles only
zapatos shoes
zona comercial shopping area
zona de aparcamiento regulado "ORA" "pay and display" parking
zona de carga loading bay
zona de carga y descarga deliveries only
zona de descanso rest area
zona de no fumadores non-smoking
zona peatonal pedestrian zone/precinct/crossing
zona residencial residential zone
zona urbana builtup area
zoológico zoo
zumos de fruta fruit juices

Numbers

GRAMMAR

> Larger numbers are built up using the components below: e.g.
> 3.456.789   **tres millones, cuatrocientos cincuenta y seis mil,**
>   **setecientos ochenta y nueve.**
> Note that from 31 to 99 **y** is used between tens and units, but never
> between hundreds and tens.

0	**cero** _thero_	20	**veinte** _baynteh_
1	**uno** _oono_	21	**veintiuno** _baynteeyoono_
2	**dos** _dos_	22	**veintidós** _baynteedos_
3	**tres** _tres_	23	**veintitrés** _baynteetres_
4	**cuatro** _kwatro_	24	**veinticuatro** _baynteekwatro_
5	**cinco** _theenko_	25	**veinticinco** _baynteetheenko_
6	**seis** _says_	26	**veintiséis** _baynteesays_
7	**siete** _seeyeteh_	27	**veintisiete** _baynteeseeyeteh_
8	**ocho** _ocho_	28	**veintiocho** _baynteeyocho_
9	**nueve** _nwebeh_	29	**veintinueve** _baynteenwebeh_
10	**diez** _deeyeth_	30	**treinta** _traynta_
11	**once** _ontheh_	31	**treinta y uno** _traynta ee oono_
12	**doce** _dotheh_	32	**treinta y dos** _traynta ee dos_
13	**trece** _tretheh_		
14	**catorce** _katortheh_		
15	**quince** _keentheh_		
16	**dieciséis** _deeyetheesays_		
17	**diecisiete** _deeyetheeseeyeteh_		
18	**dieciocho** _deeyetheeocho_		
19	**diecinueve** _deeyetheenwebeh_		

40	**cuarenta** *kwa<u>ren</u>ta*	twice	**dos veces**
50	**cincuenta** *theen<u>kwen</u>ta*		*dos <u>bethes</u>*
60	**sesenta** *se<u>sen</u>ta*	three times	**tres veces** *tres <u>bethes</u>*
70	**setenta** *se<u>ten</u>ta*	one half	**la mitad**
80	**ochenta** *o<u>chen</u>ta*		*la mee<u>tath</u>*
90	**noventa** *no<u>ben</u>ta*	one and a half	**uno y medio(-a)**
100	**cien** *thee<u>yen</u>*		*<u>oo</u>no ee <u>medeeyo</u>(-a)*
101	**ciento uno** *thee<u>yen</u>to <u>oo</u>no*	half an hour	**media hora** *<u>medeeya ora</u>*
102	**ciento dos** *thee<u>yen</u>to dos*	half a tank	**medio depósito** *<u>medeeyo</u> de<u>po</u>seeto*
200	**doscientos** *dosthee<u>yen</u>tos*	half eaten	**a medio comer** *a <u>medeeyo ko</u>mer*
500	**quinientos** *keenee<u>yen</u>tos*	a quarter	**un cuarto** *oon <u>kwar</u>to*
1,000	**mil** *meel*	a third	**un tercio** *oon <u>ter</u>theeyo*
10,000	**diez mil** *dee<u>yeth</u> meel*	a pair of ...	**un par de ...** *oon par deh*
35,000	**treinta y cinco mil** *<u>trayn</u>ta ee <u>theen</u>ko meel*	a dozen ...	**una docena de ...** *<u>oo</u>na do<u>then</u>a deh*
1,000,000	**un millón** *oon meel-<u>yon</u>*	1997	**mil novecientos noventa y siete** *meel nobethee<u>yen</u> tos no<u>ben</u>ta ee see<u>ye</u>teh*
first (adjective)	**primer(a)** *pree<u>mer</u>(a)*		
second	**segundo (-a)** *se<u>goon</u>do(-a)*	2001	**dos mil uno** *dos meel <u>oo</u>no*
third	**tercero(-a)** *ter<u>the</u>ro(-a)*	the 1990s	**los noventa** *los no<u>ben</u>ta*
fourth	**cuarto(-a)** *<u>kwar</u>to(-a)*		
fifth	**quinto(-a)** *<u>keen</u>to(-a)*		
once	**una vez** *<u>oo</u>na beth*		

Days Días

Monday	**lunes** _loones_
Tuesday	**martes** _martes_
Wednesday	**miércoles** _meeyerkoles_
Thursday	**jueves** _khwebes_
Friday	**viernes** _beeyernes_
Saturday	**sábado** _sabado_
Sunday	**domingo** _domeengo_

Months Meses

January	**enero** _enero_
February	**febrero** _febrero_
March	**marzo** _martho_
April	**abril** _abreel_
May	**mayo** _mayo_
June	**junio** _khooneeyo_
July	**julio** _khooleeyo_
August	**agosto** _agosto_
September	**septiembre** _septeeyembreh_
October	**octubre** _oktoobreh_
November	**noviembre** _nobeeyembreh_
December	**diciembre** _deetheeyembreh_

Dates Fechas

It's ...	**Estamos a ...** _estamos a_
July 10	**diez de julio** _deeyeth deh khooleeyo_
Tuesday, March 1	**martes, uno de marzo** _martes oono deh martho_
yesterday	**ayer** _eye-yer_
today	**hoy** _oy_
tomorrow	**mañana** _mañana_
this month	**este mes** _esteh mes_
last week	**la semana pasada** _la semana pasada_
next/every year	**el año que viene/todos los años** _el año keh beeyeneh/todos los años_
at the weekend	**el fin de semana** _el feen deh semana_

Seasons Las estaciones

spring	**la primavera** *la preemabera*
summer	**el verano** *el berano*
fall/autumn	**el otoño** *el otoño*
winter	**el invierno** *el eenbeeyerno*
in spring	**en primavera** *en preemabera*
during the summer	**durante el verano** *dooranteh el berano*

Greetings Saludos/Felicitaciones

Happy birthday!	**¡Feliz cumpleaños!** *feleeth koompleaños*
Merry Christmas!	**¡Feliz Navidad!** *feleeth nabeedath*
Happy New Year!	**¡Feliz Año Nuevo!** *feleeth año nwebo*
Best wishes!	**¡Un abrazo!** *oon abratho*
Congratulations!	**¡Felicidades!** *feleetheedades*
Good luck!/All the best!	**¡Buena suerte!** *bwena swerteh*
Have a good trip!	**¡Que tenga un buen viaje!** *keh tenga oon bwen beeyakheh*
Give my regards to ...	**Salude a ... de mi parte** *saloodeh a ... deh mee parteh*

Public holidays Días festivos

January 1	Año Nuevo	New Year's Day
January 6	Epifanía	Epiphany
March 19	San José	St Joseph's Day
May 1	Día del Trabajo	Labor Day
July 25	Santiago Apóstol	St James's Day
August 15	Asunción	Assumption Day
October 12	Día de la Hispanidad	Columbus Day
November 1	Todos los Santos	All Saints' Day
December 6	Día de la Constitución Española	Constitution Day
December 8	Immaculada Concepción	Immaculate Conception Day
December 25	Navidad	Christmas Day
Movable dates:	Viernes Santo	Good Friday
	Lunes de Pascua	Easter Monday (Catalonia only)

Note: There are many local variations.

Time ¿Qué hora es?

Excuse me. Can you tell me the time? | **Disculpe. ¿Puede decirme la hora?** *deeskoolpeh pwedeh detheermeh la ora*

It's five past one. | **Es la una y cinco** *es la oona ee theenko*

It's ... | **Son las ...** *son las ...*

ten past two | **dos y diez** *dos ee deeyeth*

a quarter past three | **tres y cuarto** *tres ee kwarto*

twenty past four | **cuatro y veinte** *kwatro ee baynteh*

twenty-five past five | **cinco y veinticinco** *theenko ee baynteetheenko*

half past six | **seis y media** *says ee medeeya*

twenty-five to seven | **siete menos veinticinco** *seeyeteh menos baynteetheenko*

twenty to eight | **ocho menos veinte** *ocho menos baynteh*

a quarter to nine | **nueve menos cuarto** *nwebeh menos kwarto*

ten to ten | **diez menos diez** *deeyeth menos deeyeth*

five to eleven | **once menos cinco** *ontheh menos theenko*

twelve o'clock (noon/midnight) | **doce en punto (de la mañana/de la noche)** *dotheh en poonto (deh la mañana/ deh la nocheh)*

220

at dawn	**al amanecer** *al amanether*
in the morning	**por la mañana** *por la mañana*
during the day	**durante el día** *dooranteh el deeya*
before lunch	**antes de comer** *antes de komer*
after lunch	**después de comer** *despwes de komer*
in the afternoon	**por la tarde** *por la tardeh*
in the evening/at night	**por la noche** *por la nocheh*
I'll be ready in five minutes.	**Estaré listo(-a) en cinco minutos.** *estareh leesto(-a) en theenko meenootos*
He'll be back in a quarter of an hour.	**Volverá dentro de un cuarto de hora.** *bolbera dentro deh oon kwarto deh ora*
She arrived half an hour ago.	**Llegó hace media hora.** *l-yego atheh medeeya ora*
The train leaves at ...	**El tren sale a las ...** *el tren saleh a las*
13:04	**trece horas y cuatro minutos** *trethe oras ee kwatro meenootos*
0:40	**cero horas cuarenta minutos** *thero oras kwarenta meenootos*
10 minutes late/early	**diez minutos más tarde/diez minutos antes** *deeyeth meenootos mas tardeh/ deeyeth meenootos antes*
5 minutes fast/slow	**cinco minutos adelantado/atrasado** *theenko meenootos adelantado/atrasado*
from 9:00 to 5:00	**de nueve a cinco** *deh nwebeh a theenko*
between 8:00 and 2:00	**entre las ocho y las dos** *entreh las ocho ee las dos*
I'll be leaving by ...	**Me iré antes de las ...** *meh eereh antes deh las*
Will you be back before ...?	**¿Estará de vuelta antes de ...?** *estara deh bwelta antes deh*
We'll be here until ...	**Estaremos aquí hasta ...** *estaremos akee asta*

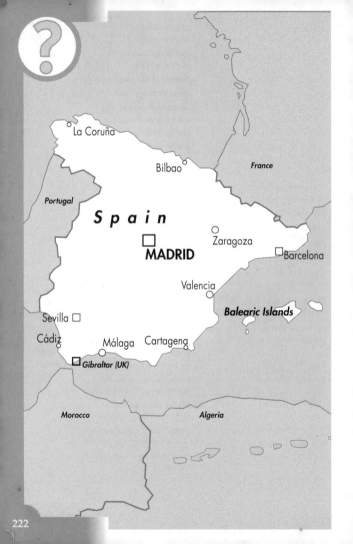

La Coruña

Bilbao

France

Portugal

S p a i n

☐
MADRID

○ Zaragoza

☐ Barcelona

Valencia ○

Balearic Islands

Sevilla ☐

Cádiz

Málaga ○   Cartagena ○

☐ *Gibraltar (UK)*

Morocco

Algeria

222